TWENTY THOUSAND ROADS

VILLARD / NEW YORK

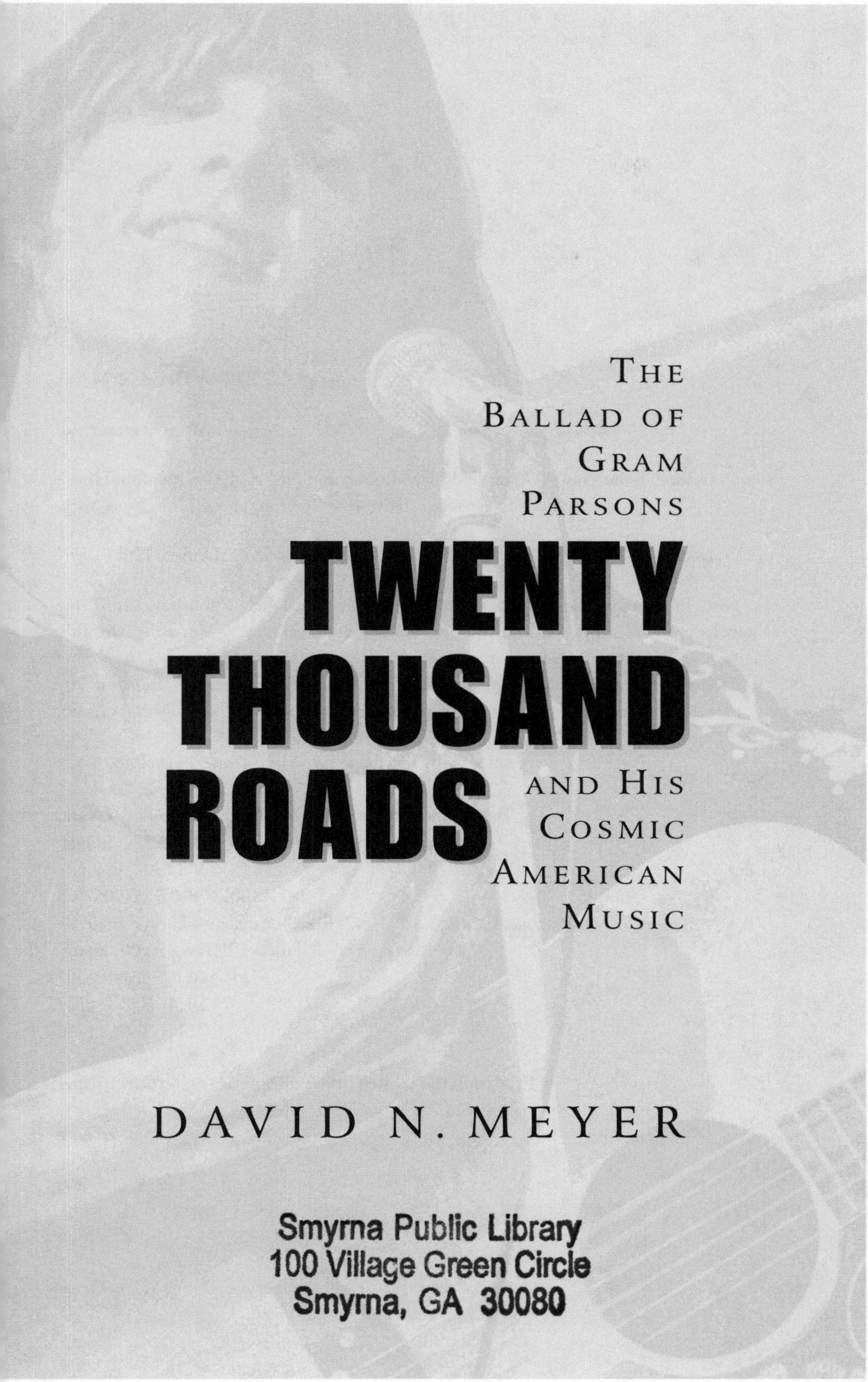

THE
BALLAD OF
GRAM
PARSONS

TWENTY THOUSAND ROADS

AND HIS
COSMIC
AMERICAN
MUSIC

DAVID N. MEYER

Published in the United States by Villard Books, an imprint of The Random House
Publishing Group, a division of Random House, Inc., New York.

VILLARD and "V" CIRCLED Design are registered trademarks of Random House, Inc.

Grateful acknowledgment is made to Rowman and Littlefield Publishing Group for
permission to reprint excerpts from *Faithfull: An Autobiography* by Marianne Faithfull,
copyright © 1994 by Marianne Faithfull; excerpts from *Desperados: The Roots of
Country Rock* by John Einarson, copyright © 2001 by John Einarson. Reprinted by
permission of Rowman and Littlefield Publishing Group.

LIBRARY OF CONGRESS CATALOGING-IN-PUBLICATION DATA
Meyer, David N.
Twenty thousand roads: the ballad of Gram Parsons and
his cosmic American music / David N. Meyer.
p. cm.
ISBN 978-0-375-50570-6
1. Parsons, Gram, d. 1973.   2. Rock musicians—United States—
Biography.   I. Title.   II. Title: 20,000 roads.
ML420.P275M49 2007
782.42166092—dc22
[B]   2007021748

Printed in the United States of America on acid-free paper

www.villard.com

1 2 3 4 5 6 7 8 9

First Edition

Book design by Susan Turner

Just because we wear sequined suits doesn't mean we think we're great, it means we think sequins are great.

—GRAM PARSONS

Anyway, it is said that during the gestation of *Remembrance of Things Past*, the author gradually became convinced of a frightening psychological truth: Contrary to popular belief, people do not learn by experience. Instead, they respond to a particular stimulus in a predictable way, and this repeatedly. Again, again, again, and again this undeviating, compulsive response may be observed. Again, again, again, and again, generation after generation, the dismal message reappears like writing on the wall.

—EVAN CONNELL,
 Son of the Morning Star

So try to understand the pain
It takes so long when I explain
Please, don't you forget
How much I've lied

—GRAM PARSONS,
 "How Much I've Lied"

PROLOGUE

"Is he the famous?"

Though New Orleans is renowned for having the most beautiful graveyards in America—urban death museums featuring bodies buried aboveground in ornate marble mausoleums—Gram Parsons lies far from the center of town and its elegant boneyards. His charred remains rest in a lush, green, and perfectly conventional cemetery a mile from the airport, twenty miles from the heart of the Crescent City.

Today the roadway to Gram's graveyard remains grim as death, an industrial four-lane gauntlet of auto wreckers, towing yards, and cement plants. How isolated and remote the place must have been when Gram was buried in 1973, how un–New Orleans and lacking in glamour. But if the setting is drab, Gram Parsons' grave itself was, until recently, unabashedly low-rent.

The grave marker is a six-inch-round stone disk with a connector-like snout protruding from the center. The engraved circular inscription is too small to read when standing. If you kneel and slowly rotate your head you can barely make out the tiny dirt-filled letters. Just behind the marker stands a small yellow plastic square mounted on rusty rebar—an aid to the death tourists who come ten to the day on weekends. A black plastic arrow glued to the yellow square points down. If you didn't know it was a grave, you'd swear that black arrow marked a sprinkler hookup for the grounds crew. I certainly did.

New Orleans cabbies talk a lot—they like to connect. A cab ride of any length usually features some bizarre intimacy. As we roll out of town through a pounding March rain, my cabbie grills me on my mission. Five minutes outside the French Quarter, we stop in frozen traffic. At the intersection ahead, a hundred-odd dancers in feathered outfits leap and swirl, knotting up the streets and drawing the locals out of the two-story red projects that line the corner. It's nowhere near Mardi Gras; this is a neighborhood impromptu. Traffic stretches behind us as three New Orleans cops lean on their cars and watch the scene. No one seems to mind the gridlock or the rain.

My cabbie wants to chat. He insists that he's Moroccan; his unspoken concern is that I might take him for a light-skinned Louisiana black man. His French accent makes him sound like a mixed-race Louisianan—but he's adamant that he's not from anywhere around here. Bloodlines and gradations of whiteness apparently still matter in these parts, and he's sensitive to misidentification. Pedigree, class, and family identity matter, too, and all exerted a strong force on Gram's life. Given that his journey relentlessly produced its own inescapable metaphors, it's no surprise that my cabbie grants me the necessary metaphorical context for a graveside visit.

Pedigree and gradations of whiteness used to matter to me, too. I was raised in a desolate hick town in north Georgia that was not much bigger than Gram's hometown of Waycross, down in the southern, swampy part of the state. And from tenth grade on, when the music I listened to became my self-definition and moral compass, I pretty much tuned out white music. Especially country. Country music incarnated everything I loathed about my hometown, the South, and all they represented: violence, racism, small-mindedness, desperate conformism, knee-jerk patriotism, oppressive Christianity, and blind obedience. Not to mention high school football.

Rejecting all this music (and an entire race) was not as idiotic a position as it might sound, even for a tenth grader. During the day, my hometown radio played only the lamest and most commercial country. After midnight, otherworldly possibilities floated through the mountain air from the blessedly clear WLS-AM in Chicago. At the time, music was as segregated as my high school. You could get beat up over what you listened to, and in other parts of the state—like Atlanta, where actual hippies were reputed to exist—you could get murdered for having long hair.

All I knew of country music was the TV show *Hee Haw* and the twenty-times-a-day rotation of "Okie from Muskogee." Buck Owens' red, white, and blue guitar gave me the creeps, as I'm sure Buck intended it should. For me and many others (and a lot of them were country musicians), country incarnated the forces of reaction. It made a point of being pathologically anti-hippie, pro-Vietnam, pro-authority, pro-Jesus, and pro-Nixon. Music was a collection of willfully exclusionary fortresses, each policing its own vision of morality, making sure its message got out and ensuring that no infiltrators watered down its values. Country, psychedelic guitar rock, radio pop, soul . . . you picked your tribe and stuck with it. As for blues, old-time white rural string music, John Coltrane, or the Velvet Underground, I didn't have a clue. How could I?

So I raised myself on soul music and was lucky to be in high school during the perfect era to do so. Otis Redding, James Brown, Stax-Volt, and Motown were my salvation. I grew up convinced there was no insight or worthy emotion to be heard from anybody white—except maybe Gregg Allman, who didn't exactly sound black, but who clearly had soul.

Then one day in Chapel Hill, North Carolina, Gram Parsons' voice came floating out of a dorm window onto the quad where I was throwing a Frisbee with my long-haired Southern soul-obsessed friends. And that was it: As Martin Sheen says in *Apocalypse Now* about the voice of Colonel Kurtz, "It really put the hook in me." Gram Parsons' voice was then, and remains today, the most moving white voice I know. For me, for my soul, Gram Parsons' voice lives with the voices of Robert Johnson, Patsy Cline, Furry Lewis, Lou Reed, Otis Redding, Joey Ramone, Charley Patton, Alex Chilton, Townes Van Zandt, Lowell George, George Jones, Brian Wilson, Dennis Wilson, Carl Wilson, Son House, Gregg Allman, James Booker, and Chet Baker . . . American voices that transcend any rational discussion and, really, anything rational at all.

Gram Parsons' voice led me to the world of country, to the world of white rural American music, and thus, years later, into recognizing how few categories or separations or genus-naming make any sense at all when you listen, truly listen, to the music of America. Gram preached his idea of "Cosmic American Music," a holy intersection of unpolished American expression: gospel, soul, folk, Appalachia, R&B, country, bluegrass, blues, rockabilly, and honky-tonk. That sound remains difficult to define but has become, in large part because of Gram Parsons, easy to recognize. Gram Parsons' music convinced me that Cosmic American Music exists. His voice led me to the America where it does.

I tell my cabbie why I'm going out to such a godforsaken cemetery on such an awful morning. He says if I take no more than twenty minutes, he'll hang out and help me search. He swears I'll find no cabs in the middle of nowhere on a monsoon Sunday. I believe him. His curiosity does not surprise me. For one thing, it's Southern, and for another, everyone drawn into Gram's orbit ends up seduced.

Outside the gates the street looks like any other near any airport in America. Towers of crushed cars, massive, foreboding tow trucks, and the spires of a concrete plant frame a check-cashing store sealed off for Sunday behind iron grates. We swing through a gated concrete wall, and the cemetery reveals itself as a sprawling, pleasant place with overhanging trees, Spanish moss, and a stream meandering through endless headstones all lying flush with the ground. The office, a mock Swiss chalet, is locked up tight. I assumed there'd be some sort of guide to Gram's grave—a map, a sign, a marker, something. There ain't.

The warm soft rain falls in sheets. The cabbie and I walk over who knows how many dead, looking for a large marker near a tree. An earlier book on Gram's life had planted a clear mental image of Gram lying in Byronic repose under quintessentially moss-hung, leafy branches. But there's no sign of him near any of the oaks. We switch to checking out the larger monuments away from the trees; still no Gram.

It's almost lunchtime, and several other couples stumble through the rain staring at the ground. I talk to one or two; they're all looking for Gram and they haven't a clue either. After twenty minutes we give up and roll out under the blue-black thickening clouds. My cabbie promises to be at my hotel door at ten the next morning.

Monday the rain thickens and the graveyard office is open. Running the place is a fiftyish woman who looks like the evil hotelier in a film noir. Her steely hair is piled up over her head in a roadhouse bouffant and sprayed solid. An unfiltered cigarette flexes in the side of her mouth as she speaks with clenched teeth and a hardscrabble accent; the front of her black dress, which fits her formerly va-va-voomish figure closely enough to sculpt her potbelly, is scattered with ashes. Even twenty-eight years dead, Gram remains surrounded by mythology and archetype.

★ ★ ★

GRAVEYARDS ELICIT SENTIMENTALITY and grand thoughts. I wish I were immune. In the company of so many corpses, Gram Parsons' life might appear as a litany of archetypal reductions, so many easy solutions for someone wanting to sing his ballad: the Poor Little Rich Boy, the Child of Suicides, the Tortured Dionysian Genius, the Lost Prince Born in the Wrong Century, the Underappreciated Artist Who Suffered from Being Ahead of His Time, the Coolest Guy in the Room, the Singer-Songwriter Too Sensitive to Live in This World, the Guy Who Could Do More Drugs Than Anyone (except Keef), the Man Who Refused to Get Out of His Own Way, and (as Neil Young epitaphed the self-murdered-by-overindulgence Danny Whitten) "He tried to do his best, but he could not."

In Gram's case, all the archetypes are true but none tell the truth. In tracing his story, I discovered that the man himself, as befits a walking catalog of archetypes, was an archetype magnet of the first degree. And so he posthumously remains.

The archetype in charge here is the Southern, pursed-mouth, nasty-redneck Dragon Lady. She rails at a cowering Bartleby-like employee, who scuttles away clutching his buttoned-up cardigan to his chest. When I take a graveyard map from a desktop stand, she snatches it from my hand and scribbles incomprehensible directions all over it. When I reach for another, she moves between me and the map rack. I ask her outright for a pristine copy to reproduce in this book, and she turns her back. She's in the midst of monologing to herself about the inconvenience of Gram grave seekers when I head out the door.

Gram Parsons' death and his subsequent slow-building legend have generated all sorts of classically American obsessions. On one hand there are, in the priceless phrase of novelist Dana Spiotta, the Bitter Lieutenants: those who played with Gram at one time or another and who may have surpassed him in money, fame, and achievement (or not) but who remain hard-hearted and unhappy about all the fuss attending him today. No matter how much they've been given or earned (or had taken away) in the rock/country/fame salt mines, only the most spiritually generous of his contemporaries can bear to give Gram Parsons his propers. The rest are sick of hearing about him and even more tired of talking.

The yin to the Bitter Lieutenants' yang are the possessive necrophiliacs known as the Grampires: those who know they have the handle on Gram Parsons' life and music and will brook no other viewpoint. The longer and more religiously they've pursued the Parsons mythology, the less likely they are to welcome anyone into the clubhouse. The graveyard proprietress represents all that collective resentment, all that conviction that anyone else who might appreciate Gram Parsons is an interloper and a fraud. Her illegible marks on the map represent everybody who wants to make sure it's their incomprehensible directions that get followed, that it's their version of Gram's story that gets told.

The cabbie drives me to the necessary quadrant. I could swear I walked this ground yesterday, squishing ankle-deep in the rain-soaked lawn. We pace back and forth over the same ten rows of flat-laid headstones, peering straight down. I read some stones, scan others for a recognizable word. The smaller ones I skip. It seems impossible that Gram Parsons wouldn't have a monumental monument. I turn from the map to the world it claims to show but see no correlation. I'm getting soaked. And frustrated: *Shit-fire!* I think. What if I've come all this way and can't find his goddamn grave? It's the biographer's dilemma in a nutshell.

A big-ass John Deere tractor comes inching along the paved circular drive. Sitting on its fenders, blank-faced in the rain, are four African American men in piercingly yellow pants and hooded slickers: the grounds crew. I wave them down and ask for help. All four climb down and walk slowly, gravely, over. They appear to be between forty and sixty years old. Maybe they're family: They have outsized heads with similarly pronounced, oversized features, and all four are dark, dark black—African tribal black with not a hint of American brown. Their darkness and solemnity makes the moment even more Southern gothic.

Their black skin stands out against the living green of the graveyard lawn and the flaming yellow of their head-to-toe rain suits. They enclose me in a tight circle. The cabbie shies away, pretending to examine more gravestones. I ask after the grave by name, number, and marker quadrant. The eldest, with an air of deep church authority, consults the plastic-covered pages of his own more detailed map book. Rain spatters off the diagrams and the backs of his enormous hands. As I did, he looks from the page to the world and back again. He asks me to repeat the name.

When I do, the youngest of the crew says, "Is he the famous?"

I nod. The crew boss takes one more look at his pages and raises his huge hand to the sky like Moses calling down Yahweh's judgment. I thought he was going to deliver a benediction. Instead he lowers his hand slowly and his long, strong fingers arrange to point. The hand stops. His rock-solid finger aims at the tiny round stone beneath the black plastic arrow on the yellow plastic square. When he sees that I see it, he drops his hand and claps his book shut with a solemn air of Here Endeth the Lesson.

I thank him and turn away. The crew clambers back onto the tractor without a word. The cabbie leans under my small umbrella and there it is, six inches across, with Gram's name engraved around the curving circular rim in microscopic letters. Below Gram's name are words even more difficult to make out. I tiptoe a tiny arc around the tiny marker as it fills and overflows with rain, striving to make out the characters. GOD'S OWN SINGER, they read.

Myth and archetype define Gram Parsons, along with that most seductive of biographers' prisms: tragic irony. But being on guard against the seduction of tragic irony doesn't make the various tragedies surrounding Gram Parsons any less ironic. Or, if you prefer, doesn't make the various ironies any less tragic.

The official version for years has held that Gram's stepfather, Robert Parsons, chose the remote graveyard, the tiny marker, and the misplaced epitaph. He thought, the story goes, that he was choosing a quote from a song by Gram. But Gram Parsons never wrote that phrase. It was composed by Gram's Flying Burrito Brothers bandmate, Bernie Leadon, a future member of the Eagles, the band that most blatantly co-opted Gram's intentions and that Gram despised with a special loathing. More recent evidence suggests that someone other than Robert Parsons—a semisecret admirer, possibly a former lover—chose GOD'S OWN SINGER and did so with full knowledge of who wrote the song. So even the tragic ironies surrounding Gram exist in the smoke and mirrors of sorting myth from history, fact from truth.

I snap a couple photos of the absurdly small marker and shoot a few minutes of video. The isolated graveyard, the misinformed epitaph, and the confusion that accompanies trying to find this final resting place leave me unbearably sad. As in so many other instances, Gram Parsons deserved better. And if Gram Parsons was foremost in treating Gram Parsons worse than he deserved, that makes his grave no less heartbreaking.

Seeking to sort out and hold on to my feelings, I ask the cabbie to drive slowly around the cemetery on the way out. He tries, but steers us into construction, then into a dead end, and then has to drive in reverse a half mile to the cemetery gate.

It's difficult to maintain a grieving sense of transcendent connection while weaving backward at forty miles an hour through a graveyard while a cabbie curses under his breath in (supposedly) Moroccan French with a

Southern accent. Finally even he recognizes the lost spiritual momentum and is embarrassed into silence. We don't say much during the forty thunderstorm minutes back to my hotel. He promises to pick me up the next morning in time for my plane, but when I hit the street at eight A.M., he's nowhere in sight.

I'm on my own.

(A couple of years after my visit, an ornate bronze plaque featuring a bas-relief portrait of Gram with his guitar was laid on the grave site. On it, Gram's birthday is listed as November 7. His birthday is, in fact, November 5.)

CONTENTS

INTRODUCTION

GRAM PARSONS' LIFE IS A BIOGRAPHER'S DREAM AND NIGHTMARE, A WEALTH OF poetic contradictions and mythological motifs: suicidal parents, family wars over money, great talent undermined by inherited wealth and inherited addiction, innate genius at war with self-hatred and laziness, immense charm wasted in the service of unspeakable selfishness, rock-star sex, drugs and gossip, the most happening scenes of the era, feuding wives and lovers, a mysterious death, and a bizarre aftermath.

Gram's life raises the classic questions of the American wanderer: Where is my homeland? What is my tribe? How to assimilate when I'm overwhelmed by alienation? What if the voice that seems most natural is not the voice of my birth? Will changing my exterior ease the pain inside? And can that pain be transcended by its expression?

Was Gram Parsons' self-destructive life a search for answers to these questions, or an unrelenting effort to evade them?

The simple facts are these: Gram Parsons looked like a movie star, sang like an angel, wrote like a poet, slept with every woman he wanted, took the most and the best drugs, hung out with the coolest people, and set the musical trends for the next two generations.

Gram Parsons had everything—looks, cool, charm, charisma, money, style, genius, health, poetry, soul, chops, rapacious sexuality, and good fellowship—and threw it away with both hands, every minute of the day. As a musician, Gram was blessed with a high-lonesome tenor, the longest fingers anyone had ever seen, sufficient skills on piano and guitar, a discerning ear, a willingness to learn, an appreciation of history, an unerring instinct for the right place at the right time, and, according to Keith Richards of the Rolling Stones, "better coke than the mafia."

Gram's family wealth ensured he could do whatever he wanted. He never had to earn a living, and with his talent he should have left a large body of work. Sadly, only six heartbreaking albums testify to Gram's genius and to his propensity for wasting it.

Gram's determination to obliterate himself existed in direct proportion to his blessings. His urges were the hammer and his gifts the anvil on which his self-destruction was wrought.

Gram did not become increasingly, tragically romantic as drugs, self-destruction, and anomie took hold. He became something much more interesting than a wasting Byronic angel. Gram Parsons became an unregenerate, unrepentant dick: careless of his talents, faithless to his women, heartless to his friends, and heedless of his professional responsibilities. He abandoned his wife, cheated on his girlfriends, left every band he ever started, and made certain that no one could depend on him for anything. By Gram's own admission, if his lips were moving and he wasn't singing, he was most likely lying.

Yet even at his worst, everyone recognized the tragedy Gram embodied and everyone spoke of how sweet he was. Gram found that the most talented musicians in America would do anything for him, would tolerate all his whims and bullshit, just for the chance to hang out and be part of his music.

When Gram died at the age of twenty-six in the isolated Joshua Tree Inn near Joshua Tree, California, of an overdose of morphine and barbiturates, he left all the heartbreak and frustration in his wake that any tragic figure might. The other rock martyrs of his time—Jimi, Janis, and Jim Morrison—stand as icons, but each exists today as the representative of a musical genre that includes only themselves. Gram's influence ranges wider than any of theirs. Given the ever-increasing cross-pollination of musical forms, the enduring market dominance of country rock and country pop—and of the alt. country that emerged in reaction to them—it can be argued that Parsons exerted greater influence on our national musical taste than any other single musician.

Yet unlike Jimi, Janis, and Jim, Gram was not slain by the excesses of success. He never experienced real success. His demons were of his own making, formed out of the dysfunctional horrors of his family of origin and his own infinite carelessness.

TWENTY THOUSAND ROADS

ONE

COON DOG CONNOR
AND AVIS SNIVELY

GRAM PARSONS SPRANG FROM RICH WHITE TRASH AND RURAL GENTILITY. THE antecedents of Ingram Cecil Parsons, né Ingram Cecil Connor III, were pure Faulkner, his upbringing a catalog of Southern dysfunction. The critical pathway of his ancestry brings together the moralistic complacency of small-town wealth and the hunger of the small-town hustler: two key routes to the American dream, played out in their most lurid Southern form. Out of generations of wanting sprang a man who never pursued anything because he was too busy fleeing from himself.

Gram came from money, vast amounts of it, and alcohol, in equally vast amounts. He had three parents—his father, Ingram Cecil "Coon Dog" Connor; his mother, Avis Snively; and his stepfather, Robert Parsons—and amid all their differences and conflicts, pedigree, money, alcohol, and self-destruction ran through their lives like the helix of their doomed Southern DNA.

COON DOG CONNOR came out of his sky. He tilted the shark-painted mouth of his black Grumman P-40 Warhawk into a blinding shaft of glare and dropped straight down from the sun. When he thumbed the red button centered on his joystick, the wing-mounted .50-caliber machine guns made the whole plane shudder. The balsa-wood Zero in his crosshairs exploded into flinders. Dead Jap aviators floated like eiderdown through the soft warm air over the far southwestern Pacific. Turning his fighter back to the sun in search of new prey, Coon Dog Connor never saw them splash.

When he touched down on the clanking metal airstrip, his canopy was already shoved back. Coon Dog's mechanic ran alongside the plane in the crushing jungle heat, leaped onto the still-moving wing, and passed Coon Dog his celebratory bottle of Jack Daniel's . . . or maybe it was Rebel Yell or Maker's Mark or homemade jungle hooch; who knows?

Coon Dog Connor shot down numerous Japanese pilots over the Pacific Ocean in World War II, bombed and strafed even more of them when they were on the ground, and consumed vast quantities of whiskey, in the process becoming an Army Air Corps flying ace, a genuine war hero, and a certifiable alcoholic. After two years of aerial combat, Coon Dog sailed from New Guinea for Australia on a hospital ship. There he was treated for the malaria that eventually sent him stateside for good in 1944.

His specific flights, number of kills, and the date and route of his rotation back to the States vanished on July 12, 1973, when the Defense Department's World War II archives in East St. Louis, Illinois, went up in flames as all-consuming as those that broiled Coon Dog's airborne enemies. What we do know is where his unit served and in what battles they fought, and there's no question of Coon Dog's prowess, courage, or fightin' want-to.

Ingram Cecil Connor was bred to the military. He and his brother, Tom, attended their father's high school, Columbia Military Academy, in Columbia, Tennessee. Cecil's folks were native Tennesseans. His father was born in Mount Pleasant in 1887, his mother in Columbia in 1889, and both would outlive their son by more than a generation.

Cecil's dad came from a well-to-do farming family. His mom's father was a lawyer. Amid the rolling hills and small lakes of eastern Tennessee, that placed both families solidly in the haute bourgeoisie. Though the two families had been in the South—and well off—for more than a hundred years, and though they had illustrious ancestors who fought for the Confederacy in the Civil War, surviving family members insist that none of the Connors ever owned slaves. On this they are adamant.

After graduating from Draughn's Business College in Nashville, Cecil's father settled in Columbia. He worked as a sales rep for two Nashville hardware companies, Gray & Dudley and Keith-Simmons. He traveled for work and was seldom home during the week. He made an excellent living and provided a good life for his family.

Cecil, his younger sister, Pauline, and his brother, Tom, grew up on a dead-end street in a big formal house with an entrance hall, four bedrooms, and front and back porches. The front room held a piano and all three kids took lessons. Cecil's mother's side of the family supplied the musical genes. Cecil's maternal grandmother, Ella Dotson Kelly, played the organ at Columbia's First Methodist Church for thirty years. Grandma Kelly was always at the piano in the Connor parlor, playing but never singing. Cecil Connor never sang, either.

Pauline Wilkes, Cecil's sister, recalls three kinds of music in the household: hymns, classical, and big band. She remembers Tommy Dorsey, Jimmy Dorsey, Glenn Miller, Artie Shaw, and especially "Moonlight Serenade." The children took classical lessons three times a week, but their relationship to music was lighthearted. In high school and college Cecil clowned around with an old ukulele. When brother Tom attended Vanderbilt University, he followed in his grandmother's footsteps and played organ in church. "We never listened to country music," Pauline Wilkes says.

Cecil, Pauline, and Tom were raised in the old-school, small-town Southern manner, a manner that lingered well into the sixties. "We answered a question with 'sir' and 'ma'am,'" says Pauline Wilkes. "We stood up when an adult entered the room; that was good manners. We never questioned anything our parents told us to do. If they told us to do something or not do something, that was all that was necessary. That was the way children were brought up in the South. My children were raised the same. Gram was raised that way too, until his father died."

Columbia prospered as a mill town. When Maury County, of which Columbia is the county seat, was found to be full of phosphate, Monsanto and other big chemical companies built plants. The county's economy was rock solid and thriving. Cecil's father was on the road five days a week, but his family enjoyed their leisure.

Cecil's dad had grown up on a gentleman's farm; he was bred to the woods and loved hunting and fishing. As soon as his sons were old enough, they were given .410 shotguns. The .410 is a small gauge with a light kick, light enough for a young boy to shoot. Cecil Connor loved guns; he was an avid hunter and an excellent shot. In Columbia he hunted dove and quail, wandering through the fields with the family dogs; when he was stationed in New Guinea he wrote home of wild boar hunts in the jungle.

Their father bought the boys an Indian canoe in which they plied the local Duck River, paddling and swimming. Cecil had a best friend, Van Shapard, whom he met at the age of five; they stayed best friends for life. Together they took the canoe to the local landmark, Big Rock, for overnight campouts. Big Rock was known as the place where only boys swam. No girls were allowed.

Pauline Wilkes recalls lazy summer evenings with the neighborhood adults gathered on the deep shaded porch after dinner, watching their children play Kick the Can and Capture the Flag. Kids and parents always gathered at the Connor house.

All of Cecil's people concur: For all the good it did him later, Cecil Connor, a beloved son in a loving family, lived a sheltered, privileged, stressless childhood and adolescence. Life came easily to Cecil, as it would to his son.

Cecil was a Boy Scout. And when he left the Scouts in his teenage years his passion turned to cars and airplanes. Cecil's folks drove regular old vehicles, but Cecil dreamed of a red convertible. His other dreams centered on flight. He and his pal Van Shapard were always talking about planes and how they would learn to fly. When Cecil (and Shapard) entered Columbia Military, his ambitions were all about the Air Corps. The school closed after World War II, but for the time it had a demanding curriculum.

As a young man Cecil's eyes seemed to slant a bit, so the first nickname he acquired at Columbia Military was "Chink." That was the name everyone in town, children and adults, called him. "Chink" was in the old Southern manner, too.

Pauline Wilkes remembers her brother as "an extremely popular boy. He was a good-looking boy all his life. My friends would come over just to be with him." Although Cecil dated often, he had no great love in high school. Already Cecil manifested the same quality of relaxed separateness that would mark his son.

Cecil grew to be manly, affable, charming, and socially at ease. At Columbia he became a student leader and the alpha of his social pack, pulling out his ever-present ukulele at parties and taking it on dates. In school he devoted himself to the Reserve Officers' Training Corps (ROTC) to ensure that he would join the service as an officer, because it was officers who became pilots.

When Cecil graduated, he and Van Shapard set off for Alabama Polytechnic Institute in Auburn. Established in 1856 and made coed in 1892, the Polytechnic is today better known by the name it took in 1961: Auburn

University. Van Shapard and Cecil studied aeronautical engineering and both were officers in the ROTC. Cecil's family says he graduated in 1939. Auburn University disagrees; he attended Alabama Polytechnic, but no record exists that he left with a degree.

In any event, when Cecil was done with college, his and Van Shapard's paths diverged. After joining the Army Air Corps together, Cecil stayed in the Army while Van Shapard opted for the Flying Tigers. Cecil would end up in the Pacific Theater; Van Shapard would fly "over the hump" from India to China over the Himalayas.

Cecil took his aviation training at Kelly Field in Texas. During training he drove around Kelly Field in the red convertible he'd always wanted. On May 11, 1940, he graduated flight school and was commissioned a second lieutenant in the Army Air Corps. His proud mother pinned his flight wings to his chest.

Cecil remained at Kelly Field until March 1941, when he transferred to Wheeler Field near Pearl Harbor in Hawaii. There Cecil Connor did not live like an ordinary officer. His life aligned more closely with the languidly structured peacetime pleasure dome depicted in *From Here to Eternity*. Cecil rented a house on Diamond Head and acquired another red convertible. In addition to being tall, handsome, socially adept, and well-to-do, Cecil was also a pilot, which at the time was among the coolest, most badass identities a man could earn. He lived in the most beautiful place in the world and he tore around that paradise in a new red convertible. Cecil Connor did not live like an Army Air Corps second lieutenant—he lived like a rock star.

The rock-star life came to a halt when the Japanese bombed Pearl Harbor on the morning of December 7, 1941. Asleep on Diamond Head, Cecil was awakened by explosions—he could see Japanese planes over Pearl from his house. He leapt into his red convertible and raced to Wheeler Field. When Cecil got there, the base was a shambles. Bomb craters littered the runway, planes were burning on the ground, and the few hangars still standing were in ruins. There was nothing Cecil Connor could do. After the war, he told a coworker, "I didn't even get up to my plane to get it cranked up . . . but I made up for that later on." If in civilian life Cecil was sometimes regarded as a hard-drinking laggard with an overdeveloped gift for indolence, during the war there was no questioning his sense of duty or adventure.

With Wheeler Field destroyed, Cecil's 6th Pursuit Squadron of the 18th Fighter Group shifted to Kahuku on Hawaii and later to Kipapa Field until they were sent overseas late in 1942. The 6th Pursuit had trained as interceptors, meaning they flew close support for bombers. In May 1942 their name was changed to the 6th Fighter Squadron, and later to the 6th Night Fighter Squadron. Their mission changed with their name. They would still escort bombers, but they were also turned loose to pursue aerial combat and to execute bombing and attack runs on their own. The 6th Night Fighters were sent to the Pacific to be aggressors.

In honor of their new name, their emblem became a gray skull outlined in black, the outline forming the hub of a spinning propeller blade in black on an orange background. Painted on the side of each plane below that emblem was the squadron's nickname: the Flying Vampires.

Here history gets a little murky; surviving records address the Flying Vampires as a unit and not Cecil specifically. At some point in late 1942, the 6th Night Fighters headed out of Pearl Harbor to war. In January 1943 they spearheaded an extended attack on Japanese forces centered around Munda Airfield, on the island of New Georgia, in the Solomons. Cecil's group attacked a Japanese transport at sea; they bombed an airfield on Bougainville Island; they assaulted Munda field repeatedly. All this was in support of the U.S. Marines' invasion of and attempt to secure Guadalcanal Island.

At some point while fighting the war, stationed somewhere in the Pacific—most likely New Guinea—and bombing jungle airfields at night, Chink Connor became Coon Dog. And Coon Dog he remained for the rest of his life.

While *coon* was the South's vilest, most hateful racial epithet during Cecil Connor's time, there's no evidence that his nickname derived from that slur. Cecil was a well-bred, civilized Southerner, and no one remembers him ever using or condoning that kind of language. But raccoon hunting was, and remains, a popular slice of backwoods Southern culture. And if you're going to hunt raccoons, you got to have coon dogs. There are two ways of hunting raccoons, and neither could exist without the dogs. In one variant, the dogs track the scent of a raccoon, find the beast, harry it through the woods, and, if the raccoon outruns them—if it doesn't turn and fight—chase it up a tree. When the hunters catch up to the dogs, which can take a while, they shoot the raccoon down so the dogs can rip it to shreds. Another method is more amiable: The hunters send their dogs out to find a raccoon somewhere in the summer night and sit around a fire drinking and listening as the dogs' voices cut through the humid darkness. An experienced dog handler can tell when his hound is on the scent, when it's on the chase, when it's treed a raccoon, and when it lies down to sleep at the bottom of the tree. Dawn finds the dogs loping back into the camp from however far off they might have treed their prey.

It's probably from those hounds that Coon Dog got his name. He became Coon Dog in New Guinea and never told anyone why. Raccoons, however, can be mean sumbitches when brought to bay. So coon dogs necessarily must be tough themselves. And fearless. And besotted with the hunt. Coon dogs are also Southern to the core; blessed with loping strides, gentle natures, and big, soft, brown eyes. As was Cecil Connor.

The Flying Vampires bombed enemy installations at Rekata Bay. They strafed Japanese bunkers while providing air support for ground troops on Guadalcanal. They ran a night raid—well out over the ocean—on Munda once more. On January 15, 1943, they attacked a flotilla of enemy destroyers at sea and shot down twelve Japanese floatplanes that rose to intercept them. The Flying Vampires, roaming over tiny island fortresses and vast waters, were ass kickers.

With Coon Dog in their midst, the Vampires kicked so much ass that the Japanese took personal notice. Throughout the war, the Japanese war ministry operated a propaganda radio show that broadcast war news (accurate when it reflected their gains, distorted when it did not) with a signal strength that could be received all over the Pacific. Marines at their bases, pilots at their fields, sailors on their ships: Everybody tuned in. The main draw was the voice of the broadcaster, a woman's voice, almost completely free of Japanese intonation or accent, Americanized, feminine, sultry, and full of promising insinuation—what today we might regard as the perfect phone-sex operator's instrument. This was Tokyo Rose, who every night went on the air to mock the American war effort. And every night the Americans listened.

Tokyo Rose allowed the Japanese to demonstrate, for a while anyway, their remarkable intelligence work and sometimes astonishing knowledge of the personal lives and habits of their enemies, whom they named on the air. More than once Tokyo Rose mentioned Coon Dog by his nickname and cited his fight wing, the Renegades. She named the targets Coon Dog hit and added, "But now you had better watch yourself. We know who you are and where you are and we're going to get you."

But the Japanese did not get Coon Dog. In July 1943, after being promoted to major, Coon Dog received the Air Medal. His commanding officer, General George G. Kenny, wrote to Coon Dog's mom back home in Tennessee: "I would like to tell you how genuinely proud I am to have such men as your son in my command and how gratified I am to know that young Americans with such courage and resourcefulness are fighting our country's battles against the aggressor nations. You, Mrs. Connor, have every reason to share that pride and gratification."

Mosquitoes accomplished what the Japanese could not: Coon Dog's flying days were ended by malaria. In August 1943, Coon Dog, wracked by blinding headaches, bone-shaking fevers, drenching night sweats, delirium, loss of weight, and the psychological punishment of being physically unable to fly (or get out of bed), was hospitalized in New Guinea. He left New Guinea by hospital ship en route to a long recovery in Australia.

He returned stateside in '44, assigned as an air inspector to Bartow Field in central Florida. Upon arrival at his new station Coon Dog got another red convertible, a Buick. He did not discuss the war with his family. "I heard that most soldiers were changed emotionally," his sister says, "but he didn't talk to me about that. I don't think he would talk to any of the family about anything sad."

She adds, "Malaria certainly zaps your strings, and he had a hard time. It took him a long while to get his strength back, and he was as sweet as ever. If there was anything wrong, we certainly didn't know it."

While Coon Dog was down in Florida, he sent his family a letter telling them he had met a girl. That girl was Avis Snively. She and her family lived in Winter Haven, the town adjacent to Bartow Field. Avis was "a nice girl," Coon Dog told his sister. But she was more than that. The Snivelys were one of the wealthiest families in the South. In Winter Haven, a center of Florida orange growing, they were outright royalty.

COON DOG came from people who stayed put, who had taken root in the rolling hills of middle Tennessee before the Civil War and had never strayed. Avis Snively's ancestors arrived in America even before Coon Dog's—by the time Avis was born to the Snively empire, her bloodlines had been American since before America existed—but the Snivelys showed more restless spirit, more entrepreneurial hustle.

The first Snively on these shores was Johan Jacob Schnebele, who fled Switzerland for Lancaster, Pennsylvania, in 1714. Genealogical records in Polk County, Florida—home to the Snively family seat of Winter Haven—record that Johan Jacob "came to this country to escape religious persecution and availed himself of the religious freedom guaranteed in the province of William Penn." He became a Philadelphia citizen in 1729 and had one son, to whom he gave the English version of his own name, John. John begat two boys and christened the older one John as well. At some point Schnebele became Anglicized to Snively, and naming the firstborn son John became a Snively tradition.

Johan's progeny were ambitious and headed west straightaway, establishing themselves in Ohio in the late 1700s. The Polk County records describe one of Avis' eighteenth-century Snively forebears as "a woman of strong character, as family tradition tells us, who combined the habitual thrift of the German Swiss with the energy of the American pioneer." Habitual thrift had leached out of the Snively gene pool by the time Avis came along, but not the strong character.

Johan's great-great-grandson John A. came from the Ohio Snivelys. Or maybe the Pennsylvania branch; the documents are contradictory. His family lived on one side or another of the Pennsylvania-Ohio line. John A., born in 1889, worked for the railroad, and his regular run took him to Akron. There he met Dorothy De Haven, a member of a storied mid-American family. Dorothy's ancestors, four brothers, loaned George Washington $450,000 in 1777 to help the government defray the expense of fighting the British. After the Revolution, the De Havens were offered restitution in (useless) Continental dollars and, prudently, refused. De Haven descendants are still dunning the U.S. government for a debt they claim has reached—with two-hundred-plus years of interest—something like $105 billion.

John A.'s family lived a few rungs lower on the social ladder. He courted Dorothy for five years before she agreed to their marriage, which took place in Akron on September 13, 1911. For their honeymoon they drove to Winter Haven, Florida, in the middle of the state, to visit Dorothy's Aunt Florence, who had moved south for her health. Aunt Flo had so many visitors that her house gradually expanded to become a hotel, the Florence Villa. The De Havens dictated that the newlyweds should move to Winter Haven to look after Flo, so they did. Soon after their arrival, John A. purchased a twelve-acre orange grove.

Citrus had loomed large in Florida ever since the early 1500s, when the Spanish, or rather their Indian slaves, planted citrus groves around St. Augustine, Florida, the oldest city on the continent. A severe freeze in 1835 drove farmers to the warmer central part of the state, but even there the vagaries of the weather made citrus a boom-and-bust business that required perseverance and deep pockets. And it bred leisure, at least for those who owned the groves: Growers routinely took off the months of May to September.

Snively's entry into the citrus business coincided with state efforts to stabilize the industry. In that same year, 1911, Florida introduced regulations that made it illegal to sell immature trees. Other rules that followed created standards for a properly ripened orange. (At the time, grapefruit were considered a backyard decorative fruit, something that looked nice hanging on a tree rather than destined for a table.) The new regulations meant statewide inspections and thus more standardization—a boon for large operators but not for small family farms.

John A. had only a fifth-grade education but no lack of the Snively pioneer spirit. Family members, business partners, and employees describe him as charming, shrewd, ambitious, domineering, and hard-assed. By the age of twenty-three he had become the family patriarch. His younger brothers, Thomas Vinton and Harvey Bowden Snively, moved to Winter Haven to work for their brother. Thomas came south in 1917 and Harvey in 1919. John ruled his brothers and two generations of subsequent Snivelys with an iron fist. He didn't bother with the velvet glove. He was famous for his method of choosing business associates. A former partner describes John A.'s technique: "When a salesman, a fruit buyer, or whatever would come into his office, John A. would tell him: 'Don't say a word. Sit down on the couch.' And he'd study him for a while, do a little business on the phone, keep looking at him a bit. Then John A. would say: 'I don't like you. Get out of my office.' Or, 'I like you. We're gonna do some business.'"

John A. and Dorothy's first child, a son, was born in 1915. Baptized John, the boy was known as John Junior and his dad became John Senior or Papa John. (The Snivelys and their cousins go by a confusing blizzard of nicknames. "Coon Dog" wouldn't have fazed them for a second.) Dorothy De Haven Snively was called Haney all her life. Their older daughter, Evalyn, known as Dede, was born in 1919. Avis followed on June 8, 1923.

At first John Senior sold fertilizer and worked as a grove caretaker. Like a Horatio Alger hero, he learned the orange business from the ground up and worked hard. Unlike a Horatio Alger hero, he had backing. The money came from "Yankee investors" and his De Haven in-laws. As early as 1924

John Senior created Haven Villas Corporation, a land-development business. Haven Villas developed a pair of successful two-thousand-lot subdivisions. One, Florence Villa, was built right across the street from Haney's aunt's hotel and named in its honor. In 1925, brother Harvey cofounded the Snively-Giddings Construction Company, which built homes for subdivisions. Meanwhile Thomas Snively began as a field foreman and graduated to running the trucking department in the grove he supervised. He hired out planting groves and started a fruit-hauling business.

Freezes in 1917 and 1927 and the appearance of the dreaded Mediterranean fruit fly hit citrus growers hard. The apocalyptic freeze of 1927 drove orange prices up but the price of groveland down; small growers went bust all over central Florida. In 1928, exploiting the bust, John A. Snively bought a half interest in an eight-hundred-acre tract of orange groves. A few years later, with the Great Depression in full force and prices at their lowest, John Senior "bought everything in sight," recalls Evalyn "Dede" Snively's son, Rob Hoskins. "He was sitting in the driver's seat. And when the country started coming out of the Depression he had property, he had income, he had a way of building a fortune faster."

Where others failed, John A. Snively and his brothers prospered, buying out competitors as the Great Depression wiped them out one by one. They didn't just buy groves. In 1934 John Senior and Thomas opened a packing house and incorporated as the Polk Packing Association. Twenty years later John Senior recalled that move in *Snively Groves*, a self-published book detailing his history in citrus. "Up until 1934 I spent my time selling fertilizer, taking care of groves for other people, and making groves for myself," he wrote. "At that time business was so bad that I came to the conclusion that the only way to exist was to have a packing house of my own. Thus in 1934 I built a small unit on the present location and a great many of the people who are working here now helped to build that packing plant. Most of the lumber came from trees around the edges of our own groves. Many times that lumber was a green pine tree in the morning and part of the packing house that night."

Another Snively acquisition was an undeveloped swamp that would become the lakes and gardens of the quintessential fifties tourist resort, Cypress Gardens.

Cypress Gardens made its money from Yankee snowbirds who came to experience elaborate tropical gardens festooned with beautiful Southern girls in antebellum dress. The main draw later became waterskiing stunt shows, with tanned, blond Floridians leaping off ramps and doing airborne tricks. The famous finale of the Cypress Gardens show was the appearance of their equivalent of the Rockettes: four handsome men and six young women waterskiing in a pyramid. The classic Cypress Gardens pyramid pose—head turned to show a gleaming smile, one arm straight out holding the towrope and the other straight overhead (sometimes grasping a flag)—became an icon for 1950s and early '60s Florida tourism. A Cypress Gardens beauty in that pose would one day adorn the label on every can of Snively Groves orange juice and concentrate. But instead of a flag, the beauty on the label held aloft a can of Snively OJ.

Legend has it that in 1932 John Senior and waterskiing pioneer Dick Pope spent a drunken night betting on what they were seeing in the moonlight across a swampy lake. Was that a duck? Was it a manatee? After betting, the men jumped into John Senior's boat, sped across the lake, and found out who was right. After Pope whupped John Senior in a few wagers, he said: "Lease me this damn swamp for ninety-nine years for a buck, and I'll show you what I can do with it!" John Senior was game. He leased the lake and its surrounding lands—thirty-seven acres all told—to Dick Pope for ninety-nine years for the sum total of one dollar.

John Senior also loaned Dick Pope his start-up money and was repaid through a secret arrangement that granted John Senior 20 percent of Cypress Gardens' stock. The Popes' and Snivelys' respective empires, Cypress Gardens and Snively Groves, would be intertwined for the next forty years, and in the end both dynasties would come to ruin in the hands of the founders' firstborn sons. But Pope's enterprise, absurd as it seemed at the outset, outlasted John Senior's by twenty-some years: Cypress Gardens opened June 7, 1936, and drew tourists under its various owners until it finally closed on April 12, 2003.

On opening day, admission was twenty-five cents. Pope took a lot of grief from local papers for opening a tourist garden in an undeveloped swamp. They called him "the Swami of the Swamp" and "the Maharaja of Muck." As Pope proved the skeptics wrong, those names faded and Pope became—possibly at his publicist's behest—Mr. Florida. "Cypress Gardens," says a spokesperson from the Central Florida Visitors and Convention Bureau, "put Polk County on the map in the 1930s." And it's arguable that Dick Pope is single-handedly responsible for the popularity of two mainstream American pastimes: waterskiing and going to Florida to visit a themed tourist park.

Florida's image as a paradise playground was key to John A. Snively's business, too. A former Cypress Gardens pyramid lovely, Cornelia Snively Wallace, married John Snively III, John A.'s grandson. (She later became the second wife of former Alabama governor and controversial presidential candidate George Wallace.) Cornelia remembers how John Senior attracted investors: "He played golf with all the Yankees. He told them if they wanted to invest in orange groves, they should pay for the land and he would grow the trees, tend the groves, and pick. The Yankees all wanted groves in Florida. They never seemed to care if they made money, and I don't know if John Senior ever sent them any or not. Later John Senior would golf with richer Yankees, and he talked them into making loans to him. Because of the loans, his books never showed any profit, and he never paid any taxes."

In 1938 John Senior built a house as a gift to his wife, Haney. Fashioned in a New Orleans mode, it was a two-story redbrick mansion with elaborate ironwork balconies and railings and faced with large white Tara-style columns. "Five bedrooms, five baths, a fireplace in the living room, dining room, master bedroom, and den, a sun porch downstairs, and a Florida room," recalls grandson Rob Hoskins. "Fourteen-foot ceilings. The entry foyer had a spiral staircase, and every year a giant Christmas tree was in that entry. In the center of the house was a huge atrium with windows looking out at the lake." (The Snivelys' private lake, of course.) "Eat-in kitchen as big as a small house, and the master bath upstairs encompassed two-thirds of the kitchen. It had the first shower I ever saw with five shower heads."

The family fortune was secured in 1945 with the development of the technology to make orange juice concentrate. Concentrated OJ became an American staple. Processing concentrate required a lot of oranges, and demand went through the roof. With that demand came the planting of ever-increasing acreage, the development of hardier, juicier oranges, and the building of more processing plants. More oranges also meant more boxes. John Senior merged Polk Packing with Snively Groves in 1956, creating one of the largest citrus operations in Florida.

In 1950 the entire complex was destroyed by fire. John Senior's family and his business associates expected him to take the insurance money and move on to other investments. Instead he rebuilt everything, declaring both his determination that his empire continue and his concern for his workers. "He was a hard-ass, but he had a heart of gold when it came to his employees," recalls his grandson Jack Snively. "He was a shrewd businessman but believed in taking care of his people." In 1949 John Senior donated land down the street from the Snively Groves offices for an elementary school in the farming town of Eloise (now incorporated into greater Winter Haven). In 1959, after his death, the school was named the Snively Elementary School of Choice. A wing of the Winter Haven hospital also bears John Senior's name. So does Snively Avenue.

As John Senior's business grew, so did his local prestige. He invested in real estate and became a director of the Exchange National Bank of Winter Haven and a director of the railroad. There was no such thing as a Southern businessman of that era who wasn't active in the Rotary Club, and John Senior became the Rotary's local leader. He was a city commissioner, a Master Mason, a director of the Florida Citrus Exchange, and cofounded a powerful trade association, the Florida Citrus Mutual. It's credited with "stabilizing the industry," which presumably means setting prices, discouraging newcomers, and keeping the workers in line.

The Snivelys became the financial engine of Winter Haven. From late September to May, the Snively Groves employed upward of two thousand people, with fifty in accounting alone. Most of what comprises Winter Haven today beyond the downtown core was once all Snively Groves. Naturally, the family dominated the town's social life, too. "The Snivelys were perceived as the crème de la crème," says Dode Whitaker, one of Avis' younger Winter Haven cousins. Although the admiration "centered on Haney and Papa John, the rest of the family was included. They lived like it, too. I remember when Haney got the first air-conditioned Cadillac. It was the only one in town and you had to go all the way to Tampa to get it. . . . If you saw that Caddy, you knew who it was."

John Senior exerted his power at home as well, meddling in every aspect of his children's lives. "He considered himself strictly a railroad man," Cornelia Snively Wallace recalls. "He forbade any of his children to ever ride in an airplane. My father-in-law, John Junior, never set foot in one. He even rode the train to New York City to show his horses."

Rob Hoskins tells the story that after his birth, his parents and grandparents were sitting in the den with the newborn when John Senior asked daughter Evalyn what her new son would call her. "Mom, I guess," answered Evalyn. "He'll call you Dede like everyone else!" thundered John Senior.

"And I did," Hoskins adds. "I was sixteen or seventeen before I ever called Dede 'Mother.'"

John Senior routinely intervened between his children and grandchildren. "When my mother divorced my father, John Senior gave him a handful of cash and an ultimatum," Rob says. "He disappeared and I never heard from him until I was twenty-one years old."

Younger generations of Snivelys describe Rob's mother, Dede, as the brains of the family. Later, everyone knew how frustrated she was when the Snively kingdom passed to her much less capable brother, John Junior. "John Senior was smart enough to know that Dede should have been the one to run the company," cousin Dode Whitaker says. "She had a fantastic business brain. But he couldn't leave it to her. She was a female and he wasn't going to leave Snively Groves to a female."

The universe Dede and her younger sister, Avis, grew up in regarded men as leaders and women as ornaments. All of Avis' life, her money would be under the control of men, starting with her father. She was groomed to spend it in the style befitting her station as not just a Southern belle but a Snively princess.

She was sent to the Gibson School, a private girls' school in Winter Haven. The curriculum centered on horseback riding. The Snively driver took her to and from school each day. Later Avis boarded at a finishing school, the Southern Seminary, in Buena Vista, Virginia.

During her high school years, Avis grew into a Southern beauty. "She didn't walk, she floated," Dode Whitaker remembers. "She had a bit of an accent, was caring, gracious. She was almost like Princess Grace. She didn't demand attention but you wanted to give it to her."

Avis attended Fairmont College in Fairmont, West Virginia, then transferred to the University of Alabama in Tuscaloosa, where she spent most of World War II. She joined the Phi Mu sorority, becoming president of the house her senior year. "Our house wasn't the most frivolous," her roommate and friend, Rosina Rainero, recalls. "We weren't thought of as the best social house. Girls actually cared about getting good grades. Avis was the only girl that was loaded." Haney, Avis' mother, came up to Tuscaloosa to visit. She donated, in Avis' name, an ornate silver coffee service to the sorority. The other girls were stunned by the lavish gift.

Avis finished school in 1944 with a bachelor of arts degree in home economics. Rosina Rainero says, "She could have been anything at all, but she had no interest in a career."

❋ ❋ ❋

AVIS CAME HOME AFTER GRADUATION and met Coon Dog. While stationed at Bartow Field, near Winter Haven, he and seven other pilots, including his hell-raising buddy Whiskey Jack, rented a Mediterranean-style mansion from an heiress to the Packard automobile fortune. They called the mansion the Purity Palace. Avis and her girlfriends visited the Palace because they'd heard it was full of crazy pilots. Avis and Coon Dog soon became as inseparable as the service and Coon Dog's antics allowed.

"She told me about him right away," Rosina Rainero recalls. "She was crazy about him. I said, 'Well, when do you think you're getting married?' She said, 'Oh, he hasn't asked me yet.'"

In 1945 Coon Dog was transferred to an airfield in Perry, south of Tallahassee, where he served as an intelligence officer instructor. There he made do with less luxurious accommodations. One drunken night he and Whiskey Jack played "chicken": They both wanted the same parking place and each thought the other would back off. Neither did. Coon Dog drove his red Buick convertible right through the wall of his barracks. Whiskey Jack smashed his dark blue Oldsmobile convertible through the wall next to Coon Dog. Both ended up restricted to base.

During the week Coon Dog went to the movies alone every night. On weekends Avis made the two-hundred-mile drive from Winter Haven up to Perry. She never missed a single weekend while Coon Dog was confined to base. They went to on-base movies; there was nothing else to do. But it's not unimaginable that Coon Dog snuck off the base on some weekend nights. Avis stayed in town at a hotel. That she even drove up from central Florida alone in her own car, never mind got her own hotel room and perhaps met her boyfriend there, suggests the kind of free, wild spirit Avis possessed.

"And then," Coon Dog's sister, Pauline Wilkes, remembers, "he called us one night to say he was asking her to marry him."

The wedding was set for March 22, 1945. Pauline Wilkes rode the train from Columbia, Tennessee. She stayed with the Snivelys for a week of luncheons with the girls and family dinner parties, some at the homes of Snively friends, others at restaurants. There were cocktail parties every night and dinners after the parties. Coon Dog's parents and brother came down right before the wedding. When they met the Snivelys, the Connors were amazed. Coon Dog had not told them about the Snively mansion or the endless acres of Snively orange groves or the phalanx of liveried Snively servants or the millions and millions and millions of Snively dollars.

The Connors, typical of the Southern small-town genteel elite, put great store in quiet, insular confidence. They avoided displays of ostentation as they would scandal. The Snivelys were one of the wealthiest families in the South; they made no secret of their love of display.

Aside from the opulence of the Snively lifestyle, Pauline Wilkes was struck by their fondness for alcohol in a time and place where many among the genteel regarded drinking as sinful and uncouth. "I didn't have alcohol in my home, and when I went down there it was the first time I was exposed to it being in the home," Wilkes says. "I was surprised by how much there was and how freely it flowed. Avis and I were the same age. She was drinking cocktails before dinner and that sort of thing. I was unaccustomed to cocktails every night. The Snivelys were big into alcohol."

Coon Dog had grown into something of a patrician in bearing: He conveyed confidence, worldliness, and expectation. He did not seem awed or seduced by the Snively millions. But as it turned out, Coon Dog was outgunned. The Snivelys did not regard themselves as patricians. They regarded themselves as deities. No one in their solar system had their money, prestige, or power.

Coon Dog was marrying into the family as it was rising to what turned out to be the peak of its wealth and prominence. The Snively view of the marriage was not that the two families were blending, but that Coon Dog was coming under the auspices of the Snivelys. "My family were always suspicious of anyone who married into the family and what their intentions were," says Jack Snively, the son of Avis' brother, John Snively Junior. "My family viewed most outsiders as gold diggers. [A marriage] wasn't because they were in love with someone but because they wanted the money. Especially if they didn't come from a wealthy background."

Given that attitude, "under the Snively auspices" could be an oppressive place.

Coon Dog and Avis were married at the Snively mansion. "Avis was absolutely gorgeous at her wedding," Snively cousin Dode Whitaker says. "Porcelain skin, dark hair. She was on the grand staircase with her gown trailing down . . . swirling around her." The *Winter Haven Sentinel* society columnist's write-up of the "exquisitely simple" ceremony was suitably breathless, describing the banks of calla lilies, the bridal gown of heavy ivory slipper satin, and the reception, in which "the dining table of antique inlaid mahogany was covered with Belgian linen and filet lace and centered with the three-tiered wedding cake. Rolls filled with creamed chicken, mints in the shape of wedding rings and orange blossoms, salted nuts, wedding cake and champagne were served the guests."

After the wedding the newlyweds moved to Perry for a few months until Coon Dog served out his time. He was honorably discharged from the Army Air Corps on August 20 with the rank of major. He had spoken of a career in civil engineering, but the Snivelys had other plans.

TWO

WAYCROSS

As late as 2004, those arriving in Waycross, Georgia, by automobile from the south were greeted by a full-color billboard of Adolf Hitler standing tall with his arm outstretched in the Nazi salute. Below, in big black letters, is the legend ALL THOSE IN FAVOR OF GUN CONTROL, RAISE YOUR RIGHT ARM! Other roadside signs pertain to Jesus and his return. Waycross, like every Southern town, has a poor black section, a poor white section, nice suburbs, and middling neighborhoods in between. Tall, slender pines dominate the more expensive areas; almost every yard features a few. The local forests make for good bird hunting, if you don't mind the snakes.

Waycross' preeminent tourist attraction, the Okefenokee, is the largest swamp in North America, a seven-hundred-square-mile web of cypress and mangrove, alligators, mosquitoes, deer, bear, panthers, all manner of birds, towering trees, and shimmering mirror-black water. The acres and acres of grasslike plants that look like turf but float on the water's surface give the swamp an eerie quality. When the wind blows or the gators swim by or the humongous catfish jump, the "ground" appears to move. *Okefenokee*, a Seminole Indian word, translates as "land of the trembling earth."

In 1943 Snively Groves, driven by the need for a nonstop supply of slat-framed wooden orange crates to transport oranges from grove to processing and worried about wartime threats of a wood shortage, purchased a box-manufacturing plant in Waycross, at the time a dreary hick town of thirty-five thousand, surrounded by pine forests. While he was still stationed with the Air Corps in Perry, Coon Dog was made president of a Snively fruit-box manufacturing plant there. When he was discharged from the military, the Snivelys put him in charge of the Waycross plant. They sent him and his new wife to the swamplands of southeastern Georgia.

"It was never Coon Dog's idea to live in Waycross after the marriage and work that job," Avis' younger cousin Dode Whitaker says. "Papa John did it to him. When Coon Dog first was interested in Avis, Papa John looked for a way to control it. That's why he told Coon Dog where he had to work. If Coon Dog had gone out to do something on his own, Papa John would have had no control. Papa John wasn't threatened by Coon Dog; it was his way of taking care of the family to micromanage. Avis was always the favorite and he felt the need to protect his family."

Waycross was a failed railroad hub, a backwater. Surrounded by pine forests, it was the perfect place for a box-manufacturing plant. It was isolated (ten hours' drive from Atlanta), devoid of culture, and brutally hot, even by Georgia standards. Winter Haven might not have been Paris, but it had all those Snivelys and plenty of other orange-rich folks to play around with and show off to. Waycross had the box plant and the swamp.

Being posted to Waycross wasn't exile, but it was close.

There are two schools of thought on why the Snivelys sent their new son-in-law to Georgia. One holds that the Snivelys loved and respected Coon Dog and gave him a prestigious assignment that was easy to fulfill, a life of leisure with just enough work to preserve self-respect. Further, this theory states, the Snively Groves needed an uninterrupted supply of boxes and wanted to show the Waycross employees that their plant—the Snively holding farthest from Winter Haven—was a valued part of the Snively empire. It was so significant that the Snivelys sent their treasured son-in-law to make everything run smoothly.

A variant of this view argues that the Snivelys didn't think much of Coon Dog and put him out of harm's way by giving him a sinecure that nobody could screw up. This seems unlikely: If the Snivelys lacked respect for Coon Dog, they were about the only people who did.

The second and more credible theory—always expressed with vehemence—is that the Snivelys found Coon Dog too intelligent for their liking.

They shipped him off so that he could neither participate in nor comment on their machinations. By giving him a no-work job in Waycross, they hoped to short-circuit any misguided ambitions he might have had about actually putting his hands on a significant part of the Snively business. Or telling any of the Snively men how they should handle the money that so affected his wife's life.

Both theories have their adherents. The Snivelys insist the Waycross job was a mark of respect. Coon Dog's pals, a couple of his coworkers, and Gram's Waycross childhood friends believe the opposite. By the time Avis and Coon Dog moved to Georgia, Coon Dog was already a hard drinker, an everyday, daytime drinker, a young alcoholic. He exhibited traits that would later manifest in his son: a kindly remove, an ambivalence about the world of ambition, a winning charm that drew people toward him but left them baffled as to his essential nature, a love of fun and taking risks, a tendency to addiction, a surprising lack of common hypocrisy when it came to pursuing his pleasures, and a Southern gift for doing very little but doing it with grace.

Like his son later, Coon Dog was willing to go along to get along. That was especially true where his in-laws were concerned. Ben Smith, a state court judge in Waycross and a contemporary of Coon Dog's, describes him as "a well-liked, handsome fellow" who "was out of the loop there in that company." According to Judge Smith, Coon Dog "never participated at a high level. They just gave him a job so he'd have something to do."

THE NIGHT THAT Coon Dog and Avis first arrived in Waycross, the Hotel Ware, the best place in town, was full. But as it happened, the former movie theater manager from Perry Air Force Base, of all people, was running the Ware. He recognized Coon Dog and wangled the newlyweds a room.

The Connors moved to 514 MacDonald Street, a redbrick apartment building in the middle of town, and Coon Dog went to work at the box plant. He and Avis began building a house in Cherokee Heights, a new subdivision. When the Connors moved into their house, most of the side streets were still dirt. The subdivision was laid out in straight lines and eighty-foot lollipop pine trees stood guard over every house. These were the sort of trees that fed the Snively box plant: tall and lean, with no branches below fifty feet and then a thick cluster all the way to the top that made them sway gently in the slightest breeze.

Their new home at 1600 Suwannee Drive was a one-story ranch with a low peaked roof, a white brick façade, and stucco around the sides. It epitomized the 1950s ideal: three bedrooms, a living room, a wet bar, a large kitchen, and a Florida room with jalousied windows. The house was more Connor than Snively in its lack of ostentation. Avis' college friend Rosina Rainero recalls that the Snively princess toned down her lifestyle for Coon Dog. "When she went up to Waycross she was not given a lot of money, because Coon Dog wouldn't have been happy about it," Rainero says. "He wanted to live on what he earned. Once, we all went shopping [during a visit to Winter Haven] for matching shoes and purses and Avis wouldn't buy a thing. I said, 'Why don't you spend more on yourself?' She said, 'I don't need 'em. I don't want to make Coon Dog feel bad.'"

The young couple were hardly ascetic. Coon Dog was as car-crazy as ever. He got himself a white Thunderbird that first year in Waycross and he drove a new one every year thereafter. Avis always had a new Chevrolet station wagon.

In the Southern small-town way, Coon Dog and Avis had both grown up spending every daylight hour of their lives with a family of black servants. They maintained that tradition in their own household. Christine Dixon worked as the Connors' housekeeper, and later her younger brother and sister helped care for the Connor children. Johnny Barnes served as the household's chauffeur and handyman. On Saturday mornings Barnes would polish the shoes and then start on the sterling silver. "Everywhere you looked in the house there was silver," recalls Dickey Smith, who frequented the house as a child. "Silver serving sets sitting out, so they had to be polished. Johnny Barnes worked for the railroad on weekdays eight to four—that was the best-paying job [an African American] could have—but evenings and weekends he worked for the Connors."

The Connor house, along with the local country club and its pool and eighteen-hole golf course, became the social hub of a group that was select, insular, and hard-drinking. "These people were all well-to-do and many were the leaders of the town, young leaders," recalls Judge Smith. "They liked to dance; most played golf. I would say they were . . . I hesitate to use the word *wild*. They did drink and have what they called fun. They had wild parties and sure weren't your average churchgoing crowd."

"They were a popular couple and would entertain quite a bit," says Waycross attorney Edmund Pedrick. "Their parties were wonderful— Southern. In the kitchen everything was delicious. Drinks prepared ahead of time and all."

In Waycross, drinking was enough to stamp the Connors and their friends as daring. A family friend described the local culture's built-in hypocrisy by recalling a typical wedding that featured two receptions: a tee-total affair and, "for our close friends who liked to drink . . . another reception afterward."

Dickey Smith still remembers the wet bar in the Connors' living room and the awe it inspired in the neighborhood kids. At the time Waycross, heavily Southern Baptist, was reputed to have 140 churches and only six bars. "You know, in the South, and still to this day, a lot of these Southern Baptists try to hide their drinking," Dickey Smith says. "The story goes that Southern Baptists invented the drive-in liquor store so they wouldn't be seen getting out of their cars." In Waycross in the late forties and early fifties, he said, "partying" meant "taking a drink in public and admitting it. In this part of the woods everybody else went behind cover."

The Connors partied hard; they were tight with their friends. Coon Dog was a natural-born hell-raiser and Avis never developed much restraint in any sphere. According to some in Waycross, things in the Connor circle went a good deal further than merely enjoying a few cocktails. "Well, ye heard about the shoe parties, ain't ye?" one longtime resident said. When told no, he muttered, "Ohhh, if you ain't heard about the shoe parties, I cain't be the one to tell ye." A Coon Dog contemporary describes the "shoe game": "Have a party, your wife throws her shoe into a pile on the floor. A man picks up the shoe and your wife leaves with the man who picks it up. It was just the local version of wife swapping." In a Deep South Baptist town in 1947, shoe parties were way beyond hell-raising. They were positively avant-garde.

Others who knew Coon Dog and Avis dismiss such talk as vicious gossip. But everyone agrees that play—drinking, partying, hunting, driving his Thunderbird—meant a lot more to Coon Dog than work. "He drank a lot and he was more of a playboy type than a businessman, but he was a good man," says O. J. Cowart, Coon Dog's second in command at the box plant. Cowart had been hired when the plant opened in 1943, then went away to war and found Coon Dog nominally in charge when he returned. Cowart resumed running the place day to day. He traveled around south Georgia buying timber, had the timber shipped to Waycross, and supervised the cutting of the boards, the building of the boxes, and the shipping of the finished boxes to Winter Haven.

When Coon Dog arrived in 1945, the plant employed 160 people and, according to Cowart, "was the biggest employer in town after the railroad and the hospital." Larger than a football field, the plant included a covered outdoor storage space for logs and gigantic doors that opened for the trains that ran right through the building to be loaded with boxes. At its peak the plant produced a train-car load of roughly eight thousand boxes every working day.

"The Snivelys had to have somebody in the front who knew something about business; Coon Dog knew a little business but he couldn't tell one tree from another when it came to timber," Cowart says. "He was an easy boss. When he was first there my brother come over and we were wantin' to go fishin'. I went and told Coon Dog I wanted the day off to go fishin' and he said: *I'd* like to have the day off, too. But he never told me not to go."

A Waycross employee describes Coon Dog as "a real friendly boss who wasn't around too much. I know one morning he come out drunk and I went to him and said, 'Coon Dog, you don't need to be out here in this condition,' and he said, 'I guess you're right.' I led him back into this office and he was willing to go. He knew he shouldn't be out there 'cause he was subject to fall into one of the machines or something. But he didn't drink much at work as a rule. He seldom stayed around too long. He liked to show up in the mornings. He'd come out onto the working floor, watch for two or three hours, and then he was gone . . . that's all you'd see him."

The same man hunted with Coon Dog. "We used to go quail hunting," he says. "He got a golden retriever and we're walking along on this fella's farm and I said to Coon Dog, 'You ever gone hunting with this dog?' Coon Dog said, 'No, but he's trained and everything.' Once or twice this dog perked his ears up and a couple times a quail went into the sky. But we never got a shot off and I asked him again if he'd been hunting with that dog and Coon Dog said, 'No, he's trained, he's good, he just didn't show it today.' Coon Dog raised his gun up into the air and fired, just to shoot it. When he did that, that dog run off and we chased it all day and didn't get back to the car until after dark."

People liked Coon Dog. His status as a gentleman boss, both enviable and pathetic, and his easygoing charm made him approachable. He could hunt and fish with the rednecks and still hang at the country club. Avis was something else. Her Winter Haven friends cite her good heart. In Waycross Avis seemed to intimidate anyone outside her intimate circle. Her gravest sin in Waycross—a mortal sin in any small town—was that she was in it but never of it. When people there remember Avis, it's either as the most glamorous hostess in town or as a wild and arrogant girl, if not the village harlot.

A Waycross native who believes the "shoe game" rumors says, "There was a lot of that going on then. Avis was having some affairs with the higher society people. That's all she would hang out with anyway." In this way she was different from her husband. "Avis kind of looked down on normal people. Coon Dog didn't. Coon Dog was a down-to-earth fellow; that's what you'd find out if you talk to anybody that knew him at any point in his life."

Avis made an effort. She did civic good works, joining the Community Concert Association and the Service League, Waycross' version of the Junior League. But she was strong-willed and confrontational. She didn't hide what she thought any more than she hid her drinking. Like her daddy, she could shift from charming to hard-assed in a heartbeat. Avis moved through Waycross as if she were above it all and untouchable, which she was.

"She participated in a conversation when she thought it was worth listening to," Dode Whitaker recalls. "She never spoke out something that flashed in her mind. She felt a woman should be respected for the person she was, the mind that she had, the children she raised. Avis insisted on that respect; she knew who she was and she was content with who she was."

"She was a strong woman," says Avis' nephew Jack Snively. "She was opinionated and had no problem voicing her opinion. She made no secret of wanting things her way."

INGRAM CECIL CONNOR III WAS born on November 5, 1946. Avis went back to Winter Haven to give birth. She wanted her own doctors and she wanted to be near her family. Gram's birth, less than a year after the Connors moved to Waycross, established a pattern: Avis began going back and forth between the two towns. Most of the time Coon Dog stayed in Waycross.

Five years after Gram was born, Avis gave birth to his sister, also named Avis, on April 16, 1951. The daughter was known all her life as Little Avis, and her mother became Big Avis. Family and friends describe Gram as closer to his dad, while Little Avis was particularly attached to her mom.

Coon Dog and Big Avis are remembered as affectionate parents and a loving couple. The atmosphere in the Connor household made a strong impression on Gram's friends, including Dickey Smith. "I'd never seen a closer couple," he says. "I wish my parents would express affection like they did. They were both good-looking; he was handsome and she was very attractive. They were physical; they'd kiss Gram, they would kiss their little daughter a lot, if they were going somewhere they'd kiss good-bye. They'd tell each other 'I love you' in front of the children. Few families around here behaved like that at the time."

Coon Dog Connor, Gram, Little Avis, Big Avis Snively Connor. (Courtesy Pauline Wilkes)

A doting father, Coon Dog led Waycross' Cub Scout and, later, Boy Scout troop. He enjoyed spending time with his children and their friends. Waycross attorney Edmund Pedrick remembers, "Gram was a good boy and his daddy was so good with all the young boys. He was a scoutmaster and took them hunting and fishing." Coon Dog acquired an old open-top Model T Ford and drove Gram and his friends around town. His sister, Pauline Wilkes, recalls, "Coon Dog bought the car to amuse the children. He would take a few kids from the neighborhood and ride them all around Waycross. He wouldn't drive the car any other time; it was only for the children."

Coon Dog taught Gram to hunt and shoot, and they went out together often. Henry Clarke, another of Gram's childhood friends, remembers getting his first tutelage in weapons from Coon Dog: "We would go out in the woods at some of the property the Snively box company owned or were buying timber from, and Coon Dog would show us how to shoot pistols and rifles. He would teach us properly how to handle and respect the firearms. Any time that he could, Coon Dog would take us with him; he'd let us come out to the mill and watch them make fruit boxes."

"Work was not Coon Dog's life. His family was his life," Rosina Rainero says. "He wasn't a great PR man. He wasn't a dynamo trying to achieve big stuff. He was a fine person. He was kind and wonderful to Avis; I never heard him be ugly to anyone. He never raised his temper. They paid him well, he had a nice house, he enjoyed his friends. He was devoted to his children. . . . He was a real man-father to Gram and he just idolized Little Avis. She was his baby girl. He talked real well with Gram . . . he talked sense. He'd take him hunting and did men things with him, you know. He encouraged Gram's music very much, too."

Every Christmas the Connor family returned to the Snively mansion in Winter Haven. Dode Whitaker remembered Big Avis' station wagon filled with presents that Coon Dog brought down for all the Snively children, and Coon Dog moving among the kids, showing them how to assemble and use their toys. "Coon Dog and Avis were in love," she says. "I can remember them walking around the house with their arms around each other during the holidays, and Coon Dog bouncing babies on his knee."

Coon Dog and Big Avis may have been loving parents, but like other Southerners of their class and time, they left most of the day-to-day child rearing to the help. White professionals in Southern towns of this era typically had daily black household employees. The Connors just had more of them.

Louise Cone, née Dixon, housekeeper Christine Dixon's younger sister, was only twelve when she was hired as nanny-cum-playmate to Little Avis. Her older brother, Sammy, served the same role for Gram. Throughout her junior high and high school years, Louise Cone spent weekends with the Connors. She lived, played, and slept with Little Avis in the little girl's room. Even by the standards of the time, this was an unusual intimacy.

"It seems strange to say to this day that I would sleep in a white person's house next to the bed on the couch, but I've done it," Louise Cone remembers. "Strange because Waycross was like it was everywhere else: Blacks stayed in black places and whites went with whites.

"But even though we were in a prejudice town, I did not feel any prejudice that went on back in the 1950s and '60s because of who we were working for. The Snivelys and the Connors protected their workers. If you worked for them, you were sheltered. I mean, we were careful, you know?

But other whites would have respect for you if you worked for the Connors. And in Florida [with the Snivelys], the same thing. If you worked for them you weren't run over. You weren't pushed around. And I did not have to call the children Miss Avis and Mister Gram. They were Gram and Avis to us."

Cone describes the Connors as "sweet people" who allowed their black servants to sit down and eat with the children in the kitchen instead of making them go into a back room, and who gave generous gifts on birthdays and Christmas. "I wanted a bedroom set for my bedroom," Cone recalls. "[Big] Avis told me, 'Go on down to Shriver's and pick it out.' She said, 'You can pay me a little bit at a time for it.' But after I'd paid so much, Avis said, 'Forget it. It's a gift for you.'"

The Connors enjoyed giving presents to their children as well, gifts that reflected Coon Dog's own love of play. "Gram had tons of toys and gadgets and games," recalls Dickey Smith, who lived half a block from the Connors and became one of Gram's best friends in grade school. "In his backyard, he had a little roller coaster! You'd sit on a little wooden thing with wheels and it'd go up and swerve you. It would go about forty, fifty feet. He had this big wheel, you'd get in, put your feet and your hands in slots, and it would roll over and over and over. I mean, the toys he had were unbelievable. He had a little car that you controlled with a whistle; blow the whistle and it would change directions."

Gram's other close childhood buddy, Henry Clarke, has similar memories. "Gram had his own room, and a big toy closet. He had things we'd never seen, like Polaroid cameras." Gram's family was also remembered for having the first television with a remote control and the first yard with an automatic sprinkler system.

"I never told my parents much about that stuff," Dickey Smith says. "My mother would always say, if I ever complained about anything, 'I believe you've been over to the Connors' too much.' Meaning if you don't straighten up, you don't get to go back. So I left what I knew at Gram's house."

Smith never quite understood the way the Connors operated as parents. "They were loving parents, but in a different way. They had their maids, to take care of Little Avis, you know. They didn't spend what I'd call quality time with the children. They were always around, but not around with the children. My family was more, 'Let's all get in the car and go to Dairy Queen and get a Dilly Bar.' But his was more, 'Gram, you all need to go in the back; we're having company tonight.'

"Usually when Gram's mother drank she stayed on him about behaving and stuff like that. She'd get on him for running through the house or not having nice manners. When she wasn't drinking she pretty much left him alone."

Nevertheless, the evidence is that Gram, despite all his freedom, was usually well mannered. Dode Whitaker says, "There was no comparing the way Gram and Little Avis were raised with the rest of the Snively children. The others were indulged and grew up with no discipline. They didn't have the respect that Gram and Avis were raised with."

Dickey Smith remembers, "Gram was never disrespectful to his parents. Occasionally, if he really, really wanted something, he may talk back to them a little bit. But I can assure you, Coon Dog would straighten him out.

"He could be a little rowdy; he might take the mattresses off the bed to make a fort. He might tear up the room, but in the end nothing would be destroyed. We never did anything bad, but I could never even do *that* at my house.

"About the rowdiest thing we did, starting around fourth grade, we'd steal two cigarettes from his mother and his daddy and go down to the canal in the woods to smoke them. Kents, usually, though a couple times his dad had Home Runs. That first time we like to never got back, they were so strong. But we took a pair of smokes every Saturday and I've been smoking ever since."

Like other small-town upper-class Southerners of his time, Gram was raised to be a gentleman. His childhood was unfettered but contained within a world of carefully defined mores. "Most of us took dancing lessons," Dickey Smith says. "We went on Thursdays for eight weeks during the school year, to the Jordans'. They owned a furniture company and upstairs they had an empty warehouse. We learned to jitterbug and slow dance and do all sorts of fancy dancing. Card dancing: You have a little card and put each girl's name on it, so your first dance is with Karen and your next is Violet and so on. You'd be in the middle of dancing and someone would holler, 'Snowball!' which meant you had to change partners."

Gram's intelligence revealed itself early on. "I'll never forget how well he could read," Dickey Smith says. "In the second grade he was already an excellent reader. He made good grades without even trying. I think it was fourth grade, every day after lunch our teacher would read a book to us out loud. But at some point she let Gram do the reading every day; he read *Robinson Crusoe* to the whole class."

If it's possible to have a turning point in one's life at age nine, Gram experienced his on February 22, 1956. Daphne and Diane Delano, fourteen-year-old twin daughters of Fred and Thalia Delano, close friends of Coon Dog and Avis, took Gram with them to the City Auditorium in Waycross. There, with no adults to restrain his joy, Gram saw Elvis Presley—only a few weeks before Elvis' first hit single, "Heartbreak Hotel," would go number one on the pop, R&B, and country charts—open for country singer Little Jimmy Dickens. Gram saw Elvis so early in his career that Elvis had yet to break nationwide; he would not appear on *The Ed Sullivan Show* for another six months. After the concert, as was the custom then, the kids waited outside the stage door for Elvis' autograph. Gram got his and was smitten.

"Gram was a sweet child as long as you let him be Elvis Presley," Louise Cone says. "He loved Elvis Presley, imitating him and playing the piano. Even as a little boy. Our favorite thing was waiting for *The Ed Sullivan Show*. Gram would crawl onto the floor and watch and get up and go right along with Elvis. He had his guitar and he got right along with him. He'd shake his hips; he was an Elvis imitator, one hundred percent. Gram came up with Elvis in his heart."

Henry Clarke remembers that Gram's room was decorated with record jackets—"all Elvis." But Gram did more than imitate and admire. "Gram's fingers were long and thin," Dickey Smith says, "while mine were short and fat. He was made to play the piano. He took music lessons several times a week, always at four o'clock. He liked the faster songs, because normally when he played the piano it seemed like everything was fast."

He was a quick study with a good ear. "Gram was amazing," Clarke says. "He could hear a song on the radio or record and in a few minutes could sit down at a piano and pick it out."

"One time Gram came to my house," Dickey Smith recalls. "We had a piano. Nobody knew how to play it; it was furniture. My mother was in the kitchen and Gram said, 'I want you to listen to a song I've written.' She walked into the living room and Gram said, 'I call it "The Gram Boogie."' He started playing that thing and my mother sat down and listened to the whole song. And he couldn't have been more than third or fourth grade at the time."

FROM EARLY ON, music and women were central in Gram's life. Dickey Smith remembers, "During the school year, almost every Saturday we'd go to

Gram's house to play records and dance. This was in fifth grade, 1956, and rock and roll had hit its peak. Man, that was the thing. That's all we cared about. We jitterbugged. The girls might dance with each other, but when we played Johnny Mathis or something slow, the girls would dance with the boys. They were Gram's records but we let the girls pick the songs. We were always trying to butter them up."

The ritual Saturday dances at the Connors' were preceded by a ritual of preparation: buying records. That meant biking to downtown Waycross or being chauffeured. As Henry Clarke recalls, "Johnny Barnes would drive us down and stand around outside waiting for us."

The town was too small to have a music store. Instead the boys went to Ware Tire and Battery, where locals bought auto parts, bicycles . . . and records. "It was a service station where you could buy stuff, small appliances and such," Henry Clarke says. "Mr. Lipsey owned the old service station, and his wife enjoyed music so much they started selling it. There wasn't another record store in Waycross."

"The one time Elvis came to town, that's where they hung a poster for the show," Dickey Smith says. "They had little padded closets where you could go and listen to the 45s. Gram would get anywhere from ten to fifteen 45s a week. Coon Dog had a charge account and Gram picked up whatever he wanted.

"Gram bought a lot of Little Richard, Fats Domino, what I called the boogie-type records, real fast, like Jerry Lee Lewis . . . and all the Elvis. For Gram it was Elvis, Elvis, Elvis. He loved Elvis. Now Gram, in my opinion, looked like Elvis when he was young. He had dark, tan skin and dark hair. And Gram used Brylcreem—'A little dab'll do ya'—and he'd slick his hair back like Elvis."

Gram dressed sharp, too. "You could see that Gram always dressed a little different from us," Dickey Smith says. "Lordy, he wore white buck shoes. He had flowered shirts and we were wearing blue jeans and plaid shirts."

Most Saturday nights, Gram's friends remember, Big Avis and Coon Dog were not at home. Christine Dixon looked after the kids (more of that old Southern manner) while their parents spent their weekend evenings at the country club, drinking hard. Sometimes the kids' dance parties included playing spin the bottle. "When we did it at Gram's house you'd take the girl around the block," Dickey Smith says. "We called it a prom, like promenade. We were at an age where we were trying to get up the nerve to kiss the girls. We'd walk around the block and hold hands, and if you had the nerve you'd kiss 'em.

"We knew where all the dark streets were. The section we lived in had real big pines and five main roads and the rest of the streets are off to the side. In those days you didn't have a streetlight at every corner . . . we knew which streets were undeveloped and that's where we ended up."

As in music and reading, Gram was a prodigy at spin the bottle. He was never nervous around girls. He never assumed they wouldn't like him. And he was seldom rebuffed.

"It didn't bother Gram, kissing a girl," Dickey Smith says. "Not at all. I almost had to get him to kiss mine for me. I remember one time going with him to Florida around fifth grade and he was making out with some girl. He had a girlfriend at Cypress Gardens named Ginger. She'd sit on a bench in these big old skirts, Southern dresses, to make everything look pretty. She was probably sixteen or so when Gram was eleven or twelve. There were certain times of day where they'd go off in the little gardens and I'd kill time skipping rocks.

"Another time we went over to this girl's house and she had a pool. Gram and this girl were making out right there in the pool while I was practicing my backstroke."

ONE OF THE MOST surprising things about Gram's idyllic early upbringing is that as the best-dressed, smartest, richest, biggest-talking, and most toyed-up teacher's pet in Waycross, he apparently never got picked on or beaten up. In a small Southern hick town of that time, where all—white—economic classes shared the same public school and playground, this seems inconceivable. Was it Gram's charm that led him to be spared, or the awe his various gifts evoked, or the power of his family's status in Waycross?

In addition to everything else, Gram talked about himself—a lot. And what he said often seemed too fantastic to be true. "Gram tried to impress people," Dickey Smith says. "And he stood out. This seems horrible coming from a second grader and a male, but Gram was good-looking. But he told tales that were so far-fetched nobody would believe him. We always thought, right from the first, that Gram was a big fat liar. That he made things up. That his grandmother had this or his grandfather had that, from chauffeurs to pools, and nobody believed him."

Most of the other kids "tagged him as a liar," Smith says. Then Smith went along with Gram to Winter Haven one summer and saw that most of what Gram said was the truth.

"Around fourth grade he invited me and I went down with him two years in a row for around two, two and a half weeks," Dickey Smith says. "It was like winning the lottery. Travis the chauffeur would show up in a long green Cadillac, right at the house, and drove me and Gram to Winter Haven. And anytime we wanted to stop and buy anything, Travis would pay for it. He ate peanuts all the time; he thought they kept him from falling asleep.

"The second year I went by railroad, by train. We had to go to Nahunta, Georgia, to catch the train, to ride the Snivelys' private car. Everybody had their own bedrooms on the train. Mine and Gram's were joining, and they had brand-new toys waiting for us for the ride. I remember that Coon Dog was on this trip because Gram wanted to talk to his parents and we had to search for the bar car at the end of the train to find them.

"Gram's grandfather's house . . . that house was another world. First off, where we stayed, it was huge—to a fifth grader, there was no telling how many rooms it had. There was an Olympic-sized swimming pool, and the pool house was bigger than my house at home . . . Every morning we'd order whatever we wanted for breakfast by intercom. 'Did we want to come down or eat it in the room?'"

In Winter Haven even more than in Waycross, the adults busied themselves with their own pursuits and left the children in the care of the help. "In the daytime we'd swim in the pool," Dickey Smith remembers. "It had a huge sliding board into the deep end and a trampoline. We'd leap from the trampoline right into the pool. We swam a lot after we got snorkels and goggles and fins at the toy store. At night we'd go out and play Putt-Putt golf; Travis [the chauffeur] would take us. He would take us to the toy store to buy whatever we wanted. But I didn't take advantage of that. My parents would kill me if I came home with a bunch of toys.

"When we wanted to go skiing, they called somebody from Cypress Gardens to take us out between shows and teach me how to water-ski. They tried all afternoon to teach me and I never could get up. Back in Waycross my big brother bought a boat and we got a pair of skis and doggonit, the man who tried to teach me, Alfredo Mendoza, his name was on the skis! I had been taught by the world champion slalom skier!"

When Gram's parents were around, it was an occasion. Dickey Smith remembers, "The last time I went down there, in fifth grade, we went deep-sea fishing in the Gulf of Mexico in the family's forty-two-foot boat. We went tarpon fishing, and that's the only time I can remember doing anything with his folks. . . . Mr. Connor went with us this time; usually he stayed in Waycross all but two weeks of the summer working. Mrs. Connor spent the whole summer in Winter Haven but she didn't come on the fishing trip."

Dickey caught a fifty-pound tarpon. "They're no good to eat, and they asked me if I wanted to mount it. I said my mother and father probably don't want to pay to have it mounted. I mean, we weren't poor, but we didn't have fish on the walls in our house. My father always wanted a Cadillac but never bought one because he was afraid people would think he was making too much money. . . . So we cut the line and let it go. I mean, that's the kind of life it was down there. And it was fun for me, even though I was always told before I left, 'Now, don't come back spoiled.'"

No parents went along another day when the two boys were taken hunting. "I don't know what we were hunting for, doves or something. They took us out in an open jeep, which was unusual. I'd never ridden in a jeep. It had a two-way radio. We didn't see any birds so we shot every tin can we could. When we eventually did see some birds we were running out of shells. The driver radioed, I swear, and in about fifteen minutes a helicopter flew out with shotgun shells."

THREE

As superficially idyllic as Gram's childhood may have been, unhappiness was eating away at the Connor family. Big Avis began to suffer from depression and added pills to her heavy consumption of alcohol. It's not known what her prescription was: Given the era, most likely she was taking Seconals, or "mother's little helpers," amphetamines.

Coon Dog and Big Avis remained a charmed couple in the eyes of many around them. "If she left the room, he would always give her a big ol' Doris Day–type kiss," Dickey Smith says. He remembers how Gram's mother treasured a little wooden carving of a coon hound. "She could never go to bed without it. One time we were in Florida, she didn't have that coon dog, and she spent half the night searching for it before she could go to bed."

"I don't think that work was [Coon Dog's] forte, necessarily," Rosina Rainero says. "He didn't like it the best, but he was always happy with Avis and he always came home." She adds: "But Coon Dog drank a lot. He always drank a lot."

The Connors' friends may have been oblivious to the family's economic dynamic, but the help knew what was going on. Little Avis' nanny, Louise

Cone, remembers, "We always used to say that the rich person super-rules the ones that don't have as much. Avis was rich and, you know, the boss, more or less. [Coon Dog] had to do what the family said to him to do. But I stayed in my place. I did not get in their business."

Cone does not believe Big Avis exploited her advantage over her husband. "Avis was one of the most sweetest persons you'd ever want to know," she insists. "She was a lovely person, beautiful. . . . She knew how to carry herself. And everyone talks about her drinking, but I never saw her in a place where she didn't know what she was doing." The Connors' drinking "was all done at home. They weren't street people. They weren't rowdy. They weren't people who were all out and public with their stuff."

Cone minimizes Coon Dog's drinking as well. "Mr. Connor drank a little," she acknowledges. "But he was such a sweet person that when he drank he never hurt anybody; didn't hurt her, didn't hurt us. I can't ever remember him saying an unkind word to us. He never got riled up; he was never a riley person. He was a good person and loving to the kids. When he'd get like that [drunk], he'd go to his room."

In 1956, the Connors sent Gram away to Bolles, an expensive military academy in Jacksonville, Florida, about seventy-five miles away. "I guess his parents didn't think he was getting a good enough education locally," Dickey Smith says.

The decision to send their son away to a military academy when he was only ten years old indicates that the household was under strain, or that the Connors' hands-off parenting style was becoming even more distant. Nevertheless, Coon Dog and Big Avis visited Bolles frequently, often taking Gram's friends with them. "They usually went down to visit him a lot on weekends," Dickey Smith says. "I can remember going down there and shooting baskets in the Bolles gym." Gram did not return to Bolles the following year. He resumed attending public school in Waycross.

Things were not getting better at home. Coon Dog was under increasing pressure from Big Avis' always overbearing family. His sinecure at the box plant was a misery; the Snivelys bossed him around from afar, never asked for his opinion or acted on any of his ideas. More and more they treated him like hired help.

O. J. Cowart remembers a trip he took with Coon Dog to another Snively box-manufacturing plant in Baxley, Georgia. "He stopped at a liquor store and bought a pint of Old Forrester to drink in the car. We went up there to talk about expanding, doing different things with the mill. We had put up a building and had a big sawmill on that site. We had a foundation up there and talked about putting a new building on the foundation, something like twenty-four feet high, to stack the product in there." As always, the Snivelys weren't interested in what Coon Dog had to say. "Nothing ever come of it," Cowart says.

A few in Waycross claim something else was weighing on Coon Dog: Avis was stepping out on him. One of the box plant's employees was eager to share the wife-swapping stories: "I know they swapped wives. Something about the wives would put a house key somewhere and a bunch of them would go and get it. Whoever got the key got that wife." But he'd also heard that Avis had gone further, that she'd had a love affair with a local doctor. "A fella told me he caught this doctor with Mrs. Connor around five different times." Several other sources describe this putative affair. Edmund Pedrick, the Connor family attorney, says such stories are nonsense. "You have to understand that this absolutely did not happen with Avis," he insists. "It's ridiculous. That did not happen." But affair or no, Avis was unhappy and Coon Dog was clearly under great strain. Photos from this time show a man who looks a generation older than his years.

Coon Dog did not talk about his marriage or his troubles at the box plant, but those who worked with him knew he was not happy. Once he told the supervisor that he had quit drinking "just to prove to myself that I could quit. I wasn't trying to prove it to nobody else." Coon Dog stayed sober for a month. He told the supervisor that the reason he went off the wagon was because "his wife kept on drinking and so did all their friends."

Years later, Judge Smith shakes his head over the toll alcohol took on the Connors' crowd. "They had a circle of friends and nearly every one of those people has come to grief," he says, "had violent deaths or divorced or split up. And both of those people"—Coon Dog and Big Avis— "are dead."

DURING THIS TIME the Snively empire was reaching what turned out to be its apogee. By the late fifties the Snively holdings included eighteen thousand acres of orange groves; the family controlled fully 20 percent of the citrus industry in Florida and operated the largest family-owned, privately held citrus company in the world. The Snivelys made fresh orange juice; they were pioneers in marketing concentrate; they had their own fertilizer plant. They made tens of millions of dollars. Tens of millions of 1950s dollars. Their social prominence and high-flying lifestyle earned them comparisons to the Kennedys. And this family-owned, family-run dynasty featured all the outward unity and vicious infighting that dynasties breed.

Avis' father, John A. Snively Senior, had built all this with his own hands. In 1957, looking toward his own death, he predicted what would befall the Snivelys who survived him. "I'm leaving my family a whole hell of a lot of money," he told Travis, his wife's driver, "and in ten years it will all be gone."

He was pretty much right. Like many kings, he left behind an empire that would not outlive him by much. Dode Whitaker says, "He predicted the year of the demise of his family . . . how far the business would go down, and who wouldn't get what they were supposed to."

Snivelys not getting what they were supposed to would dominate family interactions for the next two generations. Nobody thinks they did, and who got what remains a sore subject to this day.

"John Senior was one of the richest men in Florida," Rob Hoskins says. "When he died, his fortune in today's money was probably between two and three hundred million dollars, and there ain't none of it left!"

John A. Snively Senior died in January 1958 of age, drinking, and disappointment in his offspring. John Junior was more interested in show horses than business. Spending, not building, had become the family passion. John (Jack) Snively IV says of his great-grandfather, John Senior, "He started small and kept reinvesting. When he rebuilt the packing house in 1950 it was the largest packing house in the world. He did it through hard work and being frugal. Unfortunately, the generations after him were not so frugal, and they lost it all." Nothing fuels disappointment like alcohol, and John Senior was a dedicated drinker. Jack Snively says, "The one thing that destroyed my family was alcohol. My great-grandfather was an alcoholic, my grandfather was an alcoholic . . . when you look at the history of the family, alcoholism is rampant. Alcohol is what created all the divisions in the family."

Dode Whitaker recalls that during family gatherings, "Papa John stayed back in his den. There was a bar next door to the den . . . the other men spent most of their time in that bar. Papa John was back in his office." Rosina Rainero remembers, "If you ever wanted to see Papa John, you had to go back to find him in that den. He stayed in there and insisted that people come back to talk to him." Despite all the parties and the nominal family closeness, Dode Whitaker says, "within the group there was such isolation. Isolation from all that drinking. Alcoholism was a problem with the entire family."

Heavy drinking was institutionalized in the Snively universe. Dickey Smith remembers visiting the orange-processing plant during his sojourns in Winter Haven with Gram and seeing special concentrate, made only for the Snively family's use, that combined orange juice and alcohol—ready-made screwdrivers. "The way you could tell was the Cypress Gardens orange juice [the commercial product] had a picture of a man skiing with a lady riding on his shoulders holding a flag. Well, for the family's OJ screwdrivers, that lady was topless. I remember them showing that to me."

Avis had been Papa John's favorite. His death hit her hard. She spent even more time in Winter Haven with her children, leaving Coon Dog on his own. The demise of the family patriarch stirred up the surviving Snivelys and increased the pressure on Coon Dog. Though he might have been a Snively Groves vice president, in the family view he was nothing but Big Avis' consort.

When his wife and children were off in Florida, Coon Dog's life had little purpose. O. J. Cowart offers a grim memory: "He spent a lot of office time making a special stock for his rifle. He had a regular piece of glass that he sharpened, and he'd shave that stock down. He spent hours on it, and most of the time he spent out at the plant he spent working on that gun stock. He had a stool he sat on and had that thing in a vise where he could shave it, and he worked on it I don't know how many hours."

Had Avis told Coon Dog she was going to file for divorce after Christmas, as some have claimed? Or did she love him more than ever and carry a small hand-carved coon hound wherever she went? Did her family poison her connection to her husband with its meddling and belittling; had Avis come over to their view? Was she sleeping her way through Waycross, as a chorus of anonymous sources insists, or was she a devoted and loving wife? At this distance it's hard to say. What's clear is that by the end of 1958, just after Gram turned twelve, Coon Dog had had enough.

THAT YEAR Coon Dog bought a special Christmas present for his son. Recognizing Gram's love of music and music-making, Coon Dog bought him a reel-to-reel tape recorder. Given that home reel-to-reels were about as common in Waycross as remote-control TVs, it was a grand and esoteric gift.

On December 21 Coon Dog drove Avis, the kids, Johnny Barnes, and Louise Cone to the Waycross train depot. They set off for Winter Haven and Coon Dog went home. He told them he would drive down to Florida by himself on the twenty-third.

Later that day he phoned Gram's friends Dickey Smith and Henry Clarke. "Gram was getting a reel-to-reel tape recorder," Smith recalls. "It was going to be his big gift. Which was a big deal back then, and [Coon Dog] was getting it so Gram could make music on it. His mother, sister, and Gram went on down to Florida—his father stayed up in town to work. He called me and Henry, called us by the house to tape a message to Gram wishing him a Merry Christmas."

Coon Dog then went to a local photographer and made arrangements for an eight-by-fourteen-inch color photograph of himself to be mailed to his mother. In the photo Coon Dog wore a suit and tie and a big, happy smile.

His mother had recently been to Waycross to see him. "He called my mother three weeks before and asked if she'd come down and visit," his sister, Pauline Wilkes, remembers. "I was taking care of my children, so Tom [Coon Dog's brother] drove my mother down and they stayed I guess about a week in the house. Tom said he felt Cecil seemed happier than he had in years and years and years. He just seemed perfectly happy because he told Tom, 'Things are all working out.' Tom didn't know what he meant by that. Tom said he'd read later that when some people make the decision to commit suicide, they feel like they've solved all their problems."

On December 22 Coon Dog went to the plant and had a long discussion with O. J. Cowart. "I'd been up to the plant in Baxley," Cowart remembers, "and I come in and he was sitting. He was in the office by himself, leaning back in his swivel chair with his hands behind his head. I sat and talked to him for about thirty minutes. Then we both went home. He said his family was leaving, gone to Winter Haven for Christmas, and that he would drive down the next day. Then he says, 'We have some fruit we can give out; the truck will be down tonight with a load.' The company gave all the employees fruit for Christmas then. He says, 'I'll give you a list of who to give it to tomorrow.' So the next day, twelve o'clock, and I hadn't seen Coon Dog. But I knew who got the fruit anyway. So I told them load up the fruit, carry it on out, and give it away. So they went on and gave everybody the fruit."

On the twenty-second Coon Dog also called Freddy Barker, an exterminator. Coon Dog's golden retriever had brought ticks into the house and Coon Dog made arrangements for Barker to come over and fumigate the next day. Coon Dog told Barker he would be leaving for Winter Haven in the morning; the house would be empty and safe to work on. He insisted that Barker not come before five o'clock.

On the morning of December 23, Christine Dixon came to clean up. She was the last person to see Coon Dog alive. Sometime between her departure in the late morning and Freddy Barker's arrival in the late afternoon, Cecil "Coon Dog" Connor shot himself in the head with a .38-caliber revolver. Freddy Barker found his body when he came to fumigate, as Coon Dog intended he should.

The Waycross Journal-Herald ran the story on its front page on December 24:

> Coroner A. J. Willis said Connor was found lying across his bed and had been shot in the right temple. A .38 caliber pistol was found near the body. An inquest will be held at a later date on completion of an investigation, the coroner said.
>
> Connor, vice president and manager of Snively Groves, had been active in the Boy Scout movement in the Waycross area for a number of years. He served as neighborhood commissioner of the Central District, chairman of the Central District, member of the Okefenokee Area Council and vice president of the 23-county regional council. Several years ago he organized and was scoutmaster of Troop 80, sponsored by Grace Episcopal Church. The troop was given the same number as Connor's squadron in WWII. He was instrumental in the development of Camp Tolchee at Little Blythe Island. He was a member of the Brotherhood of the Order of the Arrow, the highest honor conferred on an adult scout leader.

The story goes on to note that funeral arrangements were "incomplete." That's because there were none, at least not in Waycross. The Snivelys had Coon Dog's body whisked to Winter Haven as soon as the inquest into his death concluded. Like his son, Coon Dog is buried far from home.

ROSINA RAINERO REMEMBERS, "When Coon Dog killed himself it was so awful. . . . We were waiting there in the living room. We thought every car that came in the drive was him. Then her brother came in and said to Avis, 'Are you a big girl?' She said, 'Sure, I'm a big girl.' And then he proceeded to tell her what had happened."

"A pall came over the whole estate," Dode Whitaker says. "Everyone was in disbelief, and then came the realization that we had to face that it was true. I remember Haney's driver, Travis, a lovely man. . . . I remember seeing him holding Haney and Avis and rocking them as they all cried. When they heard, they turned to Travis in a little upstairs sitting room and the three of them were sobbing."

Louise Cone recalls, "Oh, I was hurt. 'Cause when we left to go to Winter Haven for Christmas I can remember he said to me, 'Take care of my Avie.' That's what he called out: 'Take care of my Avie, now.' And I said, 'Yessir, I sure will.' And we left and the kids and I were upstairs playing whenever that call came that he had done this."

Avis decided to withhold the news of their father's death from Gram and Little Avis until after Christmas Day. Gram spent the holiday quietly, away from his Snively cousins. The adults and the help were either crying or subdued. Dode Whitaker remembers, "That whole Christmas was terrible. They were trying to keep things light for the children, but it was rough. . . . They told the kids their dad was not going to be there for Christmas. And all this time [Avis and Gram] thought he'd be driving in any time."

Avis' brother didn't wait to call Coon Dog's family with the news. "I was at home, with my husband and our two children," Pauline Wilkes says. "John Snively Junior called and he told us there'd been an accident. That Cecil had been shot and was dead. He told us Cecil was cleaning his pistol and it went off. He asked if we would tell our mother and father. We got in the car and drove up to my mother's and my husband said, 'You're in no condition to tell them. You stay in the car and let me do it. You come on in in a few minutes.' So I sat there and he went into the house and he told Mother and Daddy and in a few minutes I came in. We all four were in shock, just sick at heart, with no way to describe the feeling."

Gram did receive his big Christmas gift from his father, the reel-to-reel tape recorder. Family legend has it that after making a few nonsense recordings on one side of the tape, Gram turned the reel over and played the other side. His father's voice emerged from the machine saying, "Just remember I will always love you." Evidently Coon Dog—knowing full well what he was about to do—made the recording as his farewell to his son. In this family, the story is just *Twilight Zone* enough to be true.

"When they finally told them," Dode Whitaker says, "Gram yelled out, this bloodcurdling scream. Everything in the house was hushed, and normally it was loud and everyone cheerful . . . so you could hear him scream. Of course their mother was lost and crushed, not knowing what or why or where she was going, how she was going to continue. I remember her saying, 'I don't know what I'm going to do. Where am I going to go? How am I going to go on?'"

As part of her effort to give her children a happy Christmas, Avis postponed the funeral until a few days later. "I think it was December 27 we left here," Wilkes says. "The four of us went down on the train. We got to Winter Haven and the Snivelys met us and we stayed in a hotel that night. We didn't want to stay at the Snively house; there was too much emotional confusion."

Back in Waycross, the official story was that Coon Dog's death had been accidental. "I'd been up to Baxley that day," O. J. Cowart said. "So when my wife called me to say that Coon Dog had killed hisself, I said: 'Don't start nothing 'round here!' And she said: 'I won't.'" Cowart knew instinctively that the Snivelys would never admit that one of their own— even kin by marriage—could commit suicide. But he adds: "I don't know whether they were having problems or not. I did hear—and this was all hearsay, gossip—that when he was going down there at Christmas she was going to put in for a divorce. But he never said nothing to me about it."

Marital problems seemed to many the likely explanation. "Everybody was shocked," Ben Smith says. "I think he was unhappy in his marriage; obviously he wouldn't have taken a gun to his head and pulled the trigger. It was quite a sensation for Waycross at the time."

Dickey Smith remembers, "Maybe a day or two after his daddy shot himself, or accidentally shot himself, the police played the tape and they called me and Henry Clarke and they questioned us. You know, did we see anything unusual, et cetera. . . . I've thought a lot about his death and changed my mind from suicide to accident many, many times. If I had to say, I don't see how he could accidentally shoot himself. He was a sportsman, a veteran, he was used to guns and I think something was going on between him and his wife. Even though I will sit here and say I've never seen a more devoted couple. But it has always been hard for me to swallow that he could have shot himself by accident."

The Snivelys made sure they were represented when the official verdict on the death was handed down. Attorney Edmund Pedrick says, "The Snivelys called my law partner, Kontz Bennett, and asked him to attend the inquest. I don't know what occurred there, but they quickly came away with a verdict of accidental death, which is not unusual. It's so the insurance will be paid and so forth." (Most life insurance policies will pay in cases of accidental death but not of suicide.) The Snivelys did not need insurance money. The inquest's decision seems to have been more about propriety and control of history.

Baffled by the Snivelys' insistence that Coon Dog's death was accidental, his sister went to the funeral home and demanded to be shown her
brother's body. She stood over him in his casket, turning his head this way
and that, carefully examining the hole in his skull, searching for motive,
for proof.

The author Stanley Booth, a native of Waycross and a great chronicler
of rock and roll, described his hometown with that excess of gothic spirit
that sometimes characterizes Southern writers who have spent a lifetime
worshipping whiskey and William Faulkner. "Waycross is a place with a
strong vein of Manichean madness," Booth wrote. "It is populated by
people who know the flesh is evil. It's important to know that, to understand
the Deep South, and its peculiar dynamic." And in a funeral home in central
Florida, a proper, genteel, heartbroken Southern sister stood face-to-face
with her dead brother, proving Stanley Booth correct about a certain Southern emphasis. Pauline Wilkes was searching for truth in the one place it
could not be concealed: the flesh.

"We got in a taxi and went to the funeral home. Daddy was so distraught that he and my brother's wife stayed at the hotel. I went over and
talked to the funeral director. I told him I wanted to know exactly what happened and he said, 'Well, he shot himself.' 'Why do you think that?' I asked
him. He said, 'Definitely, because of the position of the wound. If you'll go
in there and look at his body, I've covered it up as best I can, but if you look
you'll see a hole.'

"It was right there above his right ear, and I wouldn't have seen it if the
funeral director didn't tell me about it. There was a hole above his right ear
that had been filled in. If you were cleaning a gun and it accidentally went
off, you wouldn't be holding it at your head. It had to be intentional."

The Snivelys had Coon Dog's body brought down to Winter Haven for
burial. Gram and Little Avis did not attend the funeral; shielding children
from the fact of death was standard procedure in that time and place.
According to Snively cousin Susan Alexander, a contemporary of Little Avis,
"We were sheltered kids as far as death . . . so we were not encouraged to go
and participate in funerals. Death was never discussed with us."

Coon Dog's siblings and parents were at the funeral. When they came
back to the Snively house afterward, they were stunned to find a cocktail
party in progress. The event had already been scheduled, Avis' sister Evalyn
told Pauline Wilkes, and there seemed no point in canceling it, since
"everyone was coming over anyway."

Big Avis decided to move back to Winter Haven and her parents' house. She postponed returning to Waycross even temporarily. "The shock was terrible," Rosina Rainero recalls. "She stayed home [in Winter Haven at the Snively mansion] a good while before she decided she would go to Waycross and pack her things. I'd say she stayed home for about a month. When she finally figured she had to go up [to Waycross], I came to help her pack her stuff. Naturally, she would have her times of crying. . . . She was questioning why, why, why did this happen? But we never could come up with any answer."

For Gram and Little Avis, the shock was even greater because Coon Dog's death was apparently never discussed with them. They had to contend with the sudden loss of their loving father and the complete upheaval of their lives.

Avis packed up the house in Waycross and she, Gram, and Little Avis were installed in the Snively mansion. The house at 1600 Suwannee Drive was sold to the sheriff of Waycross, improbably named Robert E. Lee. Attorney Edmund Pedrick remembers, "Ware County [where Waycross is located] takes its politics seriously, and one year on election night when no one was home, somebody bombed the house and it was demolished. Blown up, blown to pieces, completely destroyed. . . . So that was another wiping out of the Connors' memory in Waycross, you might say." The house was, in fact, not completely destroyed, and was moved to another location in Waycross a few years later.

At the Snively mansion, space was tight. John Junior, his wife, their two older boys, and their two girls, Susan and Martha, had already joined the household following the death of John Senior. John Junior's boys were off at boarding school, which made for some breathing room but not much. Little Avis shared a room with her cousin Susan. Gram and his mother shared another in a recently built addition. Even in a house that big, quarters were close; family members got a good look at one another.

Gram became increasingly withdrawn after learning of his father's death. "It was a turning point," says cousin Susan Snively Alexander. "They had to leave their *Leave It to Beaver* home. In Waycross they had a great house in a smaller town with close friends. It was ordinary, nice and warm. There was a whole other dynamic in Winter Haven. Life was never as low-key and carefree as they had known. Gram was never the happy-go-lucky boy [I knew] in Waycross."

Martha Snively, Susan's sister, says, "His mom lost her father, and eleven months later her husband committed suicide. The motherly attention Gram needed wasn't there, because Avis was going through her own grief process."

Little Avis' response to her father's death and a new home was to spend her time as physically close to Gram as possible, holding on to him, sitting in his lap, following him wherever he went. Gram did not shoo her away.

Susan Alexander says, "In Waycross, Gram was a typical adolescent boy, but Gram and Little Avis were still deep; they almost never spoke. It's like they were throwbacks to another time. [Little] Avis' spirit had a quietness about her even as a little girl. I cannot see an aspect of their life that mirrors anything in the lives of other members of their family."

"[Big] Avis was a moody person," Martha Snively says, "but Gram was quiet. You knew where he was: When he was happy he was happy, and when he was sad he was down."

In the aftermath of Coon Dog's death, Big Avis and Gram reversed roles. Big Avis came to depend on Gram, to need his constant company. With her father and husband gone, Big Avis became increasingly childlike and needy toward her twelve-year-old son. And family members noted how willing Gram was to take responsibility for his mother.

At the same time, Avis became stricter and more punitive, readily angered by conduct that had never been an issue in Waycross. Gram stole cigarettes daily and snuck out into the yard for a smoke. When Gram got caught, he was sent to appear before the only father figure remaining in the house, Avis' brother, John Junior. Whatever Gram got caught doing, Avis would march him to John Junior's office, saying, "He was bad. I want you to give him a spanking."

"My dad was always the bad guy to Gram," Martha Snively says, "because if he wasn't correcting Gram or giving him a spanking, Gram never saw him except for Christmas and Thanksgiving." To make matters worse, Avis had her brother inflict discipline on Gram with wide time gaps—hours or even days, depending on John Junior's schedule—between the boy's infraction and his punishment. Gram shouted every time, "You're not my daddy and you can't tell me what to do!"

Gram also faced physical discipline at school. In Winter Haven he attended a Catholic school, St. Joseph's, for seventh and eighth grade. A convent across the street housed the nuns who taught there and enforced a classic, rigorous discipline. For talking in the bathrooms or any other violation, the nuns would smack students with a ruler.

Anger that wasn't evident in Waycross now came to be part of Gram's character. "He was a good kid, but get him out by himself or with his tight friends and he was nothing but a fuck-off, a cutup," says one of Gram's Winter Haven classmates, Dubie Baxter. "One time we were in Sunday school at the Episcopalian church. They had a brand-new Sunday school teacher and we were going to break her in. Gram stole or picked or took her purse and started passing it around the table while she was up there teaching Sunday school. Gram left it on the church stove in the kitchen, where it melted, and that was the last time we ever saw her."

Rob Hoskins, Evalyn Snively's son, was Gram's first cousin. "Gram's IQ was up in the genius level," Hoskins says. "His wit was quick and sarcastic. He tended to be a little sadistic with his tongue. He could cut you so fast you didn't even know you'd been cut and miss the whole point of what he had in mind."

Sadistic not only with his tongue. "Back when we were kids messing around, he could never stand the sight of blood," Hoskins remembers. "But one day he put a firecracker in a frog's mouth and blew up the frog. He found out he couldn't stand his own blood but he could stand the sight of the frog's. The quote that came out of the deal—it became our pet saying—was, 'unfortunately for the frogs.'"

Soon another link to their late father was stripped away from Gram and Little Avis. Relations with Coon Dog's family had remained cordial until the summer after Coon Dog's death, when Pauline Wilkes and her family went down to visit Gram and Little Avis. "Avis announced that we would not be able to see the children anymore," Wilkes said. "We were already there, but she said, 'Do not come over to see them.' Our family had a pleasant relationship with all the Snivelys until my brother's death, at which time they decided that we would not be allowed to see Gram or Avis anymore. My parents were devastated." They did not see their grandchildren again until five years later, when Gram called them and invited them to his high school graduation.

FOUR

ROBERT PARSONS

BIG AVIS SNIVELY CONNOR WAS BEAUTIFUL, RICH, AND HURTING. HER CHARMS and her vulnerability drew constant suitors. "She was pursued by men in the dozens," Susan Alexander says. "Everyone was concerned that she wasn't hurt by other people." The Snivelys were also worried about fortune hunters.

A few months after the death of her husband, Big Avis met Robert Parsons and fell for him, hard. Parsons was exactly the kind of man the Snivelys feared most.

Parsons was a silky dresser, a smooth talker, a polo-club charmer with shaky finances and a personal style right out of the Playboy Advisor: ascots, a Jaguar convertible, and even a pet ocelot.

In the late fifties Parsons was living in Cuba, working in the citrus industry there, although exactly what connection he had to Cuban citrus remains, like so many things about his business career, a mystery. And like so many chapters of Parsons' life, this one involved romance. He had recently been thrown out of his first marriage, leaving behind two young daughters, after his wife discovered he'd been spending most of his time with another woman. He ventured to Cuba, possibly to work for a large citrus company.

There he took up with a society heiress—married, according to one version of the story, and planning to leave her husband for Parsons. "Bob had a lot of charisma and he always went first-class," says someone in Cuba at the time. "He associated with the most prominent people in Cuba. His girlfriend was tall, beautiful, could have been a model. She was crazy about Bob and vice versa; they had a hot romance going."

Some unspecified social complication—perhaps an angry husband—put Parsons under pressure to break up with her. Then, according to Parsons' own version of his legend, he had to leave Cuba in a hurry after Fidel Castro and his guerrilla army seized power from the island's pro-American dictator, General Batista, at the end of 1958 and the beginning of 1959. As Parsons told it, he oversaw getting his employees and their key business files out of the country. After shepherding the final group to safety, Parsons claimed to be one of the last Americans out of Cuba. He told of sitting in a plane with its engines running. The new regime's enforcers boarded again and again, each time yanking someone back from the brink of escape. Nine times soldiers came on the plane, and nine times they took someone off by force. At last the door closed, the engines revved, and the plane started up. Before it could begin taxiing, the doors opened once more and the soldiers returned. Parsons was certain they had come for him, but this time they seized no one and the plane took off. Parsons later said he'd never been so happy in his life. "Did you jump up and down?" he was asked. "No," he answered. "But boy, did I get drunk."

Shortly before leaving Cuba he met and befriended Big Avis' uncle, Thomas Snively Junior. Snively was researching the political and business climate with an eye to opening a Snively Groves processing plant. Like so many others, he was charmed by Parsons, and the two men, both dedicated drinkers, had a raucous time bonding in Havana.

Even before the Castro coup, the Snivelys decided that Cuba wasn't going to work out, but they saw potential in Parsons. They invited him up to Winter Haven to talk about managing a plant in Florida. Sometime in early 1959 Parsons arrived and spent a week as the Snivelys' guest. That's when he met Avis.

Years of dealing with Parsons has left the Snivelys with an uncharacteristically unanimous opinion of him. Rob Hoskins sums it up: "That man is pure evil. Like having 666 tattooed on the back of your head."

Gene Leedy, a longtime friend and, by his own admission, "one of only two guys in Florida who liked Bob Parsons," gives a more positive description.

"He was one of the most classy guys I've ever known. Tall, handsome, wore elegant clothes. . . . He worked in a men's store, and that's where he got his taste in clothes. He wore Brooks Brothers suits and custom shirts. He could wear a pair of khakis and be elegant."

Even Dode Whitaker, who hated Parsons, acknowledges his glamour. "He was dapper, the affluent gentleman. He had that down pat. Absolutely the top-notch attire for whatever occasion; he was a good-looking man. From what I could see, at first he was caring, like, 'You want some more iced tea?'—whatever it was. . . . He certainly kowtowed to Avis' every whim."

Rosina Rainero claims Parsons was on the make from the get-go. "When he met Avis he was Mr. Gallant," she says. "When he got here he didn't have a change of underwear. He only had the clothes on his back, honey. Avis sent him down to Gentry's, which was a real nice store, to get some stuff. He had to have the best of every kind of clothes. I said, 'Didn't he bring his own clothes with him?' She said, 'No, it was a spur-of-the-moment thing.' I knew right then he didn't have a penny to his name. He was a con man with all the tricks of the trade. He thought he was Mrs. Astor's pet horse."

"The Snivelys didn't like Bob," Leedy says. "His elegance was the main resentment the family had toward him."

Susan Alexander says, "In my family, all the women were considered to be protected by the men. Now, Haney"—Big Avis' mother, the clan matriarch—"was not happy with Bob Parsons. But there are times when every lady in our family thinks, 'Have I got any worth at all that's not monetary?' Because we were always warned, and we might've picked up the fact that nobody would love us except for our money. The older generation feared Bob Parsons would marry Avis for monetary gain. And that was drummed into her like it was drummed into all of us. And you get to the point where you think, 'Well, do I not have worth? Can't any of you see any reason this man would want to marry me besides money?'"

The nature of Bob Parsons' relationship with Avis, and with her money, varies drastically depending on whether the witness is a part of the Snively crowd. To them, Parsons was a grifter, if not the devil incarnate. People outside the Snively circle describe him as a loving, sincere—albeit vague and perhaps shady—guy with aspirational tastes who lived at the mercy of his relatively benign appetites for women and the high life. While these views may be contradictory, they are not necessarily mutually exclusive.

Someone who knew Parsons in Cuba and spoke on condition of

anonymity pointed to Parsons' Havana romance as evidence of his sincerity in Winter Haven. "He was involved with a fantastic woman in Cuba and she was worth ten times what the Snivelys had," this source contends. "They were engaged, planning to get married and everything. If he were after money, he damn sure would have married her. But he met Avis and fell in love." And Avis fell in love with him.

Dode Whitaker describes Avis as shattered and confused, defenseless against Parsons' charm offensive. "It was still so early she didn't have her feet on the ground. . . . He was an opportunist who knew how to come in at the right time and get what he wanted. I don't think she ever saw . . . well, after they were married, how could she?"

"I never thought she was in love with him like she was with Coon Dog," Rosina Rainero says.

But as Gene Leedy saw it, Avis became obsessed with Parsons because he demonstrably loved her and took care of her. Avis told Leedy that "when she was little she always felt insecure. She said her parents were always off someplace and she used to pay the maid to sleep in her room because she was lonesome. Bob made her feel secure."

Parsons was also eager to father Avis' two orphaned children. "Bob was basically a family man," Gene Leedy contends. "He wanted a family. He felt that [Little] Avis and Gram needed a father, so he jumped right in and treated them like they were his own kids."

Just how starved for parenting Gram was is clear from the reminiscences of Jim Carlton. Jim and Gram met at St. Joseph's when they were in the eighth grade and became lifelong friends. From the start, Gram made an impression on the other boy because he was called "Gram" at a school where the kids otherwise used only last names. Jim at first assumed the other boy's surname was Graham and asked his first name. When Gram answered, "Gram," Jim said, "Gram Graham?" He realized then that Gram was different from the other kids. "That was his name," Jim recalls. "He demanded respect. He wasn't overt about it, but he had a certain charisma or magnetism even back then."

Gram's family was different, too. The first time Jim visited the Snivelys, he waited with Gram to be picked up after school. A station wagon driven by a black man with a black woman in the front seat pulled up. "I wonder who they're here to pick up?" Gram said to Carlton, then leaped into the car. Carlton hesitated, wondering what was going on. He later learned that Travis and his wife brought Gram to school every morning and picked him up every afternoon. When Gram came through the front door of the Snively mansion, he grabbed an air-powered foghorn that stood by the door and blew a long blast. He did that every time Carlton came home with him. "He was saying, 'Gram's home, Gram's home,' but he was announcing it to an empty house," Carlton says. One Friday night Carlton's mother drove Gram home after the boys went roller-skating. She brought Gram to the door of the mansion and the butler let Gram in. Carlton's mother realized that Gram would be rattling around the mock-antebellum house alone for the rest of the weekend. No family—just Gram and the servants.

Even when the adults were home, Gram and Little Avis didn't get much positive attention. Before Parsons arrived on the scene, the only fathering Gram could look to was the harsh discipline and emotional distance offered by his uncle, John Junior. Parsons was both affectionate and an ally. John Junior's daughter, Martha Snively, says, "Bob Parsons didn't help Gram's feelings about my daddy because Bob Parsons hated my dad. And my dad hated him."

Parsons was eager to encourage Gram's musical talent. "Bob was not mean to Gram," Rosina Rainero remembers. "He supported his music. He was good to Little Avis. Those children did not have a rough life." But to Rainero, this confirmed Parsons' shadiness. "He was always doing the little things, like taking Avis to dinner and bringing home flowers. He had time to do that because he never worked. He never worked a lick."

To the Snivelys, even Bob's affection for the children was a strike against him. "I didn't like him; I never liked him," Martha Snively says. "You know how children have a sixth sense about people? He was too nice. He was too nice to the kids. He always wanted to get the kids on his side."

Rob Hoskins, the son of Avis' sister, Evalyn, says, "My mother tried to warn her, but Avis told her to mind her own business." Others apparently bought Bob's rich-guy act, at first anyway, and were glad that Avis had found someone who made her happy. "The family presented him as financially independent," Dode Whitaker says. "That he was going to be a protector for Avis and her family. Those were early reactions that changed pretty quick after they were married."

Whitaker claims to have been suspicious of Bob from the start. "It was a tough time for Avis, and Bob came into the picture early. One reason I resent him so much is his early thrusting himself upon the family," she says. "I thought he saw a gravy train. I would try not to be near him. That got me in a lot of trouble with my family; it wasn't the Southern custom to be rude. That is not being a good host."

After he and Big Avis became engaged, Whitaker says, Bob cornered her in a way that went well beyond flirtatiousness. Whitaker was in her mid-teens at the time. She says that when he encountered her upstairs at a dinner party, he pinned her to the wall between his arms and pressed against her. She ducked under his arm and fled. "I tried to tell my mother, but she was raised as sheltered as I was. 'You must have misunderstood,' she said. He always made me uneasy, but Bob always had an answer, and his answer was always perceived as correct no matter what. He was a wealthy know-it-all and you better listen."

Whatever his motives, Bob's courtship of Avis was lightning-quick. They were married within eight months of meeting. "Well, I wouldn't say they eloped," Gene Leedy says. "They just went off and got married, you know?"

The wedding took place sometime in 1959, but no one knows where or exactly when the ceremony was, what Avis wore, or who said the vows. No one seems to have attended, or to remember being there if they did.

ROBERT PARSONS WAS BORN IN New Orleans on September 4, 1925, to William Reginald Parsons and his wife, née Lillian Gibert. His mother, born in 1902, was one of four children. Like Coon Dog Connor's mother, Lillian Gibert would outlive her son by decades.

Exactly how she connected with William Parsons remains unknown. She grew up in New Orleans and met him when he came down there from the north—specifically Flint, Michigan. The Giberts, a well-respected New Orleans family, never much cared for William Parsons, in the beginning mostly because he was a Yankee, though he would later give them a sounder reason to loathe him. The family opposed the match; Lillian Gibert and William Parsons left New Orleans to have the ceremony in another parish. They, too, went off and got married.

Lillian gave birth to Robert and, in 1932, a daughter, Denise. Later Lillian never spoke of her marriage, but the one known fact is that one day in 1937 William Parsons walked out.

Decades later, Robert Parsons' first wife, Alice Barre, took a writing course at Louisiana State University late in life and sketched what she knew about her ex-husband's family in a journal. "I have never known the circumstances," she wrote, "but the marriage terminated not by divorce but simply because the husband must have grown tired of it all and went out to buy the proverbial pack of cigarettes."

Lillian's family members, proven right about their misgivings, were not helpful. Her brother, a well-respected New Orleans architect, suggested that Lillian put her children up for adoption. He did not offer to assist his sister financially, and Lillian, with her Gibert pride, refused to ask her family for anything. Raised a Catholic, she never sought a divorce. According to family lore, Lillian kept contact with her blood kin on holidays, but these meetings were always strained.

Alice Barre and Robert Parsons' older daughter, Becky Gottsegen, recalled that her grandmother Lillian always insisted that William Parsons had died long before and never discussed his desertion. Neither did her son. William Parsons may have worked as a pharmacist in Birmingham, Alabama, and family lore suggests he might have made it all the way to California. But there is no debate about how he left.

Becky Gottsegen, speaking of the grandfather she never saw, says, "He literally abandoned them. He never wrote, never sent money. He came by one time, showed up at the door, and my grandmother wouldn't let him in." The young Bob Parsons answered the doorbell. Standing behind him, Lillian Gibert told Bob's father they had no use for him.

The family was living on Audubon Street in New Orleans when William Parsons took off, leaving Lillian and the children with no source of support. Robert Parsons got a paper route. His mother became a clerk at the First National Bank of Commerce. Lillian stayed at the bank her entire working life; she retired a vice president. Despite the family's reduced circumstances, Lillian Gibert never lost her pride or her sense of the importance of style. She was admired for her manners; she set the table for dinner with place mats and tablecloths. She and her children ate with sterling silver flatware off fine family china. Lillian was devoted to her son—family members use the word *worshipped*. Her emphasis on self-definition through style was imprinted on Bob as an imperative moral force.

Bob graduated high school during World War II and immediately enlisted in the Air Force. He served as a tailgunner on B-57 bombers. During the war, his mother and sister shared Lillian's sister Odette's home on Frenchman Street; Odette sheltered them when Lillian's wealthier brother refused. When Bob returned from the war, he and his mother and sister moved into government-subsidized housing near Kraus Street. Their neighbors were Louisiana State University medical students or outright poor. There was no escaping the stigma of living in public housing. "A government project apartment was the very best [Lillian] could manage and the only thing going for it was that it was new and clean," Alice Barre wrote in her journal. "In the vernacular of the South, it did include a large percentage of poor white trash."

Bob went to work at Kraus' Department Store. There began his lifelong appreciation for fine clothes. Becky Gottsegen says, "He was a fabulous dresser. Always." He also took advantage of the G.I. Bill's program of college aid for returning servicemen and signed on at Louisiana State University in Baton Rouge. When the school year began, Bob moved to Baton Rouge, where he worked at the more upscale men's store Welsh & Levy and learned about fine fabrics and tailor-made suits. Even as a young man Parsons insisted on being perceived as a gentleman. He always believed in the power of presentation. He couldn't afford a car; during his student years in Baton Rouge he hitchhiked home to see his mother. In the colder season he traveled in a Welsh & Levy cashmere coat. When he got in a car, Parsons would fold the coat over his arm so the driver could see the Welsh & Levy tag and know that the hitchhiking student was no bum.

He met Alice Barre, whose family lived in Baton Rouge, on a blind date arranged by her college roommate. Years later she wrote in her journal that she was immediately "smitten." "He was highly intelligent, an avid reader, and, though I didn't know it then, had a great deal of trouble separating the right and the wrong way of doing things," she wrote. "He had the kind of personality that could charm anyone and he never lacked for invitations. He could have easily been born with the well-known silver spoon and never did anything to refute anyone's assumption that that spoon was his."

Alice's father owned and ran a sugarcane mill. The family lived in the best part of Baton Rouge and was established socially in New Orleans. By the exacting three-hundred-year-old standards of Louisiana they may not have been old money, but they were certainly money. They were not thrilled with their daughter's romance. They felt Alice didn't know Bob well enough and they weren't pleased that he came from a broken home and, worse, that his mother lived in the projects.

The two dated for three years, and time did not endear Bob to the Barres. Nevertheless, Bob studied hard at LSU and finished in three years. LSU has no record that he ever graduated. The story goes that he lacked a key gym credit. It's plausible; Bob Parsons was not a guy to bother with gym. Alice Barre recalls, "He joined Sigma Ki, where he worked hard to make his grades. He passed all his courses and I had three years before I graduated, during which time we decided to be married. Bob worked at a fine men's store"—Welsh & Levy—"and went to classes, too. After my graduation he continued to work there. I got a job in construction and loved it."

The decades-long prosperity that the Barres had enjoyed was coming to an end; their sugarcane mill fell on hard times and the Barre fortune began to evaporate. When Alice's older sister graduated college, she got a swanky car as her present. The family business was doing so poorly by the time Alice graduated that no such gifts were forthcoming. Bob Parsons joked that Alice's sister got the Rolls-Royce and Alice got the Volkswagen. Alice's father later ran a Ford dealership in Bunkie, Louisiana.

Alice graduated LSU in 1947. She married Bob in 1948. A wedding photo shows the couple running to the car as their friends throw rice. Parsons is tall and thin—six foot three inches and 160 pounds—and wears a beautiful suit. After the marriage, Alice's family disowned her.

The newlyweds moved to New Orleans for a year. Alice became pregnant and they returned to Baton Rouge. "Bob started his big agriculture job planting cotton and living on a farm where he was going to make a million dollars," she wrote. "Ha! There was a cute overseer's house on the property and we made it comfortable to live in. We painted, shined floors, and used everything we had to make it cozy."

Their daughter Jan Parsons was born in 1951. Becky Parsons (now Gottsegen) followed the next year. His million-dollar scheme having apparently fallen through, Bob found work as the district manager for Penn Mutual Life Insurance Company. Walter Lanaux, a young lawyer, met Bob while looking for office space and became his best friend in Baton Rouge. Lanaux was struck by Bob's style and remembered he'd seen Parsons working at Welsh & Levy.

"The Eisenhower campaign was in full force then, and I was a Republican and so was he," Lanaux said. "We became friends instantly. We knew a lot of people in common in Baton Rouge: the Young Republicans crowd, et cetera."

Lanaux and Parsons were politically active and ambitious. Bob's ambitions never squelched his sense of fun, which tended toward the juvenile. He and Lanaux were responsible for setting up a fund-raising party at a "camp"—a weekend estate—on the Amite River. Hundreds were invited. Bob and Lanaux posted arrow signs along the road as guideposts. On the afternoon of the party, when they drove out to check on the food and liquor, Bob said, "Let's have some fun," and turned the arrows to face in every direction. "Everyone found their way," Lanaux recalls, "but they all arrived cursing. 'Who turned those damn signs around?' and so forth. Bob stood there smiling."

The Young Republican social scene served as Parsons' introduction to the Baton Rouge that ran Baton Rouge. "Baton Rouge was a small town," Lanaux says. "The professional people all joined the same country club. Everybody pretty much knew everybody they thought mattered. Alice's family, the Barres, were included in that category. Through the club and her, Bob was used to associating with people of means." Socially, Bob was the star of his marriage. Alice was regarded as less compelling, less charming. She was bright and opinionated, not sought-after qualities in a woman in that circle.

"Bob then was not like he ended up," Lanaux says. "In those days he was an active guy, not a drinker. One day, out of the blue, he said, 'I want to take a canoe down the Atchafalaya River from Krotz Springs to Morgan City,' which is a stretch through the swamp. A big, big swamp about seventy, eighty miles. We did it; camped on the bank at night, listened to the alligators cough, swiped mosquitoes. I made fishing trips with him to various places on the coast. He loved adventures. But in our time together he never hardly—I say never—discussed his father. It was years before he would even mention his father."

In his first marriage and throughout his life, Parsons deployed unfailing seductive charm directed at everyone in the room. He was always planning to "make a million dollars," and never quite succeeded. He craved social attention, particularly from women. In that he was more successful.

"My grandmother [Lillian] was not a warm and fuzzy person," Becky Gottsegen says. "How could she be? She was in survival mode; she was working and raising her kids all on her own. And my dad's flaw was that he could not pass up the attention of an attractive woman. He needed to be loved."

"And the women loved Bob," Lanaux says. "They truly did. . . . If he had a diversion in life, that would have been it. I was around him a lot and, you know, some guys have it and others don't."

In the mid-fifties, the Parsons family moved back down to New Orleans, to a house on Valenz Street. "We moved because of a job in New Orleans," Alice wrote in her journal. "I had a job at Charity Hospital working for the head of pathology. I loved the job but was more and more concerned with Bob's behavior. I found he was seeing a young woman with whom he spent most of his time. I decided to leave him because I was filled to the brim with him as he paid less and less attention to me and the girls."

Alice's father, glad to see Parsons shown the door, offered to help her if she wanted to leave. She and her daughters moved to Baton Rouge, where her family bought her a house on Zeland Street.

Even with her family's support, divorce was a courageous step for a Southern woman of her era. At the same time, Alice prided herself on never speaking badly to her children about their father. She didn't try to turn the girls against him. She also never discussed the particulars of their divorce.

After the legalities were done, the girls visited Bob in New Orleans. As befitted his personality, he did not encourage his kids to call him Dad, Father, or Papa. Becky Gottsegen says, "We called my dad Bob his whole life."

Soon afterward, Bob left for Cuba. Once again he was looking for the opportunity to strike it rich, to find a career that could support his champagne tastes. And once again he failed. But that trip to Cuba led him to Winter Haven, the Snivelys, and Big Avis.

SOMETIME AFTER THEIR WEDDING, Bob adopted Gram and Little Avis. Both took his name. Jim Carlton remembers that Gram told him, with great solemnity, "I am no longer Ingram Connor. I am now Ingram Cecil Parsons." Gram, Carlton says, seemed pleased.

The Snivelys and their friends see a dark motive. Some of them insist Parsons finalized the adoption in New Orleans in order to take advantage of Louisiana law, which they claim gave him greater control over the children's portion of the Snively estate. The Snivelys cite the byzantine and singular Napoleonic code that governs Louisiana. They contend that Parsons played that code like a pinball machine to get his hands into the Snively till.

Susan Alexander says, "The family checked into child-custody types of things and I remember hearing how the laws of Louisiana were different. That the family had no control or power over the children. The Louisiana law tied the family's hands from being able to help Gram and Little Avis."

The trouble with this version of events is that there's no evidence Bob ever took Gram and his sister to New Orleans, or that Louisiana law would have given him any special privileges if he had. The persistence of these stories reveals more about the Snivelys than Bob Parsons.

The newlyweds were by all accounts happy. In Gene Leedy's telling, Bob was the nurturing male any poor little rich girl might dream of. "He waited on her hand and foot. He was always buying her presents and he did most of the cooking at home. She was crazy about him. I never saw them fight."

Leedy describes Bob as "a good husband. Plus he was a tremendous chef—he could have worked as a chef anywhere, he was that good. Many times we'd be over at the house and he'd say, 'Avis, it's a Saturday night. Call up about thirty people and let's have a dinner party and I'll cook.' They had a maid and she'd help Bob, and goddamn!—Bob would cook up a meal that on short notice you couldn't get at the Four Seasons. He liked company and would have all the Snivelys over for dinner."

Shortly after he and Avis were married, Parsons brought Becky and Jan, his daughters from his first marriage, to Winter Haven. Jan was Little Avis' age, Becky a year younger. Becky Gottsegen remembers, "Our first visit, the neighbors and friends had a party for me and Jan. Welcoming us to Winter Haven and so everybody could meet my dad's two children. I don't remember at that time anyone ever having had a party other than a birthday party. I'd never been to a party that was just in someone's honor." Parsons loved his daughters, and he never needed a reason to fill his house with people.

Leedy adds, "The Snivelys loved eating his food and visiting his house and going to his parties, but they were ambivalent toward him. They liked him, but they thought he was a con man because he spent so much money."

The money belonged to Avis. Bob used it to ensure that his front was larger than life. His attention to detail, now backed by ready cash, led Bob to extremes in pursuit of style. Even his enemies agreed he had a genius for it. In a town filled with status-mad orange-juice millionaires, Bob stood out.

He drove a 1960 3.8 British racing-green Jaguar and later a silver Jag with white wheels. He smoked only Cuban cigars, which he somehow managed to have shipped to him. He bought an ocelot and kept it as a house cat. The ocelot grew from a kitten to a three-and-a-half-foot-long predator. It monopolized two sofa cushions as it spent its days lounging on the couch.

Bob was determined to show the Snivelys that he was more than just a high-living gold digger. Nor did he want to be beholden to his in-laws. "He was ambitious," Gene Leedy says. "He didn't want to sit back and do nothing and live off her money." But where Leedy saw commendable go-getting, the Snively camp saw larceny. Says a family member who isn't willing to be named, "Bob was spending a lot of Avis' money, an immense amount of her money—illegally and certainly immorally."

Bob procured—or Avis procured for him—an interest in Leap Engineering, and with it an office in Lakeland, Florida. According to Gene Leedy, then a local architect, "Leap Engineering invented prestressed concrete and was known in the profession." Bob wanted to highlight the company's product by building a prestressed concrete house in Winter Haven. Thus began his lifelong friendship with Leedy.

"I met Bob and Avis at a cocktail party, was impressed with Bob and had a great conversation," Leedy recalls. "The next day he called and said, 'I'd like you to do a house for us.' He told me he was working with prestressed concrete and I said, 'Man, you want out of that shit.' But he said, 'I own this company and I need you to work with it.' I got interested in [the material] through Bob. I found out what you could do with it, became heavily involved, and consulted in the industry for years."

Gene Leedy proved it was possible to make a nice living from prestressed concrete. Bob Parsons proved the opposite. Whatever Bob's good intentions, he fell prey to an apparently inescapable pattern: All that Snively money drove those touched by it to hedonistic passivity or bad financial judgment or both.

Bob wanted to expand the company by building a prestressed concrete manufacturing plant in Colombia. Leap Engineering would supply know-how and supervision. Gene Leedy remembers, "Bob had a lot of pride, and if all the stuff had gone good he'd have made a fortune. What he wanted was to go down [to South America], make all that money, come back, and tell the Snivelys to go to hell because he had more money than them."

Bob needed seed capital. Drawing against the family trust fund, Avis financed Bob's concrete company, Preconsolidé de Caribe, and paid to build a prestressed-concrete plant in Bogotá. Bob made frequent trips to Latin America, trying to get the project off the ground. But his business strategy was risky: He was buying an inferior, cheaper grade of concrete from Cuban suppliers for resale to the Colombian government. Bob walked a tightrope. As an American it was illegal for him to do business with Cuba. He was in violation of the trade embargo that the United States imposed following Castro's revolution. Another Snively source describes the inevitable denouement: "When the Colombian government discovered they were getting second- and third-grade product, they nationalized the company, took it over, and put him out of business. And since the company was nonperforming, it caused a lot of [family] problems. Avis was getting the money from the family trust."

This same source adds, "Avis would be all upset because Bob was flying back and forth, contracts were supposed to be coming in, and business would never happen. And Bob was stuck somewhere; he'd fly from Bogotá to New York to get to Winter Haven. Then it would turn out he was in Miami Beach shacked up at the Fontainebleau [Hotel]."

Complaints about Bob shacking up at the Fontainebleau may have been legitimate. But Snively complaints about Avis using family trust money to set up Parsons' business are disingenuous. The Colombian plant debacle appears to have been less a hustle than a display of incompetence. "Bob ran into all these political problems," Gene Leedy says. "He had to pay everyone off down there and the plant was never finished." Parsons and Avis' investment evidently disappeared into the money swamp that so often traps Yanquis doing business in Latin America.

At least Parsons had a chance of making money. If Bob's schemes had worked out, his success would have added to the Snively trust's value. During the same period, family patriarch John Snively Junior was investing Snively trust money in buying and maintaining his show horses—just one aspect of his mismanagement that would soon help erase the family fortune. Here, too, though, the Snivelys insist that Bob Parsons was the real villain of the story.

FIVE

WINTER HAVEN

PARSONS AND AVIS SETTLED IN A ONE-STORY RANCH HOUSE AT 324 PIEDMONT Drive in Winter Haven. Gram had a bedroom at the end of the house, off the family room. Originally designed as maid's quarters, the room became Gram's private universe. Most houses in Winter Haven's newer, upscale neighborhoods were built with maid's rooms, although these were not intended as places for a maid to live or even stay overnight. They were expected to be used as changing and nap rooms—maids typically worked twelve-hour days. More important, the rooms always had a maid-only bathroom attached so employers would never have to share a toilet with their help.

In the Parsons household, the maid's room was Gram's exclusively. It shared only one wall with the rest of the house and had its own bathroom and a separate outdoor entrance. It was an adolescent's paradise. Gram furnished the room with his turntable, his guitars, and an upright piano and decorated the walls with album covers. He spent most of his time at home there, listening to records and playing his instruments. When his friends came over they'd retire into Gram's lair.

"That room had a double door to isolate and insulate," Jim Carlton remembers. "He had a piano, a television, his own bath, a fridge. It was his own world with his own entrance. He could come and go as he pleased. As far as privileges, he had lots, and responsibilities, he had few. So there was obviously some irresponsibility on the part of his folks."

Susan Whitehead, one of Gram's girlfriends during this period, describes the situation this way: "His mother stayed at the other end of the house, drinking. He had lots of instruments, and that's where he hung out with all his friends. He had a private entrance and didn't have to go through the main door to get into the house. At his age, most kids did not have it so easy to get out of the house."

"It was neat," says Grant Lacerte, a Winter Haven High classmate, musical collaborator, and friend. "We'd show up at one in the morning and be totally secluded. We'd play the piano all night."

That back room provided Gram's entrée into playing live music in a place that was uniquely alive with musical opportunity.

GRAM WAS BORN with an unerring instinct for the zeitgeist. He always recognized the coolest, most significant band or musician in whatever scene he encountered. When he wanted to, he effortlessly partnered with that musician or became part of that band or that scene. Every scene accepted him as an equal, someone who belonged. The roots of this phenomenon appeared in Winter Haven.

Winter Haven and nearby towns in Polk County proved to be cultural anomalies of their time. While other small-town white teenagers in the rural South immersed themselves in race baiting, hot rods, and high school football, the kids in the towns scattered between the lakes of Polk County were forming bands at extraordinarily young ages. Lots of bands. What should have been just another orange grove–covered, redneck, central Florida county was weirdly alive with musicians. That hotbed of local bands had a powerful influence on popular music that continues to this day.

One musician who grew up in this milieu was Bobby Braddock, who became one of the premier country songwriters of the last thirty years: Among his thirteen number one country records are Tammy Wynette's "D-I-V-O-R-C-E" and George Jones' "He Stopped Loving Her Today" (cowritten with Curly Putnam). A couple years older than Gram, Braddock was raised in the smaller outlying Polk County town of Auburndale and attended high school there rather than in Winter Haven. "Polk County encompasses the size of six normal Florida counties," Braddock says. "It's twice the size of Rhode Island, almost as big as Delaware. In a place so large the mathematical chances of having some talent increases."

Polk County was a Southern melting pot because Southerners of all backgrounds flocked there to work in the orange groves. Cotton and peanuts were the two main agricultural employment opportunities in the areas from which Polk County's immigrants came; Braddock credits Polk County's influx of working-class whites to the depredations of the boll weevil on small cotton farms and to the desire to escape the stoop labor of harvesting peanuts. The citrus groves offered better pay, a more pleasant living environment, and much easier work—no more endless bending over rows of cotton or kneeling to pull peanuts out of the dirt.

The immigrant influx came primarily from southern Alabama, northern Florida, and southern Georgia, with a leavening of Texans and a few Midwesterners. Braddock says, "They were strangers from similar backgrounds who had music in common."

For all its size, Polk County was not purely farmland. The biggest city in the county was Lakeland (population 61,350, circa 1960), and small towns predominated: Winter Haven, Bartow, Haines City, Auburndale, Lake Wales, Eagle Lake, Highland Park, Dundee, Lake Hamilton, Lake Alfred, Hillcrest Heights, Davenport, Fort Meade, Frostproof, Mulberry, Gibsonia, Poinciana, and Polk City. The population was not isolated in single-family farms or hollers, as might have been the case in Appalachia. In the cities, communities—whether musical or religious—formed more readily. The ease of outreach helped develop a musical culture based on bands, rather than fiddling alone on the front porch. That these towns were growing fast and were essentially suburban meant a predominance of one-story ranch houses with that key architectural aspect of any burgeoning band scene: the garage.

Regardless of how many small towns sprouted, the culture of Polk County remained rural and working-class: politically conservative, pro-segregation, and "cracker," the latter term being the linguistic forebear of "redneck"—the folks Alice Barre had called "poor white trash." Southern religion and the emphasis on church, with its organ and choir, brought music into every household. Polk County had no shortage of quintessential Southern churches: Baptists, Pentecostals, Methodists. And until recently, music had been the traditional form of home entertainment. "We couldn't get TV signals around here till the mid-1950s," recalls Dickie McNeer, a classmate of Gram's and the scion of another wealthy Winter Haven citrus family, "so there was always a lot of music, a lot of singing in people's houses."

Bobby Braddock traces the musical roots of Gram's generation: "In the early 1950s there was a radio program in Winter Haven called *The Polk County Express*. It was a mix of pop music and what we called 'hillbilly.' Most of the kids I went to school with split themselves between the two. Course, when rock and roll came along everyone loved rock and roll. Right before rock and roll came in, my older brother and his friends stopped listening to hillbilly or country and discovered black music. That happened to a lot of kids across America; rock and roll was born because of the appetite of white kids for black music. That's where Elvis came along. And that's pretty much the music we listened to."

"Country was not an accepted form of music here in Polk County," says Dickie McNeer. "Even though it was roots music for us. Nobody listened to country except the lower-class people that we didn't know, who were at the honky-tonks after picking fruit all day. Back then the pickers were all white. And they were listening to a hell of a lot of that stuff."

No matter how strong Polk County teenagers' interest in black music might have been, local venues remained strictly segregated. Braddock remembers, "The star of a show at Club 92 was Texas Ray. Texas Ray was black; he played harmonica. Being the star, he appeared onstage for only the last half of the set. The rest of the time—this was 1959—he stayed in the kitchen because he wasn't allowed out front." Given how difficult it could be to see black acts perform, local bands were more likely to model themselves after white rockers, guitar twangers, or hillbillies.

Florence Villa, one of the early subdivisions built by Gram's grand-father, John A. Snively Senior, had become an all-black neighborhood. In the early days of the Florida land boom, "Florence Villa was a place new-comers could buy land," explains Dubie Baxter, one of Gram's Winter Haven classmates. "Later on, when the boom burst, Florence Villa became the black section of Winter Haven. We called it the Quarters. Or 'the Nigger Quarters' is what some of us called it growing up. That was how some of us were raised; not Gram, just some of us. We loved 'em to death, believe me, and they loved us. We were close, but they were black and we were white. They were niggers and we were whatever—God almighty, the things we were taught."

Another Southern tradition that held strong in Polk County was that it was a tough place to get a drink. Liquor was illegal; Polk County was one of the largest, most heavily populated dry counties in the South. Until 1964, the only legally available alcohol was 3.2 percent beer. To lawfully purchase liquor required a trip across a county line—and in a county so large, that meant some traveling. With the legal drinking age twenty-one, high school kids had to know someone old enough to both drive and buy. Gram's classmate Grant Lacerte remembers, "Everybody's folks had their monthly run over to the county line. You went north to Orlando or east to Osceola County, or Hillsborough County going west. There were big liquor establishments right across the county lines." Dubie Baxter says, "Everybody beat feet to the county line. All the adults went to Tony-Mike's in Plant City or the Palms in Kissimmee in Osceola County. Tony-Mike's was in Hillsborough County. Rob [Hoskins] and Gram and everybody we knew went on rides with their parents to go get liquor."

The distance to legal liquor and the dry laws meant a ready supply of homemade moonshine, also known as boot liquor. As was often the case in the rural South, fundamentalist Christians, knowingly or unknowingly, supported bootleggers by preventing the county from voting itself wet. A strong bootleg market thrived on a network of corruption: tipped-off raids, clubs that served in full knowledge of the sheriff's department, and so on. Of course locals with clout—white locals—were always allowed to serve: The American Legion Hall, the Benevolent & Protective Order of Elks, and the country club all ran bars for their members.

The Bluebird Restaurant in Winter Haven specialized in slaw burgers (beef patties topped with cabbage slaw), but was also known as a place to buy boot liquor. Customers would drive up, give the password, and order "a bottle and a burger." The moonshine was kept hidden in back of the restaurant in the hollow of an orange tree. The burger was delivered through the car window along with a bottle in a paper bag. "It wasn't the genteel that bought bootleg—they didn't have to," explains Grant Lacerte. "It was the fruit pickers and near indigents who had no other supply."

The difficulty of buying alcohol helped divert Polk County teenage energies, which in more urban counties might have gone toward getting wasted, into music. Conversely, once kids got into bands, they discovered previously unknown access to getting wasted: They played nightclubs, adults gave them beer, truckers gave them Benzedrine. Incentives to be in a band abounded.

The bands performed in the youth centers that were ubiquitous in central Florida. Every town had one. They were community recreation centers with outdoor basketball or tennis courts and one big high-ceiling room for entertainment. Kids would go to the youth centers to hang out for the most ancient of all hang-out reasons: There was no place else to go. "The youth centers promoted a lot of kids picking up instruments," Grant Lacerte says. "You'd make a little money—not a lot—but you were a hero performing in front of your peers, and that was cool." Jim Carlton recalls, "It was a *Happy Days* culture without a Fonz."

Between garages and youth centers, places to practice and places to perform, Polk County became fertile ground for bands. On Friday nights bands would play, punch would be served, and kids would get to know the musicians. Planning well and driving hard, one band might perform their five-song set at several youth centers on a single Friday night. Bands that became more popular—bands made up entirely of high school kids—graduated to playing at nightclubs. If a band played a single gig at an establishment where liquor was served, pretty much the definition of a nightclub, they'd be banned from playing at the youth centers. This meant a regular supply of bands moving up and out, and new bands coming in to take their place.

Grant Lacerte's rockabilly band the Blazers led the way. They were regarded as too wild for the teen venues; as sophomores they were banned from playing sock hops at their own high schools. The Blazers played night-clubs and gained a reputation as drinkers. Playing nightclubs meant meeting truckers. Meeting truckers meant gaining access to the various forms of amphetamine—speed—that the long-haulers used to stay awake. "The truckers were heavy," Grant Lacerte says. "I didn't even realize what ben-nies were. But it was Benzedrine; that's what they gave us. I never knew I was doing drugs, but we were all popping bennies. Our drummer was so damn good when he'd pop a few of them—his licks were three times faster."

Grant first met Gram at a youth center when Gram approached him about finding players to form a band. Lacerte remembers a kid of fourteen with braces, "a lot of presence and bright." Lacerte and Gram would later become close friends, but in that first encounter the gulf between the sixteen-year-old Lacerte, already earning a hundred dollars a week playing in dives all over the county, and fourteen-year-old, practicing-in-his-room Gram loomed too large.

Gram joined the Pacers, his first band, in 1960 as their lead singer. He was in the eighth grade. Thus began Gram's lifelong pattern of being the youngest guy in the band. The other Pacers were Martin Clevenger on bass,

Skip Rosser on drums, and Jimmy Allen on guitar. Rosser and Allen were two years older than Gram, sophomores at Winter Haven High, and had been playing around in different outfits. Rosser picked on Gram a bit, ordering him around and taunting him. He was famous locally for having cut school to attend the State Fair in Tampa. When the high school principal spotted Rosser at the fair on television, Rosser claimed he had been kidnapped and taken on the Ferris wheel against his will.

Clevenger, the oldest, graduated high school at sixteen. "We were all trying to learn music," he recalls. "If we heard of a guy in town that could play better guitar than us, we'd go to his house and learn everything he knew and go on to the next guy until we were better than all the guys. It wasn't so much about bands as we were a bunch of guitar players and bass players and we played with everybody." Kent LaVoie, who led a rival band, the Rumors, says, "There was no ranking. There was: Can you do anything? If you can, come on."

That ethos would be echoed years later when—under the influence of Gram and twenty-odd other musicians—country and rock came together in Los Angeles. The rock musicians who wanted to learn more about traditional American music and the traditional country musicians who wanted to move into rock sought each other out. As in Winter Haven, groups would coalesce, break up, and re-form as new constellations, all the time swapping ideas and expertise.

Jim Stafford, the most determined, serious guitar player on the scene, was a key member of the Polk County learning-and-playing free-for-all, and a player Gram admired. He would be part of Gram's next band, the Legends. But Stafford was, according to Jim Carlton, "not in the moneyed social clique." It was a distinction with big implications. "My family was always on the edge of money, but played as if they had it, so we hung out in the moneyed circles," Carlton says. "We were members of the country club; we hung with rich people even though we weren't. Jim's family ran a dry cleaner's. He was into his guitar; he'd bring crib notes on songs to school. He lived in this little part of town with little houses and traveled in about as far away a circle from Gram Parsons as you could be."

Carlton's careful parsing of the money hierarchy in Polk County is telling. High school kids in Polk County were thoroughly attuned to nuances of class. Winter Haven's singular concentration of the super-rich, surrounded by concentric rings of the less well-paid citizens who depended on the rich families for their livelihoods, created some singular dynamics. Karen Goodman Lacerte, a classmate of Gram's who married Grant Lacerte, says of the Winter Haven public-school world, "We had people with no shoes and people whose maids were pulling up and delivering them to school. It made for a complex environment."

Citrus was king and the Snivelys were the most important citrus family in Florida. Most of the lakes in Polk County were encircled by orange groves, and those groves belonged to the Snivelys. So did the groves covering the rolling, low-lying hills that surrounded Winter Haven. The Snivelys sat atop a wealthy clique of more or less ten families that owned and ran Winter Haven. The clique had its own network of dances and cotillions. Ten extended families made for an incestuous but sizable social population, with enough numbers to employ a significant percentage of the rest of Polk County. They were local royalty and treated as such. The Snivelys, and later Bob and Avis, were part of the town's social elite. The cliquish and cloistered social world of Winter Haven partially explains the widespread distaste for Bob Parsons, this outsider, this interloper, this well-dressed, smooth stranger who showed up out of nowhere and married the prize catch from the county's richest family.

The focal point of the local noncitrus economy was Cypress Gardens. It was a rite of passage for Polk County high school kids to work there, waterskiing, driving boats, being decorative in antebellum dresses, or selling in the concession stands. The Gardens were a source of local pride and identity, and the Gardens partly belonged to the Snivelys, too.

A signifier for members of the wealthy clique was a big main house for the family and an ornate boathouse somewhere out on one of the seventeen lakes that lie between Polk County's various small towns. A local who asked not to be identified guesses that there were about a dozen of these lake cabins: "The cabins were used for poker and bachelor parties, but they were also rendezvous places for extracurricular kinds of things." Using the cabins for romantic trysts was a social tradition among the wealthy of Polk County. Because the families lived on or had boathouses on the various lakes, it was natural for everyone to get around by small powerboats. Since these required no license to operate, the richer kids of Polk County were old hands at navigating the lakes and their connecting canals by the time they were ten or twelve years old.

"We used to go to Cypress Gardens at night in our boats and cut the engines," Dubie Baxter says. "We let the boats drift while we took our gas cans in. We'd swim, dog-paddle, pushing the gas cans in front of us, and steal gas from the Gardens. On these islands in Lake Summit they had gas pumps they never turned off. Nobody ever locked their doors here, nobody turned off gas tanks. We'd fill up our tanks, go back out, and run on the lakes all night."

Grant Lacerte recalls, "The rich had the money and they knew how to party, and you didn't have to be one of the moneyed ones if they had taken you in as part of their entourage. You partied with them all the time. At the same time, I went to school with kids that didn't wear shoes or shirts."

The class system affected all aspects of social interaction, and it marked Gram's adolescence at St. Joseph's and Winter Haven High as a huge change from his childhood. In Waycross he could be special but still one of the gang. In Winter Haven he was a Snively. Gram would spend much of his adolescence in the company of teenage redneck musicians of genuine ambition who were looking to use music to escape the class they were born to.

For the local band members, the Winter Haven melting pot incarnated the emerging, class-destroying meritocracy of rock and roll. The teenage audiences represented the growing democracy of rock-and-roll fandom, whether they came to listen from cotillions or trailer parks, whether they were driven by the maid or showed up without shoes.

In Winter Haven, as later in Hollywood, the effect of the family millions on Gram and his companions could never be eradicated. Those with an ax to grind bring up Gram's money in any conversation regarding his life and music. In Winter Haven, as in Hollywood, Gram's disgruntled survivors keep raising two seemingly contradictory grievances. The first is that Gram, with all his money, didn't have to try—he could have had any career he wanted. The second, usually spoken in the next breath, is: Given all Gram's money, why didn't he do better?

The Pacers, who practiced—when they did—at Gram's house, spanned a broad class cross section, from Gram to the more rural Martin Clevenger. They played country clubs, teen centers, and Jack & Betty's, the local dog 'n' suds drive-in. Gram played piano and some guitar. His guitar was an attention-getting and expensive sunburst Fender Stratocaster. "Gram played piano like Floyd Cramer," Martin Clevenger recalls, referring to a key country piano stylist who linked classic honky-tonk and a smoother, more modern sound. "We were playing Ray Charles, the Ventures, Chuck Berry—three-chord, easy stuff. People ate it up." In deference to Gram's wishes and popular demand, the Pacers also played "a lot of Elvis."

Grant Lacerte saw the Pacers a few times and was impressed with Gram. "We didn't have that many people around town with real talent. Everyone wanted to play with him. Especially when he did his piano stuff." Anyone who remembers the ruthless age dynamics of high school will understand how remarkable this was, given that Gram was an eighth grader playing with upperclassmen.

Gram didn't always take Floyd Cramer so seriously. Jim Carlton says, "I played this version of 'Steel Guitar Rag' for him and he said, 'What the hell are you doing?' and started playing this Floyd Cramer country piano, mocking me, making fun of country music. Gram did not cut his teeth on country music; his dad wasn't a country singer. He was no shit kicker—he was an urbane, polished kid and he bought pop music like James Moody as well. His record collection had a lot of Ray Charles, the Ventures, even Neil Sedaka. Most of it was music we were trying to deal with in the band.

"We were all learning. Gram wasn't the greatest guitarist in the world and Lacerte didn't play all that well either. It was a high school band of kids who'd only been playing a year or two. A garage band, and that's why garage bands by definition are rotten, 'cause they don't know anything."

Carlton had reason to be more aware of technique than his classmates. His father was a professional guitar player who had moved to Winter Haven from Chicago to play in the Florida Citrus Commission's orchestra. The Commission sponsored a weekly radio show; the orchestra worked the show as well as live gigs at various industry or tourist events all over the state. Gram, dissatisfied with the Pacers, wanted Jim Stafford and Carlton to play together. He engineered guitar lessons for Stafford from Carlton's dad. Carlton's father, impressed by Stafford's work ethic, practice habits, and natural ability, did not charge for teaching.

"One of the little trade-offs was that I was learning bass at the time," Carlton says. "Stafford was with Gram, and my daddy knew the best thing for a kid is to play with other musicians, so he said to Stafford, 'I'd like my son to be in your band.'"

The Pacers are remembered as "not much of a band," and Gram's time with them was short. In 1961 the musical aggregation the Legends was born: Stafford on guitar, Carlton on stand-up bass, Gram on guitar and piano, and Lamar Braxton on drums. The Legends featured a pickup horn section three or four players strong, usually anchored by Grant Lacerte on trumpet. "I played in the Legends, became friends with Gram, hung out with him, and we wrote songs together," Lacerte says, "but I was more committed to the Blazers because I was making a hundred dollars a week and that was a lot of money. I was playing adult gigs and the Legends were playing mostly for teens, so they did a lot of gigs as two guitars, bass, and drums."

The Legends were a step up in professionalism from the Pacers. Bob Parsons bought a collection of red blazers, and whoever was in the Legends that week wore one of the blazers onstage. Others who played with the Legends included Buddy Canova, Lloyd Morgan, Bill Waldrup (who replaced Stafford on guitar), Jon Corneal, and Gerald "Jesse" Chambers. Their repertoire included meat-and-potatoes rock and roll: "Johnny B. Goode," "Night Train," "Harbor Lights," "Guitar Boogie Shuffle," and plenty of Elvis.

It would be nice to have a definitive listing of the famously loose-knit Legends' members and repertoires. Jim Carlton explains why that's not possible: "People contradict one another about who was in what band when. There were a lot of offshoots and ad hoc groups that never rehearsed very much. It was all such a Raggedy Andy outfit—a bunch of guys hanging together."

Gram was too young to drive, so his high school friend Dougie Wiggins drove him and Carlton to see shows at the Lakeland Civic Center. They saw Roy Orbison, the Four Seasons, Jerry Lee Lewis, and other touring acts of the age. And when he was only fifteen, Gram himself promoted a regular battle of the bands at the Armory in Winter Haven. The Legends played these battles, as did most of the teen bands in the county. "Promoting" might be an overstatement: With Bob Parsons' help, Gram made the phone calls that would gather various Winter Haven bands in one spot and thus bring more kids to the Armory.

Bob Parsons was relentlessly supportive of and involved with Gram's music. In this, as in so many things, he was at odds with the Snivelys. The family thought Parsons pushed Gram and took too much pleasure in Gram's playing. They viewed his approach to Gram's after-school fun as unsuitably professional. John Junior wanted Gram to get a real job, like most teenagers in town, although no other Snively offspring came under any such pressure. Still, at holidays and family visits the Snivelys would gather around the piano as Gram played. His cousins still remember him playing a rollicking version of "Jingle Bell Rock" at Christmas, with all the servants clustered in the doorways, listening.

Bob Parsons demonstrated his flair for style and forward thinking by buying a Volkswagen bus to haul the Legends around. In 1961, VW vans in

Winter Haven were about as common as remote-control televisions and backyard roller coasters had been in Waycross. Dougie Wiggins was the usual driver. He was a kid from the wrong side of the Winter Haven tracks who was raised by his single working mom. More or less adopted by Gram and Big Avis, Dougie accompanied the Legends everywhere. Bob paid to have THE LEGENDS painted on both sides of the bus. Kent LaVoie, the older guitarist who led the established local band the Rumors, says, "He couldn't even drive it, and it was brand-new! Do you understand how hip that was?"

The VW gave the Legends a Gram-related boost in status—and a boost in other bands' resentment as well. Gram's parents liked to have whatever band Gram was playing with at the moment perform at their parties. Bob Parsons' socializing gained Gram's band access to country club dances around the state. The Legends played teen clubs and proms at public and private high schools. Their widespread network of venues, and their VW bus, enabled the band to occasionally spend a night on the road, religiously building beer-can pyramids in their motel rooms. The band earned good money and appeared regularly on *High Time*, a Saturday-afternoon teen dance show on Channel 8 that was Tampa television's local imitation of Dick Clark's *American Bandstand*. The Legends played the infamous Club 92, where liquor was openly served. Gram pulled rock-and-roll privileges to get his underage (though no younger than himself) girlfriend, Susan Whitehead, into the club. "She's with me," he said, and through the door they flew. In ninth grade, Gram already knew how to behave like a star.

Gram met Whitehead at a bowling alley in Winter Haven. She remembers him as always in the back of the room, always brooding. "My first impression was that he was really cute, really talented," she says. "Those puppy-dog sad eyes . . ." Whitehead admits that she also liked him because he was a Snively. "This may sound snobbish, but they were *the* family in town. Kind of like the Kennedys. And that impressed me. But Gram wasn't a snob. He was well liked at our school. He fit right in with anybody. In the South then, it was charming for a girl to be a Southern belle, so the boy had to be a Southern gentleman. And he certainly was that—he opened car doors, never forced himself on me. He was a regular guy who happened to be talented and rich."

Whitehead's mother insisted that they go together to her Methodist church for their first date. Gram said to her, "This is boring," Whitehead recalls. "And I said, 'Well, I'm sorry.' He said, 'You got a piece of paper?' I did, and he started drawing. He drew the choir director and then the band bus. He drew it with women's underwear hanging out of the windows as if they were a bunch of wild boys, and I don't think they were at that point. The fact that he could draw that in church made me laugh. I couldn't believe he'd do something so sacrilegious."

Gram and Susan Whitehead went out for around eight months. "Even though he was fun-loving," Whitehead says, "I could tell music came first for him. He was practicing and playing every day. He was serious."

The Legends' main competition was Kent LaVoie's band, the Rumors. LaVoie and his band were three years older than Gram, from Auburndale, and considered themselves tougher than the sissy city kids from Winter Haven. Their main lineup was LaVoie, Ashley Hale, Ronnie Tieg, Billy Waldrup, and Danny Cocher. The Rumors launched their career at a talent show at Winter Haven High. The band did not yet have a name. LaVoie remembers, "The moment our drummer started playing 'In the Mood,' with the exception of no screaming, it was exactly like the Beatles for the first time at Shea Stadium. Most of Winter Haven High had never heard a live band before. Auburndale was ahead of Winter Haven then. At that moment I could see the future—I could see what the music did to people."

The Rumors' material was nearer to the hillbilly end of the spectrum, or what passed for it among high school bands of Polk County. They played Gene Vincent's manic rockabilly and the pure country of Conway Twitty. Their song choices suggested an older, less affluent audience than youth center teenagers. Like the Blazers, the Rumors played a lot of bars.

LaVoie met Gram at the Parsons house on Piedmont Street. LaVoie was friends with Gram's cousin Rob Hoskins. Big Avis, according to LaVoie, liked to encourage kids to hang out at her house in order for Hoskins to have some friends; Gram's cousin apparently had trouble being popular on his own. "Rob was a little abrasive, is the best way I can put it," LaVoie says. "Gram would be there, always lurking in the back of the room. But at fourteen he had a Martin guitar. Now that was eerie. None of us would have considered buying an acoustic guitar. If one of us had picked up a Martin, we'd have tried to play Chuck Berry and said, 'This doesn't sound too good.' But Gram was into that Martin sound, which was an insightful thing to be into at his age and to already understand where he was going."

Still, LaVoie didn't think of the Legends as tough competition. "We always considered them a follow-up band," he said, "the Rolling Stones to our Beatles."

LaVoie became friends with the Legends' Jim Stafford after the bands began performing together. "We weren't musicians," LaVoie says. "We played in bands. Stafford was already a musician. His parents were so dedicated to him doing it they had his stuff set up in the living room of this tiny tract house. He was miles ahead of any of us at playing a guitar." Gram and Stafford joined the Rumors for a gig or two, filling in. LaVoie insists that he never once played with the Legends. Grant Lacerte also sat in on a few Rumors shows.

LaVoie, Gram, and Stafford attempted to form their own group. But LaVoie, frustrated by what he saw as Gram's lack of discipline in rehearsal, pulled the plug. "He always had an air of indifference," LaVoie explains. "He would say about rehearsing, 'I'll get there when I do.' He was lackadaisical about it." What motivated LaVoie to put up with Gram was hearing Gram play LaVoie's father's Baldwin organ in the LaVoie living room. "I was dumbfounded," LaVoie says. "We were all kids with guitars and here's Gram playing like that. I'd never heard anything but cocktail music and standards on an organ. I knew 'Palisades Park'"—Freddy Cannon's 1959 hit, famous for its swirling organ sound—"but this was the first time any of us had heard an organ used live. 'Palisades Park' was the number one record. I said, 'We've got to do this record.' I was so excited I couldn't stand it. Our one rehearsal, when I counted off and Gram started singing, was astounding. I couldn't wait to do it onstage. We were going to be the coolest thing in the world. The problem with the Baldwin is hauling it around, but Gram had the Volkswagen van."

The Rumors had a job at a teen club in Cocoa Beach, the Tiger's Den. LaVoie remembers, "It was an armory, okay? They called it a teen club but it was an armory." The boys rehearsed "Palisades Park" and a couple of other numbers with Gram. The plan was that the Rumors would do their regular set and then Gram would join in for the organ songs. Dougie Wiggins drove Gram to the LaVoie house, and the Rumors helped load the Baldwin into the van—no easy feat. The Rumors headed off to Cocoa Beach, leaving Dougie and Gram to catch up in the VW. The Rumors arrived in Cocoa and set up. The opening bands performed and the Rumors' time drew near, but Gram still hadn't showed. The Rumors were scheduled to perform at eight o'clock. The Cocoa Beach high school teacher running the show told the Rumors they could go on with their missing band member or without him, but they had to go on at eight. "Seven, no Gram. Seven-thirty, no Gram," LaVoie says. "He was so laid-back about everything—we knew it was him screwing off."

The band went on. At eight-thirty Gram appeared at the side stage door. LaVoie says, "We wore these white shirts and white ties and coats. I could see the blood on his shirt. His tie was loosened and he was distraught-looking. We were in the middle of a song, so I had about ten seconds to give him. I know he has some half-assed excuse why he's late. I'm pissed. We stopped playing and—you have to remember that in 1961 people didn't cuss the way they do now—and he said, 'Don't be mad at me. We hit a cow, we hit a fucking cow.' I said, 'What?' and he said it over and over, like it was all he could say: 'We hit a fucking cow. We hit a fucking cow.' I was so determined we were going to play that song I ignored him. We go wrestle that organ out and the front of the bus is mangled. I remember some piece of a cow—some ear—stuck in the grille, and I realize: 'They really did hit a fucking cow.' That guy Dougie—there's no front in these vans, no motor, no protection—he had a broken foot. He couldn't even move.

"My mind-set was: We're going to goddamn play 'Palisades Park.' We get the organ onstage and Gram keeps saying, 'I don't feel so good.' We count off, Gram's singing, 'Last night I took a walk in the park,' and he's about green. We do the song and everyone's impressed. Gram says, 'I don't feel so good.' We do one more and he says, 'I can't do it.' And off he went with Dougie to the hospital. It turned out he had a cracked rib and an injured arm. So he should have gone to the hospital, but it was cool he didn't go before he played."

Bobby Braddock remembers Gram from this time: "He was a Snively, of course. You never forgot that Snively was the richest man in the county. Gram was kind of quiet, seemed nice, a little nerdy. He was already regarded as a good musician. Everybody seemed to respect him for that." Jim Carlton recalls, "He'd go home and learn rough guitar for whatever we were doing. Most of it was pretty easy. You're talking the rhythm parts to 'Walk, Don't Run.' Gram had enough talent to cover anything that needed to be done. But he didn't have the burning desire to be a great guitarist that Jim Stafford had. Gram had the burning desire to be a star. He was always grooming himself for that. And it was his demeanor to be a star, his natural demeanor."

Though it's a cliché to say that someone who became a star always intended to be one, remember that Carlton is describing a tenth grader—and his best friend. Jim Stafford, a junior in high school, was already dedicated to his instrument, with his family's backing. It speaks to the differing class aspirations of both families that Stafford trusted in craftsmanship to provide a future. He chose the path of hard work and dedication. Gram looked to what the Snivelys and Bob Parsons regarded as their natural birthright: the first place at the table, the first place under the lights.

As for a musical career, even as young as the band members were, some already knew where they were headed. Jim Carlton's father sat Carlton and Stafford down to lecture them on what a miserable racket the music business could be. He told them every horror story he knew. "For three days," Carlton says, "we were so depressed neither of us could pick up a guitar. Then we got over it and began practicing again. My father said, 'If anyone can talk you out of show business, then you shouldn't be in it. But you've got to want it. Music is the best sideline in the world, but if you want to be a pro you better want it bad.'"

Bobby Braddock's parents took a more typical view. "My father thought nothing would ever come of me being in music," he says. "I never had the encouragement of people who thought of themselves as musicians."

Stafford, Carlton, Braddock, and LaVoie all made a success of show business—testament to the extraordinary musical environment that Gram Parsons was born to.

Braddock, as noted, became a hit songwriter. Carlton went on to be a jazz guitarist and comedy writer for the Smothers Brothers, David Letterman, and many others.

Kent LaVoie cut a series of records under his own name. In 1971 he wrote and sang the cloying but unforgettable soft-rock smash hit "Me and You and a Dog Named Boo" under the stage name Lobo. A series of hits followed, and although his career in the States waned in the mid-eighties, Lobo remains, as they say, huge in Asia. Lobo tours Japan and Southeast Asia annually and his various best-ofs sell well there and in Germany. With forty albums released, including at least ten best-ofs and *Lobo Golds* and Asian-specific karaoke, instrumental, and Malaysian-language-version LPs, Kent LaVoie has sold over twenty million records worldwide.

Jim Stafford released "Spiders and Snakes" and several other hit songs in the 1970s and parlayed his easy sense of humor and virtuoso guitar playing into a gig hosting his own TV variety hour, *The Jim Stafford Show*, in 1975. More hits followed, including "Turn Loose of My Leg" from the soundtrack of Clint Eastwood's second orangutan epic *Any Which Way You Can*. In 1990 Stafford discovered Branson, Missouri, and was one of the first to build his own theater in what has since become the family Las Vegas for retired Christians and their RV-driving grandchildren. Stafford, now billing himself not inaccurately as "the Victor Borge of the Guitar," sells out his eleven-hundred-seat theater every day, seven days a week.

SIX

VANGUARDS
AND LEGENDS

AS WOULD PROVE THE PATTERN IN GRAM'S LIFE, HIS HOME BECAME THE CENTER of his social world. 324 Piedmont Street was a happening scene. His bandmates and friends hung out there, welcomed by Bob and Big Avis, who liked having the kids around. They encouraged Gram and his friends to perform for their more or less constant house parties. Jim Carlton recalls, "Gram was a real ham. And Gene Leedy and Bob Parsons and the whole crew would gather around. We loved hanging out with the adults. They had the alcohol. They were high. They had money, they had great stories. Of course we hung out with them. Our friends were boring compared to the adults."

"We all looked at [Bob Parsons] as the playboy of the Western world," Dubie Baxter says. "He was forty-one when we were in our teens. He had money and had married a Snively. He was from New Orleans, someplace that to us could have been France." Grant Lacerte adds, "There was a lot of booze and merriment." So much so that a number of Gram's classmates were forbidden by their parents from visiting the Parsons home, which no doubt made it an even more appealing place to go.

Aside from the truckers' bennies, alcohol was the drug of choice. Gram, Carlton, and Lacerte found classic ways to subvert the dry laws and the age limit. "We would go into Florence Villa," Carlton says, "find a guy on the street, give him an extra buck, and he'd get us a six-pack." Not surprisingly, Grant Lacerte, Dougie Wiggins, and Gram were getting reputations as bad boys—bad tenth graders. "It was the Snively family's reputation as much as Gram's," Lacerte says. "The Snivelys were considered a fast-running group, and here was the upcoming generation doing the same old shit. Gram's reputation was earned fast: He was only fifteen. The family was known to be heavy drinkers and to have affairs and Gram was only following the adult lead."

Moreover, there was plenty of turmoil within the family.

One origin myth traces the trouble to Little Avis' growing love of horseflesh. Her cousin Susan Snively (later Susan Alexander) inherited a passion for show horses from her father, John Junior. Little Avis became enthralled with them, too. While Gram immersed himself in music, Little Avis spent her nonschool hours at a riding club in Lake Regis, becoming a dedicated horsewoman.

"My father-in-law"—John Junior—"spent all the family money on show horses," says Cornelia Snively Wallace. "Avis could not get money from John Junior to buy Little Avis as fine a horse as John's daughter Susan was show-ing. That's why Avis sued the Snively family. That and Bob Parsons."

Ever since John Senior died, the wheels had been coming off the Snively empire. John Senior had put the family's wealth into a network of trusts. Once John Junior ascended to the throne, he indulged his expensive show-horse habit with family cash. John Junior was apparently too genial to run the business that his father had built up through hard-assed hard work. Gene Leedy says, "He was generous and all his friends used him. Anytime they needed money they borrowed from John. Some of the biggest citrus folks in Polk County got their start on his money."

Between lending money and selling off pieces of the business to satisfy the family's insatiable need for cash, John Junior slowly dismembered the family holdings. Most of the sales he made were either below value or ill-timed. Jack Snively says, "He sold off our groves during the worst land-market slump in Florida history." Gene Leedy adds, "John Junior went into some nebulous, questionable deals. He was a bad businessman. He bought a chicken farm and way too many citrus groves with the [family] trust's money, and through the years it dissipated. He'd have to sell off one overpriced acquisition to hang on to another. He wasn't a crook, just over-generous, and he had bad judgment."

Hastening the collapse was the decision by Big Avis to sue her family to gain control over her share of its wealth. Her relatives blame her second husband. "Parsons talked Avis into suing the family," Rob Hoskins says. "Into breaking up the holdings. However laws work about jurisdiction and being able to handle children's money, the most liberal in the country [are] in Louisiana. He moved them to Louisiana during that first summer after his marriage to Big Avis so he could have more control over the kids' money."

Again, there's no evidence that Parsons moved his new family to Louisiana nor that Louisiana law had anything to do with the lawsuit. But it is true that the suit, in combination with John Junior's ineptitude, damaged the Snively fortune.

Gene Leedy's version of the story is that he and Parsons had the idea to resurrect Parsons' Colombian concrete company by building a prestressed-concrete commercial structure as a showpiece. The budget came in at around three hundred thousand dollars. When Avis went to the family piggy bank to withdraw enough to commence construction, the funds were lacking. That discovery triggered her lawsuit against the Snively family trusts.

The claim was that John Junior hadn't provided Avis with what she deserved. At the time of the suit other Snivelys felt the same way—about themselves. They sued as well. What everyone wanted was to have certain family trusts under John Junior's control broken into assets that could be divided out piecemeal, with the possibility of selling those assets immediately for cash. Big Avis won her suit and thereby gained access to a smoother flow of ready money. As Big Avis' husband, Parsons managed to insert himself into most subsequent Snively deals. The suit produced several cotrustees—Parsons, ostensibly representing Avis' interests, among them.

"Parsons talked Avis into suing the family to break up the family trusts," Rob Hoskins says, "because every bit of family property had been put in those trusts before John Senior died. Bob wanted the cash. He didn't want money on a yearly or monthly basis—he wanted cash in hand. Avis sued to break the trust. They won in court and split the trust into three sections, Avis' being the largest.

"Hers was about $2.5 million. All sorts of Snively assets had to be sold to generate enough cash money to create these three large trusts; nobody wanted to take property as value. Everyone wanted cash. The trust was all based on orange groves, groves that had made everyone a lot of money over the years. But it was a bad time for citrus and nobody wanted to get stuck with the groves. Parsons wanted cash to go back to South America and start investing there. He couldn't do that, the way the trust was set up—he couldn't get his hands on cash or property. So he sued."

Gene Leedy insists that the impetus for the suit originally came from Big Avis. "It was Avis' idea to sue because it was her money," he says.

Even Dode Whitaker, much as she loathed Bob Parsons, acknowledges that the lawsuit preserved some of the fortune for the next generation. "The one good thing he did was to get trusts set up for the grandchildren," she says. "Not just Gram and Little Avis, but Susan, Martha, John III, and Rob."

The lawsuit played out in the Snivelys' world with typical surreality and denial. "They went to court," Gene Leedy says. "And the funniest thing happened—this is pure Tennessee Williams—they were all testifying and everything. Avis was suing her own brother, her sister. After being on the stand all day, Bob called and said, 'How about you and Marjorie [Leedy's wife] come over? I've had a hard day in court and I'm going to fix dinner.' Shit, here were all the Snivelys, and I couldn't believe it. They were all drinking and talking and having a lovely time. Drinking and laughing like nothing ever happened."

Nevertheless, the lawsuit took its toll. "It was the distress in Avis' life and it split her family up," says Buddy Freeman, who came into the Parsons orbit in 1961. "[Her] brother and a sister and her were all at odds because of Bob. When Avis was in that temperament she didn't eat." Freeman remembers Big Avis as a small-boned, immaculately turned-out woman. "She was getting all her calories from the alcohol," he says. "It wasn't that she drank that much; it just didn't take much to do her harm."

Avis' mood wasn't improved by Bob's continued business troubles. Despite the infusion of cash, his efforts to strike it rich in Latin America and Mexico bore little fruit. Avis traveled with him to Cartagena as he tried to set up other projects. His deals were wrecked on the shoals of laws that seemed designed to fleece outsiders. Bob was well into a large construction job, likely in Mexico, before he discovered that import laws forbade him from bringing in the structural steel he needed to finish. Once again he abandoned a project and all the money he and Avis had invested.

Avis' moody ups and downs didn't faze Bob. Leedy claims that instead of getting into fights with her, Bob would avoid conflict. "Later, the only arguments they ever had were over her drinking too much. When she was sober she was a delight. But drunk she was always fussing at him, mean as a snake."

Susan Alexander recalls, "She drank much more heavily after she married Parsons." Rob Hoskins says, "Her drinking changed after the marriage. She drank in the morning and then all day."

"Just try to stop a Snively from drinking," Gene Leedy says. "That's the family disease."

IN THE SUMMER OF 1961, Big Avis introduced Gram to Buddy Freeman. The encounter was typical of the interconnected high-society Snively world. Buddy, twenty-two years old, was a show-horse competitor. He met the Parsons family through the horse trainers working with Little Avis. Little Avis, then ten years old, was flying to Greenville, South Carolina, where Buddy lived, to compete in a show. Little Avis' trainer asked Buddy to pick her up at the airport, take her to the arena, and look after her. "She was the cutest kid, full of enthusiasm for horses and the horse business," Buddy recalls. "She was a good rider, too. Fearless. She was being all adult, dining out and watching the show from box seats. Kids have the freedom of the grounds, and that's a big deal to a ten-year-old."

Little Avis felt well looked after, and Big Avis wrote Buddy an effusive letter of thanks. Shortly after, he met Big Avis at a competition in Chastain Park in Atlanta. Buddy won his event. With her usual impetuous extravagance, Big Avis insisted on throwing a catered party that night in Buddy's honor and told him to invite whomever he wanted.

Buddy sat next to Big Avis and met Gram. "For a fifteen-year-old kid he had the best-looking clothes," Buddy recalls. "Tailored, handmade shirts, khaki slacks, a striped shirt and a blue blazer. He had a model's body, and clothes hung on him well. I later learned that he and Mr. Parsons had their clothes tailored at Rosenbaum's in Jacksonville. They became my tailor, too.

"Gram was bored to tears. He didn't know anything about horses and could care less about horse shows. He didn't know anybody there except his mama and little sister. I tried to engage him in conversation but he didn't want to talk." Gradually, coaxing out every word, Buddy learned that Gram was a musician. Buddy promised to get the restaurant manager to allow Gram to play the big piano in the bar after the party. Gram brightened and insisted on seeing the piano immediately. After dinner, he sat down to play.

"The main thing," Buddy says, "was he didn't have that long look on his face anymore, like he would drop through a hole in the floor. It was good to see his mother enjoying him, too. You could tell she was proud."

Gram went to visit Buddy in Greenville for a few days, playing guitar at Freeman's parties and his neighbors' barbecues. He sang the current folk hits "If I Had a Hammer" and "Puff the Magic Dragon" along with, incongruously, Frank Sinatra's "It Was a Very Good Year." Gram loved pop treacle as much as he loved Elvis, and he never lost his taste for either. The image of Gram at fifteen crooning, "When I was seventeen . . ." speaks to his devotion to performing and his affection for córnpone.

Buddy was impressed and so were his friends. Thanks to word of mouth generated at the parties and Buddy's own efforts, a local television station sought to interview Gram. "At this time folk music was a hot, big item," Buddy says. "Peter, Paul & Mary, the Journeymen, the Limeliters, the Geezinslaw Brothers, Glenn Yarbrough, the Christy Minstrels—they had hit singles and were hot groups. Gram played some folk songs; they set up a nice little prop background, and Gram was photogenic. He had a lot of charisma. He was a hit, and they wanted to tape some segments for future broadcast on noontime for an everyday show. Gram was delighted."

Gram went back to Winter Haven, and Buddy's phone started ringing. "A couple people called me from a restaurant in Fort Lauderdale, wanting to talk to Gram's manager," Buddy says. "I ran Gram down and asked him about it. He said, 'Oh, I know. I gave them your name and number. I want you to act as my manager.' I said, 'Now, Gram, you know I can't be your manager.' He said, 'You don't know it, but you're going to be.' I told him I would help him but had no idea where this was all going."

IN SEPTEMBER 1961 Big Avis gave birth to her third child, Diane. She was named for Bob Parsons' sister, with whom she shared her birth date. A year later, Big Avis arranged another new addition to the household, nineteen-year-old Bonnie Muma. Bonnie had been babysitting for a Winter Haven society family, who referred her to Big Avis. She hired Bonnie to be Diane's nanny. Within a few years Bonnie became Bob Parsons' lover, and his third wife.

A Snively cousin, who would talk about Bonnie only under the cloak of anonymity, calls her "that little skinny girl from the trashy side of town who was ugly as a mud fence." Dubie Baxter has a different memory of her. "Bonnie was a bombshell, but in a real low-key way," Baxter says. "She was upper middle-class, with strict parents. A quiet beauty. Smart but never flaunted anything. Absolutely gorgeous. She was about five foot seven, light brown hair, blond in the summer, had a hell of a body, but was so quiet I don't think anybody noticed."

Bonnie, five years older than Gram, grew up on Lake Summit, one lake over from Cypress Gardens. She graduated from Winter Haven High and spent a year at the University of Maryland.

She found the Parsons household a surprise. In her home the family ate their meals together at a long table. Over Bob Parsons' objections, Big Avis exiled the children to the kitchen. Little Diane ate her meals in a high chair there, alone with the maids. Bonnie recalls that when she took Diane on a visit to the Mumas' house, the little girl was "in shock" for the first five minutes, amazed by the sight of the entire family eating as one.

Bonnie, for her part, was awed by the Parsons family and its way of living. "When Bob walked in he filled up a room," she says. "Avis was always his focal point. Bob would go to Avis first, no matter who was there—and there were always people in the house. Friends of hers, friends of his, friends of those friends. Bob loved people in the house."

Bob seemed always up, always generous, always magnanimous. But his relentless hosting had an air of mania. His daughter Becky Gottsegen says, "So much of his life was spent caretaking other people. So when I hear about what a snake he was, I always think, Who are they talking about? Bob had the disease to please, and he always found a way to entertain other people to the detriment of his own family."

Avis and Bob's social habits brought out the hard partyer in each of them. Bob's old friend Walter Lanaux recalls, "Avis said to me, 'Oh, we're having such a wonderful time. We wake up in the morning and have a bottle of Piper-Heidsieck.' I thought, 'Bob Parsons drinking in the morning? In bed?' That was hard for me to believe. But he changed his gait—he changed his speed."

The drinking led to ugly scenes. Becky Gottsegen recalls screaming fights every time she visited Winter Haven as a child. One night when Bob had been out carousing, Avis greeted him at the door in a rage. She threw her ever-present glass right through the windshield of Bob's car. That such craziness occurred in front of Bob's adolescent daughter speaks to the passions roused in Avis by Bob Parsons and alcohol. Yet her anger, and the alcohol that fueled it, also led Avis to become increasingly withdrawn. She kept her husband at a distance, retreating into her social world or into her glass. Often she was in too much of a stupor to connect with anyone.

Bob adored his new daughter. When he came home from work he'd go straight to her room. He liked to brush her hair and throw her over his head while she giggled. He loved to give her whatever he was eating, be it caviar or salmon or steak. Bob rained presents on her. One Christmas he came back from New York with a load of toys from FAO Schwarz for Gram, Little Avis, and Diane, including the classic gigantic FAO teddy bear for Diane. On Christmas morning the bear, ignored, rested under the tree while the little girl pushed a milk carton around the floor as Bob looked on, smiling.

Bonnie would arrive at the Parsons kitchen every morning around eight and spend her days with Diane. She and her charge bonded strongly—hardly surprising, given how emotionally absent Diane's mother was. Big Avis would usually be hungover and slow to start the day. Bob rarely appeared in the mornings, and Bonnie became Avis' breakfast mixologist. After her employer pushed a few drinks back at her with the command, "More vodka," Bonnie understood just how strong Avis needed her start-up to be.

Bonnie remembers Avis spending little time with Diane: "She'd come by and pat her on the face, or pick her up quick. She was a society mother. She'd have that drink in the morning and was always gone to luncheons or the women's clubs." Bonnie says that Big Avis was never a bad mother. "But she was unapproachable. She drank from morning till night."

IN 1962 Big Avis invited Buddy Freeman down to Ponte Vedra, Florida, a high-end beach community on the east coast, south of Jacksonville. She had rented a house on the beach near the Ponte Vedra Inn so the kids could use the hotel pool and the children's beach club. They took a few meals at the hotel as well. While Little Avis went to Gainesville every day to ride, Buddy spent time with Gram and Big Avis, trying to sort out Gram's intentions.

"She welcomed me graciously," Buddy says. "She did everything with grace. She had a full staff at the house. She had Ida, who cooked, and another black lady who cleaned, and then a white girl, Bonnie, who looked after her youngest daughter, Diane. Every morning Ida would say, 'Would you like fresh grapefruit or fresh orange or fresh-made tomato juice? Would you like a Bloody Mary?' First thing in the morning . . ."

Avis, in Buddy's words, "held Gram's feet to the fire" to make him say exactly what he wanted Buddy to do and to stop spinning stories. "Gram was trying to lead us all on, his mom included. He told her he had written some things he had not, like 'It Was a Very Good Year.'"

While staying at Ponte Vedra, Freeman arranged a contract for Gram to play a solo folk-rock gig at LeCollage, a beatnik-style coffeehouse in St. Augustine. Buddy found a Ponte Vedra society photographer to shoot promo portraits of Gram and posted them outside the coffeehouse. Gram played Friday and Saturday night. Buddy negotiated five hundred dollars for the two shows. That was a giant leap from a hundred dollars a week gigging with the Legends. And the spotlight did not have to be shared. Buddy took no manager's fees: "I was doing this for Gram and his mama. Avis had been generous to me, and this was my payback." The coffeehouse crowd ran from fifteen to thirty-five years old. Friday night a hundred people came, Saturday, 150, standing room only for the LeCollage. Gram played about forty-five minutes, including his folk repertoire, "Blue Velvet," and "It Was a Very Good Year." Buddy recalls, "He was smart enough to blend in lots of ballads."

During that Ponte Vedra visit, Gram tried to use Buddy as an influence with his mom. "Gram wanted to write music, and he asked me to talk to his mother about some better instruments," Buddy says. "She said, 'I spent a thousand dollars on a Stratocaster electric guitar and he's going to have to choose. He can play this kind of music [rock with the Legends] or that kind of music [folk acoustic]. He can get rid of the Stratocaster and we'll talk. But we are not going to collect guitars.'" Where Bob Parsons unfailingly indulged Gram, Avis could be either more sensibly parental or totally vacant, depending on her level of intoxication.

Some of the tension at home may have explained the melancholy that Gram's girlfriend at the time, Pam Cairns, detected. "He was introspective," Pam says. "He was more serious than a lot of our friends because of his music. . . . He was intelligent but a loner. He spent a lot of time writing and thinking. The Legends and music became his life, and school became secondary to him."

Pam noticed how attached Gram was to his baby half sister, Diane. He would pick her up and sing to her. With Little Avis often gone, traveling to horse shows or working with her trainers in northern Florida, Diane seemed to be a touchstone for Gram in his relatively deranged household.

A girl who readily accepted the mores of her place and time, Pam wasn't a particularly good match for Gram. "He was a moody guy. He could be real up and happy one minute and down and depressed the next," she says. "He would stare down and pick up that guitar and strum it. And that was the time I'd pick up and leave. I don't like to be around people when they're in that kind of mood. If there's a reason, I'll be the most sympathetic and empathetic person, but to have no reason at all to switch moods like that—I don't have any tolerance for it."

Pam also noticed another side of Gram: his thirst for the spotlight and the thrills that went with it. "He loved for other girls and other people to give him attention, and that wasn't in my makeup," Pam says. "When girls were flirting with him, he was always happier than he was with me. And my parents didn't want me hanging out with his group. They didn't want me in that bus and leaving the area.

"Gram was leaning toward the wild side. I was pretty straitlaced. I played by the rules and would never consider not playing by the rules. Gram was always trying to find the edge. He wanted to live in a way that was more thought-provoking and have different experiences than other guys that age. He was willing to take more risks than most of my friends. We did not last long." Gram broke up with Pam after a couple of months. Proving what a small world Winter Haven could be, Pam later married Bonnie Muma's brother Lester.

As the Parsons marriage became increasingly combative and liquor-soaked, Gram gained more and more freedom. It was not uncommon for him to take off in the middle of the night, leaving a note, if that. When Gram turned sixteen, Bob Parsons, playing the James Bond father figure to the hilt, bought Gram a red Austin-Healey Sprite—a rare, bug-eyed, English two-seater sports convertible. Like Coon Dog in Hawaii, Gram tore ass around the county in his red convertible with the top down. When Gram got grounded for six weeks and was denied use of the Sprite, Jim Carlton took over the driving, taking Gram where he wanted to go. "Gram was raising himself," Grant Lacerte says. "His mother was a serious alcoholic. I recall Avis with her big jug of Jack Daniel's before lunchtime. My parents might have taken a drink every night with dinner—and that was unusual in the South at that time. I never saw my folks drink in the daytime. But if Avis went to visit her sister, she had to take a drink with her in the car."

Lacerte also recognized the pain that underlay Gram's wildness. "I was fond of Gram to the point of feeling sorry for him. I knew all he was lacking, all he had lost. He was brave in his way. He knew what his mother was about. He had to cope with things none of us had to. I heard about what happened to his father from somebody else. I never heard him discuss it."

"He would go to his room and hope his mother would stay out," Susan Whitehead says, "because she could be a monster when she was drinking. I remember her one time knocking on the door. She wasn't in the mood to have kids running in and out of the house. She said something ugly to Gram about how she wanted everyone to go home and leave her alone. That was the only time I saw her come in. Most of the time she disappeared. It was common knowledge that she was an alcoholic. She'd come to the door to let me in with a drink in her hand. My parents, and most parents, almost never touched alcohol. And Gram would say, 'Yeah, Mom's at it again.'"

With Big Avis less present both physically and emotionally, Gram's relationship to Bob Parsons grew closer. Being treated as an adult—even by an overgrown adolescent like Bob Parsons—was no doubt a pleasure compared to being snarled at by his drunken mother. "Bob and Gram got on beautifully," Bonnie Muma says. "Gram wanted to be a Parsons; he didn't want to be a Connor. He was glad to have been adopted." Jim Carlton says, "I liked Bob Parsons. Gram liked Bob Parsons. It was like having Hugh Hefner around. He was a debonair, distinguished, sophisticated guy, and he was fun. His secret was treating us like adults. That's irresistible to a high school kid. We wanted to be included, we wanted to be mature. That's exactly how he treated us, and he honestly respected Gram's talent."

Becky Gottsegen believes Bob was fascinated with Gram because Bob wanted a son. She maintains that Bob was noticeably more attentive to Gram and Little Avis than he ever was to Becky and her sister, Jan. "Gram was important to Bob," Bonnie Muma says. "Probably more so than Little Avie. He was the boy. Bob wanted Gram to have everything. And Gram emulated him. They would have boy talks."

One of their boy talks arose when Gram, who was not a big guy, came home frightened. He'd been in the town hangout, a diner across the street from Winter Haven High. Some enormous Winter Haven footballer took offense over something. The footballer, remembered by Jim Carlton as "a big lummox," slapped Gram and promised to beat the shit out of him the next morning. According to Carlton, "This huge guy pasted Gram right in the face." Gram asked Bob what he should do. Bob's response was immediate. "You have to stand up to him," he said, "or he'll constantly be on your ass." He told his stepson to push for a showdown. "When you go in there you say, 'I'm looking for that sonofabitch.'"

Later Bob regaled Gene Leedy with the story. "Bob grew up on the tough side of New Orleans," Leedy says. "He told me, 'That night I taught

Gram some cusswords he never heard of.'" Bob told Gram of the fights he'd had growing up and advised him to fight back no matter what. "You'll probably get your ass beat, but make sure he's hurt, too," Bob told Leedy he'd said. "Don't back down."

The next day Bob came home early. He wanted to be there when Gram walked through the door. Gram came in all smiles. He told Bob that as he walked into the place he said, "Where's the sonofabitch who's going to beat my ass? I'm here to see what he can do." It turned out nobody liked the bully. In Gram's version his friends gathered around and pounded the guy. Gram told Bob, "I didn't even have to touch him. I gave them all the courage to stand up to him."

This tale provides a preview of Gram's future default problem-solving method: Gram standing to the side as events unfold, taking no part in the dirty work, being happy to claim the credit. The bully story forms a small triumph, but it bears an ominous undertone of Gram observing rather than participating in the key moments of his own life. And it points to another pattern: Gram's readiness to embroider, fib, or lie outright.

There's a further wrinkle in this tale: Carlton does not remember a crowd jumping the lummox, and suspects Gram told Bob a happy ending because Gram couldn't help but bullshit. "Gram often got picked on by guys whose girlfriends hit on him," Carlton says. "He learned to take a punch, so I never remember him hitting the ground. This kind of thing happened fairly often. I don't think Gram ever hit back."

Gram's disassociation from the truth increased as he became more and more the family star. "Gram's tendency to bullshit was common to the previous generation of Snivelys," Grant Lacerte says. "A Snively might say, 'I killed a fifth of Courvoisier last night,' when you knew he only had a sip. Gram was always trying to impress you with what he'd been exposed to. I would call him on it, and Karen would call him on it worse. Karen would always say, 'Are you going to try to bullshit *me*?' And Gram was never combative or reactionary about it. He'd cease that line and go on to some *other* bullshit.

"It had to have been about insecurity. He would exaggerate things he never needed to. He didn't have to exaggerate about his intellect or things he'd done, but he always did. Karen finally came right out and said, 'Gram, you don't have to brag. You've got plenty to speak about for real that's exceptional.' And that was about the only thing that annoyed me. He was a good friend, a loyal friend. But watch out—he did not suffer fools." What puzzled Gram's close friends—Jim Carlton, Grant and Karen Lacerte—about his compulsion for talking shit was that they found him sincere, insightful, and dependable when he was doing instead of talking. "One time after hearing him play, and it was beautiful," Karen Lacerte says, "he started talking as soon as he came offstage, and I said, 'Gram, we are not impressed. There's not a thing you can say to impress us more than what we've just heard.'"

THE 1961 LEGENDS lineup mutated into the 1962–63 version: Gram on vocals and rhythm guitar, Jim Stafford—who was proving something of a prodigy—on lead guitar, Jesse Chambers on bass, and Jon Corneal on drums.

Gram had met Dickie McNeer when the Pacers played a battle of the bands in 1960 at the Lions Club Center in Lake Albert, Florida. It wasn't until 1962, at the beginning of their junior year at Winter Haven High, that Gram and Dickie became friends, fellow inebriates, and musical partners. Dickie was the same age as Gram, attended Winter Haven High, and grew up in a wealthy citrus family, part of the Winter Haven country club, big-house-and-boathouse set. Like Gram, Dickie had a passion for folk music.

In the late summer of 1962, Jim Stafford and Jim Carlton played on a Bobby Braddock demo recording. The same summer, Gram formed a typically off-the-cuff Winter Haven guitar-and-vocal-harmony group with Dickie McNeer, Grant Lacerte, and Dougie Wiggins. They performed for Snively family functions and a few country clubs, most notably the Tampa Yacht and Country Club. That gig came from Gram's social connections with the yacht club kids.

Gram continued playing shows with the Legends and doing solo acoustic performances set up by Buddy Freeman, but Gram and Dickie McNeer also spoke of forming a folk group. They listened to Peter, Paul & Mary, the Chad Mitchell Trio, the Weavers, the Kingston Trio, the Limeliters, and the Journeymen: commercial, easy-strumming, harmony-dominated, melodic light folk with roots not in protest music but traditional song. What political content might exist ("If I Had a Hammer," for instance) was universal, never cause-specific, and featured none of the outrage or anger that appeared in the later advocacy folk of Bob Dylan or Phil Ochs. McNeer insists that they never even understood that folk could be political. "Folk has always been the common man speaking out about his grievances," he says. "And our school wasn't even integrated then. We didn't connect the civil rights movement with that kind of music at all."

Gram and Dickie had, for the time, remarkable access to current folk music. WSIR-AM in Winter Haven played rock and then folk music for an hour a night. WGTO-AM, which broadcast from Cypress Gardens, played folk music as well. Again, Winter Haven proved an anomalous center of musical hipness; at that time there were few other small cities in the South where folk music could be heard on local radio.

Dickie, as a class equal, takes an unsentimental view of Big Avis' problems. "Avis was an alkie," he says. "Most of our families were alkies; that was the way of life back then. I didn't pay much attention to it. One day she was in a bad mood and the next happy as a lark. Bob Parsons, though, I didn't like. He was an asshole, a yeller. Anything that pissed him off, he would start yelling."

Dickie also experienced Gram's careless relationship with the truth. "Gram was a loner, not a joiner, and I think that's how we hooked up; I wasn't a joiner either. He had that lost-puppy-dog look. He knew how to talk and he could make you believe damn near anything he said. Gram was good at embellishing the facts. We were at his house playing this song, 'Sister Mary's turn to throw the bomb / The last one was thrown by Brother John,' and Gram told me he wrote it. A few weeks later the Legends were playing out at the country club, and here's the damn song on the jukebox by whoever." (It was likely the 1963 novelty number "It's Sister Ginny's Turn to Throw the Bomb" by the Glencoves, a Long Island folk group.)

Gram's photo in the 1962 Winter Haven High yearbook. (Courtesy Grant and Karen Lacerte)

Gram and Dickie brought out the hell-raiser in each other. They scored Dexedrine (another form of speed) from truck drivers, and they drank. They pursued the drug myths of their time: smoking crushed aspirin in a cigarette to get high, putting aspirin in a girl's Coca-Cola to send her into extremes of sexual eagerness. They used a syringe to inject oranges with vodka and ate the oranges with their school lunch. Egged on by Dickie, Gram began raiding Big Avis' medicine cabinet, a treat they allowed themselves a couple times a month.

"She had little red pills, little yellow ones, black ones," Dickie McNeer says. "We had no idea what we were taking. 'Ah, this looks good.' Gram would reach in, grab a bottle, and say, 'Let's try these.' We'd take it to see what the hell would happen. Sometimes it felt good, sometimes it didn't. This wasn't something we did every day. We were teenagers experimenting, and we happened to have access to a larger supply than everybody else.

"We drank Bob Parsons' beer, rum, and bourbon, Bacardi, Jack Daniel's,

Wild Turkey. We went to the barbershop in Florence Villa to buy liquor. Every white kid in Winter Haven went to that barbershop or to Parnell's Grocery. Parnell's was a store and boarding house; it had bunk beds in the back for fruit pickers. Parnell was a nice man and would sell liquor to us kids. Marijuana we didn't know about."

Gram and Dickie jammed on their acoustic guitars and formed a folk trio: the Village Vanguards, named for the famous Greenwich Village jazz club. The third member was their classmate at Winter Haven High, the beautiful Patti Johnson.

Gram and Patti were already dating when she was invited to join the band. The only folk band in Polk County, the Vanguards modeled themselves after Peter, Paul & Mary. Dickie McNeer recalls, "We asked Patti because she had long blond hair, was good-looking, and could sing. She could carry a tune, she could harmonize, and she had the look onstage, that long, straight blond hair."

A relative of Gram's insists that "Gram was head over heels for her. But he was young, and I'm sure the reason is that she would sleep with him." Patti was a year ahead of Gram, a senior when he was a junior. Her reputation at Winter Haven High was quite different from, say, Bonnie Muma's. Patti was intelligent, popular, a cheerleader, and got good grades. She was famous, in that high school way, for dating older men—men who had already graduated. She bore the social burden of being rumored to have gone all the way. It's almost automatic in the South at this time that the best-looking, most reclusive girl would be thus characterized.

Dubie Baxter, proving that there's nothing as timeless as the way girls get talked about in high school, says, "Today it would be nothing. She'd be a laggard by today's standards. But back then, believe me, nobody got laid until their senior year. She matured early, that's what it was. She was athletic and she had a sensuality that you never saw in somebody that young. She was reticent about being sexy. We used to laugh about it and say, 'Patti doesn't even know what she's got.'"

In other words, Patti was a star: beautiful, smart, and elusive, with a deliberately conceived public persona that was the subject of sexy but unsubstantiated rumors. Who else would Gram be head over heels about?

"Patti was the hottest chick until Karen [Grant's future wife] came back to town," Grant Lacerte says. Grant dated Patti briefly, or rather he served as her beard so Patti's parents wouldn't know that she was seeing an older boy with a bad reputation. Grant would pick Patti up at her parents' house and drop her at the Winter Haven make-out spot known as the Orange Grove, where her real boyfriend awaited. Then he'd sit at Jack & Betty's drive-in alone for two hours, pick Patti up, and drive her home.

Following the style of the polite pre-Dylan folk groups of that time, the Vanguards wore matching outfits. Gram and Dickie had light-green three-piece suits with little lapels and carried cane umbrellas. Patti wore a light-green form-fitting dress in the style of Mary Travers from Peter, Paul & Mary. Gram and Dickie went to the Winter Haven homecoming game in the fall of 1962 wearing their green suits. Patti was on the field in her uniform leading cheers. The boys brought a cooler with a bottle of carbonated grape juice wrapped in a cloth like champagne and champagne glasses. They sat in the stands toasting one another with grape juice. Their cooler-than-thou moment came to an end when Gram got yanked down to the concession stand, where, as a junior, he was required to work. For the rest of the game, Gram sold hot dogs in his green three-piece suit. Afterward, Dickie and Gram barely avoided suspension, and the cheerleaders were not happy with Patti due to Gram's poor show of school spirit.

Dickie at first played a Gibson ES175 guitar that he found ill-suited for folk music. He traded it in at a pawnshop for a Goya 20. Gram played a Gibson L4 guitar. Unlike the Legends, the Village Vanguards actually practiced. They rehearsed in Gram's room three or four times a week. "It all came easy to Gram," McNeer says. "He was a good piano player, one of those guys to whom music came readily no matter what it was. He was a good singer; he wasn't the greatest guitar player. We never did get the intricate fingerpicking down—that syncopated, claw-type finger work. But we had our facsimile of it for 'Puff the Magic Dragon,' 'Where Have All the Flowers Gone?,' and 'Don't Think Twice, It's All Right.'" The Vanguards played Journeymen songs, Merle Travis, Gordon Lightfoot, Tom Paxton, and Ian and Sylvia's "You Were on My Mind" and duplicated the Smothers Brothers' comedy routines. Patti sang lead and, as Dickie puts it, "snapped her fingers." Gram and Dickie sang harmony parts and occasional lead vocals. The Vanguards were proud of their intricate Peter, Paul & Mary–style harmonies.

Dickie, like everyone else, was in awe of Gram's living situation. "We all went: 'Damn, I wish I had a place I could come and go as I pleased and my folks would never know the difference.' Gram had the first Sony reel-to-reel tape recorder I'd ever seen. We made a few tapes in that room."

The Vanguards played the Almond Steak House on Garden Road in Winter Haven, during breaks between amplified bands at dances in high school gyms or women's clubs, and at house parties and talent shows. They performed during intermissions of Legends shows. The trio sang over the school intercom in the mornings and during lunch breaks. Between the Legends, his solo shows, and the Vanguards, Gram had little time to spend being a high school student. Karen Lacerte remembers "Gram doing no schoolwork at all, none, zero. He didn't attend class and he didn't seem to get in any trouble for it."

THE ADULTS IN GRAM'S LIFE had other things on their minds.

When Big Avis got drunk and angry, as happened frequently, she often accused her husband of running around on her, a charge that his enemies in the Snively camp insist was justified. Bob was a relentlessly charming schmoozehound and a tireless flirt, and women found him extremely attractive. "Women were after Bob all the time," Gene Leedy says. "Even some of his in-laws made overtures."

But it's impossible to find one woman of their circle who claims to have had an affair with Bob during his marriage to Avis. Nor can anyone name someone in their circle who slept with Bob. In a community as incestuous and gossipy as the wealthy of Winter Haven, it seems fair to demand smoke as evidence of fire, and no smoke appears.

But there is one woman who admits to sleeping with Bob while he was married to Big Avis: baby Diane's nanny, Bonnie Muma.

In the spring of 1963 Bonnie took a vacation with a girlfriend to Aruba. "We took off for two or three weeks, looking for boys, and both of us found one," Bonnie recalls. "And the four of us were on the beach and I heard footsteps behind. I knew it was Bob. There was a boardwalk there, and I don't know how I knew, but I knew . . . maybe from hearing his footsteps when he came into the house at home. Hearing his steps and knowing: Here it comes. He asked me out that night and I said no. He said, 'What about lunch tomorrow?' and there it started."

Bonnie never was able to find out if Bob followed her to Aruba or was there on business and just happened to run into her. "I asked him and he smiled. We went out several times and it grew more serious. I admired him. By the time he came to Aruba I had begun to see how rough it was between him and Avis. [In Aruba] he would go off during the day to do business. At night we'd go dancing, sailing, walking on the beach. But no sex. I was careful about that."

Once they returned to Winter Haven, Bob stepped up the courtship.

Little Avis, Bonnie Muma, Robert Parsons, on a fishing trip off Ponte Vedra, Florida. (Courtesy the estate of Robert Parsons)

Things came to a head that summer, when Bonnie accompanied the family to the beach house at Ponte Vedra. "One night I got up for a glass of water, and he was in the kitchen and he kissed me," Bonnie says. "I was saying no and he was saying yes. . . . Here's this man that's so bigger than life and associated with the Snivelys. Kind of like in New York being associated with the Rockefellers. And he was paying attention to little old Bonnie Muma? It was an awkward summer."

Bob Parsons went back to Colombia in search of more business. He called Bonnie, told her he needed her, and sent her a ticket. She flew to meet him. Bonnie says, "And that's when Avis called [my mother]. I don't know how she found out, but she did."

Big Avis confronted Bonnie when she returned from Colombia. The younger woman decided she had to break it off and leave town. "I do have a head on my shoulders," she says. "I knew I needed to get away. I enrolled in Palm Beach Junior College."

Big Avis assured Bonnie that there had been plenty of others. She gave the clear impression that for Bob, Bonnie was just one more out of many. But who were these many? Where are they? "Anything negative that anyone ever said about Bonnie was about being vindictive," Becky Gottsegen says. "And anyone saying those things about [Bob Parsons] either didn't know him or they have a personal vendetta against him."

Bob inspired fierce loyalty in those close to him and bitter hatred from everyone else. The story of his time with Bonnie Muma prior to their marriage has been much misinterpreted. Parsons' detractors describe him as a heartless, scheming Machiavelli. But his affair with Bonnie reveals a relatively simple—if neither brave nor straightforward—man in love.

After Bonnie left town, Bob wasn't willing to let her get away. He followed her to Palm Beach and pursued her diligently. After a series of dinner, lunch, and beach dates, Bonnie knew she was in love. Bob found her an apartment in Fort Worth and bought her a used station wagon. She drove home in that wagon to visit her folks in Winter Haven. She insists that their romance remain strictly a Palm Beach affair, and claims that in Winter Haven "we never, never fooled around at all."

Although Bob continued the affair, he did not have any intention of leaving his marriage. "He was honorable," Bonnie says. "He respected Avis. He probably enjoyed the money. He never talked about divorce. He wouldn't have. If Avis had lived longer he would have stayed with her."

How much Avis knew and when she knew it remains a mystery. But whatever she thought, her response was to drink even more. Avis' daily routine consisted of Bloody Marys in the morning, gin and tonics through the afternoon, and martinis starting at six at night. Bob's affair became common knowledge, as was Big Avis' drunkenness. As Karen Lacerte puts it, "The dad's screwing the babysitter and the mom's screwing Jack Daniel's." Susan Alexander remembers, "It was a bad scene as far as the kids were concerned. Avis knew, Little Avis knew, Gram knew. We all knew Bonnie; she was the babysitter and lived right down the street from my brother. I don't remember fights at the house about it. No one ever said a word. It was the elephant in the corner of the room."

In the midst of the ever-increasing tension, Gram and Patti Johnson staged a commotion of their own. The Legends played a women's club in Lake Howard, and the Vanguards performed during the Legends' intermission. During a break, Gram and Patti announced to the ten to fifteen teenagers assembled in the anteroom that they intended to elope that night. In the Snively and Parsons family tradition, Gram and Patti were going to run off and get married. By the standards of the time, there could be only one reason to do such a thing: Everyone assumed Patti must have been pregnant. Gram and Patti drove off right after the announcement, leaving Jim Carlton to fill in for Gram on guitar.

A fog of gossip has enveloped this incident ever since, shrouding whether Patti was actually pregnant.

Was the pregnancy an after-the-fact high school rumor-mill embellishment of Gram and Patti's simple desire to go get hitched? The more hostile a witness is toward Patti—the wanton, one-year-older-than-Gram blond cheerleader—the more lurid the details become. Cops get called, young lovers are nabbed moments before they escape, an irate father locks the car as Gram and Patti race toward it. An especially sophisticated twist, asserted by a family member hostile to both Gram and Patti, holds that Patti was pregnant but that the baby was not Gram's.

In fact, Patti was never pregnant. The two sweethearts did not run off. Nobody got married. Patti's parents stepped in before anybody went anywhere. In retrospect, the whole scene plays as a routine high school elopement drama, staged for maximum impact. A plaintive scene, clearly observed through the windows at Patti's house, followed: Gram sitting meekly on the couch beside Patti as Patti's father paced back and forth, ranting. The Johnsons' response was predictable: Patti was yanked from the Vanguards.

A friend of the pair describes it this way: "[The Johnsons] weren't thrilled with their daughter's name and reputation being fodder for scandal. [Gram and Patti] weren't forbidden from seeing each other—both came from privileged families who rarely imposed much discipline on their kids. They kept dating and even used my house when I was away on my vacation. They might have gone to the prom together—I do remember that Patti was chosen the best-looking girl. It was nothing more than sweating out a teenage girl's late period—how many millions have done that?"

Even Bob and Big Avis took notice, although they didn't react with the same fury as the Johnsons. "They wouldn't have wanted them to marry," Dickie McNeer says. "They were concerned, of course. It didn't upset them as much as it did Patti's parents. Patti's mom jumped me bad because I said something to someone else about Patti being pregnant. 'Wait a damn minute,' I said. 'They told the whole goddamned world!' It wasn't something that was being kept under wraps. Everybody knew because they *told* us."

Gram's friends felt Gram was as much in love with Patti as he was capable of being. The relationship didn't survive after the brouhaha died down. Gram became sexually active after his time with Patti. He borrowed Jim Carlton's Rambler for dates because the Rambler's front passenger seat would fold down flat. One girl became Gram's regular Rambler lover. Jim Carlton recalls lending Gram the keys to his house when his family took a weekend trip to the west coast of Florida: "When I got back, there was evidence of him fooling around. The bed was unmade, the ashtrays were full, and the turntable was still going. I had to clean it all up before my parents got home."

As a corollary to the Patti Johnson scandal, Gram failed eleventh grade. This was hardly surprising; he did no work and seldom showed up for class. Gram's days of coming and going as he pleased ended with a thud. Bob and Big Avis were compelled, for once, to behave as responsible parents. They decided that come the fall of 1963, Gram would be packed off as a full-time boarding student to the same institution he'd attended years earlier, the Bolles School in Jacksonville.

SEVEN

THE BOLLES SCHOOL

WHEN GRAM WAS SENT TO BOLLES DURING HIS SIXTH-GRADE YEAR, IT WAS A military school. In 1963, when Gram returned, Bolles was in its first years of shedding its military past. The school had been nowhere near as harsh as the more hardcore Southern military academies. Now uniforms were replaced by gray slacks, blue blazers, and ties. Faculty members retained their titles of rank, but few other trappings remained. Bolles continued to serve as a finishing school for the young gentlemen of Florida and, in a few cases, Latin America. Discipline now manifested in social pressure, conformity, noblesse oblige: a keen sense of class-appropriate behavior.

A small, expensive school, Bolles was made up of four hundred boys evenly split between boarders and day students. It began as the San Jose Hotel, which had opened as a bay-front resort on New Year's Day 1926. The main building is an elegant stucco affair, grand in the Mediterranean style, with four-story castlelike towers, arched roof walkways, and planted central plazas.

Like everything else more than fifty years old in Florida or connected to Gram Parsons, Bolles has a colorful history. A certain Richard J. Bolles had grown wealthy mining silver in Colorado and trading on Wall Street. His secretary and companion, Agnes Cane, was given authority over Bolles' estate when he died in 1917. She financed the San Jose Hotel and held the mortgage. The place thrived for two years. When the Florida land boom went bust in 1928, tourists stopped coming and the hotel failed. Ms. Cane foreclosed the mortgage and took over the property. She married a much younger man, Roger Painter. Together they enticed the Florida Military Academy to leave its former campus across the St. John's River, move into the empty hotel, and start paying rent. The academy did well enough until the Depression hit in 1931. After that, few could afford to send their sons to boarding school. Agnes Cane, now Agnes Painter, evicted the FMA, and the school moved to another failed hotel in St. Petersburg. The Painters decided to open a school of their own and to name it in honor of Mrs. Painter's benefactor.

With fourteen boys enrolled, the Bolles School opened in January 1933. Three Florida Military Academy students had so disliked leaving the grand hotel for St. Petersburg that when they heard a new school had opened on their old campus, they hitchhiked from St. Pete to Jacksonville to enroll. Or so the legend goes. One of those legendary three was Sidney Register, who became Bolles' first graduate.

In the mid-sixties, with Vietnam looming, parents were less keen to have their sons receive military training. The upper classes were running away from military service, not toward it. The Bolles board of trustees worried that the school was losing top-notch academic students to Andover and Exeter. To entice smart Florida boys to stay in Florida, they initiated the change from military to civilian culture. The market for a civilian school was stronger. And there was the issue of Bolles' sister school, Jacksonville's all-girl Bartram Academy, which was thought to give its students greater social advantages than Bolles. Bolles' headmaster, Major Hoover, was a driving force for maintaining it as a military school, but he was retiring. The time was right for change.

Longtime Bolles instructors speak of the transition years as a difficult time. The older instructors were accustomed to being saluted and addressed with a certain formality. Newer, younger teachers wanted no part of such nonsense. The school also had concerns about keeping the boys busy after class if military drills no longer filled their time. Bolles' always strong athletic culture was supplemented by an upsurge of after-class clubs and organizations. Though they'd been created mainly to give idle hands something to do, the clubs and organizations were taken seriously by the young men of Bolles. While it was nominally civilian, Bolles remained tightly regimented. It was hard to shed those forty years of military tradition.

"People like Gram loosened us up. Gram and his friends," says Quinn Barton, a teacher and administrator at Bolles for much of his adult life. "And we began to acquire new faculty during that time. Faculty who had not been in the military, who did not understand or appreciate structure, much less regimentation. And that brought on change. But we still had an all-male faculty. Bolles was a male world."

The boys wore light blazers in the summer, wool blazers in the winter. There was no school tie; the students favored conservative club ties. They wore blue or white or, occasionally, yellow shirts and the uniform footwear of the Southern country club high school student: Bass Weejun loafers. Military-style room inspections with white gloves endured. So did the demand for proper behavior in the dining hall. Students sat upright at the table and ate fried chicken with a knife and fork, never with their fingers. For the South at the time this was pretty much unheard of, regardless of class. Bolles was not as tough as it had been, but the fried-chicken rule suggests that it was still pretty strict.

After Gram's time there, Bolles suffered as a boarding school. When Jacksonville public schools were ordered to desegregate, an epidemic of private day schools sprang up to service whites fleeing the public schools. The new wave of day schools hit Bartram, Bolles' sister school, especially hard. The Bartram girls had uniforms, too, and that may have contributed to Bartram's commercial woes. Margaret Fisher, who was a Bartram student and a close friend of Gram's when he was at Bolles, says of the uniforms, "They were the ugliest fucking things you ever saw: a horrible blue shirtwaist dress with a clasp belt, buttons up the front, and a Peter Pan collar."

Bolles day students came from the affluent families of Jacksonville; the boarders were mostly wealthy kids from elsewhere in Florida. In describing the student body, Rufus McClure, another longtime faculty member, says, "If you do not have the endowment to offer financial aid [and Bolles did not], then it's only the students whose families can afford to send them here."

"Bartram and Bolles were prep schools," Margaret Fisher says. "They got the sons and daughters of the leading citizens of Jacksonville. They also got the throwaway kids. Kids who were inconvenient. They interfered with their parents' marriage, they interfered with their parents' drinking. They got thrown into this stew and went one way or the other. They assimilated or they were outcasts. Among the throwaway kids, Gram was unusually self-assured."

Gram enrolled as a junior. Nominally he was repeating his junior year, but since he had hardly attended class during his first time through, there was little academic material for him to repeat. He was not only older than his classmates, but considerably cooler.

Roger Williams, born and raised in Waycross, attended Bolles while Gram was there. "It was a predominantly Southern school," he says. "We had a lot of people from well-off families and we had my friend Clin Catledge. Clin was a real straight, ultraconservative guy. He didn't come from money. His dad was a state patrolman in Waycross who saved to send Clin to boarding school. And Clin was no big fan of Gram's—he thought Gram was a hippie."

Peter Henriques represented the new breed of instructor. Raised in Westchester County, New York, he went to Yale Divinity and Princeton Theological Seminary before heading to Bolles as a history professor and part-time chaplain from 1963 to 1966. "Gram was definitely on the liberal side," Henriques says, "and was shocked at some of the racist activities going on. Racial injustice bothered him, and this was a conservative school."

"Gram arrived a good-looking fellow; a touch of the effeminate, enough to make him attractive beyond the word *handsome*," says teacher Rufus McClure, unknowingly seduced along with everybody else. "Gram and his style were somewhat out of sync with the traditional Bolles style. He was unusual for his class."

Roger Williams recalls his first impression of Gram: "I wonder how he got to wear his hair that long." Williams explains, "Everybody wanted to wear their hair long 'cause the Beatles were coming in. Somebody at school said, 'He gets to wear his hair like that because he's paying his own way. His parents are millionaires but he's got some problem with them and he's paying his way.' That set him apart from everybody else. It was common knowledge around campus, but I think Parsons was blowing smoke up everybody's rear."

Hair length was becoming a cultural battleground. Military schools, public schools, and boarding schools drew the line at hair below the ears or touching the collar. Any sight of longish hair evoked the Beatles, the civil rights movement, beatniks (hippie awareness in Jacksonville in 1963 was minimal), and marijuana. It implied freedom from authority in an authoritarian culture astonished by its own obsolescence. In public schools throughout the South it was not unusual for boys to be ordered out of school until they got their hair cut to the school's specifications. In most places, any teacher, not only the principal, had the authority to make any boy cut his hair.

Williams can't explain the logic of how Gram paying his own way—which he definitely was not—would have exempted him from having longer hair. Williams cuts closer to the truth when he says, "He couldn't go up onstage with a buzz cut and have any credibility. People understood that."

James Mallard roomed across the hall from Gram during their junior year; they became roommates as seniors. "Gram was different," Mallard says. "He was extremely bright. He had long hair—longer hair than what a redneck Southerner like me was used to. And longer fingernails on his right hand. He was always thinking of loftier things. When he introduced himself he always said, 'Gram as in metric measure, not as in graham cracker.'"

Although Bolles had shed uniforms, the school strictly enforced its dress code. Yet everyone knew from the first couple of days that Gram needed his hair long, in the words of Judson Graves, "for his persona." The older faculty didn't like it; the younger, newer teachers intervened on Gram's behalf. Within three days of arriving as the new boy at a boarding school, Gram had somehow convinced the administration, the faculty, and his classmates that he actually had a persona. And they all bought into protecting it. It would not be the last time Gram worked this magic.

Bruce Talcott, another classmate, parses the class delineations: "He was proper and preppy. Even more so than most of us, except a few from West Palm Beach. He had a certain moneyed aura. He dressed well, but everybody on the campus dressed well. Everyone was well connected and well-off. Yet he was a standout."

In part that was because of his looks. "He was an attractive, good-looking guy," Talcott says. "He had a sort of bronze look—he had olive skin and dark hair." Gram was smart, too. Margaret Fisher recalls, "People were intimidated by his brains. If you messed with him he'd sneer at you. He was as smart as I was and I didn't know anybody who was. He was almost as well-read as I was, and nobody was as well-read as I was. He had presence—the jocks didn't think he was much, but they didn't pick on him."

In Winter Haven, Gram had been pegged the moment he arrived: He was a Snively. He hit Bolles as an unknown and was scrutinized as only a new boy can be. His classmates found him fascinating in a way that would be echoed when Gram hit other insular scenes in Greenwich Village, Cambridge, Hollywood, London, Nashville, and the south of France.

Gram's teachers believed the school provided a healthier environment than his disorganized home. "Gram was noticeably searching," Peter Henriques says, "with an element of insecurity. It seemed his family was wealthy but not concerned with him. He was not as well anchored as other students." Rufus McClure remembers, "Gram flourished at Bolles. Bolles enabled an inner life and supported his music. Because he had twenty-four-hour relationships here, and as a result of his distant family, Bolles became family. The guys became brothers and two instructors"—Robert Hubbard and Joe Dyess—"became surrogate parents." Fred Brown, a classmate who played guitar and sang harmony with Gram, says, "The faculty were close to us. Some lived on campus and had little life outside of their academic life. Robert Hubbard was one of those; he ran the Drama Club and became a mentor to Gram." Joe Dyess was a beloved and widely respected professor who proved another strong influence on Gram and one of his allies.

Gram hung out with two different social sets. One was kids who were into music and the other, as described by Fred Brown, "was the closest thing Bolles had to a counterculture." The latter group "would play out by the smoking circle"—a designated place on campus where smoking was allowed—"hang out in each other's rooms, swap beatnik books, and sometimes rent a hotel room on weekends. If they were lucky they'd drink a little beer. And though the counterculture set was his main friends, when you looked at him he was one of the cleanest-cut kids in school. He couldn't let himself look scruffy."

The "smoking circle" met in a little gazebo right on the St. John's River. Gram's group would gather at night after the last study hall. Roger Williams remembers, "You'd look across the St. John's River to the Jacksonville Air Station. The lights would be twinkling and we'd see the jets taking off and landing. It was a beautiful spot, with live oak trees and Spanish moss—it was a great place to play guitar and kill yourself with cigarettes."

Williams recalls that one member of the counterculture group "had his windows blacked out and a bright red light. After class we'd sit in there playing for two or three hours under that red light. We'd come out and would have forgotten it was daytime."

According to Fred Brown, Gram "never quite connected with either group" because he "seemed to feel he was always on display"—having created a persona, Gram had to live it. "There were things he wanted to shake about himself to present the image he wanted," Brown says, "yet he couldn't quite do it. He looked too slick and cared too much about keeping his hair perfect. This rebellious group," the counterculture group, "kept their hair as long as they could, they dressed sloppy, at room inspection they'd always have one shirttail out. He couldn't do that."

Fred was part of the other social set, a loose-knit group based on music and singing that included the brothers Bill and Shep Colledge. (Shep later came to be regarded as one of the best long-neck banjo players in the state.) Together with Gram they walked between classes singing harmony. They practiced constantly. A favorite song was "The Bells of Rhymney," which became a hit for the Byrds a few years later. The beautiful campus, right on the river, offered a number of spots to gather and sing. On weekends the boys played for hours, trying different arrangements for guitar and voices.

Gram began to write songs. His aspirations were obvious. He carried his guitar everywhere. He would perform anywhere more than three people were gathered. "Gram wanted to be famous," classmate Larry Slade says. "He talked about what it would take to achieve it. He loved to be the center of attention, to perform. I'm not sure he truly loved music as much as performance." Margaret Fisher recalls, "He was walking ambition. He always knew he was going to be somebody."

Gram and Fred Brown were invited to audition for a teen talent show on Channel 4 in Jacksonville. Even as Gram and Fred were rehearsing backstage, Gram astonished his singing buddies by creating three- and four-part vocal harmonies on the spot. One of the technicians on the show heard Gram singing sustained half-notes in rehearsal and asked, "Are you doing that on purpose?" After several other high school kids played their hootenanny-like folk songs, Gram took the performer's stool in his Bolles gray slacks, blue shirt, and tie. He left his jacket on the floor. He began to play "John Reilly," a long English folk lament made famous by Joan Baez. The show's talent coordinator stopped Gram to say his guitar was out of tune. Gram calmly adjusted his E string, looked up at the coordinator as cool as can be, and said, "Yeah, you're right." He started the song again without a pause. Roger Williams remembers, "I was sitting in the booth behind these guys thinking, 'They ain't heard nothing yet.' That voice of his, those high ranges, it got into your bones. As they were listening, the producer wrote on his clipboard in big letters: 'Professional!' with an exclamation point. He held it out to his buddy in the booth and the guy nodded, like, 'Yeah, I know.'"

A TYPICAL DAY AT BOLLES began when clock radios would go off all around the dorms. Most were tuned to WAPE-AM, and a song that everyone remembers waking up to was "Baby Elephant Walk," the jaunty instrumental by Henry Mancini. Classes ended at three-thirty, and at five study hall began. Between class and study hall came the various organizational meetings. Gram joined the Centurions, a service club that helped with homecoming activities but functioned primarily as a fraternity for upperclassmen. He wrote and edited the school newspaper. He appeared in his class play, *Julius Caesar.* His classmates remember him as anything but a jock. James Mallard says, "He played JV football his first year, but that was unlike him. I have this image of him in that white uniform with his long hair underneath his helmet. That didn't last long. He only played for part of the season." A photo in the Bolles yearbook suggests that Gram played in at least one basketball game.

Buddy Freeman continued to set up solo gigs for Gram. In the fall of 1963, shortly after starting at Bolles, Gram traveled to Greenville, South Carolina, to play *The Coca-Cola Hi-Fi Club Hootenanny*, a live radio talent show for folk performers. The program was a radio institution around the country, broadcast on Saturdays and featuring live local bands.

While backstage, he heard a banjo-and-guitar duo rehearsing and approached them. The guitarist was Joe Kelly. "He said, 'I see your name is the Shilos,'" Kelly remembers. "He was going to do the song 'The Hills of Shiloh' and wanted to make sure we weren't playing the same thing. We got to chatting. He asked if Paul and I would back him up on a couple things. We said we'd be happy to, and that's how we met."

Gram had met two thirds of the Shilos: Joe Kelly, who usually played upright bass in the group, and Paul Surratt, who played banjo. The third member of the band was guitarist George Wrigley, who was unwell that night and missed the show.

The Shilos were from Greenville, South Carolina. Joe and George, childhood friends, grew up playing together. Joe played the ukulele and George, the guitar. In junior high they entered a talent show; Joe had a tenor guitar that he played "like a ukulele." In junior high they played the light folk of the Kingston Trio, the Limeliters, and the Brothers Four. They called themselves the Princeton Quartet.

During the summer of tenth grade, George played in the Shiloh Singers. At that point the group was George, Paul Surratt, and Bryant Kendrick. Kendrick, a Civil War history buff, had named the band for the famous battle of Shiloh. No one seems to know what happened to the final *h*. It got dropped somewhere, along with "Singers," and the group became the Shilos.

Bryant, a couple years older, left Greenville for college, and Joe hooked up with George and Paul. Joe had not been possessed by a burning desire to play the stand-up bass. But the Shilos did not need a ukulele; they needed a bass player. Joe acquired a bass fiddle and began to learn in earnest.

The Shilos' repertoire featured commercial folk music. They played the Smothers Brothers' arrangement of "Down in the Valley." They liked to resurrect old spirituals like "Men Going Around Taking Names." They played acoustic blues numbers and even traditional country tunes. And they performed regularly in public. *The Coca-Cola Hi-Fi Club Hootenanny*'s chief competition was *Shindy!*, a local television show sponsored by Pepsi-Cola that featured regional high school talent. The Shilos were *Shindy!* regulars. They also played various area teen clubs and coffeehouses.

"The group we emulated more than anyone was the Journeymen," says Joe Kelly. They were a leading folk trio that featured sophisticated har-monies and superior guitar technique, and Gram was deeply influenced by them, too. Not as commercially successful as, say, the Kingston Trio, the Journeymen were regarded—in the moral hierarchy of folk music—as more authentic. "The Journeymen were top-flight musicians," Kelly continues. "They had a whole lot less popularity and less notoriety, but they were the best of all the groups technically."

The Journeymen were led by singer, songwriter, and arranger John Phillips. Phillips would later create and lead the Mamas & the Papas and sire famously self-destructive children, Mackenzie and Bijou Phillips among them. Mackenzie was named for Journeyman Scott McKenzie, who sang lead tenor in the group and took the guitar solos. He later sang a key sixties anthem written by Phillips, "San Francisco (Be Sure to Wear Flowers in Your Hair)." The third Journeyman, Dick Weissman, subsequently released a solo album of folk protest music and made a career as a folklorist and musicologist.

The Journeymen were intelligent, skilled musicians whose music was a reaction against the shallow pop of their time. They played sea chanteys, English madrigals, traditional songs, and aggressively white, peppy, colle-giate, antiseptic versions of country blues classics. The Journeymen incar-nated the lugubrious, perfectly enunciated, ethereal folk sound that ruled the day. Their arrangements did not stress rhythm. They focused on melody and clear, optimistic harmonies. They incarnated the old-school folk that Bob Dylan seemed determined to destroy—and eventually did.

It's surprising, given Gram's early obsession with rock and roll and his later, broader-ranging musical tastes, that he was so enamored of such an academic sound. The Kingston Trio, the Journeymen, and the Brothers Four were as far removed from the fashion-forward, black-saturated anarchy of Elvis as Perry Como or Pat Boone. Their music is devoid of soul, but pre-Dylan it was regarded as the height of musical integrity, the antithesis of radio pop and rock. By 1963 Dylan had already released *Bob Dylan* and *The Freewheelin' Bob Dylan*. Yet Dylan's ardently solo, anarchic, solipsistic, not-pretty folk seems to have had little impact on Gram.

He and the Shilos were on the same wavelength. After their brief preshow chat, Gram went onstage and blew the Shilos' minds. "He sang 'You Know My Voice, I've Heard Your Name' by the New Christy Minstrels," says Paul Surratt. "He was wearing a purple shirt. He had such a great voice we couldn't believe it. When he came down off the stage we talked more."

After Gram's performance, the three of them sang "Pullin' Away" and "Run Maggie Run." The chemistry was immediate, according to Paul Surratt; the three boys harmonized effortlessly. "As a singer he could kill anybody," Paul continues. "I was spellbound. We were going to meet the next day, and it was the first time in my life I was unable to sleep. I was so afraid he wouldn't call that I didn't sleep all night. I was so excited about meeting the guy; I had visions of us being the next Kingston Trio."

The boys made plans to meet and hone material. While Gram and the Shilos continued to play on their own, Paul and Joe traveled to Jacksonville and Gram went back to Greenville. The Shilos also visited Gram in Winter Haven. The most pressing problem preventing the Shilos and Gram getting together was not the logistics of travel; it was that they were all juniors in high school.

In the late fall of '63, Gram organized a show at Bolles so he could play with the Shilos. Soon afterward, Gram secured a regular Sunday-afternoon hootenanny show on a local AM station. His instructor and mentor, Joe Dyess, helped him get the slot. In the meantime, Buddy Freeman searched out gigs for Gram and the Shilos as a band—gigs that would not interfere with their school responsibilities.

Gram was becoming a celebrity at Bolles. He was invited to sing at the school's Sunday vespers service. "It wasn't like he would wake up on Sunday knowing he was gonna perform," James Mallard says. "He'd bring his guitar into vespers and sing every now and then. That voice of his would shake the rafters. The dining room was the only place all the boarders could sit down. The wood paneling had been in there since 1925. It would resonate those sounds. It was a great music chamber, and his voice would carry around and around."

Sports mattered at Bolles. Their swim team was top notch, and jocks had the most status. Sporting events were one of the few times the Bolles boys and Bartram girls got together; Bartram provided cheerleaders for football and basketball games, and girls were allowed to attend. But Gram's music altered the valence of the traditional school popularity hierarchy. James Mallard describes having refreshments during the break of a basketball game and "a covey of girls swishing around, choosing which corn to pick. When the girls spotted Gram, it was *Katy bar the door.* They were all around him. The girls would walk around and around, but wherever he was, they would be gathering. No lasting relationships were formed, but they definitely made a path to his door."

Gram performed after basketball games, singing songs popularized by the Kingston Trio, Peter, Paul & Mary, and the Journeymen. He struck the classic folkie pose: sitting on a stool with his acoustic guitar, wearing white jeans. Those white jeans have been burned into the minds of an entire class of Bartram girls as a key erotic signifier of their school days. "Gram sang after one game," Judson Graves says, "and there was a lot more interest in Gram's singing than in the basketball team. So much more it was kind of funny and we weren't even resentful. For Gram to supplant sports and to surmount the haircutting problem was unheard of." Judson's sister, Mandy, remembers, "He was playing at the Bolles gym after a game. Him on a stool and he had on white jeans, which I thought were so cool. He was neat-looking and mysterious. He was in the middle of the gym floor—no one else around him. The lighting was kind of dim. Just him on a stool playing an acoustic guitar—that was it. His hair was longish, not in front but over his ears, long in the back. He was facing one set of bleachers, and a lot of people stayed."

"After the girls heard him sing it was like there weren't any other guys in the room," Roger Williams says. "We were all chopped liver. They were swooning over him."

In the aftermath of one of these shows, someone stole Gram's guitar. The guitar was returned after a few days; a Bartram girl had been sleeping with it in her bed.

GRAM HAD MET HIS MUSICAL soulmates in Greenville and an entire girls' school swooned over his white jeans, but he still had to attend class. The consensus of

Gram in the 1964 Bolles yearbook. (Courtesy the Bolles School, 1964 *Turris* Staff)

most of Gram's professors was that he seldom did his best. He was regarded as one of the brightest kids in the school and was always likable. Peter Henriques taught a lesson about the Sherman Silver Purchase Act of the 1870s. One of the key players was a congressman known as Silver Dick Bland. "Gram picked up on the analogy of Silver Dick and kept making comments after I told them to settle down," Henriques says. "He might do something you didn't want him to do, but you found yourself enjoying it anyway."

Gram bonded with another professor, Robert Hubbard. Hubbard was part of the new breed at Bolles. Educated at Harvard, he came from a wealthy family. Other faculty members regarded him as an intellectual. Rumored to have once been a director on the prestigious, groundbreaking television drama *Playhouse Ninety,* Hubbard found himself at Bolles—according to students and faculty—because his alcoholism rendered him unable to function in the world. Hubbard was brilliant, well read, an inspiring teacher, a good friend to his students, and a hard drinker. "He taught the English literature class junior year—the whole year's worth," Fred Brown remembers. "He used this gigantic book compiled by Shorter College in north Georgia. It was a fifteen-hundred-page compilation of everything from Middle English to T. S. Eliot. Hubbard expected a lot from us. He expected us to learn a lot and to read a lot. He expected us to spend a couple hours every night with his course. Most of us did, because it was an enthralling experience."

"Gram was Hubbard's favorite," classmate Bruce Talcott says. "He thought a lot of Gram and it came across in class." In 1962, Gram had been given a two-volume set of *The English and Scottish Popular Ballads*, edited by Francis James Child. "It was a huge thing, eight hundred pages long, a collection of ballads from 1100 to the 1700s," Fred Brown remembers. "We used to sing songs from it. The songs lent themselves to different people doing each verse and harmonizing on the chorus, with all four of us singing. Hubbard was so supportive he taught us about the book, the collection, and about ballads. It was Gram's book, but Hubbard used it in class."

Hubbard had the boys read Eudora Welty. "Gram liked her a lot," Fred Brown recalls, "because [her stories] had a tone, an undercurrent of sadness that you can't reach in life. How there are circumstances you have to cherish even though they don't contribute to your happiness."

Hubbard didn't seem to mind Gram's lying. When Gram submitted a Bob Dylan song as his own poetry, Hubbard's response is remembered as "benign." Hubbard and Gram spent a good deal of time together. Hubbard took students to see plays in Jacksonville; Gram was always included. Hubbard crammed his car full of kids—Gram among them—to see the film *Wuthering Heights* with Lawrence Olivier. Hubbard and Gram went to several plays on their own. Hubbard took weekend groups to the public library and the beach. Gram seldom went because his weekends were filled with music.

Students knew about Hubbard's drinking. "Faculty members told faculty members that we were close to," Fred Brown says. "We were fascinated by him because there were days when he'd be sitting in front of the class with sweat rolling, stammering, obviously trying to hold it together.

"I think the faculty members who lived there who had problems with alcohol tended to shut out the world. That's what happened to Hubbard. I think he used Gram, his protégé, to escape that isolation. And he could acquaint Gram with parts of the world he lost because of his alcoholism."

Gram met a significant literary companion at Bolles: Margaret Fisher. Margaret came from another rich, eccentric family. Her parents, John Jay Fisher and Ellen Boyd Ludlick, were married in secret; that is, they ran off and got married. Margaret has six siblings; she's the second-oldest girl. Born while her dad was in medical school at the University of Pittsburgh, Margaret moved with her family to Jacksonville at four. Polio had almost killed her father, leaving him paralyzed for months, and doctors recommended a warmer climate. He recovered but never discussed his illness. Margaret's dad eventually left her mom and married four more times. It almost goes without saying that in the process he pissed away all the family money he was heir to.

"He had seven kids and never talked to them," Margaret says. "He was always gone, and when he was home he was just weird. He was like something out of an F. Scott Fitzgerald novel, but he did teach me to ride a horse."

Margaret suffered at Bartram. "I was the bottom of the totem pole. I was the girl that tested off the charts and failed everything. I made the worst grades in the entire school. And even though it was run like a 1930s girls' school or a medieval monastery, Bartram was excellent academically. But they didn't dare throw me out. I had three younger sisters coming in behind me. That meant forty thousand dollars a year to them. They gave up on me going to classes and let me be. A friend from Bartram tells people, 'She's the girl who read every book in the Bartram library.' And I did. I'd sit all day reading and then go ride my horse. I think around ninth grade I sort of woke up and started going to class again."

Margaret intimidated and baffled the Bolles boys. "She was a waif thing with long blond hair," Judson Graves says. "A sexually provocative young woman who was well ahead of the game in Jacksonville. She drank young. Her father was always gone. The home was open, fast-moving. They had a beautiful old home with a little playhouse on the river. Everyone hung out at the playhouse. Her parents never once left the big house to see what was happening there. The playhouse was a refuge, a safe haven, for us and for the Fisher kids. Margaret would smoke and cuss and was not intimidated by guys at all. She was hot."

"Margaret was a beautiful sixteen-year-old," Larry Slade says. "Long platinum hair that did not come out of any bottle, and this angelic face. She was eccentric and kind."

The Fisher house, a rambling old colonial with kids swarming around, became a hangout for a certain set from Bolles and Bartram. Margaret and her brother moved into the playhouse to escape their parents. "It was a retreat," Judson Graves says. "The rules were looser. You'd go down this long driveway, big multistory house on the right as you pull up, big trees, Spanish moss, white plantation-style house with white wooden columns, and, off on the river, this one-story playhouse." Judson's sister Mandy adds, "Her parents were unusual. They were all kind of fascinating. They had a lot of land and horses. They were all smart and fun and the mom was eccentric."

Like Gram, Margaret was left to raise herself as best she could. Weekends, everyone showed up at the playhouse. "It wouldn't have been a big tribal gathering—only the ten or fifteen who knew what was going on,"

Margaret Fisher, 1964. (Courtesy Margaret Fisher)

Margaret says. "On Fridays we didn't have to wear uniforms but everyone wore one: Villager skirt, Gant shirt, Villager sweater. The boys wore Gant shirts, Gold Cup socks, and Bass Weejuns, always Bass Weejuns. Gram finally came out. But he didn't come out much, and usually when he did we were alone. My mother, who never paid attention, felt that alarm that went off in every mother's heart when she met him. He was nice but he was dangerous.

"My first memory of him was that we were a bunch of Jacksonville hicks, but this guy knew what he was doing. The Beatles had come in and he already had long, long hair for that time. He was so cool—cooler than anything we'd ever seen."

Margaret, a year younger than Gram, met him after one of his Bolles concerts. "I was in tenth grade and somebody took me to see him. I was socially inept and did what I still do: I took a book everywhere. I went and listened to him and he was charismatic. He could sing. And really play. But every time he stopped playing I was afraid someone would talk to me, so I'd read my book, *Other Voices, Other Rooms* [by Truman Capote]. He stopped playing and I looked up and he said, 'Is that a good book?' I said, 'Yes, it is. It's wonderful.' I almost never talked to boys, and finally one had asked me a question I could answer. I went into a whole précis, like forever. He kind of looked at me and said, 'Well, maybe I should read it.' I said, 'You can have it—I've read it three times.' He said, 'I'll bring it back to you.' I told him he didn't have to, since I'd read it three times. After a minute or two of silence he said, 'Well?' and I said, 'Well, what?' And he said, 'Well, what's your phone number so I can read it and give it back to you?' I said, 'But you don't even know my name,' and he said, 'Yes, I do.'

"After that he would come out and we would talk. It was not an adversarial relationship. It was like, I know you're smart but so am I. We talked endlessly. What do adolescents talk about? How much they hate their parents; how alone in the world we feel.

"We both had a clear idea of ourselves, and that led to a lot of one-upmanship. We both thought we were cool. He wanted me to read *On the Road*. I told him it was an interesting story but not well written. He said, 'Well, Margaret Fisher, that just shows how ignorant you are.' We argued, and finally I asked that if I was so ignorant, what was he doing out there with me? He said, 'Because you and me are going to see wonderful things and most people around here aren't going to see shit.'

"He said he was going to be a star. I never had anybody tell me they were going to be anything but a doctor or a lawyer. He said he was going to be like Elvis, and I saw no reason to doubt him. I had no idea what being a rock-and-roll star entailed. I thought it just occurred. And so I thought, of course, that's what he's going to do.

"We never dated. We weren't lovers. It was a standoff; if he wasn't going to chase after me he didn't have a chance, and he wasn't going to chase after anyone. Gram and I were friends who might have been lovers, but we were both too goddamn proud. That was fine in my book. I'd date men from

Princeton, friends of my older sister's boyfriend. I wasn't going to be the girlfriend of anyone who wouldn't commit. Because that's what we did then, we had these tiny marriages. If he wouldn't commit, I'd date Princeton boys—they couldn't wait to commit."

Margaret and Gram remained soul mates and confidants throughout Gram's time at Bolles. Their bond only underscored the conviction of Gram's classmates regarding his singular nature. No other boys would even talk to Margaret; she scared them. When kids gathered at the playhouse, she and Gram would be off somewhere, heads together, talking a mile a minute or sitting in silence.

Gram stayed friendly with Bonnie Muma even after she left the Parsons household, and even though he almost certainly knew about her affair with Bob. Gram called her from Bolles once or twice in 1964. By then Bonnie had left Winter Haven and was living in Palm Beach. She remembers one conversation as the school year wound down in the spring of 1964: "He couldn't wait to get out. He told me over and over he was going to be famous. And I would say, 'Yes, I know, I know.' There was never anything about [Bob Parsons]. Gram was careful about people's feelings until later, when he got on drugs. He would never have upset me by asking, 'Has Daddy been down there?' He stayed out of my personal life."

GRAM AND THE SHILOS missed a chance to be stars on a typically cracked adventure in spring 1964. Buddy Freeman was at a friend's wedding in Raleigh, North Carolina, when he was called to the phone. "Only my mother and father and a guy doing caretaking for Avis knew where I was," Freeman says. The call was from Dick Pope, the creator, part owner (with the Snivelys), and director of the Cypress Gardens theme park.

"Buddy?" Pope said. "I've got your tickets for Chicago in the morning." Buddy told Pope there was a misunderstanding; "tomorrow" was Easter Sunday, and he'd be attending services at the First Presbyterian Church. "No," Pope said. "I sent tickets to the boys and they'll be there waiting on you." "What boys?" Buddy said. Pope meant Gram Parsons and the Shilos. Pope had already sent Gram to Chicago. Gram hadn't told Freeman a thing. Pope told Freeman they had rooms waiting at the Palmer House, a swank hotel in downtown Chicago.

Freeman called the Shilos. "Apparently the band was off to Chicago to record at Universal Studios. We'd been talking in some vague way about it, but I had certainly planned on being in on the decision-making process. I race home, unpack, pack, get an hour's sleep, go to the airport. The boys are already on the plane. They're all excited. We get to Chicago and it's seventeen degrees. I have no money—the banks are all closed. This is long before ATMs. I got the Howard Johnson hotel to cash a check for twenty-five hundred dollars. At least I had something in my pocket.

"We go to the hotel to meet Gram. He's been there two or three days and was bored and went down into the shops in the hotel. He's got a good-looking pair of cowboy boots, pants, cowboy belt, and hat. And this Sheffler's three-quarter-length sheepskin coat. He thinks it's wonderful and that it looks great on him. And it was cold.

"I complimented him on his clothes and he said, 'Well, I'm sure glad you like 'em, 'cause I'm gonna need to talk to you about paying for them.'"

Gram had convinced the store to sell him the clothes on credit. The total came to twenty-one hundred dollars. "I got a little hostile at that point," Buddy says.

The reason for the trip to Chicago remains murky. Dick Pope was furnishing music to the State of Florida to promote the state and Cypress Gardens at the 1964 World's Fair in New York. He'd booked Gram and the Shilos into Universal Studios, one of the "more extravagant, big-time studios in the country," according to Buddy. Furious about being left out of the deal-making, Buddy still had his own Chicago connections to exploit.

Buddy was friends with Jimmy Patrillo, whose dad, James C. Patrillo, was president of the American Federation of Musicians—and thus one of the best-connected, most powerful men in American showbiz. Jimmy, impressed with Gram and the Shilos, made hints about getting the boys on both *The Tonight Show* and *Ed Sullivan*. The latter was an especially big deal. *The Ed Sullivan Show* was the premier weekly variety show on television. During his heyday Sullivan introduced Elvis, the Beatles, the Rolling Stones, and, it must be said, the puppet mouse Topo Gigio to the mainstream American market.

"I so believed in these kids," Buddy says, "that I'd already been to a bank in Greenville investigating setting up trusts for the boys. I wanted them to keep what they earned."

Patrillo Senior's production company had deals with Cypress Gardens, the State Department, and the 1964 World's Fair. He'd heard about Gram not only from Buddy Freeman but also Dick Pope. Pope had his own reasons to be nice to Gram. Snively goodwill meant a lot to Cypress Gardens.

The stars seemed to be lining up to get the Shilos on national television and launch the group as the next big thing. But Gram and the Shilos weren't ready. In the Chicago studio they recorded a song called "Surfinanny," the tapes of which disappeared long ago. Patrillo wanted original material and, depending on whom you talk to, either the boys didn't have any ready to record or "Surfinanny" was original but so silly it left Patrillo questioning their professionalism. After making their recording, back to Greenville went the Shilos, and back to Bolles went Gram. With his new cowboy clothes.

That such a seemingly rich opportunity devolved into an anecdote is the first occurrence of behavior that would characterize Gram's entire career. He avoided success with great dexterity, turning once-in-a-lifetime, career-making breaks into amusing go-nowhere anecdotes. With his oft-stated determination to become famous, his voice, his charisma, the help of Buddy Freeman, Dick Pope, and James Patrillo, and a couple of original songs in his portfolio, how did Gram manage to avoid getting on *The Ed Sullivan Show*? It would be the first of many times in Gram's professional life that his determination to remain always in it, but not of it, would lead him to sabotage his own desires.

BACK FROM CHICAGO, Gram bought a Martin guitar: his signature 00-21 New Yorker. The 00-21 was a folk guitar brought out by Martin in the early sixties, when folk music was at its peak. It featured a small body with a wide neck for folk and bluegrass fingering, the classic Martin ebony and ivory on the back, and that big, resonant Martin sound.

Gram traveled to Greenville to play small shows with the Shilos, including gigs in a youth club and a bowling alley. While he was there, the band decided to record a demo. They went to the ultra-Christian, ultra-conservative Bob Jones University, which offered recording services for a hundred dollars. The band was broke, even Gram, so Paul Surratt's father put up the fee.

During the session Joe Kelly played bass fiddle, Gram played his new Martin and his twelve-string Goya, George and Paul both had their own Martins, and Paul played a Baker banjo. "It was a good product," Joe Kelly remembers. "Good harmonies. George always had ideas for picking songs and for structure. Paul's forte was being able to pick that banjo. Gram sang most of the leads. My strength was harmonies. Gram and I were responsible for the arrangements, but none of them were written down. We went, 'Okay, George, you go like this and Paul, you go like that. Gram, you sing the melody and I'll do something way up high like this. Then we'll hold that one line and repeat it.'"

The session was recorded on a single microphone. The band crowded around in the old-time fashion, modulating the volume of their voices and instruments by leaning into the mike or leaning away. "We were in the middle of this room with one old Shure radio mike, a diamond-shaped thing hung from the ceiling," Joe remembers. "It was like singing into a big electric razor. We stood two by two facing each other. We were in this ten-by-twenty radio studio with that one mike hanging down, a couple buddies in the corner, and the audio guy behind the glass wall with his knobs and switches. It was a one-hour session and we took an hour. We just ran right through it. There weren't any second takes. It was us going straight through our repertoire."

When Grant Lacerte heard the tape he was impressed. Gram "sounded professional," he remembers, "not like some kid with a little talent."

The band ended up sending their tape to *The Andy Williams Show* and other television variety shows, but nothing came of it. The recording was released in 1979 as an LP by Sierra Records under the title *Gram Parsons: The Early Years, 1963–1965.*

When the Shilos came down for a show at Bolles, Gram took Margaret Fisher as his date. "Afterward he took us all to the River Club, the exclusive meetin'-and-greetin' businessman's club in Jacksonville," Margaret says. "They didn't want to let us in. But Bob Parsons was a member, of course, and that got us through the door. We go in there, two seventeen-year-olds and three hillbillies. It was amazing—Gram talked us into the best club in Jacksonville. We had dinner and those Shilos boys put ketchup on everything except their iced tea."

When the school year ended, Buddy Freeman found Gram and the Shilos a monthlong gig in the redneck resort town of Myrtle Beach, South Carolina. The Shilos played the opening slot at Charles Fair, Fort Carolina, a historical theme park. The park presented reenactments of Indian and Huguenot battles featuring costumed local high school kids and Native Americans from Lumberton, North Carolina. The boys performed in an enormous picnic pavilion with no walls, under a roof supported by columns. Families sat all around at picnic tables. Their half-hour set was usually ended by cannon fire. The cannons told the customers that Indians had attacked the fort and it was time to watch a reenactment.

The band earned $850 a week. There were four Shilos, but each took

The Shilos: George Wrigley, Joe Kelly, Paul Surratt, and GP. (Courtesy the estate of Robert Parsons)

home only $170, one fifth. Rather than charge a standard manager's fee of 10 or 15 percent, Buddy Freeman put himself in for a full cut. For their $850, the theme park got seven half-hour Shilos shows a day, seven days a week, the first starting at ten in the morning and the last at six in the evening.

Like the Kingston Trio, the boys wore white buck shoes, white pants, and striped shirts. Their alternate costume was beige stretch jeans, yellow shirts, and powder-blue blazers. George Wrigley refused to wear the stage outfits. Every day, onstage or off, he wore a yellow oxford shirt with the sleeves rolled up, khakis, and brown penny loafers. "That's what he's worn his entire life," Joe Kelly says.

These weren't exactly Beatles-in-Hamburg work conditions, but the constant playing proved beneficial. "We could just look at each other and do something different in our songs," Joe Kelly remembers. "We were in a perceptive state. No song was ever done the same way." Gram and George worked out most of the onstage patter. "Gram did the introducing when it was the four of us," Kelly says. "When it was us three, we took turns. We might start playing in the background as Gram was talking. We'd get increasingly loud or fancy, and the instant he finished talking we'd tear into the song."

According to Joe, Gram possessed the star power he'd shown at Bolles. "Gram was a real charmer onstage. He had a soft voice with a little bit of hoarseness, a raspiness. He had a beachcomber type of look. His hair was light brown and he kept it straight back. He was suntanned all year-round from living in Florida."

The multiple shows every day honed the boys' act, and the hour breaks between shows let them work on new material. If they weren't rehearsing, the band put on uniforms so they could fight in the reenactments, or they'd ride the chairlifts across the park. The chairlifts offered the only cool breeze in the heat and humidity of summertime Myrtle Beach.

Paul Surratt had other responsibilities. He had to take summer school. Buddy Freeman found him an English 3 course at Myrtle Beach High School. The course began at eight A.M. five days a week, so Paul never played the first morning show. After the last show, Gram would hang with the band, or he might vanish. "He was comfortable with us," Kelly says, "but he was more worldly, more mature. He was one of us but wasn't one of us. He brought more baggage, he had more to him. He was sophisticated, glamorous, a lot more adult. He'd get into serious moods and become melancholy. When we weren't onstage together, he wasn't around.

"It wasn't that he didn't socialize or that he couldn't let his hair down and play pranks. But he tended to be a loner even when he wasn't alone. Gram used to go off to this little coffeehouse and play at night. We'd had enough playing during the day. We wanted to do something else."

The band's dinner consisted of discounted concession-stand fried chicken. For three hundred dollars a month, they rented a house three blocks from the beach. The house filled up with summer strays. The extra tenants weren't other kids working the fair, but older locals. One shared his car, a Barracuda. Dave the Barracuda, as he was known, kicked in a small share toward the rent. Another stray was the son of a local Air Force officer. He paid his way by buying groceries and household necessities at the base commissary at prices far below what the tourist-town markets demanded.

The house had three bedrooms. Paul and Gram shared one, Joe and

George the other. The strays shared the third, and on weekends there were Green Berets from Fort Bragg on the couch. One liked to sleep with his knife in his hand.

The intense community of living and playing together tried everyone's patience. The Shilos were not happy that Buddy Freeman drew a full share but never came to town. Buddy had a plumbing business and his show-horse competitions to attend to, but the park management took Buddy's money off the top and sent it to him directly. After two weeks, the Shilos felt they were getting as many extra gigs on their own as Buddy found for them. Tensions were building.

Buddy Freeman later insisted that he commuted to Myrtle Beach on weekends to take care of business. "But Gram had attracted this little snotty-nosed group that hung out at the house. They all went out drinking and raising hell and a lot of things I didn't approve of at their age. All these ne'er-do-wells and hangers-on and groupies were telling Gram he didn't need anybody telling him what to do. So we had an ugly split. I truly loved Avis and Gram. Gram and I had a close relationship. I tried, especially with the other boys in the band, to keep things on a business level. But I did not get a lot of support with them from Gram. Especially with those [lowlifes] around that he had picked up in Myrtle Beach. We had our ugly moments, but I didn't hate him or anything. He made a lot of things inconvenient, yet I still made sure his needs were always in my thoughts."

Buddy Freeman functioned at times as one of the surrogate fathers Gram would always attract. He was the first outsider Gram anointed and befriended—primarily for Gram's own benefit—then cast aside when his utility ended. Freeman would not be the last.

When the Charles Fair gig ended in July, Gram drove his Sprite to Georgetown in Washington, D.C., to visit friends. Paul stayed an extra week to finish summer school. Joe and George rode the Greyhound back to Greenville. Ten days later, Gram called the Shilos and invited them to his mother's rented beach house in Ponte Vedra. Gram said they'd rehearse and sort out what to do with the rest of the summer.

The band arrived on Thursday. By Sunday, their instruments were loaded into a 1964 Chevrolet rented by Bob Parsons and the boys were off to New York City.

"Gram knew these folks in New York," Joe Kelly recalls, "and he wanted to go to the Village. I called my family and told 'em, 'I'm going to New York. I'll see you when school starts.' I got a lot of resistance from my mom. But my dad drove from South Carolina to Oklahoma in 1920 for an adventure. So he wasn't as opposed."

Gram and the Shilos spent Sunday in the laundromat. They rehearsed as their clothes went round and round. That night the band performed at a country club party and made several hundred dollars for the road.

The Chevy was packed tight. The boys crammed the bass fiddle onto the shelf behind the backseat. The neck reached almost to the dashboard, splitting the front seat in two. In the trunk was luggage, four guitars, and two banjos. They drove out of Ponte Vedra at midnight, stopping in Myrtle Beach for breakfast. Gram wanted to see his friends in Georgetown again, so they hit Washington, D.C., around four in the afternoon and then got lost. They ended up having dinner in a hotel at National Airport. After dinner they used the restaurant bathrooms to wash up and change clothes. After traveling for twenty-four hours, they arrived in New York City at two in the morning.

Their arrival was stalled by an hour-and-a-half-long traffic jam at the George Washington Bridge. When they cleared the jam, Gram drove down to the Village. He headed for the apartment of the folksinger Jack Estes, a tiny studio on Houston Street. When the boys arrived, they found several other people crashed out on the floor, on the sofa, in Jack's sleeping loft. "By that time we didn't give a damn," Joe Kelly says.

Gram would stay with Jack Estes for the duration of his time in the city. The Shilos stayed with a friend, Annie Olmstead, who had a loft apartment on Delancey Street. Annie had two bedrooms and a roommate. For the Shilos, that left one bed. One guy got the bed each night while the other two curled up in their blankets on the floor.

The Shilos found gigs among the profusion of coffeehouses in the Village, playing at Café Wha?, the Town and Country Club, Hoot Night at the Bitter End, and Café Rafio. There was no question of salary; the boys passed the hat after every show.

Once again Gram demonstrated his instinct for the happening scene. New York that August was the place to be. The Beatles came to Shea Stadium, the World's Fair was crammed full of tourists, and folk music was at its height. There were crowds in the coffeeshops and decent money to be earned.

The band would play till one in the morning and then wander the Village. Usually they went to bed around four, slept till noon, and had breakfast at about two in the afternoon. "Daytime was not consequential," Joe Kelly says, "because we never had daytime till midafternoon." One memorable day they rode the subway to South Ferry and took the ferry to Staten Island at four in the morning. "And when we came back," Kelly remembers, "there was the Statue of Liberty with the sun coming up behind it."

One late night after a gig at Café Rafio, George Wrigley recognized John Phillips of the Journeymen walking down the street. Phillips knew the Shilos because the boys had often come to the Journeymen's shows. "Anytime the Journeymen were playing within two hundred miles of Greenville," Joe Kelly says, "we went to see them. We'd go backstage and talk with them—they knew who we were." When Phillips heard that Surratt and Kelly were also in town, he invited them to visit.

The boys went uptown to Phillips' apartment on 116th Street, where he was living with his twenty-year-old second wife, Michelle Phillips. The Journeymen were history; John had just started the Mamas & the Papas. Joe Kelly recalls: "That song of theirs, 'Twelve-Thirty (Young Girls Are Coming to the Canyon)'? It has the line, 'Outside my window was a steeple / With a clock that always says twelve-thirty.' John was writing that song and he pointed out his window. Right across the street was this huge clock face stuck on half past twelve. That day Michelle regaled us with her modeling scrapbooks. She did a lot of underwear modeling and she'd show us JCPenney ads out of the Sunday paper."

At the Phillips place the band also met erstwhile Journeyman Dick Weissman. Weissman and Phillips got the Shilos an audition for a management group, IPA.

When the boys showed up for their audition, Ringo Starr walked by. This was the big time. Foremost among those present at the audition was Albert Grossman, Bob Dylan's manager and among the most powerful rock managers in America. Grossman was a kingmaker. He was, at the very least, the American equivalent of the Beatles' manager, Brian Epstein.

Unintimidated, the Shilos shone at the audition. They were offered contracts on the spot. Then Grossman's people discovered that the Shilos were still in high school, were too young to tour, to play bars legally, or even to sign the contract they'd just been offered. The meeting ended quickly. Perhaps if Buddy Freeman had been involved, some professional agreement might have been reached. Instead, Grossman reacted as if he'd been pranked; IPA showed the boys the door.

The boys regarded it as a lark and were no more concerned than they had been about missing a chance to appear on *Ed Sullivan*. Gram had let a mammoth opportunity slip.

Still, the month in New York bore fruit. While playing at Café Rafio, next door to the Actors Studio, Gram met a girl named Zahariah. He always said he wrote his song "Zah's Blues" about her. During that Village summer, Gram worked his persona to the hilt. He carried a notebook everywhere and constantly jotted down notes, song lyrics, and rough poetry. He repeatedly told the Shilos that he did not intend to live past twenty-five.

Gram and the Shilos came home no closer friends than when they'd left. They were not worse enemies either. Joe Kelly remembers, "He was not the kind of person I'd have as my best friend. We met easily at a compromisable place as long as we were able to perform together. We had a common interest there. But to go out and have a good time, no."

As a band the Shilos were tighter, more willing to improvise, more confident in one another. In New York the band played for the most knowledgeable folk-music audiences, and for roomfuls of tourists as well. Gram's name reached the ears of people in the music business with whom he would later connect. The band met an assortment of weird Village characters and had the chance to hang out with their idols, John Phillips and Dick Weissman.

Now they had to go back for their senior year.

EIGHT
SENIOR YEAR

WHEN IT CAME TO "WHAT I DID OVER MY SUMMER VACATION," GRAM'S STORY was hard to top, and the rumors about what he'd been up to were even better. "When Gram came back to school the stories were scandalous," Margaret Fisher says. "You heard he smoked marijuana. You heard he had a New York girlfriend. You heard all the teenage gossip. I read beatnik books so I knew what marijuana was. But nobody else did. They were talking shit." With the drug stories came the sex rumors. "For me and girls it was about kissing and feeling them up," Roger Williams says. "Most of us were green as gourds at that age. For Gram it was a whole different enchilada."

Roger recalls that Gram was nonetheless generous to him: "We weren't tight friends. He had his entourage he hung out with. He'd always speak when we saw one another. Every now and then I'd go up to his door and he'd say, 'C'mon in.' Gram would teach me a few things on guitar.

"There were at least half a dozen people sitting around, most with guitars. I never carried mine in there because my playing was so awful. He showed me how to do some finger rolls, picking with two finger picks; he had a cool shortcut method. He taught me to never take off and reconnect the strings on my acoustic. He said, 'They'll last for a year if you just tune them down after you play.' Of course I later learned you should never do that—it puts too much stress on the neck.'"

Guitar strings were just one way Gram was exploring the pleasures of risk. He and his roommates, James Mallard and Fred Brown, often drank together in their dorm room, in defiance of school rules, even though Gram's mentor Joe Dyess lived only four doors down the hall. Robert Hubbard was even nearer but, according to James Mallard, "was always in a stupor anyway." The boys would gather in Gram's room, share a secret handshake that equaled being sworn to secrecy, and pull out a bottle. "It was an innocent culture," Roger Williams says. "It was a big deal if someone got a bottle of bourbon." James Mallard remembers, "We'd have about three big swigs and think we were a real band of brothers."

Gram and Mallard also snuck smokes in the professors' bathrooms. Gram liked Camels, Pall Malls, and Lucky Strikes. He taught Mallard to tear the filters off his Marlboros to make them stronger. Mallard and Gram were known for never closing their dorm-room window, regardless of season. The open window was the badge of the daring, constant in-dorm smoker.

Gram sometimes rented a room in the old Mayflower Hotel in downtown Jacksonville. He and his musical gang—James Mallard, Fred Brown, Shep and Bill Colledge, once or twice Roger Williams, and others—would gather to drink beer in safety and play music all weekend. "We had some beer," Bill Colledge says, "and girls would come around. There was never any nonsense, though. It was playing music and drinking beer and playing music. Gram playing songs he had written, like 'Hand in Glove.' He'd play, others would play. We're only talking about four or five people hanging out. Everyone recognized his talent. None of us had been introduced to a level of talent like that at the time."

Gram had still not assimilated Bob Dylan into his notions of folk music. He professed offense at Dylan's new electrified direction. One afternoon as the musical gang played in a Bolles courtyard someone asked Gram to play a Dylan song. Gram started "Don't Think Twice, It's All Right" but improvised his own lyrics. One verse went: "And you sit and wonder why, Bob, where your next dollar's coming from / And you sit and wonder why, Bob, you've gone and laid a career bomb."

It was typical of Gram to hold rigid moral or aesthetic positions and defend them passionately. If something changed his mind, he would defend his new views just as passionately and vehemently deny ever having thought any different.

Gram's rooming with Mallard baffled his friends. Mallard's family wasn't rich; he was a well-bred Virginia boy with a country edge. "James had no pretensions," Fred Brown says. "When he wore a suit he looked no better than if he was in jeans and a sweatshirt. Gram wanted to portray himself that way, too. What might have attracted Gram to James was that sloppiness came naturally to [James]. Gram had to work at that. Gram was a bit pretentious. He'd make up stories about himself. He'd tell people who didn't know him different tales about where he was born, where he was raised—he'd invent an upbringing."

"I always complained about how my hair would flop over to one side," Mallard says. "I wished it would go straight back like Gram's. He had black, straight hair, real fine. He had a soft glaze to his hair—mine was like dog's hair. I was always wanting it to go to the other side so he said, 'Let's try a hairnet.' To make me more comfortable, 'cause he sure didn't need one, he wore a hairnet, too. We'd wear hairnets going to bed at night. That lasted a couple months. I do remember wearing 'em down to Winter Haven. Most weekends we'd go down in his Austin-Healey. Here we were, two seventeen-year-olds on the road with hairnets, driving a fancy sports car."

With James Mallard, Gram adopted the model of Coon Dog's adult friendships. It was a pattern that Gram made his own: enjoying company, always charming, always removed. "He was open and friendly, a gregarious guy, a wonderful friend," Mallard says. "But he never went into his dark past. None of that ever came up. He was a giving fellow—he always wanted to ensure that you felt comfortable with him. He knew he was great, but he always wanted to make you feel you were part of the situation. So he never talked about himself. Never intimated anything about his childhood, about his father problem, about anything from Winter Haven, never went to Waycross. He was always wanting to be upfront and on the surface. Didn't want to go any deeper."

But Mallard and his other friends recognized the darkness that underlay Gram's charm. "There was always a pensive side," Mallard says. "I felt I needed a knife to cut through it. If I broke through the pensive side, he'd return to [the surface] in an instant."

"There was a vulnerability about him that was touching and frightening," Fred Brown says. "I thought: Here's a gifted person, but a troubled one. We had more talks of seriousness than you would normally have.

There was a certain amount of trouble and hunger that stayed with him. We'd be making plans about things away from school or in school and he'd say, 'How do I know that any of this matters?' It was always clear he wasn't sure where he belonged. Music was his attempt to establish an identity that would be sufficient to help him feel like a whole person."

Today, Fred is a psychotherapist in private practice. "Gram was smart. He was outgoing. People liked him," Brown says. "On the surface he was self-competent. He would do things most of us were hesitant to do. But he'd get frustrated when he didn't know who he was. He didn't seem to know it was okay not to have the answers. He was sweet and easygoing, but he'd have these bouts of anger, explosive anger. About anything. It might last five minutes, it might take thirty seconds. I didn't understand it then. But now, as a psychotherapist, I know those things come from an inability to feel free to express emotions that you have to express because they're so overwhelming. I've never seen someone who had these bouts and who was also, at heart, a nice person.

"Gram didn't hold grudges. But the bouts would rise up out of nowhere. He'd loan a song to someone, and if they didn't bring it back when they said they would, he would never go try to find them. Instead he'd have a tantrum for a minute and rake everything off his desk, throw it across the room. Frequently the anger would come from something regarding his family I was never privy to. Somebody was supposed to visit him or do something and they wouldn't show up."

GRAM OFTEN MADE the drive down to Winter Haven, and he seldom went alone. His friends from Bolles became a new audience for the strange ways of the Parsons household.

James Mallard recalls, "We were eating hamburgers. When I asked for mustard and ketchup, they brought each in a separate silver container. It was a crazy situation. Robert Parsons liked to trade us his Jaguar sedan: He'd jump into the Austin-Healey and we'd jump into the Jaguar and race off to these various places to do spontaneous gigs."

Mallard also vividly recalls Bob's pet ocelot. "It was the size of a dalmatian. They had a pool in the backyard, and the ocelot would claim the whole territory. When he walked around you got out of his way. He seemed friendly, but you didn't bother him."

Larry Slade, another Bolles classmate, also remembers "a big wild cat who lived in the backyard. It was dangerous to walk back there because it'd try to eat you. It was friendly only to Gram."

Avis' alcoholism had reached an advanced stage. "I remember his mother's appearance," Larry Slade says. "She looked poorly beside Robert Parsons, who was a robust guy. She had thin, spindly arms and a swollen abdomen. Of course, at sixteen I didn't know what it meant, but ten years later I knew. Gram's mother would essentially [let him] do whatever he wanted. His favorite breakfast was peanut butter on toast and Coca-Cola, and that's what he got."

When James Mallard visited Winter Haven, he recognized that the way Gram's little sister stayed by her brother's side reflected the family's unacknowledged but deepening crisis. "Gram had warm, concerned feelings for his sister," Mallard says. "He knew the situation with this family. He loved his sister and was hoping she would be able to float over the crap that was going on. When I went down with him, I saw what a little baby doll she was. She was coming into her own—she was cute as a button."

Little Avis visited Gram at Bolles on several occasions. Gram arranged dates for her. "Gram tagged her up with one of the undergraduates," Mallard says. "Someone he knew would be careful of her. Gram had a soft protective side for his little sister."

Mallard saw the darker side of the family dynamic as well: "On one of my visits Gram had a local gig. He left me at the house with Mrs. Parsons. She had an engagement with Gram's grandmother. I drove her over in the Austin-Healey. We walked into a formal, sit-down dinner. We first waited in the sitting room. I had no idea how to behave. Then the doors opened and the butler says, 'Dinner is served.' I go to the table and there's place cards all around. I've never been in a situation like that—a place card with my name on it! We start the dinner, and in comes Mr. Parsons. And in front of ten or twelve adults, Mrs. Parsons blasts at him. She knew why he was late— he was out with a paramour, apparently. She accuses him of this, that, and the other. I'm embarrassed to beat the band. Everybody else is looking at their shoes, and she's laying him out. He's smiling during the whole thing, trying to placate her. Finally he sits down to eat and that's about that. Everything calmed down and the steak was served and everybody had polite conversations."

By this time Big Avis' drinking was out of control, and so was Big Avis. Susan Alexander says, "I don't remember Big Avis as being nasty-tempered, but she turned nasty-tempered after she drank. One night I was playing with Little Avis in the Florida room. We were writing, I don't know, homework. We had pencils and we began tussling and a piece of pencil lead got into Little Avis' hand. It wasn't major—we were rolling around and it broke

Little Avis, 1963. (Courtesy the estate of Robert Parsons)

off. Big Avis came out of her bedroom, it was midmorning, and she started screaming. I had never seen her like that. She was drunk and I was terrified. She totally lost it and threw a plate and cursed me and told me she was glad her daughter was well rounded and could do something besides ride horses. She said that to make it a total attack on me. Even Little Avis was blown away. She was mortified."

Many of the Snivelys blamed Big Avis' drinking on Bob Parsons. "I began to see her with a glass in her hand in the morning," Dode Whitaker says. "And another highball at lunch. Bob kept her hand full of a drink of some kind. She'd get that halfway down, and he'd bring her another." Whitaker, for one, thought Bob was doing worse than pouring drinks. "I never saw him actually physically attack," she admits. "But I saw Avis on at least two occasions when she was heavily bruised. And another time when he threw her through a glass door. She was cut pretty badly. Her arms were bruised and her face—she had a black eye."

Yet everyone else's memories indicate that Bob was on the receiving end of Big Avis' abuse, not the other way around. It's hard not to take Whitaker's story as wishful thinking, as another example of the bottomless Snively malice toward Bob Parsons.

Whatever the tensions between Bob and Big Avis, Gram and his stepfather remained close. "As for Gram and Robert Parsons," Larry Slade says, "I don't remember an unkind word between them. They got along remarkably well for a stepfather-stepson relationship. I never heard him say a bad word about his stepfather."

Bob stepped up for Gram at the end of 1964, when it came time for him to apply to college. Gram applied to only one school: Harvard. He didn't have the grades for an elite school, and it wasn't a typical choice for a Bolles student. "We were and are still a regional school," Professor Rufus McClure says. "Though we send people to Yale, the majority of our students stay in the South. Gram always knew he wanted to go east."

Gene Leedy remembers Bob Parsons making trips to Harvard and organizing letter-writing campaigns among his Harvard friends. According to Leedy, Bob deployed all his charm and savvy to sell Gram to the college, emphasizing Gram's brains, talent, and sophistication. But Rufus McClure at Bolles had an entirely different view. "Gram's parents did not play a role," he insists. "It was a family of disconnect."

The likely truth is that Gram sicced both Parsons and the Bolles faculty on Harvard. Both would try harder if each believed they were Gram's only asset.

Peter Henriques wrote a recommendation despite his misgivings: "I wondered if he had the self-discipline to do the work at Harvard. He was the kind of kid who was borderline getting into trouble." McClure also wrote a recommendation, though he also had his doubts. "I knew Gram was perfectly capable of doing academic work at Harvard," he says. "I also knew he was already married to his music. I knew that if an opportunity arose, his music would preempt any plans for college. And I was correct. He was a calculated risk, but it was a losing calculation."

Quinn Barton, the administrator who thought Gram had "loosened [Bolles] up," wrote a recommendation as well. "He had intellectual ability and the ability to get along with people," Barton says. "He was a popular fellow and his teachers were fond of him. His teachers and I considered him to be a promising student, if not a scholar. I had a hunch that when he got out of Jacksonville and into the big city there in Boston, he would find better alternatives or higher priorities. All of us recommending Gram painted him—correctly—as an oddball. And I mean in the best sort of way. While everybody else was marching in straight lines, Gram was zigzagging."

Just before Christmas break, however, Gram violated the rules at Bolles so thoroughly that even the goodwill he enjoyed among his professors could not save him. Gram, James Mallard, and three other boys rented rooms under assumed names at the Traveledge Motel. The Traveledge was right down the road from Bolles, easy walking distance, and the rooms were for the boys and their dates for Bolles' biggest annual event, the Winter Ball. The girls came from Winter Haven and Pompano Beach for the weekend; there was a girl for every boy, five of each. When Gram and James and the others walked into the ball with their dates, they were greeted by Chase Ambler, a popular math professor. Ambler approached each boy, shook his hand, and welcomed him to the dance, addressing him by the assumed name the boy had used at the motel. "We thought we were slick and, bottom line, we were caught," James Mallard says. "It was a bad thing at the time. After the smoke cleared, after that weekend, we were hauled on the carpet to the headmaster's office, and we were in hot water."

The boys were told that to be allowed back in for their last semester as seniors, they would have to return after Christmas break with their parents. Students and parents would sit before the Disciplinary Committee. Mallard remembers, "We joked and called ourselves the DC5, the Disciplinary Committee Five. But this was a big deal." The boys stood a good chance of getting expelled, and expulsion would mean almost certain rejection from the colleges they had applied to.

Bolles was an easy place to get into trouble. Boarders had been known to take the bus into town on weekends and go on shoplifting sprees. Upperclassmen bluffed their way into local bars with fake IDs. Rowdy kids would cut professors' boats loose from their moorings and push the boats out onto the St. John's River. During Gram's time at Bolles, a group was expelled for stealing cars and sinking them in a local lake. Renting motel rooms to stay with girls was regarded as more sophisticated, and therefore dangerous. As the boys went home for Christmas, they all prepared for the worst.

BOB AND BIG AVIS paid the Winter Ball incident little mind. Gram invited the Shilos to Winter Haven for the entire winter vacation, and they flew in from Greenville. To ensure there'd be work for the band, Bob Parsons opened Gram's own personal coffeehouse.

The only place for kids to hang out were the youth centers, and those who could drive were too old for that. Knowing he had a ready market, Bob leased an old warehouse-cum-Pontiac-dealership on Avenue D and Sixth Street Northwest in Winter Haven. He had it renovated, following the dictates of his own taste rather than pandering to his teenage customers, choosing blond wood paneling and understated modern furniture. Bob named the club the Derry Down. It opened for business on December 20, 1964. Bob hired the Winter Haven High football coach and off-duty police officers to chaperone the crowd. As a teen club, the Derry Down did not serve alcohol.

The place held a maximum of two hundred people. It was mobbed on opening night, which proved a Winter Haven society event and a magnet for all of Gram's musical friends. "I remember Big Avis planning for the opening night," Dickie McNeer says. "She was inviting all these people and wanted to make sure my mom would come. It was mostly a party for the country club set."

"Bob had all these blenders going," Grant Lacerte recalls, "making fancy drinks that looked like cocktails. It was so dark that when you first came in you couldn't see a thing. There were a lot of tables. Standing room, too, but you were supposed to sit."

Gram was the featured performer, along with the Shilos. He played almost every night over Christmas break. After Gram and the Shilos returned to school, the Derry Down showcased local bands and brought in groups from out of town. It remained packed.

Bob applied the same business approach to the Derry Down that he had to the prestressed concrete business. "Bob was a generous guy," Grant Lacerte says. "At the club he'd make—he would personally make—hamburgers. And these teenagers couldn't afford to pay more than they paid at Jack & Betty's drive-in. So Bob issued Derry Down credit cards, like ID cards the kids could charge food on. The Derry Down was the most popular spot in town." Gene Leedy sums it up when he quotes Bob as saying, "It's not every restaurant owner that makes hamburgers that cost a dollar and a half and sells them for fifty cents."

Gram's friends in Winter Haven still shake their heads at the outrageousness of it: Bob built and ran a coffeehouse so Gram could have a place to play. And so Bob could have somewhere else to host.

Gram returned to Bolles. As the Disciplinary Committee had demanded, Bob Parsons came with him. Bob had not traveled to Jacksonville to see Gram punished: His aim was to smooth everything over. Apparently all the parents agreed with Bob. The meeting was less of an ordeal than the boys had dreaded. According to James Mallard, Bob "and every other parent went 'Yes, sir' and 'No, sir' and 'We'll do what has to be done, sir.' Parsons was charming, and after the charade ended the Committee said, 'Okay, all you guys can come back in.'"

Bob celebrated by taking Gram straight from the committee meeting over to San Jose Boulevard. There, amid the endless gleaming auto dealerships, Bob bought Gram a brand-new 1965 Austin-Healey convertible. This one was British racing green, like Bob's Jaguar. Gram leased a parking spot down the road from Bolles.

That wasn't the only gift Gram received. Just after getting the Austin-Healey, he learned that he'd been accepted to Harvard. He doesn't seem to have regarded either the car or the acceptance letter as anything extraordinary. "He didn't think nothing of it," James Mallard says. "Everybody assumed everybody was getting into school somewhere. And one school was as good as another, was how our weak little minds perceived it. His response shows his depth. He thought things through. He may not have acted like he did, but he wanted things clear in his own mind. He knew what he was after, he had a purpose. If Harvard suited that purpose, then fine."

Gram's friend Jim Carlton graduated high school in the spring of 1964. After graduation, he toured Florida, playing his guitar in coffeehouses. Carlton knew he was going to work as a musician and not attend college. Eager to avoid the draft and being sent to Vietnam, Jim joined the National Guard. The two friends saw each other shortly after Jim enlisted. Gram looked Carlton up and down, examining his National Guard–inflicted buzz cut. Carlton waited for Gram to say hello, but there was a long pause. Finally Gram said, "Carlton, that haircut does nothing for you."

In March of 1965, Jim Carlton set up two microphones in his bedroom at his father's house. A friend of the family was a United Airlines pilot who regularly flew to Japan. He brought back a Sony 500 reel-to-reel tape recorder as a gift for Jim's dad. The 500 was state-of-the-art at that time. Gram had accumulated a new range of traditional folk music during his month in the Village the previous summer. Carlton wanted to learn the songs. Carlton recalls: "It was a stereo machine, a two-track recorder for two tracks on one side of the tape. I had a microphone for each track. The recordings are in mono, one mike per track. Neither Gram nor I had any agenda but to get the tunes. I wasn't doing it to record Gram but to learn the songs. We did four sessions in all—it happened whenever he would drop by."

The songs recorded on March 13 were "Zah's Blues," a Gram original; "They Still Go Down" by the Journeymen's Dick Weissman; "Pride of Man," folkie Hamilton Camp's best-known song; "The Last Thing on My Mind" by Tom Paxton; and "Hey Nellie Nellie," a sing-along historical epic by David and Jonathan Fromer and Elbert Robinson tracing the evolution of civil rights. The latter is the most dated of the five songs. For the session, Gram played Carlton's Gibson B-25 flattop six-string guitar. Many years later, Jim discovered the tapes of those sessions, and they were released on Sundazed Records in 2001 as *Gram Parsons: Another Side of This Life*.

Bill Colledge thought "Zah's Blues" was Gram's best original song. Over a straightforward blues progression, Gram sings in a throaty jazz crooner's voice. He sounds nothing like a high school student. His voice is full-bodied and expressive, even if the song is a formulaic tale of how "love can't last forever" and "the night must fall." The confidence of Gram's performance and the ache in his voice on the last line, "It's just the sun coming down," gives some hint of how musically mature Gram was at seventeen. Neither the playing nor the lyrics are haunting in and of themselves. But Gram sings with conviction and an ownership of loss. Aside from the chord progression, the song is remarkably complete as an emotional entity. Gram took great care with its structure, and that adds to the song's power.

"They Still Go Down" is a new folk-music version of a traditional miner's lament. It's a narrative and Gram sings it like a story, with none of the heartfelt emotion of "Zah's Blues." He's imitating the Journeymen, with their perfect enunciation and tone of high moral reprobation. "Pride of Man," with its more rollicking dynamic, is a Pete Seeger–like Ozymandias bemoaning how man's folly produces disaster. Like "They Still Go Down," it's a time capsule presentation of the narrative and moral values of the new traditional folk. The song evokes worshipful coffeehouse audiences happy to hear songs with no personal, neurotic aspect. It's the sort of song sung with one's head tilted way back and guitar lifted high, and Gram belts it out like he was leading a hootenanny. His voice is shocking in its strength, depth, and technical control.

"The Last Thing on My Mind" stands on a middle ground between the new traditional folk and the scorched-earth personal vision of Bob Dylan. Paxton's melody is lovely and Gram fingerpicks as best he can, singing over a steady walking stride. Given that the picking takes more concentration than the singing, Gram's vocals have a surprising delicacy. Again, because it's not his song, Gram's emotions seem less sincere, but his range and attention to the feelings underlying the lyrical detail are years beyond his age.

Toward the end, his playing improves and with it the subtlety of his singing. "Hey Nellie Nellie," strummed a mile a minute, echoes "Pride of Man" and "They Still Go Down" in its unbearable sincerity. Telling of 1851, 1858, and then the Civil War, finishing with "a column of white and black folks a hundred years wide," it's the embodiment of preprotest, nonspecific, polite message music. The self-righteous chorus and big finish must have been irresistible to a high school student.

Gram at Bolles. (Courtesy the estate of Robert Parsons)

Taken together the recordings are extraordinary. The qualities that would later fill Gram's voice—self-mocking humor and mournful heartbreak—are nowhere present. And why should they be? Gram's self-possession, his assertion of his right to sing these songs as powerfully as he does, and his immersion in the singing regardless of the skill of his playing, are the hallmarks not of someone becoming a star, but of someone who already regards himself as one. Anyone intending to be a star must be fueled not by willingness but by desperation to perform. Gram demonstrates that gift in abundance. These recordings show not a trace of high school self-consciousness. Gram sounds ready to graduate.

THE SPRING OF 1965 was a time of endings. The school year was closing out, and with it Gram's sojourn at Bolles. His friendship with Margaret Fisher didn't survive that spring. "I didn't pay enough attention to him," Margaret says, "and that was that. Gram was talking to me at a basketball game and this boy came up and I sort of dumped Gram. With Gram, you betrayed him once and you never got a second chance. I was talking to this guy and Gram, he looked at me, and hucked off. He was that way. We were both children of alcoholic parents. He had been deeply betrayed somewhere earlier in his life."

Gram went to the spring prom with a girl who'd come down from New York City. "That was so cool," Margaret remembers. "She shows up in a little black cocktail dress and we're all in Southern prom costumes."

Family life in Winter Haven grew ever more dire. Gene Leedy had a dinner with Bob and Avis that revealed the new dynamic in their relationship. "One night Avis got drunk at dinner and that's when she got mean. 'Bob Parsons,' she says, 'I know you're having an affair with Bonnie, and you enrolled her in school in West Palm and set her up with an apartment and furnished it and are paying her tuition and expenses and you're doing it with my money, and I know it!' Bob sat there and didn't say a word. I intervened and said, 'Bob's old enough to be Bonnie's father, and that's crazy. It's ridiculous for you to have these ideas.' Bob and I went out back to have a drink while my wife and Avis sat there visiting. I said to Bob, 'I'm sorry you invited me to dinner and I end up chewing out your wife. I apologize.' I said, 'You didn't say anything and I thought it was ridiculous.' And he said, 'Yeah, it is ridiculous. And what makes it even more ridiculous is that it's true.'"

Buddy Freeman heard that Avis was planning to end her marriage over the affair. "I knew that Avis intended to divorce Bob," he says. "I think it was already in the works." Dode Whitaker claims to have heard the same thing. "I heard Avis talking to Haney [her mother] about Bob's abuse," Whitaker insists, "and Haney urging her to get out."

Rosina Rainero, Big Avis' friend from her college days, also believes a turning point came around that time. "Sick as she was, when she found out about this little babysitter, she was great," Rainero says. "She got her ducks in a row, and that was it." She and several other members of Big Avis' circle swear that Avis changed her will to cut Bob Parsons off without a cent—and that Bob Parsons had no idea she'd done so.

About a month after the dinner that Gene Leedy describes, and a few days before Gram was scheduled to graduate, Avis was admitted to Winter Haven Hospital. She was suffering from acute alcoholism. "It was a regular hospital—it wasn't a drying-out center," Rob Hoskins says. "I don't know why she went there. She was in there hemorrhaging and hallucinating."

Neither Big Avis nor Bob was able to attend Gram's graduation. Haney Snively went in their stead, along with Little Avis. Gram also called Coon Dog's mother and father and invited them and his aunt, Coon Dog's sister, Pauline Wilkes. It was the first time in five years the Connor kin had seen Gram and Little Avis. James Mallard remembers, "The night before graduation we all had a nice dinner. His grandparents, his sister, his aunt. They'd rented a motel suite and had dinner catered. Gram sang songs and everyone was amazed. My point is that Gram was acting as if everything was normal. I thought it was highly unusual that only his grandparents were there."

On graduation day Gram and Fred Brown suddenly realized they'd forgotten to buy a present for their faculty sponsor, Ron Hubbard. "We were talking about how hungover our class sponsor was," Brown says. "He was so drunk we wondered if he would make it through the ceremony. When we realized we didn't have a present for him, Gram said, 'Let's take my car—no one will see us.' We brainstormed about what we could afford, what we should get, and decided on a little portable color television set. In 1965, that was pretty high-tech. We blasted downtown and it was so much fun we took the long way back, driving through neighborhoods, wasting time.

"People missed us while we were gone. When we got back we heard people frantically searching for us and thought we were in deep doo-doo. We still had the mentality that we're at boarding school and they could still do something to us. We kept saying, 'They can't stop us from graduating because we went off campus!' We were kind of frantic ourselves, and nobody would tell us what the faculty wanted. Just that they were looking for us. We couldn't figure out what was going on.

"Everybody said they were looking for Gram. We assumed they'd missed seeing his car and knew we'd snuck off. We decided to split up, and if anything bad happened I'd try to bail him out. No one had seen us go off together so they didn't know I was gone. I saw him about ten minutes later; he was talking with his family seriously. I thought something must have been going on with his family, because Bob Parsons wasn't there. Gram did not come over and sit down with us during the graduation ceremony. I went hunting for him later, after graduation was over, and couldn't find him. I found Mallard and he saw the same thing I had—Gram talking to his family—but hadn't seen him after that either."

"It was the next day," Margaret Fisher says, "after he'd already gone, that I found out his mother had died."

"That afternoon was the last time I ever saw him," Fred Brown says.

"He left before graduation," James Mallard says, "and I never saw him again."

BIG AVIS DIED IN THE Winter Haven hospital the day Gram graduated from Bolles: June 5, 1965, three days shy of her forty-second birthday. And according to many of the Snivelys, Bob Parsons killed her.

The Snively version is that Bob seized this opportunity to murder his wife, unaware that he would inherit none of her money. While Big Avis languished in the hospital, Bob brought her alcohol—martinis or scotch; the story varies—knowing full well that her drinking it could be fatal.

"It's the general consensus that Bob tried to kill Avis," Susan Alexander says. "He encouraged her to drink before she was in the hospital. I always heard that he took her alcohol while she was on [an unspecified detox medication]. It's a deadly, lethal combination to drink with that medication." Rosina Rainero says that "he told the nurse to go out and get a cup of coffee. When she comes back, Parsons is gone from the room and Avis had a convulsion." Jack Snively recalls, "when she was in the hospital for treatment, he was bringing alcohol to her room, where it was forbidden." And Rob Hoskins says, "Gram's mother was dying and, pardon my French, but that motherfucker brought her a bottle of scotch into the hospital. Does that tell you what he was like?"

Bob's friends, in sharp contrast, paint him as the hapless enabler of a woman whose thirst for alcohol couldn't be restrained, even when she was gravely ill. Gene Leedy says, "I remember her being in the hospital and her saying to Bob, 'I can't stand the food here. It's awful. Would you go to the Sundown [a high-end restaurant in Winter Haven] and get me a nice dinner and a martini?' And Bob was always being kind to her, so that's what he did."

"If he made her a drink," Bonnie Muma says, "it was because she wanted a drink and would have thrown a minor fit, which she could do."

The hospital listed the cause of death as cirrhosis of the liver. The Snively family doctor, George Dorman, performed an autopsy in order, he told Gene Leedy, "to stop any rumors that Bob had killed her." Leedy reports what the doctor told him: "He said, about her autopsy, 'Her liver was bad, and if you could've seen that autopsy you'd never take another drink in your life. Avis' brain was pickled from alcohol over the years.' And her liver, too, and that's what she died from." Avis' out-of-control alcohol consumption makes that conclusion hardly surprising. Big Avis' death did not result, in Leedy's words, "from Bob bringing her martinis in the hospital." She died from the damage inflicted by years of heavy drinking.

Dode Whitaker claims that a Snively family friend, now herself dead, had repeatedly told the story that she had seen Bob right after Avis' death. "She said that the night Avis died, Parsons left the hospital and went to their house and said, 'Well, I got the old biddy this time. Last night I didn't bring enough alcohol, but tonight I did.'"

While there doesn't seem to be any medical basis to the Bob-killed-Avis stories, there is an element of psychological truth. Enablers, driven by a mix of motives in which anger and frustration may figure as powerfully as love and concern, often do terrible damage. If Bob Parsons did say that the last drink he gave his wife killed her, it could be taken as a confession of premeditated murder. It could also be the rueful, self-damning reflection of a man who, as an alcoholic himself, could not refuse his wife another drink. And discovered, to his horror, the consequences.

Avis' funeral a few days later was crowded. All of Winter Haven was there. One of Avis' pallbearers was Travis, the lifelong Snively family chauffeur and majordomo, who had held Avis and her mother as they cried on the night that Coon Dog died. Now she was gone, too.

The legend has grown that Bob brought Bonnie Muma to his wife's funeral—that his young lover and former family babysitter came as his date. Like many stories about the crimes of Bob Parsons, this one isn't true. When Big Avis was hospitalized, Bob sent Bonnie to friends of his in Asheville, North Carolina, where she stayed for several weeks. "Bob called me twice, mostly to tell me to hang in there," Bonnie recalls.

After the funeral everyone flocked to the Parsons house, where Bob was in full host mode. "He wasn't cavalier, he was trying not to show his grief," Jim Carlton says. "The funeral was the Gene Leedys and the normal crowd, and Bob was jovial and pleasant and fending off the well-wishers. The sense of, 'Oh, I'm so sorry for you'—he didn't want much part of that."

Gram, too, used manners as a shield. "While we were waiting, he showed such grace," Jim recalls. "He answered the phone and to some relative he said, 'Well, she had been declining for quite a while.' . . . Gram's stock line when people would say, 'Oh, I'm sorry,' was, 'It happens to everybody.' That's it. That's all he would say.

"He was probably numb. And, as always, cool. Not in a not-caring sense, but in not willing to break down. He was determined to handle it in stride, and did he ever. There was no obvious grief. His mother was gone, and he dealt with the situation. He handled himself beautifully."

Susan Alexander says, "We all ended up back at the Parsonses' home afterward. There was a lot of food and cocktails and the house was packed. Avis and I went into the living room, where we usually didn't go. It was empty. Everybody was off in the Florida room. Avis and I sat down. Big Avis' portrait hung on the wall. Little Avis sat there looking at her mother's picture. I don't remember tears. I only remember quiet."

NINE

CAMBRIDGE

AFTER AVIS DIED, THE TRUST SITUATION WAS UNCERTAIN AND BOB PARSONS needed cash. He approached his friend Gene Leedy and insisted that Leedy buy his treasured silver Jaguar. Leedy told him he could not afford a ten-thousand-dollar car. Bob told him he could have it for twenty-five hundred dollars. Leedy, confused, asked what was going on. According to Gene, Bob said, "I need the money today. You want it at that price, buy it today. I need twenty-five hundred dollars to pay Gram's tuition to Harvard today." Leedy bought the car.

Shortly after his mother's funeral, Gram drove out of Winter Haven in his Austin-Healey. He spent the summer of 1965 in Greenwich Village, where he rented a small apartment off Bleecker Street. Gram played few solo shows; mostly he hung out. According to John Einarson's superb history of country rock, *Desperados*, Gram lived across the street from future Buffalo Springfield-ers Richard Furay and Stephen Stills. Stills brought Gram into a budding folk-rock group that did not develop. As that attempt fell apart, Stills left the Village for Southern California. At summer's end Furay moved to Wilbraham, Massachusetts. But before he left, according to

Einarson's account, Furay spent time with Gram swapping songs. Furay loved Gram's "Brass Buttons." "I was blown away," Furay told Einarson. "Sometimes you hear a song and you think, 'Wow. This is good.'"

During that Village summer Gram hung out with former child star Brandon De Wilde; rumor has it they met buying marijuana from the same dealer. Brandon was a bit older than Gram, languid yet charismatic, glamorous in an effortless, natural way, and now a budding singer-songwriter. He and Gram became instant friends.

Brandon had become famous, if not immortal, playing young Joey Starrett in the 1953 western *Shane*. Shane's a gunfighter who drifts into town and protects Joey's family. At picture's end Shane rides off into the high lonesome, as wanderin' heroes must. Little Brandon runs after Shane, like every boy after every vanished father, crying, "Come back, Shane! Shane, come back!"

Brandon's blond good looks typed him as a Norman Rockwell kid. As he grew to adulthood, De Wilde developed a reserve, an observing aspect that made his screen presence more profound and unsettling. Ten years after *Shane*, lean and lanky at age twenty-one, Brandon played Paul Newman's distant, too-knowledgeable younger brother in the hard-bitten contemporary western character study *Hud*. The year he met Gram, Brandon costarred in a large-scale war epic, *In Harm's Way*, playing John Wayne's estranged son. Like Gram, Brandon manifested a constant, visible emotional pain; it makes his performance in the film almost too honest, especially next to Wayne's bluster.

A measure of the power of the Village scene is that a young man with Brandon's movie career would try to redefine himself as a troubadour. "Brandon was getting into music," says Gram's soon-to-be bandmate Ian Dunlop. "He was a good-looking guy—he could play and sing. He was into the Beatles and would try to write the new pop music of the time."

Ian Dunlop's use of the word *new* is revealing. The "new pop music of the time" meant something heretofore unseen. It meant pop stars who, as critic Robert Christgau pointed out, wrote and arranged their own songs. White pop stars, that is. Black performers from Robert Johnson to Louis Armstrong to Duke Ellington to Louis Jordan to Chuck Berry, Bo Diddley, Little Richard, and Fats Domino had always written and arranged their own material. But the payola scandals of fifties radio—over bribes paid to radio stations and DJs to guarantee airplay—and the backlash against black music driving white teenagers berserk with its jungle rhythms forced the market ascendancy of pop music that emphasized melody over rhythm and polish over soul.

Ground zero of this movement—the old pop music—was New York City, and specifically the Brill Building on Broadway. Starting in 1960, the Brill Building became home to the pop songwriters and producers Carole King and Gerry Goffin ("Locomotion," "Will You Love Me Tomorrow?"), Jerry Leiber and Mike Stoller ("Stand by Me," "Save the Last Dance for Me," "On Broadway"), Neil Sedaka ("Where the Boys Are," "Breaking Up Is Hard to Do"), and Barry Mann ("I Love How You Love Me," "We Gotta Get out of This Place"), who wrote with Cynthia Weil ("You've Lost That Lovin' Feeling") and with Weil and Phil Spector ("Walkin' in the Rain"). Songs were written with no idea who might sing them; groups could be made up of whomever happened to be in the studio or available that afternoon.

The Brill Building system was the antithesis of the folk movement, whose cherished self-image was preservationist and anticommercial. Brill pop was carefully designed, orchestrated, and produced—gleefully, passionately artificial. Its roots lay in vaudeville, Broadway, and Tin Pan Alley—not just urban traditions, but specifically New York Jewish traditions. That was about as far from Appalachia as you could get. Or so thought the more censorious folkies. Elijah Wald makes a convincing case in his excellent revisionist history, *Escaping the Delta: Robert Johnson and the Invention of the Blues*, that many rural musicians utilized ideas about showmanship and personality marketing drawn from vaudeville and Tin Pan Alley in their quest for larger audiences.

The writers and producers of the Brill Building created a mythology of teenage life that existed only in their songs. Their three-minute melodramas stood in stark contrast to folk music about God, family, plowing, rambling, liquor, women, and labor troubles. The Brill songs, whether or not they realistically reflected the lives of American teenagers, became the formative universe for the emerging mass market of teens nationwide. As with psychedelic rock, punk, and hip-hop, the audience culture conformed to the songs, not the other way around. The music's pervasive and enduringly popular message—regardless of the songs' content—was that to be an American teenager was a melodrama. A scorching melodrama. And that every moment of teendom—going to high school, finding a date, arguing with your parents, learning the newest dance—was imbued with grand passion. Brill pop codified an identity of separateness for teenagers and ensured that teens or their parents would pay for that identity—for clothes, for cars, and for more and more music.

The songwriter-producer lock on the charts was threatened, and soon would be eradicated, by three other musical movements. The first would be the Beatles, the Rolling Stones, and the rest of the British Invasion. The Beatles and Stones wrote much of their own material while also scoring hits with cover versions (as did the Who, the Kinks, the Dave Clark Five, and others). While they may have been as carefully managed in presentation and image as their Brill Building counterparts, the Beatles and Stones were, unlike the Dixie Cups ("Chapel of Love"), real bands. They were friends who played and lived together. Hip scenes coalesced around their professional circumstances. Swinging London, for example, grew as the music (and the associated drugs and fashion) proved that there were customers and money for this new pop direction.

The second movement eroding Brill pop domination was Berry Gordy's Motown hit factory (the Four Tops, the Temptations, Marvin Gaye, the Supremes) in Detroit and its Southern equivalent, the Stax/Volt label (Otis Redding, Booker T & the MGs, Sam and Dave, Eddie Floyd) out of Memphis. The songs they produced were not teen melodramas but raceless, ageless emotional odysseys with roots in R&B, black church music, and the blues.

The third assault on Brill pop came from folk rock, which was rising on a path paralleling that of the Beatles. By the time Dylan went electric at Newport in the summer of 1965, two months before Gram arrived at Harvard, the Byrds' folk rock and wholly electrified version of Dylan's "Mr. Tambourine Man" had already hit number one. Richie Furay remembers Gram playing the Byrds' debut album as a galvanizing event: "I thought, 'I'd like to be part of something like this. I gotta find out where Stephen Stills is and get ahold of him.'" After his brief stint in New England, Furay moved to Los Angeles, where he and Stills formed Buffalo Springfield.

Ian Dunlop's use of the phrase *new music* also suggests the perceived difference between what folkies regarded as worthy music and what they considered the putrid wreckage of plastic American pop crap.

The folkies loathed the post-Army Elvis (gone was the sexed-up white black man; in his place appeared a Bing Crosby wannabe), the Brill Building, and Pat Boone (who symbolically castrated Little Richard by hitting number one while crooning Little Richard's anarchic piano rock into smooth vanilla pudding). Not that they were all that crazy about Little Richard to begin with; folkies hated harmony groups in matching suits and processed hair. They disliked urbanity and found its pop manifestation inherently false. Here their reasoning may have been extreme, but it wasn't entirely unsound. Most pop manifestations of urbanity *were* bogus: bands thrown together for a song or a tour, total strangers onstage for a night, payola dominating radio . . . but folk wasn't immune to the corrupting influence of mass-market image-making either.

The avatar of folk plasticity was the much-reviled Kingston Trio, who had five number one hits. The Kingston Trio wore matching striped shirts and flattop haircuts, sang in antiseptic barbershop harmonies, and were regarded as vile popularizers aiming for the lowest common denominator. Any neophyte who showed up in the Village in a new work shirt with his guitar and harmonica holder and started up a Kingston Trio song would be laughed out of Washington Square Park.

Still, the Kingston Trio can be credited with creating the college-student mass market for LPs. Prior to their success, kids bought singles; the Trio launched the endlessly self-renewing culture of college kids sitting around dorm rooms, nodding thoughtfully as an entire record plays.

One reason the hardcore folkies hated the Kingston Trio may have been that for most, the Trio was the first folk music they ever heard. As ears grew more sophisticated, that introductory music came to seem cruder and more emblematic of the listener's own unsophisticated past. It was easy to blame the messenger.

For those who controlled the conversation in the Village, the moral high ground continued to be held by what was deemed the honest expression of (presumably) unsophisticated rural folks, black and white. The unknowing inauthenticity embedded in this urban yen for rural simplicity was summarized best by Rodney Dillard. Rodney played with his brother Doug, a banjo virtuoso who later toured Europe with Gram and the Byrds. Dillard told author Richie Unterberger (for Unterberger's excellent history of folk rock, *Turn! Turn! Turn!*):

> "I came from a rural area, grew up on a farm with no electricity and no bathroom until I was fourteen. We were coming out of that music which had been around like dogs in the yard. These intellectuals who discovered bluegrass were coming from an intellectual/educational/social approach. At that time, everyone was wanting to put bluegrass in a museum, keep it the way it was, look at it once in a while, and protect it so it didn't change.

Our first album, *Back Porch Bluegrass*, had echo on the record. And one of the critics from one of the little back-East rags said, 'Since when did they have echo chambers on back porches?' Well, that guy had probably never been off of his block. Because you sit here on my back porch right now and you get nothing but echo, because I live up the side of a mountain."

Primitives were supposed to remain primitive and thus support widely held preconceptions about an anticommercial vox populi. The seminal text for those notions was collector and rural music historian Harry Smith's *Anthology of American Folk Music*, released in 1952. Smith's six-LP set included murder ballads, country blues, Hawaiian slack-string guitar, jug bands, mountain folk songs, and Southern gospel. It seemed a paragon of rural authenticity, but there were deceptions galore even in this fantastic collection of American weirdness.

Many of the twenties, thirties, and forties down-from-the-hills/up-from-the-hollers musicians the folkies so admired were not consciously preserving a back-porch tradition. They wanted radio play and popular success. It did not seem to register on their future listeners that these hillbillies might have deliberately altered their seemingly primitive style in search of more airplay and bigger sales. Similarly, for the staunch folkies, Dylan's decision to go electric was a betrayal because it meant he was superficializing his music, willfully reaching out to the rock mainstream. Dylan had only done what most of the musicians in Smith's *Anthology* had. Or would've, given the chance.

Typical of movement-driven shifts in popular entertainment—the early days of punk, for instance—perceived authenticity meant everything. Who had integrity and who did not and who made such judgments determined the moral ascendancy in the folk community.

Demonstrating folk's market penetration at the time, Joan Baez appeared on the cover of *Newsweek* in November 1962. Folk popularity peaked in 1963; ABC ran a weekly *Hootenanny!* show that fall. Then the Beatles were introduced to a mass American market by their first appearance on *The Jack Paar Program* on January 3, 1964. A month later, on February 9, they appeared on *The Ed Sullivan Show*. Fifty thousand people applied for the 728 seats in Sullivan's studio. That was the beginning of the end of the folk movement, and of the flattop haircut along with it.

Jerry Yester of the Modern Folk Quartet (who would later join the Lovin' Spoonful) also spoke to Richie Unterberger:

"We rented a motel room to watch *The Ed Sullivan Show* 'cause we wanted to know who the hell the Beatles were. We watched the show and it was like a bolt of electricity. That was it. No more haircuts. Within a month all the pawn shops were cleaned out of electric instruments. Chip got an electric bass, I got an electric guitar, and in less than a year we were a rock band. And all the little folk clubs became rock clubs."

Sales of electric guitars in America tripled in the two years following the Beatles' television debut. America turned into one big Winter Haven: Everybody started a band. In 1964, Roger (then known as Jim) McGuinn—longtime folkie, future cofounder of the Byrds, and future Gram bandmate—began to feature Beatles songs on his twelve-string acoustic during solo gigs at the folk club the Troubadour in Los Angeles. A year before, McGuinn had been a thirty-five-dollar-a-week Brill Building songwriter in the employ of Bobby Darin.

As a capper, Dylan obsoleted the whole idea of folk authenticity by turning into a rocker. He sidestepped integrity issues by doing something unprecedented: Dylan entered the mainstream by writing hermetic, self-referential, literary material set to rip-ass amplified blues forms. And he raced up the charts doing it. No wonder the old-time Village hardcore were so pissed off. Never mind content or market share; even as implicit protest against plastic pop crap, folk had been totally outmaneuvered.

Gram's taste lay somewhere in the middle. While he was conscious of what was regarded as righteous and what was not, it did not affect what he played. He was strongly influenced by Fred Neil, a folksinger-songwriter legendary for his dark, brooding voice, skill on the guitar, and charisma. A commanding presence, Fred was widely admired in the folk world. He, too, had once worked as a songwriter in the Brill Building. He befriended Dylan when Dylan first came to New York. Everyone sought his company, but Fred preferred the quieter folkie-hippie scene of Coconut Grove, Florida (the scene that nurtured future Byrd David Crosby), and left the Village for Florida in 1965.

Gram also liked a bit of schlock, as his fondness for the Journeymen and the songs he recorded at Jim Carlton's suggest. He had little interest in protest music. Even in late 1965 he was still writing in a folksy, post-(acoustic)-Dylan idiom, with complex literary metaphors set against familiar folk chord changes. His hostile response to Dylan's shift in styles seems more like a one-night complaint than a philosophical objection. Gram was no ideologue, not politically or aesthetically.

In August 1965, James Mallard and Larry Slade came to New York for a visit. Though they stayed in Gram's apartment, they didn't see much of him. On Tuesday, August 23, Gram went with Brandon De Wilde to catch the Beatles at Shea Stadium. It was the first time that an American stadium had been used for a rock concert: The new paradigm was arriving on the wings of huge cash outlays by teenagers and their parents. No one who craved center stage the way Gram did could have remained unmoved while surrounded by fifty thousand screaming teenage girls.

"Gram was gone that whole first weekend," James Mallard remembers. "Larry and I were in the apartment cooling, eating pastrami sandwiches and cheesecake. In walks Gram after the concert with Brandon De Wilde. They bring some hashish. We sat around and sucked on that pipe all night long. We laughed and giggled, had a great time. While we were there we mostly talked and slept; talked late into the night and slept all day. Gram took us to little bars and dives and we drove around in his Austin-Healey. It was parked on the street up there and getting beat to hell in short order."

Gram's time alone in New York was a period of concentration, of listening to others and focusing on songwriting. He performed less because he was creating a body of work and getting his chops together for Cambridge, Massachusetts.

FOLK DOMINATED CAMBRIDGE, but Cambridge was not Greenwich Village. Cambridge was hardly even Boston. Although it had become a center of folk music in America, Cambridge, unlike the Village, was no melting pot. The community of students who lived there was white, well-to-do, and young. After the hat-passing, cold-water-flat, floor-sleeping ambience of the Village, Cambridge was a leafy safe haven, the Bolles School with longer hair, wilder girls, and drugs. Lots of drugs. And the emerging model of hippie house sharing . . .

Piano player David Barry remembers, "Halfway between Harvard Square and Central Square was a residential area of two-story houses that hippies and artists and freaks moved into. It was no good to be in a house by yourself, because the neighbors were hostile. They were Irish rednecks and they hated, hated, *hated* Harvard people, and long-haired hippie Harvard was loathed with a special loathing. So musicians gathered in protective enclaves. Times being what they were, it was often unclear whose place a place might be. People managed to get the rent paid, but there may have been four or five people living there."

Cambridge offered Gram a milieu he understood. Surrounded by wealthy, sophisticated kids, few of whom had to worry about working for a living, Gram found himself in the heart of the East Coast kindling that would shortly ignite the counterculture explosion nationwide. Inevitably, Cambridge harbored plenty of doctrinaire musical factions.

The hardcore folkies, who were determined to re-create every scratch and pop on a vintage 78, remained adamant that the best modern folk exposed the least of the singer's personality or inner self. Their aspirational models were the antiseptic harmonies of the Journeymen. They were fast running out of cultural currency.

In addition to plenty of time and few responsibilities, the young people of Cambridge had the Harvard Library and its Library of Congress Anthologies of folk and blues music, recorded in the field by Alan Lomax and Harry Smith. Many Cambridge kids had complicated record collections and encyclopedic knowledge of American roots music, black and white. These knowing few knew too much to become ideologues. They listened to everything not to determine a moral hierarchy but to discover how primitive American musical forms nourished one another. And because they dug it.

Cambridge offered numerous bars and coffeehouses in which to play. Folk clubs ringed Harvard Square. The main folk coffeehouse was Club 47 off the Square. In Boston, just across the Charles River, the Berklee College of Music produced a never-ending stream of students with developing chops who wanted most of all to play. They were eager to take what they'd learned in teaching studios and honed in practice rooms and show it off in front of an audience.

Larry Piro, Gram's Pennypacker Hall roommate, remembers Gram's arrival: "I had been there a couple of days and had staked out the room, wondering when my roommate was going to be arriving," he says. "I registered along with everyone else at Memorial Hall. It must have been some time in the afternoon that registration for freshmen was about to close. There was about fifteen or twenty minutes left. All of a sudden he appeared, top down in this green sports car, looking at least five years older than his picture . . . zipping up in the Austin-Healey 3000, tearing off to Memorial Hall to see if he can register, getting in under the wire. Typical Gram Parsons. He was like that: a lot of flourish, a lot of unusual."

Gram enrolled in Harvard's core curriculum. Majors were not declared until sophomore year, so Gram's course load centered on the natural and social sciences and French. Though he seldom went to class, Gram formed a lifelong friendship with Harvard's freshman advisor, James E. Thomas, known as Jet. Jet, who subsequently became dean of freshmen, reminded future Gram bandmate Ian Dunlop of a character in a John Updike novel— "you know, the alternative college-type crowd of that period"—or the avuncular prof portrayed by Donald Sutherland in the movie *Animal House*. "He was a caring professor," Ian summarizes. "Open, and occasionally smoked pot."

Jet's fields were linguistic philosophy and philosophical theology, but he and Gram found common ground in their roots. "Both being from the South, Gram and I had a connection right off the bat," Jet says. "It turned out we liked the same kind of music: old-time country like [Faron Young's] 'Hello Walls,' gospels, old hymns. He'd bring his guitar to my room almost every night and play and sing new songs he'd written. He kept them in a composition notebook, like a student notebook. Gram started talking to me about everything and quickly I got to know about him and his concerns. Money was a problem in Gram's life the entire time I knew him. He had too much, really."

Gram appeared to fit in at Harvard, Jet says: "You wouldn't be able to tell Gram from any other prep school student. Gram was outgoing, pretty conservative. He wasn't dressing in any far-out way." But from the beginning Harvard failed to engage Gram. "He never went to classes. I'm not sure why he came to Harvard. It was clear from the moment he got here that he was interested in music. That happens with students sometimes: Harvard becomes a goal, and once they get there they don't know what to do.

"He bought his books and went through the motions that freshmen do. He had his student card, but within a couple weeks his real locus was not Harvard."

Jet and Gram's conversation ranged widely. "Gram had strong ideas about spiritual life even then," Jet says. "He never went to church of any kind the whole time I knew him. But he grew up in a Southern environment which is permeated with the language and the ideas. Those old gospel hymns—you don't have to be religious to love that music. He did love it, and listened to it and sang it a lot. It's something he absorbed with his Southern culture. At the same time, Gram was worldly oriented. His spirituality, his interest in religion, was not an interest in another world or an afterlife. He was interested in discovering the qualities of this life. That's why he wanted to create music that cut across the boundaries of people."

In 1972 Gram was famously quoted about his brief time at Harvard. "I think I was there about four hours and fifteen minutes," he said in a Warner-Reprise publicity bio. "At Harvard, you don't major, you concentrate. One thing I was hellbound to concentrate on was what Alpert and Leary were up to with LSD. But they'd left. Mainly I was turned off by the fact that I had to study all these things I didn't understand. I lasted about four or five months playing music and having good times."

Gram was compelled toward music and good times more than studying, but there's no indication that when he hit town he knew who Timothy Leary and Richard Alpert were. Those twin apostles of LSD had been kicked out of Harvard two years earlier. All descriptions of Gram at that time align with Jet Thomas' impression: a naïve, enthusiastic, preppy.

Jet Thomas dismisses Gram's later claim that Alpert and Leary had drawn him to Cambridge as a fanciful rewriting of history. "He never met any of those people!" Jet exclaims. "He never tried to meet any of those people. He and I had lots of conversations about theology, but as far as I know he was never involved with that world. Whatever drugs he was doing, he wasn't doing them with Harvard people. He was doing them with his musician friends."

Judson Graves, one of Gram's more straitlaced Bolles classmates, wasn't a close friend but visited Gram about this time. He walked into Gram's dorm and found "a group of people guarding him, limiting his access. They were newly long-haired students who looked like residents of the dorm, circling the wagons around Gram. Once they cleared my arrival with Gram, I went upstairs. He was in bed, and it was a strangely lit psychedelic scene. Gram was wrecked. He could barely string a sentence together. He knew who I was and we had a semblance of a short conversation, but he was so wrecked we could not communicate. And these guys hanging around who seemed to be worshipping him—it was the middle of the day and strange. That was one of my earliest exposures to someone who was really trashed. I came down from Dartmouth, which was a drinking school. Plus it was Gram, and I wanted Gram to succeed at Harvard. I never saw him again, and every time I heard about him or saw his image that scene came back to me and I wondered if he'd ever be able to get over it. He was in kind of a cocoon up there. Music playing. Two or three guys . . . he was all kind of tucked in."

In that encounter Graves unknowingly occupied one side of a culture clash. Maybe Gram was wrecked; maybe it was a normal afternoon of drug taking and music listening. What Graves saw would expand outward from Harvard and other cutting-edge scenes to become a standard dorm-room motif: a bunch of guys hanging out on drugs with the music blasting, protecting the one who was the most far gone.

Paul Broder, another Bolles classmate attending college in Boston, also visited Gram. "Gram got fucked-up a lot," Broder says. "He could function, but it was beyond getting high. He was solitary and distant. I remember going home with him once. We were using his Austin-Healey convertible, going over one hundred miles per hour on a little back road. I asked him why he drove so fast. He said, 'If I get into a wreck, I don't want to be maimed.'"

That Gram's star quality shone at Harvard is attested to by David Johnson's reminiscence in the *Harvard Journal*:

> In the fall of 1965 I stood near the entrance to Memorial Church, facing Widener Library. On the library steps a group of young musicians posed for a photographer from *Life* magazine. The center of attention was the group's leader, Gram Parsons, then a 19-year-old Harvard freshman from Winter Haven, Florida. Another Harvard freshman, Lawrence Piro, held one of Gram's guitars. I envied him. Up close, Parsons appeared remarkably self-possessed and confident. He was lean and good-looking, with longish dark hair. I felt awed that a contemporary could be so far along the road to the American Dream we grew up on: being Elvis.

The circumstances that gave rise to this photo shoot are lost to history, and no article or photograph ever appeared in *Life*. How typical of Gram that weeks after arriving at Harvard he would attract the attention of a *Life* photographer, and that nothing would come of it.

WHEN GRAM ARRIVED IN CAMBRIDGE he hit the ground running. "The whole experience of Harvard as a student was secondary," says roommate Larry Piro. "Gram immediately started to find other musicians here. He wanted to play, to write songs into the wee hours of the morning."

Gram put up a sign in a coffeehouse and recruited music students from Berklee. The pickup band was christened Gram Parsons and the Like. They jammed in local coffeehouses. "They were educated musicians," Ian Dunlop says. "They had been star pupils and were fantastic readers. But they were dedicated to a musical education; they weren't in it for the rock and roll. They were upset with Gram because he wanted more simple tunes, without so many chords."

Gram met Ian, a singer, guitarist, and saxophonist, and guitarist John Nuese shortly after school started. The link that connected them was Diana Dew, one of the first of several supergirls of the emerging sixties scene that populate Gram's story. These extraordinary women run through the sixties like a current: smart, fashionable, aware, absurdly cool, talented, and often connected to one another by something other than their boyfriends.

Diana was working at Isis, a fashionable Cambridge boutique. Later she migrated to New York and became a well-known designer for rock musicians. "She designed clothes that had tiny electric lights on them," says pianist David Barry, who played with John and Ian. "The Blues Magoos wore her suits in concert. She sang. She had a beautiful voice and she put together a band, Diana Dew and the Dewdrops. She hung out at Max's Kansas City. She made clothes for rock musicians that were totally out of place, because people were wearing work shirts and someone's girlfriend would embroider some stuff on it. Diana was making shirts out of sateen, like for a soul band. In Boston she was part of a hip music scene that Gram was right in the middle of."

Gram went into Isis looking for a present for Little Avis and was invited to visit the house Diana and John Nuese shared. Diana and John had been a couple, but Diana had left John to go out with Ian. There were no hard feelings; as Ian put it, "This was the sixties."

Ian had been in the Refugees, a band in Providence, Rhode Island, where Ian attended the Rhode Island School of Design. In Cambridge he and John were playing in pickup bands together. It was an era of ludicrously ornate band names. Ian and John were in Happy Pantaloon and the Three Buckles as well as Desmond and the Lagondas. Pianist David Barry was also in the Lagondas. "Desmond had a 1937 Lagonda, a sports racing car about sixteen feet wide," Barry remembers. "We actually went to our gigs in this magnificent Lagonda. We'd pack amplifiers and stuff on the running boards and the rumble seat. We'd show up at these vaguely psychedelic places and play. We didn't play many gigs. We weren't any good because the band would never practice. Ian was about the most laid-back guy in the hemisphere. He would show up an hour and forty-five minutes late for something that had a two-hour-and-ten-minute schedule. And speaking in his low, whispery voice: 'What's goin' on, man? It's all cool.' He was so totally of the era you couldn't help feeling like, 'What am I getting so uptight about?' We'd get to some gig and we'd have nothing because we hadn't practiced. And if the audience smoked enough dope, nobody would notice that we weren't together at all."

John Nuese had a reputation as a killer guitarist. Like Jimi Hendrix, John was left-handed and so played and strung his guitar upside down. He had been playing in the Trolls with Banana, a.k.a. Lowell Levinger. Levinger's later band, the Youngbloods, would become an unavoidable one-hit wonder with their lugubrious cover of the 1967 hippie anthem "Get Together" (by Dino Valenti of the San Francisco band Quicksilver Messenger Service).

When John arrived at the house, Gram was playing and singing. "We got into jamming," John says. "He produced some unique substances and we commenced to adjust our attitudes. Then we played till six in the morning. When you meet someone like that and you play for an hour or two, you know when the chemistry is right. Gram told me he wanted to put a band together."

Ian's first impression of Gram: "He was a smooth talker. He had plans and wanted to do something that included music. He was a tall, slender, fresh-faced, clean-cut-looking guy, with that charm and a Southern gentleness. I remember going over to his dorm. The drinking age was eighteen; Gram would call up a delivery service, give them a credit card, and they'd deliver to the door."

Gram, Ian, and John piled into Gram's Austin-Healey, which was built to hold two, and crossed the Charles River bound for deep downtown Boston and the Combat Zone. The Zone was Boston's red-light district, with streetwalkers, stripper bars, and, according to Boston musician Billy Briggs, "funky shoe stores, pizza joints, and clubs that stayed open till four o'clock in the morning. They were notorious for making the bands play ten sets a night, but it was a place where people went to get good. We didn't play that scene because we were already playing this new rock-and-roll stuff. James Brown and soul, the R&B-type thing, was the genre played in the raunchy places back then. You know, organs, horns, black chick singer, bass, drums, guitar playing rhythm but not a lot of lead guitar, more horns, one or two sax players."

In other words, bands in the Zone played black music, not rock.

Gram, John, and Ian went to the Zone to see Mickey Gauvin, a madman drummer with a citywide reputation. "He was in Robert Pace and the Pacemakers, a real hardworking band," Ian says. "They played horrible places like Val Beach and Baltimore, playing in clubs and lounges where sailors go to drink. Rough places—we saw him at the Intermission, a bar in the roughest part of Boston. The band was tight and they played early Motown and James Brown medleys; their front guy had a pompadour dyed bright red and all the dance moves down. They were hot. They'd do an entire set without one stop. They'd play seven nights and a matinee. As for Mickey, I never heard a guy who played as well—he hit all these strange beats and those James Brown riffs with all their weird timing."

"I was floored by the guy," John Nuese says. "We asked him to come to Cambridge and meet our scene and in a week he was there. We gave him the correct substances to take care of him and he quit the Pacemakers and said, 'I want to play with you guys.'"

Gram had a lineup he liked. He described the band as "an English psychiatrist's son [Ian Dunlop], a Connecticut judge's son [John Nuese], and some kind of anarchist from Baltimore [Mickey Gauvin]. Mickey was artistic but he kept getting busted for blowing up draft boards." It's unlikely that Mickey blew up anyone, but he had the personality for bomb throwing. He was a drummer.

The band rehearsed three times a week at Ian's apartment but played no live gigs. Ian's home was the quintessential early hipster-hippie pad. The walls were covered with hand-painted murals and found street objects stood around as sculptures. Orange-crate bookcases lined the walls. At first the band spent its time learning and arranging Gram's originals, which were rooted in folk music's chord changes and strumming. Gram played a Martin 0-16NY, a smaller guitar. That set him off from the traditional folkies, who preferred the big, boomy sound of the Martin G series.

Ian Dunlop recognized that the band came together as professionals. "I was living in a wooden tenement in Cambridge, real slumlord housing full of musicians, with lots of students and bohemians. There were always instruments set up and different combinations were always playing. We started rehearsing Gram's self-penned ditties in the living room. We had the goal of getting it together to make demos and record. It was not that everyone had an immediate indelible affinity and a clear 'You're my spiritual mate, my soul mate' about music. We were all playing and interested in doing something professional and in pursuing music in our different ways. It was all sorts of different tastes. And it suited us at the time to work on Gram's songs."

Another aspiring professional in the scene was Tom Snow, a songwriter and keyboardist from the Berklee School who recorded with Gram, John, and Ian in New York later that fall—another example of Gram's singular instinct for collaborators who would go on to great success. Snow's later career included two Oscar nominations for film soundtracks, two Grammy nominations, and recordings of his songs by Barbra Streisand, Ray Charles, and Bonnie Raitt.

Gram was maturing rapidly as a songwriter. "There was individuality and creativity in his writing," Ian Dunlop says. "It was highly romantic and lyrical, and not based in grooves or riffs as in rhythm and blues. Some of his songs were better suited to a solo performance. They were nothing like playing 'I Want to Hold Your Hand' or 'My Guy.' They grew from Gram's experience of gigging solo."

"November Nights," a Gram original from that time, occupies a middle ground between a solo guitar strummer and likely ensemble material. The band rehearsed it often. Another major influence on Gram and everyone in the band was Ray Charles' seminal *Modern Sounds in Country & Western Music*. Ian Dunlop recalled that the first time he and Gram hung out alone together, that "extraordinary album" was the music they were listening to.

Charles' version of Don Gibson's 1958 "I Can't Stop Loving You" hit number one in 1962. The B-side, another Don Gibson original, "Oh, Lonesome Me," made it to number seven. Charles' lush strings, smooth orchestral arrangements, and R&B-drenched vocal style opened up new frontiers for country and soul musicians. Charles also made clear that the emotions of country music were as potent and meaningful as those expressed in soul. For that era, it was a revelation. Charles' approach was wholly original, and no other R&B artist had yet dared produce an entire record of country music. Charles demonstrated to a skeptical world that commercial country had soul and would sell to a noncountry market.

A RECURRING CRITICAL QUESTION REMAINS: What led to Gram's fascination with country music?

Gram heard plenty of country in Winter Haven, and the early Sun Records pioneers—Elvis, Carl Perkins, Jerry Lee Lewis, and Johnny Cash—emerged from, aligned with, and shattered country forms. But the moralist folkie community, so quick to condemn any sound that did not meet its standards for integrity, held no music in greater contempt than commercial country. The emerging hippie audience had even less use for it. When Dylan was asked, "Who's your favorite living poet?" he replied, "Smokey Robinson," hailing Motown's foremost singer-songwriter and author of "First I

Look at the Purse," "Tears of a Clown," and many more. Nobody from the Village would have answered that question with "George Jones." The country audience was perceived as ignorant hicks. Country musicians' aesthetics—sequined suits, absurdly ornate hairdos, endless kiss-ass stage patter—seemed so ridiculous as to be otherworldly. Nashville's reliance on studio musicians to produce its signature polished sound went against all folkie ideas of the authentic song artifact.

"I remember Elvis and the magic of 1956," Ian Dunlop says. "And before all that was this sound that was more like country but it wasn't country. It came from the South. In the old days there were these huge stations, like, in Wheeling, West Virginia, WWVA-AM. It was country like the Grand Ole Opry. I remember getting stations like that on my AM radio at night. Even before that whole Carl Perkins, Elvis, and rockabilly Memphis sound, there was other stuff that was a countryish, rock 'n' rolly sort of thing. It was an influence to anybody who had ears. All of us were exposed through the process of random osmosis to country more than we realized. But still, the reputation of being a Southerner was embarrassing, and that stuck like bad luck."

It took great courage—and massive insolence—to deliberately imitate what was regarded as the least worthy music in America. Gram had a perverse streak and a mischievous sense of humor, but no one with Gram's ambition would focus his career on music he didn't love. Gram had never been a pioneer for pioneering's sake. The motivation seems simple: Gram and the band heard what they liked and pursued it.

"When the band got together," John Nuese says, "I was the only one with experience playing and listening to a lot of country. I take the credit for turning Gram on to this music. Because he didn't know anybody who listened to it at that time. Everybody wanted to play black music, R&B—they wanted to be black. Or they wanted to play folk music. Nobody was listening to what they'd call redneck country-western shit. Mickey Gauvin was a black, soul kind of drummer. Ian was familiar with some country, but was mostly a rock and roller, and Gram, who had been exposed to country in his formative years, was doing commercial folk music. Gram did not know what was going on in country music. He knew no Buck Owens or Merle Haggard. Nor did other members of the band. When I turned them on to these singers they all liked it and were caught up, totally hooked by the music."

"Country music formed the basis of what we played," Gram said, "but we experimented with other noises, too."

No one disputes Nuese's claim that he educated Gram about country music. He liked Ernest Tubb and Webb Pierce, but when Nuese played Buck Owens for him, Gram had been immersed in folk music for three years.

"I started right away to teach him some country music stuff and turned him on to Merle Haggard and Buck Owens," Nuese says. "It became apparent to Gram that that was the music that he should be doing. The folk stuff was nice, but it didn't have any *cojones*. Gram knew nothing about what was going on with country music in the sixties and he quickly became an avid fan of the modern country sound, which was Merle Haggard and Buck Owens. He took on that music and made it his own. He used that time period [September through December of 1965] for his formation of his roots in country music. He learned lots of Haggard and Buck Owens. Those were the two biggest influences on him."

Haggard and Owens were the exemplars of the "Bakersfield sound," a term referring to a small truck-stop city north of Los Angeles on the edge of the desert that was identified with trucker music, outlaw bikers, and methamphetamine. Haggard and Owens were singer-songwriters; Haggard wrote a certain redneck poetry, and Owens constructed songs as semi–nursery rhymes. Their sound was the antithesis of commercial Nashville at the time. It was the sound of a band playing together, a sparse sound without multiple overdubs or session musicians. Most Nashville hits were performed by studio musicians, lots of them. A Nashville hit might have seven rhythm guitar players on one track. Having numerous musicians on the same part gave the songs a weightiness, a polished orchestral sound (though the syrupy strings and horns associated with, say, producer Billy Sherrill were some years off).

Similar to the Brill Building system, Nashville had—and still has—a plethora of songwriters all turning out hits for whomever. Buck Owens and Merle Haggard had a different approach. Both toured and recorded with their own bands. The personnel seldom altered and the bands were tight. Owens and Haggard were demanding bandleaders and rehearsed their bands constantly. Both wrote their own songs in collaboration with singular, original, talented lead-guitarist-arrangers. Buck Owens' partner was Don Rich and Merle Haggard's was Elvis' guitarist, the legendary James Burton. (Burton would later play with Gram.) Their songs retained a raw feel: Owens' with roots in rockabilly, and Haggard's in traditional rural music. Both reveled in a steely guitar sound.

In November Gram and Ian spent a stoned Halloween in Gram's place in Greenwich Village. Though enrolled at Harvard, Gram had not given up his apartment. The two came down to New York to solidify plans to record demos over Thanksgiving break at RCA Studios. Gram's nominal manager was Marty Erlichman, though his relationship with the band and with Gram remains mysterious. Erlichman managed, among others, Barbra Streisand. He has attempted to disassociate himself from Gram and the band, but every surviving member insists that the RCA sessions were Marty's deal. The band traveled with their gear in a rented car. Gram stayed in his Village pad while the band crashed at Brandon De Wilde's apartment.

"Marty the Manager wanted Gram to get together a backup band, and then he said he had a record deal from RCA," John Nuese says. "Marty managed a lot of other people, like John Barry, who wrote scores for the James Bond films. As soon as we had a few tunes down we were going to go to New York to record. It was the winter of '65, and we went to a couple recording sessions and we never got to hear the tapes. We recorded with Ian Dunlop, Mickey Gauvin, and Tom Snow. The recording people in the studios either wore lab coats or corduroy with patches. This was not people in their garage. It was a bunch of scientists trying to do what they could about this musical revolution. But they were so inept and lost."

The sessions were straightforward. The band set up, the lab coats miked them, and they played four songs live, no overdubs. Even the vocals were live. Included was "November Nights," a Gram original that appears on *Another Side of This Life*. The tapes have since been lost. Or not—there's dispute as to whether they rotted for years in the basement of the house owned by Brandon De Wilde's wife, Susan, or were thrown out by RCA.

After the New York sessions, Gram and the band made plans to move full-time to the city. "We got more into the New York scene and realized there was a lot more happening," John Nuese says. "We also went down to play with Brandon. He figures heavily in the history of the band. He was close to everyone—an unofficial fifth member." Brandon had chops and, like Gram, a gift for harmony. He and Gram sang high harmonies modeled on the Everly Brothers.

Though Gram's business relationship with Buddy Freeman had ended with bad feeling on both sides, Gram had kept in touch. He proved reluctant to relinquish contact with older male figures all his life. He told Buddy that he was moving to New York. "He said Harvard was boring but Boston was interesting, particularly musically," Buddy remembers. "He said he thought he'd take a sabbatical, and then he laughed because he had just gotten there. But he had enough money to do what he wanted, and that's what he did."

"Gram had two choices," Jet Thomas says. "He could stay in Harvard and do music after. Or he could leave. I'm an academician. My typical speeches were, 'Why don't you finish Harvard and then do your music? It'll be better; you'll be better educated.' I'm sure Gram got more than one of those speeches. It became clear that his real commitment was to the music. I told him, 'You can't do both at the same time because you're flunking out.' By the end of the fall semester he had decided."

The thinking that led Gram to his decision is hinted at in a letter he wrote to his sister Avis, dated November 8, 1965. He never spoke about the deaths of his mother or father with his Cambridge friends, but in this letter he addressed his pain and lost identity:

> I wish there was one thing I could tell, some clear advice or magic spell to whisk away all the things that are bothering you right now—the problem is obviously not entirely a growing pain. Besides, they're not only for your concern they're our concern, your mine and Diane's and I'm afraid they will continue for some time yet. The best thing we can do is learn from the past and live our lives the right way, so in time, when we can do something to change things, we will be real people. Not sick and haunted by what life has done to us. Above all—believe in yourself and other people—they're the one thing that is real. I'll write as often as I can. Until then—live your life as you see it—as best you can—give it a solid foundation for the future.

GRAM SPENT CHRISTMAS BREAK in Winter Haven, mostly hanging out and recording in Jim Carlton's basement. "Gram had all these work shirts; he was a folkie and he had nothing but blue shirts as a wardrobe," Carlton remembers. "He and guys from the band would hang out and smoke hash and play here and there at parties."

The songs Carlton recorded in his living room are also available on *Another Side of This Life*. The tracks, recorded the day after Christmas 1965, include a Fred Neil song, "Another Side of This Life," "Searchin'" by Leiber and Stoller, "Candy Man" by the Reverend Gary Davis, "High Flyin' Bird," which became a signature song for Richie Havens, and four Gram originals: "Wheel of Fortune," "November Nights," "Brass Buttons," and "I Just Can't Take It Anymore."

"Wheel of Fortune" is archetypal second-level folkie material and shows the influence of Peter, Paul & Mary in its earnest lyrics and Gram's rendition. He sings in an overly gentle voice until he hits the surprisingly hooky chorus, which he belts in a rockier style. The others cut on this date show a more refined and structural songwriting sensibility.

"November Nights" opens with Gram explaining to Jim Carlton that the song is "Bach-ian." It's no more Bach-ian than early Paul McCartney, with Beatlesesque changes and rueful lyrics. Despite a chorus that blatantly copies the Beatles, the words evoke Dylan. It's hard to imagine the song structured as a country piece. It's willfully adult, deliberately self-challenging.

"Brass Buttons" wouldn't be recorded properly until Gram's 1973 album, *Grievous Angel*. Though sung in the Carlton session with a constant folk strumming, it's structured as a country song and contains the adult pain and bittersweet yearning that would become Gram's trademark. It's his most mature work to that point. He avoids the clichés of structure that make his other originals seem lightweight or temporary. Initially, his folky quaver is at odds with the moving lyrics. When he sings in a more restrained tone, the song reflects a lover's haunted memory, cast in Gram's preference for archaic imagery: "Brass buttons, green silks, and silver shoes."

"I Just Can't Take It Anymore" is a throwaway, a hard-strummed cop of Dylan's many see-how-angry-I-am-with-my-former-lover songs, set to the chords of Dylan's "Chimes of Freedom."

When Gram returned to Harvard after Christmas break, he packed up and left Cambridge for New York City. The band came with him.

TEN

The International
Submarine Band

WHILE THEY LOOKED FOR A HOUSE TO SHARE, THE BAND CRASHED IN BRANDON
De Wilde's apartment on West End Avenue on the Upper West Side of
Manhattan. They found a well-kept duplex with high ceilings at 195th
Street and University Avenue in Kingsbridge Heights in the Bronx, on a
tree-lined street in a mixed Jewish, Italian, Irish, and black neighborhood.
The local main drag, Kingsbridge Road, bustled with butchers, candy stores
with soda fountains, Jewish delis, and pizza joints that charged a quarter for
a slice. Gram left his Village apartment to move in with his bandmates. He
and Mickey took the second floor, Ian and John the first. They lined the
attic with cardboard egg crates to make a soundproof rehearsal studio.

The boys decorated the house in their own sign-of-the-times way. Ian
kept a Moto Guzzi motorcycle in his room and painted a pop-art Camel
cigarette pack on his door. He built a humongous pyramid of orange-juice
cans, placed found objects everywhere, and painted multicolored stripes
radiating out from his ceiling. Mickey decorated his room in mad psychedelic swirls. "We did a bit of destructive stuff," Ian Dunlop says, "but it was
actually more creative." One night Ian, Gram, and Brandon came home to

find black smoke pouring out of the kitchen stove and a foul smell filling the house. In their absence, Mickey had fed Gram's plastic portable record player to the oven and turned it up to three hundred degrees. Ian rescued what was left: a molten slab of black plastic. "He decided to put it in the oven," Ian says. "And it came out all melted." Mickey never explained why. He was, after all, the drummer.

Marcia Katz was sixteen years old when the boys moved in down the street. "One day I'm hanging out in my room and I see these guys walking across the street," she recalls. "They all had longish hair. It was the most unusual sight—in a Jewish, Italian, Irish neighborhood, none of the boys I knew had long hair." Marcia summoned one of her friends to join her on a reconnaissance mission. "We went walking by the house and hear music blaring. I said, 'Come on, let's check it out.' She's like, 'No, no.' We marched up the stairs, rang the bell—Gram answered the door. I go, 'Hi. My name is Marcia, I live right down the street. We heard the music and thought you might be a fraternity or something.' He looks at me, not knowing what the hell to think, and goes, 'Wait a minute.' He vanishes, running up the stairs.

"Then one by one they each come down to check us out. Finally, after the last one eyes us up and down, we get invited in. We go upstairs to the top floor, bypassing everything, upstairs to this studio, and they were playing. And of course we're being grilled. I looked like a little teenage girl. My friend was voluptuous and much more bad-looking than me. We got invited to come back."

The friend had "a momentary hookup with Gram," Marcia says, and then never returned. Marcia kept coming back: "I was like their kid sister that lived up the street. I was never romantically involved with any of the guys, even though I had a little crush on Ian. The place was a magnet. The music was good and the vibration was good. I grew attached to them."

According to Marcia, the four bandmates' living situation echoed their personal and musical styles: "John was private—you never went into his room unless you were invited. You would walk by his room and sometimes hear him playing guitar. Mickey would go off and do whatever Mickey things there were to do. Ian would be in his room drawing. He was always drawing or writing letters, into creating. Gram would be playing a little music, tinkering around, or reading. Gram read. He was quiet at first, cautious, secretive. He would test you. When you got to know him he was more outgoing. As he got to know himself, and became more and got more exposed, his personality picked up and he became more at ease."

Her visits usually led to the studio: "They'd start rehearsing. The next thing you know they'd be jamming. They'd play off into the night and have a great old time."

Marcia's enthusiasm for the household reflects how the era's hippies-to-be responded to a lifestyle—a big cheap house, communal living, home-made art, music room, nothing but leisure—that they would soon be adopting themselves. Buddy Freeman, from a different generation, had a predictably different reaction.

When Buddy came to New York for an American Horse Show convention at the Waldorf, he made the trip up to Kingsbridge Heights to visit. While everyone young who visited found the house clean and welcoming, Buddy calls it "dismal." "His parents lived in good style and accommodation," Buddy says with distaste, "and this place was dreary, cold, and dank." Buddy was put off by more than the décor: "Gram came downstairs with no shirt. He looked a mess. He'd kept us waiting for thirty minutes and he had no shirt and didn't have his shoes tied. We sat on the sofa and chitchatted. By this time we had wasted a lot of time. You know, it took a long while to get way out to the Bronx in the first place. The visit left a bad taste: Gram had a better upbringing than to come downstairs to meet anybody with no shirt and no shoes."

Despite an atmosphere of what looked like sloth to a disapproving grown-up, Gram and the band were working hard. They rehearsed every day, and to do so they didn't need to leave the house. In the attic they had a Wurlitzer organ, a drum set, and Telecaster guitars with small Fender amps.

Mickey Gauvin kept the band motivated. "Mickey came out of a severe music ethic, from being in an on-the-road band with long hours and endless stints," Ian says. "He didn't like to sit around." And John Nuese's professionalism set a standard for the others. He could play, and his ability made a deep impression on Gram. John's style was country and his mode was professorial. He'd play the band a song and then teach them how it was made. "We did a lot of flattop guitar playing," John says. "And I was able to teach Gram that country rhythm. The style was similar to what he already knew. I enlarged on it by emphasizing the backbeat."

The band did a lot of listening. The four shared a record collector's curiosity. They'd sit for hours around the record player, swapping music, listening attentively, trying to play what they heard. The listening sessions led to jamming. The band would move from song to song, each figuring out where he belonged in the tune.

A primary influence remained the Ray Charles country albums. "Ray changed the feeling from being cowboy stuff into more dance," Ian says. The band also played Buck Owens' "Just as Long as You Love Me" and an Owens instrumental, "Buckaroo." They played soul music, too, like Wilson Pickett's "In the Midnight Hour" and songs by seminal rockers like Little Richard. "We didn't play that sort of stuff when we were rehearsing in a formal way—when we were in a room with instruments trying to write songs," Ian says. "We'd play casually, or it would be two of us."

In addition to working on songs they wanted to add to their repertoire, the bandmates explored the farther shores of the country-music spectrum. "We sang a lot of country ballads and songs that were so weird they were funny—ultra-obscure Americana," Ian says. "Gram had not been to the white-trash world of pure country. This strange Americana was about the heart of America, and that's where a lot of country music came from. The passion and the cheating and the drinking. We were discovering the depths of how impassioned that music is. It's magnetic and terrifically poetic. It's the human condition exposed."

The boys' fascination with country came as the commercial end of the genre was facing difficult times. "The country industry was going through this terrible softening and dumbing down of the Nashville sound," Ian says, "which was big production, orchestras, and violin sections. All that earlier 1950s honky-tonk was raw. It wasn't quite like punk, but it was hot, raw, electric, writhing, bluesy white stuff. All of the early-fifties people—Hank Williams, Lefty Frizzell, Webb Pierce, and Ray Price—they were a lot more hard-edge than people think.

"We were searching for this raw country stuff, which was all pretty vulgar, with a lot of vulgar sentiments. That vulgarity was out of fashion in Nashville. Nashville had become boring and dead."

Another influence came from Barry Tashian and Billy Briggs of the band the Remains. Tashian and Briggs started the Remains in 1964. Their sound has been described as a "fusion of the Beatles and the Zombies." The Remains opened for the Rolling Stones in 1965 and were the Beatles' opening act during their American tour that year. Has any opening band in the history of rock ever been regarded with less interest or greater impatience? The Beatles tour left the Remains broke and aimless, despite their four singles on Epic Records. Their morale was shot.

Barry had grown up with John Nuese in Westport, Connecticut. He and Billy came to the Bronx to visit John and met the band. The two ended up spending a lot of time at the house.

"I sat in at their rehearsal studio," Barry Tashian says. "They played 'Waiting in Your Welfare Line,' 'My Heart Skips a Beat,' and 'Buckaroo' by Buck Owens and 'Six Days on the Road.' It was great—it opened my ears to a new kind of music: country."

"We'd go out in the afternoon, get high [on marijuana], and play till we dropped," Billy Briggs says. "Then we'd raid the fridge and try to find something else to get high on. Then sleep. We'd go there for days at a time and play in a little room. I had a keyboard up there and we rocked. Gram showed us songs he'd written, and played the more obscure country stuff. Barry would sing harmony. I'd sit in on the keyboard or play background guitar. Gram did things that in later years I found out were classic country licks.

"I showed Gram a few things on the keyboard. He liked my Hohner Clavinet. I needed the money, so I sold it to him. After the Beatles tour we were destitute. They didn't have anything either. They never had any food in the house. The house was bare. And cooking hot dogs, there was like one hot dog between us. It was brutal. No gigs at that time—we were just jamming up in the attic."

To Billy, Gram was just another guy who wanted to make music. He was impressed by Gram's hard work more than his star quality. "I always thought he was a good player, but I didn't get the feeling he was special back then," Billy says. "He made himself special, which always intrigued me. He attacked with an artistic vengeance and he learned to play country music— that isn't easy."

Drugs were part of the scene, but not as big a part as they would later become. "We'd drive out there and smoke pot," Billy says. "Nobody had a lot. It would piss you off 'cause you wanted more, but there wasn't that much around. I remember going into the back room and mixing up some nasty drug. They made it on a cookie sheet. It was probably horse tranquilizer. It would take your frickin' head off. It had a metallic taste and would make you hallucinate like crazy. I'd have seizures and roll around the floor. It was not fun to do. But we did it anyway.

"And nobody drank."

"Mostly we used pot," Barry Tashian says. "But psychedelics were around. The weird drug was bovine tranquilizer, into which you dipped your cigarette. When you took a drag the rush supposedly approximated a two-minute acid trip. This sounds quite extreme to me today."

"Gram was not a druggie," Ian Dunlop says. "We frequently smoked grass, but I never saw hard drugs during the time I knew Gram. It was more dabbling in psychedelics and grass and maybe the odd pill."

In addition to drugs, Gram was exploring the psychic and spiritual quests that would always intrigue him. Barry Tashian remembers, "Gram had come back from a consultation with a psychic, Jacques Honduras. Gram tape-recorded the session and played it for the band. Gram was talking about energy, how if you put your fingertips together you'd complete the electrical circuit in your body."

Gram was deeply into unidentified flying objects and what they might mean for his spiritual pursuits. Gram's lyrics reflect so much intelligence that his interest in UFOs and psychics seems incongruous, but it was a legitimate passion and never flagged. Aliens and the paranormal seem too adolescent, too brainless for someone of his apparent sophistication. Gram's fascination seems an offshoot of his interest in various spiritual quests, and tied to his theological bent.

Plus, marijuana was an undeniable factor.

GRAM'S PRIMARY FOCUS remained music. Previously he had followed what he liked: Elvis at nine, the Journeymen at sixteen. His musical life had been about meeting other musicians with similar tastes and pursuing those tastes for a while. But the Shilos, among others, had found how short Gram's attention span could be. Before Gram moved to New York, his passion had been more for performing than for the material he performed. That changed in the Bronx. There Gram developed a life not unlike that of the students at Harvard he had never once hung out with: He found what he loved and studied it diligently. Gram had never before shown such determination, had never manifested such a work ethic. His curiosity for listening matched his enthusiasm for playing. His diligence was apparent in his devotion to writing as well. He carried a notebook everywhere. He jotted down idea fragments, conversational snippets, phrases, and couplets.

Gram was finding his voice. Poised between esoteric Americana and raw country, Gram and his bandmates found a path to an original sound, a sound no one else was playing.

Barry remembers the day Gram came in and said, "I wrote this last night," and began to play his song "Luxury Liner." "There was something compelling about the stroke of those strings, the way he played them," Barry says.

"Luxury Liner" is Gram's first fully mature song created in what would become his signature style. The lyrics are catchy and surprisingly witty. The structure is classically country. The subject is loss and solitude. The upbeat presentation contrasts with the lyrics. As with Gram's most moving songs, the lyrics can be taken lightly and the wordplay viewed as only that. Or when listened to with greater care, his lyrics become heartbreaking. The fundamental contradiction in Gram's songwriting—first seen so clearly in "Luxury Liner" and repeated in his best work—is the ease with which his language flows around a profound and unbearable sadness.

Here Gram—free of all responsibilities, living in a house full of friends, playing all night, with neighborhood girls knocking on his door, finding his niche and purpose—describes himself as a lost soul. He demands not to understand others but that everyone understand him ("Everybody ought to know what's on my mind"). His travels in the world ("I've been around") have not granted him connection. He looks at himself from the outside in, asks if the world sees him clearly ("You think I'm lonesome?"), and owns the truth of his situation.

The luxury liner of the title is that staple of country songs, the locomotive. The song's chugging beat and shuffling drums suggest the railroad sound that comes not from trains but from country and bluegrass music evoking a train. The train is a recurring, deeply American image in folk, bluegrass, country, and blues. It's a symbol of fleeing from trouble, moving on to better things, or the inability to do so. In Johnny Cash's "Folsom Prison Blues," the narrator hears the train "rollin' 'round the bend" and sings that he hasn't seen the sun "since I don't know when." Cash uses the train to emphasize his immobility and as a metaphor for the time that ticks by as the trains roll on. Gram, by contrast, doesn't address the train directly at all—he cites it as a symbol, evokes the wealth of railroad mythology, and then drops it. But with all its loneliness and chugging beat and the image of a locomotive as big and sleek as a steamship, "Luxury Liner" is a train song sure enough.

It is a bleak and cunning document for a nineteen-year-old, surprising for its structural sophistication. It has a great, memorable hook. It's no folk song, with narrative verses separated by a repeated chorus (like Dylan's work of that time). It's made to be a hit country single, with a building intro, a fast leap into the lyrical message, a brief solo, one choral repetition, and out, with a lingering harmonizing honky-tonk flourish at the close.

"Luxury Liner" may not be purely autobiographical, but it hits like self-portraiture. Gram's not singing about all tomorrow's parties or a leopard-skin pill-box hat or being a nowhere man or having a nineteenth nervous breakdown or whether all the leaves were brown and the sky gray. Folk rock had a strong presence on the charts in the spring of 1966, with "Homeward Bound" by Simon and Garfunkel, "California Dreamin'" by the Mamas & the Papas, and "Daydream" by the Lovin' Spoonful in the top ten. Gram ignored all that. With the fervor of a new convert, Gram absorbed what his scholarship had shown him and arose, newly born, in the country tradition. Lyrically he hews to the country master of unbearable self-inflicted suffering, George Jones. Musically, "Luxury Liner" is a Bakersfield ditty after Buck Owens.

"I'm so lonesome I could cry," Hank Williams sings, right after citing "the lonesome whistle" of a train. Gram's narrator never straightforwardly identifies his pain as does Hank's. Partially concealed by the jaunty shuffle beat, the narrator's awful mental state hits as a punch line. Hank Williams describes his current position; he sings in present tense and thus suggests that maybe one day he might not be so lonesome. Gram offers no such hope. Like Hank singing his lonesomeness or Cash his imprisonment or Jones his drunkenness, Gram's first-person presentation soars beyond the pain of the singer and into the heart of whomever might be looking into the mirror as the song plays. The authorial "I" becomes "me" for its community of listeners.

The song was not recorded until a year and a half after Gram first played it. It remains a startling suggestion of his capabilities. When contrasted with the work of the Beatles, Stones, Byrds, and Velvet Underground, it's shocking for its incongruity. Nobody but nobody from a noncountry background was writing such willfully country material. Nobody so embraced the core of pure country: a straightforward presentation of the singer's emotional pain.

WITH THEIR CHOPS COMING together and a solid repertoire of original material and covers, it was time to gig. To gig, the band needed a name. In keeping with the time and mood, Ian Dunlop came up with a pseudo-psychedelic, unbearably twee handle for the band—a twee name with a worthy pedigree. It was the International Submarine Band, after the International Silver String Submarine Band formed by the kids in the *Little Rascals*. The *Rascals*, a Saturday matinee staple from the 1920s through the early '40s, had become a fixture on Saturday-morning television. Ian found the symbolism of the submarine evocative. "It means *beneath*, it means under the mainstream or subversive," he says. "I did a painting on the bass drum with the band name on it. I was Jasper Johns–influenced at the time in art school, and so I painted stars and stripes in a submarine type of thing on the drum skin." The Beatles' "Yellow Submarine" had no bearing on Ian's inspiration; the song was not released until later, in 1966, the film in 1968.

The International Submarine Band found regular gigs at the Village clubs the Night Owl and Café Wha? and the uptown jet-set hang Ondine's. The Night Owl kept its doors open to the streets, and the squares wandered in along with the regulars. The crowd might have been Gram's Village clique or out-of-towners who had no idea what they were hearing. The International Submarine Band often shared a bill with the Blues Magoos, a proto-garage-psychedelic band who'd had a hit with "(We Ain't Got) Nothin' Yet." Two bands were usually booked for a night and switched off, set to set.

Peppy Castro, the Magoos' madman lead singer, met Gram during their shared Night Owl gigs. "The ISB were one of the many bands that were in the Night Owl," he says. "This rich kid from Palm Beach [sic], running around the Village, he's got bucks and he's a good-looking guy and he's got this twangy band and everybody in the band is as nutty as a hatter. That crazy house in the Bronx—when we used to visit them, those guys would be wrecked out of their minds." Peppy was something of a drug neophyte. He adds, "Gram was the first person to ever turn me on to pot."

Drugs figured largely in the networking among musicians. Peppy remembers the Bronx household's drug connection. "The guy had a loft with a huge brick wall opposite which was a huge fireplace," Peppy says. "You could only get up there by an elevator, which he controlled. It was an old loft building, before any of the downtown area had been gentrified. He had tons of drugs stored in a library case on wheels, so if anybody tried to pop him he'd push the whole thing into the fireplace. I was the baby of the scene—the other guys were a little older and were carrying on a lot more than I was." Billy Briggs remembers Muddy Waters and blues virtuoso Michael Bloomfield hanging in the same dealer's loft.

Ian Dunlop maintains that the ISB's drug use was sporadic. "We didn't take that much [acid]. You hear about some people taking it constantly. We did it a few times, and I remember Gram and I taking mushrooms.

"We couldn't have done all those drugs in New York. We worked a hell of a lot. We were dedicated. I remember reading some article on the twenty-fifth anniversary of Gram's death. It made me so angry because it said the ISB lived in a drug stupor and a haze of LSD. That we were wallowing around New York in this lost period. I thought, Christ, it wasn't like that. We were rehearsing hard, we were gigging a lot, we were traveling, getting up early in the morning. Well, early in the morning New York time. You know: noon.

"So maybe we were walking around in a bit of a stupor in the morning, but we weren't in a complete haze. We were busy. We did residencies on a rotation. We'd do a week at a club and then we'd do another place, and that's like six nights for that week. It wasn't conducive to hanging out and having a social life. None of us had girlfriends or anything in New York. We were single-minded. More single-minded than you'd think."

Onstage the band was high-functioning, and the Night Owl audience came to understand what they were after. Comfortable there, the ISB developed a bit of an act. Ian was the onstage card. He liked to banter. Mickey might join in, but never John Nuese. He always treated being onstage as serious business.

"They did cover versions that never sounded like the originals," Peppy Castro says, "and obscure covers. To a normal kid coming up on rock and roll, it sounded like a new slant on things. It grabbed me because it was electric and not so predictable." Part of the ISB magic was John Nuese's upside-down guitar playing. Peppy recalls, "I would play with John and go, 'John . . . how do you fucking do that?' Seeing him play gave me a weird vibe, because everything he played was like coming in through the back door. It wasn't recognizable, so that got into my head when I listened to them."

The band covered Otis Redding as well as the Buck Owens and Merle Haggard material that few in their audience had heard. "We played the music we wanted to play," John Nuese says. "We were connected to the sound we felt was happening in country music, this strong, powerful sound. The set we played mixed R&B and country tunes. The R&B the audience knew and the country stuff they had never heard before. Ever."

Dance music, as it was then understood, was not in their repertoire. The band auditioned for a booking at Trude Heller's, a club in the Village. "Tourists went there who were seeing New York, people from Ohio and Kansas," Ian says. "It was not a hip place." Pianist David Barry says, "It wasn't a hip place, but it was a happening place. If you played there you had to play dance music. And the currency, at least in 1966, for dancing in a New York club was James Brown. James Brown was a bitch to play if you hadn't grown up with that stuff. It's hard. The band had gotten an audition at Trude Heller's and they didn't dress right. The bands that played soul stuff were white bands that imitated black bands. They wore narrow-legged suits and ruffled shirts. You can imagine how much Gram didn't do that.

"The ISB showed up wearing what they wore. And I don't know what they were wearing, but the punch line was when Trude Heller said, 'Okay, do your James Brown.' And Gram said, 'We don't know any James Brown.' And Trude said, 'What?' and they did a Buck Owens tune. And it was instantly: 'Take a hike.' I remember looking back on that, not too long after, like, wow, that's a damn interesting thing to do: going into Trude Heller's and not having a single thing to play that she wants. And that was Gram, I guess."

One imperative even Gram couldn't ignore was the military draft. Dropping out of Harvard meant the end of his student deferment. In that era, avoiding the mandatory two years of military service—and the overwhelming likelihood of being sent to Vietnam—was the major life drama of any young man not intending to enlist.

It was a binary situation: Fail the physical and live as you please. Pass the physical and go to Vietnam, to jail, or flee the country. Lives changed direction and careers were thwarted in the interest of avoiding the draft. One option was to join the National Guard, as did Gram's Winter Haven bandmates Jim Stafford, Kent LaVoie, and Jim Carlton. Joining the Guard meant six months of basic training and serving one weekend a year for six years. The upside was a guarantee of never being sent to Vietnam—at the time, Guardsmen pulled duty near their homes.

Jim Carlton served in Charlie Battery, the artillery unit in Winter Haven. (Tony Pervis, Roy Orbison's bass player, ended up in Charlie Battery as well.) Jim regarded the Guard as "summer camp." "We had a unit full of musicians who didn't want to fight," he says. "We'd entertain the troops almost every evening. Jim Stafford took control. He blossomed with his guitar in hand and became a celebrity among the National Guard. All these other battalions wanted to hear us play. It was Tony Pervis, Buddy Canova—a Winter Haven saxophone player—Stafford, me, and whoever else could play. It still didn't excuse us duty. We still had to pull KP and all that business, and that was a drag."

Gram had no intention of being tied anywhere one weekend a month for the rest of his youth. He was determined to beat the physical. When he received the dreaded induction notice, with its order to appear for a physical exam, he stayed up for three days and nights before the appointed date. The morning of the physical he took LSD. "Gram dropped a little bit, not a big whackered dose—enough so he was completely spaced out and dozy and looked bad," Ian Dunlop says. "His skin was glaring and his eyes were scarlet and he couldn't answer a question." Following the usual procedure, Gram was ordered to take a clipboard with his personal data through one room and into another. Gram wandered off in his underwear and waited out most of the day crouching in a trash cellar. When he was finally discovered he was belatedly taken through his interview and physical. "They thought he was some sort of street person, really out there," Ian says. "They concluded he was disturbed."

A designation of 1A, fit for immediate duty, meant a quick trip to Vietnam. Gram received the draft dodger's cherished 4F, which meant unfit for service under any circumstances. The acid ploy worked for Gram in 1966, and for several musicians he would meet on the West Coast. At that time the Army did not seem to realize that certain young Americans would do anything to avoid Vietnam. Nor did it understand the pervasiveness of the drug culture or the pharmacological expertise of its adherents. The Army learned slowly, but it learned. By 1968, the LSD gambit wasn't so effective. If Gram had tried the same strategy two years later, he would almost certainly have been sent home so his dose could wear off, and then run through the process again.

But it was 1966, and the nerve-racking trial was over. Gram could never be called up again, never reexamined. He was free.

In March 1966 the ISB booked a one-week tour of Florida. Ian, Diana Dew, and Gram crammed into Gram's Austin-Healey and drove from New York straight to Daytona Beach. The tour was typical of the time. A short-lived pop sensation, Freddy Cannon, needed other bands to entertain the teenyboppers before he appeared. (Coincidentally, one of Freddy Cannon's hits had been "Palisades Park"—the organ-driven song Gram played with Kent LaVoie the night Gram's van hit the fucking cow.) Thrown to an indifferent audience, much as the Remains were presented to Beatles fans, the ISB was in a unique position. They didn't have to worry about pleasing anyone. They could develop their stage chops in big arenas before large crowds with no fear of failure.

"We went down well," Ian Dunlop says. "We were out of New York! We had New York clothes. We were sharp. Mickey had a bright-red velvet jacket. I had this unusual thing I found difficult to wear because Florida was so hot. It was a ridiculous designer custom outfit with a cape and a big fur collar and boots that came up to here. Almost Russian empire, like an early prerevolutionary Russian military guard, and I mean we looked good. We looked different. The boys in Florida hadn't seen anything like it."

A new manager surfaced. The boys' earlier arrangement with Marty the Manager had come to nothing. After the recording session, RCA had never been heard from. "Suddenly there was this funny guy called Chester Fox, and Chester thought we were great," Ian says. "He said, 'I want to be your manager. I'm gonna get you guys a deal.'"

The Freddy Cannon tour ended badly. On the last night, the opening act got booed off the stage. The ISB hurried on to perform to mostly empty seats. Freddy Cannon did one song and sulked off. Back at the hotel, the band found their new manager huddling furtively with the tour's promoter, who was responsible for the band's hotel rooms. Someone told them to pack up their gear and sneak out. "And we did," Ian says. "We did a flit, a bunk, a scarper, like running out on your rent. We loaded up and drove across Florida in the middle of the night."

The band headed to Gram's home in Winter Haven. But Gram's immediate family no longer lived there.

After Avis' funeral, Bonnie Muma returned briefly to her parents' house in Winter Haven, and then went back to college in Palm Beach. She and Bob Parsons kept their distance for a couple of months. Bob, cut out of Avis' will, moved Little Avis and Diane from the Winter Haven house to a new home in Winter Park, Florida, about an hour away. The new house, a sprawling suburban with a huge expanse of ugly concrete driveway, represented a serious comedown from Snively life. Five months after Bob and the kids moved into the house, Bonnie got her own apartment in Winter Park and found a job as a dental assistant. Their relationship began again. "He wanted me to move in, but I wouldn't," Bonnie says.

Little Avis had never liked or accepted Bonnie Muma. The fifteen-year-old girl was not ready to see her mother replaced. "She had gotten mad at me because she thought I was going to take her daddy," Bonnie says. "And I said, 'I won't if you don't want me to. You're the important part. I love your father but I will walk away if you feel that strongly about it.' She said, 'You saw my daddy before my mommy died.' And I said, 'Yes, I did.' And then I told her that I had stopped. And she said, 'Yep.'"

Bonnie and Bob lived separately for a decent interval—a year. During that time, Bob left Florida and Bonnie behind. He moved the children to New Orleans. And he kept asking Bonnie to come to see him. In response, she gave him an ultimatum: Propose or forget about her. Bob flew back to Winter Park and asked Bonnie to marry him.

"I'm probably not what Bob would have married, because I didn't have any money," Bonnie says. "Bob liked to live high on the hog. But with Bob we always laughed a lot. He said, 'I'm not sure I'm good marriageable material, and there's the age difference.' I told him it didn't matter."

The night Bonnie arrived in New Orleans, Diane told her that "Daddy had gone out with a lady." Looking around, Bonnie discovered a desk full of unpaid bills. When Bob got home, late as usual, Bonnie was ready to fly right back to Winter Haven. He convinced her that "the lady" was only a friend. Bonnie decided to stay and take over the family's finances. Bob set Bonnie up in an apartment on St. Charles Avenue. They spent five months planning their wedding.

"Bob said he had married money and married for something other than money, and I was his Mia Farrow marriage," Bonnie says. "A lot of people thought I was too young for him and he was too old for me."

"Honestly, it's funny that no one knew much about her," Gram's former schoolmate Dubie Baxter says. "Only that she was reserved. That's why it surprised us so much when all of a sudden she marries Bob Parsons, this asshole, this playboy . . . along comes beautiful, quiet, austere, intelligent Bonnie Muma and she runs off with this forty-one-year-old guy, and he might as well have been King Farouk at eighty-five! Forty-one was too much to comprehend."

Bonnie and Bob staged a huge affair atop the Trademart Building overlooking the Mississippi River. The centerpiece of the catering was a Douglas fir, a living tree, every branch hung with gigantic boiled shrimp. A judge was on hand to conduct the ceremony, Walter Lanaux was standing by to be best man, and three or four hundred other guests were all assembled. When the time came for the ceremony to start, the groom was missing. Finally Bob strolled in, wearing a white linen suit, forty-five minutes late. The guests had attacked the champagne as they waited, and by the time Bob arrived the atmosphere was as he liked it: relaxed. He walked through the crowd like a superstar, went right up to the judge, and said, "Let's do it." "Without one word of apology to anyone," Walter Lanaux says. "When I asked him later where he'd been, he said, 'I got here as soon as I could.'"

Bonnie Muma wore "a white dress with little blue flowers on it. Bob loved low-cut dresses, and this dress was low-cut. I put something over the top to cover me up, but when he got near me he began poking it down."

Little Avis and Diane attended the wedding, but Becky and Jan, Bob's children from his first marriage, did not. Their mother refused to permit it.

Bob so enjoyed the wedding party that he and Bonnie missed five consecutive flights to New York. "I cried all the way on the plane because I was so tired," Bonnie says. "I was ready for a good bed, and Bob was ready to hit the town." A friend had arranged for a limousine to meet the couple at the airport, and they were whisked straight to the restaurant 21.

Bob and Bonnie stayed at the Pierre Hotel, Bob's New York home away from home. Gram did not come to the wedding, but he visited Bob and Bonnie during their honeymoon in New York. They went to hear him play at a Village club and Bob tried to convince Gram to consider returning to Harvard, without success.

"I think he wanted the best for Gram, I really do," Bonnie says. He appreciated his music, but Bob was not an aficionado. He was more into classical and waltz music, although he could also do a mean rumba. He believed in [Gram's music] in theory; he just wanted an education behind it."

WHEN HE AND THE BAND arrived in Winter Haven, Gram called on the hospitality of the Snively side of the family. Ian Dunlop describes Haney's mansion as "like a big movie set, overlooking a lake. But that was Crackerville. That was the Old South. It's got a bunch of character, but it's a hillbillyville."

Gram's arrival was celebrated with that Snively family ritual, a cocktail party, thrown by his uncle, John Snively Junior. "The host was this cracker, overweight, and an archetypal Southerner," Ian says. "He had an investment that went wrong. He planted a whole lot of watermelon and a big wind blew them off. He said that a lot of the people in the family were bad at investments and that they usually fucked up."

Gram enthusiastically brought Jim Carlton up to date on his new musical tastes. "When Gram was into someone he was into them," Jim says. "He threw himself into Merle Haggard, Tammy Wynette, Buck Owens. There was a little diner in Winter Haven; we went there because they had Owens' 'Heart of Glass' on the jukebox with a lot of other great country. Gram loved Don Rich." Don Rich was Buck Owens' guitar player and arranger, a key figure in the Bakersfield country sound.

Gram arrived in Winter Haven with a supply of drugs. This was either brave or foolhardy, since a matchbox of hashish would have gotten him twenty years (or not, depending on how vigorously Bob Parsons went to bat for him). But here as throughout his life, Gram was lucky where drugs and the law were concerned. He suffered few close calls. "Gram always had the best hash," Carlton says. "He got it in the Village. His acid came on sugar cubes. He'd made a little pancake batter with the Sub band [to put the sugar on]. We used to go to the Snively mansion and do that."

Carlton could see the effect of acid on Gram's conversation: "He got metaphysical. He'd sit on the edge of his bed and outstretch his fingers back and forth and say you can pick up energy. He talked about astral projection quite a bit and experiences like that. No matter how much he tripped, he always had his faculties. He was always in control. I never saw him wasted."

Chester Fox, the enthusiastic manager guy in Florida, proved to be an assistant to Monte Kay, who represented a powerful roster of black entertainment including comedian Flip Wilson and actress and singer Diahann Carroll. Kay became the ISB's manager and snagged the band a contract for one record. In April 1966 the ISB signed to cut a promotional single for the Norman Jewison film comedy *The Russians Are Coming, the Russians Are Coming*. The band had only one afternoon in the studio to record the instrumental, which was written by Johnny Mercer. "We simply did an instrumental rendition of the melody of the theme," John Nuese says. The flip side was the roadhouse staple "Truck Drivin' Man" by Terry Fell. The latter was later released on the remastered and expanded double-CD set of the Byrds' *Sweetheart of the Rodeo*. Mickey Gauvin does nicely with the shuffle beat that was to become a default songwriting rhythm for Gram. John Nuese credibly plays country chicken-scratching rhythm guitar and takes two Byrdsian leads that foreshadow his later work with Gram.

The single, released on the Ascot label, did nothing. As was expected; it was a throwaway. Monte Kay arranged to have the band sign with Columbia. The Columbia recording session left the band less than satisfied.

"The Columbia session was rushed, underproduced, skeletal," Ian says. "We thought, Wow! Columbia, that's a real record label! We went into Studio B in New York. The engineer, wearing a corduroy jacket with leather patches, puffing on a pipe, said, 'This is Columbia, guys, don't waste our time tuning up,' and, 'Oh, my God, look at those needles! Get the drummer to turn down!' I have no idea what they usually recorded.

"We cut an original credited to John and Gram, 'Sum Up Broke,' and a pumpy fast country blues, 'One Day Week.' Some DJ in Boston played it and that was it." Originally released as a Columbia single and now available on the remastered *Sweetheart of the Rodeo*, neither song reflects anything Gram would do later.

"Week" evokes young, musically ambitious Americans imitating the Beatles and the Dave Clark Five in precisely the style of that moment. The compressed and slightly distorted vocals especially evoke the Dave Clark Five, as does Mickey Gauvin's driving energy. The song is catchy, well played, anonymous, and forgettable. "Sum Up Broke" is a bit more ambitious. It sounds like a cross between the early Who, the Blues Magoos, and Paul Revere and the Raiders. The clean production and earnest vocals keep it out of the realm of the garage rock of the time. "Broke" sounds too sincere to be from the Standells/Shondells/Music Machine end of the post-Invasion continuum. The song opens and closes with nice ornate guitar work from John Nuese and ends with a recognizably Gram sentiment. Throughout the song he complains to a lover who's rejected him. The song ends:

> *You should have done better*
> *Like I care*

(Words and music by Gram Parsons and John Nuese)

The single was released and nothing happened, but not for lack of trying on the band's part. Monte Kay found them numerous promotional opportunities. Cousin Brucie Morrow, a well-known DJ on powerhouse New York WABC-AM, brought the ISB into a showcase in Palisades Park. The band appeared on *The Zacherley Show* on a local New York City station. Zacherley—who billed himself as "the Cool Ghoul"—dressed like Dracula, showed old horror movies, and did comedy bits between commercials. The ISB played during one of the movie breaks. Ian describes the show as "the *American Bandstand* of Newark, New Jersey." It speaks to the band's ambition, or desperation, that they took any opportunity to find an audience, no matter how ridiculous.

A club date in Kenmore Square in Boston with folkie Phil Ochs showed the band what their decision to pursue country music might cost them. Ochs was a Village contemporary of Dylan's, a subtle singer-songwriter best known for his intelligent lyrics and the protest anthem "I Ain't Marchin' Anymore." The audience that came to see Ochs hated the Sub Band, with its country sound and electric guitars. "By the second night we got the flavor of what was happening," Ian Dunlop says, "and this perverse devilment came out of us. We dropped the easygoing, recognizable music and started playing obscure and bizarre country music we would [usually] only play at home or for a laugh. Most featured heavy Christian lyrics like 'Satan's gonna get you if you don't watch out / You better praise the Lord and give his name

a shout.' They hated it, and we loved that. They couldn't believe that someone would get up in the cosmopolitan North and come out with this wacky
Christian shit."

Monte Kay did find the band some worthy gigs. In the summer of 1966
the ISB opened for white soulsters the Young Rascals in Central Park. Fifteen thousand fans turned out for the Rascals, who had hit number one with
"Good Lovin'." The Central Park crowd was the biggest audience the ISB
ever saw.

NEW YORK'S SWELTERING SUMMER made rehearsing in the attic uncomfortable. Brandon De Wilde had a remote little farm with a cottage and a barn
near White River Junction, a village in the hills of Vermont. With Brandon
and his wife, Susan, the band fled to the mountains. The Beatles' *Revolver*
had been released and was always on the cottage turntable. Everyone did
acid together and lay around looking at the sky. "The ISB would go up to
Brandon's house, drop acid, and make home movies," Barry Tashian says.
"Long shots of blades of grass and weird zooms into their instruments set
up in the living room."

"Brandon loved the ground Gram walked on," Marcia Katz says. "They
had a million stories to tell each other—they were best friends hanging out.
Brandon was conservative-looking, but he wasn't conservative at all. He was
married to Susan, a beautiful blonde. Brandon was outgoing and quite the
charmer. He'd come over and Gram and Brandon would snort coke. It
wasn't a serious thing, but it was an introduction. I could hear the chop-
chop-chopping."

Shortly after the summer Vermont trip, Brandon visited Los Angeles.
"We were restless and ambitious," Ian Dunlop says. "It was clear the entertainment industry was shifting to the West Coast. Brandon's career had
ground to a halt. He went out to visit and made a snap decision. He sold his
New York place and moved to Los Angeles, just like that. Once he got there,
Brandon was on the phone to Gram all the time, saying, 'Hey man, you gotta
come out here, you gotta come out.' Gram was interested, so he went."

Gram stayed with Brandon in Los Angeles for three weeks in November
1966. Brandon introduced Gram to Dennis Hopper and Peter Fonda and to
the younger, long-haired LSD crowd that had taken over the Hollywood
hangout Ciro's. The restaurant had been haute Hollywood's prime gathering
place in the forties and early fifties. Following Ciro's renovation in 1964, the
Byrds established a gigging residence. They played their first Ciro's show

before the April 1965 release of the "Mr. Tambourine Man" single, which reached number one in America and the United Kingdom.

After that first single the Byrds enjoyed such consistent, stunning success that many regarded them as the American Beatles. June 1965's "All I Really Want to Do" (another Dylan cover) went to number forty in the U.S. and number four in the U.K. The B-side, "Feel a Whole Lot Better," hit number 103. October's "Turn! Turn! Turn!" provided their second number one. Dylan joined the Byrds onstage in late '65 to crown the early phase of their residency.

January 1966's "Set You Free This Time" reached number sixty-three and March's "Eight Miles High" hit number fourteen. June's "5D" got to number forty-four; September's "Mr. Spaceman" hit number thirty-six. Their albums also did spectacularly well: *Mr. Tambourine Man* made number six, *Turn! Turn! Turn!* number seventeen, and *5D* number twenty-four.

The Byrds attained a rare combination of popular and critical acclaim. They had a purely American, wholly original, guitar-driven rock sound that owed little to the British Invasion, the Brill Building, or soul music. They were prime movers in the shift of folk music to electrified rock and the shift of folk rock to psychedelia. They were young, good-looking, and stylish. They ran with, and drew to Ciro's, a glamorous new Hollywood crowd whose regulars included Peter Fonda, actor Sal Mineo, and comedian-philosopher Lenny Bruce.

Jim Dickson, who produced "Mr. Tambourine Man," describes part of the madness of the Ciro's scene. "Vito the Magnificent, a.k.a. King of the Hippies, and Karl Franzoni, a.k.a. Captain Fuck, would bring their crowd to Ciro's to dance to the Byrds. They established a kind of hippie dress that blossomed on the Strip. The dancers attracted as much audience as the band. They dressed like freaks and were very colorful. It was like a big party every night. There were lines of three hundred people waiting to get in."

Brandon brought Gram to Byrds singer-songwriter-guitarist David Crosby's house on Beverly Glen Drive. Crosby, the son of a Hollywood cinematographer, had been a Village folkie and a drug and songwriting partner of Fred Neil's in Coconut Grove, Florida. When Brandon and Gram came to call, Crosby was gone on a road trip with Peter Fonda. Brandon introduced Gram to Crosby's live-in girlfriend, Nancy Ross.

"Their eyes met," John Nuese says, "and that was it."

Nancy was an exquisitely beautiful Santa Barbara society girl out on the Sunset Strip scene. She had married Franklin and Eleanor Roosevelt's grandson Rex at sixteen. The marriage lasted two years. Nancy had a torrid affair with Steve McQueen. She left McQueen for Crosby, whom she had known from their similarly comfortable upbringings in Santa Barbara.

Nancy's leaving McQueen for Crosby highlights the paradigm shift in coolness and credibility sweeping Hollywood in the mid-sixties. McQueen was a fifties version of the World's Coolest White Man: tough, crew-cut, monosyllabic, a drinker, a race-car driver, macho, a movie star. David Crosby was a longhair, a drug fiend, captained a sailboat, made a living off his sensitivity, dressed as an icon of the new hippie style, and performed live. He was a rock star. He was also a famously prodigious seducer; his nickname among his fellow Byrds was Tripod.

Gram and Nancy were instantly smitten. The day after they met, Nancy moved out of Crosby's house (which he had bought at her demand) to be with Gram. She was nineteen.

When Gram returned to New York, Nancy followed close behind. "He came back a different guy," Marcia Katz says. "He said, 'I met this girl and she's fantastic. Her name is Nancy and she'll be here soon.' I was walking down Kingsbridge Road shortly after, and coming around the corner wearing this white fur coat, with long black hair, was this absolutely beautiful girl. I knew right away it was Nancy. Her face looked like Natalie Wood. She was so striking, with fantastic eyes. . . . You didn't see women like that in the neighborhood."

Gram was eager to move to Los Angeles. Nancy was only one reason. Another was that the band's hard work did not seem to be paying off in New York. "We ran into some blind alleys," Ian Dunlop says. "There were a few places in Manhattan we could play and they liked us, but after a while it was a merry-go-round. We were running out of options. . . . It was getting claustrophobic, and California became interesting because it was new."

Brandon De Wilde felt the same way. According to Ian, he thought his New York management "had him pigeonholed." California offered new opportunities. "He came back excited," Ian says. "Gram was already thinking we were in a rut. We had had two record deals and nothing had happened. Even though the Columbia single got airplay, there was no follow-up or promotion. We played the clubs we could play, we made the records, and our management was out of ideas."

Gram convinced the band to come to the West Coast. The others felt some misgivings. "Gram was always seeing something else that distracted him," Ian Dunlop says. "I knew that there was a certain amount of disagreement about going to L.A. I don't know about the other guys, if they felt like, 'Look, we got a management deal in New York and a record deal.' Gram was young. He wanted instant gratification. That's the thing that plagued his whole career."

Nancy's role in Gram's decision-making didn't sit well. "A lot of people at the time thought Nancy was nuts," Marcia Katz says. "They thought she was weird and a little wigged-out." Marcia and Nancy became friends. "I thought she was an incredible woman who had evolved spiritual thinking," Marcia says. "She and Gram together—their chemistry was indescribable. Women were jealous of her, and men didn't know what to think."

Gram and Nancy flew to Los Angeles in March 1967. The other band members decided to drive so they could go via Nashville and search for obscure country records. Gram and Nancy rented a Tudor-style apartment at 821¼ Sweetzer Avenue in Hollywood. It was part of a bungalow complex that had been built as an investment by Charlie Chaplin. Ian, Mickey, and John rented a house on Willow Glen Road in Laurel Canyon, which John describes as "this huge, fancy Hollywood house in this little private canyon." Gram subsidized the move and the rent on the Willow Glen house. At Nancy's urging, Marcia Katz followed six months later, staying with Gram and Nancy until she found her own place.

"Some of the guys weren't that open to Nancy," Marcia says, "because it took Gram's attention away from them. Things change when you fall in love. Not that you're taken away from your friends, but you don't have time for them. They all liked Nancy. But she had her female influence on Gram, and they were jealous. Gram was living with Nancy and the guys were living in their own house up in the Canyon. They wanted Gram for themselves. Everyone wanted Gram for themselves."

The rest of the band thought of their California sojourn more as a vacation than a relocation. They held on to the house on 195th Street. "We kept the Bronx house thinking it was going to be a quick trip," Ian says. "That it might not work out. We had a management deal in New York and a record deal, and maybe they'd want us to do more recording one day. . . . But we got to Los Angeles and, being new and enthusiastic, we got picked up. We had a lot of interest immediately with a booking agent who put us on constant local Southern California tours."

"The Sub Band called us up one day, said they were going on tour and giving up the house," Peppy Castro says. "Did we know anybody who wanted it? We already had a hit record ["(We Ain't Got) Nothin' Yet"]—we were the Magoos, up and running! We said, 'Oh, we know that house! That house is nutty!' We thought the house was haunted. We would get whacked and strange things would happen in that house. I don't know if those strange things seemed to happen because we were all so wrecked or if they really happened. We'd open up the door and a black crow would fly out at us. And I actually saw the aura of a ghost in the house. I know I was smoking a shit-load of weed, but I know I saw an aura."

ELEVEN
Los Angeles

During their time in the Bronx, the International Submarine Band never complained about Gram's willingness to work or his commitment to the band. He wrote constantly, rehearsed hard, and played their many sets with dedication. Gram's time in Los Angeles would be marked by periods of passivity, a disinclination to rehearse, pissed-off band members who regarded Gram as a lazy prima donna, and canceled gigs. Gram would have periods of intense commitment in L.A., but they were not the norm.

Gram's hard work in New York might have sprung from the excitement he felt being in a community of great players, living and working full-time with a real band. Youthful enthusiasm doesn't provide a sufficient explanation, because Gram didn't outlive his youth by much. The obvious culprit in Gram's eroding work ethic would seem to be drugs. In New York, Gram had smoked a lot of pot, dropped a disputed amount of acid, and spent the odd afternoon puffing cow tranks and rolling on the floor. In L.A. he would discover barbiturates and heroin. While on those, he never worked with the drive he showed in New York.

The band's fast start in California seemed to augur well. Their new

The International Submarine Band, newly arrived in L.A.: Ian Dunlop, John Nuese, Gram Parsons, Mickey Gauvin. (Courtesy Marcia Katz)

booking agent, Ronnie Herrin, placed them in prestigious opening slots in Long Beach, the L.A. Palladium, and clubs in Southern California. The ISB packed their gear in a van and drove from gig to gig. They opened for the Doors, those darlings of the Sunset Strip, whose first album had just been released in January 1967. They opened for Iron Butterfly, whose "In-A-Gadda-Da-Vida" wouldn't be released until 1968, when it would spend eighty-one weeks in the top ten. The Butterfly were the quintessence of a jamming band; "In-A-Gadda" et cetera, all seventeen minutes of it, took up the whole first side of their second LP. Together with the amped-up English blues band Cream, the Butterfly could be held responsible for the plague of drum solos inflicted on concert crowds for the next seven years. Their onstage ramblings provided an extreme contrast to the ISB's three-minute version of "Buckaroo."

As the ISB opened for successful bands with clear-cut identities and crafted stage shows, they were coming undone. In New York the band worked well together. Their separate Los Angeles lives ate into rehearsal time and gave rise to an indulgence that did them no good.

One night they opened for Love at a two-thousand-seat arena in the San Fernando Valley. Love's single "Seven & Seven Is," had reached number thirty-three but the band had a far-reaching influence not represented by its chart position and performed tight, well-written songs. For their part, the ISB gave a hysterically disjointed performance that demonstrated the fissures opening within the group. Their set began with the usual repertoire of Buck Owens, a couple of Gram originals, "Six Days on the Road," and soul covers. Then the band branched into a disastrously free-form jam. Gram played organ. In addition to his drums, Mickey had a theremin, an early electronic instrument played by moving one's hands between two antennae, creating an eerie ululation most readily associated with soundtracks from low-budget fifties sci-fi movies. As the music unfolded, bereft of any structure, Ian assembled a sculpture onstage. The theremin jam and sculpture erection evoke a scene out of *Spinal Tap*. Drug-fueled misunderstanding and bad judgment might be the explanation, but Ian Dunlop painted the show as an earnest effort to stretch out—and a reflection of diverging interests. "While it could have been an interesting departure," Ian reflects, "it underscored the dispersal of the band."

The ISB was losing momentum. The boys rehearsed less frequently and, when they got together, tended to jam rather than polish their songs. They would set up and play casually at Brandon's house in Topanga Canyon, where Peter Fonda was a regular visitor. Life in the Bronx house had hardly been monastic. It came to seem rigorously focused compared to the temptations of L.A.

Fonda became a countercultural star for his role as the sensitive Hell's Angel leader Heavenly Blues in Roger Corman's 1966 biker-exploitation drive-in movie classic *The Wild Angels*. Featuring episodes adapted from Hunter S. Thompson's *Hell's Angels: A Strange and Terrible Saga*, Corman's film costarred Nancy Sinatra, Bruce Dern, and several members of the Hell's Angels San Bernardino and Oakland chapters.

Fonda's portrayal of the conflicted, violent-yet-poetic Blues produced the first true counterculture movie hero. Blues is a sixties update of the macho cowboys and tough warriors of the post–World War II era. *Wild Angels* set up Fonda's starring role in the Dennis Hopper–directed (and Fonda-financed) *Easy Rider* three years later. *Easy Rider* grossed a hundred million dollars and, like the 1969 Woodstock music festival, demonstrated the shocking market power the counterculture possessed. More than the Beatles, it was *Easy Rider* that taught Middle America how grossly uncool it was to not have long hair, to not smoke marijuana, and to not be nice to hippies. *Easy Rider* is only one example of the artifacts tossed off by the originators of sixties aesthetics and style that were seized by the slow-moving mass market as beacons lighting a new road. While the masses embraced these new archetypes, the originals who created them had already moved on, hunkered down, burnt out, or cashed in.

Fonda met Gram when he was starring in Roger Corman's LSD film *The Trip*. The screenplay, credited to another Corman regular, Jack Nicholson (though Corman did not shoot Nicholson's script), sought to re-create the experience of an LSD trip. *The Trip* reflected Corman and Fonda's evangelistic fervor about the drug. Fonda had taken acid with the Beatles and told them of a childhood near-death experience, repeating, "I know what it's like to be dead." The Beatles re-created that conversation in "She Said, She Said" on their album *Revolver*.

The movie star and the musician hit it off—"Gram was kind, and that's a rare quality," Fonda said—and Fonda featured Gram's band in *The Trip*, putting them onstage in a scene shot in a club. Gram wears a turtleneck and jeans. He lip-syncs to the music of the Electric Flag, an all-star psychedelic blues band featuring guitarist Michael Bloomfield, drummer Buddy Miles, and keyboardist Barry Goldberg, who would later write songs with Gram. "I wanted to give the ISB any exposure I could," Fonda continued. "John Nuese was a fine guitarist and Mickey was a hell of a drummer. A fast foot— that boy had a fast foot."

Gram paid for a Sub Band recording session at Gold Star Studios in Hollywood. The ISB cut Gram's original composition "Lazy Days." Featuring the driving cut-shuffle beat that Gram picked up from the Bakersfield sound, it's a witty seduction song, with Gram promising, "I think I'll teach you how to relax." The lyrics also reflect Gram's emerging comfort with life in L.A.

"Lazy Days" was intended for *The Trip*. Roger Corman rejected the song as "not acid enough." Fonda was more taken with Gram's "November Nights," the "Bach-ian," Beatlesesque folk number he'd recorded at Jim Carlton's house. A wordy, rueful look back at a former love, "Nights" reflects Gram's early inspirations (Dylan and the Beatles, mostly). The best moments foreshadow Gram's mature, harrowing, confessional songs. In the song's most personal lines, Gram sings, "You think you were taken for granted / You're probably right."

Fonda told Gram it was terrific. "He taught me to play it," Fonda said. "I practiced and practiced and practiced. Then I went out and cut it. Gram was thrilled." Fonda's producer was the black South African expatriate jazz trumpet player Hugh Masekela. Best known for his instrumental hit single "Grazing in the Grass," Masekela was perhaps not the first choice that comes to mind to produce a strummed-guitar folk song. Masekela had also produced the "Lazy Days" sessions, so he was at least acquainted with Gram's music.

Fonda recorded with Masekela on trumpet and a standard four-piece backup band. Masekela's label, Chisa Records, released the single with a B-side of Fonda singing Donovan's "Catch the Wind." It's an astute pairing on Fonda's part: "November Nights" has a certain Donovan feel. The record never got any airplay nor made a dent in anyone's attention span at the time.

Gram was pulled away from the band by the time he spent with Nancy exploring their shared spiritual interests. "She opened spiritual doors for him that words could not provide," Marcia Katz says. "He was so thirsty. He was seeking inner knowledge and higher thought. The two came together not just as soul mates but as spiritual beings that had come from some other higher place. They knew each other well. They were as kindred and of like kind as you could get."

Gram and Nancy, at this stage in their relationship, spoke of one another in precisely those terms. They briefly attended Scientology meetings. Both also became intrigued by a spiritual movement known as Subud, founded in the twenties by an Indonesian guru, Muhammad Subuh Sumohadiwidjojo, and introduced to the West in the late fifties. It focuses on an experience of surrendering completely to the divine rather than on specific religious dogma. Roger McGuinn, cofounder and leader of the Byrds, was an avid follower. Adherents of Subud hold that changing one's name can be an aspect of spiritual development; McGuinn changed his first name from Jim to Roger at the urging of his Subud guru, who believed a name starting with *R* would "vibrate better in the cosmos." Much later in life, McGuinn became a devout Christian.

Gram's Harvard advisor, Jet Thomas, also moved to Southern California. He attended Pomona College, doing postgraduate work in Heidegger, Wittgenstein, and the philosophy of language. "Gram got me to go with him to this Subud guru guy," Jet says. "It was a quasi-Hindu thing. I don't think it was dangerous. It was a little sect personality group around this person. We talked about it afterwards, but Gram was smart and had a good sense of skepticism. He would flirt with these things and had interest in them, but he never got involved with them."

Gram burrowed deeper into his relationship with Nancy and pursued other interests. The ISB became less of a priority. "After the initial activity and getting gigs, things tailed off," Ian says. "We were meeting with A&R people trying to get a deal. We weren't doing much writing. Record people would occasionally come to gigs, but they didn't want to take a chance on us. We stagnated. Not getting an opportunity definitely wore on us. I wanted to do more than sit around and wait."

The problem wasn't that Gram lived separately from the band or that he was in love. He also lived in a different economic reality. Despite the financial difficulties of the Snivelys, Gram's portion of the Snively trust was intact. Though the figures are in dispute, Gram most likely received around thirty to forty thousand dollars, two times a year—a fortune in 1967. Gram never had to earn. If he wanted to let music slip to focus on love or spiritualism, he would eat no worse. That was not true for the rest of the band.

BILLY BRIGGS AND BARRY TASHIAN followed the ISB to L.A. With the band in disarray, Mickey and Ian regularly rehearsed with the two former Remains. They shared an interest in Fats Domino and what Billy describes as "rocking out." After a successful audition at the Topanga Corral, a watering hole for long-haired musicians and their crowd, the four began to play more often than the ISB. Gram sometimes joined them onstage. So did a collection of Topanga music luminaries including Taj Mahal guitarist Jesse Ed Davis and legendary saxophone player Bobby Keys. Once a member of Buddy Holly's touring band, Keys would later play with Joe Cocker's Mad Dogs & Englishmen and with the Rolling Stones on *Sticky Fingers* and *Exile on Main Street*. Keys played with a singular, ripping tone and was as famous for his prodigious appetite for liquor, drugs, and hell-raising as for his music. As required of anyone who hung with the Stones year after year, Keys was gifted with an apparently indestructible constitution. As of 2007, he was still touring with the band.

The most luminous of L.A. luminaries joining the band onstage was pianist, guitarist, and songwriter Leon Russell. Russell is an intersection unto himself in rock's history: Many other artists' careers pass through his. He studied guitar under James Burton (Elvis' guitarist, Gram's future guitarist, and a legendary player), produced hits for Gary Lewis and the Playboys (Russell's band played all the instruments on Lewis' hits), and was part of the famed Wrecking Crew, the collation of L.A. studio musicians who provided music for Phil Spector, Brian Wilson of the Beach Boys, the Byrds, and the Mamas & the Papas among hundreds of others. Russell played on hits as diverse as Ike & Tina Turner's Phil Spector–produced "River Deep, Mountain High," the Byrds' "Mr. Tambourine Man," and Herb Alpert's "A Taste of Honey." Russell wrote "Superstar," a number one hit for the Carpenters; formed Joe Cocker's band Mad Dogs & Englishmen, led the band, and starred in the movie of their tour; recorded two influential records of Southern, gospel-inflected rock in 1970 (*Leon Russell*) and 1971 (*Leon Russell and the Shelter People*); appeared onstage and in the film of George Harrison's all-star *Concert for Bangla Desh*; and wrote "This Masquerade," which soft-jazz guitarist George Benson took to number one in pop, dance, and R&B.

Russell was also responsible for the Shindogs, the house band for ABC's weekly rock showcase, *Shindig!* Their lineup included guitarist James Burton, Elvis' keyboardist and arranger Glenn D. Hardin, bassist Joey Cooper, and drummer Chuck Blackwell. Burton and Hardin would later play with Gram, Blackwell would tour with Russell and Cocker in Mad Dogs & Englishmen. Also in the lineup was guitarist and singer Delaney Bramlett. Delaney, a white Southern blues-gospel-country shouter, pursued, in his own chaotic, random way, the synthesis of American roots that Gram would later call Cosmic American Music. Delaney had an in-depth knowledge and repertoire of blues, traditional country, mountain folk music, gospel, and rock. Eric Clapton fell in with Delaney—for better or worse, Delaney's credited with convincing Clapton to sing—and toured with him and his wife, Bonnie. Clapton was in search of musical roots that, as an Englishman, he felt he did not possess. The core of Delaney's band, and of Russell's, went on to back up Eric Clapton on his *Layla* sessions as Derek and the Dominos.

Leon Russell incarnates key ideas of Gram's Cosmic American Music. He was a one-man melting pot, playing commercial pop, country, white roots, R&B, and his signature original sound, which owes much to Jerry Lee Lewis, Oklahoma church music, and the L.A. studio obsession with killer chops and sellable pop structure. The power and breadth of Gram's influence on American commercial and underground music took years to mature. In the late sixties and early seventies, Leon Russell *was* California-white, commercial pop.

Russell taking the stage with Billy and Barry and Mickey and Ian at the Corral gave them instant credibility. His presence also speaks to how well they played.

The new group felt the need of a handle and, following the disaster of the name the International Submarine Band, came up with something even worse: the Flying Burrito Brothers. Both Billy Briggs and Ian Dunlop take credit. "We went to some funky Mexican restaurant-stall place in the Valley," Ian says, "and I said, 'Look, let's go out and do some gigs and we'll call the band, I don't know, anything—the Flying Burrito Brothers.' I said it just like that."

"Ian will tell you that he invented the name the Flying Burrito Brothers," Billy says. "But I invented the name, and the way I can prove it is that handwritten on the back of this poster for the Topanga Corral I have all the permutations of the possible ways to have it"—Flying this and Brothers that. "I finally came up with Flying Burrito Brothers. Maybe Ian thought of the word *burrito*."

At times the band called itself something even sillier, as bad a name as the annals of rock provide. According to John Einarson's *Desperados*, they occasionally gigged as the Remains of the International Main Street Flying Burrito Brothers Blues Band. By that standard, the Flying Burrito Brothers is a masterpiece of branding.

The Burrito Brothers played comedy material, western swing, older rock and roll, soul, and country. "Suddenly Mickey and I were busy," Ian says. "We were doing gigs, and the other thing seemed to be floundering or had gone a bit stale."

Gram sometimes sang with them and played guitar when they played country. He began to woodshed with Barry Goldberg, one of the pioneers in the early-sixties movement of white musicians playing the Chicago and Detroit style of amplified blues. This represented a departure from the folkie movement of re-creating Delta or acoustic blues. The Chicago sound was urban, hard-edged, and raw. Exemplified in its original form by Howling Wolf, Sonny Boy Williamson, Muddy Waters, pianist Otis Spann, and harmonica player Little Walter, it was an inspiration for the Rolling Stones among countless others. Goldberg played piano and organ with Charlie Musselwhite, a white blues harmonica player who modeled his style on Little Walter's, and can be heard on *Stand Back!*, Musselwhite's best record. Goldberg also played with Michael Bloomfield and the Paul Butterfield Blues Band. Gram and Goldberg tinkered around and together wrote "Do You Know How It Feels to Be Lonesome?"

Fred Neil came to town and stayed at Denny Doherty's house. Denny had been a member of the Village folk group the Mugwumps with Cass Elliot and Lovin' Spoonful cofounder Zal Yanovsky. Denny hit it big with

Cass as half of the Mamas & the Papas. Gram visited Fred Neil at Denny's and there met Bob Buchanan, an old-school folkie who'd played with the New Christy Minstrels. "Whenever you go to Fred's," Bob Buchanan says, "there are guitars out. Gram had his and of course I had mine. Gram and I figured out that we had the Everly Brothers in common. It was a marriage made in heaven."

Bob describes Gram at that time as "a pretty mellow fellow," but with a lot of presence. "He was casual—he'd wear slacks and a button-down shirt, shoes and no socks. He held himself when he was out and about like he was a commanding kind of guy. He wasn't shy, he was sure of himself. He knew who he was and he knew he had an agenda. We weren't sure what it was, but Gram was unto himself. That was his agenda."

Gram was searching out the context of the music that attracted and intrigued him. That meant heading into a nightlife that other musicians of his age and milieu avoided. Gram and Bob played impromptu gigs at the Corral and the Palomino in North Hollywood. The Palomino was a country bar, a redneck dive. Gram and Bob showed up for open-microphone talent nights; their repertoire included George Jones, Buck Owens, and Everly Brothers covers. They played or hung out at the Bandera on Ventura Boulevard when Delaney Bramlett had a regular gig there, the Rag Doll in North Hollywood, the Corncrib in Monrovia, and others.

A favorite was the Aces in City of Industry, a louche industrial zone next to Los Angeles. It was the site of a jam session that pianist Earl Ball had originally run as an all-night, Friday-evening-to-Saturday-morning party at Okieville, a country bar in Fontana, home of the original chapter of the Hell's Angels. "All those people doing all that speed needed someplace to go," Earl Ball says. "And there were a lot of Okies and Arkies that liked to party late." When Okieville shut down in 1967, Ball's jam moved to the Aces.

It took courage for Gram to venture into country bars like the Aces. They were cultural enclaves—ghettos—in which the lines were clearly drawn: hippies on one side (suburban, likely middle-class, long-haired, dilettantes when it came to country music, anti-Vietnam, and pro-marijuana) and non-hippies on the other (working-class, defiantly short-haired, devoted to country music, likely veterans or self-anointed patriots, drinkers, and amphetamine users). In 1967, the relative rarity of long hair meant that anyone who dressed a certain way was automatically an ally. "If you played in a blues or a psychedelic or an English rock band," David Barry says, "you had long hair and you were a hippie. You walk into a psychedelic club and

The Aces after-hours club. (© Andee Nathanson,
www.andeenathanson.com)

everybody likes you because you were a hippie. Period. You listen to FM radio, you've got underground newspapers, you read *Rolling Stone*. You were hermetically in your own cultural universe—you could live in and work in it, at least in a few big cities.

"And that was not true if you were into country music. If you were a hippie, you walked into a scene out of *Easy Rider* every time you wanted to play."

In 1967, longhairs who stepped outside their own milieu could look forward to verbal and often physical harassment. In a noisy drunken room where hippies were rare, hostilities were more likely to surface. Gram was undaunted; he had been venturing into forbidden places since he went into black Winter Haven looking to buy liquor. He and Bob competed in the Thursday-night talent shows at the Palomino. Contestants would sing a song of their choice backed by the steel guitarist (and guitar technology innovator) Red Rhodes and his band, the Detours. Rhodes could play: The Country Music Association voted him Steel Guitar Player of the Year from 1965 through 1968. He played on Elvis Presley's records and joined the Wrecking Crew when they needed a pedal steel. It speaks to the enclosed world of country music and to the status of the Palomino that a musician of Red Rhodes' reputation and influence would run a house band.

Pedal-steel player Jay Dee Maness had played in the house band at Okieville until it closed. He occasionally sat in with the Detours at Palomino's. "Talent night at the Palomino was always Thursday nights," Jay Dee remembers. "Anybody who wanted to sing or play would sign a list up to a certain number. Many of the same people showed up every week. The MC would go, 'Let's hear it for so and so, come on up!' and they'd do one song only. Usually it was average or horrible. People didn't have good timing, and the band got to where we could follow them no matter where they came in or out of a song. That was our challenge. So talent night was popular, especially with the musicians."

"Gram usually went in a T-shirt, a pair of jeans, and slightly long hair," Bob Buchanan says. "My hair was longer. So they thought we were from over the hills in Hollywood—that we were the enemy. We'd always come in second to the guy in the wheelchair who did Johnny Cash impersonations.

"Gram kept going out there after I stopped. He got into a fight with some Marines and got his ass whupped. Gram couldn't keep his mouth shut, even in the wrong situation."

In a last attempt to hold together, the ISB cut a demo. Gram financed the sessions, hoping to emerge with product he could take to record labels. The band cut six songs at Gold Star Studio. "We recorded a mixed bag that was heavier, with not so much country," Ian Dunlop says. "Gram played a big Hammond organ. We had a big, fat sound. I sang 'Hooked,' a slightly obscure Bobby Marchan number, and Gram sang a more bluesy soul thing, a cover of Little Milton's 'Feel So Bad.' It was a good session. It was full of energy, with little angst. There wasn't anything at risk, wasn't any anticipation of disappointment. It was good fun."

L.A. scenester Suzi Jane Hokom heard about the band. After producing Kitchen Sink, a band from Amarillo, Texas, Suzi was looking for another project. She was well connected: Her boyfriend was the producer, arranger, songwriter, and hit maker Lee Hazlewood. A tough-ass Texan who'd written songs and produced for a number of smaller pop acts, Hazlewood built his reputation working with seminal guitar twanger Duane Eddy. In 1966 Hazlewood hit the big time by writing and producing the Nancy Sinatra smash "These Boots Are Made for Walkin'."

Suzi convinced Hazlewood to sign the Sub Band to his Lee Hazlewood Industries label. Gram's dealings with Hazlewood would produce nothing but trouble: Being the pet project of a powerful man's girlfriend seldom proves a good career move. The upside was that Hazlewood came from

Texas, knew country and hillbilly music, and was rolling in money and clout from his Nancy Sinatra hits. The downside was that Lee Hazlewood International was not RCA or Columbia.

Ian Dunlop wasn't happy: "The ISB seemed to be floundering. We had interest from major labels and none of them panned out. Signing with Lee Hazlewood happened because the big-league labels passed. Gram was full of frustration. He was a big fish in a small pond in Florida. He showed so much promise and expected to get somewhere faster. Now we were doing a deal with LHI [Lee Hazlewood Industries] and making a country album? Lee Hazlewood didn't sound interesting or adventurous to me. I was the only one who felt that way. That's when I decided it wasn't working."

In June 1967, Ian officially departed from the International Submarine Band. He wanted to focus on the Flying Burrito Brothers, and Mickey Gauvin went with him. Their repertoire swung back to Mickey's roots: soul music. They added a horn section and gigged like mad.

Ian and Mickey did not play on the ISB's LHI sessions in July. John Nuese stuck with Gram's vision: "Gram and myself felt country music was the thing to do." He also found much to like about the L.A. lifestyle. "It was a different era," he says. "It was the age of free love. The male-female relationship criteria were considerably different than they are now. At Shady Grove, Peter Tork's estate [Tork was a Monkee and nationwide teen heartthrob], I lived in the pool house by this huge swimming pool. Every morning I'd get up by nine o'clock, and there'd already be eight or ten naked women sunning themselves at the pool. Every single woman that came to Peter's estate eventually took off her clothes. Brandon [De Wilde] and I would take bets. 'I'll give her ten minutes, I'll give her half an hour . . .' Women in those days in that era wanted to show off their bodies, and they were beautiful. There hasn't been anything like the sixties in California, with the love-ins and everyone getting high. This was similar to the promiscuity of the 1920s. The sixties were even possibly more pronounced. The age of free love."

GRAM SIGNED WITH Brandon De Wilde's manager, Larry Spector. Spector was pure Hollywood, with a pure-Hollywood career history. His mother had been Dennis Hopper's bookkeeper. Hopper had a meeting at 20th Century Fox and felt vulnerable showing up without an agent or manager—so he ordered Spector into a suit and took him along as a prop. As could only happen in L.A., Spector parlayed his propdom into an actual career as a manager. Byrd David Crosby was Spector's entrée; Crosby then introduced Spector to Peter Fonda, Brandon De Wilde, and other members of the Byrds. Byrds manager Jim Dickson quotes Hopper saying of Spector: "His only asset was a college education and that his mother was a bookkeeper. He winged it constantly and didn't know anything about the business at all."

Spector is remembered as an operator's operator. He was a master of paperwork transfers, mysterious mortgages, providing assets without fronting cash yet still finding a way to take a cut. He shifted his clients from one house to another, from one car to another. When one client moved up to a Porsche, a less successful client would end up with his cast-off Pontiac. "Something happened with Bob Denver," Ian Dunlop says, referring to the actor who played Gilligan on the hit TV series *Gilligan's Island*. "He either got richer or poorer. Larry Spector got Brandon to take over Denver's house in Topanga Canyon. That was the Wave View Drive house. It was your classic L.A. house with an empty swimming pool. It came complete with Berber rugs and pseudo-Kline paintings. All that shit stayed in the house. Denver out, Brandon in."

Bob Buchanan moved into an apartment in the Sweetzer Avenue complex, where Gram was living with Nancy. "Gram and I were often at his or my place playing Everly Brothers, George Jones, and Buck Owens," Bob says. "Gram wasn't doing any folk music. Not one folk song. Not one protest song. Nothing. And when it came to Buck Owens, or George Jones, I was lost. I never listened to that as a kid. I was totally in love with it: the sincerity and the heartbreak. We were jamming on that and Gram says, 'We're getting a band together.'"

In *Desperados*, John Nuese tells Einarson, "Our approach to country music was from a rock end of things. We weren't like a bunch of rednecks from Dixie, straight arrows with a quarter inch of hair. We were longhairs playing country music, so from that angle it was new to the longhair audience. It took a little bit of acclimating to, but once they heard it they got into it and liked it. To our knowledge, we were the only people playing hardcore country around L.A. at that time."

Gram took Nancy for a visit to Winter Haven. Gram went fishing with the husband of his cousin Martha Snively, and insisted Martha cook Southern dishes including the traditional New Year's Day good-luck meal, hoppin' John, a mixture of rice, ham hocks, and black-eyed peas. Gram played piano, organ, and guitar at the Snively big house.

Martha thought Gram and Nancy "seemed to be in love. Not the huggy-kissy kind of love, but our family was not that way. We were not outwardly affectionate." Gram's friend Jim Carlton wasn't so sure. "Nancy was a lovely woman, beautiful," he says. "Over and over she and Gram said, 'Marriage is a piece of paper you don't need,' et cetera, et cetera. But it felt like game playing. Gram wasn't ready—he was twenty-one. Nancy was smart, but they were both too young for any kind of marital relationship, to settle down and have kids. Nancy was glamorous, and they were into the glamour and the rock and roll of it. She was sophisticated about their relationship, in the sense that Gram was certainly not faithful to her. Gram said, 'Aw, we're past all the cheap physical stuff.'

"I didn't get the feeling he was that attached to her. He was fooling around with anyone he could at the time. Love the one you're with, that kind of thing. He liked having her around when there was no one else, 'cause she was a gorgeous woman. She was lovely, but she was like those gals on album covers—just beautiful women, ornaments.

"Nancy was into him, but every woman he ever met was into him. Women found him attractive. Always did. And you look at him, he's not a great-looking guy. He doesn't have classic features. But you put all the pieces together and whatever that synergy is, he certainly made it work."

Jim joined Nancy and Gram at the Snively mansion. "We were at the big house all alone," Jim says. "The family had gone, so we were hanging there for a long weekend, doing acid. Gram was entranced by Ringo's version of 'With a Little Help from My Friends.' He played it incessantly. He loved the song, he loved the version, he loved the feel. And he had that record on the turntable constantly, that one cut."

After Nancy left, Gram and Carlton went to breakfast in Cypress Gardens. As they walked out of the restaurant, the waitress came running with Gram's sunglasses, which he'd left at their table. Gram told her: "You're a very nice country lady." He showed the glasses to Carlton. "They were the sunglasses Fonda wore in *The Wild Angels*," Jim says. "Gram got custody of them. They were a gift from Fonda and Gram was proud of them. Of course, he wouldn't announce it. It had to come up in conversation."

Jim recalls that Gram talked a lot about his new movie-star friend, however. "He brought home this grass called Icebag that Fonda kept buried in his yard. It was smuggled into the States in ice bags and was legendary smoke back then."

Jim and Gram frequented a Winter Haven lounge where Buddy Canova played. Gram got up to sing, and someone insisted he do "I Left My Heart in San Francisco." Gram stumbled through it, then followed up with a rendition of Porter Wagoner's "A Satisfied Mind" that brought down the house. Afterward at the lounge, Gram bragged to his high school friends that he was making a hundred dollars a day in Los Angeles as a session musician. No one but Jim Carlton knew enough about the music business to contradict him, and Jim let it pass.

While Gram went to call Nancy long-distance, a waitress approached Jim to ask if acquaintances of his across the bar were old enough to drink. Carlton shook his head, meaning he didn't know one way or the other. The acquaintances, who couldn't hear the exchange, took Carlton's gesture to mean that he'd snitched them out to the waitress.

"Somebody onstage asked, 'Where's Gram? Will he come sing a song?'" Carlton says. "I said, 'I'll go get him.' These guys followed and ambushed me. I knocked on Gram's phone booth and said, 'They want you to sing another.' I turned around and one of these guys got me right in the neck with his fist. My glasses flew off and fell over this balcony down by the pool and I could not see. I yelled to Gram and he came out and the two of us took care of those guys. It was great. Gram had no qualms about jumping in and getting hurt. There wasn't any of his pretty-boy crap. He could have gotten his teeth knocked out. So we took care of them, and Gram went down to retrieve my glasses. It was like the cavalry showed up. . . . Somebody told the manager, and he wanted to get the police. We were like, 'No, no, no,' 'cause we were underage, too."

This fight contradicts the persistent "rich pussy" stories that paint Gram as a tough-guy poseur. Such talk originated among Gram's more macho Winter Haven former bandmates. On the scale of redneck fighting men, Gram may not have been number one, but that didn't automatically make him a "rich pussy." Later, when Gram began to ride motorcycles that he could not handle, his harder-core motorcycle buddies in L.A. would resurrect the phrase.

Jim saw firsthand how Gram financed his lifestyle. "One night Gram told me, 'You don't know that I have this fund.' He had collected his stipend and had thirty or forty thousand dollars laid out on the bed," Jim recalls. "I didn't know what to say . . . I was terribly broke. I had a '57 Ford that needed a battery. I had to leave it running in the parking lot so it wouldn't quit on me. Gram handed me twenty dollars and says, 'Go buy a battery.'

"And every day he'd buy lunch. Paige was one of the Snively family secretaries. She'd drop by every day and bring a bond, a matured savings bond from way back when. Gram would buy lunch with that. I'd say, 'Well, jeez, thanks for lunch,' and he'd say, 'Don't worry about it. It's on some old relative.' Gram had little hundred- , two-hundred- , five-hundred-dollar bonds, whatever, they were rolling in. . . . Chump change in addition to his stipend from the trust fund."

While Gram was in Winter Haven, Bob Buchanan was in Coconut Grove, recording with Fred Neil. Gram visited them in the Grove and brought Bob back to Winter Haven. The two took a train from Winter Haven to Chicago, where Bob gave Gram a tour of Chicago's folk scene. They rode the *Sante Fe Chief* from Chicago back to Los Angeles, occupying a private compartment, singing train songs and working on new tunes the whole way. Together they wrote "Hickory Wind" and talked about their mixed feelings about returning to California. "We had family and locations that were very familiar," Bob says, "and now we were going back to the City of Angels that was killing all the angels. I think deep down inside we both had this resentment for that Hollywood thing. Sucks people in and spits them out. He and I were aware of that, so we were both getting very cynical at our young age."

Gram was coming back not only to Los Angeles but to his girlfriend. Nancy, feeling neglected, dramatized her upset with a range of attention-getting techniques. Tensions increased when Nancy became pregnant, in March. None of Gram's friends believed he'd intended to become a father.

It's an old story in rock that band members have little patience for girl-friends. Notwithstanding this tradition and the shortage of slack that Nancy would have got from Gram's musician friends in any case, the tensions between Gram and Nancy during her pregnancy were real.

"We were having a meeting at my house with a couple of big-time guys, record executives," Bob Buchanan says, "and Nancy took my car. Suddenly Nancy's had an accident. She went four blocks and totaled it. 'Come and save me!' So the meeting's over, and we had to go save Nancy. It was outrageous. I'm sure she didn't try to do it on purpose, but she'd get herself in predicaments. Running up a bill here, or forgetting to do this, and Gram was busy being Gram. She had depth and stubbornness, so they were like two roosters in the pen."

Nancy was accustomed to a certain level of drama. "She thrived on craziness," Bob says. "Anybody that was hanging around with Steve McQueen and David Crosby and Gram Parsons had to be nuts. Nancy was outrageous on her own and she liked the excitement. She had an agenda: to be the famous one next to the famous one. She wanted to be Gram's wife instead of girlfriend. She went to the point of trying to get him to come home and not be out running around all over the place being a musician. But she couldn't get her way, and she was as stubborn as they come. Without meaning to, she could be quite a destructive force."

Gram made no apparent effort to soothe Nancy or prepare for fatherhood. "Say Gram was trying to help somebody who OD'd," Bob says. "Nancy would rather preach to the person who OD'd: 'It's not good to use needles, it's bad for you,' with the guy dying in front of her. She didn't know how to deal. She'd call the ambulance or the police, and those were the wrong people to call. You don't want the guy to die, but you don't want everyone to go to jail, either.

"At this time Gram was not using needles, but I certainly was, and Fred Neil and Tim Hardin, a lot of people. All I saw Gram do was smoke his pot and once in a while he'd snort a little heroin. Gram liked his pot, but he was nowhere into needles."

GRAM CONTINUED TO SEARCH for and hang out in the roughest country bars he could find, seeking the essence of the music. Like any serious mystic, he was convinced of the link between the magic and the setting. He became a regular at the Aces. "The Aces was rough," David Barry says. "Everybody had a gun in their car. And a posse of L.A. sheriffs [sat] in the parking lot waiting for the inevitable brawl—those guys would shoot anyone.

"The toughness was part of the beauty of it. I loved it. Gram did, too. The City of Industry"—where the Aces was located—"was one of the worst places on the planet. The Aces club was the toughest place around, because not only Anglo rednecks but Mexican rednecks went there. The Mexican rednecks had plenty to fight about amongst themselves, but you put them together with the Anglo rednecks and you had a nice mix goin' on.

"Of course the Aces had a country band. Country musicians tended to be crazy in a way that rock musicians weren't, because the country drug was amphetamines and the country guys were always wired. To get a fight going was easy, and that was the scene. The Aces was the ground zero of country music in L.A. County.

"Gram described sitting outside that club. He'd been playing with David Crosby at an open mike. He described this strange hostile beauty and the sun coming up orange over the San Bernardino Mountains behind the oil derricks. He was so lyrical about it. That was his metaphor for his love of country music. He knew the shit-kicker mentality that produced the mix that all this music came out of. Gram knew the mentality informed the playing. That was not true of a lot of the guys who played country rock. Gram did not want a rock-diluted version of country music. He was into the real thing."

To record the album that came to be called *Safe at Home*, Gram and John Nuese set out to put together a band that would manifest that reality. While in Winter Haven, Gram tried to recruit local bass heavy Gerald Chambers. Chambers didn't want to move to Los Angeles. Gram ran into drummer Jon Corneal, a man who knew country music. "I was down for my yearly visit home to see the orange blossoms," Corneal says. "I had already moved to Nashville in July 1964. In 1965, Gram had a folk group [the Shilos] and he made fun of me for playing country. When I ran into him in 1967 he said, 'Man, I've got some music I want to play you, some stuff I've discovered.' And he had a reel-to-reel tape full of George Jones, Merle Haggard, Buck Owens, and Loretta Lynn, like he had discovered them. I had come off some Grand Ole Opry–style jobs. I had worked for the Wilburn Brothers for a year, Roy Drusky, Kitty Wells, and Connie Smith. I was leaving Connie Smith when I ran into Gram. I'd come off the road with the Wilburn Brothers." Corneal was willing to relocate. He was in.

They hunted down steel-guitar player Jay Dee Maness. "Jay Dee had a DA haircut," John Nuese says, meaning a duck's ass, a high-topped, greased-back 1950s shit-kicker roll of hair ending at the back of the neck with a feathered, tapered flip like the hind end of a duck—"pointed shoes, and a skinny tie. He was leery of us hippie types, skeptical at first. I didn't know him well, but what a player! He developed his own style and was one of the best steel players of all time. So we got him and Earl Ball, a piano player. Jon Corneal played drums and Chris Ethridge played bass. He's from Meridian, Mississippi, and a great R&B bass player."

"I started playing the pedal steel when I was eleven," Jay Dee Maness says, "and was playing bars by age fifteen. My dad said, 'If you always play that instrument you won't ever go hungry. You'll always be able to work.' He was right."

Jay Dee leaned on Gram and John to bring in Earl Ball on piano. Gram was reluctant to have any piano on the record; he wasn't intending to play himself. He wanted a purer Bakersfield sound: rhythm and lead guitar plus steel, bass, and drums. But Jay Dee nagged until Gram gave in. Earl Ball remembers, "Jay Dee Maness came to me one night and said, 'There's this bunch of hippie guys and they're trying to do country music downtown. They've got me hired to play steel guitar, and this guy plays the piano, but says he'd rather have a real country-music piano player if I knew one. I told him about you, so you come on down and do the session.' That's how I got connected with Gram."

Earl Ball was the real thing. He first played on Jimmy Swan's radio show in Hattiesburg, Mississippi, hitchhiking into town from the family farm for the show and hitchhiking back afterward. He played Ray Price and Hank Williams songs and made ends meet working door-to-door as a Fuller Brush salesman. Earl hooked up with a Johnny Cash soundalike, Danny Ray. Their travels took them to Los Angeles, where Earl became house pianist at Olie's Bar, which later became Okieville. There Ball came to love the sound of Bakersfield honky-tonker Wynn Stewart and added rockabilly to his country playing. After a year at Olie's, Earl became the house pianist at the Aces. "The ISB was the first people I ever heard of with that look," Earl Ball says, meaning hippies, "that wanted to play country music."

Earl and Jay Dee, whose standards were rigorous and unyielding, regarded Gram as something of an alien. "I thought, 'This is a young guy and he sings pretty good,'" Jay Dee says. "He was never a great singer. But he wanted to be and he worked at it. What I call a great singer is George Jones or George Strait. Gram was always kind of in the middle, which became the trademark country-rock thing. None of them were great singers—they sang the way they felt it. Like the Rolling Stones. Those guys do great but they're not great singers."

Jay Dee and Earl's reactions suggest the musical and cultural gulf that Gram was attempting to bridge. Gram wasn't the only one hanging out in scenes he found seductive yet foreign and unsettling. "I went to his house one time when they lived on Sweetzer in Hollywood," Jay Dee says. "It was quite an eye-opener. That was my first introduction to what we called hippies. It was like going into a garden. There were plants and strange things hanging on the walls. I hate to use the word *hippie*, but it wasn't like going to a normal person's home where you sit down to a meal. It was like going to a museum or thrift store. I thought, 'They actually live like this?'"

Earl believes that it was drugs, rather than music, that eventually led the country and rock musicians to understand each other. "The country players took up marijuana," he says, "and the rockers started in with speed." In 1967 that magical rapprochement was still a couple of years off.

John and Gram rehearsed at Suzi Jane Hokom's Laurel Canyon house.

It turned out that she, with the blessing of her boyfriend, Lee Hazlewood, was going to produce the ISB sessions. John taught Gram flattop guitar parts with an emphasis on the chugging country backbeat. The band went into Studio B of Western Sound Studios in Hollywood in July 1967. Two songs were cut, both Gram originals: "Blue Eyes," a shockingly accurate attempt at a Buck Owens domestic-bliss romance ditty (with a perfectly executed Buck Owens kindergarten chorus), and "Luxury Liner." LHI Records released the two songs as a single.

The culture clash between rock and country was manifest in the studio. "We didn't record the way I usually do," Earl Ball says, "because I tried to have my band be a little more polished. I was older, only twenty-seven, but still older. I thought it was kind of rough, but maybe that's the way the kids needed to hear it, a bit more rock and roll, in a looser form than Nashville."

It was Gram's first exposure to the way of country studio musicians as exemplified by Jay Dee Maness. "Jay Dee had a little problem with the whole long-haired hippie thing," Bob Buchanan says. "He thought it was weird. Everybody on break going out and smoking a joint. Jay Dee would stay inside and drink coffee. . . .

"He was used to working with great names; Jay Dee was a classic for-hire studio musician. Those guys hung around Nashville at these open-all-night restaurants sipping coffee and taking speed, waiting for somebody to come in and say, 'Hey, so-and-so had to go home, you want to fill in?' These guys were incredible players, and there would be anywhere from three to thirteen of them waiting all night to do a session. That was their livelihood, and it was good money. Once in a while they'd go on the road with a band, but they would rather be home with their family.

"Jay Dee was far and away a great steel-guitar player. He came to work like punching a clock. But he was not in his element. He'd say, 'What do you want?' Gram would say, 'Do something you feel,' and Jay Dee had a hard time with that. He wasn't used to doing what he felt. All he was supposed to do was play the steel."

If Jay Dee Maness stood for working-class professionalism, Earl Ball represented the universe of Southern California roadhouse honky-tonk speed. "I was a beer man," Earl says. "Beer and uppers. Because I did those long jam sessions, I'd try for balance. I'd drink a good whiskey with those uppers, a bar whiskey, Kessler's bar whiskey, and those round speed tablets you could get back then with the smooth edges. . . . That was the hillbilly music culture. The rock guys or hippies were doing more pot and a little

LSD. But I went to this doctor one time, told him I wanted to do some LSD, what'd he think, and he said it would eat my brain up, so I said, 'Well, okay, I won't do that.'"

For a band with such diverse views on drugs, the ISB managed to produce a cohesive sound. With no thanks to Suzi Jane Hokom, whom the band considered a meddling amateur. "She was bossy in the studio and insisted on a piecemeal recording," John Nuese says. "We were at loggerheads because she didn't understand the procedure we used, which was to get everyone together and get a sound. Then you do the song."

"We had some real difficult times making that album," Suzi Jane Hokom said. "We had to do it in about two weeks because Lee [Hazlewood] didn't want to spend a lot of money. I had big problems with John Nuese. He hated me. There was nothing I could do to make him like or accept me. It was a battle with him every day."

Though she and John Nuese disagree on every aspect of the sessions, one thing is clear: They battled constantly. John's complaints about Suzi's preference for recording piecemeal referred to doing a lot of overdubs. John had problems playing live and preferred to overdub his parts. Nevertheless he was reluctant to relinquish control. Gram was, too, even as he held back from firmly taking charge.

"Suzi Jane Hokom more or less had charge of things," Jay Dee Maness says, "but musically we did what we wanted. We didn't have a direction. We just played. Gram would go, 'Here's a song I want to do,' and we'd look at each other and go, 'Okay, you play the chorus and maybe you play the . . .' Or we'd all start playing and it would fall in place. We'd develop it on the spot." Bob Buchanan recalls, "It was the Gram Parsons Show. Suzi Jane Hokom had no idea what sound anybody was after. The sessions were like a toy. Lee Hazlewood's a producer and he wanted to give his girlfriend a gift, a band to play with. But we didn't know what sound, either. John Nuese and the band knew it was Gram's show. They went in and played what he wanted."

In addition to the stress of working with a producer who could neither guide the band nor help them find what they thought they wanted, tensions were emerging between Gram and Jon Corneal.

Jon had hoped to record his own originals for the album. He told the others he was a better singer and guitar player than Gram. He complained that Gram had promised him a chance to cut his own songs and felt he'd been lured to California by false promises. Jon had been in L.A. less than two weeks when Gram told John Nuese, "I have some reservations about having invited Corneal." Moreover, Corneal proved too much of a shit kicker for the band's social vibe. Or perhaps his shit-kicker behavior lacked the cool veneer that came naturally to shit kickers like Earl Ball and Jay Dee Maness. Corneal felt out of his depth in L.A. and took offense easily. Not having a girlfriend, Corneal was reduced to tagging along after Gram.

Gram brought the band to a few high-end Hollywood parties in the hills. At first people were amused by Corneal, who wore overalls and "fart kicker" boots and talked, as one bandmate put it, "like a stone-kicking farm boy." When the sophisticates realized it wasn't an act, the amusement soured. "You knew he wasn't going to make it for long," Bob Buchanan says.

Alone among the band, Jon was impressed by Suzi Jane Hokom. He insists that she played the ISB's record for George Harrison when the Beatles were looking for artists for their Apple label. Suzi told Jon that Harrison wanted her to produce an ISB record for Apple, but that Lee Hazlewood wouldn't allow it.

The band took a break after the release of the single. "Money was not a problem to Gram," Jon Corneal says in *Desperados*. "He had plenty of it. But I had to work for a living. We needed to be gigging, but we weren't. Gram and I used to go out and play places. We actually could have performed, but John didn't want to, so Gram and I would go sit in at the Palomino. It was kind of a strange situation. But I knew I could go back to Nashville and get work." According to Einarson, Corneal went back to Nashville and returned when the recording sessions picked back up.

Sessions resumed in November with little structure. "I'd walk in," Bob Buchanan remembers, "and Gram would say, 'We're gonna do "Strong Boy."' And we'd run through it once or twice by memory. 'Bob, why don't you try singing an octave below me or a harmony?'" When Buchanan and others sang harmony with Gram, Suzi Jane tweaked the volume in their headphones, making it sound as if the others were as loud in the mix as Gram. In fact, the harmonizers were reduced to background vocalists without their knowledge. "So it wasn't a band," Bob says. "It was a Gram album with the band behind him. They called it the International Submarine Band, but Gram picked the songs and the harmonies. It was all Gram. Even Suzi Jane was obligated to get along with him. John would say, 'Let's do this part in the break,' and if it sounded good to Gram, fine. If he didn't like it, he would tell you and it wouldn't happen. There was no equality in the band. Gram was the show."

Glen Campbell came by to play guitar and add tenor vocals. Poised on the edge of stardom himself, Campbell at the time was a highly regarded L.A. session musician with credits on Brian Wilson's *Pet Sounds*, among others. The session men, like Earl Ball, got along fine with Gram. They were not dependent on him for their home or their food.

Gram pursued a different dynamic with everyone else. He wasn't afraid to bully the band. When John Nuese and Gram argued, John usually backed down. In the words of one of the session players, John Nuese "didn't want to get in the way of the Gram Parsons machine. If Gram had an idea and Corneal didn't like it, Gram would say, 'Leave the session. I'll get another drummer.' Nuese and Corneal were upset. They both thought it was going to be an even band. There was not a lot of happiness. Of course Gram would never do that to Glen Campbell. Gram was in awe of the people who were good. If you earned Gram's respect, you had it."

The dissatisfaction spilled over at the band house. When Jon Corneal couldn't take it anymore, he said those classic rock-and-roll band-breakup words: "Who does he think he is?" The inevitable realization followed: "I haven't any money. I don't have any work here. I'm broke. I'm going home."

The overdubs were recorded by Hokom and Gram and whoever was necessary, day by day. "We were there several weeks for the first stint," Bob Buchanan says. "Then we realized there were some weak points. We overdubbed some of the rhythm guitars and harmonies. By that time I had distanced myself from Gram. I went in, but I was in bad shape with my drug addiction. I wasn't able to do the rhythm guitar parts. They had to get another guy."

Gram showed a new level of assertiveness, a drive and a sense of ownership over the music. Musically and emotionally, Gram was a collaborator only to a degree. After years of wanting the spotlight, he did not waste his opportunity. Patterns were established that would hold true in all his recording sessions: a distaste for structuring his material before going into the studio; a preference for playing live with the tape machine running; not much interest in listening to a producer; ruthlessness about finding the best player for the part, regardless of whose feelings might get hurt; and a sense that everyone was laboring in the service of his vision.

In fairness, Gram drove himself to a standard that made it reasonable for him to be ruthless with others. At first listen, an outstanding aspect of *Safe at Home* is the skill with which the band apes then-current and traditional honky-tonk forms. To seek to capture those forms was a revolutionary, not evolutionary, step in 1967. There were no longhair rockers exploring these sounds with Gram's accuracy and attention to detail or his fealty to the cultural mythology underlying the music. The album is pure City of Industry honky-tonk, executed with loving gusto and hell-raising sincerity, even on the joke songs.

"There are those that say the best thing Gram ever did was the International Submarine Band record," John Nuese says. "The singing is great. It's better than his later singing. He wasn't drinking, he wasn't taking hard drugs, he was concentrating. And that's one of the things that made that album hold its position over the past thirty-seven years."

Also evident on *Safe at Home* is Gram's quirky, bemused genius for picking cover songs and his music-archeologist's attention to aesthetic detail in performing them. He shows an astonishing grasp of the idioms in which he wrote originals as well. With his connoisseur's ear, Gram demonstrated that he technically, emotionally, and musically understood the tiniest difference between highly specific country styles and traditions.

At the same time, he proved to have a tin ear regarding some material: His covers of Johnny Cash's "Folsom Prison Blues"—which medleys into Arthur Crudup's "That's All Right Mama" (an early hit for Elvis)—and "I Still Miss Someone" are throwaways. They show little insight into what makes Cash's minimalist delivery so potent. Alone on *Safe at Home*, these three covers lack soul. Jon Corneal overplays in the shuffle version of "Folsom/All Right." The band is reaching, trying to infuse energy into arrangements that work against them. A stronger producer, or maybe any producer at all, might have imposed some needed discipline.

Another cover, Merle Haggard's "I Must Be Somebody Else You've Known," shows much more exuberance than Merle's world-weary delivery. The song slows in the middle and never recovers its pace—perhaps two different takes were spliced together. There's a palpable joy in Gram's singing and great, understated tempo comping in a Floyd Cramer style from Earl Ball. Gram's love of wordplay and puns (evident from his early song "Sum Up Broke" to the double meaning of *Safe at Home*) is clear in how much he enjoys singing the title line.

Porter Wagoner's "A Satisfied Mind" had been covered by the Byrds on 1965's *Turn! Turn! Turn!* The Byrds performed it as the classic folkie's lament about the perils of chasing after money (like that other folkie fallback, "The Ballad of Richard Cory"). Wagoner's own version is right out of the hymnal. It's lugubrious and echoes the slow-motion sincerity of the

Louvin Brothers. Porter sings with such churchy sadness, you can almost believe the message: Be grateful you're poor. Gram's vocals are never equal to the song; his focus on singing with feeling keeps him from feeling whatever emotions he's seeking. It's hard to imagine that "A Satisfied Mind" was any fun for either the Byrds or Gram. The song is such a lesson. It's as if Gram was determined to demonstrate his broad grasp of the canon: a couple Johnny Cash songs, a Merle, and a Porter Wagoner. Given that no one on earth can sing as slowly as Porter Wagoner, covering "Mind" in Porter's style is a fool's errand.

Even so, Earl Ball and Jay Dee Maness shine. The pedal steel is a virtuoso's instrument—fretless, scaleless, and requiring two hands and feet. On "A Satisfied Mind" Jay Dee takes the steel through all its roles: lead guitar seizing the spotlight for a solo; string section providing a smooth road down which the other instruments travel; a horn section adding rhythmic punch; and that ineffable Greek chorus steel-guitar commentary, wherein the great players somehow manage to be within and without the song—moving it along and telling us about its themes at the same time.

"Cowboy" Jack Clement's "Miller's Cave" demonstrates Gram's cunning at choosing unlikely covers and his glee in singing them. "Miller's Cave" is that staple of the country charts, the story song. Some are historical narratives, like Johnny Horton's "Battle of New Orleans" and "Sink the Bismarck"; Jimmy Dean did Homeric epics like "Big Bad John"; Ray Stevens made his name with the low comedy of "Ahab the Arab."

"Miller's Cave," first brought to the charts by Hank Snow, historically aligns with Porter Wagoner's "Cold Hard Facts of Life." Both feature O. Henry or de Maupassant endings: an unexpected twist reveals the song to be told in flashback by a narrator who's in big trouble. Gram altered the first line in the song to change its setting to "Waycross, Georgia." He understood the original sufficiently to bring in a big, booming Mitch Miller–style multitracked male chorus for the final verse. Of all his faithful renditions of lower-brain-function country, this is the most deadpan and fun. Gram strives for emotion on the more canonical covers. This joke song seems his most sincere.

"Luxury Liner" demonstrates, in the arrangement as well as the lyrics, the future of Gram's songwriting, the power he would find in his own pain. Part of the shock of the music of singer-songwriters George Jones, Lefty Frizzell, Wynn Stewart, and other honky-tonkers lies in their straightforward descriptions of their fucked-up lives, inability to love, life-altering romantic mistakes, and distanced self-perception. Their view of self is always through a prism of anguish. Country pain is expressed often without metaphor, simply and plainly. At first the expression seems crude and comical, but once the force of the music hits, it's the bottomless emotional torment, and the singers' naked confession thereof, that make raw country so moving.

"Strong Boy" is one of the last times Gram would tout his strength, rather than his weakness. Again relying on the shuffle beat, Gram tells off someone competing for his woman's affections. It's a brag song and seems incongruous, but he sings it with gusto. Earl Ball takes a cheerful, galumphing solo until Jay Dee Maness comes in with a real showpiece solo.

Safe at Home ends with Gram's most straightforward and mournful song. "Do You Know How It Feels to Be Lonesome?" addresses the alienation that plagued Gram and describes depression with clinical precision. Andrew Solomon, author of *The Noonday Demon*, describes the salient aspect of depression as the constant illusion that one is alone and disconnected. The band treats the lyrics as typical honky-tonk: Earl Ball loses himself in tinkling Ray Price solos, and Jay Dee stretches the end of each lyric line with lingering, sorrowful wails. Though a chorus of almost-Nashville girl singers provides a soft bed of "ooooohhhs" under Earl Ball, the attempted sweetening only emphasizes the isolation of the singer. From this song onward, Gram's best lyrics would place him on the outside looking in at the world and at himself.

Do you know how it feels to be lonesome?
When there's just no one left who really cares

(Words and music by Gram Parsons)

Peter Doggett wrote in his exceptional history *Are You Ready for the Country: Elvis, Dylan, Parsons and the Roots of Country Rock*: "Ironically, the same isolation from the times which marked *Safe at Home* as a historical dead end is its greatest artistic strength." Yet time has proven that *Safe at Home* was not a historical dead end: The ISB's enthusiasms were simply alien to the rock-and-roll culture of the moment. Just as hippies walked into country bars with a wholly reasonable fear of being unwelcome ("And all they seem to do is stare"), country music was equally unloved and misunderstood by the larger rock audience. Gram and John Nuese loved the pain, the sincerity, the raucous ecstasy, and the deceptive simplicity of country music. They burrowed into its forms with an acolyte's devotion. Corneal, Ball, Maness, and bassist Chris Ethridge didn't need to learn. They were living it.

The most argued and least interesting question of Gram's legacy is whether he invented country rock. Anyone immersed in the history of American popular music understands that almost nobody invents anything. (Miles Davis' psychedelic period might well be the exception that proves the rule. Ditto Sun Ra and Mr. Cecil Taylor.) Sounds emerge as synthesis, in evolutionary steps; musical styles bleed into one another; musicians at different ends of the continent have similar ideas at similar times.

Almost four decades removed from the moment, though, it's hard to remember how radical a breaking down of walls, a liberating of ghettos, *Safe at Home* proved to be. In 1967 there was nothing like it being recorded in rock and roll. The combination of rocker exuberance, roadhouse scholarship, and Nashville session tradition generated a new form.

In 1972, Gram told Chuck Cassell, an A&R man at A&M records, that *Safe at Home* "is probably the best country album that I've done. Because it had a lot of quick shuffle, brilliant-sounding country. Once in a while in the Burritos I'd run into some freak who had nine copies of it. Nobody else had ever heard of it. I had, like, four songs that I'd written on it that were good. I was real young and I got carried away. It was all recorded in a week. Mixed in one day."

The album was not recorded in a week or mixed in a day. And in his conversation with Cassell, Gram sounds high as a cooter. Their interview occurred during a phase when Gram was most full of bullshit when talking to journalists or A&R types. His clear affection for *Safe at Home* still comes through.

Recording finished in early December of 1967. The wrap-up of the album coincided with the birth of Gram and Nancy's daughter, Polly.

Having completed his first album and fathered a child, Gram abandoned his band and showed little interest in parenting. Shortly after their album was in the can, Gram left the ISB and charmed his way into a new band that offered greater fame and much more poisonous group dynamics.

TWELVE
The Byrds

THE BYRDS WERE A NEST OF VIPERS, *LORD OF THE FLIES* WITH GUITARS.

They began as a mix of self-reliant pros who came together out of ambition and the sense that they were wholly of their moment. They knew how to seize that moment, and their success led them to hate, distrust, and scheme against one another. They never shared a house, hung out as friends, or—after the early days—rehearsed with diligence. They were famous for their mediocre live performances. They gathered in the studio and fought like dogs over whose songs would be recorded and who got to sing lead.

Even now, each surviving original Byrd insists that he's preeminent in Byrds history. Chris Hillman, the bitterest of the Bitter Lieutenants, has had little to say about Gram and now declares himself "all Grammed out." Of his bandmate Gene Clark, the principal songwriter for the band, Hillman maintained for decades that "Gene didn't add that much." In the past few years, Hillman has been giving Clark more his proper due. Roger McGuinn, speaking reluctantly of Gram, says, "Remember, you're only talking about a guy who was in my band for six months."

The men who formed the core of the Byrds had been wandering troubadours in the early-sixties mode. Gene Clark met McGuinn in 1964 after McGuinn opened for Hoyt Axton at L.A. folk nexus the Troubadour. Clark was writing songs with folk structures and themes and wanted them set to a rock beat. McGuinn and Clark started working together. David Crosby heard them playing in the stairwell of the Troubadour and sat down to sing harmony. Crosby had been recording demos with producer Jim Dickson, a veteran of the L.A. folk scene who had produced banjo genius Doug Dillard, Odetta, and the Southern California bluegrass ensemble the Scottsville Squirrel Barkers. Under Dickson's guidance, Crosby, McGuinn, and Clark performed as the Jet Set, yet another example of the laughably lame names that have plagued Southern Californian bands, a curse culminating in the Eagles.

Dickson recommended Squirrel Barker mandolin player Chris Hillman as a replacement on bass for Crosby, who was an indifferent guitarist and no bassist at all. By training and inclination, Crosby was a lead and harmony singer. In attitude, Crosby was a star; he told the other Byrds, "I have the best voice in the world." The drummer, Michael Clarke, was an habitué of the Sunset Strip. Clarke was invited to join because he had the best Brian Jones bowl haircut in L.A. He could barely play.

McGuinn led the band. After studying at Chicago's Old Town School of Folk Music, he accompanied the Chad Mitchell Trio and the Limeliters in the early sixties. McGuinn toured in Bobby Darin's band and came to New York at Darin's request to work in the Brill Building. Seeing the Beatles was a revelation for McGuinn, prompting him to add rock covers to his folk-club performances. The hardcore folkies in the Village considered this heresy. McGuinn left New York for Los Angeles and regular gigs at the Troubadour.

Gene Clark was born in Missouri and raised on a family farm. In 1963 Clark joined the New Christy Minstrels. As would prove the story of his life, Clark was too shy to assert his place in the group. Relegated to the background despite his songwriting abilities and weary, pain-racked voice, Clark left the Minstrels in 1964. Clark proved to be the songwriting engine for the early Byrds. He wrote "I Knew I'd Want You," the B-side of the Byrds' number one single "Mr. Tambourine Man." Thanks to his songwriting royalties, Clark was the first of the Byrds to see money rolling in. The others never forgave him.

Chris Hillman had joined the Squirrel Barkers as a teenager. They cut one album. Guitarist Bernie Leadon, a future Flying Burrito Brother and

Eagle, sat in with the Barkers after two members failed to avoid the draft. At seventeen, Hillman joined another bluegrass outfit, the Golden Boys, who then changed their name to the Hillmen. The Hillmen featured the Gosdin brothers, Rex on bass and Vern on guitar. In 1963 Jim Dickson produced their one album, *When the Ship Comes In,* a collection of bluegrass standards and the Bob Dylan song of the album title. Dickson had a relationship with Dylan and access to Dylan's catalog of unreleased songs. The Hillmen broke up after the album's release. Hillman moved to L.A. and played with the Green Grass Group.

Michael Clarke was a kid from the Strip with a great haircut.

Clarke aside, the Byrds had all been committed musicians from their early teens. They knew the folk and bluegrass circuit. They had played big halls and shitholes. They were ambitious. In those early days Dickson worked the band hard in rehearsals (their frequency of rehearsal was inversely proportional to their success). After several months in the studio, the Byrds auditioned for Columbia Records doing "Mr. Tambourine Man." Dickson's friend Miles Davis helped secure the audition. Terry Melcher, the son of iconic fifties film and singing star Doris Day, produced the sessions. Only McGuinn played on the record. The rest of the music was supplied by the cream of L.A. session musicians, including Leon Russell.

"Tambourine Man" was an instant hit and exacerbated the competitive vibe within the band. "Gene Clark was nervous," Jim Dickson says. "Chris Hillman was sullen. Michael Clarke was like Tom Sawyer. McGuinn isolated himself. He didn't hang out much with anybody.

"The group as a group never spent time together outside the music. They were never buddies. Sometimes on the road they would get along. They got down to business and were spectacular. It was so much fun with the chicks and groupies that by the end of the night everybody would get along great. Next day they would come in like five guys that didn't know each other.

"McGuinn was aloof, but he had recorded before and knew that the leader got double what the others got. So he wanted to be the leader. Gene Clark became the leader in reality but he never directed what the other people did. Chris Hillman had been the last one to join. He never tried to assert any authority and he never sang. He kept saying he wanted to sing. I'd tell him, 'Sing!' but he wouldn't sing.

"Gene Clark was originally the lead singer. David [Crosby] talked him out of singing. So McGuinn, in order to keep the peace, said he'd sing.

David was a troublemaker. David crippled the Byrds at every turn. He had an essential voice and he made everybody pay for it."

Gene Clark's songwriting royalties paid for a limitless supply of drugs and new Porsches. The other Byrds were envious. They had little patience for Clark's demons and never protected him from Crosby. Clark was long, lean, and handsome as a cowboy; Crosby was short, squat, and self-conscious about it. He never let up on Clark. Crosby banished Clark from guitar, forbade him to play even the tambourine, and finally prohibited Clark from singing lead on his own songs.

Clark quit the band after the release of "Eight Miles High." According to Byrds biographer Johnny Rogan, "Although McGuinn was nominal leader, Clark was regarded as the central figure in the group. He stood stage center as the tambourine man and was apparently the only member capable of writing an album's worth of songs. He presumably left because of his fear of flying; he freaked out before takeoff on an L.A.-NYC flight to appear on a television special hosted by NYC radio personality Murray the K. When asked by Murray where Clark was, McGuinn responded, 'He broke a wing.' The press instantly dubbed Clark 'The Byrd who could not fly.' "

Crosby was the next to go. The precipitating incidents were a near-fatal OD in a New York hotel room followed by the public punching of road manager Jimmi Seiter onstage at the Fillmore East. Crosby didn't jump like Clark; he was pushed. McGuinn and Hillman drove to Crosby's house and fired him.

Michael Clarke left shortly after. The classic Byrds were done—the quintet was now a duo, Chris Hillman and Roger McGuinn.

The Byrds' three years of animosity, jealousy, petty power struggles, and shameless ego horseshit produced six top-fifty albums and eight top-forty singles from 1965 to 1968. During that time, along with the Velvet Underground and the Beach Boys, the Byrds were arguably the best band in America. (Bob Dylan was a guy, not a band. Motown was a factory.)

Like the Velvets and the Beach Boys, forty years later their recorded output remains instantly identifiable, wholly original, and fun to listen to. No matter how many bands imitated them over those forty years, the Byrds' sound remains their own. Yet they thrived on hostility and competition. Among their traditions, after big chiming guitars and three-part harmony, mutual distrust was foremost.

To replace Michael Clarke, Chris Hillman brought in his cousin Kevin Kelley. Kelley was the former drummer of the Rising Sons, a band featuring blues scholar Taj Mahal and slide-guitar virtuoso Ry Cooder. After Crosby's firing, Gene Clark tried playing with the Byrds again. He lasted three weeks. Clark couldn't bear the stress of flying or of being onstage, where he was famously awkward.

McGuinn, Hillman, and Kelley gigged as a trio, but a trio couldn't do justice to their studio material. They needed a fourth player before embarking on a major tour.

In February 1968 the Byrds, in the person of McGuinn and Hillman, signed a new seven-year deal with Columbia Records. "The Byrds were a good brand name and I have a built-in perseverance," McGuinn said. "Chris and I needed a rhythm section, but we weren't looking for partners. Anybody we got would be a sideman."

THERE IS NO UNIFIED THEORY of how Gram first met the various Byrds. Several versions exist, all contradicting one another. Gram and Chris both told of meeting in a bank-teller line when, according to Gram, "we were both wearing the same blue jeans and the same look on our faces." In an interview with the Long Ryders' guitarist and Gram chronicler Sid Griffin, Hillman said, "Gram and I had the same manager-accountant [Larry Spector]. I knew Gram. I ran into him in a Beverly Hills bank and asked him if he wanted to join the Byrds. He passed the tryout and became a member." In a later interview, Hillman said, "I'd heard of the Submarine Band without hearing them. But I knew their guitarist, Bob Buchanan, and I found Gram to be charming and motivated. So I said, 'C'mon down to rehearsal tonight and see what works out.'" It's a tidy story, but nothing was ever that simple with the Byrds.

Late-seventies Betty Boop soundalike chanteuse Genevieve Waite claims that her husband, Mamas & the Papas founder John Phillips, recommended Gram to Roger McGuinn. Road manager Jimmi Seiter maintains that bank-line meetings were hardly necessary: "We already knew Gram. We had met him at parties and social things. I had seen him sing at the Palomino. Gram didn't fit where the music was at the time; he had a different feel. He was introduced to the band as a potential player, but there were problems with Lee Hazlewood. Gram wasn't a hundred percent free.

"But he seemed like a natural for two reasons: The first was financial. He was under contract or pseudo-contract to Hazlewood, so he wasn't free to sign and that was an advantage." An advantage for the Byrds—Gram could not demand to be made a full partner. "McGuinn was Machiavellian,"

Seiter says. "McGuinn preferred a guy who couldn't or wouldn't sign a contract." The second reason was that Hillman's manager, Larry Spector, also represented Gram.

Gram, along with guitarist Clarence White, had filled in for Clark at a few local L.A. shows. McGuinn was looking for hired sidekicks, a role that neither Gram nor White was keen to fill.

Chris Hillman had known Clarence White since they were teenagers. Hillman's Scottsville Squirrel Barkers were playing a similar round of venues as White's bluegrass combo, the Kentucky Colonels. In late 1966, Hillman invited White to the sessions for *Younger Than Yesterday.* White provided a country feel on two Hillman songs, "Time Between" and "The Girl with No Name." After the Colonels, White made a name for himself at the rough country bar Chequers. He was a singular stylist and guitar innovator and a fingerpicker of blinding technical facility and speed. At the same time, he produced a unique tone and played with great soul. Rare among lightning pickers, White disliked showing off and was known for his restraint. He seldom changed expression onstage and stood dead still, inscrutable, as his fingers flew.

White also coinvented, with future Byrd drummer/banjoist Gene Parsons, a B-string bender that enabled an electric guitar to sound like a pedal steel. The Parsons-White String Bender attaches to the back of a guitar and allows the player to bend a string up an entire tone.

"We did some rehearsals and there were ongoing gigs booked," a source remembers. "Clarence White filled in on a couple, but McGuinn wouldn't commit to Clarence as a partner. He wanted to pay Clarence, Gram, and Kevin [Kelley] as salaried musicians. Clarence didn't want to do that. He was fabulous from the first moment that he walked into rehearsal, but they couldn't work that out because McGuinn was being stubborn."

Gram didn't mind being salaried. He had money; he wanted the biggest possible platform for his ambitions. "At the time Parsons auditioned for the Byrds," Johnny Rogan writes, "McGuinn was still intent on projecting the group into the area of future electronics and jazz. Parsons thrilled Chris Hillman by singing Buck Owens' 'Under Your Spell Again.' While ignoring Parsons' other qualities, McGuinn accepted him solely on the strength of his keyboard abilities. 'When I hired Gram Parsons, it was as a jazz pianist. I had no idea that he was a Hank Williams character. He pretended to be a jazz player.'"

Interviewed by Jan Donkers in November 1972, Gram said, "It wasn't a replacement they were looking for, they needed another musician, a keyboard man. I'd come out [to L.A.] because Peter Fonda had recorded a song I wrote and I got connected to the same business manager. So they said, 'Why don't you come down and try playing our stuff?' They liked it. Chris and I immediately got together as far as country music, because he had been wanting to do something like that."

"We hit it off right away," McGuinn says. "I was looking for a piano player. He sat down and played and it sounded pretty good—I was thinking of going in the direction of 'Eight Miles High,' that jazz-fusion direction. He played Floyd Cramer–style and thought he could learn to play like McCoy Tyner. I had no idea he was a singer and songwriter. It went for about two hours of Gram being Gram the piano player to pulling out his Gibson guitar and playing his fave Merle Haggard songs. I thought, 'This guy's got talent.' Not knowing that he and Chris were in cahoots and going to sway the whole thing into country music."

"I knew this music," Hillman said. "I was playing in hardcore country bars south of L.A. with a fake ID when I was nineteen. But Gram understood the music, too, and he knew how to sing it. Roger and I were a little jaded at that point, having been around the block. But Gram was ambitious, full of vinegar and ready to go.

"I sang harmony with Gram and I went, 'Wow!' So I said to McGuinn, 'I think we should hire this guy.' Gram came in with such a strong love of country music that that's when we made the decision to go to Nashville and cut *Sweetheart of the Rodeo*."

If McGuinn is telling the truth, he's the only musician in L.A. who was impressed by Gram's piano playing. Gram could never play on the level of John Coltrane sideman McCoy Tyner. He was an average musician at best. But at that moment Gram was perfect for the Byrds.

The Byrds were a great empire in decline. They had ruled the world, launched countless bands by inspiration, demonstrated new directions and inflections for rock and songwriting, either created or popularized the L.A. hippie style that would become America's hippie style, and sold a shitload of records. But now, without songwriting machine Gene Clark or harmony god David Crosby—and without Crosby's insufferable but motivating willpower—McGuinn and Hillman were unsure of their next step. Gram knew what he wanted. His desire gave McGuinn and Hillman direction.

"We were in limbo," Hillman said. "We were looking at each other thinking, 'We're the last guys left and we don't know where this is going.' And here comes Gram."

"Gram's selling point was that country sold worldwide, in massive numbers," McGuinn said. "And because he was a rich kid, Gram had this confidence that he could do anything he wanted and people would go along. He was used to getting his way."

"Along comes Gram, hopping and skipping." Jimmi Seiter says. "He didn't realize the level of animosity between these guys."

"Roger and Chris had an aggressive negative energy going with them all the time," Byrds roadie Carlos Bernal says. "Gram was always laid-back. He had the songs, he was a singer, but he only had to play acoustic guitar. It was the other guys' band—he never had anything to worry about. If he brought an idea up, it was only a suggestion. If Chris and Roger said no . . . then oh, well."

Hillman was thrilled with Gram's understanding of country. Chris and Gram played songs from Hillman's bluegrass days, and McGuinn gave up on his original idea for the group's next album, which was more like stoned musings than a workable plan. McGuinn had conceived an album reflecting the history of the twentieth century in music, running from old-time string songs to an electronic finale. McGuinn said, "My original idea for *Sweetheart of the Rodeo* was to do a double album, a chronological album, starting out with old-timey music—not bluegrass, but pre-bluegrass, dulcimers and Appalachian stuff. Then get into the advanced 1930s version of string music, and move it up to more modern country, the forties and fifties, with pedal-steel guitar. Do the evolution of that kind of music. Then bring it up into electronic music and a kind of space music, and go into futuristic music." McGuinn's description is oddly reminiscent of the International Submarine Band's concert featuring the theremin and onstage sculpting.

In an interview thirty-five years after recording *Sweetheart of the Rodeo*, McGuinn said, "It wasn't my intention to do a full-out country band and never do anything else . . . part of the fun of the Byrds was changing the musical direction all the time. We started with folk rock and raga and put in the Moog synthesizer. Some people called it psychedelic but I thought of it as Coltrane and [sitar master Ravi] Shankar. I was into experimentation and did not want to get involved with pure country."

Unsurprisingly, Hillman's version places himself at the forefront of the idea of a country album. "People forget things," he complained to Sid Griffin, insisting that he was "doing country things" with the Byrds long before

Gram showed up, including using Clarence White's guitar playing on the two songs on *Younger Than Yesterday.*

"When Gram came into the group," Hillman went on, "I had an ally in country music, someone who understood and grew up with it. He did help us into a full-out attempt at doing country." The Byrds recorded a country song on their second album in 1965, "A Satisfied Mind." Hillman insists that it was "a Porter Wagoner hit I brought into the group. I was always trying to get the band to play country songs, but David Crosby always objected."

Hillman's protestations only underline how pervasive yet boring the contest to claim the title of First to Play Country Rock can be. His examples do not make a strong case. The two tracks on which he used Clarence White, "Girl with No Name" and "Time Between," sound like Beatles-inflected Byrds songs, in straight-ahead 2/4 time with trademark folkie Byrds harmony. The down-home aspect comes from Clarence White's instantly recognizable guitar noodling as he fingerpicks bluegrass banjo lines on his Telecaster. "A Satisfied Mind" is arranged as a folkie dirge and has no perceptible country flavor.

Hillman does give Gram credit for connecting to the soul of country. "There's a certain way to play it, a certain lifestyle you have to feel and understand," he said. "It's an easy form of music from a technical stand-point. But you've got to feel the music, and that's one thing about Gram Parsons. He understood. He felt it. He knew what it meant."

With typical bravado—and in typical denial of how the real world functions—Gram dropped by Hazlewood's office in February 1968. Gram told Hazlewood that he had joined the Byrds and would record no more for Lee Hazlewood International. Hazlewood cited Gram's signed contract. He refused to release Gram without compensation and drove a tough bargain. Hazlewood demanded Gram relinquish all royalties from *Safe at Home* and rights to the name International Submarine Band. Gram agreed not only for himself, but on behalf of his bandmates as well. Hazlewood fleeced Gram and the band but good.

Gram went into the meeting with no attorney, no apparent concern about being paid for his labors, and no apparent understanding that the issue didn't have to be settled that very day. By giving up the Sub Band name, he left his former bandmates unable to tour as the ISB, with no way to support their own album. Gram's money protected him from the consequences of his whims; his bandmates had to pay the price of his folly.

"Hazlewood heard about [Gram sitting in with the Byrds] and threatened Gram with a lawsuit," John Nuese says. "Gram said we could alleviate the suit by relinquishing the name ISB and giving the album rights to Hazlewood. We were reluctant, but there didn't seem to be much happening with the album. Hazlewood canceled the publicity. So even though 'Blue Eyes' was getting airplay in New York, we were left without an album."

"Gram used the ISB as a stepping stone," Bob Buchanan says. "That was the bad side of Gram—he didn't think of the rest of the band."

With even the most elementary strategy and a halfway decent lawyer, Gram could have done better. He wanted instant resolution, and Hazlewood gave it to him. Gram feared any delay in working with the Byrds. He made a bargain with the devil to save time and protect his opportunity.

"Gram was enthusiastic and happy," Ian Dunlop says. "It was a major move forward. Being promoted to the Byrds came at the right time for him. I was amazed. I felt, 'Holy mackerel, man, you haven't finished the goddamn record with the other band!' The Byrds were big but still . . . Gram would jump on anything new until it didn't pan out or the novelty wore off. Of course, the ISB were left sitting on a dud and were trying to figure out what to do.

"With Gram's energy and enthusiasm, you could see how he made the sale [of more fundamental, straight-ahead country] to the Byrds. His enthusiasm was contagious, because he always went into everything believing without reservations."

"There was a unity as well, a love for this music," McGuinn said. "We got into the whole country thing: playing poker every day, drinking whiskey, wearing cowboy hats and boots."

"Chris and I, both being into country music, formed an alliance and persuaded the others that the Byrds should start playing country," Gram said. "McGuinn, being a perceptive fellow, saw that it would help the act, and he started sticking me out front."

McGuinn wasn't entirely convinced. He had been the avatar of at least two influential rock movements: folk rock and what became known as raga rock—rock with Indian or spacey influences, a precursor to the psychedelic explosion. He feared losing power to Hillman if the music went in Hillman's direction.

The Byrds were under contractual deadline for a new record. March of 1968 found them in Nashville preparing to make *Sweetheart of the Rodeo*. Driven by newfound passion and Gram's meticulous sense of detail when it came to style or presentation, the Byrds were determined to record country as authentically as possible.

THE BYRDS HIRED a diverse team to run the control board. Gary Usher came to Nashville as their producer. Usher had cowritten surfer and hot rod anthems with Brian Wilson and produced *Younger Than Yesterday* and *The Notorious Byrd Brothers*. The engineers were Charlie Bragg and Roy Halee. Halee produced four influential folk-rock albums for Simon and Garfunkel including *Bridge over Troubled Water* and *Parsley, Sage, Rosemary and Thyme*. Bragg engineered *John Wesley Harding*, Bob Dylan's 1967 foray into Nashville session recording, and 1969's *Nashville Skyline*, Dylan's country-rock album.

Part of the lure of Nashville for McGuinn was the opportunity to work with Charlie Bragg. In opposition to the usual lush Nashville soundscape, Bragg had helped create a clean, stripped-down, "live" sound for Dylan. "Nashville was where Bragg did all of his work," Carlos Bernal says, "and you don't want to take a guy away from where he's comfortable—the studios he's used to, the sound boards, et cetera. So we went."

"We were the first rock band to record in Nashville," Jimmi Seiter rightfully claims. "Bob Dylan used Nashville players. We went there as a band and used only a couple Nashville session guys. It freaked everybody out when we showed up in their backyard. There were no longhairs in Nashville but us. Gram didn't even have long hair then. His hair was to the ears, not much longer."

In a sign of respect and sacrifice that may be difficult to properly appreciate forty years later, the Byrds cut off their hair. The band wanted to be accepted by Nashville. Hillman's visual trademark was a huge halo of rising, Dylanesque curls. They were gone. McGuinn looked like he was back with the Limeliters, and Gram had shorter hair than during his senior year at Bolles. The haircuts were a powerful act of solidarity with the country scene. They meant shedding identity and that instant connection to anyone else with long hair. It meant masquerading as part of a political and social culture the band despised, or at least had built an identity reacting against.

Not that anyone in Nashville showed appreciation for the gesture. As much hair as they cut, it still wasn't enough. "Their hair was long enough," Carlos Bernal says, "to where there were situations that caused trouble from the hair."

The band recruited fiddle, banjo, guitar, songwriting, and producing savant John Hartford to play guitar and banjo on the sessions. Hartford wrote the hit "Gentle on My Mind"; Glen Campbell's version won four Grammies and a lifetime of financial freedom for Hartford. He was a regular on Campbell's and the Smothers Brothers' TV variety shows. Like Clarence White, Hartford was an unpretentious picker of limitless ability and steady mien. He moved easily between the country and rock worlds.

Lloyd Green was hired to play pedal steel. A lifelong Nashville session man, Green played with Faron Young, Ferlin Husky, Porter Wagoner, Charley Pride, and George Jones. He was accustomed to as many as five hundred session dates a year. "I was aware of their popularity," Green later recalled of the Byrds gig, "so I knew this was going to be special." Roy Huskey came in to help on bass. Clarence White's brother Roland, who played mandolin and guitar with Bill Monroe and with the Kentucky Colonels, was also on hand, though he is not credited on the album. Roland served as a keeping-the-scene-cool presence and jamming partner.

Jimmi Seiter was skeptical of the whole enterprise. "Gary Usher wasn't a country producer," he points out. "He was a pop producer who produced a bunch of pop shit in L.A.," including records by the Hondells, the Surfaris, the L.A. Teens, and the Castells. "He wasn't into country music, so he didn't understand it, whereas Gram and Hillman did. McGuinn didn't understand it either, so it was a new bag for him. It was a new bag for the producer, and here we were. We did it anyway."

According to Carlos Bernal, Usher knew how to work with the band: "He had a lot of experience. When problems came up, he was good at greasing the tracks to make things move forward as opposed to joining in some difficulty."

Nashville cut the newcomers no slack. "In Nashville the engineers come in at nine A.M.," Jimmi Seiter says, "and at ten the band is all there and by ten-fifteen they've got a track done. That's the way they're used to doing it, and it wasn't that way with us. I tried to explain, but these guys didn't get it until it actually happened. I told them the band probably wouldn't show up until twelve-thirty or one o'clock. They're like, 'What!? That's a whole session!' At lunchtime the engineers just left. I would turn around at twelve-thirty and couldn't get into the control room. They locked me out and were gone."

Other differences between L.A. and Nashville emerged. "The technical capability of the facilities was not up to the L.A. scene," Seiter says. "The equipment was backward. They didn't know how to use it, either, which was weird for us. Engineers kept sneaking in to see how we were doing things, because the Byrds were renowned for their recording technique."

"There was some snobbery," Carlos Bernal says. "When we first walked into the studio, it was awkward and rigid. Here were city kids coming into country and bluegrass land. There was all this music and noise going on in the studio when we walked in, and then all of a sudden it was quiet. There we were . . . silence. When Roland White broke the chill by starting to play, it was like, Welcome home."

McGuinn brought no original songs to the sessions. "I didn't have any country songs," he later explained. McGuinn had two unreleased Dylan songs, 'You Ain't Going Nowhere' and 'Nothing Was Delivered.' Both were first recorded during the 1967 sessions with Dylan and the Band that were released eight years later as *The Basement Tapes*. A Dylan bootleg, *The Great White Wonder*, released in 1968, contained both songs, but the tracks were new to all but the most fervent Dylanites. McGuinn sang lead on both. As Hillman noted, "The Dylan songs usually went to Roger."

"Nowhere" and "Nothing" serve to bookend the album. Both are arranged as slightly more complex versions of the drums-bass-guitar-pedal-steel simplicity of Dylan's (and Charlie Bragg's) *John Wesley Harding*. "Nowhere" should suggest stasis, but Lloyd Green's steel lines carry too much joy and optimism for that. The "Nowhere" of the title, through the usual Dylan alchemy, becomes a center of domestic bliss. There's a jaunty happiness that suggests contentment. But it's the end of the last verse that properly introduces the album: "Strap yourself to a tree with roots," McGuinn sings. And on the songs that follow, the band does just that.

"Nothing Was Delivered" is a different story. Reputedly the tale of a drug messenger who failed to show up with the goods, "Nothing" rumbles along with an ominous feel. McGuinn's quavering vocal demands retribution. The closing chorus finishes the album on an unsettling, contradictory note. While embracing nihilism ("Nothing is best") over the transcendence of music, it closes as parody of the smarmy we-love-you-God-bless finish to every country concert: "Take care of yourself / And get plenty of rest."

Even McGuinn, it seems, was not immune to the irony-driven ambivalence of Gram's aesthetic. Although McGuinn picked the Dylan songs, they align perfectly with Gram's embrace of pleasure and doom.

There was little strife in the studio. The sessions were set up to go quickly. Gram seized the momentum. "There was never an aggressive or over-the-top dynamic that I saw," roadie Carlos Bernal says, "and I was there all the time."

"We got along okay—we were like brothers, that give and take, that flowing friendship that goes in and out," McGuinn says. "It was like a sibling relationship. There was no power struggle. I was the leader of the band and the big brother, but Gram grew more convinced it was his territory as things went along. He convinced Chris to go along with him."

A decision was made to record only rough vocals in Nashville. The instrumental tracks proved rigorous enough. In the town of Nashville cats, where everyone sitting in an all-night coffee shop could play, the band wanted to show they could stand on their own. "Players are players," Jimmi Seiter says. "At the time, Hillman was the best player in the band and he messed around on the mandolin with Roland White. They realized that McGuinn wasn't a guitar player, that Kevin Kelley wasn't that good a drummer, and that Chris wasn't a good bass player—he was better on the mandolin. And Gram . . . he wasn't a player at all. The word had gone out. The Nashville musicians knew the truth, but they also knew the guys were real and nice."

Since in the Nashville view the boys were suspect players, they gained what acceptance they could by not coming off like stars.

On March 9 the band recorded Dylan's "You Ain't Going Nowhere" and the song that Gram had written with Bob Buchanan, "Hickory Wind." "Hickory Wind" would prove as pure a distillation of Gram's songwriting themes and forms as he ever wrote. "The psychology of Gram sliding into Roger's position started happening," Seiter says, "because, hey, this was Gram's world. As 'Hickory Wind' proved the first day."

The song, set in 3/4 waltz time, features dense steel guitar and moaning dobro, with John Hartford's bedrock fiddle. "Nashville sessions are regimented," says pedal-steel player Lloyd Green. "I was used to doing an intro to a song, laying out for eight bars, then filling in different spots. It was pretty formulaic. My first question to Roger and Gram was, 'Where do you want me to fill in?' And in unison they said, 'Everywhere.' I said, 'Are you serious? Nobody ever asked me to do that!'"

"Wind" begins as an expression of nostalgic yearning, a yearning for a place that most likely never existed, the piercing ache for a homeland of the soul. Proof that the place yearned for lives only in the imagination is the rending lyric, "I always pretend / That I'm getting the feel of hickory wind." The singer is so far from his roots, real or imaginary, that he must pretend to feel the gentle breath of wherever passes for home.

As with the Gram songs that ring most true, "Wind" shifts to honest autobiography. The song's narrator finds perhaps more of a dead end in decadent pleasures than did Gram at the time. The song ends as country classics do, with the supposedly unsophisticated country boy realizing that the big city—the necessary universe for his ambition—has corrupted him irredeemably. In the final lines Gram calls out for a simpler time. The heartbreaking music makes clear that simplicity is no longer available to him. Only the yearning remains.

The alternative take released on the remastered two-CD *Sweetheart* set features stripped-down production with no Hartford fiddle or breathless, Nashville-backing choir on the chorus (or is that Chris Hillman?). The only musicians are the Byrds quartet with Lloyd Green's steel. Hillman's thick, plucked bass dominates the mix; he plays lead lines that intertwine with McGuinn's strummed acoustic guitar. The effect is rock and roll, and much less moving. The song's hurt requires the Byrds' mix of ferocious, subdued picking and Nashville lushness. The choir, the dobro, the fiddle, and the more decorative pedal steel metaphorize the rich emotions of the lyric. They add sentiment, but not sentimentality, to the singer's anguish.

On March 11 the Byrds cut Gram's "Lazy Days"; March 12, Woody Guthrie's "Pretty Boy Floyd"; and March 13, the traditional Appalachian holler "Pretty Polly," arranged by McGuinn and Hillman, and "I Am a Pilgrim," another traditional bluegrass number arranged by the two founding Byrds.

"Pretty Boy Floyd" is an outlaw narrative with a Guthrie populist theme. The Depression turns Pretty Boy into an outlaw and he wages war on the corrupt bankers. It's a Robin Hood folk tale that McGuinn understands perfectly; he does a stellar job on the vocals. John Hartford picks the banjo with a steady driving clip-clop that evokes the pure Nashville picking of guitarist Chet Atkins. Hillman, singing over a mournful bluegrass arrangement of guitar, bass, fiddle, banjo, and dobro, embraces the spiritual yearnings of "I Am a Pilgrim." Hillman later complained about his vocals on this record, but they're moving and appropriate. Chris Hillman is a deeply underappreciated singer; he has a gift for straightforward lyrical statement with an undercurrent of ambivalence that suits the old-timey material well. Hartford's understated fiddle on both songs anchors them to their respective traditional roots. The last line of "Pilgrim" functions in emotional contradiction to its meaning: "I've got a home in that yonder city, good Lord / That's not, not made by hand." The last words, sung a cappella, illuminate the entire record, reminding the listener that, whatever heaven may be like, here is a world of handmade music.

★ ★ ★

THE NIGHT OF MARCH 13 featured one of the band's more public culture clashes with the world of Nashville: their appearance on Ralph Emery's radio show. "It was horrible," recalls a member of the band's entourage. "CBS insisted that we do this fucking interview with this guy because that's what you had to do to get on the radio. You had to talk to this prick to get on the Grand Ole Opry."

Emery began as an all-night DJ on the fifty-thousand-watt clear-channel powerhouse WJM-AM, which could be heard all over the South, especially at night. Ralph interviewed, and hosted impromptu jam sessions with, Merle Haggard, Loretta Lynn, and everyone else in commercial, establishment country music. He was Country Music Disc Jockey of the Year six times—and in country-music culture, that award meant commercial and cultural clout. Emery's best-known country-music television talk show was *Nashville Now*, which aired on WTBS-TV.

To the Byrds Emery was, in the entourage member's words, "a redneck motherfucker, made no bones about it, and he hated us." When Emery expressed his disdain, "Gram took him to task on the air," although exactly what Gram said has been lost to time. Ralph Emery's collected radio interviews, all forty-six discs' worth, do not include the Byrds appearance.

Gram fared better in the Nashville demimonde than he did interacting with its most mainstream DJ. After work in the studio wrapped, Gram would sneak off to perform solo in country bars around town. "Gram would go to this club down the street from the hotel," Jimmi Seiter says. "They had an open mike every night, and Gram would get up and sing. Hillman was with him one night and he was like, 'Holy crap! He's gonna sing.' And I was like, 'Fuck, yeah, he sang last night. He'll sing again.' We had a strict rule in the Byrds that whatever music we were recording in the studio was never played live until the record came out or we did it at a live show as a group. It was a hard rule and Gram knew it. I'd go down and there'd be Gram. He'd know half the people in the place. He was singing George Jones and all kinds of country. I don't think he ever sang any of his own stuff."

However welcome Gram was in the seedier nightspots, taking Ralph Emery to task on his own show just wasn't done. Emery was supposed to play the rough-vocal track of "You Ain't Going Nowhere," but refused. Eventually he relented and broadcast the song, but he made sure the band and his audience knew he didn't like it.

The incident showed the Byrds how far they were from the mainstream of the music they were trying to play. The next day, on March 14, perhaps feeling how poorly they'd been served by Emery, they recorded Tim Hardin's "You Got a Reputation." The stress of working so far from L.A. in every sense was starting to take a toll. Someone present says, "Gary Usher, our producer, didn't travel well. He was taking some weird kind of pills to keep him awake, and it caused him to totally space out. After five days in the studio recording, suddenly he wakes up. He says, 'Let's play back some stuff.' And I play back and he looks at me and says, 'When did we record that?'"

"Usher was on codeine," Carlos Bernal says, "but everyone was whacked out all the time. Usher had a bad cold and took medicine prescribed by a doctor. These things happen."

Doctor-prescribed pharmaceuticals weren't the only forms of mind-altering the band preferred. "We went to the Exit/In," Carlos says, "which was a restaurant, night club, bar [later featured in Robert Altman's film *Nashville*]. It was a teeny place with a fifteen-stool bar. They had a pool table, but mainly the action happened in the parking lot out back. Guys would show up and we'd play pool and have drinks and, of course, because we were the Hollywood boys they'd mess with us. 'Oh, you think you can play fast? Take one of these mini-whites.' 'Wait till you snort this! Then you're gonna play fast.' They opened up the trunk of a car and wrapped in a towel was this glass jug. In that glass jug was real white lightning, moonshine. We freaked, looking around for cops. They said, 'Shut up! Shut up! Calm down, calm down.' Apparently moonshine was a bigger nondeal in Nashville than having other drugs anywhere else. So they bust it out and unwrap it. It was one of those classic jugs that you throw over your shoulder. I asked what we were supposed to do, because I was always naïve and a couple of steps behind. Roland White said, 'Well, what you do is you take one shot and you won't like it. Then you have another shot and you still won't like it. But when you have the third shot you'll like it, and then you've got to stop.'

"So we did that, and it was amazing. The first one was unbelievable. It was like drinking kerosene. The second one didn't change that much, but the third one was not so abrasive. The next thing I know—after having enjoyed several of them—they pulled the bottle from me and I woke up the next morning in the hotel." On awakening, Bernal learned that he had filled the hotel hallway and the sound engineer's room from floor to ceiling with fire-extinguisher foam. Carlos had no memory of the deed. "So I don't drink white lightning anymore," he concludes.

On March 15 the Byrds made history. They performed on the legendary Grand Ole Opry stage. They were the first rock band to perform in Ryman Auditorium and the first to be broadcast on the Grand Ole Opry radio show. The atmosphere was hostile. The Opry had little use for hippies and less for country usurpers or pretenders. That the Byrds were successful and famous in another idiom only made their reception in Nashville that much more guarded.

"The Grand Ole Opry was cold—we were interlopers and they were leery of us," McGuinn says. "They didn't know what we were about. They didn't know if we were sincere or making fun of their music. They knew we were hippies, and there was a good deal of polarity. It was like the stigma of the McCarthy hearings—you were a pinko and dangerous to have around. Columbia Records was able to leverage it—they had country artists. Gram was ecstatic—his grandmother used to listen to the Opry all the time. For him it was like going to Nirvana."

"To let you know how hostile the audience was," Hillman says, "they were shouting things like 'Tweet tweet' and 'Cut your hair!'" Jimmi Seiter recalls, "Roland White was backstage to support us, and Lloyd Green came to make sure the other musicians treated us decently. We only had these two players in the whole Nashville scene to hang out with us and let everyone know that we were good old boys and to leave us alone." Hillman adds, "As for Lloyd Green, it took a lot of balls to get up onstage with a band of long-haired weirdo strangers in town, knowing his friends and neighbors were so antagonistic."

"We had relatively short hair at the time," McGuinn says. "Short by L.A. standards, but long by New York standards and insane by Nashville standards. We were wearing suit jackets, and I played Gram's Gibson [acoustic] guitar so as not to freak anybody out with Rickenbacker guitars," the iconic folk-rock twelve- and six-string electrics that were a trademark of the Byrds' look and jingle-jangle sound. "We were told to do Merle Haggard songs and agreed."

Jimmi Seiter recalls that Tompall Glaser, a singer-songwriter who was acting as master of ceremonies, came over "like he's our old friend. He shakes hands and says, 'What songs are you going to do?' And they tell him." The band was supposed to do Merle Haggard's "Sing Me Back Home" and "Life in Prison." Glaser announced "Sing Me Back Home" and the band performed to an unimpressed, blank-faced crowd. Lloyd Green heard booing. "I was so embarrassed I wanted to crawl off the stage," he recalls. "I didn't believe they'd get such rude, redneck treatment. I felt sadness that people would do that to musicians because of their hair."

Glaser came back out to announce the second song. The song list was sacrosanct. The Opry went out live, and song lengths were key for scheduling other songs, commercials, and the skits and interviews that came between. Nobody messed with the Opry's schedule.

"Gram took the reins," Hillman says. "He was right smack into that: Here I am on the Opry! I'm Hank Williams! And he went with it. He played the role out." McGuinn says, "At the last minute Gram changed his mind and said, 'This is for my grandma. We're gonna do a song I wrote, 'Hickory Wind.'"

"You could see Glaser turn red from the neck up," Seiter says. "He was fucking livid. He thought we told him the wrong songs on purpose. It was a big deal for us to be on the Opry, of course. Everyone was excited about it. And a little bit nervous. But Gram took over."

"Gram decided, out of nowhere, to do 'Hickory Wind,' which I thought was interesting," Hillman says. "But it incensed Tompall Glaser, and he screamed at Gram afterwards. They were taking themselves way too seriously, and they still do. We played and sang good, and Gram was dedicating a song to his grandmother, which was right on the money for the Opry."

On the most hallowed stage in country music, Gram's instincts for nailing the moment did not fail him. He made the Byrds and the Opry do things his way. Gram made sure that he played his song, his original, at the Grand Ole Opry. The shameless courage of the moment, the hubris, only adds to its legendary stature.

Like most of Gram's cultural breakthroughs, the aftermath proved an anticlimax. The audience did not rise as one, shouting and applauding, recognizing with a lightning bolt of illumination that this hippie boy had true country soul. Nor was there a riot of anti-Byrds tomato-throwing. The band left the stage and another took its place. That night echoed the many firsts in Gram's career: None brought him any greater commercial success or acclaim. All added to his myth once he was dead.

Today that moment is a cornerstone of Gram Parsons mythology. Even the Opry places his performance at number thirty-three among the Eighty Greatest Moments in Opry History. At the time the gig was nothing more than a curiosity.

The Byrds: Kevin Kelley, Gram Parsons, Roger McGuinn, and Chris Hillman onstage at the Grand Ole Opry. (© Michael Ochs Archive)

THIRTEEN

SWEETHEART
OF THE RODEO

AFTER THE OPRY, THE BYRDS LEFT NASHVILLE FOR A TOUR OF EAST COAST college shows. Interviewed at the time, McGuinn insisted that he was still in charge. "Gram has added a whole chunk of country and we're going to let him do his thing," he said. "But Chris and I are still there. We're the containers of the old sound, and the new members augment that sound."

In an interview with Pete Johnson, McGuinn described getting a standing ovation at Michigan State and "good reviews" at other schools. He praised Gram, saying, "He likes to work with us, and we like to tour with him. I never had more fun than we had this last tour." McGuinn was still clinging to his idea about the final shape of the new album, telling Johnson that it would be a double LP with a total of twenty-two songs. "The first half will be bluegrass with banjo and the second half will be modern country," McGuinn said. "Then we'll move to the Moog synthesizer with voice for the third quarter, so it'll be a chronological structure, from old-time to modern to space-age."

As McGuinn talked about album concepts that no one else in the band shared, the Byrds watched Gram emerge from his chrysalis. "When he first came to the Byrds, Gram had short hair and looked collegiate," Jimmi Seiter says. "He started to change immediately. He had never been out there like this before. He'd never done anything successful. It was the first time he'd been onstage in a big environment, and he didn't do it all smoothly. He was nervous, but he dealt with it."

Another member of the Byrds' entourage says, "Gram played electric piano and slowly creeped over to acoustic guitar. Roger didn't want that, because he was the only guitarist and didn't want to compete.

"They played 'Tambourine Man' with a piano, which they had never done before. Slowly but surely Gram picked up the acoustic guitar and sang. It was quite good, but you could see McGuinn's uneasiness about this upstart country guy stepping up. McGuinn was trying to hold on, and Hillman was trying to pull it away from him by making the Byrds a country band. Gram was right in there with Chris. Kevin [Kelley, the drummer] was a country player and Chris' cousin, so McGuinn was losing control. He always tried to push the other side, the folk side, the Byrds side, so it wasn't a bad mix. But Gram didn't like doing the Byrds songs. That was obvious from the first day.

"For many people, if somebody said, 'Would you like to be one of the Byrds?' Fuck! Of course! Who wouldn't jump at that? But in Gram's case it was a step. He was a bit in awe of being onstage with that many people in the audience, but he wasn't in awe of being in the Byrds."

"He did a few shows and slowly his style changed," Carlos Bernal says. "He started with a scarf around the neck. It was the beginning of the guy emerging. He comes in wearing turtlenecks and nice shirts. And all of a sudden his hair is going wild. But McGuinn made it obvious to Gram that he didn't want him stepping up."

"I thought I hired a piano player," McGuinn says. "He turned out to be a monster in sheep's clothing. And he exploded out of that sheep's clothing. Good God! It's George Jones in a sequin suit!"

The band returned to L.A. and spoke to T. Wilym Grein about recording in Nashville and their new sound. According to Grein, Gram, munching on "the remains of a five-hour-old hamburger," explained that the band's main objective was its own musical development, which "includes exposing ourselves to every possible type of music—pop, rock, classical, and country." The band described their performance at the Opry to Grein as something of a triumph, and Kevin Kelley called country "probably the biggest and most honest [facet of music] we have today." The band expressed eagerness to break away from the clichés and *longueurs* of the Los Angeles rock world. "I'm terribly disillusioned," Hillman complained about Southern California's ubiquitous herd followers who put style ahead of musicianship. "They think because they wear an Indian morning coat that they're saying something, that they're making the scene."

"That's right," Gram chimed in. "To be honest about wearing an Indian morning coat, you must be an Indian in the morning."

On March 28 the new Byrds lineup debuted at Ciro's, with Jay Dee Maness on pedal steel. The gig was a good-bye party for rock PR agent extraordinaire Derek Taylor, who had managed the Byrds' public relations from the beginning. The set list included classic Byrds material: "Chimes of Freedom," "Mr. Tambourine Man," and "Eight Miles High." Gene Clark clambered onstage for a couple of numbers. "Gene was drunk," Derek Taylor says. "He sang a few songs with them but stayed up there too long."

"McGuinn's old lady was tugging on [Gene], trying to get him off the stage," recalls one of the roadies. "She lost hold of him. He slipped, fell backward over an amplifier, and his head hit hard on the stage. The look in his eyes was incredible. He jumped up, ran off the stage, straight through people, and gone. We didn't see him for months after that. Gene's life was shattered when he left the group. All of a sudden he was walking around Hollywood and he wasn't a Byrd anymore. That hit him hard. He came to many gigs drunk as a skunk. He had to be kept away from the band when they were onstage."

Jerry Hopkins mentioned Gram in his favorable *Rolling Stone* review of the show, even if he didn't spell his name right: "They appear secure in their country milieu. Graham sings often and sings well, sharing lead voice with Roger."

A member of the Byrds backstage crew introduced Gram to a key L.A. rock drug connection. "I turned Gram on to the Beverly Hills doctor," the crew member says. "He had clients like John Phillips. In later years he got busted for selling cocaine in huge amounts. You went into his office and he'd have his prescription pad in his hand and would say, 'Okay, what do you want?' I was introduced by the Byrds office. They said, 'He's with the Byrds. He needs some drugs to take on the road.' I got uppers and downers and Valiums and Placidils. Quaaludes weren't happening yet. The idea was you'd leave his office and go to multiple pharmacies. He used to sell me bottles of pills. It was a cash-only deal. Gram would go every month. He loved this pill that was blue on one end, red on the other"—Tuinal, a barbiturate sold as a sleeping pill. "This was when Gram started doing that stuff."

On April 2 Columbia released the single "You Ain't Going Nowhere," with vocals by McGuinn, backed by "Artificial Energy" from the Byrds album, *The Notorious Byrd Brothers*. The single peaked at number seventy-four. In a publicity interview for the single, McGuinn said, "If you want to go into the psychological reasoning behind it, it's sort of a backlash from the psychedelic scene, which I'm tired of. We were influential in starting that stuff before it was appreciated, and a year later other groups made a great success with it. I think that we can offer country music with what we know from other fields. It's basically a simple music but will accept a little change every once in a while. Gram worked with us on this last tour and he was great. The audience loved him."

In Southern California the Byrds fell into their normal schedule. They did shows in Santa Barbara or San Francisco and recorded in L.A. They appeared on *The Glen Campbell Goodtime Hour*, *The Smothers Brothers Comedy Hour*, and a local TV pop show, *Ninth Street West*. Gram was already proving less than reliable. "A couple of times Gram didn't come," Jimmi Seiter says. "He was not real aggressive about being on time. I'd have to call him and call him. Then I finally put it on Hillman: 'Hillman, get that fucking guy!'"

The *Sweetheart* sessions continued. On April 4 the band cut "Life in Prison," a favorite Merle Haggard song of Gram's. Gram and McGuinn each recorded solo lead vocals. On April 15 they recorded "You Don't Miss Your Water" by William Bell. Though he's not credited on the album or the remastered bonus-track CD, Clarence White plays on "Water." Again, both Roger and Gram cut solo lead vocals.

Perhaps McGuinn and producer Gary Usher suspected there might be legal trouble from Hazlewood over Gram's contract. Or maybe Usher just wanted to hear who sounded better. As always, there were issues of band power politics. "Whoever sang lead on the songs was there not because of what we could do legally," Usher says, "but because that's how we wanted to spice up the album. McGuinn was edgy that Parsons was getting too much out of this thing. McGuinn wanted to keep the Byrds in the Byrds' pocket, which at that point in time was him and Chris. McGuinn didn't want *Sweetheart* to turn into a Gram Parsons album. You don't take a hit group and inject a new singer for no reason. It was also a question of how long Gram Parsons would be in the group . . . he had stars in his eyes. I knew he'd be there for the album, but he didn't seem to be the one who could fit into that framework with McGuinn and Hillman for long."

"He was a rich kid," McGuinn later said, "which meant that he was already a star. It was as though Mick Jagger had joined the band."

For the L.A. sessions, Gram brought in Earl Ball and Jay Dee Maness. Earl Ball found it disorienting to go from working with Buck Owens in the afternoon to the Byrds in the evening. "When you drive over from Capitol Studios to Columbia," he says, "you had to make an adjustment mentally. I was going from a high pressure—I had to dress up for the Owens sessions—to a loose kind of thing.

"With Buck Owens we had to get at least three songs done in our three-hour period. Then I'd go over and record with the Byrds, where if you got one song all night you were doing good. And Don Rich [Buck Owens' guitarist and arranger] was insistent about everybody being in tune, everybody having the intros together, and checking the tuning. Ken Nelson was producing. The two of them were real perfectionists. I'd get over to the Byrds, and first thing they'd do was get high and try to tune their guitars. That was a challenge. I'd show up when I was supposed to show up, and sometimes me and the engineer would be the only people there.

"But I adapt to my surroundings pretty well. I would have smoked some pot with them but I thought, 'I'll be lost, too.' So I would stay straight, because there were enough people over the edge without me getting there with them."

"There were people setting up the studio, getting things ready to go," Jay Dee Maness says. "I guess the band was the darlings of that label at the time, and they let them do as they pleased. They would literally show up in a Volkswagen bus. Like you see in the movies—they'd have their arms hanging out the windows, hollerin'.

"But I learned something important from that record: that steel guitar can fit into any kind of music, if it's allowed."

Maness retains contradictory memories about who was in charge. "Roger McGuinn was the leader of the Byrds, when I was with them," he said in one interview. "He knew what he was doing with the twelve-string, and we'd fall in behind him. He helped hold things together."

But Maness told John Einarson that "Gram was the boss of the whole thing." Hillman he dismissed as "only the bass player," saying that Roger and Gram effectively ran the band. He added, "Gram was calling the shots. He wasn't nasty about it. He was a strong personality."

On April 17 they cut "You're Still on My Mind" by Luke McDaniel, with Gram and Roger singing separate lead tracks and Clarence White on guitar. Jay Dee Maness insists they cut sixty takes of "You're Still on My Mind"; the version that appears on the remastered CD is take forty-three. "There were a lot of takes, a lot of overdubbing," Earl Ball says. A week later they recorded Cindy Walker's "Blue Canadian Rockies," which had been a hit for both Gene Autry and Jim Reeves. Hillman sang lead, with McGuinn on harmonies. On May 1 the band cut the E. D. Hewitt–R. J. Ledford instrumental "All I Have Are Memories." Clarence White plays on the track. The remastered CD features a version with Kevin Kelley adding lead vocals. On May 27 they cut "One Hundred Years from Now," a Gram original.

As THE BYRDS WERE RECORDING *Sweetheart*, Lee Hazlewood released the Submarine Band's *Safe at Home*. Gram was not above pulling a prep-school gag on Suzi Jane Hokom; the album sleeve lists her last name as Hokum, a polite Southern word for bullshit. Jay Dee Maness' credit reads "Good Ole Jay Dee."

"It was a great crossover opportunity had it not been for the problems between Gram and Lee," Suzi Jane Hokom says. "It came down to an ego thing. Lee had a difficult time with this bright and articulate young man. Gram was too smart and too talented. Lee didn't like him. We threw a couple of huge parties and everybody was hot for the band, but the LP never got promoted. Lee didn't know the finer points of marketing and promotion."

The LHI press release accompanying the record did break new ground in one respect, introducing the term "hippie-billy." It touted the album as "unique and interesting," faint praise indeed. The release goes on: "We would like to emphasize that we believe this LP has a great deal of Pop potential. It was not intended for C&W stations only. Lee Hazlewood has believed for some time that hippie-billy was going to be a trend in the music industry. This is in part borne out by the recent Byrds and Bob Dylan albums. We feel that the International Submarine Band belongs in the same category." It closes by begging for "your consideration and open-minded audition."

Chris Hillman dismissed the record as a beginner's work. "I look at that album as being fluff now, lightweight," he says. "Gram had not quite developed into the soulful guy he was going to be." The few reviews the record received were respectful. *Los Angeles Times* writer Pete Johnson wrote, "Here we have a youthful quartet restyling existing songs and enriching the medium with their own writing . . . done up purty authentic with a vitality not always found in traditional country performers. . . . Parsons has appeared with the Byrds on several recent occasions, bolstering their incursions into country music, a liaison which could cause difficulty for the ISB." When Johnson wrote his review, he didn't know that Gram was a Byrd and the ISB was history.

Hit Parader magazine wrote, "The band is dealing with country-and-western music honestly. No gimmicks. Although the Buckaroos are much more exciting, the Submarines [*sic*] band is at least exploring an area that most groups wouldn't touch."

A year after the album appeared, Robert Christgau wrote a rueful assessment in *The Village Voice:* "The cover depicted a typical rock group, four smiling longhairs, but inside was skillful country music. The album was an assertion of continuity from Arthur Crudup to Gram Parsons, with country music and all its simple virtues square in the center. In retrospect it seems a good record and a brilliant conception. Yet at the time I listened to it twice and filed it in the closet. Parsons, with his deep respect for country music, played it too straight. He needed the canted approach of the Byrds, who combine respect with critical distance."

Safe at Home never broke into the top two hundred. There would be no live gigs for promotion: The ISB no longer existed. Gram wouldn't earn a cent from its sales and the label, the one party with a vested financial interest, was immobilized by incompetence or hostility. The International Submarine Band was finished.

The Byrds discovered that country was a hard sell to rock audiences. "People didn't take to the band's sound," says Jimmi Seiter. "Obviously the band could make the hits sound like the hits, but people weren't too thrilled with the country thing. Nowadays people talk about it like it's no big deal, but it was a bold step. It was taking its toll on McGuinn. All of a sudden *Sweetheart of the Rodeo* wasn't a McGuinn album, and he didn't care for that. Nowadays it's a big deal, but then it was like, 'Country album? What are they doing?'"

"Our fans were heartbroken that we'd sold out to the enemy," McGuinn says. "Politically, country music represented the right-wing redneck people who liked guns. We were the pioneers—with arrows in our backs."

Gram's response was to push deeper into country. He wanted to add a pedal-steel player to the Byrds' live shows. McGuinn resisted, but he was under pressure from Hillman as well. Gram asked Jay Dee, but Maness had a gig at the Aces and preferred his burgeoning L.A. session career to weekend gigs on the road. Hillman and Gram lobbied McGuinn to bring in "Sneaky" Pete Kleinow.

"Gram and Chris took over at that stage of the game," McGuinn says. "They brought it into the country thing. That wasn't my idea, but I went along with it because it sounded fun. It was totally their trip. They actually wanted to fire me and get Sneaky Pete in my place. In essence, they later did this by getting the Flying Burrito Brothers."

"Slowly Gram started, I won't say taking over, but nudging Roger aside," says a member of the band's entourage. "Gram was a dynamic performer. He could make you cry at the drop of a hat. At the same time he could piss you off. He had that way about him. McGuinn had a different kind of charisma. Gram was the center of the stage and Hillman was stage right, where Hillman always was. Chris several times tried to get between Roger and Gram to keep their personalities apart, but he never succeeded."

The power shift happened behind the scenes, but was driven by the band's onstage behavior. "David Crosby used to talk [onstage], but he would say bullshit," the same source explains. "When David was gone, McGuinn had to fall into that role, and it took him a while to get to it. Gram pushed him, because Gram would talk. I never heard Roger say anything to Gram about, 'Back off, you're the new guy.' I never heard that and if [Roger] did it, I don't think he would have done it in front of anybody. McGuinn would have had Hillman do it."

Along with bad feelings, the Byrds were awash in drugs. "I had a snifter of cocaine," Carlos Bernal says, "and Gram asked me if I had powder. I had a bottle with a little glass cap and a long glass tube. We called them high hats. They were about an inch and a half high. I gave him my high hat to go to the bathroom to have a snort. He comes back from the bathroom and gives me the bottle and it was empty. He said, 'Oh, man, it fell in the toilet.' The bottle wasn't wet, but there was no blow in it. He took it. He snorted all my blow or put it in a thimble or something.

"But it didn't matter, because I had a whole briefcase full of coke. That was during a time when there was money for promotion and tours. That stopped during the late seventies. The shows themselves had to make a profit, but at that time we flew around first-class and in limousines. My briefcase never had less than three or four bottles of prescription Dexedrine and a California Turnaround, a black pill—mainly speed, but with these little black dots in it to level you off. You could drive from Los Angeles to New York and then turn around and drive back to L.A. That's why they called it a California Turnaround. Ask any truck driver. . . . We always took *The Physician's Desk Reference* on the road, so we could read about our pills."

The Byrds flew to Paris in May 1968 to begin their European tour. Roger McGuinn and Chris Hillman brought their wives. Gram refused to let Nancy travel; he insisted she stay home with Polly. "They started to drift apart when Gram began hanging out with music and musicians more than his newfound love," Bob Buchanan says. "And Nancy produced a baby, which Gram saw as a burden. Nancy wanted to go on the road. Gram convinced her that the baby shouldn't be away from home. Nancy wanted to be around famous people. She wanted to be in the center of things. She sought attention and Gram wasn't giving it to her."

The band played Paris, Rome, and London. McGuinn had prevailed: The Byrds did not tour with a pedal-steel player. Longtime Hillman associate and Gene Clark bandmate Doug Dillard came along as a "temporary member." Gene Clark and Dillard had been recording together in L.A.; their first record would be released in the fall of 1968. "I used to say Doug was the best banjo player in the world," Jim Dickson says, "and he'd say, 'You gotta stop saying that, Jim. I'm about fourth or fifth.' He was phenomenal." Jimmi Seiter says, "He's a wonderful guy and he could drink anybody I ever met under the table."

Dillard was another Southern California virtuoso looking for a new idiom. His band the Dillards included his brother Randy on guitar. In 1969 he would record the seminal new-grass country-folk-rock album *The Fantastic Expedition of Dillard & Clark*, with Gene Clark singing, Hillman on mandolin, and ex-Byrd Michael Clarke playing drums. *Fantastic Expedition* would prove a pervasive influence on the emerging Southern Californian country-rock scene.

"You Ain't Going Nowhere" was released as a European single in support of the Byrds tour. The song features a steel guitar, but Gram's participation was minimal. On a May 2 gig at the Piper Club in Rome, McGuinn can be heard saying sarcastically after almost every song, "Thank you, country-music lovers." Out of a ten-song set, Gram sang lead on only two: "You Don't Miss Your Water" and "Hickory Wind."

Gram, Kevin Kelley, Doug Dillard, Jimmi Seiter, and Carlos Bernal hung out together as the tour traveled by train; Hillman and McGuinn had their wives for company. Gram would take his guitar to the bar car and play for whomever was riding along. "Gram would perform," Jimmi Seiter says, "then go back to his first-class cabin to work on songs. We'd smoke hash, open the windows, hang out. We had a great time."

McGuinn and Hillman were interviewed extensively about the "new sound" by the European rock press. Gram was given short shrift. It was a tough discovery for Gram that his creative leadership in the studio meant nothing to the outside world. Byrds chronicler Johnny Rogan describes McGuinn revealing to the press that he was the only Byrd to play on the group's smash "Mr. Tambourine Man": "In this way, McGuinn asserted his importance as the man who formulated the group's sound, and nobody could doubt that he was still King Byrd."

Tour audiences wanted to hear the Byrds' hits and were politely indifferent to the new country songs. This helped solidify McGuinn's feelings of control. By dipping into the band's back catalog and demonstrating the range of their material, McGuinn presented the Byrds as a historic force in rock. Gram was the new boy, a momentary aberration. As McGuinn's confidence returned, he kept Gram on a tighter leash onstage. Playing the older material meant McGuinn sang lead.

IN MID-MAY, the Byrds played the Middle Earth, a significant London rock venue. Housed in a large basement warehouse space, the Middle Earth featured a light show, an audience dressed in cutting-edge hippie-rock style, the foremost bands, and a lot of drugs. The Byrds played their usual set and included Buck Owens' "Under Your Spell Again" and "Excuse Me (I Think I've Got a Heartache)" by Owens and Harlan Howard. The show was fateful for Gram because the Rolling Stones were in the audience. "I was really going to see Roger," Stones guitarist Keith Richards says. "Gram was with him and we hit it off right away."

That was the understatement of the era. Keith and Gram became instant best friends, music collaborators, and drug partners.

At the heart of the Stones had always been the struggle to be Keith's best friend. Brian Jones and Keith were the band's core until Mick Jagger slowly usurped Brian. By the time Gram met the Stones, Brian—almost permanently high and musically ineffectual—was on his way out. Mick wanted no outside collaborators and was ferociously protective of his friendship with Keith. The Stones were in flux. Their musical direction was slightly uncertain. Their venture into psychedelia, November 1967's *Their Satanic Majesties Request*, was a forced effort and sold poorly. The band regarded it as an unsuccessful sellout, a mistaken side step from playing the music they knew and loved. Psychedelia did not suit them. The Stones, in ethos and expression, were not hippies. Peace and love were not their métier. The Stones moved toward a darker, blues-based, stripped-down, acoustic sound for their next album, November 1968's *Beggars Banquet*. Keith became intrigued with American roots music that was not born from the blues.

After the show, Mick Jagger and Keith took the Byrds in their Rolls-Royce to Stonehenge. Photographer Michael Cooper, who shot the covers for both *Sgt. Pepper's Lonely Hearts Club Band* and *Their Satanic Majesties Request*, came along and took psychedelic portraits. They spent a rainy, cold all-nighter among the megalithic monuments. All reports of the evening list Johnnie Walker Black whiskey as one ingredient; others cite LSD as well.

Jagger and Richards tried to talk McGuinn and Gram out of an upcoming Byrds tour of South Africa. To protest apartheid and South Africa's racist policies, most aware American and U.K. music acts were boycotting the country. McGuinn claimed to have his reasons for going. He was friends with black South African expatriate vocalist Miriam Makeba; she had told him about apartheid and he wanted to see the country for himself. Gram was surprisingly ignorant of the issue and listened to Keith avidly. "Gram was like a puppy dog with them. It was sort of embarrassing, like bringing your kid brother on a date," Chris Hillman says.

Keith remembers it differently. "He was a lovely, warm, down-to-earth guy," he says of Gram. "He didn't know much about the situation in South Africa, so Anita [Pallenberg, Keith's exquisite, glamorous, somewhat viperish German-Italian girlfriend, an intimidating force of fashion, street smarts, and pure sex] and I explained it to him."

"Gram immediately fell in with Mick and Keith," Hillman says. "He was obsessed with the idea of being with the Rolling Stones, if not actually in the band."

"Since we obviously hooked right away as friends, the next thing, being musicians, we started to find out what music we both liked," Keith says. "Gram had a great love for Lefty Frizzell, for Felice and Boudleaux Bryant. A lot of time was spent talking about songwriting and what a song was supposed to do."

Keith and Gram became inseparable. If he wasn't working with the Byrds, Gram was with Keith. "He has a great ear for country music and basically producing and playing guitar and getting sounds out of the studio," Gram enthuses. "Keith is great."

"The reason Gram and I were together so much more than other musicians is because I wanted to learn what he had to offer," Keith continues. "Gram and I shared this instinctive affinity for the real South."

Keith biographer Barbara Charone writes that Gram profoundly affected Keith, "teaching him countless guitar tunings and rare country songs belonging to his heritage." As with the Byrds, Gram's trust-fund-baby status set him apart from the usual hangers-on. "Parsons was one of the few people who had no calculated reasons for depending on the Stones," Charone writes, because he "was a wealthy boy who never needed to ask the Stones for financial favors like so many before and so many after him. It was quite easy for Richards to believe that Parsons' friendship was quite genuine."

The Byrds hung out with London's rock elite in a series of all-night clubs. Tony Sanchez captured the atmosphere in *Up and Down with the Rolling Stones:* "I was sipping a scotch in a dark London nightclub called the Speakeasy, waiting for my girlfriend, a nightclub dancer, to show up. It was two in the morning, and the club was crowded with the young and beautiful men and women who had turned London, momentarily, into the hip capital of the Western world. 'Swinging London' may be a dusty cliché now. But then it was a reality we were all working hard to perpetuate. At clubs like the Speakeasy everyone tries to appear supercool but spends most of the evening looking around for famous faces. You can tell when a star arrives because everyone—even the dancers—starts gaping."

"There would be music all the time and wonderful food and great booze and drugs and handsome guys and beautiful girls," Carlos Bernal says. "It was models and rock and roll. Drugs and booze. Chop up some rails, drink some Courvoisier, and be visited by good-looking people. The sun never came up and never set on those nightclubs."

The Byrds did a show at Blaises, a private basement club and a center of the groovy London scene. "I had heard that all the guys in the music industry in London would be there," Jimmi Seiter says. "And they were. Everybody in every band was there. The Who were there, the Kinks were there. The dressing room was one of those little storage rooms where they keep the trash cans. It was underneath the grates in the street above. People are standing waiting to get into the show and we're down below tuning up and getting ready. We did the Middle Earth in London and there was hardly anybody who mattered [in the audience] because they all came to Blaises. It was intimate. It was cool."

It was druggie. Carlos Bernal tells of a British guitarist who arrived to bring everyone "high hats" of heroin and cocaine, "but he left forgetting to give out the cocaine. The band didn't realize they had heroin in the high hats. The show was puke city. I don't remember which night this was, but it was like Gene Clark always said, 'Serve the song well and the song will not let you down,' so the only net to grab on to was the song. They played and they puked. The audience was thrilled. The songs were a little slower, but the magic was never gone. Everybody took turns [being sick]. The music was extremely loud and the people were screaming, so it wasn't a big deal for the [the various musicians] to stop playing for a few bars."

"They were playing all kinds of stuff," Jimmi Seiter says. "Stuff I hadn't even heard. Chris and Gram would go, 'Let's do this,' and the band would be like, 'What?' It came out pretty well. McGuinn knew those songs. They were doing traditional country songs and Dillard knew them all, so that was cool."

Gram seemed to neither chase girls after gigs nor turn them away. "He seemed initially a quiet, polite, country gentleman," Carlos says. "He was a wonderful vocalist, wrote great songs, was a beautiful talent on stage. But later on it seemed like he was a little dull. He poured all his energy out in writing great songs. The girls thought he was pretty and they were always coming around, Gram this and Gram that. But as far as to hang out with, to have a good time and do anything interesting and exciting, he wasn't the guy to do it with.

"On dozens of occasions we were roommates on the road, two guys in each room. He was a magnet onstage, but afterwards in the hotel room, when the girls were around, he didn't know that much. About how to chat a girl up—what to say, what to do. I had to show him a couple times—'Gram, you have to be a little more aggressive, say something. Start with playing them the song . . .' But I guess he wasn't experienced that way. If he didn't have that songwriting, guitar playing, he'd be kind of a dull guy. I mean even an amoeba knows what to do when a cute amoeba grabs him by the amoeba parts. He wouldn't take the lead."

Gram expected women to come to him. Maybe he never explained his technique to Carlos, who mistook Gram's *le jet majesté* as indifference. Gram's preference for cocaine and Tuinals could have added to both his reclusiveness and to what Bernal naïvely regarded as passivity.

Gram and McGuinn couldn't have gotten along too badly in London. They took the time to write a serious fuck-you song about Ralph Emery, "Drug Store Truck Drivin' Man." It would appear on *Dr. Byrds and Mr. Hyde*, the follow-up to *Sweetheart of the Rodeo*, with McGuinn singing lead. Though they're listed as coauthors, the nasty wit seems more like Gram's sensibility than McGuinn's. The song expresses bafflement that a man as immersed in country music as Emery could be so prejudiced, stiff-necked, and stupid. Gram never recorded the song but often played it live.

After the tour on the flight back to New York, Gram discovered a small brick of hashish in his guitar case. Reluctant to crumble it down the airplane toilet, he opened Jimmi Seiter's briefcase as the road manager slept and hid the hash inside.

In New York, U.S. customs found a gift-wrapped switchblade Seiter had bought for a friend. That was enough—along with Seiter's long hair— to trigger a strip and cavity search. As customs went through Seiter's bags, the band abandoned him, piling into a rented limo and heading for their hotel. They knew Gram had stashed the hash on Seiter and wanted to be far, far away when it was found.

Customs found bottles of prescription drugs and a great deal of cash. Happily for Seiter, the cash was in an envelope with band contracts and pay-ment checks. As part of the search, all the linings were torn out of his lug-gage. Somehow customs missed the hashish. Seiter wasn't arrested. He was turned loose and caught a cab to the band's hotel. "I get to the hotel, check in, and have them take the luggage up to my room," Seiter says. "I'm barely inside when there's a knock on the door. It's Gram. 'So?' 'So?' 'Did they find it?' 'Did they find what?' 'Did they find the hash?' 'What hash?' 'I put a block of hash in your briefcase.' 'You did what? You mother-fucker!'

"Hillman's right there with him. All they want is the hash. I said, 'You think I'm gonna give you the hash? That I brought into the country? Go fuck yourself!'" It turned out that through a lucky accident the hash, a small block about two by three inches, had fallen into one of the envelopes in Jimmi's briefcase, the only one customs hadn't opened. "It was a miracle," Seiter says. "I would have been in jail in New York for twenty years. The next morning I went to this Halliburton shop nearby and bought a combination-lock Halliburton aluminum briefcase. And I changed my combo weekly."

In this tale lie the roots of the *Spinal Tap* cliché of the road manager with his inevitable Halliburton aluminum briefcase. The Halliburton apparently exists not to protect its contents from the outside world, but to protect the road manager from his band.

Gram came home to California to find Nancy in the throes of post-partum depression. She needed his support but also pushed him away. Bob Buchanan was living next door and recognized the building tension: "She was pretty strung out because there she was with a baby and Gram needed a nurse. He needed somebody to take care of him because he was outrageous but helpless. Totally helpless in a lot of areas. So Nancy knew that what she envisioned—a wedding, a home life, et cetera—was not coming true. Gram was off flitting around doing the Byrds thing. She was having constant arguments with him on the phone. I could hear her yelling."

As he neglected Nancy and his baby daughter, Polly, Gram ramped up his drug intake. Nancy not only wanted more attention from Gram but also feared, legitimately, that his late nights and increased drug use were endangering him. The first cries to "rescue Gram from himself" began to be raised among his L.A. friends.

"As far as Nancy and the baby, as far as how to take care of them, Gram had no clue," Bob Buchanan says. "Give her some money and tell her to go shopping. Yell at her when she got in trouble. She got in trouble a lot because that brought her affection. He was too busy with his own self. If there was something that he enjoyed or someone that he liked, he'd give them attention. Nancy and the baby were a load to bear."

With the release of *Sweetheart of the Rodeo* imminent, Columbia Records insisted that some of the vocals be rerecorded. The official Byrds version of the rerecording, the explanation that originated with McGuinn, is that Lee Hazlewood International threatened Columbia with a lawsuit because Gram was still under contract to Hazlewood. The result, this version goes, was that Columbia told the Byrds to erase Gram's vocals. By the time the parties settled, only the original vocal tracks for "Hickory Wind" remained.

McGuinn broke the news to Gram. Gram never fully believed that erasing his vocals was Columbia's idea; instead he blamed McGuinn. "He thought it was Roger's own idea," Byrds producer Terry Melcher says. "But Parsons had a lot of things in life distorted. He and McGuinn were not friends for a while because of this."

"Things came out well until this thing about the lawsuit," Gram said. "They had to pull a few things out of the can that we weren't going to use. Things like 'Life in Prison' and 'You're Still on My Mind.' Those are great songs, but we did them as warm-up numbers. We could have done them a lot better. They were about to scratch 'Hickory Wind' when somebody ran in with a piece of paper. It was the last one they saved."

The early-eighties discovery in the Columbia archives of two more Gram lead vocals undermines the credibility of McGuinn's explanation. These outtakes had not been purged. Gram's vocal tracks for "Life in

Prison," "The Christian Life," and "One Hundred Years from Now" were also found.

In *Are You Ready for the Country*, Peter Doggett observes: "Roger didn't help his case when he revealed that he'd also dubbed a vocal onto 'Hickory Wind' but elected to use the original instead. Presumably Gram's renditions of 'You Don't Miss Your Water' and 'The Christian Life' could also have been included. . . . Twenty years after the sessions Gary Usher rekindled the controversy. In his revised account, LHI's claims were raised during the March '68 sessions in Nashville and had been settled by the time he and McGuinn assembled the final album."

"It is true that some of Parsons' leads were overdubbed because of legal problems, but those problems were resolved," Gary Usher says. "Once we were down in Nashville, the attorneys back in Los Angeles were able to work that out."

Later, both McGuinn and Gram acknowledged that the legal issues were a cover for the real struggle over the band's direction.

"There was genuine concern that we would be sued if we kept Gram's vocals," McGuinn says. "We put mine on and then the contractual dispute went away, so we got Gram's back and kept some of his. Basically it was a misunderstanding. I wouldn't have had any involvement at all if it had been up to Gram. I would have been a harmony singer. He was taking over the band, so we couldn't let that happen. That's why I sang a couple of songs anyway. That was the balance."

In a 1972 interview, Gram said, "Columbia had thought that for some reason they were going to get sued because of my release [agreement] with Lee Hazlewood. And so on a few songs they overdubbed completely things that shouldn't have been overdubbed, and my voice was used in the background as a guide. And it gave it too much of that old Byrds sound, which we were fighting against at that time. Not because it wasn't any good, but because there was all this other stuff to work with and you didn't need to look back, as Bob Dylan once sort of said."

A Byrds insider doesn't buy the McGuinn version. "It becomes pretty obvious that McGuinn was threatened by Gram," he says. "On the Grand Ole Opry, Gram sang both songs. All throughout that whole album he shined. But did they use his vocals? No. They used a bullshit excuse that he was signed to Lee Hazlewood and therefore they couldn't, blah blah blah."

Many years later McGuinn offered a little of that old-school country humble: "I didn't enjoy [overdubbing the vocals]. It was trying to fill in, and that's why we put them on the Byrds box set and the *Sweetheart* reissues. I always knew Gram's vocals were better. I was a parody of that."

No great album is made without its share of petty backbiting, credit-stealing, and turning the other guys' tracks down in the mix. The erasing of Gram's vocals on an album of such historic and aesthetic importance demonstrates how threatened McGuinn and his allies were. Whether McGuinn's motive was protection against a lawsuit or protection against being usurped, wiping Gram from the tracks is, even by the tawdry standards of rock and roll, an astonishing attempt at artistic murder. It's even more astonishing when viewed through the prism of the times: McGuinn had no idea of *Sweetheart*'s importance when he recorded the record. From his descriptions, he regarded the record as another piece of product, one with a new direction. McGuinn's paranoia over Gram seems all the more mean-spirited given that another Byrds album would be coming down the pike in six months.

The erasing of Gram's vocals either helped exacerbate or caused the growing tension in the Byrds. Gram got into more and more arguments with McGuinn and even Hillman. The band rehearsed less and less. Some think the Byrds' lazy attitude toward rehearsal solidified Gram's increasingly poor work habits. Others think Gram's poor work habits helped encourage the other Byrds to be even more lax about rehearsing.

"The Bay Area bands thought we were a 'Hollywood band' because we never rehearsed," a member of the Byrds organization says. "Those Bay Area bands [the Grateful Dead, Jefferson Airplane, Quicksilver Messenger Service, Steve Miller Band, Moby Grape] always rehearsed, always played together. We tried [before Gram joined], and it ended up a fistfight. . . . The first time they had rehearsals [again] was when Gram joined."

The Byrds' lack of discipline dovetailed with Gram's growing narcissism. Jimmi Seiter's characterization reflects the complaints of all of Gram's future bandmates: "Gram's the kind of guy you could not get to do anything because he's got millions of dollars in the bank coming to him every six months. It would take something or someone to motivate him. Otherwise he would do nothing. He didn't mind rehearsing as long as it was a song he wrote. He wanted his songs to be good on the stage. Beyond that, when things bored him he would walk away. He did it time and again. He would only do something as long as it pleased him. There was no drive for him to succeed at anything. He entered the Byrds because Larry Spector put him there. Gram kind of fit, but he kind of didn't. And as soon as Gram started to become Gram, McGuinn took it personal."

Gram had the gift of charm; he had an equally powerful knack for irritation. "Gram had a beautiful [Gibson] J-200 guitar," Carlos Bernal says. "There was an argument in rehearsal—Gram was saying something to Chris, Chris was saying something back, and I guess maybe Gram was being a little more stubborn. Gram said one more thing and Chris punched him in the guitar.

"I had to take it to the Art Valdez guitar shop. He put Gram's J-200 back together, but for quite a while it had Chris Hillman's fist hole in it. Gram played it anyhow. Gram was lucky that Chris didn't punch him in the face. Gram was a thin, younger guy. Chris was the same age but a more roughed-out, tougher, stronger, bass-playing sort of person."

With the album's release approaching and their upcoming European tour to be followed by the South African shows, Gram made demands. He wanted more money—he was still on salary—and even suggested he get individual billing. "They had had number one records," Carlos Bernal says, "and he's in the middle of all of this and thinking, 'I want more. I deserve more. I am more.'"

In June 1968, when Polly was six months old, Gram and Nancy visited Bob and Bonnie in New Orleans.

Bob had settled into a new groove. After several fruitless trips with Bonnie to Cartegena, Honduras, and Guatemala, he recognized that his pre-stressed concrete empire had no future. He took a public relations job with the Bechtel Corporation, which offered a steady income and the means to entertain as he preferred. Bob bought a big house on Pine Street near Ottoman Park with an expansive, fenced-in backyard and a swimming pool. Every Saturday and Sunday, fifty to seventy-five people gathered in Bob's yard. The mix included friends from Baton Rouge, routinely a senator or a governor, and a pool filled with children and surrounded by lounging grown-ups. Bob kept a commercial refrigerator full of steaks and had the kitchen redesigned for large parties. No matter how many guests filled the yard, Bob would prepare steak for everyone. He prolonged his parties by blackmailing his guests with the mirage of an impending meal. If a dinner was planned for eight o'clock, the food usually wouldn't be served until ten-thirty. "Everybody came, and everybody complained, 'When are we going to eat?'" Bob's friend Walter Lanaux says. "Bob served late because he knew when they ate, they'd leave. And he liked having them around."

Bob's penchant for exotic pets was still in force. In addition to two Welsh corgis and a cat, he acquired an otter. "I could have killed him when he brought that home," Bonnie says. "In fact, he didn't bring it home. He said, 'Look in the paper, they've got otters for sale.' I told him, 'We are not getting an otter.' He said okay and called me that evening to meet him for a drink at the Lake Pontchartrain Hotel. I went down and he had this otter on the bar. Of course the otter was having a ball."

The otter, Sebastian by name, took up residence in the Parsons back-yard. He had the run of the pool, playing with the kids and nipping at their toes. If Sebastian got too aggressive, the children would carry him upstairs and leave him in a full bathtub while they swam. Bob put a dog door in the kitchen for the otter, who would make his own way into the house for break-fast. The Parsons later discovered that Sebastian had another morning rou-tine: He had tunneled a path under the backyard fence, and every day after breakfast would wait out front for the mailman. Sebastian would "sort of hump down the sidewalk," Bonnie says, and follow the mailman along his neighborhood route. His chore completed, Sebastian would hump home and rest by the pool. The mail route proved to be Sebastian's undoing. A young girl asked the mailman if she could have Sebastian. The mailman, apparently not knowing to whom the otter belonged, said yes. The girl took Sebastian out to the country, where her not-so-domesticated farm dogs killed him. "He was party-oriented," Bonnie Muma says. "Everybody would feed him little tidbits, and he would go right up to anyone or anything. He thought he was a dog."

Bob also had a mynah bird that was famous for saying, "Saints tickets for sale, Saints tickets for sale," referring to the National Football League franchise in New Orleans. Bob liked to take the bird out of its cage at parties and let it travel from shoulder to shoulder throughout the evening.

The day they arrived in New Orleans, Gram and Nancy announced they were going on a weeklong cruise and asked the Parsonses to look after Polly. "Bob and I had talked about it, and we thought the trip was to try to heal their relationship," Bonnie says. The discord between the two was obvious. "Nancy was harder on him than anyone else," Bonnie recalls. "She was protective of the baby. If he'd pick Polly up when she was asleep Nancy would say, 'Put her down.' They were nipping at each other all the time."

Bob drove the couple down to the dock and saw them off. "It was a cruise, on one of the cruise boats," Bonnie says. "They were supposed to be gone a week.

"And then they showed up three months later. Of course the baby was fine. I remember Bob being mad, but I knew Gram was going through a rough time then."

Where Nancy disappeared to remains unclear. The Byrds were returning to England prior to their scheduled South Africa tour, so Gram went to London. Nancy neither accompanied him nor returned alone to New Orleans to reclaim their daughter. When Gram returned, they traveled together to pick up Polly.

On July 7, the Byrds, with Gram, played Sound '68, a charity event at London's Royal Albert Hall. The bill included the Move, the Easybeats, Joe Cocker, and the Bonzo Dog Doo-Dah Band. The audience featured more headliners than the stage; watching the show were Brian Jones, Mick Jagger, Keith Richards, two of the Beatles, and Jimi Hendrix.

The Byrds opened with "So You Want to Be a Rock and Roll Star." They played "Eight Miles High" and Gram sang "Sing Me Back Home." "Chimes of Freedom" closed their set. The glamorous crowd greeted them with cheers. "There was a tremendous reception for the Byrds," Nick Logan wrote in the *New Musical Express* under the headline BYRDS' LONG FLY WORTH IT, adding that "a good selection of the 4,000 audience was there to see them alone, and let them know it."

The next day, the band was scheduled to leave for South Africa. Gram did not want to go. He insisted his newfound understanding of apartheid—provided by Keith—made it impossible for him to play there. "Something people don't know about me is that I was brought up with a Negro as a brother," Gram later told the *Seattle Helix*. "Like all Southern families, we had maids and servants, a whole family that took care of us. Sammy Dixon was a little older than me, and he lived and grew up with me, so I learned at a real close level that segregation was just not it."

Despite the high motives he invoked, everyone understood Gram was not going to separate from Keith Richards or do anything Keith disapproved of. "He said that he didn't want to go to South Africa because of the segregation," Roger McGuinn later said, "but what he really wanted to do was hang out with the Rolling Stones."

Carlos Bernal agrees. "The way he left was interesting," he says. "We were checking out of the hotel and loading our cars to go to the airport. Gram's clothes and luggage and everything was in the car, and everybody else was in the car, too—Chris Hillman, Kevin Kelley, Roger McGuinn, and myself. I'm looking around: 'Where's Gram?' Roger, Chris, and Kevin say,

'Where's Gram?' And I say, 'Well, I don't know. All of his stuff's here. Let me go find out.' I go up to his room and Gram says, 'I'm not going.' I mean, the motor's running and we are on our way to the airport and I say, 'What do you mean you're not going?'

"'I'm going to stay here,' he says. I said, 'Well, okay.' I went down and let Roger and Chris know that he wasn't coming. I guess they must have had a feeling, 'cause it didn't take long for them to say, 'Okay, screw that. We'll go without him.' I said, 'What about his luggage and all that stuff?' They said, 'Put it on the curb.'

"We put Gram's stuff on the curb, drove off, and went to South Africa."

Gram was off the tour and out of the band. He was done with the Byrds and they with him.

The way Gram quit was notable. He did not march into McGuinn's hotel room with a declaration, as with Lee Hazlewood. Gram left the Byrds by omission. He quit passively—by refusing to leave his room.

In a contemporaneous newspaper account, Gram painted himself as a noble protester standing up to his ex-bandmates' corrupt commercialism. "I knew right off I didn't want to go. I stood firmly on my convictions," he said. The other Byrds "thought it unprofessional of me not to go to South Africa," he added. "I thought it was shortsighted [confirming the tour], without finding out about the South Africa situation first." The article noted that Gram had already formed a new group that he described as a "Southern soul group playing country- and gospel-oriented music with steel guitar." According to the article, "Roger (Jim) McGuinn and Chris Hillman" had no comment. And that their South African tour enjoyed "the approval of the [South African] Government."

"Gram pulled the race card and said he didn't want to go," McGuinn says. "He flew to England with that in mind. So he quit—leaving us with three guys. Carlos Bernal, our road manager, who was not a proficient guitar player [stepped in]. The results were less than professional. Gram painted me as a racist. It was a dirty trick."

Whatever their good intentions might have been, the Byrds ended up playing to segregated audiences only. The tour lost them a shitload of money. Gram's passive-aggressive ducking out at the last minute still rankles the band. "He thought he was more important than the Byrds," Hillman says. "He knew we were going to South Africa long before England. Why the sudden announcement?"

A gossip item in a teenybopper magazine highlighted the band politics that lay behind the geopolitics. After reporting that "short-term Byrd" Gram Parsons was out of the band and that Clarence White would fill in, the anonymous writer added, "I sometimes wonder why they don't call themselves McGuinn and Hillman and hire backup musicians for gigs and records. That's essentially what they've been doing."

GRAM'S TIME with the Byrds was over, only six months after it began. The Gram Byrds era was no different from any other in terms of power struggles and internal resentments. If Gram quit the band like a fifth grader, McGuinn was no more mature in his response to Gram. That half year of battling yielded a seminal work of art, one that changed so many perceptions: of what country music could be, of how the walls between American musical forms could be torn down, and of the likely future of rock now that psychedelia had run its course. *Sweetheart of the Rodeo* would bring a new white-roots and rural consciousness into rock and roll. This consciousness remains dominant not so much in rock but in recent commercial country. Following the trail blazed by *Sweetheart*, country music moved ever closer toward rock, as rock began to cannibalize country.

Sweetheart of the Rodeo is, of course, a masterpiece. As befits a masterpiece whose power endures, it ain't perfect. The human striving to make the art is clear throughout—the loose arrangements, the mix of skilled playing and fervent groping, McGuinn's reaching vocals on songs he clearly did not fully understand.

McGuinn's quest to record the twentieth-century arc of white American music is partially achieved. There's a credible mountain madrigal ("I Am a Pilgrim"), a heroic banjo-driven ballad ("Pretty Boy Floyd"), inexplicable folk poetry (either Dylan song), and perverse gospel ("The Christian Life").

Whatever his frustrations with band politics, Gram realized his ambitions in the lineup of songs and arrangements alone. He achieves—as no one ever had—his dreamed-of synthesis of the Nashville and Bakersfield sounds. The songs with full-band accompaniment—"Nowhere," "Pilgrim," "Christian Life," "Water," "You're Still on My Mind," "Hickory Wind," "One Hundred Years from Now," "Blue Canadian Rockies," "Life in Prison," and "Nothing Was Delivered"—feature Bakersfield honky-tonk piano and the raw, aggressive pedal steel of the roadhouse. Yet the production is Nashville rich and smooth, filled with backing choruses and comfy sofas of floating, supportive keyboard and pedal-steel chords. That balance— achieved, one assumes, instinctively—is matched by the perfect scale between instrumentation and lyrical weight. No track is a triumph of songwriting over arrangement; no arrangement has to make up for weak lyrics.

"The Christian Life" probably suffers most from losing Gram's vocals. McGuinn follows Gram's tracks religiously, but he sings the song as if it were a joke. McGuinn sings as if he were removed from the faith of the lyrics and commenting on the poor suckers who would believe such a thing:

> *I won't lose a friend by heeding God's call*
> *For what is a friend who'd want you to fall?*

Gram's rendition is more tender and sincere. "The Christian Life" is Gram's homage to one of the most significant influences on his conceptions of harmony, expressions of sorrow, and lyric writing: the Louvin Brothers. Perhaps the greatest white harmony singers in country history (and a powerful inspiration for the harmonies of another Gram influence, the Everly Brothers), Ira and Charlie Loudermilk came from the Alabama Appalachians; for some reason they regarded Louvin as a more promising stage name. Charlie was the guitarist and the dominant force. Ira played mandolin and became a serious alcoholic. They modeled themselves after other brother acts with stunning two-part harmony: the Monroe Brothers, the Callahan Brothers, the Blue Sky Boys, and the Delmore Brothers. The Delmores were a profound influence; the Louvins recorded a tribute album of Delmore Brothers covers.

The Louvins wrote several songs that became standards, including "The Family Who Prays" and "Broad-Minded." Their shift from gospel to secular came when the tobacco company sponsoring the Grand Ole Opry told the Louvins, "You can't sell tobacco with gospel music." "When I Stop Dreaming" was a top-ten hit in 1955 and was followed by their number one, "I Don't Believe You've Met My Baby," in 1956. They had three other top tens in 1956 and released their album *Tragic Songs of Life*. No record was ever more accurately titled. The naked expression of punishing destiny and broken hearts makes it almost too sad to bear. The Louvins combine a natural gift for hooks and hummable choruses with a merciless Southern Baptist concept of Old Testament punishment. Their embrace of cruel fate and hard-nosed redemption proved a powerful influence on Gram's songwriting.

The Louvins charted steadily through 1962, but never hit number one again. Ira's drinking, Charlie's intransigence, and demands from the label that they try rock and roll led the brothers to go solo in 1963. Charlie released over thirty singles. Ira's alcoholism led to a domestic disagreement with his third wife that ended badly: She shot him. Once recovered, he toured with his fourth wife until they were killed in a car crash, echoing another of the Louvins' unbearably tragic songs, a cover of Roy Acuff's "The Wreck on the Highway."

The Louvins' wackiest, scariest record, *Satan Is Real*, features the brothers on the cover in white evangelist suits with arms outstretched. Behind them a pile of burning tires (Charlie's idea) represents the flames of hell. Towering over the tires, a huge red cardboard Satan stands guard, ready to welcome sinners. The cover would be funny if the brothers' ideas of inescapable damnation weren't sung with such conviction. The music on the album is even more singular and arresting—weirder and more moving—than the cover.

Gram brought "The Christian Life" to the sessions as his connection to a strain of terror and religiosity in traditional country. And as an expression of his dark humor and willingness to mess with people's heads. McGuinn's rendition shows no grasp of the abyss beneath the lyrics.

"Life in Prison" has a kinder fate. Gram's vocals transform the song. The mix of pain and exuberance in his voice suggests a deeper meaning to the lyric than perhaps even Haggard realized. Haggard's version is a straightforward prison lament:

> *My life will be a burden every day*
> *If I could die my pain might go away*

Over Hillman's old-school walking bass line, Earl Ball's deranged whorehouse piano, and Jay Dee Maness' spacey theremin-like steel lines, Gram finds increasing release in the bleak lyrics. He briefly turns into a prep-school boy with his English "rawther" pronunciation, but roars back in full voice to change the song's meaning in the final verse. When Gram sings, "My life will be a burden every day," it's clear that at age twenty-two he has cut to the heart of country music's inescapable pain. It's the pain of self-loathing, the prison of being inside one's own head when one's own head offers no kind of refuge. Gram turns "Life in Prison" into Samuel Beckett: The life that burdens him is his own, the prison his identity. The only release is death: "If I could die, my pain might go away."

The glee that accompanies this discovery is downright perverse, as is the perky pedal-steel finish that belies the horror Gram sings. It's hard to distinguish Gram's joy at singing Merle from his joy at discovering the full extent of his existential trap. The worst has happened, and it turns out not only to be funny but worth celebrating.

The double-CD remastered *Sweetheart* set, like most directors' cuts, only underscores the worthy results that limitation produced. By adding extra cuts to disc one, the producers dilute the impact of the original lineup of songs. Most of what's added proves compelling only as archival material and as a glimpse into the recording process. The one new gem is Tim Hardin's "You Got a Reputation," a taut, stinging put-down driven by a New Orleans backbeat pulse on the organ and a piercing dobro guitar. It's more aligned in sound and theme to the initial release of the album than the other extra cuts.

Gram's version of "You Don't Miss Your Water" is especially lugubrious. McGuinn sings it far more convincingly. As sung by McGuinn, the song is no longer the soul shouter's anthem that Gram strives to re-create, but a folk-country lament, an updating of an Appalachian holler. "Water" was an R&B chestnut and can be moving or tedious depending on the singer. Otis Redding cut the definitive version on 1965's *Otis Blue*. The Byrds could not compete with Otis for emotion. Who could? Wisely, they didn't try. Arranging the song as a country waltz was a masterstroke. Unlike Gram or Hillman, McGuinn did not use his voice to express emotion. He sang deadpan and let the lyrics express a song's feelings. But on "Water" he sounds, for one of the few times in his career, genuinely sad. Odd, given that the song was a Gram favorite and focuses on one of his favorite subjects; bitter regret. Still, McGuinn sounds more connected to its essence.

"One Hundred Years from Now" showcases harmony from Gram and McGuinn. Gram was supposed to sing solo, and McGuinn follows Gram's inflection syllable for syllable. The song is a new leap forward in Gram's writing. It's conceived as rock and roll, not country. It's not only the structurally perfect chorus and verses, nor the killer hook (Gram's song craft is well understood; it's his pop craft that's underappreciated), nor the off-kilter backbeat intro that provides the song's unexplainable emotional wallop. "Years" marks a trend in Gram's songwriting that would be further reflected by "Sin City" with the Burrito Brothers.

Gram's lyrics make little rational sense yet generate profound emotions. The mind might not know what the song's about, but the heart feels it plainly. It's a song for wallowing in heartbreak and for celebrating newfound love. The arrangement is full of life, McGuinn's vocals tamp the exuberance down, and Lloyd Green throws Nashville restraint out the window. These contradictions give it great power. It took Wilco to capture the pure rock-and-roll energy of "One Hundred Years" on *Return of the Grievous Angel: A Tribute to Gram Parsons*.

The "You're Still on My Mind" refrain of "An empty bottle, a broken heart, and you're still on my mind" is so associated with George Jones that it's a surprise to learn he didn't write it. Luke McDaniel, an obscure rockabilly singer, achieved his greatest glory with the tune. Gram does not try to sound like Jones. He makes the song his own. McGuinn harmonizes beautifully, and the band lays back to let Earl Ball tromp along with some classic honky-tonk plonking. Ball gets a nice solo chorus, but it's his accents under Gram's voice that link the song to its rockabilly roots.

Among the extra cuts are two oddities. "Pretty Polly" was a bluegrass standard that Gram wanted to include as an homage to his daughter. Hillman thought the song had been done far too many times. His arrangement reflects his intense lack of enthusiasm.

Kevin Kelley sings lead on "All I Have Are Memories." His hesitant, wimpy vocals and the meandering, unfocused arrangement sadly predict the future of most L.A. country rock. The tough soul and bitter heart that the Byrds and Gram unearthed would slowly devolve, through ever-slicker production and more self-consciously "sensitive" singing, into a blander, cleaner, more accessible, more commercial, and gutless product.

FOURTEEN
THE FLYING
BURRITO BROTHERS

THERE IS A SMALL GROUP OF NOW AGING HIPSTERS WHOSE PLEASURES BECAME, in the sixties, the model for an entire subculture. Members of this demimonde knew of a certain basement club in Rome, a bar in Kenya, a hotel in Tangiers; they were citizens of the world, fearless travelers, at home with dope and sex and post-Beat chic and lifelong feuds. They tend to tell stories in one long breathless sentence, like this one from the daughter of a famous man: "I was in Morocco with Brian [Jones of the Rolling Stones] and Anita [Pallenberg, who was Brian's girlfriend before she dumped him for Keith Richards], and that young count, you know, the one who sold Pamela the dose in Paris that killed Jim. [She means Pamela Courson, Jim Morrison's wife, and takes it for granted that everyone knows not only that Morrison died of a heroin overdose—as opposed to the official story that he suffered a heart attack brought on by alcohol and barbiturates—but that the dose that killed him was provided by Count Jean de Breteuil. Breteuil was Pamela's boyfriend and is also known as the man who sold Janis Joplin her lethal dose.] Marianne Faithfull showed up with Keith, and I hated her because she told everyone she fucked my father. But I got back at her, because a couple of weeks later I was in London doing threesomes with [Faithfull's boyfriend, Mick] Jagger."

This was the scene that Gram, by dint of hanging out with Keith, fell into just as it was peaking, in 1968. He felt at home there. The louche depravity, the sense of privilege, and the willful expression of any urge to pleasure fulfilled his notions of what rock stardom should be. The entitlement and exclusivity must have evoked an infinitely more glamorous version of his life among the Snivelys in Winter Haven. His American friends feared he was playing out of his league.

Director and London scenemaker Tony Foutz first met Gram while working with the Stones and Sam Shepard on the script for *Maxagasm*, "a distorted western for the soul and psyche" that was never filmed. "I had gone up to London for the weekend and was staying at Jagger's rented house on Chester Square," Foutz says, "a three-floor Regency pile with next to no furniture. I was with Anita Pallenberg—an old friend from Rome, where I was living at the time—and we were met by Marianne Faithfull as we came in, who announced, 'I've found this most beautiful boy . . .'

"And there he was: dressed in white, propped up on an elbow, all stretched out on a creamy carpet like a poolside parvenu in *Paradise Lost*, a fetishlike necklace of turquoise and feathers at his throat. Man-child musician in the fold of newfound friends. I recall the mischief in his eyes, the lazy-boy smile. It was July of 1968 and he'd walked away from the Byrds' tour to South Africa. He was on the corrosive threshold of his run down fame's gauntlet and ruptured recognition as a gifted individual artist. The future was fatally bright."

"Gram was ripe," Faithfull says in Victor Bockris' *Keith Richards*. "He was like an apple waiting to fall off a tree."

Foutz had come up to London from Redlands, Keith Richards' estate in Sussex, ninety minutes south of London. He returned there with Anita and Gram. The house had been the site of an infamous drug bust the year before. Keith and Mick had been in jail briefly. The tabloids raised hell because the police had discovered not only drugs but also Marianne Faithfull wearing nothing but a bearskin rug. Rumors persist that the cops delayed their raid that night until Beatle George Harrison left the grounds.

Keith and Gram played together nonstop as Gram taught Keith, in the latter's words, "the mechanics of country music." The two discussed the fine points of Nashville versus Bakersfield, the styles of George Jones versus

Merle Haggard. "We sat around the piano for ages trying to figure out little licks," Keith says.

The focus on country reflected their shared fascination with American roots music. One song that obsessed them both was "Love in Vain" by Robert Johnson, the then obscure avatar of Delta slide-guitar blues. Keith and Mick loved everything about the song and wanted to record it. "Gram and I started searching for a different way to present it," Keith says. "There was no point in trying to copy the Robert Johnson style or version. We tried it more country, more formalized. We felt we had to do this song, one way or another."

On August 9, 1968, Gram came back to Los Angeles with Keith and Anita. Three years later Gram told an interviewer: "Keith had to go to L.A. to mix *Beggars Banquet*. And I was broke. [The Byrds] had left me penniless and Keith said, 'Well, that's okay—come on. I'll fly you there.' And we came back to L.A."

They were picked up at the airport by Phil Kaufman, the Stones' Los Angeles procurer and gofer. Kaufman, who'd been introduced to the band by Tony Foutz, was an ex-convict known around town as King Con. His role was to ensure that the Stones got to the studio, or anywhere else, when they were supposed to. Given the distractions available, it was a full-time job.

When Gram returned to L.A., Nancy moved with Polly to Santa Barbara. Marcia Katz followed her friend to the small resort town about ninety-five miles up the coast. "Nancy was getting despondent about what was going on between her and Gram," Marcia recalls. "She was so immersed emotionally. . . . She needed time to herself desperately. They were in the middle of having this big separation. Nancy had given up. And Gram wasn't making changes in his life that needed to be made."

It's unclear if Gram was chasing other girls, bored with Nancy, or simply starstruck. The limitations of fatherhood and Nancy's emotional demands could not compete with Gram's new rich, charismatic, world-famous friends.

"Gram would come to visit Santa Barbara once in a blue moon for all of thirty minutes or an hour," Marcia says. "He and Nancy were more or less over. He would use seeing Polly as an excuse to see Nancy. But he was not motivated in the father area. He just wasn't."

While his responsibilities as a father failed to engage him, Gram pursued his spiritual quest with greater energy. That included frequent trips to Joshua Tree, California, often with Keith, Anita, and other members of the Stones scene. Joshua Tree National Monument, about 140 miles east of Los Angeles, is a desert like no other. Joshua trees are large, slow-growing yuccas that are remarkably humanoid in shape and evocation. Some in the park are over thirty feet high and almost two hundred years old. With their thick, bulbous stalks and multiple branches that reach into the sky like upraised arms, the trees have an air of timeless suffering. Dotting the park are enormous piles of softly rounded boulders that, like the Joshua trees, seem somehow animated. They form phantasmagorical shapes against the park's infinite blue sky and deep silences. Joshua Tree feels like the end of the world, but a benign one. There is no escaping that the park is a magical place. As guitarist Bernie Leadon puts it, "Joshua Tree is everybody's power spot." The consumption of LSD or other psychedelics could only intensify this feeling. Gram developed a profound attachment to the landscape.

Somewhat less magical was the town of Joshua Tree: a short row of cheap motels, bars, and restaurants along Highway 10, an east-west truckers' artery. The summer heat in Joshua Tree is paralyzing; the winters are pleasant. In the late sixties the town was home to a small community of hippies and desert rats. When Gram visited, he usually stayed at a roadside motel called the Joshua Tree Inn, an L-shaped, one-story, flat-roofed joint of no distinction. The Inn offered the advantage that its pool and courtyard were invisible from the road, so that guests could do as they pleased. Perhaps for that reason, the motel had a reputation as a haven for fifties Hollywood libertines.

Gram discovered its charms via Ted Markland, whom he'd met hanging out in Topanga Canyon. Markland is a character actor who'd had roles in Burt Lancaster westerns, any number of TV series, Peter Fonda's acid western, *The Hired Hand*, and Dennis Hopper's psychotic (though compelling) western deconstruction, *The Last Movie*. Markland discovered Joshua Tree in the early fifties when he came out to the desert to attend a Spacecraft Convention at nearby Giant Rock. He returned frequently and eventually hauled a swivel chair to the top of one of the park's mountains so that he could enjoy panoramic views in comfort.

The area has a long history of attracting seekers. Native Americans regarded Giant Rock—a huge freestanding boulder—as a sacred spot. In 1953, an aircraft mechanic named George Van Tassel was meditating under the rock when he received a telepathic message from denizens of Venus, who later visited him and showed him techniques for reinvigorating human cells. On their instructions Van Tassel built the Integratron, a three-story-tall dome he claimed was able to fight gravity and "recharge the cell structure." During the fifties and sixties, Spacecraft Conventions at the dome drew thousands of people, including UFO contactees and mad scientists of all stripes.

The acceptance of crackpot ideas and the pursuit of seemingly forbidden or concealed knowledge were key aspects of the counterculture—and of living in Los Angeles—that Gram embraced. Joshua Tree enabled him to marvel at an apparently spiritual natural beauty and to imbue it with outerspace qualities. Blending the two seamlessly provides a portrait of a certain early-hippie mind-set. As part of that mind-set, Gram showed little self-consciousness about espousing his thoughts on UFOs. Despite his social sophistication, Gram was only twenty-one years old. Instead of the education he and his Joshua Tree regulars skipped in order to rock, Gram had enthusiasms. He and his fellow UFO seekers made a belief system out of being willfully naïve and wacky. Soon hundreds of thousands of Americans would follow their example.

"I showed Gram this whole area, and he went a couple of times up on the mountain," Markland told the *L.A. Weekly* decades later. "Then, through Phil Kaufman, I brought the Stones up there. Marianne Faithfull was with them. Mick kept comparing Joshua Tree to Stonehenge, or various Druid sites he'd been to."

Gram and his friends would go out into the desert with an array of stimulants and spend the night searching the sky for extraterrestrials and blowing their own minds. "They all seemed like one endless night," Richards later recalled. "It took a thousand years, but it was over too quick."

"We had binoculars, loads of blankets, and a big stash of coke," Pallenberg says. "That was our idea of looking for UFOs! Did we believe in UFOs? Well, it was all part of that period. We were looking for something."

The group also experimented with mescaline and peyote "and tried to talk with the local Indians," in Keith's words. In emulation of Markland's chair-topped mountain, Gram and Keith dragged an old barber chair to the top of another peak they claimed as their own.

"It was wonderful," Faithfull says. "Staying up all night, driving out to Joshua Tree and walking along as the dawn came up. We would leave the cars somewhere and go off. We didn't bring anything—food, water, nothing. In that state we could have gone off in the wrong direction and gone around in circles forever, but somehow we didn't."

One night as the moon came out, Faithfull heard "this unearthly sound, a sound I'd never heard before. It was so thrilling, like being in India with the wolves howling." What is that? she asked Gram. He answered, "Why, Marianne, don'ja know that's just a little old coyote?"

SWEETHEART OF THE RODEO was released on August 30, just weeks after Gram returned to Los Angeles. The illustrated cover, supposedly designed by Geller & Butler Advertising, features an illustration by artist Jo Mora from a 1933 catalog for rodeo gear that included the phrase that became the album's title. "We never had a working title while we were in Nashville," Byrds road manager Jimmi Seiter says. "I bought the [Mora] poster at some funky shop. I took it to the studio and showed everybody. They said, 'Ah, nice name!' And boom—it's the album title. Of course, the album got panned."

"They try to sing country, I think," one British newspaper wrote. "Let's hope they don't try it again."

Another reviewer demonstrated the deep confusion the album wrought: Country was redneck music, and the context of *Sweetheart* had to be explained before anyone could enjoy it. Painstakingly describing various connections between the Byrds' earlier efforts and Bob Dylan on the one hand and country and western on the other, the review concludes by warning that "in a super hip society" the album "will be accused (in fact it already has been accused) of being a put-on. Tragically, this indictment mirrors a callous code of savoir faire whose essence sounds a death knell for all but a Dadaist aesthete. This is a great album in spite of the fact you might enjoy it."

The album charted at number seventy-seven, down thirty from the Byrds' previous LP, *The Notorious Byrd Brothers*. In the face of negative reviews and disappointing sales, McGuinn disclaimed responsibility. "We've always dabbled in country music, but we ran into Gram Parsons, who wants to be the world-champion country singer, and he hung out with us for a couple of months," he said. "He was going to be in the group, but it didn't work out. While he was with us, he led us into this direction headlong which we would never have done. We were afraid to commit ourselves. It was a little foreign to us."

Sweetheart didn't receive the acclaim it deserved, but the times were catching up to Gram's ideas. As he returned to Los Angeles, the country-rock scene was beginning to coalesce.

Richie Furay, whom Gram had first met in Greenwich Village two years before, had gone on to form Buffalo Springfield with Stephen Stills, Neil

Young, Bruce Palmer, and Dewey Martin. Buffalo Springfield is best known for their hit single "For What It's Worth." The song's spare arrangement and almost-spoken solo vocal track does not reflect the signature Springfield sound of multiple-voice harmonies and intertwining lead guitars. Their final LP, 1967's *Last Time Around*, featured pedal steel. By then the group had exploded; no two band members played together at the same time during the recording.

Now Furay was putting together Poco, which was conceived from the first as a country-rock band. (He'd originally planned to call the group Pogo, after the brilliant daily newspaper cartoon by Walt Kelly. Pogo's copyright holders objected, so Furay changed one letter.) Furay joined forces with Jim Messina (guitar), Rusty Young (pedal steel), and Randy Meisner (bass). Meisner would later play in the Eagles.

Furay invited Gram to audition. "Gram turned me on to George Jones," Furay says, "and I thought, 'Man, this guy is absolutely phenomenal.' And we were into the Bakersfield influence, the Buck Owens kind of thing. Gram and I had the same love for country music and we wanted to incorporate that into a more acceptable thing on the rock-and-roll side. Country music had its influence, but there were definitely dividing lines with rock and roll and long hair on the rebel side. We wanted people to see this thing work. Both of us wanted to see if there could be acceptance between the two."

First Gram had to be accepted by the rest of Poco. Jim Messina, whose cheesy pop sensibility would find full flower with Loggins and Messina, says: "I saw Gram as a talented young man, but there was an edge about him. Even back then it was destructive. It came across when we were auditioning him. I felt he would have been a disruptive element, and Richie naturally sensed that."

"Gram was trying to surround himself with the best country band he could," Rusty Young adds. "There was us trying to get our trip together. There was all sorts of country rock going on: Doug Dillard and Gene Clark, Hearts and Flowers [with guitarist Bernie Leadon], and the Byrds. Everybody knew what everybody else was doing. Everybody was trying to beat everyone else to the punch.

"Gram decided he was going to be in Poco instead of having his own separate thing. It didn't work out because he didn't like Jimmy Messina. They had a confrontation. Jimmy was our friend and Gram was a little strange, so we told Gram that we would stick with Jimmy. He went off and got the Flying Burrito Brothers rolling."

After his problems with the Byrds, and finding that he couldn't dictate terms to Furay, Gram gave up on being in anyone else's band. As he later told an interviewer, "You can't go on as Billy, Buzzy, and Boppy without losing part of your mind."

Things were no more harmonious for the Byrds with Gram gone. McGuinn wanted to reassert control. "When they came back they were a trio again," Jimmi Seiter says. "McGuinn hired [drummer and banjoist] Gene Parsons and Clarence White. It was Roger's way or the highway."

Chris Hillman's frustrations with the Byrds peaked after a Rose Bowl show, when manager Larry Spector told the band they had no money because the South African promoter had refused to pay up. The band had been vilified for playing to all-white crowds when they'd been assured their audiences would be mixed races; now they weren't even going to get paid.

Hillman pinned Spector to the dressing-room wall, turned him loose, picked up his bass, and smashed it on the floor. "I don't know how I got stuck with this fucking thing in the first place!" yelled Hillman, who had built his reputation as a mandolin player. Hillman meant that Jim Dickson's early formulation of the Byrds made Hillman a bassist rather than something more exalted, like a guitar player.

Hillman and Gram started talking to each other again. In Hillman's words, "we made our peace." "At first Chris wouldn't speak to me because of the rough time they had on that tour," Gram later said. "At the time we split we were bitter enemies. But when he left the Byrds we got back together and began jamming in country bars." Hillman recalls, "He told me about the new group he was forming, and because of the various business-financial hassles with the Byrds, I decided to go with him."

Hillman was done playing the bass. In Gram's new group, that job would go to Chris Ethridge.

Ethridge was long, lean, and quiet, a sensitive Southerner with an inclination toward soul music. He'd played bass on the ISB's *Safe at Home*. "My daddy wanted me to read the notes and I wanted to play [Ray Charles'] 'What'd I Say?'" Ethridge says. "I started in little bands around the Mississippi coast in the early sixties. Johnny Rivers [a pop crooner with sophisticated taste in covers who had a hit with "Secret Agent Man"] came to town. He had an argument with his bass player, who left. Johnny was stuck; he took me back to California with him in 1965." Ethridge played in folk warbler Judy Collins' touring band and on her album *Who Knows Where the Time Goes*.

Gram and Hillman made the rounds in L.A. looking for players. They sat in with the Main Street Blues Band, a jamming group of session musicians. It included Leon Russell and J. J. Cale, a guitarist whose "After Midnight" was a hit for Eric Clapton and whose later solo albums made him a reclusive star. Gram and Chris' first choice for pedal steel was Pete Kleinow, a distinctive stylist who was also an animator for the cartoons *Gumby* and *Davey and Goliath*. When they were both in the Byrds, Gram and Hillman had lobbied McGuinn to bring Sneaky Pete on tour. McGuinn had refused. "I was playing in a lot of clubs—the Palomino, the Lazy X," Sneaky Pete says. "Chris and Gram had been in to hear me play and asked if I wanted to join the group. I decided that it would be fun."

"Sneaky uniquely played an eight-string Fender cable pull steel," Bernie Leadon says, "tuned to B6 instead of the more common C6. He played [a] usually more jazz or swing tuning in a style that most other players use an E9 tuning for. His rationale was: B is the 'five chord,' or dominant chord, to the key of E. This resulted in absolutely unique-to-Pete steel licks. And no one else thinks like him anyway."

Country is a music of traditional forms; Sneaky Pete played a classically country instrument in an entirely new way. He deliberately avoided standard pedal-steel tuning. There was a logical method to his madness. Musicians heard his tuning and recognized its power. As Bernie Leadon's description suggests, musicians were at a loss to describe that power to a nonmusician.

Sneaky Pete's approach required typically Gyro Gearloose pedal-steel-player musical mathematics. Using his signature tuning allowed Sneaky to play in a more modal style, and to produce a sound that was familiar yet unorthodox. It took a musical historian like Gram or a virtuoso like Leadon to understand and savor what Sneaky Pete was attempting. Sneaky took country roots and—utilizing his weird tuning and rococo playing style— made the pedal steel cosmic. Cosmic as in the Sun Ra sounds he emulated, cosmic as in the modal free jazz of John Coltrane and others, cosmic in the sense of psychedelic, and cosmic in the Gram Parsons mode: basing a new sound on a scholar's knowledge of roots.

By way of contrast, Lloyd Green—who played with, among others, Charley Pride—is a master of clean, sharp notes and quick lines. He evokes the era of Bob Wills and provides a shimmering accompaniment. Buddy Emmons also plays with glistening clarity, but a close listen reveals the Hawaiian slack-string, bar-guitar music of the twenties and thirties that— along with bluegrass dobro and blues slide guitar—lies at the heart of the history of pedal steel. In addition to eschewing the understatement of his forebears, Sneaky Pete also ran his steel through fuzz boxes and other effects. His rich, enormous, occasionally distorted sound made him more of an aural sculptor than an accompanist.

"Pedal steel is a strange instrument. Steel players are eccentric," L.A. session musician John Beland says. "They're strange people, like drummers. They have always been weird characters. I have never met one steel player who wasn't off his nut."

GRAM HAD A BAND. He appropriated the Flying Burrito Brothers moniker. "I borrowed the name from my friend Ian Dunlop," he said. The next thing he needed was a record deal.

Warner Bros. and A&M both showed interest. The latter label was the brainchild of Herb Alpert and Jerry Moss. Alpert played trumpet and led the Tijuana Brass, a mariachi-influenced horn band that played peppy, accessible instrumentals with killer hooks; their music existed in a middle ground between a slightly hipper Henry Mancini and a slightly less ethereal Sergio Mendes. They sold a lot of records. The Tijuana Brass provided A&M a significant, reliable cash flow.

"The Tijuana Brass had a hit or two on each album," Jim Dickson says. "They made a lot of money with this one thing. Jerry Moss was the business guy. He was aggressive and strong. Alpert was a shy musician." While A&M was making money, its principals realized they were missing out on the market for "hippie music." "Jerry Moss got Chris Hillman and Gram and gave them a shot," Dickson says. "He did the same thing with Dillard & Clark."

Michael Vosse was in touch with music scenes Alpert and Moss knew nothing about. As an A&R man at A&M, Vosse's job was looking for bands to sign, making the scene, and keeping tabs on what was happening on the Strip. Within A&M he was known as the Company Hippie or Resident Freak. "That company hadn't been in business long and they already made a shitload of cash," Vosse says. "They bought the Charlie Chaplin studios. They weren't throwing money around like crazy, but they were loose."

Vosse knew Chris Ethridge from Ethridge's stint with Judy Collins. Ethridge sold Vosse on Gram and Hillman's new band. "Chris told me the Burrito Brothers had a couple ex-Byrds," Vosse says. "I didn't know who Gram was, even though he played on *Sweetheart*. I knew Mike Clarke and Chris Hillman."

Ethridge told Vosse that the band was talking to Mo Ostin at Reprise, a division of Warner Bros. "My first thought was, Well, too bad. We're not going to get them. Everyone who had been signed by Mo loved him," Vosse says. "But I told Chris our company would be interested and that Jerry Moss was a cool guy. They said something about a big advance and started talking limos and all that. They wanted the rock-star things. Two of them [had been] in the Byrds and that's what they were used to.

"Then it got icky. They talked to Mo again and something happened. They said, 'A&M is great, but we're going to Reprise,' and then all of a sudden they didn't. I think the decision [not to sign] was made by Reprise. So they signed with A&M. They asked Reprise and A&M for fifty thousand dollars. I know it doesn't sound like much today. But we turned down Santana because he wanted fifty thousand dollars."

Gram's band did not get fifty thousand dollars either. Gram, spinning the facts of the A&M signing, said, "There were a lot of record companies eager to sign us—and anything we wanted, they were willing to do. But we happened to sign with A&M because of Mike Vosse, who came and got us. He didn't set up appointments for us to see him—he came and saw us. Tom Wilkes, in the graphic-design department [a renowned graphic designer responsible for numerous iconic sixties images, including the graphics for Monterey Pop and the original, banned cover for *Beggars Banquet*], was a friend of Chris'. So we had a personal contact and they had a personal interest in us. It's not the big executives like Herb Alpert. Who cares about the big executives? Who knows where they're at anyway? Herb Alpert's a nice cat, he's a brilliant cat, got a beautiful smile, and that's all I know."

What he really knew was that no other label was interested.

Gram had little animosity toward Chris when he quit the Byrds. Chris was enraged with Gram and felt deeply betrayed. Apparently he got over it. Those who have never been in a band might find it curious that Gram and Chris would so willingly partner up right after such a fraught separation. As the history of Southern California rock suggests, though, such feuds, and far worse, could be easily suppressed if the music was good enough. Suppressed for a while, anyway.

Gram and Chris Hillman rented a three-bedroom ranch house together on DeSoto Avenue in Reseda, way out in the San Fernando Valley, a deliberately long way from Hollywood and the Strip. "It was a bachelor pad with motorcycles," Bernie Leadon says. They spent their days writing songs. Pamela Des Barres, the queen-bee groupie of the Sunset Strip and later the author of *I'm with the Band* and *Rock Bottom*, described the house: "Chris had a fur bedspread. They had pillows all over the living room. It was kind of sparse. Instruments all over. A real bachelor pad, but clean. Pretty tidy for two guys. And a lot of great clothes."

"There was never anything in the refrigerator," Jet Thomas says. "I remember one morning opening it to make some breakfast and there was only, like, half of a cold potato. They had this old funky upright piano that was great, that they played on all the time. There were times they would have a joint for breakfast and I would criticize them for that, but there wasn't much of that going on as far as I can tell."

Gram's relationship with Nancy was more off than on and Hillman was getting a divorce. Music provided solace and a bond. Gram and Chris were born to collaborate. "To this day, [that was] the most productive time I have ever had," Hillman says. "We woke up in the morning and would write as opposed to the usual being out until five in the morning. We wrote 'My Uncle' [about Gram's draft notice]. 'Sin City' was about our manager who had robbed us. We were writing every day on a spontaneous schedule. I've never peaked like that, working with other people. I've written a lot of songs, had a lot of fun and success, but for writing, [Gram's] the guy."

Gram and Hillman were in perfect sync as coauthors. Hillman would toss out a lyric and Gram would answer with the next line. There was little formal separation of tasks—little of one writing the music and the other fitting lyrics to it. "It's being familiar with your partner, knowing and anticipating what Gram was thinking about, because we were sharing a common thing then," Hillman later said. "We were sharing a divorce thing and we were firing a manager. That's what caused our creative working condition."

It was around this time that Gram befriended the legendary country-music tailor Nudie Cohn. Nudie, who had arrived in America from Kiev as Nuta Kotlyarenko, designed and created the ornate sequined suits that were de rigueur for country music stars. Roy Rogers' Nudie-designed and -sewn shirt featured white leather trim and a sequin portrait of Bullet, Roy's German shepherd; Porter Wagoner's Nudie suits sported enormous spangled wagon wheels on the front and a covered wagon in rhinestones and sequins on the back. Nudie also designed for Buck Owens, Hank Williams, and Roy Rogers' wife, Dale Evans. A celebrity in his own right, Nudie drove a customized Cadillac with three-foot cattle horns on the hood, toy pistols for door handles, and leather seats hand-tooled like saddles.

As he did with the Byrds and the Stones, Gram walked into a select and demanding scene—Nudie's shop—and found himself right at home. Gram recognized Nudie's Rodeo Tailors as the nexus of true country style.

L.A. piano player David Barry, who played with ISB guitarist John Nuese, understood the difference between the Sunset Strip idea of country and the real thing. "The hippies in Southern California were cowboy-oriented," Barry says. "Everyone wore boots and cowboy shirts and blue jeans. I told this girl that I was going to meet at the Troubadour, 'I wear blue jeans, a suede Levi western jacket, Peter Fonda glasses, and a Butch Cassidy cowboy hat.' She said, 'Great. How will I recognize you?'

"One of the differences between country music and the world that all of Gram's friends came from was the way country musicians dressed. I had long hair, and those country pickers didn't like Peter Fonda glasses at all. They all wore rodeo outfits and satin. They looked like a Las Vegas joke.

"But that was what the real guys wore, and if you wanted to be authentic, that's what you wore. People like me wore jeans and boots, which is exactly what real country stars didn't want to wear because it suggested they came from country's poor white roots. They wanted to deny that and have a guitar-shaped swimming pool in Nashville."

Gram's emerging idea of glamour—custom sequined Nudie suits coupled with a Mick Jagger androgyny—would, in the perceptive words of author Dana Spiotta in her novel *Lightning Field*, "invent the style period in America that came between Hippie and Glam."

"Nudie was a character," Chris Ethridge says. "He was a little Jewish guy—originally a lingerie salesman in New York—who moved to California. When someone said to Nudie, 'I'm a Sagittarius, Nudie. What's your sign?' he'd say, 'My sign is the dollar sign. Let me give you my card.' And he'd pull out a stack of dollar bills with his picture instead of George Washington's. He used to sing these dirty old songs. He would play the mandolin and he would get me and Gram and whoever was in there to play the guitar. He had Nudie guitars. They were Japanese guitars with 'Nudie' stamped on the back."

Nudie's shop was a hangout for old-time showbiz cowboys. "Those old cowboy movie stars and singers would sit around and tell stories. It was fantastic," Ethridge says. "There was no telling who you would meet when you went to Nudie's.

"Gram really, really loved Nudie. He identified with him and Nudie liked Gram. Gram trusted him. Nudie watched after us, in a way. When we would play at the Whisky he'd show up in his Cadillac with the horns and the guns on the doors and the saddles on the seats."

A Nudie suit brought Gram to the attention of Pamela Des Barres and her compatriot Mercy Peters, better known as Miss Mercy, at the opening of the Beatles movie *Yellow Submarine*. The two women were members of the GTOs, Girls Together Outrageously, the queens of the groupie scene that revolved around the Whisky a Go Go. The GTOs' adopted uncle and karmic guardian was guitarist and bandleader Frank Zappa, who produced their one album, 1969's *Permanent Damage*. On it the girls sing short nursery-rhyme ditties like "Rodney," a tribute to the scene maker, club owner, and DJ Rodney Bingenheimer. They also chat with groupie Cynthia Plaster Caster—whose specialty was taking plaster casts of the erect (or in some cases, semierect) cocks of rock stars—and rate various musicians in terms of their "groupie cred." Zappa had the most groupie cred of all because, according to the GTOs, he never tried to sleep with them. The GTOs dressed in a mixture of hippie and Victorian style, danced prominently in front of the stage at Ciro's and the Whisky, and offered themselves to the rock stars of their choice. Among their claims to fame are Miss Mercy's appearance on the cover of the sixth issue of *Rolling Stone*. She was also a star of one of the most controversial of the magazine's early issues, Number 27, which was devoted to groupies.

Miss Pamela and Miss Mercy arrived at *Yellow Submarine* in a Hudson Hornet, a bulbous fifties car painted like a yellow submarine. Gram was there wearing a red Nudie suit covered in yellow submarines. "Pamela had a connection to the Byrds because of Hillman," Miss Mercy says. "She had a longtime crush on him. She kept hitting me in the shoulder and going, 'Oh, God, it's Gram Parsons.' And I'm going, 'What? Who? How?' Like, 'Oh my God, he's cute, isn't he?' We started hanging out with him from that point on."

In the eighties Miss Mercy won an *L.A. Weekly* journalism contest with an essay about Gram. When she first saw him in his submarine suit, she wrote, "I was captured and spellbound from here to eternity because he was so real he was unreal. . . . He was true glitter-glamour rock. The rhinestone suit sparkled like diamonds, it was submarines all over the suit outlined in rhinestones and the color was scarlet red. His Nudie belt hung on his hips like a gunslinger. Pamela always raved on about Gram and I'm the only GTO that listened. She was always in contact with the special earth angels . . ."

In an interview, she recalled their first visit to Gram and Chris' house on DeSoto: "We drove to the outskirts of the San Fernando Valley, to a modern cowboy ranch with wagon wheels paving the driveway. We entered the house and a shy Chris Hillman and the cat in the Nudie suit greeted us with a grocery bag full of grass. Gram was so down-home dazzling with Southern hospitality it slayed me. These are the first words I recall him speaking to me: As he leaned over his pile of records and put on an old George Jones album, a tear fell from his eye and he said, 'This is George Jones, the king of broken hearts.' Imagine crying over a hillbilly with a crew cut."

The girls invited Gram and Hillman to the recording session for *Permanent Damage*. The visitors ran into Frank Zappa's well-known insistence on control. "He came to the studio with Hillman and they wanted to be on our record," Pamela says. "And Frank said no! And Mercy and I are looking at him like: 'Oh, my God! These are our heroes and they want to be on our record.' Gram even said, 'I'll play the tambourine.' And Frank said no!

"They became my social scene for a while. I was a wild freak when I started hanging out with them. Gram was in a lot of ways a reserved, old-fashioned guy even though he was living a wild life. I tempered my nuttiness with a cowgirl look. You know, vintage cowgirl shirts and cowboy boots and stuff. I was trying to fit in visually, but it was easy to fit in musically. I got right into the sound. Gram turned me on to Merle Haggard, George Jones, Waylon Jennings, Willie Nelson, all those people, and it's impacted my life to this day. Thank God he turned me on to that music, because before that time I considered country music lame. I wouldn't even consider listening to it and he opened my eyes, ears, heart, soul to that music."

Pamela Des Barres knew every significant rocker, and she would become lovers with a number of them. For others she existed as a surrogate mother, part-time muse, helpmate, and confidante. Because her books are willfully straightforward (*I'm with the Band*) or specialize in the sensational (*Rock Bottom*) and because she's known foremost as a groupie, Des Barres does not get the credit she deserves for her musical understanding and discernment. To understand Gram's quest for country, to be open to country music period, and to get the whole Gram package—clothes, persona, musical taste, vocals, ambition, and careless lifestyle—made Des Barres extraordinarily perceptive for that moment in L.A. She thought Gram, with whom she was never lovers, and Hillman, with whom she was, were just it. If anyone on the Sunset Strip was in a position to know it when they saw it, Pamela was.

"He had a sweetness and a weeping-willow-tree genteel Southern mentality that I hadn't been around much," Pamela says. "Then at the same time this incredibly brave, brave-new-world kind of focus about what he wanted to do. Nothing was going to stop him. He was on a mission. I was impressed by both of them. Chris and Gram together invented this music, and Chris is often left by the sidelines because he lived and Gram was more the upfront singer. I was so impressed with their determination. Especially Gram's resolve to get this sound out there. The merging of the music was important to him. He saw no boundaries in music."

Pamela accurately describes the Hillman Dilemma: Hillman cowrote with Gram, sang beautiful harmonies with Gram, put together and ran the band with Gram. Yet Hillman still has not gotten the credit he deserves as a singer, songwriter, bandleader, or picker—at least not for his work in the Burritos. He remains foremost among the Bitter Lieutenants, but has good reason to be.

THE NEW FLYING BURRITO BROTHERS were preparing to go into the studio. As they readied songs, Gram loved to round up his friends to go hear Delaney & Bonnie. An addition to his circle was Andee Nathanson, a lovely photographer who, like filmmaker Tony Foutz, had been part of the hip scenes worldwide that had helped to create the counterculture. Andee dated Denny Cordell, the producer of Procol Harum's "Whiter Shade of Pale" and Joe Cocker's *With a Little Help from My Friends* and co-owner, with Leon Russell, of Shelter Records. She also dated English actor James Fox, who portrayed a tormented gangster in the echt end-of-the-sixties movie *Performance*. Fox's costar was Mick Jagger. When asked how Gram comported himself in a room filled with English rock and movie stars, Andee said, "He hung back in a chair, taking it all in and smiling. Gram knew how to hang—to sublimate his ego. He was a very cool cat."

Delaney & Bonnie and their core group of musicians, which included Cordell, Russell, bassist Carl Radle, and J. J. Cale, were generating a scene of their own. "They would play at the Brass Ring in the Valley," Andee says. "We would dance all night—it was so hot. We all went crazy! Gram got everybody down there. He loved all the musicians.

"Gram had these after-hours clubs, those weird places he discovered like Aces. He loved it. He loved the real people who lived outside of Hollywood, who would give him a whole different kind of feedback. If you could make it at Aces, your music was good. If those people liked you and didn't break a bottle over your head, you were good. He would jump up there somewhere around three o'clock in the morning and play his little heart out."

"The sixties is when Bobby 'Blue' Bland, James Brown, and real good R&B was still making hits," Chris Ethridge says. "That's when Stax came out with Otis Redding. It was a great time for R&B music. 'Knock on Wood' . . . 'Midnight Hour' . . . Wilson Pickett . . . all those were such great songs, and Delaney & Bonnie were an R&B band. That's why Gram loved them: He had a strong love for Southern music. Even though a lot of the people talk about Gram being all country, he loved R&B and gospel. Delaney was real gospel oriented, too. That's why we were such big fans."

October 1968 saw the release of a single from *Sweetheart*, "I Am a Pilgrim" backed by "Pretty Boy Floyd." The former was sung by Hillman, the latter by McGuinn, and neither was written by Gram. Save the Dylan covers, these two have the strongest old-Byrds feel of any on the record.

When the Burritos went into the studio their lineup was Sneaky Pete Kleinow on steel, Ethridge on bass, and Gram and Chris on everything else except drums. If the successful Byrds were lazy about preparation, the nascent Burritos were much worse. Sessions went slowly, stretching into January 1969.

"There were no rehearsals, nothing. I didn't know the material," Sneaky Pete later said. "Gram and Chris had written some songs. We didn't really have a drummer."

Under the familiar rubric of spontaneity and authenticity, the Burritos sidestepped any studio techniques that required discipline—like knowing their parts well enough to overdub.

"Everything was recorded live, singing and playing at the same time mostly," Hillman says. "A couple of tracks were overdubbed, but that's all. We had some rough times in the studio, when we couldn't get together, like any other group. But there's magic in the group when it's together."

"Larry Marks was a staff producer at A&M," Michael Vosse says. "He was a good guy, but he wasn't a good match for them. He was completely flummoxed by their behavior. They were less prepared and less conscious of money and time than he was used to. There was a lot of wasted time and a lot of crap. There were also a lot of good sessions."

"I think Larry Marks did a good job of giving us the range on the first album to get the group started," Gram said.

In other words, Marks had no control over the band.

"A&M opened their own studios inside their huge sound stages," Vosse says, "so that was the place to record. Henry Lewy, by luck of the draw, was the Burritos' engineer. Henry Lewy is, or was, God rest his soul, one of the most serene people on the planet. He was one of the first people in the rock scene into meditation. Even before the Beatles. Henry Lewy was friends with Brian Wilson and got Brian to go to meditation. He was good at bringing people down to earth. He wasn't into people fighting with each other. He didn't buy into the cocaine flashes. He kept people cool. He was the glue that held together the disparate elements of the making of the album."

"To do the album in L.A., we had to close ourselves off," Gram said. "When the smog was heavy we had to wear tanks of oxygen, and luckily we were blessed with a fellow named Henry Lewy who can cool out. Henry's an engineer unlike any engineer I've ever worked with, and projected an attitude of 'We're not in L.A., boys, we're together.'"

"There was a lot of wasted time," Vosse says, "but when they started clicking they started clicking and things got better and better. During the time that things were not going so well, Sneaky Pete and Ethridge were always ready to rock. Pete was squeaky-clean and Ethridge was a highly disciplined recording musician. He did not go into the studio in any condition where he couldn't work. Those two guys were always ready to lay down the tracks and the other two, not always. They would get fucked-up in the studio or get fucked-up ahead of time. Cocaine was the big bugaboo. They'd get fucked-up on cocaine and fight and get mad at each other. Larry, the producer, would get mad, so Henry would come in and Zen everybody out.

"And that's how *Gilded Palace of Sin* got done."

The getting done cost the band a drummer a month. "The original [drummer] was Eddie Hoh," Gram says. "He only wanted the advance money and then he scored and left town. We found out Eddie was going to split and we were gonna get Morris 'Tarp' Tarrant. He played for Jerry Lee Lewis. But he never came through. I always felt the Burritos had a drummer problem."

The band booked only one or two sessions a month. In order of sessions played, the drummers were Eddie Hoh, Jon Corneal, Popeye Phillips, and Samuel Goldstein. A drummer would last one or two days—which meant one or two sessions—and then leave or be replaced. The fast, ragged work ethic was hard on drummers but produced a vocal sound that reflected more Gram's key influences than Hillman's: the Everly and Louvin Brothers. He and Chris sang harmonies in firsts and thirds, Everly style. "We did those live and sang them live," Hillman says, "so there's a lot of leakage [voices or other sounds being picked up by the microphone]. But the feeling is there."

The Burritos knowingly brought country and western together with the soul sound associated with Otis Redding's Stax-Volt label and singers like Percy Sledge and James Carr. "That was the merging of the black and white blues," Hillman continues. "The crying out . . . taking those R&B songs and putting a light country-and-western arrangement to them." Ray Charles' country-and-western work provided a noteworthy influence as well.

Sneaky Pete did not like to record live with the band. As befitted an animator's piecemeal method and love of process, he preferred to come in after the others had gone and painstakingly build his pedal-steel parts phrase by phrase. "Sneaky Pete provided magic on the first album," Gram said. "I think Larry Marks had a lot to do with that, because he let Sneaky go with some of the weirdest ideas. I mean, there were times on the first album when I wanted to quit because I couldn't understand this guy doing like eight steel overdubs over himself. But I liked it."

Despite their half-assed schedule, the band could feel the record coming together. The Burritos were creating their own sound and they knew it. "We went through 'Hot Burrito #1' and '#2' and we saw we had the high polished musical thing by the nuts," Gram said. "We had it and we could do it. My piano playing and organ playing came back to where it used to be before I was with the Byrds. I started getting funky again, and everybody started getting funky again. It was time to do 'Hippie Boy,' and it was time to end the album."

"Hippie Boy," the record's final cut, features Chris Hillman speaking softly over ever-swelling down-home Southern church music. Aping the fake-soothing tones of a radio evangelist, Hillman tells of coming down the street and meeting a hippie boy, one of the "strange breed" with "stringy hair." The hippie boy tells the redneck narrator his sad story of a dead brother. It's impossible not to visualize everyone in the control room falling over in stoned hysterics as Hillman recites his sermon with total deadpan conviction. Set in the Chicago "police riots" during the 1968 Democratic convention, when an army of policemen went berserk on unarmed protestors, "Hippie Boy" recounts the tragedy of an innocent child cut down in the melee. It's a cracked stoner narrative that ends with the mock-profound spoken lesson, "Never carry more than you can eat."

Gram claimed in interviews that the song was a protest against Chicago. What comes through more than any protest is the deranged piety of the Louvin Brothers filtered through Gram's dark humor and his connoisseurship of Southern evangelists. It was a supreme, easily misunderstood goof. Freed of its immediate context, "Hippie Boy" remains utterly strange and yet moving. Under the final lines of Hillman's solemn sermon are the swelling voices of Andee Nathanson, Miss Pamela, and Miss Mercy singing the traditional hymn "Peace in the Valley." Gram insisted they sing off-key for a more authentic feel.

"We kept saying, We got to do a song called 'Hippie Boy' about Chicago, and it's got to be a narrative song, and Chris Hillman has to do it," Gram said. "He has to drink a fifth of scotch before he does it to feel the whole thing. He can't smoke an ounce of grass. He has to drink a fifth of scotch and do a narrative. And let's see somebody else do that. Let's see McGuinn do that. It was the toughest challenge on the album."

As THE ALBUM CAME TOGETHER, Gram and Nancy struggled over the terms of their relationship in a counterculture context that called into question every traditional idea of relationships. In December 1968, Nancy and Polly started visiting Gram more frequently. Pamela got along well with Nancy. "Nancy became an instant dear friend," Pamela says. "We were so open to each other. We bonded in a female way. It was a real girlie take-care-of-your-man type bond, as the girlfriends/wives of men we loved so much." Pamela was seeing Hillman, though she wrote in her journal that he had "92 other girlfriends." "Nancy was a stunning brunette with the biggest green eyes and was so in love with Gram I could smell it on her skin," Pamela says. "She called him 'her old boy,' and I was a little in awe of her, as I was with all wives and nearly wives. Nancy was smart and very cosmic. She loved astrology and we were into occultish things together and were spiritually minded, both of us."

After recording Andee and Pamela singing the chorus on "Hippie Boy," Gram sat down at the piano and played them "Hot Burrito #1" and "Hot Burrito #2." "Before he sat down," Pamela says, "he looked at his longest of long fingers and said, 'Sometimes I wonder where these hands came from, I keep expecting to see stitches around my wrists.' His hands were thin, long . . . the most elegant hands I have ever seen. He cried while he sang a sorrowful song for Nancy. I figured they were having problems I didn't know about. I was right."

The role of "wife or nearly wife" was a spectacularly difficult but typical one in that time and place. Gram and Chris were living the sixties rock-star life at the DeSoto house, which came to be known as Burrito Manor. The men were irresponsible and the women devoted. "Nancy was a flower child like me," Pamela says. "We were caught between the fifties and sixties. We wanted to be free feminist women, but we also wanted to take care of our man the way we watched our moms do. We connected that way.

"We did everything. Clean the house, cook the chicken, make the shirts, take care of the guys. It was old-fashioned and Southern. I was a nineteen-year-old girl. I was trying to do what they wanted: clean up and stay out of their way while they play poker. But I always felt connected to them. Even more connected when I was there doing for them. I loved to go to Burrito Manor and clean up. Make it nice for them. I was so enamored with them, their lifestyle. Brandon De Wilde wasn't that way. He had a much more open view about women and their role. I learned a lot from him about equality of men and women, but [Gram and Chris] were old-fashioned guys. They had an old-fashioned view of women. We were coming into that era where women's lib had started and it was a new concept. I sort of combined the two by doing what I wanted. Taking care of a rock star instead of a regular guy."

The double standard extended to the substances the household indulged in. Soft—and less expensive—drugs were for girls. The more high-line substances were for boys. "We smoked a lot of pot," Pamela says. "There was cocaine around, but they didn't want the girls to do it. They would be playing poker and Nancy and I would be with Polly in the other room. They did not offer us coke. I'm sure I did it with Gram a few times, but it wasn't a big deal. It wasn't something he did a lot in the Burritos [at home]. On the road he went insane. When I was around him there was a little coke, but a lot of pot. He wasn't a big drinker.

"We were such hippie freaks—we were always getting stoned and every day ran into the next. It was such a free, easy, peaceful, frolicsome time. We were all hanging out . . . one big, I hesitate to use the word *party*, but it was one big love-in almost. Each day bled into the next and the nights . . . no one knew what time it was. I'd find myself at Burrito Manor for three days. All of a sudden it would be the next week and I'd be at Brandon's place in Topanga."

Around this time—late December 1968—Gram asked Nancy to marry him. Polly, their daughter, was a year old. It was sink or swim for their relationship. Whatever his reasons, Gram and Nancy set a date for late January.

Gram never intended to go through with it. It's not clear whether his proposal was an instantly regretted, guilty-conscience whim or something more self-serving. The most credible and consistent version of this disputed event, and the one least flattering to Gram, appears in Pamela's book *Rock Bottom*: "One afternoon Nancy gaily announced that Gram had proposed to her, but the gaiety was short-lived. Unbeknownst to Nancy, Gram had devised a publicity scheme, reminiscent of Hank Williams marrying one of his wives onstage in between concerts. Gram would invite all of his showbiz pals, play a set, and maybe even get his wedding on television! He told Nancy that the invitations were being made up and to create her wedding dress with good old Nudie, and leave the rest of the plans up to him. She did as she was told . . . and waited. And waited."

Nancy went to Nudie's and learned that Gram had never paid for her dress. She became convinced he was using her as a publicity device. "I knew already that it was a big, awful, horrible joke," Nancy recalls. "The fact that he would set up this elaborate ruse—this man I loved with my immortal soul—one hand beckoned me forward, the other one pushed me away."

Neither the concert nor the wedding ever happened. Nancy refused to go along, and Gram realized the media weren't interested. It faded away as did many of Gram's plans, with explanation of neither the genesis nor the collapse of the idea.

No one in Gram's circle remembers the proposal as that cruel a prank or even that big a deal. "It was pretty harrowing, but they were kids," Pamela says. "We were all kids. You know, it was dramatic. Gram had to still sow some oats. He was too young to be tied down in a marriage as much as he loved her and Polly. He was too young in that life situation."

Pamela's forgiving view that Gram was too young to be married hardly addresses what drove him to put the mother of his child through a painful and humiliating ordeal. Gram taught Nancy a lesson that he taught his bandmates and others: Don't count on me. And the more you try to pin me down, the more hostile my response is likely to be. He put Nancy through the charade rather than simply tell her he could not be hers alone.

Nancy resorted to a simple, old-fashioned form of revenge: She slept with drummer Mickey Gauvin. "I didn't have to sink to that level," Nancy says, "but remember the sacred sexuality, the ancient temples? I wasn't getting back at Gram, I was fulfilling myself with a temple boy!"

"Gram was on his way to go beat up Mickey Gauvin," Miss Mercy remembers. "I was sitting in the Laurel Canyon Country Store with Johanna, who was this incredible-looking woman [when Gram drove by]. Gram stopped the car and said, 'Oh, I've got to meet her when I come back, but I gotta go do something now.' So he went up there and did what he had to do. . . . When he came back Gram and Johanna had some kind of fling."

It's not clear whether Gram ever did beat up Gauvin, or that he could have if he tried. What he could do was make a huge scene out of being upset over Nancy being untrue. Given how often Gram took other lovers or claimed they were free to do as they pleased or told his friends that he and Nancy were "above" the "cheap physical stuff," his scene-making seems plenty disingenuous. Still, Nancy's fling marked the end of their once-intimate connection.

FIFTEEN

THE GILDED
PALACE OF SIN

GRAM TOOK THE BAND TO NUDIE'S TO GET CUSTOM SEQUINED SUITS FOR THE album cover shoot. Knowingly or not, A&M footed the bill. Chris Ethridge's suit was tailored in an Edwardian cut with a below-pocket-length, double-vented white jacket. It had high lapels and was covered in ornate roses: Red blossoms climbed up each leg; red roses on green stems decorated the sleeves, chest, and lapels; yellow bouquets provided accents. The back featured a huge three-stemmed red rose and two yellow free-floating blossoms above.

Sneaky Pete got a black velvet pullover shirt with a gold pterodactyl in full flight on the front and twin Tyrannosaurus Rexes rampant on the back. The shirt matched his plain, full-cut black velvet pants. "I designed my own," Pete says. "I was a motion picture special-effects guy, so I figured dinosaurs, wow, that'd be great."

Chris Hillman's screaming neon-blue suit had a business cut, with peacocks of gold and green on the chest and sleeves. The back was a golden sunburst. The pants had red sequin peacock feathers and vines unfurling up his legs.

The Gilded Palace of Sin *photo shoot: Chris Ethridge, unidentified, Gram Parsons, unidentified, Sneaky Pete Kleinow, Chris Hillman.* (© Barry Feinstein, www.barryfeinsteinphotography.com)

Gram's suit, a garment of legend, hangs in the Country Music Hall of Fame. It reflects his passions and contradictions, Gram's brazen sense of humor and his insistence that his most outrageous statements be grounded in country traditions. The belled pants are jean-cut and hang low, with scarlet flames reaching up the legs and poppies on the front pockets. Poppies cover the back pockets, too. A naked woman, rendered as an old-school sailor's tattoo, adorns each lapel of the belt-length, silk motorcycle jacket; red poppies embellish the shoulders. Growing up the chest are carefully articulated, deep-green marijuana leaves. On the sleeves are embroidered Seconals, Tuinals, and a sugar cube representing LSD. In blazing contradiction to the women and the drugs, the back of Gram's jacket is covered, top to bottom, by a flaming red cross surrounded by radiating shafts of blue and gold light.

"The first couple of times I played the Palomino I nearly got killed," Gram said. "There I was in my satin bell-bottoms, and the people couldn't believe it. I got up onstage and sang, and when I got off a guy said to me, 'I want you to meet my three brothers. We were gonna kick your ass, but you can sing real good, so we'll buy you a beer instead.' Thank God I got up on that stage."

"They thought he was out of his mind," Miss Mercy says. "They were like these conservative rednecks, right? And they're goin', 'What the hell?' Big cross . . . he had the big Nudie cross on the back of his suit. They thought it was anti-religious. It was absolutely hilarious. People didn't get it."

For the album cover shoot the band posed in Pear Blossom, California, in the desert east of L.A. They stood in front of a tiny shack meant to represent a whorehouse, the Gilded Palace of Sin of the title. Two models lounge against the shack and, on the back cover, in the arms of Gram. Gram and Ethridge wear their suits with aplomb. Hillman's suit appears to be wearing him, and Sneaky Pete might as well be wearing pajamas. The band looks uninterested and high, save Sneaky Pete. He looks intense and strange, like a pedal-steel player.

The *Gilded Palace* recording sessions ended in January. The Burritos were unveiled in all their glory at a promo show at the Whisky a Go Go, the center of the late-sixties Sunset Strip. A small club with a high ceiling, the Whisky was dominated by a postage-stamp stage seven feet off the floor. Tables and a dance floor curved around the front of the stage, and a shallow standing-room balcony wrapped around above. The proximity of the audience to the stage, and the crush of the crowd at a well-attended show, turned the Whisky into a cauldron of sweat and energy.

The opening act, which had been booked by Warner Bros., was Van Morrison—then and now a notoriously difficult guy. "The place was packed," Vosse says. "Van was drunk—no big surprise—and he was not about to stop. Long past where the first set was supposed to end, Van kept going and going. The Burritos were getting agitated because they wanted to get onstage. The people that we had gotten to come see them were like, 'Jesus Christ, I've got to go.' I remember yelling at people from Warner, saying, 'Get this fucking guy off the stage!' They said, 'You don't understand. There's nothing we can do!'"

When Morrison finally stopped, the Burritos went on an hour late and nervous. "I cannot tell you for the world whether they were good or not," Vosse says. "It was a nice evening and it accomplished what it was supposed to accomplish."

Vosse adds that the band's club performances were rarely stellar. "Usually they were underrehearsed. All it took was for one or two of them to be on coke and not on the same page.

"It was never horrible, because Sneaky Pete could save anything. You'd turn to Pete during a bridge and let him do a solo and take the lead and songs could come back together again. Gram could sing when he was fucked-up, that was the other thing."

"I cannot recall one performance where I was not embarrassed to tears," Sneaky Pete says. In his recounting of that evening at the Whisky, Jerry Moss and Herb Alpert were sitting in the audience, waiting to see A&M's new band. "Gram was so stoned he couldn't play the piano. Chris Hillman, of course, was right up there plugging, but Chris Ethridge had smoked a little too much of something." Ethridge grew progressively more disoriented until he passed out. A roadie scooped up his bass and stepped in to replace him. "The suits got up from their table in midconcert and walked out," Pete says. "We thought we were finished. It was typical."

"On Monday nights the Troubadour had a Hoot Night, which was an open-mike night," guitarist Bernie Leadon says. "You had to sign up and be approved by the guy who ran it. The Burritos showed up wearing their Nudie suits. There was quite a buzz about them. I sat there and couldn't believe what I was seeing because they were so bad. It was atrocious. It was as if they had never met. Nobody had electronic tuners, and they were out of tune. They didn't stop and start at the same time. They didn't sing in tune. I couldn't believe it. I went, Wow, there's something here, but I can't make it out."

A thorough listen to most live bootleg tapes from 1969—before Bernie Leadon joined the band—reveals the Burritos to be unbelievably sloppy, even by the lax standards of live shows at that time. They could occasionally nail the moment, as their blistering set at 1969's Seattle Pop Festival demonstrates. The Burritos' consistent inconsistency makes it clear how seldom they rehearsed. Bakersfield music isn't hard to play. Buck Owens turned it into an art form by performing his simple compositions with rigorous Zen discipline. There's no question the Burritos were skilled musicians—except for drummer Michael Clarke. The Byrds' original drummer joined the Burritos officially. He could not keep time. His beats are ragged. Sneaky Pete zings his deranged Sun Ra–like steel lines across every minute of every song. The band was too disorganized for Sneaky to play carefully placed accents. The absence of lead guitar meant the soloing fell to him. Gram sounds more high than anything else, disconnected from the songs and singing with all his might. It's difficult for any band to pull off live shows that reflect their true abilities. The Burritos' laziness makes their performances painful.

The addition of Michael Clarke, who'd been playing with Dillard & Clark, didn't help the band. Gram biographer Rick Cusick refers to Clarke as the King of Common Time, meaning that all Clarke could play was 4/4. "I know Jon Corneal played on tracks on the album. But he looked like a schlump. And the Burritos wasn't about that," a member of the Burritos organization says. "The Burritos had to be pretty. Corneal didn't fit. They didn't even put him on the cover. They needed someone pretty. Michael Clarke—for all of his bad points, chicks dug Michael Clarke."

HILLMAN AND GRAM conceived a band tour by train, like the old-school country stars. Lacking a proper manager—Larry Spector had been fired—they hired Keith Richards' factotum Phil Kaufman as their road manager. Michael Vosse came along for the hang. "I didn't work for the Burritos," Vosse says. "I worked for A&M. It was a promotional tour. It was easy to go. It was cheap. A&M was paying for it."

The day after the going-away party that launched the tour, Pamela Des Barres wrote in her diary, "Gram was practically stuffing [cocaine] up people's noses on the train last night—big globs of it. I had the feeling at the station that Gram wanted to be wild and free. Brandon and I are driving up tomorrow to see Nancy." They wanted to console her; she was still suffering over Gram's wedding ruse.

The train tour was bound for Chicago, Detroit, Boston, New York, and Philadelphia. Reliving Gram's trips from Waycross to Winter Haven, the band had its own car and everyone had his own compartment. In Phil Kaufman's book *Road Mangler*, Kaufman reports that he insisted all the musicians give him their drugs. He argued it was safer to have all the dope in one place, and for each person to come ask him for their drugs, than to have six separate stashes scattered about the train. "It was debauchery personified," Kaufman writes.

Michael Vosse did not like Kaufman. He thought Kaufman had no idea how to manage a tour. Cocaine was Kaufman's drug of choice, he says, "because the Burritos would give him money to buy drugs. Still, the baseline was marijuana. People were happy getting high on marijuana and it was easy to get. Everyone was always smoking a joint except for Sneaky Pete. I never even saw him drink."

"Things were always going wrong with the Burritos," Hillman said. "We toured before the album was out, so audiences didn't know what to expect." The band arrived in Chicago to discover they had no promotional appearances booked. Michael Vosse knew the Chicago journalist Studs Terkel (author of *Working* and *Hard Times*) and asked if the band could appear on Terkel's popular radio show. Terkel, unsurprisingly, had never heard of them. He listened to their record and agreed. "Gram and Hillman were good," Vosse remembers. "Ethridge and Sneaky were pretty quiet."

The band stayed in a small hotel with an expensive, highly regarded restaurant on its ground floor. "The band found out that they liked the lemon soufflé, so late at night they would order dozens," Vosse says. "They would hoard the soufflés and eat them. It was this panic situation with the soufflés, like somebody might wake up at three A.M. and have to have one."

Gram was drinking heavily and doing a lot cocaine. "I never saw Gram do that shit out in the open," says a Burritos source. "One of the reasons was Michael Clarke was an addict. And if you had powder, as he called it, he would be all over you. Gram didn't want Michael to know he had powder. He'd sneak off to another room and maybe take Hillman with him. Michael would come around and say, 'Where's Chris?' And he would nose his way into the bathroom. If you had an ounce, Michael would do an ounce and a half. That was his m.o."

Sneaky Pete did no drugs. He seldom socialized with the band after shows. He liked to go back to the hotel and call his children. Sneaky was the one Burrito with a real job—animation. "Woe unto anyone who would be mean to Pete," Vosse says. "The one person everybody thought was most important for the sound of the band was Pete. He was so fucking good and awesomely hardworking. If the guys were having a bad night, he was not having a bad night. He didn't have bad nights. He had nights where he would get irritated because things weren't going well. He wasn't a junkie or a drinker. So when they would go to the hotel to do coke and go over the show, he was nowhere to be seen."

In Boston the Burritos shared the bill with the Byrds. The prospect of being outplayed caused the band to be more sober—or at least less fucked-up—for that show than for any other on the tour. The Burritos' set included "Close up the Honky-Tonks" and "Sing Me Back Home."

After the show, Gram took the band to visit Jet Thomas. "He had a little apartment on Harvard Yard," Vosse remembers. "It was so wonderful. It was snowing and we all got invited. He had a collar, which he had unhooked. I think he had just done vespers or some bullshit. He had this dream apartment with plenty of books and nice leather chairs and pipes. He was so hospitable and polite. Scholarly people smoked pot. He had this fishbowl full of pot and Ethridge did nothing but look at it. Ethridge was just, 'Ahhh.' He had this big smile and his eyes were real big and he didn't know what to do about it and he said, 'Michael? Do you think that that's pot? Do you think he'll give us some?' It was as if Chris had walked into the enchanted forest. He'd never seen anything like that in his life, plus the guy was in a collar and we were at Harvard. After we left we talked about it for hours. It was like [imitates Chris], 'We're in Boston, Massachusetts . . . we're at Harvard University, that person is a priest [*sic*], and there is a big bowl of marijuana on his coffee table?' Chris thought that this meant the world was going to be fine."

The first show in New York City was to be at Steve Paul's Scene, a cramped, happening basement in midtown Manhattan. A snowstorm canceled flights from Boston to New York. Kaufman failed to organize transportation and each band member made his separate way. Anarchy ensued. One Burrito (the source for this story wouldn't reveal which one) rented a car with a friend, dropped acid on the road, got hopelessly lost, and showed up in New York a day late. As a result, the band—A&M's big new signing, featuring two ex-Byrds—did the unthinkable: They missed the gig.

A&M was infuriated. They regarded the New York Scene performance as the whole point of the tour. The Burritos' lack of professionalism made A&M look ridiculous. The label worked to get the New York rock press to the show. There was no show for them to see. A&M blamed Vosse; Vosse blamed Kaufman. The Burrito whose absence caused the problem was "all coked up," Vosse remembers, "and angry that anyone made an issue out of it."

To make matters worse in the eyes of A&M, Vosse had shifted the band to a more expensive hotel only hours before the missed gig. A&M had been readying costly support for the Burritos. Jerry Moss was trying to get David Geffen (creator of Asylum and Geffen Records and later co-owner of the film studio Dreamworks SKG) and his partner to manage the band. Geffen had signed Crosby, Stills and Nash and so was reluctant to help the Burritos. Between the missed showcase and the indulgent hotel, A&M lost patience with the band. They wrote the Burritos off as a bad investment.

The band did manage to make their second scheduled appearance at the Scene. *Billboard* writer Fred Kirby reviewed the band's one show in New York: "Country-style music landed at Steve Paul's Scene on Tuesday in the person of the Flying Burrito Brothers [who] brought the act in splendidly. . . . [The band], whose first A&M album is due early this month, would seem to have a bright future with country music becoming one of the day's in sounds."

In Philadelphia Gram bought everyone turbans to wear onstage. They were both ridiculous and an obscure homage to the crazily dressed soul singers of the past. "In Philly the shows were great," Vosse says. "One night they opened for Three Dog Night and one night for Procol Harum. Procol Harum's road manager was Nick Brigden, who has since become a big shot at Bill Graham Presents. He was the sweetest and most professional guy. That night everything got done well because Bridgen took care of it. I hadn't been on the road much and I thought, 'Oh, my God, this is the way it's supposed to go.' It was all done simply and professionally. They got the equipment ready and did a sound check, and none of this was being done with Phil.

"The band felt good because it was a much bigger crowd. Three Dog Night was huge then. It was a good audience, and they played well at both of those shows. They weren't intimidated, but goaded that this crowd would expect them to do a good job. We went to Philly from New York—from catastrophe to that."

An entourage member remembers the groupie habits of the Burritos on tour: "Philly was the only place on the tour I remember Gram not sleeping with floozies. The rest of them would go for groupies except for Ethridge. He was chaste. Gram never did groupies. He would go to bars and pick up [hardcore bar girls] who were older than him. Keith Richards talks about these hardened bar girls in Topanga Canyon who would cry when Gram sang. Gram was drawn to these people. They were soulful to him. And they didn't have an agenda. They didn't know who the fuck he was and he was drunk by the time he made his choice anyhow. They would be in their thirties and not particularly beautiful. You wouldn't see them. They would be gone the next day.

"On the road, Hillman always had your prototypical groupie. They almost all looked the same . . . the long hair . . . find a picture of a little hippie girl from that era, there you have it. Ethridge, no. Pete, no. Michael Clarke, sure, but it would be whoever was willing to go home with him because he was so drunk. Gram separated himself from everybody. I never saw him at the hotel playing poker. The others would keep their girls around, but not him.

"But in Philly, Gram had a little filly. He had a little blond colt. And things got way out of control. She was like sixteen or something, and people had to get her the fuck out of the hotel. Flash forward to the next night backstage: I was called back to the door because there she was with her parents to meet Gram. We kept it away from him. That was the only time that I remember him going for a groupie that came up after the show—she was really, really cute. I remember saying to someone, 'What the fuck? Is that a twelve-year-old?' [Usually] he didn't dabble in that area because he'd get drunk and couldn't tell about age. Gram would go to a bar and find some hardened woman with a face all lined with sorrow and he'd be happy."

On their last night in Philly the Burritos played a local TV dance-party show. They wore their turbans and Nudie suits and mimed to "Christine's Tune (Devil in Disguise)." Chris Ethridge and Michael Clarke switched instruments; Chris faked the drums and Michael the bass. Footage from the show can be seen in Gandulf Hennig's Gram documentary, *Fallen Angel*.

The tour ended unhappily. "We got to New York and discovered that the managers hadn't gotten the right work permits," Gram said. "So we had to turn around and return to L.A., starving and in debt. We burned a lot of bridges when we left, like leaving unpaid phone bills and stuff." The work permits reference New York musicians' union requirements, but Gram was finding any excuse for the catastrophe of the tour. Between the bills for drugs and expensive hotels and the missed showcase in New York, A&M had had enough. They canceled further support and promotion for the band.

CHRIS HILLMAN FOUND another house to share with Gram, a new Burrito Manor, on La Castana Drive in Nichols Canyon in the Hollywood Hills.

Hillman also asked Byrds road manager Jimmi Seiter to work for the Burritos. After the nightmare of New York, Gram wanted Seiter to comanage the band with Phil Kaufman. Seiter was reluctant. "Gram insisted that Phil and I be partners in managing the band," Seiter says. "I didn't want that. Hillman didn't want that either. The management contract was signed by everyone but Gram. He didn't sign it when it was time. Gram didn't want to sign anything with anybody because of his bullshit with Hazlewood."

The Gilded Palace of Sin was released in the midst of the tour, in February 1969. It reached #144 on the charts. It's estimated that fewer than forty thousand copies sold.

Despite the crap sales, some contemporaneous critics recognized the worth of the album. "This album quite clearly stands as a complete definition of the term *country rock*, using a heavy instrumental approach combining

Gram, Bonnie Muma, and Robert Parsons. (© Andee Nathanson, www.andeenathanson.com)

strong country roots," John Firminger later wrote in *Country Music Review.* "The lyrical content showed a departure from the more traditional subjects and involved topicalities like drugs, draft dodging, and sex, matters that the younger generation could readily identify with as part of their life styles." When *Rolling Stone* asked Bob Dylan to name his favorite country-rock band, he answered, "The Flying Burrito Brothers. Boy, I love them. Their record instantly knocked me out." Allan Jones, writing for the influential British rock weekly *NME* (*New Music Express*), raved, "Let me discourse on the sheer magnificence contained within the micro-grooves of *Gilded Palace of Sin.*"

Stanley Booth, writing in *Rolling Stone*, showed greater prescience and understanding than any critic of the time. He so captured the valence and intent of *Gilded Palace* that his arguments have framed the critical discussion of Gram's music ever since. After citing *Sweetheart of the Rodeo* as "one of the best records of last year," Booth wrote that *Gilded*, though possessed of "less surface charm," "is the best, the most personal [music] Parsons has done." The album, Booth noted, is about the temptations of urban life and the suffering of a man who finds himself at home neither where he came from nor in the city he has escaped to. Exploring these themes in a song-by-song analysis, Booth concluded that the album's final cut, "Hippie Boy," "summons up a vision of hillbillies and hippies, like lions and lambs, together in peace and love instead of sin and violence, getting stoned together, singing old time favorite songs."

Despite Booth's rave in the most important rock magazine in America, airplay was hard to come by, especially with no support from the label. The common wisdom of the album's poor commercial reception is that the rock audience found the Burritos too country and country music listeners dismissed them as too hippie and rock and roll. There may be some truth to that view. The album's slapdash production and cheap, tinny sound did not help. Among all the records that remain such major influences on the course of American rock and roll, *Gilded Palace* is the most shoddily produced.

Gram, playing the street-tough artist, told *Fusion* magazine, "They've let us follow our concept. They are in it for the money like every other record company, and if people start buying our records they'll let us run with the ball. If I have to pay more dues I'm willing to, because I dig honky-tonk and rock 'n' roll—and being on the street doesn't bug me at all. I don't need to have an image. So it doesn't matter, one record company or another."

Back home, the Burritos played regularly at the Palomino. They were heckled often—"Get off the stage, goddamned queers"—but their renditions of Porter Wagoner and Conway Twitty songs won the crowd over.

The band got a more welcoming reception at the hippie-oriented Topanga Corral. Byrds roadie Carlos Bernal was there. "When the Burrito Brothers hit the stage with 'Six Days on the Road' at the Corral in Topanga, the girls were beyond themselves," Bernal says. "They left their tables as if hypnotized. They left their boyfriends. They left their drinks, they left their drugs. They had to get onto the dance floor and start dancing. It was an ocean of the cutest girls in high heels and miniskirts. Ask any other drummer and they'll say, 'Michael Clarke was a hack.' But if you ever had Michael

Gram onstage in 1969. (© Andee Nathanson, www.andeenathanson.com)

Clarke playing drums behind you, you didn't need to worry about a thing. He was a performer's drummer. You never had to worry about the beat not being right up your ass. It was a driving force. The girls were in a frenzy. Our frenzy was country rock at a loud level. It was a sexy sound."

Around this time, Earl Ball ran into Gram at the Palomino. "He wanted to talk and I wanted to talk to him so we leaned up against a car and chatted," Ball says. "I looked at his suit. He told me, 'I've been over to see the Rolling Stones and I'm getting them interested in country music.' He was telling me he was going to pull this off . . . the youth was ready for it and it was going to be the next big thing. It was going to happen. He had the Rolling Stones on his side. He was real positive."

In March 1969 the Burritos opened for the Grateful Dead in San Francisco. The Dead and their consorts were well-known for dosing those around them with LSD. It was unwise to eat or drink anything in the Dead's proximity that you didn't bring yourself. The San Francisco show was going well until someone gave Sneaky Pete a Coca-Cola that was, unbeknownst to him, laced with LSD. Of that there is no doubt. What happened next is disputed. A less reliable source claims the acid hit Sneaky in mid-set, that he freaked out onstage, crying, "Whoop, whoop, whoop!" as he played the steel, and then walked from the Fillmore to Marin County and back. A more credible source reports: "It was scary. Pete went from never, ever doing drugs to being fully dosed with acid. He had to be taken to an emergency room and given downers."

Gram was not thrilled to be compared to the San Francisco bands. When asked if his group shared communal housing like the Dead and the Airplane, Gram answered, "No, we're not wife swappers and we're not faggots, so why live all in the same house together with the same old ladies with all those temptations hanging around?"

Gram and Hillman wrote "The Train Song" during the tour. Back in L.A. they called in Larry Williams and Johnny "Guitar" Watson to produce it in a one-song recording session. Gram and Chris wanted an old-time R&B authenticity for "Train Song." What they got was a hard lesson.

Watson and Williams incarnated gut-bucket R&B roots. Williams' first hit was "Short Fat Annie." He followed it with "Boney Moronie" in 1957 and "Dizzy Miss Lizzie," both of which he wrote. The Beatles covered "Dizzy Miss Lizzie" and almost everyone covered "Boney Moronie." Williams' royalties enabled him to become a heavy drug user. He was shot to death in 1980.

Watson's first hit was a 1955 cover of Earl King's "Those Lonely, Lonely Nights." He played with R&B bandleader Johnny Otis (father of guitar prodigy Shuggie) and in 1962 charted with "Cuttin' In." He and Williams toured the U.K. in 1965. Together they hit with "Mercy, Mercy, Mercy" in 1967. In the seventies, Watson cut two idiosyncratic funk albums highlighting his wailing guitar and yielding the hits "Ain't That a Bitch?" in 1976 and "A Real Mother for You" in 1977. Watson was a fearsome character who pimped to support his career as a session guitarist and producer. Or, rather, he played guitar when he could be called away from pimping.

In hiring Watson and Williams, Gram and Chris sought a link to the pure R&B they loved and covered in their live shows. Clarence White and Leon Russell played on the session, which turned into a drug-fueled circus. The Burritos felt like poor hosts when they had no weed to offer Watson and Williams. After the band apologized, Watson pulled out a fat joint. Referring to a popular margarine ad in which crowns magically popped up on people's heads ("Taste fit for a king!"), Watson said, "I call this the butter. It'll make you feel like you're wearing a crown."

Watson and Williams reportedly spent their time in the control room doing drugs and ignoring the band. According to Phil Kaufman, instead of injecting soul into the proceedings, the two producers sat in the control room doing lines of cocaine and saying, "Sounds great, guys. Sounds great."

Leon Russell finally took over the board to make some sense of the chaos. Gram, as the paying customer, could have held Williams and Watson to a professional standard, or fired them on the spot. Instead, he snorted right along with them. "It was terrible! I was so embarrassed," Jimmi Seiter says. "That's the demise of the Burritos in my mind. All Gram wanted to do is have fun, party." Burritos insiders agree with Seiter. For Hillman the sessions represented the peak of Burrito excess and indulgence, the end of a pure period of writing, recording, and playing the sounds they heard in their heads. It also ended Gram and Hillman's dream of directly incorporating the R&B they loved into their music. The two worlds would not merge as easily as Gram and Hillman had thought.

Gram's behavior was characteristically passive and destructive in the face of dashed hopes. He did nothing to rein in Williams and Watson; he endorsed their antics by snorting with them. He could have taken action but instead encouraged events to spin out of control. To be produced by two obscure R&B legends was Gram's dream, but he declined to pursue the dream when it did not magically unfold.

Chris and Gram moved again, to Beverly Glen Drive. This house, too, was known as Burrito Manor, and the atmosphere was hardly different from the Manor's previous address. "Strange women coming in and out, a lot of powder, liquor," Hillman recalled later. "Gram was drunk and stupid a lot. . . . He would go up to some chick at the Troubadour and say, 'Hel-*lo*, senorita.' He had these big, sincere, brown eyes. We were hoodlums then, really the outlaw band."

Being consistently underappreciated and forced into an outsider role led the band to develop an ethos to go with their clothes and repertoire— and their refusal to be professional about rehearsal. "We were musical rebels," Sneaky Pete says. "We didn't play according to any slick concept. We played rough, as we felt it. We were an outlaw band because we weren't accepted by audiences or by our peers and contemporaries. A lot of musicians in other bands were derogatory in their remarks about us."

"We're the only true outlaw band," Gram said. "Why? Because we're treated great in one way and, on the other hand, we're completely misunderstood. Rock critics and country critics completely misunderstand—it would be the same with R&B critics if they had the opportunity."

Years later, Hillman reflected on how the Burritos' outlaw style, musical and otherwise, set the tone for other bands. Glenn Frey, soon to be a founding member of the Eagles, was half of the duo Longbranch Pennywhistle.

The other half was producer and songwriter J. D. Souther, who later formed a band with Hillman and Richie Furay. The Pennywhistle sometimes opened for the Burritos. Frey claimed he "learned a lot about stage presence and how to deliver a vocal" from watching Gram and the Burritos, according to Hillman. "Don't think Glenn Frey wasn't in that audience studying Gram. He was. And it is nothing bad. I have all due respect for Glenn and the Eagles. I think they are great. But they are an extension of the Burrito Brothers outlaw thing, an extension itself of the Byrds–Buffalo Springfield family. It's a heavy family tree."

Playing redneck clubs and low-down dives was key to the Burritos' outlaw self-image, but it was also a fact of life. The band had once loved dives; now they had few other options. The two former Byrds felt they had too much stature to go back to playing second-rate venues, however romantically low-rent they might be.

"They couldn't get booked anywhere," Jimmi Seiter says. "They're not country, they're like a bastard son. They would book us these gigs and the venue would be expecting a pop band and we're a rock band or country band or vice versa. . . . At rock festivals we were well received. But we weren't country enough to play at a country nightclub . . . Gram didn't mind playing the pop festivals, but he didn't like playing clubs. Hillman didn't like it either. Hillman had never played clubs before. When the Byrds played clubs they played the biggest clubs in Hollywood. The Burritos played shitholes, places in Colorado Springs. Hard-to-find places out in the middle of nowhere. Try to play 'Hot Burrito #1' for a country audience. They go, 'What the fuck is this? Fuzz steel guitar? Get out of here!'"

"They could play country. And a couple of times they had to redo the Burritos style and play a full-blown country set. They'd pull out the acoustic instruments and wing it. Fortunately for them, country songs are kind of easy. Like three chords and out. As long as you know the words you're cool, and Gram knew a lot of them."

"We played anywhere," Sneaky Pete says. "High schools, grade schools, junior proms, even *prisons*. They loved us at the prisons. But generally audiences didn't respond to us. We ended up in a black club that had just switched over the clientele and was not amused by our Nudie suits. They walked in and said, 'Man, what is this shit?' and then walked out."

Gram naturally put a positive spin on their circumstances. "There is a good music scene in L.A.—a lot of good musicians have been playing together lately," he told an interviewer. "But it's not so much at the Whisky and places like that as in the honky-tonks out in the Valley. Groups like Delaney & Bonnie, Taj Mahal, the Tulsa Rhythm Revue. A lot of funky people coming from the South—Texas, Tennessee, and Tulsa—coming out to L.A. to make a little dough, and they find out you can't because there aren't many clubs in L.A. to play at . . . Snoopy's Opera House, Peacock Alley, the Laurel Room, the Prelude, the Palomino, the Aces Club, and the Red Velour and the Hobo, clubs that nobody knows about in the San Fernando Valley, the City of Industry, Orange County. The clubs out in the Valley are honky-tonks and funky, nicer than the honky-tonks in Nashville, because the people are less liable to rap on you for having long hair. They see more of it and you can go out there and boogie all you want. That's the most positive thing I can think of about L.A., these places out in the Valley—the most negative thing I can think of is the Strip itself . . . with all the people addicted to carbon monoxide."

Gram was frustrated with the Burritos' lack of success and the country-rock acts springing up in their wake. Michael Nesmith of the Monkees was making authentic country records; Poco's first album, a sort of country-rock lite, was well received. San Francisco's Moby Grape had begun a Bay Area movement away from psychedelic jams toward tighter, country-inflected material. The market was starting to embrace a variety of emerging country-rock forms, but not the Burritos.

"We paid a lot of dues, but we dug it," Gram said. "While everyone else was going to the Whisky building up their egos, we were saying, 'Jesus Christ, man, nobody likes us! What are we doing?' We were going out to clubs and to forget our troubles we were getting smashed and rocking 'n' rolling every night as hard as we could. Nowadays everyone wants to get in on the bandwagon, everybody wants to say they are country, including Bob Dylan, who I dig and respect, but he's not as country as *Crawdaddy* [a national monthly rock magazine, now defunct] seems to think he is. Now [the critics and rock writers] are trying to project this country scene onto him. And Dylan isn't country . . . he's a poet."

Gram spoke to the fuss raised over their sequined suits. "We think sequins are good taste," he insisted. *"Rolling Stone,* the *Free Press*—they think that we're a bunch of show-offs and we're trying to put everything down. We're merely reflecting everything because real music is supposed to reflect reality. You can't build a reality in music, you have to reflect it. Like 'original' music was made to get people together. Like religious music, to form a bond between you and your ancestors, let's say. In church you would have music that would make you nostalgic and think of the olden times and what the reality was that led you up to right now. That's where music is at. You can't build your own reality—that's why psychedelic music is so jive. It's everybody's own bag. No, I'm sorry, you know, we're all in it together. Like it or not."

Gram was making his case for Cosmic American Music and stating the facts. Real country musicians wore sequins. Gram loved the sequins for their absurdity, and he loved them sincerely. The L.A. country rockers following Gram thought boot-cut jeans and cowboy boots were a uniform of authenticity. But in the world of real country, the blue-jeaned boot wearers were the poseurs, and Gram had it right.

"They're so uptight about our sequined suits," he said. "Just because we wear sequined suits doesn't mean we think we're great, it means we think sequins are great."

IN THE SUMMER OF 1969, Gram left Burrito Manor and moved into the Chateau Marmont Hotel on Sunset Boulevard. He shared an apartment with Tony Foutz. When Gram moved out, Chris Hillman left to share a house with Bernie Leadon in the nearby beachside town of Venice.

Eve Babitz was an astute observer of and participant in the Sunset Strip scene. Like Andee Nathanson, Eve hung out in the music and movie worlds and dated musicians. A remarkable writer, she had a column in *Esquire* when she was nineteen and *Esquire* was the best magazine in America. She became a close friend of Gram's and later portrayed him as a character in her fiction. The chapter "Rosewood Casket" from her first collection of stories, *Eve's Hollywood*, describes Gram's magical presence when Babitz first met him, and his later decline.

"When I first met Gram he was wearing a blue blazer and white pants," Eve Babitz says, "and then it was, like, cowboy boots and Indian outfits and serapes. Gram was the perfect Hollywood person. He was so beautiful and a stranger from the South. I was amazed by him. He had charisma. He was like Elvis. I never met Elvis, but Gram radiated charisma. I had seen a lot of people with charisma by that point. There's a tradition in Hollywood that we try to protect people who are going to be actors and stars from whatever's going to go wrong with them. We try to keep them safe before they either go insane or die. When people have charisma, other people take care of them around here. They could get away with murder." As for Gram's mission to bring American roots music to resistant audiences while wearing a sequined suit: "He was so beautiful he got away with it."

Gram around the time he moved into the Chateau Marmont. (© Andee Nathanson, www.andeenathanson.com)

When Gram moved into the Chateau Marmont, a room in the hotel cost only twenty-six dollars a night. "The Chateau Marmont is elegant," Eve says. "Greta Garbo lived there. It's intense and behind the scenes. Quiet. It was beautiful. Gram was perfect in it. It was as beautiful as he was."

Eve points out that the hotel was part of a cluster of old-time Hollywood landmarks. The Garden of Allah apartment complex, where F. Scott Fitzgerald, Robert Benchley, and other literary and film celebrities lived, was across the street. Down the road was Schwab's drugstore, a meeting place for old Hollywood where Lana Turner was supposedly discovered. "The Garden of Allah was torn down in the fifties and all the ghosts went over to the Chateau," Eve says. "So the Chateau had this ancient patina. Of course, Hollywood has only been here since 1903. But the Chateau seemed to have five hundred years of history."

With its separate self-enclosed bungalow apartments and thick, sound-proof walls, the Marmont offered more privacy than the average hotel. "I once stayed next door to the country-rock star Gram Parsons, a man whose consumption of drink, drugs, and women was legendary, as were his good manners," a British journalist wrote. "Indeed, he was very pleasant in the corridor, and for all the sounds I heard from his rooms he might as well have been at his prayers."

Andee Nathanson first met Foutz when she was eighteen and working as a model at Jax, the Beverly Hills fashion house. "The Chateau was hilarious," Andee says. "It was like a well-located rooming house where the inmates were running the institution."

"It was like a rock-and-roll hotel, but rock-and-rollers would change where they lived every five minutes," Eve Babitz says. "They never lived there, except for Gram. They would buy one house here, one house there. The rock-and-roll scene was in Topanga, and they were out at five in the morning. Nobody ever lived anywhere. Gram was a bastion of stability, considering."

Another worldly character in this scene was Prince Stanislas "Stash" Klossowski de Rola, son of the reclusive French painter known as Balthus. Discovered by Italian director Visconti at seventeen, Stash became an actor. In 1963 he went to Paris and played rock and roll with Vince Taylor, a performer credited as the inspiration for David Bowie's *Ziggy Stardust*. In 1965, on tour with Taylor, Stash befriended the Rolling Stones and became close with Brian Jones. It was on the same tour that Jones met Anita Pallenberg, who had been hanging with Taylor's band. Jones and Stash were busted together for drugs in 1967, further cementing their friendship.

Stash and Tony Foutz became acquainted in Rome, where both stayed at the Villa Medici. Stash moved frequently: L.A., Paris, Rome, and the Moroccan mansion of playboy John Paul Getty and his iconic bohemian wife, Talitha. Stash was one of the first prehippies to make the pilgrimage to India to study meditation.

"It was rather seedy and very much a home," Stash says of the Chateau. "The Chateau Marmont was full of artists and longtime residents. It was the Chelsea Hotel of the West Coast."

"The Chateau was a den of iniquity," Eve Babitz says. "I would always leave before things got too weird. I would figure things are falling apart and I should leave."

Even in this star-studded setting, Gram stood out. Just as he found a way to bring together the sex of rock and the pain of country, Gram combined the glitter of old-school Hollywood with the new hippie glamour. A glamour he helped create and codify.

"When I grew up, the bohemian community was in San Francisco, and L.A. was this square place where nothing ever happened," Eve says. "L.A. was as isolated as an Iowa farmer town. They believed in stardom and sequins and rhinestones. And they took it seriously."

As a connoisseur of the L.A. scene, Babitz was fascinated by Gram and recognized that he incarnated something magically, classically Hollywood yet totally brand-new.

"I was so into Gram's looks," she recalls. "I couldn't see anything else when I was around Gram. I couldn't see other people. I told him I wanted to come over and take pictures of him and he said, 'You have to wait three days so I can lose some weight.'

"I would make him get dressed up and take pictures. But his ex-girlfriends and wife would tear them up when they left."

Gram and Foutz's apartment number was 4F—as visitors often remarked, the same designation as Gram's unfit-to-serve draft status. John Phillips' wife, singer Genevieve Waite, another Swinging Londoner, recalls that the door "had these incredible graphics that said: ALL ABOUT GRAM. I had never seen graphics like that: this great printing of spacemen all over the door. It was cool."

Linda Lawrence moved to L.A. from England with her son Julian. Julian's father was Brian Jones of the Stones. Linda met Gram at the Chateau. Shortly after, Linda and Julian moved in with Gram. The affair lasted a few months. Linda later went on to marry the hugely successful folk-pop singer-songwriter, Donovan Leitch.

"Train Song" was released in July of 1969. It garnered no airplay or sales.

On August 9, 1969, the sixties came to an end in Los Angeles when Charles Manson's long-haired minions murdered actress Sharon Tate and four others at the house Sharon's husband, director Roman Polanski, had rented from Byrds producer Terry Melcher.

"It was the end of the innocence," Andee Nathanson says. "In Hollywood, in music, film, in L.A., that wasn't supposed to happen. That was the bogeyman coming out. The energy shifted, from a sense of connection to,

'Oh, my God, there's crazy people out there that can kill you.' In all this innocence and all this love, it came crashing down. The bubble burst. I've heard rock-and-roll people say, 'Let's not get too real.' But that's about as real as you can get."

Manson burst the bubble for the originators of the sixties. A few days later, on August 15, Woodstock demonstrated the market penetration of the longhair lifestyle. The size of the Woodstock audience—almost five hundred thousand strong—shocked the business world into understanding how much money could be made from the notion of a counterculture. Simultaneously, Manson's crew established that the trappings of the hippie lifestyle could be extended—for better or worse—in directions other than peace and love. As the groovier Angelenos reeled from their new perspective on the dark side, the movie *Woodstock* was about to convince the American public that the brotherhood of hippie-dom was alive and well.

Woodstock, the movie, brought the concept of an alternative community held together by rock and roll and drugs to every small town in America. At Woodstock, the festival, Joan Baez played "Drug Store Truck Drivin' Man." The song was not included in the film.

THE ROLLING STONES returned to L.A. on October 17 to mix *Let It Bleed* and prepare for their 1969 tour of America. They moved into several L.A. houses, including Stephen Stills' estate—which had earlier been home to Monkee Peter Tork and his legion of naked girls. Phil Kaufman had to eject Stills, who didn't want to leave because he was ill, and his drummer, Dallas Taylor, who was drunk.

Writer Stanley Booth, later the author of *The True Adventures of the Rolling Stones*, met Gram shortly after the Stones arrived in L.A. He and Gram both hailed from Waycross, but hadn't known each other there. In his book, Booth describes Keith and Gram coming in from a tennis game and singing country tunes together around the piano, with Mick Jagger joining in. Added Booth, "Mick didn't look sure he liked it."

"When the three of us sang together, it sounded like Gaelic music. Like the Incredible String Band," Gram said, referring to a popular English group given to sophisticated hippie sentiments and exquisite harmonies with an Olde English feel. "On one occasion at the piano with me and Jagger and Richards, there was Little Richard. 'It's all the same,' that's what Keith said. Two Georgia peaches and two English boys, stinky English kids. . . . It's far out and drunk."

"Gram was one of the few people who helped me sing country music,"

Mick Jagger recalls. "The idea of country music being played slightly tongue in cheek, Gram had that in 'Drug Store Truck Drivin' Man,' and we have that sardonic quality, too."

At Gram's urging, Mick and Keith hired country fiddler Byron Berline for "Country Honk," the countrified album version of their cowbell-driven single "Honky Tonk Women." Byron had played with the Dillards and recorded with Dillard & Clark; he and Gram met when both were recording at A&M.

As Berline tells it, the emerging country-rock scene in Los Angeles was like "a big family," with everyone playing, experimenting with, and enjoying the same kinds of music. "Country music, rock-and-rolly stuff," Berline says. "I get a phone call from the Rolling Stones. They called real late at night and were mumbling, 'Hey, we're the Rolling Stones.' I asked, 'The magazine?' 'No, the group.' Finally I figured out it was Keith Richards and Phil Kaufman on the phone. I said, 'Well, I'm gonna be out there in about six days.' They said, 'No, no, we want you out here tomorrow.' So I flew out of Oklahoma City."

Berline played the song with the band a few times in the studio. He was told, "We have this idea to give it a little ambience—we'll take you out to the sidewalk and record it there." His track was recorded on the sidewalk. Berline learned that he'd been called because, "Gram tried to talk them into doing it more country, so they decided to use the fiddle on it. That was a big shock to me. That helped my career."

The song does have a powerful outdoor ambience. It opens with the sound of wind, an acoustic guitar, and an iconic double car-horn honk as Byron spirals in the opening fiddle lick. Phil Kaufman later claimed he'd hired a woman to drive by and repeatedly hit the car horn.

Gram took the Stones to his favorite haunts. One night the crew turned up at the Topanga Corral. Gram and the Burritos played and sang and everyone whooped and drank beer. According to Stanley Booth, the evening reminded the Stones of the good old days when they had played in down-and-dirty clubs. "Now, getting ready to get back on the road," Booth wrote, "it was good to be at the Corral and see all these different types, motorcycle boots, eagle tattoos, lesbian romancers, white English [singers], Beach Boys, Georgia boys brought together by the music."

Gram, Andee, Keith, and Anita flew to Las Vegas to see Elvis Presley. It's impossible to overstate how unhip Elvis was at that point. He incarnated everything destructive about the effects of show business on rock authenticity. "Gram was so excited, he was like a little kid," Andee remembers. "I've never seen him so animated. . . . Gram was almost out of his seat, jumping up and clapping when Elvis appeared in a white outfit with sequins and all the little old ladies in front were so excited—it was electrifying. We met Elvis afterwards backstage. I think it was one of the great highlights of Gram's life, and amazing to see them together."

Gram was constantly high. "I would spend days taking drugs with Gram," Eve Babitz says. "I thought he was always on drugs. He had huge bottles of drugs—jars filled with Demerol and Placidyl [a sedative and hypnotic whose production in the U.S. was discontinued in 1999] and Dexamyl [an amphetamine combined with a barbiturate] and stuff you shouldn't be having. Stuff that would keep you up all night and all day. His friends were over and they all took them. I took as many as I could. Meth was the worst. You can write *War and Peace* but you can't sit down. I would hang around, take drugs. We would wait all day for somebody to bring the grass. . . . That's what people did in those days if they could afford it."

The creative abuse of substances was another interest Keith Richards and Gram shared. "Gram was as knowledgeable about chemical substances as I was," Keith says. "I don't think I taught him much about drugs—I was still learning myself, much to my detriment. I think we were both basically into the same thing. He had good taste. He went for the top of the line. We liked drugs and we liked the finest quality. He could get better coke than the mafia."

Throughout the Stones' history, plenty of others liked drugs of the finest quality and tried to hang with Keith. Keith's constitution is legendary, and no one who tried to match his drug consumption (or his appetite for staying awake days on end) could, in the final trial, stay the course. Stanley Booth wrote, "I decided that if Keith and I kept dipping into the same bag, we would both be dead." Booth flatters himself. If the historical record is any guide, only one of them would be.

That's not to imply that Keith bears any blame for Gram's drug use. No one ever lived on Keith's schedule for any length of time except Keith. What may have seemed like normal life to Gram was in fact junkiedom at the most taxing levels of consumption.

As for precisely when Gram added regular heroin use to cocaine and pills, no one remembers a Eureka! moment. No one describes being shocked to discover Gram using. No one suggests that Keith introduced Gram to shooting up. It struck Gram's friends as inevitable, another step on the path.

"This whole generation has been into heroin, which I'll never understand because it's the worst drug on the planet," Miss Mercy says. "Even though I've done it, I was never into it. L.A. was a wonderful place . . . but there were too many drugs. Everything was too drug oriented. At that point everyone was on downers and drinkin'. It was kind of sloppy—all Seconals and Tuinals."

In a milieu where roots and authenticity—and relentless ego competition—loomed so large, the move from prescription downers to the baddest-ass street drug was, for the committed, almost unavoidable. In the immortal words of Keith Richards, as told to John Phillips, "Pharmaceuticals are for pussies."

Well-off users assert that heroin, among the major addictive drugs, is not so bad for you. As long as you buy first-rate junk, as long as you don't suffer withdrawal or do unreasonable amounts, their argument goes, heroin is manageable. It's the withdrawing and becoming readdicted and withdrawing again that wrecks your health. That and not having the money or connections to buy clean shit. And for some, Keith Richards among them, it seems to be true. "Remember," Richards once said, "I learned to *ski* on heroin."

If your main heroin partner is a guy with those capabilities and attitude, then devoting yourself to keeping up is a dangerous decision. But Gram liked heroin, and nothing in his financial circumstances made addiction difficult for him. Gram never claimed to be a tormented addict. He often said he had no desire to quit.

Genevieve Waite came to a Stones session with John Phillips, who had drug problems of his own. "We went to the recording studio and Gram was there," she says. "Everyone was on junk and John was *really* mad at him. John said to me, 'We're getting out of here!' And I said, 'John, why do we have to leave?' And he said, 'Well, everyone is on junk.' John was trying hard not to be around it."

Miss Mercy recalls the day that Jimi Hendrix's girlfriend, Devon Wilson (the inspiration for his "Dolly Dagger"), came pounding on her door saying, "Keith sent me here for me to find Gram." Miss Mercy took them to Gram's place. "We found Gram playing with his fucking needles," she says. "He was that far gone. Taking a lightbulb wire to clean out his needles so he could fix. But he was all excited that Keith sent Devon. Devon wanted to find Gram for heroin, and the heroin was there."

"John [Phillips] was not a member of the Gram Parsons fan club," Genevieve Waite says. "He was hard on Gram, like an older brother. He loved Gram and he loved his voice, but he wasn't like a lot of people who were Gram sycophants. Gram was doing junk long before John started, and John hated it. He loved him, but he wasn't going to ease up. Gram would come over to all our different houses and John would say to him, 'What are you doing with the Stones? Why are you doing this?'"

The drugs, music, and elegant graveyard wit that Keith and Gram shared seemed only the signposts of a deeper bond. The two were so enmeshed that boundaries separating their two personalities began to erode.

"Gram and Keith were kind of in love," Pamela Des Barres says. "I'm sure they never did anything physical, but they had this incredible mutual-admiration society. They understood each other and wanted to take parts of each other and make them their own. . . . They took different pieces of clothing from each other and traded. Gram started wearing makeup like Keith and Keith started wearing Nudie belts. It was incredible to watch."

"Gram got so overtaken that he started turning into Keith," Miss Mercy says. "It was crazy. Gram was just like Keith and Keith was just like Gram. They switched accents and they switched clothes. Gram was running around stage with his wrist [flapping] and acting so odd that people would roll their eyes up in their head. We were like, 'Oh, my God, this is frightening what's happening to this poor guy.'

"He had a limp wrist. That's how influenced he got by Keith. He was acting like he was English and gay. You know the rest of the Burritos thought he'd flipped his lid. At the Troubadour, Gram started putting all this English stuff on and Keith was giving him clothes. Keith was getting more Gram-y. They changed identities, basically. Gram was almost getting an English accent and Keith was getting a Southern one. They were inseparable. Mick was annoyed."

Pamela Des Barres wrote at the time: "Keith scared me; he's like a foreign object and Gram is becoming his clone." "The time he was spending with Keith didn't have a very good influence on him over the long term," Jet Thomas says. "It made the other [Burrito] members feel left out." "Gram stuck out like a bleeding thumb in satins and nail polish," journalist Rick Cusick says. "The rest of the Burritos wondered where he got the balls." "Gram wanted to be in the Stones," Bernie Leadon says. "Onstage with us he'd take off these scarves and start dancing like Jagger—with this country band! Hillman called this Gram 'Mr. Mystique.' But I liked him. The cat had balls—he didn't care."

"Chris didn't like that—he didn't get it," Jimmi Seiter says. "One night, they played the Whisky, which was a good gig for them, and Gram arrived late, with his eye makeup on. You can't imagine. Chris had this manly thing about him and Gram showed up with makeup and Keith's scarves and belts. He started acting like Keith onstage—eventually he drop-kicked his guitar across the room, into the wall at the other side of the club. By that point Chris had turned his back."

"The Rolling Stones got in the way tremendously," Hillman says, "because Gram was like a groupie. 'Oh, sorry guys, but I've got to go hang out with the Stones now.' The times I picked him up at Keith's house were a little strange. They'd come skipping out like kids."

"Chris and I were living in this little house down at the beach, riding our bicycles and trying to be healthy," Bernie Leadon says. "Chris and Gram were living different lives."

Gram's different life was wreaking havoc on his performances and his relationship with Hillman. "Sometimes Gram was fine in that drunken, good-old-boy, sorrowful voice of his," a source recalls. "Other times it would be fragmented and you could see how angry Hillman was. A lot of shows weren't as good as they should have been. A lot of recording sessions that could have been better. But there were also a lot of recording sessions that were fine."

"[Gram and Hillman] both loved the music and worked together musically," Jet Thomas says, "and during a certain period of time they were buddies with their motorcycles and Chris' little pickup [truck]. They hung out together, but ultimately they were different people. I'm not surprised that over a period of time those differences became greater."

Gram and Keith's bonding caused strains for another partnership as well. "My only problem with Gram was Mick," Keith says. "For some reason Mick has a hard-on about me. He'll get incredibly shitty against anyone who appears to be getting too close to me . . ." According to Keith, he and Mick never spent that much time together outside of their work for the band. In Gram, Jagger had run up against what Keith called "a bigger gentleman. The biggest gent that I have ever known." Keith resented Mick's efforts to control who his friends were. Gram—as the bigger gent—reminded Keith that he had to get along with Mick.

Gram's infatuation with the Stones, and Mick's impatience with Gram, came to a head. The Burritos had a show to play, but Gram didn't want to leave the Stones' recording session. "I finally found him at the Stones session!" Hillman recounts. "I go in there to him and he's going, 'Ah, I don't want to go.' And Jagger got right in his face and told him, 'You've got a responsibility to Chris, to the other band members, and the people who come to your show. You better go do your show *now*.' He was matter-of-fact. I'll never forget that. So Gram got up and went to the show."

Jagger seemed to be the only person whose chastening made Gram behave more maturely.

Keith threw a party at Stephen Stills' house for Gram's twenty-third birthday, on November 5, 1969. One of the guests was sixteen-year-old Gretchen Burrell. She was a quintessential blond Southern Californian, an aspiring actress and the daughter of Larry Burrell, a conservative TV newscaster. Even by L.A. standards, where astonishing beauty is commonplace, Gretchen was astonishingly beautiful. She and Gram were immediately smitten.

Pamela Des Barres says of Gretchen: "She was a gorgeous model, a real beauty." Miss Mercy found her stunning. Genevieve Waite says, "I met her once. She was in Gram's room at the Chateau, sitting on Gram's bed. She seemed like a happy, smiley, beautiful blond girl. She seemed happy with Gram and to love him." Eve Babitz remembers Gretchen as happy when she first met Gram and then increasingly "pissed off." Marcia Katz says, "He was heavy into drugs when he met Gretchen, so his whole involvement with her came from a drug-related state."

In late November Chris Ethridge left the Burritos. He wanted to pursue his growing studio career. He later played with Ry Cooder, Linda Ronstadt, Jerry Garcia, and Willie Nelson. "I had never realized that Chris wasn't a country bass player," Gram says. "And it should have been obvious to me 'cause he's such a great studio musician, but he's not a country bass player. He realized it before anyone and said, 'Wow, man, I'm sorry.'

"What we needed was somebody who could play country shuffle. Chris understood that, so he split. I suppose from the time he split I got sort of disillusioned."

Even if it sounds like sour grapes, Gram's assessment is accurate. Ethridge's style inclines toward R&B and groove-oriented rock. His hands and mind are too busy for simple country bass playing. Ethridge tends to push the beat forward or lay back off it—slow-burn funk style—and neither works for country.

"I liked writing with him an awful lot," Gram continued. "It blew my mind that he wasn't the right bass player. And so when he was missing, it seemed the idea had been wrong, that we had picked the wrong people. And

I didn't know quite how to say it to Chris [Hillman] without getting in a fist-fight about it. So I tried to stick it out, make it work, but . . ."

Chris Hillman moved back to bass. Bernie Leadon took over Hillman's spot as rhythm guitarist. Leadon had played with Hillman in the Scottsville Squirrel Barkers, with the folk-country pioneers Hearts and Flowers, and with Dillard & Clark. He was a rhythm guitarist with an exceptional sense of the beat and the ability to blend driving guitar lines with the bass. He described himself as "a great utility infielder." Leadon has skills and a singular cohesion; he makes any band sound tighter, their songs more energetic. That's no small gift, and few have it. Leadon radiates an unshakeable air of purpose and bedrock sanity. Given that he later helped cofound the Eagles, one of the most popular bands in rock, remaining sane is no small accomplishment.

"The first album's momentum had been spent," Bernie says. "They had gotten a lot of critical acclaim, but they hadn't sold much. Chris Ethridge had quit and now they're a man short. Chris Hillman went back to playing bass and they call me.

"Gram was an incredibly charming, charismatic guy, and he made sure that people would look at him. He was dressed in an interesting, different way. He always had expensive clothes, scarves, and funny hats. He could afford a custom Harley [Gram had traded up from a smaller BSA] with a custom paint job and those clothes and to live at the Chateau Marmont.

"I was intrigued by all the music that Gram was listening to. He always had something on the record player or the tape player. He was the first guy that I knew that made custom tapes. He made mix tapes: He would have a bunch of different country people, R&B people, the Stones, the Impressions, Curtis Mayfield. He had a lot of obscure country stuff. He knew all these songs. He was a musicologist in that way. He knew the lyrics to hundreds of songs. He could always throw something out like, 'Hey, let's do this,' and I was like, 'What the fuck is that?' He knew all this old country stuff and obscure R&B. He could pull it out of his pocket. He would start playing, or start strumming in some tempo or some key, and we would all fall in."

SIXTEEN

Burrito Deluxe

THE NEW BURRITOS LINEUP'S FIRST APPEARANCE WAS AT THE STONES' disastrous free concert at Altamont Speedway on December 6, 1969. Responding to fan complaints about high ticket prices for their tour, the Stones added a free show at the last minute and did not plan it with their usual care. When permits for San Francisco's Golden Gate Park were denied, the gig was moved to Sears Point Raceway and, when that fell through, to the lesser-known Altamont Speedway, sixty miles east of San Francisco. The venue was chosen fewer than forty-eight hours before the concert began. Altamont was pretty much in the middle of nowhere. Nevertheless, some three hundred thousand people showed up.

Little attention had been given to the usual niceties. The stage was only four feet high. Security was provided by local Hell's Angels, brokered through Grateful Dead guitarist Jerry Garcia. Garcia had hung around with the Angels since the days of Ken Kesey's Acid Tests. In his words: "The Angels are scary." One version of the story is that the Angels were hired by Stones factotum Sam Cutler for five hundred dollars and free beer. Another holds that the Angels wanted the gig to ensure their control over drug sales at the show. At first the Angels were there only to guard the band's gear, goes yet another variant, but Cutler moved them down near the stage when they got restless.

Jacked up on speed and LSD and not so at one with the peace-and-love ethos, the Angels pounded anyone near the stage who offended them, using fists, boots, and pool cues. Among their targets was Jefferson Airplane lead singer Marty Balin, whom they knocked unconscious. The Dead refused to perform in the face of the violence. The Burritos played after the Airplane and their set is remembered as one of the few calm points of the day. In *Gimme Shelter*, the Maysles Brothers' documentary of the Stones' tour and of Altamont, Gram's back can be seen over Michael Clarke's flailing elbow. The Burritos are shown only by a camera behind the stage.

The Stones waited hours to go on, leaving the crowd restless, to say nothing of the Angels. After sundown—when the stage was more dramatic for the Maysles documentary—the Stones appeared. During their set Meredith Hunter, an eighteen-year-old near the stage, was stabbed to death by an Angel. Slow-motion replays during *Gimme Shelter* make it clear that Hunter had a gun in his hand when the Angel killed him. The Stones, who amid the ongoing chaos could not tell what had happened, kept playing.

"Gram insisted that I go with him to Altamont, which I did not want to do," Jet Thomas says. "He got me a hotel room and paid my plane ticket. He sent Sneaky Pete all the way out to Claremont to come get me. He was kind and generous about including me. For some reason he always wanted me to go. He would insist. I wish I had never gone to Altamont, but he insisted."

"That was Gram's gig because of the Stones," Bernie Leadon says. "It was a comedy of errors the way the whole thing went down. . . . By the time that we got there in the afternoon, there was inadequate everything, and they had three hundred thousand people, with few bathrooms and no concessions, no fencing, no backstage security. We had to get in and there was bumper-to-bumper traffic.

"Sneaky Pete heads onto the shoulder and he starts going forty miles an hour next to two lanes completely stopped. We looked behind us and said, 'Oh, shit,' because there were tons of people following us. Somebody in front of us got the bright idea to pull onto the shoulder, except they forgot to look to see us coming. I can't remember if Pete actually hit him or if we swerved. We went down into a ditch and luckily it was all grass apron. We basically semicrashed, and there were all these people behind us zooming by in the breakdown lane. A couple of bikers go by and Gram says, 'The Hell's Angels are in charge of security, so I'm going to stop one of them.' So he goes up and he has silk pants on and some kind of scarf and says to them, 'Hey, we're with the Stones, man, and we have to get in.' The guy says, 'Get on.' So he hops onto some guy's bike and says to us, 'Come on, guys, we'll go with the Angels,' and everybody says no.

"I said, 'I'll go.' I hop onto the second bike and we blast off with these bikers. At the head of the road where all the people came in was a big natural bowl. We came in at the top and the bikers kept going right down through the middle of this jam-packed crowd. There had to be three hundred thousand people in there. People everywhere with their blankets set up. It had a Sunday-in-the-park kind of vibe. The Angels rode right over their blankets, with everyone scattering. They rode down to the front of the stage with me and Gram on the back and parked their bikes and got off. They parked their bikes right there! It was so close that you could touch the microphone. They had pissed off three hundred thousand people! I went, Whoa. That was the beginning of it."

After Marty Balin was carried off unconscious, the Jefferson Airplane stopped playing and the Burritos took the stage. Their set included "Lucille," "To Love Somebody," and "Six Days on the Road." Gram wore brown suede pants with a wide, low-hanging, big-buckled belt and a python-patterned rhinestone Nudie shirt with thunderbirds on the front, Indians on the deltoids, and a dancing Indian warrior on the back. Beneath that shirt he wore what appears to be a truck-stop waitress' tube top that left his belly exposed. His hair, frosted with blond streaks, fell down below his shoulders. He was a beautiful androgyne, a new model of rock style, citing so many different sources and ideas in his outfit—and they all worked. No white rocker in America dressed as Gram did at the time; no one else had the chic or the balls. In her novel *Out of Africa*, Isak Dinesen describes chic as "a wild intelligence." Gram had that in spades. Only Sly Stone could equal Gram for outrageous style.

"There was real anger [in the crowd] because the Grateful Dead refused to play," Leadon says. "The Burritos played in the afternoon. While we played everyone was sort of happy because we were playing happy music. Everyone had these coffee-can lids with different colors—there were thousands of them and people were throwing them into the air like Frisbees. And people were having fun. Then [Crosby, Stills, Nash and Young] played, but there was a two-hour lull before the Stones. They didn't want to play till

Gram at Altamont. (© Robert Altman, www.altmanphoto.com)

after dark. Gram and I went to hang with the Stones in this little tiny trailer. I lasted twenty minutes."

"I was sitting on the back of the stage on the back of a truck with Bernie Leadon and Chris Hillman," Jet Thomas remembers. "The Hell's Angels started going berserk and we left before the Stones even went on. As soon as the Burritos finished we were out of there. Gram got us a nice hotel around Sausalito." Gram paid for all the band expenses connected to Altamont.

Pamela Des Barres wrote in her diary: "As a matter of extreme principle,

I left Altamont an hour before the Stones came on. Scrunge and filth unlimited! I wasn't satisfied to sit in the dirt with half a million smelly, grubby people and wait for the Stones. I thought that people would be united and brought together in a lovely way . . . but nobody cared about each other. I lasted until the Burritos were over (they were wonderful) and the SLIMY FUCKED-UP Hell's Angels started throwing beer on me and no one around me cared! I started crying and cursing and we *split.* I don't have to go through that crap to see Mick Jagger. In the first place, after seeing him so many times, I can close my eyes and see him ANY TIME I PLEASE."

Stanley Booth pushed his way to the Stones' trailer with the band's drummer, Charlie Watts. "We moved quickly, glimpsing faces painted with crescents and stars, one big naked fat boy whose nostrils were pouring blood," Booth writes. "The trailer we were headed for was surrounded by little girls, people with cameras, and Hell's Angels. Once up the steps and inside, we were in the eye of a hurricane, peaceful and redolent of ozone." Michelle Phillips of the Mamas & the Papas showed up, bringing horror stories about the Hell's Angels' violence against the crowd. LSD was being handed out wholesale and the Angels were reportedly eating it like candy. "It didn't sound good but there was no way to do anything about it," Booth writes, "nothing to do in the center of a hurricane but ride it out."

"The reason that they had started beating people with pool cues," Bernie Leadon says, "was because their bikes were right in the front of the freaking stage. So when the concert started and the crowd surged forward, they tramped on these guys' bikes. So the pissed-off, drunken Hell's Angels started beating the shit out of people because people should not be touching their bikes, while they shouldn't have their bikes there in the first place."

"There was something wrong at Altamont from the start," Jet Thomas says. "The feeling was wrong. I don't think it was the Rolling Stones' fault. It was the end of an era, as people have said. People were not cooperative. Instead of being a love-in, it was something else."

According to Booth, the Stones delayed their show because Bill Wyman hadn't appeared; his helicopter was delayed. Gram amused himself by singing Hank Williams. At last Wyman arrived, with his wife and a woman who'd worked for the Stones in Los Angeles. Charlie Watts told Booth he was impressed by the way Gram, ever the gentleman, sprang to his feet when the women entered the room.

The Stones bolted the stage the instant they finished their set. Booth describes the Stones' departure from Altamont as a last-days-of-Saigon panic. Everyone ran for the helicopter through the enveloping darkness, charging up a steep hill and climbing through a hole in a wire fence. They piled into an ambulance that drove them through the seething crowd to the waiting chopper. Booth, Gram, and Michelle Phillips were among the last to cram into the aircraft before it took off.

"Gram was kissing Michelle," Booth writes, "trying to make out with her, and she seemed to be enduring it like a high school senior trying to make do with a sophomore boy on the way home from a church hayride."

"The rest of the Burritos left early," Bernie Leadon says, "which was smart. I stayed, me and Michael Clarke, and watched the Stones with Gram. When the show was over, Gram joined their entourage—he got into the Stones' helicopter and left. Leaving me and Michael by ourselves, with our equipment gone. So we hitchhiked and stayed in a nice hotel room that Gram had paid for in Sausalito. That's what Michael and I got out of going to Altamont."

Pamela Des Barres met up with the group in San Francisco at the Huntington Hotel. They sat and talked about the disastrous concert and Hunter's death. "Mick kept saying he felt like it was his fault and maybe he would quit rock and roll forever," Pamela says. "Everyone was extremely high. I felt like some inadequate female fly on the wall, stuck in the middle of No Laughing Matter. Gram was there, leaning against the wall, wearing black leather and eye makeup, nodding out. Keith was wearing cowboy clothes. It looked like they were turning into each other."

Gram's high school confidante, Margaret Fisher, was also at Altamont. She was part of the crowd. Margaret had been modeling in San Francisco, living an aimless life as a party girl and sequential mistress to various Bay Area filmmakers and writers. "I had a terrible time," she says. "It was cold and damp. The first twenty junkies that got there locked themselves in the Porta Potties for the rest of the day and I couldn't pee. I hated it. Gram never knew I was there—he was on the stage. I read about him in *Rolling Stone*. I wasn't even surprised. I thought, Well, of course, what else is he going to do? Some of my friends said I should go up and talk to him and I said, 'I don't think so.' I'm not the type that goes up to the stage."

THE NEXT MORNING the Stones left for Europe. Gram went back to being a Burrito. The band, with its new lineup, continued to play wherever it could get an audience. "The first six months we were playing in the San Fernando Valley," Leadon says. "We would play high school assemblies. Michael and I were trying to find a place to have a cigarette. We were back in high school and were all of twenty-two, thinking, This is a trip. We mostly played club gigs, a few in California but a lot of these daytime things, high schools, prisons, a UCLA lawn festival."

Even high school gig life couldn't squelch Gram's glamorous aura. In a review of a January Burritos show, *Circus* magazine reported in its March 1970 issue that the Burritos had "cut to pieces" the other acts on the bill, including Crosby, Stills, Nash and Young and the Grateful Dead—yet the Burritos played country music. "Yes, out and out country music is what you hear," the reviewer marveled, "even though the group's spokesperson, Gram Parsons, has incredibly long hair. . . ." The audiences at the band's shows often included the Stones, Jim Morrison, Linda Ronstadt, and other stars, the review noted. At the band's show at the Palomino, "Marlon Brando and Janis Joplin were there. According to Parsons, Janis kept on saying, 'Can you believe it? That's Marlon Brando!'"

This was Hollywood, after all. Inevitably Gram found himself in front of a movie camera. In January 1970 Stash Klossowski came to town to work with Tony Foutz on Foutz's film *Saturation '70*. John Phillip Law—who starred in the 1968 Italian comic-book film *Danger: Diabolik!* and played the angel Pygar in that same year's *Barbarella*—picked Stash up at the airport, took him to an Indian guru, and drove him to the Chateau to see Tony and meet Gram.

"Gram and I had a strong connection. We adored each other," Stash says. "He was delighted with me and I with him. We saw each other every day. He was part of an intimate circle of friends comprised of the late Christian Marquand [director of the erotic farce *Candy*], the future Bianca Jagger, and all these amazing people . . . Marlon Brando, the whole French crowd: Jane Fonda, Roger [Vadim, Fonda's husband and director of *Barbarella*]. Gram had the kindest eyes and the most charming aura."

Saturation '70 was set in Joshua Tree National Monument. The action consisted of Tony's friends running around the park's magical landscape, some wearing white coveralls. There was no script. According to a press report at the time, the film portrayed "'intergalactic flower children' who travel in a flying mobile home." Foutz was coproducing with Douglas Trumbull, creator of the special effects for *2001: A Space Odyssey*. The report suggested that Roger McGuinn, of all people, had been tapped to write the film's score.

"It was about Cosmic Kitties banished to earth to clean up the planet," Andee Nathanson says. "Gram was one and I was one, Michelle Phillips was one, and Stash. And Julian Jones, Brian's son, as the little kid. They rented a Winnebago and we all went out to the desert, to the flying saucer convention at Giant Rock airport, where there was a crowd of about twenty-five thousand people.

"Tony shot great stuff and then the producer got scared and confiscated the film and nothing ever happened. It's probably in a vault. There's this incredible footage of Gram wearing his Nudie shirt. Tony was filming him while he was standing on top of a car, communing with the stars."

The group invaded a supermarket in Century City. "We Cosmic Kitties were to go in and remove the contaminated meat from the meat department," Andee says. "We wore gas masks. Mine got stuck and I couldn't pull it off. Everyone was focused on getting the shots, so no one noticed I couldn't breathe. Gram rescued me. He was like that—always so kind. He ripped it off me and got me breathing again."

Gretchen Burrell's attempt at an acting career pursued the more conventional path. Roger Vadim cast her in his film *Pretty Maids All in a Row*. Based on a novel about a high school football coach who seduces and then murders all the beautiful girls in his school, *Maids* was cowritten by *Star Trek* creator Gene Roddenberry. Rock Hudson starred as the seductive/ murderous coach; Angie Dickinson played his wife, and Telly Savalas, the policeman investigating Rock. Hollywood stalwart Roddy McDowall costarred, as did James Doohan, who had already spent one season playing Scotty on *Star Trek*.

Vadim, an arty European hack with a daunting level of self-regard, was as famous for his beautiful wives and girlfriends as for his films. He rose to fame directing Brigitte Bardot in *And God Created Woman;* his career peaked with directing Jane Fonda in *Barbarella*. His and Fonda's L.A. home became a salon for the new, young Hollywood. Prior to *Barbarella*, Vadim made an almost unwatchable short film that formed part of a trilogy released as *Spirits of the Dead*. In it, siblings Jane and Peter Fonda play lovers who slouch around abandoned castles in fancy medieval costumes, muttering. Peter Fonda appears high beyond imagining.

Gretchen's role in *Maids* consists of taking off her clothes and being murdered. She never acted in another film. Appearing nude from the waist up in a *Playboy* magazine pictorial brought her more fame than her role in *Maids*. In an accompanying article, Vadim coolly evaluated the various bodies of the young starlets who provided *Maids* with its jiggle interest. "Gretchen Burrell has the best figure in the cast," he says. "Her breasts are just right, like a happy compromise between Jane Russell and Twiggy." Given that Angie Dickinson also had a seminude scene, Vadim's endorsement was high praise.

"*Pretty Maids* was a lot of fun," Stash says. "All my girlfriends were in it."

Another Joshua Tree outing took place around this time. Andee Nathanson went to see Gram at the Chateau. He wasn't there, but Denny Cordell was. "He knew who I was," Andee says, "and was so very charming." Cordell asked if she knew "the Master of Space and Time," meaning Leon Russell. "Denny rented the entire Joshua Tree Inn for the weekend," Andee says. "It was like a rock-and-roll conference. We made music, sang songs, went out to the Integratron. We saw the sun come up and connected with the beyond, with the stars out there in the desert. It was fabulous."

"We all went up there," Stash says, "and I recall someone passing me a joint and it having this extraordinary taste of mint. It was angel dust, which came onto the scene at the time. It wasn't the devil's drug at all, at least to me—it was a mild and beautiful experience."

There were musicians in every room, singing and playing, including Russell, and several members of Russell's and Delaney Bramlett's bands. "Gram was loving every minute," Andee says. "Matthew Moore and his brother, Daniel, sang us a song they'd written called 'Space Captain.' There's a line in it that says 'Once while traveling across the sky / This lovely planet caught my eye.' That was the spirit of what was going on out there—people from completely different backgrounds and cultures coming together through the music. It was a very pure time and energy."

The jamming musicians that weekend, the partying communal vibe, the mix of Tulsa-influenced rock and roll and English rock—plus Leon Russell's band and the friends of the L.A. British rock scene—would become Joe Cocker's Mad Dogs & Englishmen tour.

It was time for a second Burritos album. Gram hoped Keith would produce the sessions, but Keith wouldn't commit. "Keith was going to produce the Burritos thing and then it worked out that he was going to be doing something else," Gram said later. "I don't know, that's the way it always is with the Stones. It's always, 'Well, tomorrow this and tomorrow that!' They have an incredible organization to put up with, so I finally realized it was too much to get into."

When clearly the band could wait no longer, Hillman approached Byrds producer Jim Dickson. "They were falling apart," Dickson says. "Chris was trying to salvage it. I had worked with Chris since he was seventeen. I brought him into the Byrds. I was the logical person for him to go to when he got into trouble at A&M. Chris told me they had spent over a hundred thousand dollars trying to promote *Gilded Palace of Sin*. They'd gone on the road and spent all the money."

Bands are advanced money against future royalty earnings—a percentage of the sale price of each record that the band receives. Until the band sells enough records to pay back the advance, they owe the record company. The hundred grand the Burritos spent on private train cars and drugs and nice hotels did not come out of Gram's pocket. It came out of A&M's, and every penny was charged to the band's royalty account. "It was a horrendous amount for them to be in debt," Dickson says. "*Gilded Palace of Sin* didn't sell enough to even scratch it."

Hillman pressed the Burritos to use Dickson as their producer and invited him to hear the band play. "One of them had taken so many sleeping pills that he fell asleep against the wall between bass drums," Dickson remembers. "People on the dance floor sort of bumped into each other— they were playing in such bad time."

"We had the Byrds rhythm section," Bernie Leadon says. "If I'm anything, I'm a good rhythm-guitar player. And Hillman is a solid bass player. We're playing with Clarke—the only thing he did was 'chugga chugga chugga.' Once he got going he couldn't stop. . . . Sneaky Pete was a great steel-guitar player. I was playing rhythm and Pete was playing leads in the fills between the verses, pretty much every solo. Gram was an ineffectual guitar player. Gram appeared to be strumming an acoustic, but it didn't matter. His guitar was inaudible. He wasn't even plugged in. Basically he would be singing."

"I brought in Eddie Tickner," Dickson says. "He realized the recordings would last longer than the band. He didn't want to get involved with them because he thought they wouldn't last much more than a year. He handled the live stuff and I recorded the band."

"The Burritos weren't making much money and I didn't have any," Leadon says. "I had to do something to pay rent. I was doing sessions and playing with Linda Ronstadt. Chris got ticked at me and said, 'Hey, man, you've got to decide which band you're in.' But the Burritos weren't working that much. So I would try to book ahead because I didn't have any money."

Rehearsals for *Burrito Deluxe* began in a studio the band rented cheaply. They kept cheaper space for additional studio time after they began working days on the A&M lot. The band consisted of Gram, Hillman, Leadon, Michael Clarke, Sneaky Pete, and Byron Berline on fiddle.

What the band didn't have was material. Bernie Leadon remembers Gram complaining, "We don't have any songs." Gram hadn't been writing—which Leadon blamed at least in part on his accelerated drug use—and neither had Hillman or Leadon.

"We started getting together—Gram, Chris, and I—at the A&M lot and trying to write songs," Leadon says. "We spent three or four months doing this. It was like pulling teeth. We knew the mechanics of writing music, but the stuff that we did were not Gram's best songs. I wrote one called 'Man in the Fog.' I came up with the guitar progression and the melody. It's a weird little song. Gram wrote the lyrics. Chris wrote a song called 'Cody, Cody.' We wrote enough songs to make a record."

"I couldn't get much cooperation out of Gram," Dickson says. "He'd show up, but there was no energy in the rehearsals. Finally, with pressure, we started recording."

"After that brief initial burst Gram and I couldn't seem to hook up again," Hillman says. "*Burrito Deluxe* was recorded without any of the feeling and the intensity of the first album."

"I think the Burritos had used up their creative surge that resulted in all those songs on the first album," Leadon says. "'Hot Burrito #1' and '#2' are brilliant songs. It's where Parsons united traditional country with traditional rhythm and blues. The first album was *brilliant*, even though it wasn't well recorded. But they had shot their wad. The record label had given them a lot of money to promote that album, and the band squandered it on wine, women, and song on the train trip. So on the second album, A&M basically said, 'You can do another album, but there's very little money.' Gram was not being creative and was not writing more of these songs. It was a fallow period."

Gram became unhappy with the Burritos lineup. Perhaps he was bored, or felt guilty for being so unproductive. He began to cast blame. "Chris [Hillman] knew all along that Sneaky wasn't the right steel player," he said. "Chris digs Sneaky more than I do 'cause he likes that *dut dut dut dut* that Sneaky could pull off. I wanted a Tom Brumley [Buck Owens' pedal-steel player, a stalwart of the Bakersfield sound who played in Ricky Nelson's Stone Canyon Band and later with Chris Hillman in the Desert Rose Band]. Then I'd settle for anybody that played slide guitar with pedals on it. I wanted a brilliant-sounding, good, fast, pedal-steel player." Sneaky seldom recorded with the band—he liked to come in later. And Sneaky did not play conventional pedal-steel lines. Gram yearned for a more rhythm-driven pedal-steel sound, but to blame Sneaky Pete for his own lack of productivity is absurd.

Conflicts in the studio were more passive, more under the surface, Jim Dickson says. There was little jockeying for leadership. Gram and Hillman continued to work as partners, but the exhilaration of the *Gilded Palace* sessions was long gone. "The sessions weren't difficult," Dickson says. "They weren't inspiring. . . . I don't believe they ever hung out together. They came there to do the gig. There was no unified spirit. People had connection with one another, but not as a group. Sneaky lived in his own world—he was an illustrator before he was a musician. Michael was always a little sloppy, but he did what he could. Michael was glad to get work. He connected best to Chris. Gram was off in his own world and Chris resented it. Bernie was the most unifying factor. That was the dynamic."

"Chris was very professional," Andee Nathanson says. "He would book sessions and want to get to work, which was good for Gram but hard to live up to sometimes. Basically they had such different work ethics—it was a challenge to both of them."

Gram had complaints about his producer as well. "[Dickson's] a good producer in one sense," he said. "He knows how to, and this is a Leon Russell quote, 'Put everything into a little box.' He can draw a series of boxes and put everything into [the right] box, and know how it goes. And either Jim himself didn't fit, or the method didn't fit. He was trying to make it commercial. He dictated to Chris Hillman, and Chris has always listened to what Jim says. I think it's because of the *Mr. Tambourine Man* album. I can't even claim to really have participated."

"We never had any big arguments," Dickson says, "but I saw the Flying Burrito Brothers as a group and Gram saw it as his backup band. One time he accused me of trying to make it like the Byrds. That wasn't true, but I did want it to be a group, partly because of loyalty to Chris. I didn't want to make Chris a sideman when they were supposed to be doing it together as far as A&M was concerned.

"Gram wanted to be the only star in the band. Gram wanted it to center on him and didn't put much energy into the songs. He said groups were done. About six months after he left, the Eagles proved that was wrong. Not that he still wouldn't be a featured lead singer, because there was nobody else that could do more than a song. But I wanted it to be a group effort, not a Gram Parsons band."

Gram responded to his own creative impasse with moping and recalcitrance. He became the sulky, balky schoolboy—if he couldn't get what he wanted, no one else would either. He blamed others and subverted the band in ways that made it difficult to confront him on his behavior.

"So Gram sulked," Dickson says. "He didn't push for what he wanted, he didn't put energy into what he didn't like. Gram never got on my case, like other musicians would have done. If David Crosby wanted something different he would create a storm. Gram would sit quiet. He wouldn't be upfront about what it was he wanted to do. If it wasn't what he wanted, he didn't cooperate. Or he'd do it halfheartedly so you wouldn't like it."

"Gram could sing the shit out of a song," Jimmi Seiter says. "There's no denying that, but trying to get him to do it day in and day out was another story."

"Some of the songs were rejects from *Sweetheart of the Rodeo*, like 'Lazy Days,'" Dickson says. "We spent a lot of time in another studio rehearsing and figuring out what songs we were gonna do and how we were gonna do them. We spent more time in that studio because it was cheap. Sometimes Gram would play the piano, but not well. Gram wasn't communicative and mostly I talked to Chris. Gram was spaced out. If there was anybody who was going to be late for the sessions, it would be Gram."

"I don't think Gram had a car," Leadon says. "He lived in L.A. and didn't have a car. Gram would always have a ride. He had to have a minder. From early on he had to be taken everywhere. I now see it as a ploy: 'Aren't I pitiful? Don't you think you should take care of me?' Somebody always had to look after Gram or he wasn't going to show up. He may have had a car at some point, but he always had an excuse to be late."

Gram's Hollywood prima donna behavior was also classic junkie passive-aggression. He made himself helpless and so turned over responsibility for his life to those willing to—though the term was not in common parlance at the time—enable.

Gram's listlessness was, as apparently intended, rotting the soul of the band. "There was not a lot of bickering—it was sort of blah," Dickson says. "Nobody put their heart into anything. We would do it over and over and try to get it. Michael would get distracted, then he'd try again. Chris would keep plowing through it, like he does, and hope that it would work out. That spark didn't come to life for Gram. When you take sleeping pills, you've no claim to life. I assumed that that was the reason.

"Chris used to get pissed off because Gram wouldn't try. We'd go out and play, in [Topanga] Canyon or something, and if enough people showed up, then he'd entertain. But then he'd come in the studio and be lifeless again. It was the nonenthusiasm from Gram that weighted [us] down."

While the band was recording *Burrito Deluxe*, Leon Russell, Joe Cocker, and the rest of the Mad Dogs & Englishmen crew were rehearsing in a big room next door. "They sucked up all the energy," Dickson says. "There were so many people, like forty people working on that thing. It was a whole lot more fun to watch them rehearse with Leon than it was to be in our session. It was like having Barnum and Bailey's circus next door when you're trying to put on a puppet show. It took the life and energy out of us. It was overwhelming."

Seeing this collective of different musical styles coming together so harmoniously next door must have been especially galling for Gram. Russell plundered Delaney Bramlett's band and brought every down-home session player from L.A. into the mix. The Mad Dogs' song list featured exactly the gumbo of roots rock and roll, R&B, and gospel that Gram had always preached. Russell's two solo albums—1970's *Leon Russell* and 1971's *Leon Russell and the Shelter People*—present a Tulsa-fied version of Cosmic American Music. No other musician came closer to what Gram sought until the Stones' *Exile on Main Street*. Russell does not use pedal steel or other country tropes; his mélange showcases more gospel and roadhouse influence. It also features more straight-up pop. Like Gram and the Stones on *Exile*, Russell recombines the American musical DNA. He had the knowledge of the breadth and depth of American musical forms to create his own sound while doing so.

Between the Mad Dogs' sessions next door and Gram's refusal to participate, the band could not focus. "We did an average of two or three takes per song," Dickson says. "They pretty much knew what they were going to do. If you do something too much and start to go downhill, you stop and go on to the next song. They recorded live and later added the vocals. It was the normal methodology for the time.

"Bernie was a nice kid and had an innocent vibe. He's straightforward and unbiased. Everybody else had attitudes, including me. I was not happy, Chris was not happy. Bernie was a rock. Through all those sessions, Bernie was the one that tried to keep it together. He kept the rhythm tight. He was the only professional at the studio. He was the only one you could count on to keep time, play the right chords, and sing at the right time in the right place.

"Sneaky Pete would want to redo his part by himself afterwards. Or put on two or three parts. He wanted to construct them. He didn't want to play them like a player. He was not cooperative. He wanted to do songs that nobody wanted to do. I ended up having to be the one to tell him no. Chris would say, 'We can't do these songs, but you have to tell him because I have to play with him.' Sneaky wanted to concentrate and not have the chaos of the session around him. He was always distant. He never said much of anything. He wanted to think about it separately and build his parts like an engineer. [Though] sometimes he'd do some great steel parts, [he] didn't help other people playing. He wasn't so country, yet he played the pedal steel.

"There was never any camaraderie from Sneaky toward anybody. He didn't see himself as part of the band. There weren't a lot of steel players around, so it was either Sneaky or they weren't going to have a steel player. He had ideas, but he was never listened to. He wanted to do 'Wings of an Angel,' and nobody wanted to do that. He had his own life and he didn't sing so he didn't have a chance to have any input. He was definitely on a different wavelength."

The Burritos' live repertoire included "Image of Me," a Harlan Howard lament. When Gram recorded his vocal for the song, it seemed the sessions had a chance. He sang with fire and conviction and was well pleased with the result. But A&M studios had a brand-new machine, and the engineer mistakenly erased Gram's vocal. "It was the first great vocal I got out of Gram," Dickson says. "He could see I had never responded to his vocals before and he was brokenhearted. He never got back to the magic he had on the first take. I was pissed, but he started responding better after that.

"He was doing so many downers, he was only about half there. When it came time to sing with people, he didn't sing so harmony singers could stay tight with him. He sounded like a sloppy Johnny Cash. You know how Johnny Cash kind of wanders around? If you don't sing on key, if you slide off of a note, it doesn't work when you've got somebody singing harmony. They can't anticipate if you're going to sing different every time. He was resisting because he wanted it to be about him. That was part of the tension that made us do songs over until we beat the life out of them."

Legend and rumor have always dogged the Burritos' recording of the Stones' "Wild Horses." Some say Gram was the inspiration for the song; others, that he contributed to the writing of it. Other folks claim a role, too. Marianne Faithfull maintained that Jagger wrote the song for her after she overdosed on downers.

A more credible notion is that Keith led the writing of the song. It's his ode to Anita Pallenberg and their son, Marlon, whom Keith had to leave behind for the Stones' U.S. tour. Bud Scoppa, writing in *Rolling Stone*, argued that Jagger wrote the song about Gram and that its chorus "describes the paradox that fueled Parsons' life and vision. . . . 'Wild horses couldn't drag me away / Wild horses, we'll ride them someday.' Unable to choose between devils and angels, Gram broke the rules and welcomed both." Today Scoppa's version seems the least likely. Why would Jagger, who was jealous of Keith's attention to Gram, write a song about his rival? Moreover, heartfelt, yearning love songs and declarations of undying connection are not, to understate wildly, Jagger's métier. As can be proven by one listen to "Angie."

How the Burritos came to cut the song is more straightforward. Stanley Booth reported that Gram had no direct influence on the writing of the song. But he heard the Stones playing a demo of "Wild Horses" while everyone crashed at the Huntington Hotel after the debacle at Altamont. He asked if the Burritos could cover it. According to Gram, Jagger gave his permission that night.

"The Stones sent an unfinished multitrack master by courier," Stash Klossowski says. "You had to play it on a special machine. They sent a temporary mix with indications for Gram to listen and play a part on it. It was Keith's idea that Gram should sing a part on the chorus. We took advantage of having the master to learn the song and sing it. I remember we set it up in John Phillip Law's garage. I don't think it worked out. When [the tapes] got back to London, [the Stones] weren't pleased with what had been put on it."

Leon Russell joined the Burritos in the studio to cut "Wild Horses." "The Stones said we could do the song but we couldn't release it as a single," Dickson says. "So we used it as an album closer to leave a good taste. We did 'Wild Horses' when the sessions were almost over. I realized how much better they could do if they were focused. They were doing something that they wanted to do. I was depressed with what we had. I wanted them to play like a group. Not like a bunch of pickup musicians."

The contrast with the Mad Dogs & Englishmen collective must have been painful for Gram. Worse was that when the Mad Dogs & Englishmen tour rolled out of L.A., Gretchen rolled right along with them—with Stash. Stash insists he didn't steal her away: "I met Gretchen with Gram when she was seventeen years old. She was one of Gram's girls. I don't know how it happened that we ended up together. Perhaps Gram had left or abandoned her at one point."

✱ ✱ ✱

THERE WAS A WORLD OF hurt brewing with Gram's sister, Little Avis. Gram was in only sporadic contact with her. Occasional letters suggest that her troubles worried him, but he did little to help her.

Little Avis adored her stepfather, according to Becky Gottsegen, Bob Parsons' oldest daughter by his first marriage. Little Avis didn't feel the same about her new stepmother. "She was angry about Bonnie's existence," Becky says. "It's the typical bringing the stepparent into the picture. Avis was young when Bonnie married my dad—my dad was the only father she ever knew. Bonnie's way of trying to reconcile was to be nice—Bonnie was always nice. But Avie hated her. She had a picture of Bonnie in her closet that she threw darts at. It was that serious. Ultimately they went to counseling. Avis was civil but they never worked it through. Bonnie continued to be nice. I have never in my life seen Bonnie ruffled."

"Avie maybe slipped through the cracks," Bonnie says. "She was a little quieter, where Diane would throw herself at you."

When Little Avis graduated high school, her problems became more serious. She took up with an older man. Avie brought him home to dinner, and Bob—following the pattern set by the families of two of his three wives—did not approve. A few days after the dinner, the boyfriend was arrested. An emotional scene at the house followed. Avis, sobbing, pleaded her boyfriend's innocence, though Bob and Bonnie remained in the dark about why he'd been jailed. Bob went down to the police station, where he charmed the police, bailed out the boyfriend, and brought him home.

The next morning, the boyfriend and Little Avis were gone. They took off with a cache of Big Avis' credit cards. Bob, with his typical inattention to mundane details, had failed to cancel them after her death. Avis and her boyfriend used the cards to finance their disappearance.

Bob and Bonnie later discovered that the boyfriend's arrest was for performing abortions, which were illegal in Louisiana. "He had been performing abortions all up and down the East Coast before he came to New Orleans," Bonnie says. "He was a dominant person and Avie was not. She followed him."

Bob called the cops and the search began. The couple first surfaced in California, then settled in Colorado. After four months, U.S. marshals arrested the boyfriend and brought Avis back to New Orleans. She came home a drug-addled mess.

"He had been feeding her pills," Becky says. Bonnie Parsons remembers, "She walked around like there was a heavy rain in front of her. All she wanted to do was climb in bed and sleep. She was thin, a lost waif. We called a psychiatrist, who suggested DePaul's," a venerable hospital in New Orleans. "It was a beautiful place. It wasn't like being locked up in some horrible insane asylum."

Bob and Bonnie had Avis committed. She resented it for the rest of her life. When Bob and Bonnie visited, they found Avis in a lockdown unit and learned that she was pregnant.

"I saw Avie when she was in DePaul's," Buddy Freeman says. "She was under house arrest, but they let her go to Bob's for Saturday brunch. It was not pretty. Avie was bitter. There was a portrait of Big Avis prominently displayed in the house—Avie wanted it and Bob wouldn't let her have it."

Avis behaved well enough at DePaul's to get out of lockdown and earn yard privileges. One day she made a call and had a friend come meet her when she walked to the corner mailbox. The friend drove Avis to a train station. She went to Tennessee and stayed with Coon Dog's brother and sister. While there, in 1970, she gave birth to a daughter, whom she named Avis.

Sometime during her pregnancy the father of her child was arrested again and sent to jail. When he was released he married one of Avis' friends.

Avis had little contact with Bob or Bonnie. Bob tried to keep an eye on her through Coon Dog's family, but they were more protective of their niece and her child than they were willing to help Bob. The Avis episodes proved punishing for Bob Parsons. His hair turned gray and his drinking, already more or less constant, grew heavier.

As soon as the *Burrito Deluxe* sessions wrapped up, the band went into another studio to cut an album of country standards. They wanted product in the can as a follow-up for *Deluxe*. "I had to get something out fast in the summer that was more fun and better to listen to," Dickson says. "We knocked out country standards that Gram already knew. Something you could dance to and wasn't so constipated. Something more positive, looser, fun. It didn't get finished."

The sessions were released in Europe in 1976 under the title *Sleepless Nights*, with a few Gram and Emmylou Harris outtakes tacked on. Among the tracks recorded were "Dim Lights, Thick Smoke (and Loud, Loud Music)" by Joe Maphis and Rose Lee, "Honky Tonk Woman" by Jagger and Richards, "Tonight the Bottle Let Me Down" and "Sing Me Back Home" by Merle Haggard, and "Together Again" and "Close up the Honky-Tonks" by Buck Owens and others.

Burrito Deluxe was released in April 1970. The cover is an at-first-sight indecipherable and then repulsive photograph of a pair of stale burritos, the upper one edged in hand-sewn sequins. The whole thing looks like roadkill. In a small photo superimposed over one of the burritos, the band forms a dance line, wearing the white coveralls from Tony Foutz's movie. Like the production on *Gilded Palace of Sin*, the artwork for *Burrito Deluxe* seems obscenely lazy and counterproductive.

"The cover was Gram's [idea]," Dickson says. "He wanted the burrito with the sequins on it. The white suits had something to do with a movie his friends were involved in. Gram thought the movie was going to be real hip, and he wanted these white overalls on, like everybody in the movie wore. It didn't make any sense to me."

"The second album was a mistake—it was a mistake to get Jim Dickson involved," Gram said. "We should have been more careful than that."

"Of all the albums I've produced, I'm least proud of *Burrito Deluxe*," Dickson says. "I don't like to think about it very much. It was an album I wanted to move on from right away. We thought that if we didn't get the album out fast the band would fall apart, but the band fell apart while we were making it."

"Nothin' on *Burrito Deluxe* was mine but the name, man," Gram later said.

Despite some critical praise for *Burrito Deluxe* ("Gram Parsons is all right, as readily proved by the new album," one reviewer wrote, a touch defensively; "the album is masterful for the most part," said another), reaction was muted. Sales proved insufficient to push the record onto the charts, let alone pay off the Burritos' debt to A&M. The album reception matched its creation: the disappointing last gasp of a band coming apart.

Several critics singled out the Burritos' version of "Wild Horses" as a high point of the album, even "the closest thing the Burritos have to a classic." In that judgment, they were dead wrong. It's hard to fault the arrangement; the Burritos copy the Stones beat for beat. But Gram strains at the vocals, forcing the long notes, which do not suit his voice or his straightforward, conversational delivery. The chorus is lugubrious and unconvincing. The Stones were never all that believable when they strived to be sincere. "Wild Horses" does not express the usual Jagger/Richards sentiments. Yet their version remains not only credible, but deeply moving. Maybe the Stones own the song so completely, no one else can cover it. Gram seems to be mouthing the words without understanding their meaning. The effort required comes through more clearly than any desired effect. The song is as complete a failure as *Burrito Deluxe* holds.

The Burritos' enduring classics—songs like "Hot Burrito # 1" and "Hot Burrito #2," "Sin City," and "Do You Know How It Feels"—make it plain how cohesive, emotional, and heartfelt the band could be. There are no classics on *Burrito Deluxe*, and that speaks to the band's decline.

The album's high point is Gram's rendition of Harlan Howard's anthem of honky-tonk guilt, "The Image of Me." "Image" shows how differently Gram sang when his soul connected to a lyric. With nothing to prove to Keith or anyone else, Gram leads a rousing Cajun stomp-waltz fueled by Byron Berline's multitracked fiddle. In the studio as in life, self-loathing proved far more accessible to Gram than declarations of love. He's so much more believable singing, "I know I'm to blame / And I feel so ashamed" than "I can't let you slide through my hands."

Cowritten by Gram and Hillman, "High Fashion Queen" exemplifies the frustrations of *Burrito Deluxe*. A brilliant narrative of any night in any bar anywhere is set to the laziest arrangement on the record. The band lurches through a painfully inept boogie, and Gram rushes the lyrics as if his dealer were waiting in the parking lot. Steve Earle and Chris Hillman resurrected this gem on 1999's *Return of the Grievous Angel*. Their Texas two-step version demonstrates the genius of the song's atmosphere, and how anyone—man or woman or both—feeling lonely in a roadhouse could nod their head in recognition. Its story resonates for the brokenhearted, the drug-addicted, the alcoholic, the recently fired, and the momentarily hopeless.

The closing lines form a perfect self-portrait of Gram at that moment, even if Hillman helped him write it:

When all those fancy lies have left you stranded in a dream
Ain't you glad you're a high fashion queen?

Earle and Hillman's rendition on *Return of the Grievous Angel* proves that Hillman's ability to harmonize hadn't suffered over the ensuing thirty years. Too bad both Burrito albums are produced like shit; Hillman's subtlety as a singer might have been more apparent. In all his solo or headlining recorded output since those two albums, Hillman has always made certain his voice is way out front in the mix. But he's never sung so well as his duet with Steve Earle.

It's impossible not to feel for Chris Hillman. He has a soulful, expressive voice, a gift for harmony, and, for a while at least, a generous willingness to collaborate. Playing Salieri to so many Mozarts (McGuinn, Gram, Stephen Stills in Stills' band Manassas, among others) had to be an exhausting career path. As a result, Hillman seldom gets the credit he deserves.

There is a British remastered collection of both Burrito albums on one CD sold as *The Very Best of the Burrito Brothers.* With bonus cuts of "Six Days on the Road" and "Close up the Honky-Tonks," the remastering shows how well played *Gilded Palace* was and how rudimentary the arrangements are on *Deluxe.* When the playing can finally be heard as it was laid down, Gram's poor-mouthing of the band seems downright offensive. The Burritos had such potential.

AT SOME POINT IN THE Bernie Leadon configuration, the Burritos appeared in a short film—a crude music video of the day—lip-syncing "Older Guys" on a small cabin cruiser motoring about a marina in L.A. The seventies comic John Byner introduces the clip, which seems to be from a comedy-variety TV show.

The band disappears behind Gram's front-man antics. Sneaky Pete wears a Hawaiian shirt, there's no telling who plays drums, Hillman looks miserable, and Leadon appears determined to be a trouper. Gram sports an odd amalgam of Southern preppie yachtwear accessorized with Rolling Stone–wannabe paraphernalia: white pants Gram might have worn for a gym dance at Bolles, a gigantic tweed newsboy cap, a garish brown blazer patterned in white squares, a yellow cashmere sweater, and two or three silk scarves. He prances around the boat aping Jagger, smiling and upstaging his bandmates like mad, hands on his hips, ass twitching. It's ridiculous and irresistible. When Leadon and then Hillman have close-ups to sing their backup "woo-woos," the contrast is telling. Leadon smiles and raises up his head like a wolf howling. Hillman looks like he's being turned on a spit.

The band toured once more, to little effect. Gram hated to fly; perhaps it was the residue of his Snively grandfather's prohibition against traveling by air instead of by rail. Gram took downers to get through the flights. "He was in a wheelchair wasted on these pills," Hillman says. "It was getting sad."

"Perhaps the country-rock sound is getting passé or else too many groups are using it," sniffed one writer reviewing a May 1970 gig at the Aragon Ballroom in Chicago. "In any event, the Flying Burrito Brothers just don't have a strong impact on the crowd here. . . . The Burritos were hurt probably by the crowd's anticipation of Joe Cocker, who topped the bill." The review mentioned only one song from the Burritos set: "Wild Horses."

How that critical attitude stung. Here the originators of country rock were being told they were passé, that they were being eclipsed by bands coming in on their coattails. To make matters worse, the only song that garnered any praise belonged to the Rolling Stones.

That same month, May 1970, Gram suffered a serious motorcycle accident. His friends had been worried ever since he moved from his smaller BSA to a larger Harley-Davidson. The big bike was part of his pose, they felt. John Phillips described Gram's Harley as "pure redneck, all buckskin and fringe." Gram decorated the bike with airbrushed outer-space scenes that Jimmi Seiter remembers as "costing almost as much as the bike."

"Gram never ever did anything mechanical to that bike except put the key in the ignition and turn it on," a Burritos insider says. "You can't ride a Harley if you don't know how to use a tool. So for him to buy that motorcycle was fucking ludicrous." Gram was almost always high on downers or heroin, and that, combined with his lack of instinct for the machine, made a wreck inevitable.

"He was a little guy and wasn't strong enough to hold it," Hillman says. "I knew his accident would happen sooner or later. I knew he would eat it on that bike."

The crash occurred through Gram's negligence. He had repaired a broken front fork with a piece of coat hanger wire. The wire came loose and the bike went down. Actress and singer Maggie Thrett was riding on back. John Phillips and Genevieve Waite were riding alongside.

"Someone was watering their lawn and we saw them scream and point," Waite says. "We saw Gram and Maggie lying in the road, and blood was flowing out of Gram's head."

As Phillips bent over him, Gram, never one to miss an opportunity for melodrama, said, "John, take me for a long white ride."

"Neither of them had a helmet on," Waite says. "Maggie was thrown differently and she was all right. Gram fell hard. The people called an ambulance. I went with the ambulance and John rode his bike home. We left Gram's bike in the road."

It turned out Gram had his Blue Cross card in his pocket. "I remember thinking that for a fucked-up musician type, he was pretty together," Waite says. "When we got to the hospital we had to go through his wallet to get his

Gram after his motorcycle accident. (© Andee Nathanson, www.andeenathanson.com)

card and they were all there neatly. Most people didn't even carry a wallet, or only have a couple of dollars."

"When I found out I was like, 'Holy fuck. Did he kill anybody?' I was surprised the girl didn't get killed," the Burritos insider says. "When the handlebars come off and the forks dig into the pavement, you are in trouble. It doesn't matter how fast you are going."

Gram had a broken leg, and his head wound required stitches. "He was full of blood and bandages," Stash recalls. Gram called Tony Foutz, who hurried to the hospital. John Phillips sent Genevieve over in a limo every day to sit by Gram's bedside. She brought *The Story of O* and other erotica, which Phillips told Genevieve to read to the invalid. "I would read them to him, but he didn't seem interested," Waite says.

"The bike wreck led him to take all those drugs because he was in a lot of pain," Miss Mercy says. "He never healed right."

"Went to see GP with Mercy and Carlos [Bernal], took flowers and all," Pamela Des Barres wrote. "He's so beaten up, such a mess. It was hard not to scream, his face was blown up like a purple-and-blue balloon. God bless him and keep him through this, maybe it will help somehow, he's been SO high all the time. I've been calling him Gram Richards. He hasn't heard from Keith, so I sent him a telegram. I hope he gets it."

By June, Gram had healed enough for the band to play at the Sound Factory in San Antonio. The show did not go well.

"We didn't have a set list," Bernie Leadon says. "Hillman would say, 'Let's start this song.' We would count it off and it would be an up-tempo song in one key, and when it came time for Gram to sing the verse, he would sing another song in another key at a different tempo. His acoustic guitar wasn't plugged in and it didn't matter if he broke a string. He had these big heavy-gauge strings so he'd beat on that thing. If he broke a string he would keep playing. It looked pretty dramatic—he had all these strings flapping off and he would still be going. He would play until he broke two or three strings. Then he'd take the guitar by the neck and he would throw it up over his body, over his head, and it would spiral down right by the drums and Michael would have to duck. It would land with a clatter on the wooden stage back behind the amp line. One of the roadies would shake his head, pick the thing up, and see if the neck was still on. He'd go slap some more strings on it and take it out to Gram."

Gram was too wasted to play guitar. His guitar playing became so distracting that the band unplugged him, harkening ominously to the last days of Brian Jones. When Jones showed up too addled to play, Mick and Keith took the strings off his studio guitar. As the rest of the band recorded, Brian would lie on his back, lost to the world, his fingers scrabbling away at his stringless instrument.

In an interview with *Melody Maker*, Gram predicted that the days of groups dominating the charts were numbered. "We may be the only group left," he said. "We're the underground group anyway, the only true outlaw band." The article was entitled "Gram Parsons, the Burrito Ego Man," and the interviewer, Jacoba Atlas, wrote that the musician's ego was prominently on display—but that he seemed oblivious to how he came across when he boasted of being a poet or a member of the only outlaw band still standing. He earnestly talked about his motorcycle accident and what he'd said to John Phillips immediately after it happened. "I must be a poet," he told Atlas. "Because I told John, 'Take me on a long white road.' I mean, I said that."

The article ends there.

In late June, at a gig at the Brass Ring in the San Fernando Valley, Chris fired Gram from the band. Leon Russell and Delaney Bramlett were in the audience. Leadon: "We were down in the Valley at some club and Gram didn't show up till late," Leadon says. "Chris was pissed and Gram was fucked up. Chris had had enough and fired him."

Hillman declared himself sick of Gram's "rock-star games" and his lack of commitment to the Burritos. "It got to the point where we couldn't work with him," he said later. "Michael and I said, 'Out!' And that's why he left."

"Gram was totally not into it anymore," Jimmi Seiter says. "They were having to drag him to do anything, everything."

"I may seem callous but we've all had family problems," Hillman says. "But of course it was tough for him, especially with money from the trust fund. But hey, people with no legs hold down jobs. I'm a team player. I like to work in groups. I like a clean team effort. But it was definitely not working out that way with the Burritos."

"Chris Hillman never got over how much more credit Gram got than he did," Jim Dickson says. "They did the same thing, but Gram was willing to put feeling into his songs and Chris never was. Gram was more interesting than Chris. He wanted to be a legend. Hillman was never willing to let himself expose his emotions or be vulnerable in front of everybody. He couldn't do it—he was always pretty tight-assed."

Pamela Des Barres was traveling in the Netherlands when she heard the news. "I found a newsstand with *Rolling Stone* displayed and, foaming at the mouth, I perused the pages rapidly," she wrote. "Much to my bitter sorrow, Gram Parsons had quit the Burrito Brothers to branch out on his own, and I grieved as though a death had occurred. I wrote to him, sobbing on a postcard, while I chewed *pommes frites* from a paper cone. 'My dear GP. I could cry that I missed you all playing together one more time. Your music has made me so happy at times I thought I would pop open with joy . . .'"

In an interview that predicts the rambling, loopy accounts Gram would henceforth give journalists, Gram told Chuck Cassell, "I waited to see if the album was going to be a freak hit. And I split. I was starting to duck out on road gigs about that time. Starting to say, 'I can't handle it. I don't want to go to Seattle for eight hundred bucks. No, thank you.'

"Chris and I always remained friends, though. He hit my guitar once, but we've always understood what the other one was going through. The old country flavor, it was always there somewhere. And finally when it became too much, I split."

SEVENTEEN

NELLCÔTE

No matter what the level of self-loathing or self-destruction, nobody enjoys failure. The desire to succeed can be perverted into a desire to fail, of course. A certain temperament might require the suffering that failure brings, or renewed proof of the validity of a tormented self-image. For the addict, failure reliably produces a good reason for another fix. If *The Gilded Palace of Sin* had sold ten million copies, would Gram have done less heroin? He likely would have done more.

But no one seeks negation, oblivion, as an artist. The drive to create, despite its tortured path to expression, yearns for success—for an audience—no matter how forcefully or unknowingly the self-hating artist might push it away.

Gram's denial took the form of insisting that nothing was his fault. He masked his refusal to get out of his own way by being increasingly dissatisfied with everyone else. He claimed to be fed up with Chris Ethridge, with Sneaky Pete, with touring, with the idea of groups, with having to collaborate. The self-loather survives his self-hatred by finding reasons that everyone else is more hateful still. While Gram worked that vein diligently, he also insisted on negating his own gifts. Even as he desired acclaim for his talents, he sought to minimize what they might produce.

Contradictions in human nature are not surprising or in themselves puzzling; contradictions are our essence. Those baffled by Gram's self-destruction in the face of his talents miss the point. Gram's sensitivity might generate paralysis in anyone. That sensitivity, combined with all Gram had lost, could make the usual internal artistic struggles well-nigh unbearable. Gram's prominent and more intriguing contradiction remains the unbridgeable gap between his gifts and his want-to. He rarely tried to improve what he produced. He seldom took the extra step, spent a bit more time, worked with greater discipline, or examined his own processes. If Gram had the motivation to do so, he seldom showed it.

Gram had more of a classic self-hater's approach to his work. He cast his gems away from him as if their existence undermined his self-definition. He seldom rehearsed, seldom prepared before entering a recording session, seldom spent any time on album production, and treated every notion however profound as a throwaway. He could justify this pattern under any number of theories of Beat, post-Beat, and hippie creativity. They held that spontaneous creation was best: that to work too hard on a moment's inspiration cheapened it. Gram cherished an image of himself as a star whose abilities could save him in any situation: playing live, the studio, whatever. He could step up at the moment and nail it. He created that myth for himself and was stuck living it out. Trying to ignore reality and keep that myth going must have been full-time work.

Mick Jagger and Keith Richards, who were as wanton, pleasure-seeking, and distractible as Gram, never let their distractions distract them from their ruthless ambition. Nothing and nobody got in their way, including themselves. No matter how fucked up they might be, they'd still rehearse for days, plan every detail of a tour, and build their songs piece by piece. The recording of a song—the final step for Gram—was only the beginning for the Stones. They reveled in the details of their own work. That's why *Beggars Banquet, Let It Bleed, Sticky Fingers,* and *Exile on Main Street* are among the best-produced records in history.

Gram fled those details, refusing to confront them, thus avoiding the rigor of making good work great and great work immortal. Among the worthy, lasting, and influential albums of the last forty years, it's hard to find one more shoddily produced or sloppily performed than *The Gilded Palace of Sin.* To their advantage, Jagger and Richards had each other as inspiration, motivation, and competition. Gram insisted on fighting the creative battles himself. It's no accident that some of his best songs were written with Chris Hillman and Chris Ethridge. Or that *Burrito Deluxe* has no worthy numbers at all; when Gram turned his back on collaboration, his songwriting suffered. He could not, it turned out, walk that lonesome valley.

Having made what he knew were two masterpieces (*Sweetheart* and *Gilded Palace*), Gram was left with nothing. He was no longer a Byrd or a Burrito. Neither record sold worth a damn. The first produced little critical understanding, the second only slightly more. The first appeared to have no supporters or followers, the second sufficient that—even though it never charted—Gram was no longer perceived as the innovator of a scene that was already outgrowing any tracing of its origins.

Gram's hard drug use had gone from recreational to life-dominating. His L.A. reputation held him to be spoiled, lazy, willful, uncooperative, a commercial liability, and in thrall to the Stones. Money he had, and girls and style. But his best work, his brief periods of discipline and enthusiasm, had come to nothing. He had reached a dead end. All around him, the L.A. country-rock scene was growing. Gram was being left behind.

He began to hang out with Terry Melcher, Doris Day's son, the former producer of the Byrds. "Terry liked witty, funny people," Eve Babitz says, "and Gram was extremely funny. They were two dilettantes together."

Terry had been a surf-rock producer at Columbia. He formed the group Bruce and Terry with Bruce Johnston, who later became a mainstay of the Beach Boys and wrote "Disney Girls." Melcher was also part of the Rip Chords, who hit with "Hey Little Cobra," a paean to an American sports car of the era. He produced "Mr. Tambourine Man" and "Turn! Turn! Turn!" for the Byrds and worked with Paul Revere and the Raiders and the Rising Sons (Taj Mahal's band, from which came drummer Kevin Kelley, Ry Cooder, and Jesse Ed Davis). Melcher performed on the Beach Boys masterwork *Pet Sounds* and introduced Brian Wilson to L.A. songwriter and producer Van Dyke Parks, who helped Wilson create the psychedelic word-poems for Wilson's never-finished opus *Smile*. (Much of the album's content was re-created and released in 2004.) Melcher later produced *Byrdmaniax* and cowrote "Kokomo," a hit single for the Beach Boys. He died of cancer in 2004.

In 1968 Melcher was involved, with John Phillips, in producing the Monterey Pop Festival. That same year Charles Manson, who had ambitions as a singer-songwriter, auditioned for Melcher through the auspices of

Beach Boys drummer Dennis Wilson. Melcher declined to sign Manson, and Manson was not pleased. Melcher had been living with Candice Bergen at the Cielo Drive house. They had moved out by August 1969, when Manson sent his acolytes to butcher the occupants. One of the killers, Susan Atkins, told the L.A. police that Manson knew Melcher no longer lived there but had chosen the house as the site for a murder to frighten him.

"Terry wanted to be hip," Jim Dickson says, "so he found his way into the world of hippies with money and privilege and musical training. He had produced the Byrds but he didn't understand what it was all about. He hired a girl from the Whisky to take him around and teach him. When I warned Gram about Terry, he bawled me out. Terry was still traumatized by the Manson thing. He was a victim. I told Gram he'd be sorry."

Terry had a great deal of money and an appetite for drugs. Gram and Melcher wanted to work together. Melcher sold A&M's Jerry Moss on the idea of a solo album with the argument that Gram was "the white Jimi Hendrix." Session musicians for the recording included Clarence White, Ry Cooder, Earl Ball, Byron Berline, and singer Merry Clayton, a former Ikette who became famous for her wailing background vocals supporting Mick Jagger on "Gimme Shelter."

"Terry loved Gram and wanted to produce him," Eve Babitz says. "But neither of them could get anything done."

Gram moved into Terry's house in Benedict Canyon. "They would think up album titles for days," Melcher's secretary, Ginny Ganahl, says, "like *These Blues Have Made a Nigger Out of Me* or *Money Honey*. The way they related to each other was like outlaws, from being born to money."

Jimmi Seiter says, "Working with Terry drained me of energy, and Gram could be the same way." Ganahl agrees: "Gram was a little punk. It was all time to kill and so he killed it." As another regular at Melcher's house puts it: "If there were ever two guys who were alike it was those two. Both wasted so much talent, both wealthy and never had to earn. When they were bored with something they didn't want to get involved."

The recording did not go well. It was these sessions from which the legend sprang of someone—maybe Gram, maybe Terry—vomiting into an open piano. "I played on two songs, 'Hand to Mouth' and 'White Line Fever,'" Earl Ball says. "I brought Don Rich [Buck Owens' guitarist and bandleader] with me. We sat around and waited to see what Gram wanted to do. . . . I've had this experience several times, working with someone I care about and want to see do well because they have a vision. But they've let their habits get in the way and are not operating at maximum capacity. There's nothing you can do about it. Terry was in the booth, but he didn't say a whole lot. He was watching. This whole thing may have been planned when Gram was in a better situation, a better place in his mind. . . .

"I don't remember how many tunes we recorded. Gram sat in a chair—he had these big purple blotches on his arm. I imagine he was shooting some kind of drug. He played and sang and then got sick."

"I got a phone call one night to go down there," one of Gram's handlers says. "Gram was on the floor of the studio trying to sing a vocal, and Terry was asleep at the console with no lights on in the whole fucking place."

"We were all kind of quiet and trying to do our job," Earl Ball says. "We were getting paid good money to be witness to a tragedy."

John Beland, a session guitarist and friend of Clarence White's, came down to the studio. "About four-thirty in the morning it started wrapping up," he remembers. "Clarence introduced me to Gram, who was loaded. Clarence said, 'Hey Gram, this is John. He plays with Ronstadt.' Gram threw his arms around me and he gives me this big bear hug. He wouldn't let go and I'm looking over his shoulder and there's Clarence with his eyes rolled. It was embarrassing. Gram said, 'I want to tell you, brother, you played your ass off tonight.' I wasn't even playing on the session. I was only listening in the control room.

"Clarence did coke and so did Gram, so they did a lot together and were legendary figures at the time and kindred spirits. They were as compatible as could be. But Clarence's life was not the train wreck Gram's was. A session player like Clarence learns to adapt. Clarence would play and do his thing, and Gram would let him. Nobody would make a scene in front of Clarence or get on his case. He had this poker face that could be intimidating—he hardly said a word—but he was the opposite as a person. He was warm and funny. Clarence would sit down and be quiet and play his guitar part. And it would probably be brilliant. They got along together, because Gram had a lot of respect, as everybody did, for Clarence's ability."

Long lost, the tapes from this session have gathered a legendary patina. Either Gram checked them out of A&M or Melcher took them. According to Jim Dickson, Terry was in the habit of taking tapes from the recording studio. He was hedging against getting stiffed by the record company after he'd put his own money into the sessions.

In the aftermath, Gram played on a few sessions around L.A. He sang on Jesse Ed Davis' album *Jesse Ed Davis*. Davis, a Native American guitarist, played with Taj Mahal and Leon Russell and did session work for John Lennon, George Harrison, Ringo Starr, Keith Moon, Jackson Browne, Van Dyke Parks, Eric Clapton, and Leonard Cohen. He produced Gene Clark's brilliant 1971 solo album *White Light*. Davis died of an overdose in a Venice, California, laundromat in 1988.

Gram was also part of the chorus on Delaney & Bonnie's *Motel Shot*. "The whole concept of *Motel Shot* was inspired by the fact that after each gig, we'd go back to the motel and sing," Bonnie Bramlett says. "Eric [Clapton], Delaney, Duane Allman, or me or whoever would sit around singing and picking and strumming guitars all night long. We thought we should try to recapture the spontaneity of those motel rooms, because that's where the real genius comes from."

The album was cut in producer-engineer Bruce Botnick's living room in one day. (Gram's insistence on spontaneity as the mother of creative soul was not an isolated view.) The word was spread among Delaney's circle that a recording session was on and that the doors would be locked at seven P.M. Those who made it on time included the cream of L.A. music: Duane Allman (the John Coltrane of the slide guitar), organist Bobby Whitlock, drummer Jim Keltner, Traffic cofounder and guitarist Dave Mason, Delaney's mother, Iva, Jimi Hendrix drummer Buddy Miles, bassist Carl Radle, Leon Russell, Joe Cocker, and John Hartford, to name the best-known—and Gram.

Gram provided a bluesy cover of "You Don't Miss Your Water" for Fred Neil's *The Other Side of This Life*. He also wrote "Apple Tree" for Johnny Rivers' album *Slim Slo Slider*. "Apple Tree" at first seems a nostalgic look at the lost innocence of youth, a recurrent theme for Gram. But it becomes a tale of throwaway regret, with the heartbreak hidden in what at first appears to be a sentimental memory of childhood summers. As in the story songs Gram liked so well, the punch line undoes all the happiness of what came before. It's the bitter taste that lingers.

> *Maybe she's lonely, needs me somewhere,*
> *Maybe by summer I won't even care.*

Released as a single by Rivers, "Apple Tree" did poorly.

GRETCHEN BURRELL'S AFFAIR with Stash Klossowski was over. She and Gram were back together. (Stash said that Gretchen told him, "I always knew I belonged to Gram.") Gram had reservations about Gretchen, or feared this relationship might deteriorate as his love for Nancy had. Gram visited the Phillips home as Genevieve Waite was putting her infant son Tamerlane to bed. Gram told her, "Don't let Gretchen see him." His reason, Waite said, was "because he didn't want her to want one."

The Stones had to leave Great Britain in March 1971. Their new financial advisor, Prince Rupert Lowenstein, determined that they needed to live outside of their homeland for a certain period of time to avoid a ruinous tax payment. Gram and Gretchen flew to England to accompany the Stones on their Farewell to Britain tour. Gram invited Bernie Leadon to come and described his own position on the tour as "sort of hanging around and playing."

During the tour Gram met author William Burroughs. Proto-Beat, author of *Naked Lunch*, heroin avatar, *halluciné* first-class, Burroughs had an exquisite presentation, with the clothes of a fifties FBI agent and the courtliness of a Renaissance prince. He was a connoisseur of drugs and deranged scenes. Gram: "I met William through [photographer] Michael Cooper," Gram said. "William is a beautiful old man who knows where all the best, cheapest restaurants are."

When the tour ended, Keith, Anita, and Gram decided to clean up, undergoing a "cure," in the language of the times, at Keith's Redlands estate. "We did detox together," Anita Pallenberg said, according to Barney Hoskyns' invaluable article in the June 1998 issue of *Mojo* magazine, "The Good Ol' Boy." "Me, Keith, and Gram, with two nurses William Burroughs had recommended. I have crazy memories of that, of Gram always running away and hiding and never being there when they were looking for him."

According to Stones errand runner and drug procurer Tony Sanchez, the cure consisted of tablets of a morphine substitute administered under the tongue, with a smaller dose given each day. Sanchez reported arriving at Redlands as the cure was completed: "Keith was battered and pale, but he had the exuberance of a man who has been freed from jail. 'Yipppppeee, fuckin' great, man!' screamed Keith. 'Got any coke?' I knew that his cure was going to be short-lived."

Gram later expressed his doubts about this cure and other forms of addiction treatment. "Methadone is *twice* as addictive as heroin. It rots your veins *twice* as fast," he assured an interviewer from *Crawdaddy*, adding that people on methadone "are impossible to cure." The morphine-substitute cure sometimes works, he said, but for most it is a scam, "like the sleep cures for heroin addiction. Nothing would please a junkie more than to . . . take enough sleeping pills to wipe himself out for three weeks and come out thinking he's cured."

In April 1971 the Stones went off to the south of France to begin recording what would become *Exile on Main Street*. Keith found himself an elegant, crumbling villa and the band moved into the surrounding area. Gram and Gretchen remained in London, crammed into a run-down Belgravia apartment, until Michael Cooper, the Stones' photographer and confidant, found them the bottom half of a smart house in Abingdon Villas in Kensington.

The Stones announced the formation of Rolling Stones Records as part of their new deal with Atlantic Records, with whom they'd signed after spending their entire recording career with London Records. "The company would be relatively small in scale, unlike the Beatles' Apple Records, which kept a number of artists under contract," journalist and Gram biographer Rick Cusick explains. "Rolling Stones Records would be limited to the Rolling Stones and solo efforts by Bill Wyman and Keith Richards and 'possibly together with Gram Parsons, ex-Byrd and Burrito.'"

Michael Cooper's assistant, Perry Richardson, took Gram to Olympic Studios, where Trevor Churchill of Rolling Stones Records listened to the Melcher A&M sessions. "I remember Gram did a version of '$1000 Wedding' on the studio piano," Richardson recalls. "And doing a little overdubbing. This went on for a few days. He turned me on to Merle Haggard, Waylon Jennings, Conway Twitty . . . his main criterion was to sing as well as Conway Twitty, who was his great idol as a singer. Gram would try to model his phrasing on Twitty."

"I did some preliminary sessions but that didn't work out," Gram later said. "Keith was right in the middle of *Exile on Main Street*, which took an awful lot of concentration and effort on everyone's part. . . . Keith didn't have the time to give me. He would have had to come back over to the States—that would have been too precious for him. He was too busy being a Rolling Stone."

This was the first time that someone who really mattered to Gram gave him a taste of his own passive-aggressive behavior. Keith never said no. He kept saying maybe until it was clear he would do nothing.

During this stay in London, Gram met the notorious Dr. Sam Hutt, who had what he called "a hippie general practice" in London. "The doctors and the patients had long hair," Hutt says. "It was in Ladbroke Grove, part of Notting Hill, and was always a bohemian area in London. The Floyd came through there, as did everyone. The Grateful Dead were patients. Dead guitarist-songwriter Bob Weir would regularly have a sore throat and that would be far out and groovy. Some geezer would say, 'I got this sore nose,' and I'd say, 'You silly fuck, you've been snorting coke, of course it's sore.'

"The clinic was started by a doctor who was interested in helping people [get] off junk. He found that doctors still had rights to prescribe cannabis in a tincture or extract form. I did that for a year and then I went on being a private doctor doing homeopathy—still prescribing cannabis. The Wooten Committee [a British government advisory body] looked into cannabis and came up that it wasn't dangerous and should be legalized. I was one of the witnesses to the Wooten Committee, and the officialdom knew that I was a smoker and the so-called underground did, too.

"I was a hippie with long hair, and that's why someone like Gram would come talk to me. If they wanted uppers or downers I'd send them to the straight doctors in Harley Street and Wimpole Street. I wasn't going to be a grocer."

Hutt was keenly interested in music himself. In part as a result of meeting Gram, Hutt subsequently embarked on a second career as a performer, singing country music under the name Hank Wangford.

When Gram and Gretchen came by the office for their first appointment, Hutt was playing a record by Fred Neil. "If you knew about Fred Neil you were in on something," Hutt says. "Gram said, 'Hey, that's Freddy Neil,' and I swung around and said, 'How did you know Fred Neil?' He says, 'Well, man, I played with him,' and I'm completely gobsmacked! 'You played with Freddy Neil? What's your name?' He said, 'Gram Parsons.' I fell off my chair. I didn't know he was Gram Parsons when he made the appointment, although I'd been listening to the Flying Burrito Brothers, who I enjoyed but didn't perceive as being country music. I thought *Sweetheart of the Rodeo* was crap.

"While I consulted with Gretchen, Gram sat on my sofa and picked up my old 1940s English-copy Maccaferri guitar [an imitation of the kind Django Reinhardt used to play]. It's not a great guitar, but Gram took to it and wanted to swap his guitar with mine. I said, 'No, fuck off.' He had a Martin.

"He played 'You're Still on My Mind,' and that for me was the road to Damascus. I was knocked out and heard the soul in country music that I hadn't before. Right then I was a convert. I understood what it was about."

As for Gram and Gretchen: "They were a certain sort of wealthy

American couple. I couldn't say they had a terrible relationship. Gram was in a bit of a state all the time. Gretchen was a real babe: blond Californian, a beauty. I remember her wearing something suede and buckskinny, good couture. Buckskins would be the kind of thing that she, being the wife of a groovy rock star, would wear. A country-rock star. He was always conscious of his appearance. He wasn't afraid to wear a groovy hat. He went for it full tilt. I'd say he was probably quite vain.

"He could be pale-faced . . . like a rocker: pale, didn't see a lot of sun. He liked to wear his suede jacket, Native American style, had fringe on it. He looked like a guy on the scene."

The doctor and his patient became friends, based on their shared musical tastes. "We'd play together and he would come over and hang out," Hutt says. "He was always sort of pointing me in the way of George Jones and Tammy Wynette. Once he came over with *We Go Together*, the George Jones and Tammy Wynette album. And that was his kind of matrix—those became his role models later for him and Emmylou. There was also the medical side [of our relationship] and his excesses. He was on a mission to wipe himself out.

"He kept his inner core to himself, and it was covered over by an awful lot of drugs. He was into the smack and booze and any sort of uppers that you could keep yourself awake to. He sang like a smack user. He had a smack voice like Billie Holiday, Ray Charles . . . Joe Cocker, and Lucinda Williams, I'd say, with all that kind of ravaged quality, quite raw."

Hutt had a treatment for getting Gram off heroin. "The chemical that people don't know about is Lomotil," Gram later explained, "which is nothing more than a paregoric. It's a cure for traveler's and baby's diarrhea. Take twelve every four hours for three weeks, then you cut down to eight pills every four hours, then stop. It doesn't do anything to you. It doesn't make you high—it takes all withdrawal symptoms completely away. All . . ."

The cure didn't take, however. As junkies do, Gram would clean up only to fall back into his habit. "I would prescribe Gram homeopathic stuff like everyone else," Hutt says. "There would be occasions when I would have to give him heroin antidotes. I didn't have to do that frequently, but there were a few times when I'd have to go sort him out. It was usually a basic first aid of getting somebody out of an impending coma. He was taking a lot of whatever drugs he could take and a lot of times he was taking too much, and I would be the person he would call when he was scared and had to be looked after."

Sometimes Gram was "slightly shamefaced" about his drug use and "sometimes there would be a naughty-boy thing," Hutt recalls. But Gram didn't express much interest in giving up drugs. "He said, 'I do it because I like it. I'm not stupid. I do it because I like it.'"

IN JULY, GRAM AND GRETCHEN moved to Nellcôte, the villa Keith rented in the south of France near Cap Ferrat. "I dug their music, and I called Keith and said, 'Can I come over to your place?'" Gram later explained. "And he said yeah. So I went over and stayed at his place for a while in London and later on in the south of France [near] Cap Ferrat. It would be eighty degrees there in the summer and we'd all sit around drinking hot toddies . . ."

Nellcôte is a white palace on a hill overlooking the harbor of Villefranche-sur-Mer, a small town on the French Riviera. Elaborate wrought-iron gates enclosed the gardens, which led down to a private beach; inside, the high-ceilinged rooms were furnished in grand nineteenth-century style. The rent was $2,400 a week. In 1971.

Keith set the schedule for the band. It was always more reliable for everyone to come to Keith than to get Keith to show up somewhere else. The band and their hangers-on rented their own places around Cap Ferrat. Nellcôte was the center of activity. The Stones brought in a truck filled with a quarter-million dollars of equipment, and the palace's dank basement rooms and the wandering corridors that connected them became the recording studio. "They were all of a sudden not in the studio," Gram said, "but playing in Keith's basement!"

In May, Mick married the Nicaraguan jet-set beauty Bianca Moreno de Macias in St. Tropez. Gram was not invited; neither were most of the old-line Stones entourage. Their union caused no small tension in the band.

"I had a 1969 Rolls-Royce Phantom that I drove from Rome to Nellcôte," Stash Klossowski says. When he arrived, "Keith took me aside and he said, 'First thing I want to know is, what is your take on this marriage? How much do you think this will cost us?' He was furious. He was quite prophetic.

"Mick and Bianca had a villa some distance off. Charlie was far away. Nellcôte became headquarters. Keith would emerge in the late morning, early afternoon, and go waterskiing. At night everyone would come [to play]. I remember Keith playing 'Rip This Joint' standing in the middle of the Nellcôte living room and blazing away at the guitar. It was the best version of that song that I had ever heard. I've never forgotten it."

The band fell into Keith Time, sleeping most of the day and staying up all night to play and record.

Keith needed heroin. Tony Sanchez described one way they got it. He and Keith ran into Count Jean de Breteuil, who introduced himself as a friend of William Burroughs. De Breteuil's fashion signature was red suspenders, leading Keith and Sanchez to refer to him as Johnny Braces. Learning that Keith was looking for a connection, de Breteuil returned, at the wheel of a Bentley, with heroin that Sanchez describes as looking and smelling "like pink talcum power. Pure Thai heroin."

Impressed with the quality of the goods, Keith expressed interest in a steady supply. When de Breteuil got back to London he called his dealer, a Corsican based in Marseilles, and asked him to arrange regular deliveries to Nellcôte. Tony Sanchez describes the arrival of the first batch: "They were two burly Corsicans, perspiring profusely in their Daks lightweight suits and carrying identical black fiberglass executive attaché cases. After a brief exchange of pleasantries the stouter of the two clicked open his case to reveal a polyethylene bag approximately as large as a two-pound sack of sugar. . . . Keith cautiously snorted the mixture and after a few minutes lapsed into unconsciousness. When he came to, he said, 'Okay, I'll take the lot.'"

The kilo cost four thousand dollars. The heroin was so pure that Keith cut it three-to-one with glucose. The stepped-on kilo lasted the household less than a month.

According to Sanchez, the cost of running Nellcôte included an average of a thousand dollars a week on alcohol and a thousand a week on caviar, lobster, and other edibles. Remember, these are 1971 dollars. "The food and drink were consumed with locust-like avidity by swarms of visitors who descended on the house," Sanchez writes. "Marshall Chess [of the Chess Records family] stayed for a while; so did Eric Clapton, little Michele Breton from *Performance*, and numerous passing strangers. Keith enjoyed having people around him, even though he knew that the impression of friendship and bonhomie they produced was purely illusory. Most of the houseguests were interesting, creative people."

Some, of course, were junkie scum.

Tensions mounted between the spongers and those who were working on the recording. There was jockeying for position between the primary band members and those with lesser functions. A courtlike hierarchy developed, with Gram in an uncomfortable middle position. He was truly Keith's friend and could pay his own way, so he was never considered a leech. Still, he was one of the many who lived in the house but were left behind when the band went downstairs to record.

"If you couldn't play and be part of [the recording sessions]," Stash says, "you were relegated to this other circle of people who were caught in between with not much to do. Yet it was almost frowned upon if you weren't in attendance.

"A lot of people came from England or America. They had taken cabs and now they were stuck. You could barely walk anywhere from Nellcôte. With the constant playbacks and recordings, people couldn't sleep well. At first it sounds exciting, but the music's going on all night long, and if you're not participating or actually playing, with the constant drugs it could be iffy."

That Stash—Gretchen's former lover—was on hand added to Gram's discomfort. Worse, Gram showed that he was bothered.

"In those days we considered that you could not be jealous," Stash says. "It was unthinkable. We all had horrible attitudes. First of all, never talk to girls except to sleep with them. We didn't talk to them. If you met someone else's wife, you never addressed her or talked to her. Girls were objects. It was a strange thing. You weren't allowed to be jealous. It was unthinkable to complain—you were automatically classified as out. So this jealousy of Gram's was not welcome. I don't think anybody was sympathetic to his perceived plight. He was with Gretchen, but he was still resentful about what had happened a year before."

While some maintain that Gram can be heard on the chorus of "Tumbling Dice" and "Sweet Virginia," Keith has been adamant that Gram is not on the album. "He was on some of the workups," Keith said later. "But Gram was too much of a gent to impose himself that much."

Gram and Keith still played together every day. Photographs from the time show Keith and Gram in their bathing suits, sitting around a vast baronial dining table under a chandelier, guitars in their hands. They look like what they were: the two coolest guys on the planet. Gretchen and Anita Pallenberg sit with them, wearing almost nothing. Anita lolls in her underwear and high-heeled sandals. Gretchen looks ravaged and gorgeous. The atmosphere is of drug decadence and almost impossibly casual glamour.

That Gram and Keith had a profound musical, drug, and soul connection is apparent at a glance. The *Exile* sound clearly grew from that connection. Gram introduced Mick and Keith to much American music. He championed the idea that supposedly disparate American sounds could be conjoined.

He showed Keith the path down which *Exile* travels. But Gram wasn't invited to play on the sessions. No matter what the bonds, there were Stones and not-Stones. Gram would never cross that divide. It was a hard reality and required a thick skin.

"There was music going on nonstop," Stash says. "It was a weird atmosphere. Keith was in this extraordinary state because he managed all of it. He had a boat and he was thriving on this whole thing. He worked beautifully, he sang brilliantly, he played hard, and he slept a great deal. But if you weren't one of the people actually doing the recordings, there were all these weird little tragedies that went on. This guy went insane. There was this ex–racing driver who was there with his kids"—he reportedly had smuggled a kilo of cocaine into France by strapping it to his children under their clothes—"who had mysterious schemes. There were these weird floating characters."

Stash had no aspirations to be a Stone. He was an aristocrat with his own wealth and other places to hang that were as cool as Nellcôte. That gave him a kind of independence most of the other Nellcôte hangers-on envied. "Since the atmosphere got a bit heavy with Gram," Stash says, "I lived a completely different life. Not Keith, but other people resented the fact that I had that freedom and I was able to just go off."

The belief in the otherworldly that was so popular among Gram's set provided one explanation for the darker side of life in the castle. Nellcôte had a foreboding atmosphere: Believing was not difficult. "I was playing guitar in one of the rooms one day," Stash says, "and suddenly I felt this strange presence next to me. But there was no one there. It was like the moment where your hairs start to rise, this weird, uncomfortable feeling. I put the guitar down and went downstairs and found Elizabeth, a woman who had lived and worked in Nellcôte for some time. I asked her in French, 'Is this place haunted?' She said, *'Mais oui, monsieur.'* She was deadly serious. She said, 'No one has ever been happy here.'"

The easy comings and goings of junkies and leeches reached its logical conclusion when the Stones awoke one morning to find their instruments stolen. The Keith method was not working out. A housecleaning was in order, and Gram was to be swept away.

Trying to keep up with Keith while having no musical focus took a terrible toll on Gram. Those who were there remember that he was "zonked out of his skull" much of the time and in such bad physical shape that many were worried he might die on the premises. Jo Bergman, the

Stones' majordomo, took care of the nondrug functional aspects of the Stones' world. Bergman later said she was told, "Okay, you will take Gram to the airport and you will put him on a plane *out of here*."

"WHEN I STARTED to hang with Gram, it did alter my relationship with Mick," Keith says. "He may have been a little bit jealous, because Gram and I were working together a lot and playing a lot of country music, which Mick is as intrigued by. I don't know if Mick felt shunted aside because Gram and I were tight for a while."

Anita Pallenberg laid the blame for their ouster on Gretchen, describing the California girl as "moany and reproachful—always reproaching Gram for being who he was." Gretchen blamed Mick for coming on to her constantly, hoping to drive Gram off: "He wouldn't leave me alone," she later said. "He was a little overbearing with me, and that would get Gram's goat, I think. I don't think it was about me, that's for sure. It just seemed too obvious."

Among the legends that sprang from this time is one that has a ring of truth and plenty of supporters, but no direct confirmation: that Keith sincerely feared Gram was doing an unhealthy amount of heroin. It hardly needs saying that if Keith Richards is running your intervention, you're in trouble.

Even before he left London for Nellcôte, Gram had been pushing his limits. "There'd be times when he'd be taking overdoses where he'd look appalling," Dr. Hutt says. "That's when people turn blue and they die. There were a couple times when he was looking close to it and pulling back from it.

"You worry and you get angry. Angry at being manipulated when somebody takes themselves that far out on the edge. You feel they're wanting to know how much you love them. How far will you come out and save me? To see if you can catch me and bring me back. Gram had that feeling."

At Nellcôte no one, not even Keith, saw rescuing Gram as a project that had much chance of success. Tolerance for his self-destruction had run out. The Stones had an album to record. Gram provided inspiration for much of what ended up on the record, but he had become a drag. It was time for him to go.

According to Barney Hoskyns, when Gram realized he was being booted he became as ill-mannered as he was capable. Perry Richardson heard that as Gram and Gretchen were packing to leave, Keith asked Gram to perform some chore and Gram replied, "Well, I don't know if I can do that." "I don't know that it was particularly Keith and Anita's fault," Richardson says. "There's a history of people getting pulled into that Stones vortex. . . . According to Gretchen, it was a crushing blow to Gram.

"It was easy to get caught up in the world that surrounded the Stones, and Gram did. The thing people forget so easily was that Keith had his own life and his own problems. And I know that Gretchen was young to be in that situation and found it difficult. A pattern had been set whereby Gram would take whatever was around, probably more than anyone. Michael Cooper phoned me up from Cap Ferrat saying, 'Look, Gram and Gretchen are gonna arrive back in London, and they're gonna ask you for the keys to the Holland Park flat. Can you tell them you've lost the keys?'"

Gram called Richardson minutes after Cooper told Richardson to bar Gram from the London flat where he expected to stay. Being denied that small sanctuary was a slap in the face. Keith and the Stones circle had turned their back on Gram, and that was that. Having witnessed others with lesser claims to a rightful place in Stones World be cast out, Gram knew his time in Eden was over. Barney Hoskyns asserts that Gram attempted suicide by willfully overdosing on heroin in London. But Gram was routinely doing so much smack that it's difficult to distinguish between a willful OD and the almost inevitable accident.

Gram and Gretchen had nowhere to stay. All their London friends were either in Nellcôte with the Stones, knew from the Stones to turn a cold shoulder, or had heard about Gram's behavior and were less than welcoming. After visiting with Dr. Hutt in an attempt to get clean, Gram reached out to his former bandmate Ian Dunlop.

Dunlop was living with his wife and their infant daughter on a small farm in the village of Tregidden in Cornwall. "I had started living an entirely different life," Dunlop says. "I was healthy and outdoorsy. I had dropped out—I wasn't quite living off the grid, but pretty close. Gram loved it here. He was considering wanting to drop out himself and have a breather. There was a little cottage nearby that we went over to look at, and Gram and Gretchen were considering renting. He thought it would be nice to live away from everything for a while."

"England's a place I've always dug for its simplicity in lifestyle," Gram said. "Maybe I wouldn't be able to find the right musicians there, but at least I wouldn't be taken off on some side trip. I could develop my own trip and then make up my mind about things."

"We were doing a lot of outdoor things and going on walks and going to the sea and riding on a motorcycle. I had a motorcycle and a sidecar," Dunlop says. "Gram and I played music and went to the pub for a few pints. Nothing excessive. We weren't smoking dope. He wasn't carrying on in any abusive way at all. He had been to a doctor in London before he came. I remember Gram helping me cut firewood and chop logs. We went on long walks and hikes on the coastal cliffs, what they call the footpaths, on the edge of the sea. My wife and I, we had had the first baby, a couple of months old, and we were all going to bed at ten o'clock at night. It was not like L.A."

Or Nellcôte.

Dunlop was meeting Gretchen for the first time. "She was skinny and had a cone-shaped hat and wore a furry vest," Dunlop says. "She was cordial and nice." Dunlop was shocked to learn about Gretchen's dad: "He was on this notorious right-wing television station [in Los Angeles], Channel 5, KTLA. The news had an amazing right-wing slant. I practically choked when she told me. I think Gene Autry owned it. At the height of Vietnam there was glorified coverage [of the war] every day. It was a station we used to watch like it was comedy. It was so blatantly, ridiculously right-wing, and all the rest of the programming was so trashy."

Dunlop regarded Gram as "penniless" when he arrived in England. Gram and Gretchen stayed on the farm, keeping a low profile and nursing their wounds. Being thrown out of Nellcôte meant starting over entirely.

Then the phone rang. "There was some manager from L.A. saying, 'Get your ass down here,'" Dunlop says. Gram's country idyll was over. He got his ass down to L.A.

"The first thing everyone said when Gram got back [to Los Angeles] was, 'Gram is *fat*,'" Eve Babitz said. "It was like saying he was dead or had cancer. He looked terrible, like a mean Southern cop."

EIGHTEEN
GP

AFTER A BRIEF STAY IN LOS ANGELES, GRAM AND GRETCHEN FLEW TO NEW Orleans to get married. No one from their L.A. community came along. Jet Thomas performed the ceremony. Despite her difficulties with Bob and Bonnie, Little Avis attended. So did Gram's stepsisters, Becky and Jan. "He was a little removed," Becky Gottsegen says. "He wasn't the Gram I knew growing up. He had gone into that alternative lifestyle. The handsome, clean-cut young guy was changed into a long-haired hippie. He didn't look healthy."

"Gram was fat," Jet Thomas said. "Fatter than I'd ever seen him. He told me he was fat because he was off drugs."

Gram kept saying he was clean. No one believed him. Several members of his family were convinced that Gretchen was also using heroin, but no one reports having seen her shoot up.

Bonnie Parsons couldn't tell about either Gram or Gretchen, since she wasn't familiar with druggie behavior. "I wouldn't have known it if I saw it," she says. "Gretchen slept a lot—so did Gram. Gretchen was too hotsy-totsy for me. She thought she was perfect. Bob [Parsons] didn't think she had much upstairs. She had a good body—though not enough boobs for him—but not much upstairs."

Gretchen wore a traditional long white wedding dress. Jet Thomas spoke a simple nondenominational service of his own creation. It ended with a blessing.

"Gretchen knew exactly what colors she wanted," Bonnie Parsons says, "and that was red and white. We toned it down to red sashes on all the white dresses and had a big bash in the backyard with tons of people, mostly Bob's friends. I don't think anybody came from California."

"The stepfather had arranged for this big fancy thing out by the swimming pool with an ice sculpture," Jet Thomas says. "It was a beautiful wedding and simple, elegant. Bob had an old Southern house with the slave kitchen downstairs. It had commercial appliances and lots of servants. They flew in caviar, because that was one of the things that Gram wanted. We had a nice ceremony out by the pool and a reception afterwards. Few of Gram and Gretchen's friends came. It was mostly older people and Gram's family. There was a big fuss because they invited some of Gram's black friends."

"Gram was in lust," Bonnie Parsons says. "He couldn't keep his hands off Gretchen. They were always kissing and hugging and rubbing bodies. Nancy hadn't been that way. Gretchen was flamboyant and showy about affection. Gram would grab her and pick her up off the ground and kiss her on the mouth to the point where Bob and I said we were both going to throw up."

Jet Thomas, who was more likely to see past the sexual to the emotional core of things, says, "Gram and Gretchen did okay. They didn't seem to be close. It was almost like a business relationship. But Gram was not that close to anybody."

For their honeymoon, Gram took Gretchen to Disneyland in Anaheim. "I guess if you're stoned or something, it may be fun," Bonnie Parsons says. Chris Hillman said, "He took her to Disneyland on their honeymoon—that's the boy I knew." It hardly seems possible, but everybody swears that's where they went.

GRAM PATCHED THINGS UP with Hillman sufficiently to tag along with the Flying Burrito Brothers on their East Coast tour in October 1971. It's a mark of Gram's aimlessness that he would travel with the band that had kicked him out. And a mark of his charm that they let him.

Singer-songwriter Rick Roberts (whose later band Firefall hit with

"Wildfire") had replaced Gram in the Burritos. In Washington, D.C., Roberts and Kenny Wertz (former banjo player in the Scottsville Squirrel Barkers, who replaced Bernie Leadon in the Burritos) discovered the folk-singer Emmylou Harris playing in a local club. They raved about her to Chris Hillman, and Hillman suggested that Gram hear her sing.

Byron Berline was also touring with the Burritos. "Gram met us down in Virginia and he looked pretty good," Byron remembers. "He said he wanted to do duets with a female singer. We had just run into Emmylou Harris in D.C. at the Cellar Door. Chris gave Gram her phone number."

"Rick Roberts found Emmylou and he dragged me down to watch her play," Hillman says. "She was doing Joni Mitchell and Joan Baez and some country songs. She sat in with the Burritos and I said, 'You should do more country songs, they're magical.' We parted company and I told her it would be great to do something with her someday. . . . Gram was back from England and ready to do a solo record. I said, 'There is this girl in Washington you've gotta meet. She's perfect for you.' I got her on the phone and got her to talk to Gram. It took me an hour to talk him into driving there and meeting her."

Emmylou Harris was born in 1947 in Birmingham, Alabama. Her father was a Marine. Her family, as service families will, moved often. Emmylou competed in beauty contests as a teenager and graduated as her high school valedictorian. In 1965 she enrolled at the University of North Carolina at Greensboro and majored in drama. Enthralled by Bob Dylan and Joan Baez, she dropped out of college and moved to New York in time for the tail end of the Village folk scene. She married songwriter Tom Slocum in 1969 and released a solo record, *Gliding Bird*, on the Jubilee label in 1970. *Gliding Bird* includes Emmylou's cover of "Everybody's Talkin'" by Gram's friend Fred Neil.

Jubilee declared bankruptcy shortly after the record's release, and *Gliding Bird* didn't sell. Emmylou moved to Nashville with Slocum while she was pregnant. They divorced after the birth of their daughter, Hallie. Emmylou struggled in Nashville and ended up living with her parents in the rural suburbs of D.C. She gigged at clubs in the area with her boyfriend, bass player Tom Guidera, and guitarist Gerry Mule.

When she met Gram, Emmylou was living in a shared house near the freeway with her daughter. She subsisted on food stamps and what came in from passing the hat at her shows.

"I was pretty jaded at that point," Emmylou says. "I didn't expect anything to ever happen to me. I was cautious and extremely reserved about the whole thing . . . people had said to me over the years they were going to do this for me and they were going to do that for me. I realized I didn't have any of those hopes anymore. . . ."

"Chris told me there was this girl singing in this club in Washington, D.C.," Gram later recounted, "that she was 'pretty good, but needed some work.'"

"I got this phone call—this long, drawled-out voice," Emmylou recalled. "Gram was in Baltimore, which is about a fifty-mile drive. He wanted to hear me, and to hear how we sounded together, and would I pick him up? I said, 'Hell, no! It's raining and I gotta work tonight and do you realize how far it is?' I'd been knocking around for a long time and I was pretty cynical. I was vaguely familiar with the name Gram Parsons, but I didn't listen to a lot of music, and I wasn't familiar with his work.

"He and Gretchen took the train and I met them at the station. We drove down to this little bar called Clyde's. He got up and played with my bass and guitar players. We did 'I Fall to Pieces' and 'That's All It Took.'"

When Gram heard Emmylou sing he was "knocked out," he said later. To test her "country phrasing and feeling," he proposed singing "That's All It Took" because "it's one of the hardest country duets I know. . . . Emmy sang it like she was falling off a log. I never lost touch with her after that."

Emmylou had a slightly different reaction. "To make a confession, when I first heard Gram sing I wasn't too impressed. He hadn't sung for a long time. . . . It's amazing how much he changed with me. It's probably easier to make it with somebody than it is to sing with somebody and get it right."

Gram told Chuck Cassell: "I found a chick singer who's good who I wanna sing with. I like that idea. I've always had a problem with guys who can't sing high enough. Singing with chicks always seems to work out, at least half good. And if you get a really good chick, it works better than anything. 'Cause you can look at each other with love in your eyes. If my wife can put up with it, it would be the perfect solution. She's a gas. Her name's Emmylou Harris. I won't say where she lives. I don't want one of these Mustache Petes around here to go steal her away."

Gram still hoped that Keith would finally confirm a deal with Rolling Stones Records and produce his solo album. "I don't know if I'll wind up recording for Rolling Stones Records or some small company," Gram said. "I'm thinking of recording with a smaller company where I can be more of a big fish." Keith continued to not come through; he wouldn't say yes, he wouldn't say no. However hurt Gram must have been by Keith's years of stalling, he never complained.

Gram made a prodigal return to Mo Ostin at Warner Bros. "I went with my hat in my hand and said, 'Mr. Ostin, sir, I sure am sorry about that deal I pulled a few years ago. What do you think about me doing an album now?'" Gram said. "He said, 'Great.'" Ostin signed Gram for two solo records. Merle Haggard was to produce the first. Having Merle as a producer would be a coup and a blessing: It would give Gram the purest of country credibility.

"Warner Brothers arranged a meeting at Haggard's Bakersfield home, and the two musicians seemed to hit it off," Rick Cusick wrote. "Parsons played with Haggard's massive model train collection, and Haggard agreed to handle the production of the album. Unfortunately, Haggard backed out. The day before they were scheduled to begin recording, Haggard refused the project and wouldn't explain why. Parsons had the impression that marital troubles were forcing Merle's hand, but it's possible that GP's reputation for less than professional behavior had something to do with it."

Gram's first hire was Eddie Tickner, formerly the Byrds' manager, who took charge of organizing the sessions. "Merle was stashed in the Holiday Inn on Highland Avenue," Tickner said, "and I'd stashed Gram in the Roosevelt Hotel. Keep him away from everybody . . . sometimes known as 'drying out.' The afternoon before the first session, Merle cancels. I trot over to the Holiday Inn and he won't come out of the bedroom. I went back to Gram and said, 'It's off.' He went right for the bottle."

Merle's wife had left him; he was too distraught to work. His departure was a crushing blow. "Merle not producing Gram was probably one of the greatest disappointments in Gram's life," Gretchen said. "Merle was very nice, very sweet, but he had his own enemies and his own demons."

Plans for recording stopped cold. Years later, in 1980, as cantankerous as ever and trying to protect his own reputation as a hell-raiser, Merle spoke disparagingly of Gram. Dismissing the idea that Gram had been "wild," Haggard said, "He was a pussy. Hell, he was just a long-haired kid. I thought he was a good writer. He was not wild, though. That's what was funny to me. All these guys running around in long hair talking about being wild and Rolling Stones. I don't think someone abusing themselves on drugs necessarily determines how wild they are. It might determine how ignorant they are."

Merle's contempt for the hippie lifestyle is well known; his "Okie from Muskogee" was the national anthem for anyone who wanted to beat up longhairs and feel righteous about it. Merle despised the entire longhair, drug-taking, country-music-usurping culture and was happy to say so. Merle knew from wild: He had done time in San Quentin for robbery. Rich kids with long hair on drugs cut no ice with Merle; he'd done his share of country-musician speed and didn't have to invent a subculture to justify it. By that standard, no, Gram was not wild. But he was "a good writer." And that's about as much praise as anybody can expect from Merle Haggard.

From December 1971 to May 1972, the Stones were in L.A. adding overdubs to *Exile* at Sunset Sound Studios. There is no record of contact between Gram and Keith during this time. There would be no deal with Rolling Stones Records. There would be no producing by Keith. There would be no more invitations into Stones World.

After hiding away for some weeks, Gram and Gretchen went back to England in June of 1972. The idea was that Gram would collaborate with bassist Rick Grech on a Grech solo album. Gram had met Grech during the Byrds' 1968 tour of the U.K.

Born in Bordeaux, France, and trained as a classical musician, Grech switched to "beat music" in 1965 after he heard the Beatles. He played bass and violin in a Leicester band, the Farinas. When singer Roger Chapman joined they became Family and signed to Reprise Records in 1967. Grech left Family in 1969 to play bass in one of the first "supergroups," Blind Faith. Blind Faith included organist and vocalist Steve Winwood, late of Traffic, and Eric Clapton, then regarded as the world's greatest guitar player after his stints with John Mayall's Bluesbreakers and Cream. Clapton brought along Cream drummer Ginger Baker. Blind Faith made one album and was known for its lugubrious live jams, during which everyone in the band save Baker seemed to stare off into the distance in a druggy haze. Clapton dumped Blind Faith after their U.S. tour to play with Delaney & Bonnie. Grech joined Traffic when Winwood re-formed the band. He was sacked for drug use in 1971 after the release of Traffic's *The Low Spark of High Heeled Boys*.

Gram and Gretchen stayed with Grech and his wife, Jenny, at their estate in Surrey. "Hippie doctor" Dr. Sam Hutt was there, too. He had gotten in touch with Grech and had presented a bunch of country songs he had written. "Rick was hot to make a country album," Hutt says. "We called Gram and he came over that summer."

"Gram always followed Rick's career as he moved from Family to Blind Faith to [Ginger Baker's] Air Force to Traffic," Jenny Grech said. "Rick was making a solo album here in England with Sam Hutt. Gram and his wife, Gretchen, came to stay with us. Rick and Gram went through this rebonding process. They were riding go-carts round the roads, drinking too much, but also starting to write songs."

"We unsuccessfully started to record some demos," Hutt says, "but nothing ever happened. It dissolved into a smacky haze and I was outside the club. I was not a user. The two boys would get out of it and Rick would fiddle with his recording equipment, but he was too stoned. The recording gear proved to be something Gram did not know how to use."

With the project in disarray, Gram and Gretchen left Grech's estate in Sussex and moved to a small house in the Belgravia section of London. Their circle included Perry Richardson, William Burroughs, and his sometime collaborator, the Beat painter and poet Brion Gysin, who had introduced Brian Jones to Moroccan music.

Joan Baez's performance of "Drug Store Truck Drivin' Man" at Woodstock hadn't made it into the 1970 movie of the festival, but it was included on an extended soundtrack album of the film. Out of the blue, a songwriter's royalty check from the soundtrack found its way to Gram at his London house. His friends remember Gram literally jumping up and down with happiness.

That check was the only royalty payment Gram ever received.

"We'd had great times in London," Gretchen said, "and pretty bleak times—very bleak times. By the time we were in Belgravia, Gram had started to deteriorate."

In the midst of his deterioration, tragedy struck. Gram's friend Brandon De Wilde was dead. On July 6, 1972, Brandon was driving alone through the rain in a suburb of Denver, on his way to perform in *Butterflies Are Free* at a theater at an amusement park. His van skidded on the wet road and hit a parked truck. Critically injured, Brandon died in the hospital a few hours later.

RICK GRECH'S ALBUM was going nowhere. Gram and Grech decided that Grech would produce Gram's solo record. Gram and Gretchen went back to Los Angeles with Rick and Jenny. Gram was determined to find session players and make his record happen. Eddie Tickner was commissioned to get the project going and hired Phil Kaufman.

"Eddie Tickner arranged the whole thing," Kaufman's then-girlfriend, Kathy Fenton, says. "He was managing Gram and had worked with Philip before. Eddie said, 'I've got a new act that I am managing, and I want you to be the road manager.' . . . Phil wasn't working, so he said yes. About fifteen minutes after Philip accepted Eddie's job, somebody called representing the Band"—Bob Dylan's backing group.

Kaufman had evolved into an L.A. character, the Executive Nanny—an indispensable figure on the upper end of the rock lifestyle. Short, squat, strong, and crude, Kaufman both protected and procured for his clients. When they needed to be off drugs Kaufman fended off dealers and parasites. When they needed drugs, Kaufman helped facilitate. Though not quite as competent or in the know as he claimed to be, Kaufman made things happen and made happenstances go away. His strengths were his loyalty and discretion, his refusal to be impressed by stardom, his outlaw-biker hard-assedness, and his determination to see the job through. He had no desire to join anybody's band or compete for women, status, or drugs. He understood his role and his place and stuck to them. He and Gram moved beyond any client relationship—though Kaufman stayed on Gram's payroll—and became genuine friends.

"Phil was an unusual person," Barry Tashian says. "He had this humor you had to get used to . . . very in your face. Nothing was sacred." Jim Dickson, who has a great affection for Kaufman—and Kaufman inspires loathing or affection, and nothing in between—tells of Kaufman dressed in a striped convict's costume, carrying a ball and chain, standing on the road near San Quentin Prison, trying to hitch a ride.

Kaufman had a darker aspect. He claimed that when he was arrested on a drug charge in 1967, he shared a jail cell on Terminal Island with Charles Manson. After his release, Kaufman lived with the Manson family for two months. Mainly, he later said, because Manson had a fleet of young girls under his command who stole food and were available for sex on demand, twenty-four hours a day. After the Tate-LaBianca murders, Kaufman said, in *Road Mangler*, "I realized I'd had sex with every one of those murderesses." Following Manson's conviction for masterminding the killings, Kaufman released Manson's jailhouse album, *LIE*. Kaufman also arranged the famous *Rolling Stone* interview with Manson. Kaufman was proud of his Manson connection, and in his world it granted him perverse street cred. It certainly burnished his claims of being the baddest motherfucker in the Valley.

Gram asked Barry Tashian to come from Boston to play on the sessions. Tashian slept on Gram's couch at the Chateau Marmont for two weeks until he found an apartment. Emmylou came west and got her own room at the Chateau. The developing band rehearsed at the Chateau and at Byron Berline's house. "We would hang out and sing harmony in Gram's living room at the Chateau," Tashian says. "He'd play records for us and we'd sing songs like 'I'm Still Feeling Blue.'" Eddie Tickner ran the rehearsals at Byron's house; the sessions were recorded but later erased.

Tashian suggested a number of songs to Gram: "I Can't Dance" by Tom T. Hall, "Burn That Candle" and "Rocking Chair" by Bill Haley, "Cry One More Time" by Peter Wolf and Seth Justman of the J. Geils Band, and "Streets of Baltimore" by Harlan Howard and Tompall Glaser—the Byrds' nemesis during their Grand Ole Opry appearance. Gram was already familiar with "Streets" and intended to record it.

"Gram was getting more fucked-up, to a greater degree," a member of the band says. "One night he was so blithering high that you couldn't relate to him. Rambling, not paying any attention to others, preoccupied. He seemed angrier. The addiction was growing."

"Gram never tried to clean up," Gretchen said. "And his mental health became precarious. He was ill, and you can only beg someone so many times, 'Please don't bring these people over, please don't give him anything, water down the drinks.' There would always be someone going, 'Hey, Gram, lemme buy you a drink . . . hey, look what I got for ya.' I couldn't fight it. If I'd been an octopus swinging my tentacles in all directions I couldn't have fought it."

"[Those rehearsals] were what I called the pickin' and pukin' party," Jenny Grech later said. "The combination of Gram and all the substances he was using, and these lovely but incredibly straight country musicians."

"There was plenty of drinking and drugging," a band member says. "We went out one night to see the Country Gazette at McCabe's in Santa Monica. We drove down in a black Cadillac, Grech, Gram, and I. Gram was driving, pretty drunk. We'd stopped at Jack in the Box and gotten burgers. We were opening them when Gram ran a stop sign and got pulled over. He stopped so suddenly the hamburgers went flying all over the dashboard.

"Gram started berating the policeman. They were trying to get him to walk a straight line and giving him the sobriety test, which he failed. Phil had to go down and bail him out."

Phil brought Kathy Fenton to the Chateau. "Gram was hungover, disheveled," Kathy recalls. "He was a good-looking and troubled young man. He had a good heart and I immediately liked him. He was down-to-earth, a real person. He didn't treat you like he was any better than you were. Gretchen was at the Chateau. She was loaded out of her mind, coked up, drunk. I remember instantly not liking her."

Margaret Fisher with Sin City jacket. (© Robert Altman, www.altmanphoto.com)

Gram reached out to his high school friend Margaret Fisher. Margaret was living a drifting, marginal life as a beautiful girl on the scene in San Francisco. She did some modeling (she appeared in a Levi's print campaign), sold marijuana, and waitressed in a hippie restaurant. She was friends with Francis Ford Coppola, the jazz trumpeter Chet Baker (an avatar of self-destruction and wasted gifts), satirist Paul Krassner, and the Beat poet Lawrence Ferlinghetti. Margaret and Gram reconnected after Gram saw her photograph in L.A. Margaret had auditioned for director Donald Cammell (cowriter and director of the 1970 film *Performance*); Margaret wanted to play actress Jean Harlow in Cammell's L.A. production of Michael McClure's play *The Beard*. Gram contacted her through the production company. She refused to see Gram, didn't get the part, went back to San Francisco, and enrolled at U.C. Berkeley. Gram called her regularly, and eventually she took his calls.

"Gram started calling from the Chateau Marmont," Margaret says, "and he didn't sound good. He'd say, 'Remember me?' and I would say, 'Shoot, yes! You know you're one of the coolest guys I ever met.' We talked about high school. It got to the point where he was calling like every other night. I would be going to Berkeley in the daytime and coming home and trying to study. He'd call and I'd talk to him. He'd say, 'Things are terrible.' I'd say, 'Nah, they aren't that bad.'"

For his solo album, Gram wanted the core of Elvis Presley's band: James Burton on guitar, Glen D. Hardin on piano and organ, and Ronnie Tutt on drums. Gram, Gretchen, and Rick and Jenny Grech went to the Hilton International in Las Vegas to watch Elvis perform and to hire his band. "We flew out to see Elvis play," Barry Tashian says. "Gram and Rick stayed up all night and went backstage and sat with the band, and that's when he talked to them about doing the sessions."

Rick Grech and Glen D. Hardin got kicked out of the casino for drunkenness (and having long hair). Glen railed at the casino employees and told Grech, "Let me apologize on behalf of the United States for the way these assholes are treating you."

"We went back to L.A. the next day and the sessions started the following week," Tashian says.

Warner Bros. refused to foot the bill for such expensive talent. Gram paid out of his own pocket. Choosing Elvis' band was a brilliant outsider's move. Despite their abilities, they were regarded by L.A. rockers as campy hicks for wearing matching Vegas stage outfits and backing the King. They performed as a show band, which was held to be ridiculously inauthentic. Everyone knew Elvis' song list was a joke. The Vegas setting, the orange jumpsuits, playing "You Made Me a Mountain," all obscured the musicians' brilliance to any but the most observant.

Their image worked against their credibility. The rock world did not take them seriously. It didn't help that they had backed the country-music attempts of Ricky Nelson, who was seen as an early-sixties bubblegummer striving vainly to overcome his teenybopper past. Gram was a connoisseur; he knew the truth. Gram had a vision—he wasn't much good at detail, but he saw his own myth in broad strokes. Playing with Elvis' band was a key part of it.

Something had galvanized Gram into action. Perhaps he finally accepted that Keith would not swoop in to save him. Perhaps the collapse of the Grech sessions in London frightened him. Or perhaps the arrival of his first and only royalty check gave him the single shred of validation none of his other work had produced. Gram, loaded or not, wanted to work.

Gram could see his influence on the culture. He could hardly miss it. The Burritos had unleashed a plague upon the land of ponytailed young men in snap-button shirts doing variously lame versions of "Six Days on the Road." More worthy California (and English) bands had shifted from jamming to highly crafted country, country-inflected, or roots material.

After the ethereal acid meanderings of 1969's *Live/Dead*, the Grateful Dead—the most jam-centric band in America—put out *Workingman's Dead* in 1970. Their style had altered drastically. *Workingman's Dead* features brief, spiky Bakersfield-style guitar leads, carefully constructed harmonies, and pedal-steel guitar. The album spans a variety of American roots music, from Bakersfield country to folk to roadhouse blues; the Dead left psychedelia behind. Critics were quick to cite *John Wesley Harding* and the Band's *Music from Big Pink* as influences. Few recognized the profound effect the Burritos had on the Dead.

The Dead's follow-up album, *American Beauty*, was even more country-inflected, produced with a stoned, San Francisco version of the Nashville glossy sound. A side project of *American Beauty* were Dead buddies New Riders of the Purple Sage, whose first album was released in 1971. Calling themselves "psychedelic cowboys," the New Riders specialized in a wimpy, pretty, overproduced sound that echoed Richie Furay's Poco. Gram was surrounded by watered-down versions of his own originality.

The greatest affront had to be the June 1972 release of the Eagles' self-titled debut, which went platinum (that is, sold at least one million units) and hit number twenty-two. The single "Witchy Woman" went to number nine, "Take It Easy" to number twelve, and "Peaceful Easy Feeling" hit number twenty-two. A band offering the most pallid rendition of country rock was a smash—with Gram's former bandmate Bernie Leadon at its core. Eagles drummer Don Henley said of himself: "I have a high tolerance for repetition." Gram lacked this quality. Henley's abundance of it helped provide the Eagles' music with its soulless, overrehearsed, antiseptic, schematic, insincere, sentimental core. The Eagles managed to deny every roots-music source of their sound. Their country rock—with its self-satisfaction, misogyny, absence of pain, junior high emotions, pop hooks, and facile faux virtuosity—was more than dumb enough to please the broadest American audience. And still is. The Eagles were and remain arguably the most consistently contemptible stadium band in rock. Gram famously referred to their music as "a plastic dry-fuck." He bore the Eagles a special loathing, as any sane listener might.

As the Eagles vigorously superficialized the roots of their sound, the Rolling Stones passionately embraced roots they, as Britons, never possessed. *Exile on Main Street*, released on May 12, 1972, proved a sweeping success. The double LP went platinum, hit number one in the U.S. and U.K., and spawned two singles. "Tumbling Dice" b/w "Sweet Black Angel" was released in April and hit number seven in the States and number five in the U.K.; "Happy" reached number twenty-two in America.

Exile had to have been a bitter pill for Gram: proof it was time for him to get off his ass before his most original ideas were forever co-opted by others.

Over its four sides, *Exile* did more than embrace Gram's Cosmic American Music; *Exile* proved it existed. The Rolling Stones' route to expressing Cosmic American Music did not, like the path taken by Delaney & Bonnie, include the outright copying of existing forms. The Stones' approach was more sophisticated, more knowing. As Gram had always preached was possible, the Stones subsumed gospel, country, R&B, soul, honky-tonk, blues, roadhouse, boogie-woogie, and rock into their own sound. What they created was Stones music rooted in the broad embrace of Americana that was Gram's passion and expertise (decades before Americana came to mean the alt. country or No Depression music of the late 1990s and early 2000s). The lyrical choices and song structures were new for the Stones. They featured a deceptive lack of polish, a raw expression of the heart of the musical forms they digested. Following the precepts—if Gram's thinking can be described as having precepts—of Cosmic American Music, the Stones manifested, devoutly, the musical stew Gram described. Gram pursued this stew directly—covering obscure but resonant country and R&B classics, writing new country tunes whose heartbreak was shot through with irony—the Stones did it obliquely.

One of the two covers on *Exile*, a honking, metallic stomp through Robert Johnson's "Stop Breaking Down," sounds nothing like the acoustic original. Neither does it sound like the overly constructed, orchestral version of Johnson's "Love in Vain" on the Stones' *Let It Bleed*. "Stop Breaking Down"'s fiendish intent and swaggering vibe align perfectly with the original. There's no proof that Gram directly participated in any songs on *Exile*, but the influence of his taste and philosophy is everywhere.

The Stones were rooted in the blues from their first incarnation. Gram's mix tapes and his endless song sessions with Keith opened their ears to new worlds. Yet the sound of *Exile* owes little to Gram. The detailed, layered, revolutionary production, the ornate arrangements, the willful submersion of lead vocals into the swirling mix—these are hallmarks of musicians more experienced, successful, and confident than Gram.

Which success must have burned Gram more, spurred him more to action? The pop bubblegum country of the Eagles, or the thoughtful colonization of America by the Stones? Each had to have stung in its own painful way. A few months after *Exile* appeared, Gram was ready to work.

THE SESSIONS FOR THE ALBUM that would become *GP* ran from September through October of 1972. Gram hired Merle Haggard's engineer, Hugh Davies. The session personnel included Gram, Emmylou Harris, and Barry Tashian on vocals and rhythm guitar; Rick Grech and John Conrad on bass; drummers Ronnie Tutt, John Guerin, and Samuel Goldstein; Glen D. Hardin on piano and organ; James Burton on electric guitar and dobro; Al Perkins and Buddy Emmons on pedal steel; Byron Berline on fiddle; Alane Munde on banjo; and Hal Battiste on baritone sax.

"I went out to California in a long black beard, ripped jeans, funky old shirt, and here I was plunked in the studio with Glen D. Hardin and James Burton," Barry Tashian says. "Watching these other great musicians work was fascinating to me. I had an Epiphone Frontier guitar with cactus and a western rope on the pickguard. Gram had a small Martin and a Gibson J-200. Emmylou would sit and knit between takes. Ronnie Tutt wore Native American jewelry and sold silver during the session."

Gram had exactly the creative situation he claimed he needed. At his disposal was a supergroup of country session musicians with a strong grounding in rock and roll. The lineup speaks to Gram's relentless musicology. Since Gram was spending his own money, he could get the players he wanted. It was an intimidating bunch. Backing Elvis and playing nonstop sessions year after year, James Burton, Glen D. Hardin, and Ronnie Tutt had seen it all. Twice, at least.

"The first night Gram got pretty wasted," Byron Berline says. "We all told him, 'This isn't going to work.' He was stumbling around. He dropped a guitar pick. We said, 'We'll be ready to play with you when you are ready.' So he kind of straightened up after that. He came around."

"He got so embarrassed to do this," Eddie Tickner later said, "in front of these professional people, favorites of his for a long time, that for the next three weeks he didn't drink anymore before the sessions."

"Gram would always get good musicians," Byron Berline says. "That's the whole secret to put together a good record—get the best musicians you can get and let 'em go.

"Most of the singing was overdubbed. Gram put out a rough track and then did the vocals over. Everybody does it differently. Some people like to do everything live—vocals and everything. We had multitracks—he'd gotten into them."

One morning, Rick Grech and Barry Tashian were eating breakfast near the Chateau Marmont. Rick cried out in pain and crumpled over. An ambulance took Grech to the hospital. He had a kidney stone. A few days later he was back at work.

Some accounts of the making of *GP* portray Grech as mostly absent and of little influence on the sessions. "Rick did pass a kidney stone and miss a few days of the sessions," Jenny Grech later said, "but the rest of the time he was there and actively working on the record—playing bass and singing." Time sheets of the overdub sessions prove her right. Though not listed in the album credits, Grech played bass on several tracks. Jenny said he was not listed to avoid complications with the American Federation of Musicians, which would not have sanctioned the participation of a non–U.S. citizen.

Grech's influence on the making of *GP* has been unfairly minimized. His passion for and understanding of country music is made plain with one listen to "Kiss the Children," a Grech composition on the album. Jenny Grech said, "It was Rick's and strictly autobiographical, but Rick was always generous when it came to his music."

"Kiss the Children" is a harrowing narrative in the Louvin Brothers tradition, told by a man who recognizes his demons yet can't do a thing about them. Warning others of his own dark impulses is about as much control as he can muster. The verse that ends:

Such a shame that it's so hard for me to tell the truth to you
But by now you know the kind of man I am

evokes the theme of helpless lying and self-loathing that also appears in a Gram original, the even more harrowing "How Much I've Lied."

Gram sings "Kiss" in a quiet, restrained voice, sounding more mature and in touch with his instrument than on either Burrito album. He sings with a subtlety—a connection to the material—lacking in earlier recordings. The delicacy of his rendition contradicts the image of Gram smacked out on a recording-studio floor. The sadness in Gram's shaky voice, however, evokes it perfectly. He could be totally straight or so gone on booze and pills, so high beyond wasted, that he found a moment of sacramental clarity.

The final verse of "Kiss the Children" combines the ever-present Devil of the Louvins with the all-too-real domestic violence of the most psycho George Jones songs.

Glen D. Hardin arranges a four-voice male choir that soars at song's end, evoking both the Submarine Band's "Miller's Cave" and the smooth, melded voices of white gospel stars and Elvis backups the Jordanaires. As the choir "hmmms" the song to its close, Al Perkins follows them note-perfect with a ringing line on the pedal steel. The heavenly choir and final note plainly suggest the slippery path to hell.

Without Sneaky Pete, there is no deranged-commentary-on-pedal-steel-guitar pedal steel on *GP*. Al Perkins' style is the anodyne to Sneaky Pete's alien noisemaking. Burton, Hardin, Tutt, and Perkins all ferociously understate. Perkins does not fill every open space, like Jay Dee Maness. He adds thematic embellishment and is always attuned to the valence of the song. He and Burton have a telepathic understanding of how much solo guitar each cut can take. Both are determined to keep out of each other's way. Neither reminds us of his unlimited chops; both apply their discipline in service of the song.

As the sessions went on, Barry Tashian and Emmylou Harris realized how much Gram wanted them to sing. "At first I figured Emmylou and I were singing backups for Gram," Tashian says. "It slowly dawned on me that Gram wanted Emmylou singing more. I was playing guitar and singing sometimes. I was out there for six weeks and could see Gram still liked to get high, but he had matured after he had been in England and France. I thought he was headed in a new direction, more straight and narrow. I thought with being married he was straightening out or something."

"By singing with Gram," Emmylou said, "I learned that you plow [the overt emotion of a song] under and let the melody and the words carry you. Rather than this emoting thing, emotion will happen on its own. As you experience life and know more, then [emotion is] gonna come out almost unconsciously as you sing. You have to have restraint in how you approach a song."

Tashian suggested the J. Geils Band song "Cry One More Time." Peter Wolf, Tashian's college roommate and the lead singer for J. Geils, cowrote the song with J. Geils keyboardist Seth Justman. Wolf, who credits Tashian as a key influence in his own career, was a Boston hipster. He DJ'ed the coolest, most eclectic radio show in America on WBCN-FM before he sang with J. Geils. Wolf was fired from WBCN for refusing to conform to a management playlist. His epic dispute signaled the end of the free-form FM era, when knowledgeable DJs played music from all eras and styles for an audience presumed to be passionate about wanting to know more. On his final shift, Wolf locked the control room door and repeatedly played the Five Royales' classic of jilted love, "Think!" ("Think of all the good things / That I done for you"). Wolf's valedictory gesture numbers among the most exquisite hipster fuck-you exits in the history of American corporate media.

The J. Geils band, an amplified Boston R&B five-piece, played covers and originals and were known for their connoisseur's juke-joint authenticity. Wolf, who called himself the Woofer-Goofer (pronounced *woofa-goofa*), was a charismatic, long-limbed, almost spastic front man with an unhinged line of fifties DJ chatter and way-gone-daddy mannerisms. At the height of the J. Geils band's fame, Wolf married actress Faye Dunaway. The musical star of the band was Magic Dick, a singular stylist on the blues harmonica with an enormous Izro (a big head of kinky Jewish curls worn full-out like an Afro), a percussive Detroit sound, and lungs like a locomotive. Like George Thorogood twenty years later, the J. Geils Band were purists copying a sound they loved who broke huge and suddenly found themselves playing the blues in arenas.

Gram's cover of "Cry One More Time," a fairly standard R&B lament in the hands of the J. Geils Band, is in many ways the essence of his Cosmic American Music. Gram arranged the song to reflect both R&B and country attitudes toward this sort of lover's regret, a difficult task performed with equal credibility only by Ray Charles. A honking baritone sax leads the song, and piano triplets in the style of Fats Domino (rather than of the more expected choice, blues god Otis Spann) provide a loping New Orleans feel. Burton's steely, elegant solo drives the song into its second half, which slowly layers more and more instruments and voices in classic Nashville mode. The lyrics speak to the aching regret and hopeless yearning that were Gram's bread and butter.

> *So sad to be alone at night*
> *So sad it didn't work out right*

(Words and music by Peter Wolf and Seth Justman)

Underlying the country heartache is an ephemeral ironic wit. Gram emphasized the song's sadness and its humor, a double whammy on par with making it both country and R&B. For no discernible reason—certainly not because of the lyrics—the song brings a smile. It might be the singing. Gram understood that his voice was not the best for the material. After bitching, moaning, and sabotaging every Burrito session that didn't feature him on lead, Gram had Barry Tashian sing "Cry." Gram sang only harmony. Tashian's vocals, half conversation and half archivist R&B, suit the song perfectly. His emphasis in the line "I need another *beer*" evokes at least three different generations of white honky-tonk and black roadhouse music.

"I liked the music. I could enjoy myself," engineer Hugh Davies says. "It was sort of funky country. Not quite rock, but beyond traditional country. I looked forward to each session with Gram. He was interested in getting it recorded with the flavor and style that *he* wanted."

A witty traditional number that Gram and Emmylou made their own was Harlan Howard and Tompall Glaser's "Streets of Baltimore." Wynn Stewart cut Howard's "You Took Her off My Hands" in 1958; Howard wrote the monster hit "Heartaches by the Number" for Ray Price in 1959. Patsy Cline made a standard of Howard's "I Fall to Pieces." Howard had fifteen songs on the charts in 1961. He wrote "Streets of Baltimore" with Glaser in 1966 for Bobby Bare. A year after Glaser's 1968 run-in with the Byrds at the Grand Ole Opry, he opened a recording studio known as Hillbilly Central. By 1970 it had become a locus for the Nashville outlaw scene, an amusing turn in view of Glaser's by-the-book outrage at Gram. Glaser subsequently had a career as a musical "outlaw" but was overshadowed always by the ur-outlaws, Willie and Waylon.

"Streets of Baltimore"'s story chooses an improbable city as Babylon. The narrator finds his woman irresistibly drawn to the place: They sell the farm and abandon their kin to live in the big city. The wife falls under Baltimore's spell and the narrator heads back to his simple country life. As in all of Gram's beloved story songs, no good comes to those who abandon their roots.

In their rendition, Gram and Emmylou betray no irony toward the song. Gram speak-sings in the Wynn Stewart style; he's in good voice, projecting strongly. Playing in a loping two-step, the band sticks to a simple arrangement: Byron Berline solos over the first chorus, soaring with Emmylou and Gram's harmony. Al Perkins drops in deft accents, but the band leaves the song to the singers.

"Gram was inspiring, the way he spoke. He had charisma, magnetism, an assuredness about things," Barry Tashian says. "There was gravity to what he said about music being the saving grace for mankind. Like most of the world is so messed up, but this is the real truth. Music is what it was all about."

"I don't think showing the real side of life through song has any barriers," Gram said. "Race or age, everyone can dig it. But it's not to say that life is pointless. . . . Life has so many points. I think country music can be done [with] much more than a Baptist outlook on life. It's infinite."

"I was the audience he wanted to reach," Emmylou says. "I hadn't really heard [country]. I couldn't get past the layers and country music being politically incorrect. I grew up with rock and roll and folk and was a huge Bob Dylan fan. But Gram did bring the whole rock sensibility—not just the attitude and lyrics, but the whole culture—into this other culture."

Gram gives Emmylou center stage on the George Jones–Darrell Edwards–C. Grier lament "That's All It Took." Edwards wrote Jones' first hit, "Why Baby Why," and "That's All" features the wordplay Gram always savored. Over a shuffle beat introduced by a swing-dance steel intro, Gram takes the first verse and then trades off with Emmylou, harmonizing with her on the choruses. Byron Berline drives the first half of the song and solos as if he had a hall full of two-steppers; the steel comes in for the second half of the solo. No steel player is listed on the studio logs, but an educated guess would be that Buddy Emmons plays the sprightly, restrained lead. Like Berline's solo, it's designed to keep the dancers moving across the floor. Gram belts out the song, enunciating clearly and pausing here and there with the fiendish timing of Thelonious Monk. Emmylou stays with him through every hesitation. The song is sung from the voice of Gram's recurring musical character: an obsessive who finds himself at a loss before his urges, able to describe but never control them.

"GRAM HAD A VIVID IMPRESSION of certain people like Elvis, Merle, and others," steel guitarist Al Perkins says. "He tried to follow in their footsteps, right down to guest musicians and getting musicians to play twin parts like were heard on country records of the fifties and sixties that were no longer done."

"Gram showed me that you can bring all these influences together if you have a focal point," Harris said. "What he gave me was learning how to sing and how to phrase. I got this point of departure that I didn't have before. Gram's writing brought his own personal generation's poetry and vision into the traditional format of country music. He came up with something completely different."

The covers on *GP* are authentic, engaging, hummable—they honor their traditions and remain wholly new. It's a music obsessive's array, sure to please any contemporaneous student of Nashville and Bakersfield. The collection is also a hipster demonstrating the range and discernment of his ear.

Gram with the big rig that appeared on the inside cover of GP. (© Barry Feinstein, www.barryfeinsteinphotography.com)

The cover choices seem to dare anyone to match Gram's knowledge of American country roots.

Gram's originals on *GP* stun with their wit, songcraft, individuality, and naked expression of blinding existential pain, isolation, never-to-be-resolved longing, and self-hatred. Some songs are about Gram's entrapping, distancing, inescapable anomie; some address the hurt he sees in others.

"A Song for You" echoes "Sin City" and the Louvin Brothers: At times the lyrical subject matter is too clearly expressed to be borne. It's impossible at times to decipher the meaning of Gram's lyrics, yet the ache in the melody makes meaning irrelevant. The opening lines of "Song" suggest a combination of Waycross' Okefenokee swamp—with its acres of rippling grasslands growing on water—and the earthquakes of Southern California. That's the literal view; the poetic view is of a song opening with a howl of dislocation. There is no firm ground to stand on, no structure to trust, no nature that endures, and no building that will not fall.

Gram evokes the promise of redemption, the idea that singing to Jesus might offer the hope of navigation over the first verse's ever-shifting land-scape. But he negates that promise instantly. Gram's friends, like the land itself, can claim no home, no community, no rock on which to stand. With such disharmony without, there can only be confusion within.

Yet the end of each verse offers hope of connection, of salvation, in the continuance of the smallest celebration and assertion of identity.

Gram sings the opening lines over a picking guitar and celestial pedal-steel atmosphere. Emmylou joins on the aching choruses over Berline's fiddle. Gram's voice is weak, quavering, filled with sadness. He sounds determined to reach the end of each line before his strength fails him. Gram's gift for conversational phrasing never deserts him, even as his voice breaks in the middle of a held note. He sings the last hopeful line of each chorus alone. For the final rendition Emmylou joins him. Their harmony emerges as a prayer, a plea for something to believe in.

"Big Mouth Blues" suggests "Luxury Liner"; it's a romp, a hollerin' post-rockabilly rave-up set to a shuffle beat and backed with a sax chorus. Jerry Lee Lewis piano triplets drive the song; Gram belts it out—the song doesn't require much delicacy. His voice is strong and heartfelt. He whoops and hollers "Yeah," apparently having more fun singing this than any song on the record. The instrumental solos lag, but the lyrics are witty and self-amused.

It's telling that Gram chose "Big Mouth Blues"—a celebration of point-less striving and a gambler's self-delusion—to end the record. (With *GP* packaged on CD as a two-fer with Gram's next album, *Grievous Angel,* and with so many compilations, extra tracks, and rereleases, it can be difficult to remember his original intentions regarding song order.) On the surface "Big Mouth" is a joyous rocker, but even the happiest song on the album suggests a man with no solutions to his problems.

On a record of searing heartbreak and disillusion, the masterpiece of the form is "How Much I've Lied." Gram cowrote it with David Rivkin, then a staff writer at Irving Music, A&M's publishing division. Gram and Rivkin met at the Chateau Marmont. For reasons lost to the ages, Rivkin is credited on the album as Pam Rifkin. (On Judy Collins' *Wildflowers,* he's credited as Joshua Rifkin.) Perhaps to avoid such misidentification, he was subsequently known professionally as David Z. Under that name his production credits include Prince, Fine Young Cannibals, and Kenny Wayne Shepherd.

Whatever Rivkin's contributions may have been, "How Much I've Lied" is Gram's most revealing self-portrait. It is also a perfectly structured composition. Like a story song, the worst news is saved for the final line, and that line is never repeated. There is no verse-chorus-verse structure; the confession tumbles out in an avalanche of truths that should never be said. The singer could not possibly go back and repeat a word of what has come out of his mouth.

The French film noir director Jean-Pierre Melville said, "I like futility of effort; the uphill road to failure is a very human thing." "How Much I've Lied" is written like an uphill road to failure—the singer confesses and confesses, and the more he says, the bleaker the landscape becomes. Once past the initial impossible admission, the deepest secrets come pouring out with a bottomless self-loathing.

As in "Kiss the Children," the singer is warning his beloved about himself, telling her who he is and making it clear that he has no control over his demons. The singer loves her, yearns for her, desperately needs her love, and says flat-out that he cannot protect her. For lacerating self-disgust, the only equal might be Randy Newman's "Guilty." But "Guilty" takes refuge from its own horror in its pastoral form. "How Much I've Lied" offers no such respite. It's a clearheaded narrative of a man revealing his soul, a soul that he despises but cannot change.

On this harrowing journey, Gram does walk that lonesome valley. He sings the song all by himself. The shakiness is gone from his voice. His delivery is straightforward and conversational. "How Much I've Lied" is the quintessential Gram Parsons song; he says the unsayable clearly and simply. He embraces his own pain and sings as universal a sentiment as ever appeared in his work. The arrangement evokes the traditions he loves (a big all-male choir in the middle), but no one who came before him ever sounded like this.

NINETEEN
The Fallen Angels

GP WAS RELEASED IN JANUARY 1973. NEITHER THE ALBUM NOR THE SINGLE— "She" b/w "That's All It Took"—charted in the top two hundred. Warner Bros. may have had mixed feelings about the record and about Gram, judging by an in-house circular: "*GP* is unabashedly country. With a leavening of West Coast studio sophistication, and enough tongue in cheek to get away with it. The lyrics are fraught with 1930s melodrama. . . . Satan gets a mention; and . . . the melody hangs . . . like washing on predictable chord sequences and resolutions as common as a back fence."

In the March 1, 1973, issue of *Rolling Stone*, Bud Scoppa wrote insightfully about Gram's music. He fell prey to a couple of mythologies—Gram's Harvard education, for one—but he understood the traditions Gram worked from and was uniquely unwilling to pigeonhole the Parsons sound.

Scoppa praised Gram as an artist with a unique personal vision and called the Burritos' *Gilded Palace of Sin* a milestone that "brought a pure country sound and a wrecked country sensibility to rock." Gram's central theme, he continued, "[is] . . . the innocent Southern boy tossed between the staunch traditions and strict moral code he was born to and the complex,

Gram in the Chateau Marmont for the GP *cover shoot.* (© Barry Feinstein, www.barryfeinsteinphotography.com)

ambiguous modern world. He realizes that both are corrupt, but he survives by keeping a hold on each while believing neither."

The album has an anachronistic feel, Scoppa wrote, because of its classic country-and-western atmosphere, an atmosphere abandoned by most contemporary country music. Scoppa places Gram and Emmylou's harmony work on a par with George Jones and Tammy Wynette's, and with Conway Twitty and Loretta Lynn's—the highest possible praise. With remarkable insight. Scoppa cites Gram's absence of moral certainty (so prevalent in the Louvin Brothers' work) as the root of *GP*'s modernity, and of its distance from its country predecessors, no matter how similar it might be in sound.

GRAM PUT TOGETHER A BAND for a U.S. tour. He wanted the Elvis crew—Burton, Hardin, and Tutt—but could not afford them. Clarence White, who was playing with the Byrds, said no. So did Rick Grech. "After a few months away from Gram," Jenny Grech said, "Rick had come to see that it wasn't safe for him to follow Gram any further. He loved him, but it was too dangerous. So he turned down the chance to go on the road."

Emmylou suggested Gerry Mule, her classically trained D.C. accompanist, on guitar. Gram flew Mule to L.A. for rehearsals. Neil Flanz, a Nashville pedal-steel session player who had worked with Charlie Louvin, came aboard, joining Barry Tashian, Kyle Tullis on bass, and drummer N. D. Smart, formerly of Tashian's band, the Remains.

Neil Flanz got the call after another Nashville session player whom Phil Kaufman knew, Bobby Seymour, turned down the gig. "I had no idea who Gram Parsons was," Flanz says. "I went into work that day and mentioned it to our keyboard player. He burst out laughing. Our keyboard player was into the Byrds, while I was strictly straight-ahead country. He said, 'Take it! Grab it!' I was on a plane to LAX the next day."

Gram and Kaufman met Flanz at the airport and drove him straight to Sid Kaiser's house. Kaiser was a public relations man—Peter Lawford was one of his clients—and a pal of Gram's who always had fabulous dope. "I used to tread on my tongue when I walked out of Sid's house. His grass was unreal," Phil Kaufman said. "You had to be careful going home because you were invariably wrecked." Gram also took the band to the Palomino and to Nudie's.

"I don't usually travel in limousine circles," Neil Flanz says. "When I went out to California I gave Buddy Emmons a call and went to his house. He asked what I was doing out there and when I mentioned Gram he said, 'Boy, that's a guy who has a lot of notches on his belt.'

"As for the band, Kyle, may he rest in peace"—Tullis died of liver cancer in 2004—"was one of the most laid-back humans that I've ever met anywhere. N. D. Smart was into martial arts, and aggressive. Emmy was beautiful."

"It was a terrific band and a great bunch of people and they, at least outwardly, adored Gram," Kathy Fenton says.

Gram had GRAM PARSONS & THE FALLEN ANGELS T-shirts made; the back featured Bugs Bunny giving the finger. The Fallen Angels even had a short-lived softball team featuring Kaufman, Kathy Fenton's brother, Guy Baron, Gram, N. D. Smart, and Bill Maxim. The team was mostly Kaufman's crew.

"Gram decided he wanted to be a baseball player," Kathy Fenton remembers. "So he got a bunch of people together, a bunch of friends, and went to play softball. We would play at Ethel Street Park, not too far from where Phil and I lived on Chandler Boulevard."

Kaufman's house became Fallen Angels Central. The band rehearsed there for two weeks. "It was a beautiful old Craftsman house with a shaded front porch with big pillars and couches out there," Kathy says. "We had hardwood floors—the living room had an old fireplace. The house was falling apart.

"We had some batiks and antique furniture, a huge round oak dining-room table, and mismatched chairs. We had a church pew and an old couch that belonged in a French provincial house, with carved wood on top. A beautiful old mirror above the fireplace. Phil had an ancient wooden desk. There was a rocking chair. It was shabby. It wasn't quite shabby chic—that hadn't been invented yet—but nice old stuff. All original twenties furniture. We had beautiful old rugs that were Indian and hand-knotted."

Gram posing for a Crawdaddy *interview.* (Courtesy Ginny Winn)

"Kaufman had this country backyard disorganization of basketballs, netless hoops, broken tables, warped chairs, rusting Ford pickups, and an old Cadillac limousine," Jay Ehler wrote in *Crawdaddy* magazine.

Jock Bartley, who would join the Angels on guitar, says, "Kaufman's house was like a museum. You pulled into his driveway and on either side of the roof were the Mobil horses that were, like, fifteen feet tall that he'd gotten from some gas station that went out of business. When he plugged these things in, these winged horses would rear into the sky. His house was legendary, with all this antique stuff from gas stations, Harley-Davidson gear. Occasionally B movies would rent his house and use it for a location."

In rehearsals, the band listened repeatedly to *GP.* "They'd pick me up about noon and we'd go from one to six," Neil Flanz says. "We listened to the album for ideas, but we did not take it seriously enough to nail it down lick for lick."

"Rehearsal for Gram was playing lots and lots of songs that he liked, but we'd never work out getting an end or a middle," Emmylou Harris says. "I thought there was some mysterious process where it was all going to fall together. It started out pretty grim and Gram was not a disciplined person. He loved to sit and play. I'd never gone on the road before, so I thought, 'This is how it's done.' I thought some magical thing happened when you walked out on stage."

"As soon as six o'clock rolled around Gram'd say, 'Okay, boys. Rehearsal is over. Let's have some fun,'" Neil Flanz says. "He'd break out a whole bunch of George Jones and Merle Haggard tunes. That was the music that was dear to his heart. That's what he always wanted to play."

PHIL KAUFMAN THREW a send-off party to celebrate the start of the tour. He made a big batch of Mexican tripe stew. According to Kathy Fenton, Kaufman was an amazing cook. Beer and whiskey flowed freely. A group called the Oily Scarf Wino Band performed, playing on bedpans as well as guitars.

John Phillips and Genevieve Waite hung out. They thought Gram looked unhappy. "John said, 'That's because he should be going on the road with the Stones,'" Genevieve says. "[John] played the piano with them and he worked with them on their arrangements. And they were best friends. He didn't seem to know these people that he was going on the road with."

"There is always that anticipation and excitement going out on the road," Neil Flanz says. "Spirits were high. Of course a lot of the spirits were inside of us! Quite a few spirits were consumed at the party."

The tour started inauspiciously. The tour bus, an old Greyhound with GRAM PARSONS painted on the side, sat beside Phil's house during two weeks of rain. The day after the party, when the tour was to commence, the bus had settled up to its hubs in mud. Phil and his friends had to dig it out to get the tour under way.

"[The bus] wasn't fancy and it didn't have bunks," Flanz says. "There was an area reserved in the back where Gram and Emmy could pick their guitars. They sang and worked up stuff and practiced their harmonies. Most of the time there wasn't a great deal of socializing. It's boring riding around the country in a bus."

"They were sitting in the back singing songs and picking," Kathy Fenton says. "The guy who developed a little amp called a Pignose [a book-sized guitar amplifier of surprising sound quality that runs on batteries and is totally portable] came to our going-away party and gave one to us. We took it on the road. Gram would plug in and they would sit and pick in the back of the bus. Emmylou and I would sit in the front and do whatever we did and they would be in the back doing their thing. And Phil was walking the aisles making sure everything was okay."

The driver was nicknamed "Romance Lance" because he had a girl-friend at every stop. "Lance was secretly delivering a bunch of triple-X-rated porno movies and porno stuff from L.A. to New York," a band member says. "He was going to go sell this stash of stag films in New York and had an outlet."

The band traveled with their entourage. Kaufman brought Kathy Fenton, who hid the payment for shows in her cowgirl boots. She hung out with Emmylou and babysat Gretchen. "We had a roadie named Jerry Gottlieb," Kathy says, "who was on the softball team. He didn't know anything about being a roadie. Jerry decided he wanted to go with us, so at the last minute he got on the bus. I taught him how to string a guitar and tune it."

Michael Martin, an Australian newly arrived in the States, became part of the crew. Martin was the boyfriend of Dale McElroy, heiress to the Caterpillar Tractor fortune. Years before, Dale had hired Kaufman to clear brush on her Laurel Canyon property. She and Kaufman had become friends. McElroy traveled a sophisticated hippie trail, living in Ibiza, Spain; Goa, India; and Katmandu, Nepal. While in India she met Martin, and they returned to America as a couple. They moved to San Francisco but were in Los Angeles for the going-away party at Kaufman's house. Martin, wanting to experience America on the cheap, joined the tour as Gram's valet.

The bus got stuck in a snowstorm en route to the band's first gig in Colorado. When they arrived in Boulder for a show at the Edison Electric Company, the bus sustained serious damage. "When the bus was in the parking lot near the venue," Neil Flanz says, "some truck rammed into the side and damaged the cargo. The side of the bus—where the name 'Gram Parsons' was so beautifully painted—had a great big dent on it through the entire tour."

The first tour show was supposed to be something of a practice gig. "It was one of the most pitiful things I ever saw," Richie Furay said. "Gram looked about fifty pounds heavier—he was big, fat, dumpy. His band was atrocious. The only good thing was when he and Emmylou sang together. I felt embarrassed for him. I went backstage after the show and he was, you know, getting high."

"We didn't treat the songs with enough seriousness, so when we opened up at Boulder we weren't prepared," Neil Flanz says. "We didn't pay any attention to the arrangements on the *GP* album. There were no intros. The band wasn't tight at all, and that's putting it kindly."

"I was horrified," Emmylou said. "I went, 'What have I gotten myself into?' Gram would take himself to the limit to see what he could get away with. Then he would realize, 'Okay, this has to stop'—like the first sessions in *GP*. We ended up playing places that looked like the original setting for *McCabe and Mrs. Miller*. I thought we were all going to either get shot or knifed. People were toting guns; two women got into a fight and knocked each other down and pulled each other's hair."

"Gram was abusing himself with drugs," Sherry Reed, a Warner Bros. publicist, said. "I was concerned about him keeping up his commitments. I called Mo Ostin about it. Mo got on the phone with Eddie [Tickner] and Eddie ended up flying into Boulder to make sure Gram was okay."

"I got a call in the afternoon, after their sound check, from the manager of the Electric Company," Jock Bartley says. "He knew I was a good player and said, 'You should get down here. You might get a gig.' I'd heard *Gilded Palace of Sin* in college and the country-rock thing was fairly appealing to me, so I went down to the club. Gram and Emmylou played two sets and Gerry Mule was mostly an acoustic guitar picker, not much of an electric player. He was a pretty straight-arrow guy. He was nervous and got drunk that first night and pretty much sucked. He was not good. The band was not tight and kind of sucked, too."

"For some reason or another Gerry and I couldn't click," Neil Flanz later said. "He was basically a flamenco, classical player."

"The first night when I saw him in Boulder," Jock Bartley says, "I thought Emmylou carried the show, because Gram was slurring his words and couldn't play. I didn't know until later Gram was mostly a piano player. He was a bad guitar player, but he got by. He just strummed and they turned his guitar off in the mix because he was all over the place.

"Emmylou and Gram carried the night, but the band sounded like a brand-new band. It didn't sound like polished country-rock music. I heard that management might cancel the tour because the guitar player sucked so badly. They introduced me to Phil Kaufman, Eddie Tickner, and Gram and Emmylou, and said, 'This is the local hot guitar player around town—maybe you guys want to check him out tomorrow.'"

The Edison Electric Company canceled the second show. A replacement gig was set up at the Pioneer Inn in Nederlander, Colorado, a funky mountain bar in a log cabin where hippies fought old-school drunks on the dance floor. The band set up in a corner; there was no stage. The Pioneer was about as far as one could fall from Nellcôte.

"Gram's band invites me up to sit in," Jock Bartley says. "They put my amp next to Gerry Mule's and he's glaring at me all night, like, 'Who's this guy? What's he doing up here?' Of course I didn't know any of the tunes. I blundered my way through, and at the end of the night they had a meeting. They took a vote and said, 'Do we keep Gerry Mule or hire this guy?' They needed three things from their guitar player: a good rock-and-roll rhythm guitar player—which I was; a good lead guitar guy—which I was; and they also needed a good country picker, which I wasn't at all. Gerry Mule was zero out of three and I was two out of three. They hired me that night. It was unanimous except for Neil Flanz. He didn't vote for me because he knew I wasn't a country guy."

Gram heard that Flanz was complaining that "Jock can't play country music worth a shit." He told Flanz, "I like Jock. He's got nice hands."

After the first gig of the tour, the band shitcanned Gerry Mule and hired a total stranger. It speaks to Gram's financial situation—after paying hefty studio fees to record *GP*—and to Warner Bros.' limited support for the band, that such a desperate step was taken. Kaufman, Tickner, and Parsons must have known a hundred L.A. guitarists between them. Hiring Bartley illustrates the groping, short-term-solution style of the entire tour.

"From the first night, Gram was pretty wasted," Jock Bartley says. "He was drinking heavily. He and his wife were not getting along. They were fighting. He'd go sit in the back of the bus and she'd follow him. He'd move up front and she'd follow him—that kind of thing. I'd be in the back with Neil trying to learn songs. I attributed Gram's drinking as escaping from her, but who knows what the dynamic of a marriage is?"

"Gretchen wasn't pleasant to anybody," Kathy Fenton says. "She wasn't pleasant to Gram, which was one of the reasons he was so miserable. And she was always stoned.

"Gretchen was never nice to women. But she wasn't sexy, she was a skinny skeleton of a person, and at that time she was not attractive at all. She didn't do a good job on her makeup. Gretchen was pretty depressing."

"On the bus there were people always drinking Jack Daniel's. There were a few always smoking pot or hash," Jock Bartley says. "Sometimes we'd intermingle, but most of the time the drinkers were drinking and the smokers were smoking and Gram and Gretchen were fighting. We'd try to keep them separate. Phil would be like, 'Gretchen, go sit up front. Gram, go in back.' They were at each other's throats. Gram was not a happy boy."

In Austin, DJ Rusty Bell, on KOKE-AM, interviewed the band. Austin had become the center of a more roots-aware country-rock and outlaw-country scene. Doug Sahm, Willie Nelson, Jerry Jeff Walker, Waylon Jennings, Guy Clark, and Townes Van Zandt formed the core of the scene. Their music fell under the rubric of Cosmic Cowboy. KOKE—which played only Cosmic Cowboy and traditional country—called itself Goat Roper Radio; "goat roper" meant a stoned longhair in boots and a cowboy hat who wouldn't go near a horse or a cow or a gun. The Austin audience was knowledgeable. KOKE's listeners were better prepared to understand *GP* than any in the country. It was a perfect promotional opportunity.

Gram and Emmylou did their best to ruin the moment and alienate Rusty Bell. They insulted him nonstop. When he asked the band what they thought of progressive country, he touched a nerve. "'Progressive country' was a term Gram intensely disliked," Neil Flanz says. "At the time, progressive country meant modern country. Just when I thought modern country couldn't get any worse, with what they were playing back in the seventies, believe me, it got worse. When Rusty Bell asked Gram what he thought of progressive country, Emmylou chimed in, 'We don't do progressive country. We do *regressive* country.' That's exactly what she meant."

Gram tore the Emergency Broadcast System box off the wall of the studio. When they left, Bell thanked them for "the worst interview of my life."

"Gram saw a bunch of awards on the wall that read 'KOKE.' He thought that was the funniest thing," Jock Bartley says. "He wanted them and the station wouldn't give them up. He said, 'I'll buy it from you, how much?' He ended up taking two or three and walking out with them and suddenly the bus was adorned with memorabilia from KOKE."

The Armadillo World Headquarters was among the most significant and well-run rock venues in the country—certainly the most important that was not on either coast. Like the Fillmores East and West, the Armadillo boasted a stellar light and sound system and an in-house recording set-up. Shows at the 'Dillo drew national press attention. Despite Gram's willingness to alienate the Austin radio audience, the band prepped with unusual discipline for the show. "We made up for Boulder by heading immediately to the Armadillo three days early," Neil Flanz says. "We practiced like crazy. We had the afternoons to ourselves, with a whole sound system. The night we opened there were two thousand screaming hippies charging the stage, trying to touch us. I never saw anything like that before, certainly not at the Opry.

"Most of the places that we played weren't country-music venues. We were booking the rock-and-roll circuit. The dope-smoking circuit, if I may refer to it that way. Gram wanted to reach that audience—hippies. Pretty much everyone had long hair. All the guys did, including myself. It was a different thing. It's an attitude. A rock-and-roll attitude.

"At the Armadillo we started putting together arrangements. I did most of the signature licks from the record. We put together pretty close to what was on the record. On the live album, steel is more predominant. That's because Jock was more of a rock-and-roll player than a country player, but he was what Gram wanted. Gram and Emmylou were really performing, and my country experience combined with Bartley's experience playing rock."

"The first night in Austin the band smoked," Jock Bartley says. "We made it through and everybody seemed happy. It was pretty good and they obviously liked the band better than in Boulder.

"Emmylou had never played tambourine in a rock-and-roll band before. After the set she had a bruised left hand from banging the tambourine because it felt so good. She was like, 'Oh, God! But wasn't that fun?' I remember being backstage like, Woo! I'm the new guy, isn't this great?

"The first night we played the Headquarters I wore the one and only country shirt that I had, that I bought in some secondhand store in Boulder. Gram said, 'We need to dress you up, kid.' He gave me one of his Nudie shirts that was tie-dyed with sequins, and to this day I still have it. He was such a good-hearted, generous guy. He gave money to people. He was a sweetheart and people misunderstood. He was so screwed up he couldn't stand up for himself very well. But he was a deep guy."

"Gram did not speak a lot onstage," Neil Flanz says. "N. D. Smart did a whole lot of talking and so did Emmy. Gram would occasionally come out with a remark. Like he always introduced 'Drug Store Truck Drivin' Man' and pretty much told the same story. A brief little thing that he says at the beginning of the song. You know, 'Here is a song I wrote when I nearly had my life taken away from me.'"

"Gram ran the show in a nonchalant manner," Jock Bartley says. "The only thing that was tight was we had the set list and knew what songs we were going to play in what order."

"When he did traditional music," Neil Flanz says, "it was very traditional. Nashville, at that time and probably more so today, has been trying to citify country and water it down. Put in flowery string arrangements and loads of oohs and ahhs. . . .

"Gram's singing brought an awful lot out of me. I like to consider myself a singer's player, and the more emotionally a person sings, the more emotion I'm going to play with. We also did some old-timey, rock-and-roll, 1950s-type shuffles. Emmy has got to be one of the greatest singers I ever heard. Her and Gram together . . . had a harmony that was absolutely incredible. It was quite an experience."

The band traveled to Houston for a residency at Liberty Hall. "Gram was blasted out of his gourd, and it was pretty sad," John Lomax, a local journalist, said. "He was putting everything into his system you could get, without regard to anything.

Rocky Hill, Emmylou Harris, Gram Parsons, backstage Liberty Hall, Houston, Texas, 1973. (Courtesy John Lomax)

Kaufman had more on his hands than he could handle with Gram alone. One night Gram was so plowed he backed up and knocked Neil Flanz and the steel guitar flat off the side of the stage. Poor ol' Neil was sittin' there lookin' at his steel lying on the ground. Gram never even knew what he'd done."

"Gram's first solo record was an 'event' in my little circle of musicians," singer-songwriter Steve Earle says. "When I heard that Gram and company were coming to Texas I was off like a prom dress, down the I-10 to the big city. It was loose but it was tough. Gram's hair was frosted and his fingernails were painted red. He sang through his nose with his eyes closed while the band played catch-up for most of the night. I saw and heard Emmylou Harris for the first time. I left a little bit in love and absolutely certain of what I was going to be when I grew up."

The four-night residency brought together a hardcore group of fans who called themselves the Sin City Boys. They had custom jackets made with a Sin City logo on the back and brought a gang of friends to every show. Gram and Emmylou were both given Sin City patches, and Linda Ronstadt, who showed up on Sunday—the third night of the residency—wanted one, too. Parsons, Emmylou, and Ronstadt sang "Sin City" together that night.

"That gig was one of the highlights of my career," Jock Bartley says. "It was a sold-out affair. Halfway into our set, out from the wings walked Neil Young and Linda Ronstadt. Emmylou and Linda had never met before and I don't remember how many songs they played. It was amazing fun."

"They went *crazy* for Gram and Emmylou," Kathy Fenton says, "and at the end of the set this one person came down with an armload of yellow roses for Emmylou and laid them at the foot of the stage. It was overwhelming. It was wonderful. . . . I was so filled with joy and so thankful to be there."

An unknown local reviewer, starstruck and full of wishful thinking, wrote that "harmony" characterized everything about the band, the music, the tour, then added: "Gram also brought along his beautiful wife Gretchen, who is a perfect complement for Gram. Married life and maturity have advanced their effect . . . musically and personally. Gone are the flash and the rough edges; here is a smooth and mellow Gram Parsons, a warm and friendly Gram Parsons."

THOSE ON THE BUS had different perceptions. "Gram and Gretchen weren't happy around each other, that was for sure," John Lomax says. "I wondered why she was along at all, or what her function was."

"What was driving Gretchen nuts was every night Gram and Emmy-lou's microphones were three or four inches from each other," a member of the touring band says. "They weren't directly facing the crowd, they were turned half facing each other, singing right at each other. So here they're singing songs like 'Love Hurts' and 'We'll Sweep out the Ashes,' these lov-ing songs—and the vocal blend those two had has never been duplicated. Gram's fragile, over-the-edge kind of voice—he didn't have control, he'd be sharp or flat. He wasn't a good technical singer but he was emotional and emotive, and Emmylou was fragile, too. It was the best vocal blend you could imagine. Gretchen would be off to the side of the stage singing and trying to get Gram's attention. She was jealous, so jealous of Emmylou Har-ris. Here Emmylou was in the spotlight, and it was brewing."

"If I'd been so jealous of Emmylou, I wouldn't have had her living in my house," Gretchen said. Evidently Emmylou had stayed with Gram and Gretchen in Laurel Canyon. "If anything, it was the other way around. If anybody thought about it, that would pretty much be the obvious answer, but it doesn't make such a good story."

Emmylou Harris had no choice but to face Gram and sing inches from him. She never could have harmonized with him otherwise. Gram made no effort to merge with another singer. Emmylou had to do all the work. Gram seldom stayed on key or tempo or sang a song the same way twice. Emmy-lou had to watch Gram's mouth closely and be ready to change her vocals as Gram wandered wherever he was going.

Emmylou Harris, like Ralph Stanley, could harmonize with a barking dog and break your heart. It's understandable that Gretchen might have been jealous watching them sing. Gram and Emmylou sang such aching love songs, and with such emotion, it's impossible not to assume that they were in love.

"Neil Young and Linda Ronstadt were staying at one of the ritziest hotels in Houston and had a whole floor to themselves," Jock Bartley says. Jimmy McDonough, in his Neil Young biography, *Shakey*, reports a harrow-ing moment. Gram shared a limo with Young and legendary producer, songwriter, and keyboardist Jack Nitzsche. After checking Gram out, Nitzsche said, "You look like Danny . . . and Danny's dead." Nitzsche meant Young's friend and guitarist Danny Whitten, who had overdosed just weeks before.

"We went over to Neil's suite and got the guitars out and played coun-try songs all night," Jock continues. "They'd say, 'Hey, how about this?' and it'd be a Louvin Brothers song. Everybody of course was quite drunk and smoking dope and who knows what else. We were all totally wasted. I remember Linda and Emmylou sitting close together, harmonizing. Linda's voice was a little huskier and lower and fuller, and Emmylou's was this angelic, high, fragile, breathy voice. When the two of them sang together it was magical. They were discovering that magic and going, 'Wow.' I felt fortunate to be in the room, much less playing guitar next to them.

"We stayed up until four or five o'clock, playing songs, getting high, and drinking. I went to breakfast with Linda's band when the sun was rising, jazzed from the whole night. Gram must have played thirty or forty amazing country songs. He was like a dictionary, an encyclopedia, of country and bluegrass. The second night is when I started to respect Gram. I saw his depth. It's one thing to be a drunk guy onstage and sing. Superficially, he was an over-the-top acid-cowboy drunk, but underneath he was a sweet, sweet Southern boy, a nice human being, generous. He was incredibly talented and knew thousands of songs. I had a different relationship with him after that."

After the euphoria of Houston, the band boarded their grimy bus and set off for Chicago by way of Arkansas and Michigan. Once they got going, Kaufman declared they would not stop for five hundred miles. But by Blytheville, Arkansas, Gram could take no more.

"Gram's going, 'I got to get off this fucking bus, come on, we gotta stop,'" Jock Bartley remembers. "Lance is saying, 'Well, we're not five hundred miles yet. We're getting close but let's go a little longer.' People on the bus are grumbling. There's a sign in front of us that says Blytheville, Arkansas, next exit. We pull off and roll into the Holiday Inn. Gram started playing country songs and singing to two or three drunks in this funky old piano bar in the hotel. They're sitting at the bar going, 'This guy's pretty good.' Gram's drinking shots of Jack Daniel's and I go, 'Hey Gram, how's it going?' He says, 'Oh, fine. I gotta get away from Gretchen.'"

That night, Gram and Gretchen got into a fight. "It got a bit loud," Neil Flanz says. "Some neighbors called the police. N. D. Smart was into kung fu and so was Gram. He did some of these moves on the police when they knocked on his motel door and they beat him up and maced him. They might have actually taken him seriously. Or else they were redneck bullies, and there is a good probability of that."

Kaufman went to the Blytheville Police to bail Gram out. He heard Gram sassing the police and the police beating on Gram, with neither side willing to quit. Kaufman finally got Gram released; they went back to the hotel. Gram was in serious pain. The mace and the police choke holds had damaged his voice. Jock Bartley found him sitting in the restaurant a few hours later when he went down to eat breakfast.

"There's Gram sitting with his hat pulled over his head and he's not looking at anybody," Bartley recalls. "I said, 'What happened to you?' He had a semi-shiner and he went, 'Man, I spent the night in jail and they beat me up.' What happened was after he closed the piano bar, he got drunk. Gretchen was in the room waiting for him—'Where the hell have you been?' kind of thing. They get in a huge fight in the hotel room. She's screaming at him and he's yelling back and things are being thrown. One of the hotel guests called the front desk and complained. The front desk called the police. They knock on the door like two-thirty A.M.—*bam, bam, bam!* 'Go away!' 'Police, open the door!' Gram opens the door and the police push the door and take a step in. Gram, reacting to the aggressive police, staggers and takes a step back and launches a roundhouse right punch that misses by three or four feet, I mean it wasn't even close. And they mace him, beat him up, handcuff him, and take him out of the room to jail.

"Phil told me the next day on the bus that he gets a call at about three A.M. that they've got Gram about to go in the cell—he's in the holding pen. He's made his one call to Phil. Phil came down. [Eddie Tickner was en route to the next gig.] Phil brought a big bag of money and told the magistrate, 'Look, we're going to Chicago, we got a gig there tomorrow night. You'll never see this guy again. How much is it going to take?' He paid however much it took and got Gram out. Gram comes back to the hotel at six A.M. and sits down in the coffee shop and drinks coffee, trying to get it together. That's when I run into him. He can barely talk.

"We get on the bus. Everybody's freaked out because Gram has to be helped up the stairs—he can't talk and he's got a shiner. His face is all discolored, he got beat up seriously by two or three Arkansas cops. We get in the bus and go, 'Let's get out of this fucking place!'

"Lance gets on the freeway and literally two miles after we get on the interstate there's a big sign that says WELCOME TO MISSOURI. It's like the sky opened and suddenly the sun was shining. It was a new day and fuck you, Arkansas. The first sign we see says FIREWORKS and Gram goes, 'Pull over—I want some fireworks.' Lance says, 'We've only been on the road like four minutes. Come on.' 'Pull over! I need to get some hooch and fireworks.' We pull over and Gram buys two or three bags of fireworks that aren't sold anymore: big, long Roman candles and all these sky fountains. Those bruisers were like two inches across. Right next door was the liquor store. We're all following Gram, seeing how he's doing after being beaten up and all.

"There was this big blow-up plastic Jack Daniel's marketing standalone, a four-foot-high bottle of Jack that Gram wanted bad. And they said, 'Sorry, that's ours, we can't do that.' Gram says, 'Look, we're a country band.' He gave them an album and signed it, bought a couple bags of alcohol for the drive, and ended up talking them out of the big Jack bottle. We get back on the bus and Gram's in way better spirits because he's got a new bottle of Jack and all these fireworks. He's saying, 'I'm gonna set these things off in New York City.'

"The big bottle of Jack got hung up in the back of the bus. N. D. Smart would stand on one foot and practice his balance and punches and kicks and of course he's totally wasted like the rest of us. Now he has a punching bag, or at least something to dodge and weave with. Everybody else was doing their own thing on the bus. I'm still crib-sheeting and trying to learn more of the songs and N.D. is in the back of the bus throwing kicks at this bottle of Jack. Phil's sitting at the table talking to himself, something about the hoosegow, getting Gram out of the hoosegow. The whole thing was, we gotta keep Gretchen and Gram away from each other because she's freaking out. It wasn't Gram. Gram was an easygoing guy, but . . . on the road Gretchen was not a happy camper. Watching Emmylou sing every night was driving her nuts."

Kaufman later described the couple fighting like children, often physically, amid accusations that each had stolen the other's supplies of pills. Kaufman may have exacerbated the problem. He often hid Gram's drugs in an effort to keep his usage down.

"Phil and Gram got on well together," Kathy Fenton says. "Philip, in his weird way, loved Gram and admired him and wanted nothing but the best for him. He got disappointed when Gram would get coked out or drink too much and do something really stupid. I think that weighed heavily on Phil. He felt bad about it and felt he couldn't control it."

Bob Buchanan, who had played guitar on the International Submarine Band sessions, went to see the band—he remembers it was at Michigan State University in Lansing, though no record of a Fallen Angels concert there has survived. "I went down and sat in the front row," Buchanan says. "Phil Kaufman, bless him, saw me from the wings, came running down, and said, 'Bob, come on up after the set. Sing the encore with Gram.' Near the

end of the set I went backstage and waited. Gram came out and didn't recognize me.

"Emmy was supposed to do 'Hickory Wind.' She saw I was going to
sing with Gram and walked offstage. I walked out to replace her. Gram and
I did 'Hickory Wind.' Gram didn't know who I was. He'd seen me two years
before and he didn't recognize me. He thought I was one of the roadies or
something.

"We decided to go to a conference room at the hotel and jam. Emmylou
and Gram and myself and the musicians. Gram sheepishly admitted that he
didn't recognize me. He had whiskey and everything he needed and we
jammed till daybreak.

"Gram had no stage banter whatsoever. There was an audience out
there but he wasn't connected to them. He was so screwed up he was not
even connected to the band behind him. He had coke up his nose and booze
down his throat and his head up his ass. He had been going around like that
for a few years before I finally saw him. The damage had been done."

The bus headed for Chicago and a show at the Quiet Knight. Lance the
driver got lost looking for the hotel. As the bus drove aimlessly around
downtown Chicago, Gram made Lance stop at a cheap burger joint. He
bought bags of burgers and passed them around to everyone on the bus.
"He takes the first bite of his and it was terrible," Jock Bartley says. "He
went, 'Give them back!' At times when Gram'd be real high or drunk he'd
seem like a six-year-old kid. He went out in the parking lot of the burger
joint and took a couple of M-80s [that is, big-ass firecrackers] and did a sac-
rificial blowing up of their burgers, right in front of the place."

The band was staying at the Lake Shore Drive Hyatt hotel, which was
promptly dubbed the LSD. "After the show we went up to Gram and
Gretchen's room," Bartley says. "Everywhere we'd go he'd have people
come visit to continue the drinking and bring us good drugs. He ordered a
couple of trays of shrimp cocktails from room service. He had these two big
circular trays filled with shrimp and soup and champagne. We were shooting the shit and laughing, playing guitars. Gretchen said, 'We need to get
this shit out of here. Let's put it out in the hall.' And Gram said, 'Fuck that.'
He takes this big tray, it was about four feet in diameter and half full of
dishes and shrimp remains, and he opens the window. We all looked out.
Below us was the parking lot with a fair amount of cars. Someone said,
'Gram, don't do this.' Gram goes, 'No, no,' and gently gave the tray a nudge
and let it fall. As the tray was falling it was turning and with each revolution

the stuff that had been on it got farther away from the big tray and we watched it hit. He immediately shut the windows and curtains and said, 'Oops.'"

Crammed into the moldering bus, Gram and Gretchen fought more and more. "I basically had to keep her away from Gram," Kathy Fenton says. "If she wanted to go visit or watch them perform, I would try and figure out a way to try to not let her go. She was distracting for Gram and the situation made Emmylou uncomfortable. Gram didn't want Gretchen there at all. Phil didn't want Gretchen there at all. She made Emmylou's life miserable. Making little digs and trying to tell Emmylou how to sing. Of course she had no idea.

"Gretchen's insecure. Her actions came from insecurity. It was hard on everybody. She was drinking and slurring her words, sloshing drinks all over the place. She would always be sitting in the back with the band. Giving the stink eye to Emmylou and trying to keep her away from Gram. Gretchen thought Gram and Emmylou were having an affair. *They were not.* And she made Gram's every waking moment miserable."

"Sitting in a bar after a gig were Gram and Gretchen," a member of the Warner Bros. entourage later said. "When Emmylou came in there was a total change in his personality . . . his eyes would light up."

"I had a short period of my life when I was with Gram," Emmylou said later. "And in that period of time he was such a life force to me that I never realized the extent of his self-destructiveness. What I saw in Gram was a real kind of strength . . . a positive, positive force."

In Manhattan, the Fallen Angels played a packed Max's Kansas City, a hangout for Andy Warhol's crowd, the rock elite, and what would become the foundation of New York glitter rock. "Dave Mason [from Traffic and Leon Russell's L.A. jams] came one night and hung with Gram," Jock Bartley says. "Everybody was coming down to see him. They knew who he was, that he was a larger-than-life figure that was trying to change, almost single-handedly, the face of modern music."

Fred Kirby, reviewing the show for *Billboard*, wrote that "ex-Byrd" Parsons and his Angels were "offering some of the best in country rock" and welcomed "Parsons's country-style voice and top-notch vocal support by Marylou [*sic*] Harris." "Parsons ranged from his own material . . . to the melodies of Merle Haggard and Hank Williams," Kirby wrote, adding, "Set also includes some boogie, but its strengths are in country rock."

This was the last time Bud Scoppa saw Gram perform. "Gram was more hefty than lanky, and his voice had taken on a new heft, too," Scoppa later wrote in *Rolling Stone.* "Watching Gram and Emmylou sing 'Love Hurts' gave me the overlapping sensations of being in church and gazing through the window of a lover's bedroom." Here's how Scoppa described the evening:

> That night—for me, at least—Gram Parsons was transformed into a latter-day Hank Williams: an innovator still revering the past and proud to be bound to it, an anguished genius daring to use his pain as the foundation of his art, no matter what the consequences. He was beautiful, but there was danger in the beauty.

The post-show scene backstage was something of a coronation. "I was sitting in this big overstuffed leather chair," Kathy Fenton says, "and at my feet were Gram, Emmylou, Dave Mason, Stephen Stills, and Jackson Browne! A bunch of musicians who had come to hear him play. There must have been a dozen sitting on the floor, picking on their guitars and jamming."

THE BAND WAS SCHEDULED TO perform live on WLIR-FM in Hempstead, New York. The radio show was performed and taped at Ultra Sonic, a recording studio in nearby Garden City. The band members didn't expect that this radio gig would, years later, be released as an album.

They almost missed the show. "We had a fabulous Chinese meal before we did WLIR," Neil Flanz says. "It was right across the street from the studio. We were taking our time, drinking and eating it up gourmet style, until someone said: 'What time is it?' and we realized that we were overdue. We ran like crazy and got there just before the ON AIR sign went on. I literally made a beeline for my steel guitar. I moved Gram's bottle of Jack Daniel's conveniently a little bit away from him and toward me and partook generously. I was in great shape when we recorded that album, not realizing that it was ever going to be released. It's got some great stuff on it. A little ragged. Very raw, but hell, I think it's some of the best stuff that I ever played on a recording."

The album, titled *Gram Parsons and the Fallen Angels Live 1973,* was released on the Sierra label in 1983. The track list includes "Cry One More Time," "Streets of Baltimore," a couple of Chuck Berry numbers, and Gram originals. Ken Cole, the host for the live radio concert, sounds as if he has no idea who Gram is, introducing him as "a man who's played a lot of music for a lot of years." Gram and N. D. Smart take a long, self-amused time providing song introductions. Both sound happily wasted. Curiously,

Gram only sounds loaded when talking; his singing is on key, true to tempo and on time. The on-time part is no easy feat, given his hapless rhythm section. Gram introduces the band members as "Ohio's finest," or "Colorado's finest." For the opening of "Love Hurts" he says, "Anyone who's expecting fancy guitar intros can forget it."

Gram gives his rote intro to "Drug Store Truck Drivin' Man": "This is a song I used to sing when I was in fear of getting my life taken away from me. Sometimes all you can do is sing gospel music." The band, in their self-satisfied way, joke about tormenting Rusty Bell at KOKE in Austin. They rehash how they mocked Bell for using the term "progressive country."

Credited as producers on the record—but not the original recording—are John Delgatto, owner of the Sierra Records Label, and Marley Brant, author of *Freebird: The Lynyrd Skynyrd Story*. In 1983 Gram and Emmylou's version of "Love Hurts" from *Fallen Angels Live* was nominated for a Grammy, ten years after it was recorded. Their version is beautiful through the intro, which is sung over strummed acoustic guitar. When the rest of the band comes in, the song suffers.

And that's the album in a nutshell: Gram and Emmylou sing with clarity and intensity. The band is either struggling, high as kites, or both.

When they sing, Gram and Emmylou connect to every word. There are no lazy vocals. Gram is more on key than his busmates allege, and Emmylou hits the high lonesome as no one else can. Gram never sounds as shaky as he sometimes does on *GP*; his voice has strength and confidence.

Drummer N. D. Smart evokes Michael Clarke; he chugs relentlessly but can't keep a steady beat or play anything other than a 4/4 shuffle. He hits too hard on the slow numbers and hits too slowly on the fast ones. His stage patter in the face of his apparent lack of ability is arrogant to the point of delusion. He tells the crowd that most country music is played to a shuffle beat, and that "That's All It Took" typifies the shuffle. No one seems to have ever clued Smart in about any other beat or tempo.

The bass playing hardly matters and Jock Bartley does sometimes sound, for a measure or two, like an inexperienced country guitarist. More often he sounds like a second-rate rock soloist who just joined the band. His rhythm playing owes more to California boogie rock than country. His solos connect to the songs in neither mood nor type. Bartley's a flashing-fingers-on-the-fretboard kind of guy; he only comes into his own on the encore Chuck Berry medley. There both Bartley and Gram find liberation; Gram embraces the chorus on "Forty Days" like salvation.

The Fallen Angels were a mediocre band. The vocals are so outstanding, and for the most part the song choices so compelling, that the band is secondary to the singers. After the high standard Gram set in the studio, it's hard to imagine that these musicians could have inspired him. With one notable exception.

The revelation of the album, beyond Gram and Emmylou's vocals, is the steel of Neil Flanz. He holds the band together, playing with understatement and delicacy. Flanz has more chops than the rest of the band combined, yet never once shows off. Given the crap rhythm section, it's a testament to Flanz' genius that he so deftly accompanies Emmylou and Gram. Flanz is in a tough position: He can't trust the time of the drummer or bass player, and he can't rely on Gram's—Gram never sang a song the same way twice. All Flanz can do is listen closely . . . and he has to play as he listens. He's always seeking, and finding, exactly what the song needs: a horn chorus here, a string section there, a brief lead solo, tiny coloration.

"The majority of what we played on our sets is what you heard on the live album," Flanz says. "We didn't veer from that a whole lot. Most of it, with the exception of the Chuck Berry mix at the end—which we always closed with—was hardcore traditional, except with hip lyrics."

From the studio the band drove to Philadelphia, where they did several nights at the Club Bijou. They performed "Still Feeling Blue" on a local TV show. "It was one of those 'Hey!' energetic, dance teen things. We're going, 'What are we doing on here?' Once Gram realized that it was lip-syncing he said, 'This is bullshit,' and N. D. Smart said, 'I didn't play drums on the record [*GP*]. I'm not gonna get up there and pretend it's me playing that part.' The roadie Jerry said, 'I'll play drums.' N.D. said, 'Cool. There's a piano part on it. I'll play keyboards.'

"We played 'Still Feeling Blue,' which had Byron Berline on the record playing fiddle. We didn't have a fiddle player in the band, but Emmylou had bought an old violin at an antique shop that didn't have strings on it. Phil Kaufman strung it with this fuzzy twine and played it with a drumstick.

"By the time we got up there to play . . . I couldn't stop laughing. We were a bunch of country freaks that weren't even trying. We were making a total pimp of the show, and the crowd loved it. Jerry was strung out on downers and trying to play drums. The only two people that were serious were Gram and Emmylou as the front people. After the song the host jumps up onstage and says, 'Well, Gram . . .' and he's doing his whole thing—it's the biggest applause of the three bands. The producer said, 'We need it again,' and the crowd went 'Yay!' They were excited to see it again. Somewhere there exists two takes of us lip-syncing 'Still Feeling Blue.'"

From Philadelphia the bus headed to Boston for a week of shows at Oliver's. There poet Tom Brown approached Gram with lyrics based on one of his poems—lyrics that would become Gram's signature song, "Return of the Grievous Angel."

"Warner Brothers threw us a dinner party in Boston at Ye Olde Oyster House, where Daniel Webster wrote his dictionary," Neil Flanz says. "It was a fabulous dinner. The bill came to seven hundred dollars, most of which was for liquor expenses. I ordered myself a whole bottle of wine. . . . It came in a bottle shaped like a fish. I kept that bottle for a long, long time after the tour."

The tension between Gram and Gretchen came to a head in Boston.

"When Gram and Emmy would sing," Neil Flanz says, "Gretchen would get out right in front of the audience, right in front of the stage, and be dancing around and yelling. . . . She was actually competing with the show for attention."

"Watching Gram and Emmylou sing onstage was so magical," Jock Bartley says. "To this day when I hear 'Love Hurts' it makes me cry. You hear that stupid version by Nazareth and you want to get the shotgun out— that's not how that song should be sung. Emmylou and Gram, they had an emotional blend that was just . . . no wonder Gretchen was jealous."

"Gram and Emmylou brought out the best in each other's singing," Jet Thomas said. "Whatever else happened, that was the primary basis of their relationship."

"I never heard of Gram and Emmylou ever being romantically involved, and Gretchen was with Gram the whole time," Jock Bartley says.

"I think that Gram's commitment and passion for the music was so strong that Nancy and Gretchen found themselves competing with it," Jet Thomas says. "I don't think that's unusual for musicians."

"The fight and feud between Gretchen and Gram blew up in Boston," Jock Bartley remembers. "The first day in Boston, Gretchen freaked out. I remember her running down the corridors of the Fenway Boylston Motor Lodge right next to Fenway Park, screaming. She knew where Kyle and I were rooming and banged on our door. I made the mistake of opening the door and talking to her and she said, 'I want somebody to hold me.' I said, 'Gretchen, sorry,' and I had to close the door. She's falling and screaming and causing the biggest scene.

"Eddie Tickner was on the road with us by that point. He had flown to New York and Boston to see how things were going. Eddie and Phil decide, 'That's it, Gretchen, you're going home.' They bought her the plane ticket and she went home that evening.

"There was a baseball game going on at Fenway Park. The lights were on and you could hear the announcer. The parking lot was pretty full and somebody knocks on the door and says Gram's gonna set off fireworks. There was Gram in a robe carrying two huge bags of roman candles and fireworks—celebrating Gretchen's departure."

No one much liked Gretchen. No one in L.A. or Nellcôte or on the Fallen Angels bus cut Gretchen much slack. Nor did Gretchen make much effort to be likable.

But riding in grotty buses all day, every day, makes people bored and cranky. Hungover musicians coming down off drugs are grumpy and irritable. Being a nonmusician observer stuck in a bus full of working musicians makes people feel excluded. Watching your husband sing his heart out while gazing lovingly into the face of a beautiful, soulful young woman in front of an audience night after night after night might make someone act out, too. Cokehead or not, drunk or not, jealous or not, obnoxious or not, in fairness to Gretchen, who was dealing with most or all of these cranky-making situations, she was only twenty years old.

Emmylou Harris always insisted that she and Gram shared a powerful bond of love but were never lovers. That issue remains the holy grail of speculation in the Gramophile universe—did they or didn't they?

Watching the scant, grainy live footage of the two harmonizing, eyes locked and hearts melting into one, it's clear Gram and Emmylou shared a profound connection. Their recorded music suggests a once-in-a-lifetime union of souls. It's a poetic, emotional bond that could make anyone jealous, never mind Gram's wife. After so many years, though, the question seems increasingly irrelevant. What would it reveal about Gram's life or music if he and Emmylou were lovers? Gram never bared his soul to his lovers—as a result of *being* lovers—as he did to Emmylou through music. If they were lovers, it's unlikely Gram would have been so open when they sang.

Though all sources indicate Gram and Emmylou never consummated their love, it's disingenuous to pretend there are not strong forces at work to preserve this view. It may likely be the truth, but that truth serves several agendas. The great-love-but-never-lovers trope is a cornerstone of the Emmylou Harris brand. Gretchen, in her role as Gram's Widow, has also fought with determination, insisting that Gram and Emmylou were only friends. Given that Gretchen has a reputation for being difficult and litigious, few seek to cross her. Since this version serves both Emmylou's and Gretchen's interests, they are unlikely allies in seeing it sustained. And just because Gram and Emmylou remaining chaste serves both Gretchen's and Emmylou's agendas, that doesn't necessarily make it untrue.

The base, practical realities work against their having been lovers. Decades later, no source anywhere, even people who were with them in close quarters day after day, has ever asserted direct, first-person, eyewitness evidence of a physical relationship. Gretchen and Kathy Fenton—two people who couldn't stand each other—are equally adamant in their denials. There's also the issue of Gram's alcohol, barbiturate, and heroin consumption. Eve Babitz, speaking with rueful kindness, provided the simplest, most convincing answer: "Gram was too high," she said, "to make it with anyone."

TWENTY
"Farther Along"

The Fallen Angels tour ended in Boston. Everyone was given a one-way plane ticket to the U.S. destination of their choice.

In March or April of 1973, Gram and Gretchen moved out of the Chateau Marmont and into a house in Laurel Canyon. "The backyard backed up into a mountain and the interior was dark wood," Kathy Fenton says. "They had a fireplace, a baby grand piano, and a few bedrooms. There was a sliding glass door out to the patio and into the backyard. Gram would always be in bed when we went over there."

"Gram called and said they moved into their own house," Margaret Fisher says. "And I said, 'Good, you ought to, like, make amends.'"

"We didn't go over much," Kathy says. "Gretchen was the reason. Gram would always want to leave. He always came over to our house or we would pick him up."

"He would call and every so often Gretchen would get on the phone and yell at me," Margaret says. "I'd say, 'Gretchen, look, I'm not after your husband here.' Both of them were fucked-up. Gram didn't seem to be happy. I felt badly for Gram. I felt badly for Gretchen."

Robert and Bonnie Parsons invited Gram and Gretchen on a three-week sailing trip through the Grenadine Islands in the Caribbean. They stayed in bungalows in Grenada before the start of the cruise.

Sometime after Gram and Gretchen's wedding, Bob Parsons had become so ill he had to be hospitalized. The diagnosis was liver failure. "He had come very, very close," Walter Lanaux says. "His doctor told him, 'You're not going to get away with this twice. If you continue this abuse, the next time you won't make it, period.' Bob recovered from that and for a year he looked terrific. Then he started drinking again."

Bob had always taken his duties as Gram's stepfather seriously, in his own fashion. Whatever Bob's own problems with alcohol, he was upset by Gram and Gretchen's behavior. "Bob yelled at them after a few days," Bonnie Parsons says. "They kept going out at night and coming home stoned and then were stoned for days. We had individual little bungalows with hot tubs and secluded patios. Bob had to go to theirs to quiet them down more than once. They were pretty high all the time in Grenada."

Bob chartered a sailboat and they sailed to Petit St. Vincent, then to St. Vincent and Martinique. "We had a good time," Bonnie says. "Gretchen would help me cook lunch in the galley. We'd anchor for the night, have cocktails on the back deck before we went onshore, and Gram would play his guitar." The four slept on the boat but took their evening meals onshore.

"Gram was a quiet one. Gretchen was louder. She would want to dance around and was kind of yell-y and singing," Bonnie says. "He was mostly on his towel on his stomach."

Bob worried about Gram smoking marijuana on the boat, Bonnie says. "Bob caught 'em on the boat one time and told Gram that he was going to put him off on the next island if he didn't straighten out. He told them they were not going to smoke on the boat, period. Or do anything. He and Gram had a big fight about that. Gram said, 'Dad, you know, it's just a little bit. Just enough to get me moving.' Bob said, 'Nothing, nothing, nothing on the boat. We're in foreign waters. You could be arrested.' He was right."

After several shouting matches with Bob, Gram and Gretchen left the boat trip early. They got off in either Martinique or Guadalupe and went home.

Published sources assert that Bob Parsons, while drinking with Gram on one of the last nights of the trip, told Gram that he brought liquor to Big Avis while she was in the hospital—in effect, that he had killed Gram's

Gretchen Burrell Parsons, Diane Parsons, Gram Parsons, 1973. (Courtesy the estate of Robert Parsons)

mother. This confession could not have been news to Gram; he had likely heard different versions of it from the Snivelys for years. Still, if true, it marks a remarkable or deeply drunken desire on Bob's part to demonstrate how strongly he felt his bond with Gram. Bob's daughter Becky Gottsegen says that neither Bonnie nor Bob ever reported this conversation to her. She regards the story as highly unlikely.

Years later, Gretchen told Ben Fong-Torres that after this trip—and Bob Parsons' alleged confession—Gram started having seizures. "That's when the seizures started," she said. "He wasn't there mentally anymore." No one else has mentioned that Gram suffered seizures of any kind. Among the skeptics is Kathy Fenton. "Jesus Christ, a seizure?" she says. "That's pretty scary. . . . I don't remember anything like that, and that I would have remembered. Gram had been out there using and abusing for quite a while. He was doing a lot. It wasn't the occasional snort or the occasional joint. It was a lot."

Whether Bob Parsons "confessed" or not, his flip-flopping between anguished attempts at drunken intimacy and ridiculous attempts at parental control highlight Gram's lifelong, unsuccessful search for a father figure. First Buddy Freeman, then Jet Thomas, Tony Foutz, and John Phillips—all slightly older men whom he could come to for advice and later act out against. That his last older male advisor was Phil Kaufman speaks to the sadness of Gram's classic junkie downward spiral. Each successive figure seemed less able to keep Gram from doing harm to himself.

"Phil decided he was going to be a father figure for Gram," Kathy Fenton says, "because Gram didn't like his stepfather from New Orleans. Gram respected Philip and looked up to him and trusted him to look after him and take care of him and not rip him off. Philip took pretty good care of Gram. He was in it for himself, but I think Philip was also in it for Gram. He's not totally unselfish—he was out for himself. But he also respected Gram and, in his own way, he loved him. He wanted things right. He wanted everything to be okay—making it okay was his livelihood."

Even if the melodramatic confessional moment on the boat never happened, Gram's relationship with his stepfather worsened. Not long after the cruise, Gram joined forces with Little Avis to initiate legal action against Bob, seeking to remove whatever control he still had over their Snively trusts. It's not known why Gram and his sister took this step. But Bob—himself dying of alcoholism—had apparently been giving both Little Avis and Gram a hard time about their drug use. Maybe they were sick of it. Or maybe, as is often the case when the rich battle the rich in court, it was all about money.

In June of 1973, Emmylou came to L.A. with her boyfriend, Tom Guidera, for rehearsals for an upcoming country showcase. A four-date "pilot tour" was planned to showcase the Country Gazette, Clarence White's bluegrass outfit the Kentucky Colonels, and Gram and Emmylou. Milt Levy booked the shows, which were to be live jam sessions—hootenannies—to prepare for a more formal tour of colleges and likely European gigs in the fall. The Tower Theater in Philadelphia hosted the last date of the pilot tour. It featured four segments, the highlight of which was Gram and Emmylou backed by Byron Berline, Clarence White, Gene Parsons (the then-current Byrds drummer and banjo player), Chris Ethridge, and Sneaky Pete. Interviewed by *Grass Seen*, Byron Berline described the tour as "about the most fun thing we had done in our lives. We were all ecstatic about it." Sneaky Pete put it this way to the *Daily Planet*: "I know everybody enjoyed it because they told me so, and they wouldn't lie."

The lineup for the final Philly show added Kenny Wertz on guitar and Roger Bush on acoustic bass. Gram and Emmylou sang "We'll Sweep out the Ashes in the Morning," "Streets of Baltimore," "Hickory Wind," "Country Baptizing," "Love Hurts," and "Hot Burrito #2."

"What pure delight it was to sit there and once again hear Gram plaintively sing 'Jesus Christ' in the middle of 'Hot Burrito #2,' with Pete's piercing guitar wailing," Dennis Dyroff wrote in *Rock Ravings and Musical Madness*. "It was an evening to be remembered and savored . . . when old friends came together to create some fine music and fine feelings."

A few weeks later, in July, Gram and Gretchen's house burned to the ground. No conclusive cause for the fire was discovered; an electrical failure is one theory. Another is that someone out of it on downers or heroin fell asleep with a lit cigarette in his or her hand. Sources conflict, but Gram may have been hospitalized for smoke inhalation. He told Emmylou Harris that he had survived by jumping through a glass window. One version has it that Gram ran into his closet, passed out, and was protected from the flames by the weight of his Nudie wardrobe, which fell on top of him.

The couple moved back to the Chateau Marmont. "He called and said, 'I'm at the Chateau Marmont—my house burned down,'" Margaret Fisher remembers. "He said, 'If you don't come down here I think I will die. Gretchen set fire to the house.' I don't know if that's true. I thought with two people walking around on downers all the time, of course their house burned down."

Margaret went to L.A. with her boyfriend at the time, a lawyer. "I met Gram at the Chateau Marmont," Margaret says, "and he said, 'Why don't we take another room and get it on?' I said, 'I can't believe that. I'm here with my boyfriend. You're here with your wife. That is too tacky for words. I am surprised you would suggest that.'

"But on that same trip down there with my lawyer, I OD'd. I had been shooting [heroin] maybe two weeks. Not much—it was experimental. My friend brought me back by stuffing ice cubes up my butt."

Gram and Gretchen separated. Gretchen moved back to her father's house; Gram set up in the guest cabin behind Phil Kaufman and Kathy Fenton's house on Chandler Avenue. Gram and Gretchen began to discuss a divorce.

According to Kathy Fenton, Gram's daily routine consisted of getting up late and having a cup of coffee laced with alcohol. Shortly after, Gram would commence his drug routine for the day. He sometimes turned his attention to music. Between trying to take up with Margaret Fisher and aping his mother's worst behavior, Gram seemed to be collapsing into his own past. "He might try to write songs," Kathy says, "he'd chat with friends, at night he'd go to clubs.

"We went to the Palomino to see Linda Ronstadt. Gram went up onstage and picked up a guitar. Gram started singing one song and Linda started singing another. It wasn't 'cause Linda was wasted! Gram was stumbling around up there and it was embarrassing. He was wasted most of the time. It was sad toward the end. Poor baby. I felt bad for him."

In his book, *Road Mangler*, Phil Kaufman claims that Gram had oxygen tanks delivered; he told Kaufman that inhaling the gas helped relieve hangovers. Kaufman suspected the oxygen was a cover for pharmaceuticals that Gram was having delivered to the house.

"I don't know if it was straight heroin that he was shooting all the time, but he told me it was," Kathy says. "Heroin. We'd always find paraphernalia around the house."

Kaufman tried to manage Gram's drug use by stealing or hiding his supply. Gram was so loaded he sometimes assumed he'd used the drugs up himself. Kaufman said that Gram never suspected his drugs were being rationed. Gram always found a way to get more.

"Gram had a delivery service! I can't tell you the guy's name, but he's a pretty famous actor and he's been in jail," Kathy says. "He had a long pinky nail and he was the coke dealer for everyone in Hollywood. He would scoop his nail in the coke and stick his finger up to your nostril as soon as you walked in the door. It was the first thing that he would do. He was a bit-part actor. He's sort of famous now. He's clean and sober now and has been for many years. He dealt drugs to everyone in Hollywood. We got our coke from him. Maybe heroin, too."

Gram visited Rick Grech at the home of Jerry Allison, the drummer for Buddy Holly's backup band, the Crickets. The Crickets did their best to keep their career alive decades after Holly's death in 1959. Grech was working with the Crickets and English guitarist Alvin Lee of Ten Years After. "[Gram] was in a real state," Jenny Grech said later. "He'd got into this pattern of getting strung out and then going out to the Joshua Tree Inn to recuperate. Rick told Gram he ought to sort himself out. Almost his final words to Gram were, 'You wanna watch it, 'cause you're gonna be a legend in your own lifetime.' Great words on which to part."

"We used to hang around with Linda Ronstadt, Delaney & Bonnie, Bonnie Raitt," Kathy Fenton says. "Gram was going to the Palomino and clubs all the time to meet and greet.

"He wasn't a man about town in the kind of way that he would be going out with different women all of the time. I never got the impression that Gram was a ladies' man. He wasn't a skirt chaser. I never saw him be disrespectful. He was always a Southern gentleman. Always being respectful of women and other human beings. He rarely cursed around women. He was raised that way."

Margaret Fisher came to L.A. again. This time she spent the night with Gram. Margaret had refused to sleep with him while he was married, and refused again when Gram told her his relationship with Gretchen was unraveling. Margaret became Gram's lover when she knew he and Gretchen were living apart.

"He sent me a ticket and I went down," Margaret says. "The next day Philip and Kathy took us out to Joshua Tree. We went out and cooked out—like a barbecue—on this hillside, and we talked. Gram was doing downers and he had taken me to a doctor in L.A. and gotten me a prescription for some."

"Margaret was an airhead," Kathy Fenton says. "Ditzy. She was wonderful—a sweetheart. I liked her. She didn't have a whole lot of common sense."

"I liked Phil," Margaret says. "He's like a Yorkshire terrier. He will bite at your ankles until you stop fucking up. He's a little guy and he's tough."

"We went to Joshua Tree because for Gram it was a spiritual place. We would sit at Devil's Outlook, close to Cap Rock," Kathy remembers. "We'd walk to an outcropping of rocks and sit up there and look out over the whole floor of the desert. Sitting up there we would all Zen out. Palm Springs would be way off into the distance. It was so quiet and peaceful. Gram got a lot of his ideas there. He would go back and relax and write songs. He seldom took his guitar out of the car or the room—he'd come back from the park to write."

WHEN GRAM, Margaret, Phil, and Kathy returned to L.A., they learned that Clarence White had been killed on July 14. He was twenty-nine years old.

(Margaret Fisher and others remember events in this sequence: Gram's house burning down and then Clarence White being killed. Other accounts say the fire occurred after Clarence White's death. As ever, precise dates remain elusive. That the two events happened in quick succession is not in dispute.)

Clarence had been loading out after a Kentucky Colonels show near his house in Palmdale, California. A drunk driver ran Clarence down as he was putting his amplifier in his car. He died in front of his brothers, Roland and Eric. Roland dislocated his shoulder trying to pull Clarence out of the way.

Before and after he played with the final configuration of the Byrds (White, McGuinn, Gene Parsons, Skip Battin)—the band broke up in February 1973—White's fame had spread through his near-constant L.A. session work. He played for the Everly Brothers, Linda Ronstadt, Rita Coolidge, Jackson Browne, Terry Melcher, Maria Muldaur, Arlo Guthrie, Randy Newman, Joe Cocker, the Monkees, Gene Clark, and many others.

With Peter Rowan, Richard Greene, Bill Keith, and David Grisman, White backed up bluegrass legend Bill Monroe on a live TV appearance on February 15. Monroe's bus broke down en route to the show and the band performed a roster of bluegrass classics without him. They began gigging around L.A. under the name Muleskinner. The group disbanded after Clarence died; an LP, *Muleskinner: A Potpourri of Bluegrass Jam*, was released in 1974. The band is regarded as the trailblazers of progressive bluegrass, a term that seems even more oxymoronic than progressive country.

Earlier on the night of the fourteenth Clarence and his two brothers visited Roger McGuinn's house in Malibu for McGuinn's birthday party. They left early but promised to come back after their show.

Songwriter, and professional best friend to Bob Dylan, Bob Neuwirth says, "We were sitting around playing music and Clarence said, 'I have to go. I have a gig with Roland. I'll come back after the gig.' Now, I'd sit and listen to Clarence White all fucking day and night if I could. So we said, 'Yeah, man, please come back.'"

"Chris Ethridge called me the next day. I thought he was drunk," Byron Berline says. "He sounded real out of it. He told me Clarence was dead. I didn't believe him. After he said it again I knew he wasn't kidding."

"We were sitting at Roger's house waiting for him to come back," Bob Neuwirth says, "and at about three or four in the morning someone called up and said, 'Clarence just got killed.' We started to cry. I was there with Roger and Kris Kristofferson, and we didn't know what we could do. Except in country music there's a tradition that when something bad happens, you sing. That's what June Carter Cash taught me when Janis Joplin died. So we wrote a song called 'Rock and Roll Time.' We all recorded it eventually, all three of us. Not that it was a great song: It was our way of saying good-bye to Clarence."

Clarence had re-formed the Kentucky Colonels with his brothers after the Byrds breakup. His time with the Byrds, his session work, his coinvention of the B-Bender with Gene Parsons, and his ability to play bluegrass, rock, country, and even pedal steel (using the B-Bender on his Telecaster, which now belongs to another virtuoso picker, Marty Stuart) had earned White a hallowed place in L.A. and Nashville music circles. Attendance at his funeral, which was held on July 19 at St. Mary's Catholic Church in Palmdale, where Clarence owned a house, reflected the scope of his community of admirers.

Over a hundred musicians attended, including Kris Kristofferson, Roger McGuinn, Bernie Leadon, Jim Dickson, Chris Hillman, Chris Ethridge, Rita Coolidge, Gene Parsons, and Gib Guilbeau, a member of the then-current version of the Burrito Brothers.

"There wasn't anybody that I ever knew that didn't love Clarence," Jim Dickson says. "He was a sweet man, he was never abrasive to anybody, he was a nice guy. I was stunned that he was so casually killed. All of a sudden he was gone."

"It was a Catholic funeral, a boring, terrible service," Byron Berline says. "No music. The priest didn't even mention Clarence's name. All these musicians in there and no music! We hated that."

John Beland, a close friend of Clarence's, later joined the reincarnated Flying Burrito Brothers. "In the middle of the eulogy, Gram stumbled into the church flanked by a couple chicks," Beland says. "When Gram showed up, everyone started muttering, 'He's next.'"

Margaret Fisher was one of the women with Gram. (The other was probably Kathy Fenton.) "We went to the church and the priest was all in black," Margaret says. "It was elaborate. After the church we went to the interment and the priest had changed from black to pink."

The service was impersonal and cold; it seemed the priest knew nothing about Clarence. His friends questioned whether Clarence would have even wanted a religious burial. The mood at the graveside was somber and confused. The musicians stood by the grave, packed shoulder to shoulder, looking at one another. No one thought Clarence was being given a proper send-off, but no one knew how to respond.

Suddenly, Gram opened his mouth and began to sing "Farther Along." It's a traditional hymn that Gram had sung on *Burrito Deluxe;* another arrangement appeared on the Byrds' 1971 album *Farther Along,* on which Clarence was prominently featured. Bernie Leadon, standing beside Gram, joined in:

Farther along, we'll know more about it
Farther along, we'll understand why

"I was standing right beside him and I tried singing with him," Byron Berline says, "but nothing was coming out. I was all choked up. They sounded great together. It was so appropriate, because Clarence had sung and recorded 'Farther' with the Byrds. I appreciated those guys doing that. It made me feel good, and I'm sure that it made everyone else feel good, too."

"Everybody felt the loss," Jim Dickson says. "Everyone at the funeral was stunned. Nobody had anything to say, and then Gram sang."

Once Gram and Bernie started, those gathered joined in. Most knew the words; most sang with tears in their eyes. Their voices soared over the grave. The song was Clarence White's true, sincere, and righteous eulogy.

The moment crystallized why Gram Parsons is a legendary figure and should be. Grief-stricken, irritated by the priest, heartbroken over Clarence White's death, and loaded on pills, liquor, and likely heroin, Gram remained the one person at the grave who knew how to illuminate that precious moment. When all around him were paralyzed—and when all were likely far more competent in day-to-day problem-solving than Gram—Gram alone understood what the soul of the moment required. He understood the poetry necessary to deal with the pain. With his own profound connection to grief and loss, Gram understood how to grant the assembled throng catharsis, and Clarence White release.

After the funeral, or perhaps during it, gathered at a bar later or right there out by the graveside, Phil Kaufman and Gram made a promise to one another on which rests a cornerstone of the Gram legend. There are several different, equally credible versions of how this promise came about.

Phil Kaufman's version of the story enhances his status as Gram's best friend. He and Gram made a pact "whereby the survivor would take the other guy's body out to Joshua Tree, have a few drinks, and burn it. The burning was the bottom line." The goal was to ensure that neither would have "one of those long, family-and-friends funerals."

"Gram and Phil Kaufman sat in the pew right in front of me," Byron Berline says. "That's when Gram told Phil Kaufman, 'I'm not going through this crap—take me out to the desert and burn me. Just burn my body.'"

"We left the funeral and we went out to a Mexican restaurant," Margaret Fisher says. "Philip and Gram were drinking and they were talking about how horrible the funeral was. They decided whichever one of them died first, the other guy would take him out to Joshua Tree and burn him up. It was a way to, like, piss on their parents. It might have been something they talked about earlier. They were both drunk—I was sober."

"Gram told me, 'I don't want that to happen to me,'" Roger McGuinn said. "He didn't want to be sent back to the hypocrites in his estate who were trying to rip him off for all his money. They'd put him in the family mausoleum or something."

"It was always our intention that he be cremated and his ashes scattered in Joshua Tree," Kathy Fenton says. "It was a pact we made. It was me, our two next-door neighbors, Allen and Joanie Swerdloff, Philip, and Gram. We did one of those handshakes where you piled hands on top, like 'Break!' I want to be cremated and I want my ashes scattered. Phil said the same, Gram said the same, and I said the same. He said he wanted his ashes scattered at Joshua Tree and I said, 'Oh, yeah, me too.' We all made this pact: 'Whoever dies first, the other person has got to carry this out because this is what I want.' That's the way that happened."

"It wasn't a large group, maybe twenty or thirty people gathered around the casket," Jim Dickson says. "Nobody was [talking]—there wasn't any conversation where you'd have to raise your voice to get any attention. He said it in a quiet place where he didn't have to make it like an announcement. Everybody heard it, but it wasn't a pronouncement of ego. He said it in a normal voice and everybody heard it."

It's hard to say now whether this was a solemn pledge or drunken sentimentality. The others in the pact might have envisioned a classic cremation, an urn, a drive to the desert. No doubt Phil Kaufman was the only one who thought of doing it all himself.

GRAM TOLD MARGARET he had to pull back from their relationship in order to work. "Gram said he had to work on his album and he wouldn't be able to see me," Margaret says. "I thought that was fine. Gretchen got into trouble bringing her own personal feelings and problems with Gram into recording situations. I didn't want to make that mistake. For Gram, recording was dead serious. He cleaned up for that album—he cut his drinking. It was serious business."

Gram's resilience—his ability to bounce back into shape—was fraying. The real world forced its way into his drug haze. Gram was suing his stepfather and getting a divorce. Clarence White was gone just like that. Gram's drug buddy and supplier Sid Kaiser, a father figure of comfort and reliability, died suddenly. Pulling himself together was getting harder, but Emmylou, ever the optimist, was hopeful. "Near the end, Gram seemed constantly beset by personal problems," she said later. "Still, he managed to cut down on drinking for the sessions themselves. Everything was going great. Any fears, any misgivings I had about his health disappeared at that point. I felt like we were entering a new era."

Sessions for *Grievous Angel* began in the late summer of 1973. The personnel included the basic band from *GP*: Gram, Emmylou Harris, Glen D. Hardin on piano, James Burton on lead guitar, Ronnie Tutt on drums, Al Perkins on the steel. Byron Berline played fiddle on "Return of the Grievous Angel" and fiddle and mandolin on the "Cash on the Barrelhead/Hickory Wind" medley. Emory Gordy joined on bass and N. D. Smart played drums on "Hearts on Fire" and "In My Hour of Darkness." Gordy came from Elvis' band as well; he later joined Emmylou's Hot Band. He produced Patty Loveless' first recording efforts in 1985. Loveless and Gordy married in 1989.

New players included Herb Pederson, who had contributed harmony on the Burrito outtakes produced by Jim Dickson that became the album *Sleepless Nights*. Pederson played rhythm guitar on "I Can't Dance" and later went on to perform with Chris Hillman. Bernie Leadon added acoustic guitar on "Return of the Grievous Angel," lead guitar on "Hearts on Fire," and dobro on "In My Hour of Darkness." Steve Snyder played the vibes on "Hearts on Fire," and Linda Ronstadt sang backup on "In My Hour of Darkness." The album credit for the fake live medley boasted, "Background blah-blah on Northern Quebec Medley by Kim Fowley, Phil Kaufman, Ed Tickner, Jane & Jon Doe." Fowley was a notorious L.A. scenester perhaps best known as the Svengali responsible for the Runaways.

"[Gram] had split from his old lady and was getting it together," Ginny Winn, a photographer who worked for Warner Bros., said. "Hardly drinking and not doing dope. He was putting down three songs a night."

"There was a lot of cocaine use. A lot of alcohol and a lot of cocaine," Kathy Fenton says. "We tried not to let him use drugs and alcohol while he was in the studio, and when he was rehearsing we wouldn't let him while the whole band was there. I am sure that he went into the bathroom and dipped a little."

Grievous Angel was actually planned, unlike *GP.* Several arrangements had been worked out on the road—such as Gram's duet with Emmylou on "Love Hurts."

Gram worked with a new professionalism, hard-learned in the meandering *GP* sessions. "We laid down all the backing tracks in a week," Emory Gordy said. "Gram played us each of the songs that he had ready. Glen [D. Hardin] would already have a basic chord chart written out prior to coming to the studio. We took it from there. It was loose as far as formal arranging was concerned—we played what we thought was right for the song, and it all seemed to fall together. If anything went wrong, we heard it on the playback and rectified it with a new take."

"Every night we'd get mixes of what we'd done, the rough vocal, and we'd take them back and listen to them over and over again," Emmylou Harris said. "We'd get so excited, dancing up and down. *GP* had been a struggle, but Gram's singing was so much better after a year on the road."

"He was in good shape, Gram," Emory Gordy said. "There was a lot of energy going on in the studio for the whole of that album. Gram was bouncing all over the place and Emmy was bouncing around him. They were great, happy sessions."

"Gram's style was to start a number of songs and then delay finishing them until the last possible moment," Emmylou continued. "Often he'd work on an idea while it was fresh in his mind, and then set it aside until time demanded he complete it. In the case of 'In My Hour of Darkness,' we put the finishing touches on it on the day of the session. All I did was make a few odd suggestions in the wording of the lyric—it was Gram's song . . . a song quite personal to him, and his giving me [co-songwriter] credit was an example of his generosity—a token of friendship and an acknowledgment of my help.

"Our singing came together on two songs: 'Love Hurts' and 'Angels Rejoiced' [which appeared on the Gram compilation *Sleepless Nights*]. Those two songs should have been the starting point for whatever we would do in the future, because I finally learned what I was supposed to do. I go back now and I think about how much better I could have been, because I feel Gram deserves it. His singing is so incredible. He sings with such subtlety. And the fact that his voice sometimes suffered from the hard life that he lived gave it a vulnerable quality."

"In My Hour of Darkness" honors three of Gram's fallen friends: Brandon De Wilde, Clarence White, and Sid Kaiser, whom Gram memorialized as "kind and wise with age," a man he "loved . . . like my father."

"The song was done in maybe two takes," Emmylou recalls. "As were the rest of the tracks. We cut it totally live: everybody playing together and Gram and I were singing simultaneously. Though they were only guide vocals, which we recorded with some help from Linda Ronstadt. Gram invited her down to sing on the session."

Gram cowrote and recorded Rick Grech's archetypal "Ooh Las Vegas," about which Jenny Grech says, "None of the Americans were prepared to admit that a Brit could write a decent country tune." Barry Tashian says he had a hand in writing several lines of the song, although he wasn't credited "due to a series of mishaps. . . . That's show business."

Gram called Margaret as the sessions went on. "He said he's getting a divorce," Margaret remembers. "Every so often he'd play me something from *Grievous Angel*. He'd sort of talk about getting married, but I thought that was, like, testing me. He talked about when he wasn't married perhaps he would get married again. I would look at him and I'd say, 'Shoot, son. You ought to get divorced first before you ask a lady that question.'"

During the sessions Gram cut back on his heroin use. When the record was done he began again. "Philip wasn't home one day," Kathy Fenton says, "and a girlfriend had called from England and I was chatting with her on the phone. I heard a crash. A loud crash. And I said, 'I gotta go.'

"I went running to the bathroom and opened the door. Gram was three sheets to the wind and had fallen into the tub. He'd been sitting on the ledge of the bathtub and had fallen backwards so his legs were splayed. There was his shooting-up kit laying on the side and his arm was still tied off. I was not used to that. That was not where I was coming from. I never shot anything and I was paranoid of needles. It totally freaked me out."

Gram's "shooting-up kit" presumably contained the usual implements for injecting heroin: a syringe, a spoon or container for cooking the heroin, and a belt or piece of rubber tubing for tying off the arm prior to injection. The tying-off limits circulation, causing the veins in the arm to swell and making injecting the drug easier. Removing the tie-off releases the heroin into the bloodstream in one big rush.

"I said, 'What are you doing? What the fuck are you doing?'" Kathy says. "He was groggy and I got hysterical and started yelling at him. I said to him, 'Why do you keep doing this? You're going to kill yourself! You can't live like this. This is terrible. Don't you see the pain you're causing? It hurts me to see you like this. It hurts Philip to see you like this. It hurts everybody who knows you to see you like this. What the fuck do you think you're doing?'

"I was absolutely hysterical. I was screaming at him, 'You're a fucking asshole. Why are you doing this to me and everybody else?' He got sheepish and he said, 'I'm sorry. I will never do this again. I promise you I will never do this again.' And I was still mad and said, 'Yes, you will! You're just saying that! You're lying! You're a liar! You're a fucking son of a bitch! You're a liar!' He put his arms around me and I was sobbing. He said, 'I will never do this again. I promise you. I promise you I will never do this again. I love you. I will never do this again.'

"I kind of calmed down and thought, Okay, he promised me he will never do this again. I think he wanted to calm me down and didn't want to deal with it. God, that's terrible. I think he meant it in the moment. I'd like to think that he did."

A few days later, Gram and Margaret Fisher went out to Joshua Tree with Dale McElroy and her boyfriend, Michael Martin. Margaret and Gram drove out in Gram's new white Jaguar. McElroy and Martin had their own vehicle: McElroy's 1960 cherry-red Cadillac hearse.

TWENTY-ONE

Joshua Tree

Dale McElroy later said that going to Joshua Tree with Gram was Kaufman's idea. Kaufman thought Gram needed to spend time in the desert and that Michael Martin could keep an eye on him. Dale wasn't enthusiastic—she didn't care for Gram—but Kaufman insisted. Martin didn't seem to mind.

Gram called Margaret and suggested she fly down from San Francisco for a Joshua Tree vacation. He sounded happy. "He had his record. He played me his record a lot. He was getting ready to file for a divorce," Margaret says. "And I got the feeling—and I don't think I was wrong—that there was no chance there was going to be any reconciliation."

According to Kaufman, attorney Bruce Wolfe was drawing up papers for Gram's divorce. The plan was for Kaufman to serve the papers to Gretchen on September 20, while Gram was in Joshua Tree. Others have echoed this idea more vaguely. Kaufman remains the only adamant, published source. He and Gretchen are mortal enemies. Gretchen has denied that a divorce was imminent.

"I think Gram and I could have had a relationship," Margaret says. "I certainly wanted to take care of him. On the other hand, I would not have been tolerant of his fucking up. I probably would not have put up with a lot of nonsense. I knew his bullshit from high school. He didn't have to be anybody different, and he could be sure that if he was I would not put up with it."

Another woman has claimed that Gram was going to marry her as soon as his divorce from Gretchen was final. Margaret wasn't aware of any significant woman in Gram's life. It's not impossible: Gram compartmentalized, and was intensely secretive. Conversations with dozens of his friends, musical partners, and acquaintances never produced an identity for this mystery fiancée or any evidence that she existed.

Gram, Margaret, Dale, and Michael stayed at the Joshua Tree Inn, where Gram liked to hunker down when he retreated to the desert. "Everyone out here liked Gram," Al Barbary, the son of the Inn's owners, said. "He got into fights in bars sometimes—Gram liked to play, and if they didn't want him to play, he'd play anyway and they'd throw him out. Most of the time they wouldn't throw him out, because he was good. When he went into a bar it got crowded, and there were lots of happy people. He used to drink tequila and play all night. Since he rented most of the rooms here, he was free to do what he wanted. It was a hideaway hideout for him."

The foursome cruised around the Joshua Tree Monument, had dinner, and went to a bar. Later Gram and Margaret drove to a drive-in to see the science fiction film *Soylent Green*.

"We talked about stuff from high school," Margaret says. "We talked about having a reunion at Bolles of all the people that had gone on to be drug addicts and calling it the Bolles Track Meet. We talked about the drugs we had done. Bragging. The good ol' days. . . . He didn't talk about doing drugs with Keith Richards. He talked about Keith's son and the relationship between Keith and his son. He said he didn't see Polly enough. It felt like what he said to me he did not say to other people. But who knows? Gram could put on personalities. He could be what he wanted to be. He could be charming. He was a performer."

Dale, who was recovering from hepatitis, wasn't interested in drinking or barhopping. According to her, Gram was drinking nonstop. He insisted she and Michael come along to the local dives and be part of the audience when he sat in with the band. Dale found his behavior tiresome and his drinking obnoxious.

"We weren't using heroin. Gram was on pills," Margaret says. "He had a seemingly limitless supply of downers. Gram drank Jack Daniel's and Southern Comfort. I did not drink, so I had no idea that he was drinking a great deal. I didn't have a clue."

"That guy could consume booze," Al Barbary recalled. "He'd drink a fifth of tequila before he went out."

Michael Martin drove back to L.A. on Tuesday, September 18, to replenish their marijuana supply. He told Dale to take over his assignment of watching out for Gram. Dale told Michael she "wasn't intrigued by the antics or the personality of this obviously desperate guy."

Gram, Margaret, and Dale went out to the airport for lunch. Neither Dale nor Margaret wanted drinks. Gram ordered a series of doubles and ignored the food. He was drunk before lunch was over. Dale, disgusted, retreated to her room.

"During the day we'd go to bars and it was great," Margaret says. "These desert bars were barfly heaven. There would be these desiccated desert rats, amazing people. All of them were in there drinking because somebody had done them wrong and it took you about two minutes to get them to tell you who had done them wrong and why. It was always the same story: some woman, some man, some corporation. . . . There was one guy who was receiving radio signals through his fillings. That's why he was drinking. Because he didn't hear them when he drank.

"They had one song from Gram's first album on the jukebox, which he played incessantly. I was almost embarrassed. He played it over and over. He was so pleased. When we were out in the desert he just knew *Grievous Angel* was going to be *it*."

Here was Gram, the coolest guy in town, fresh from teaching the Rolling Stones about American music and recording with Elvis' band, enthralled at finding his own song on a jukebox in a desert dive. It's a poignant moment: Gram was astonished that he really had accomplished something, that he could savor his music outside of his own house, in the company of strangers. And that when he wasn't in the bar, people he never met might pay a quarter to hear his song.

FOR DECADES MARGARET FISHER has been the designated villain of Gram's last day in Joshua Tree. She's been accused of negligence and even complicity in the events of September 18. Without mentioning Margaret by name, Rick Grech later summed up the conventional wisdom: "Gram was surrounded by people who weren't that close to him. If they were, they would never have left him alone to die. Gram was in a crazy state because of his separation. He was out on a binge. He took too much of too many things at one time. And these 'friends' couldn't see that he was in no state to continue. When he got *heavy*, they *split*. They left him; they got afraid and let him go. It made me wary of who I got off with."

Since that night, Margaret Fisher has never spoken in detail about what happened until now. For key moments of that night, she remains the sole witness—her version is the only version. If her version suffers from a certain sparseness, it's because Margaret does not embellish what she cannot remember. On some points Margaret's memories align with Dale McElroy's; on others they diverge. But the gists of their stories are so similar that they form a reliable narrative.

"We went to a bar after dinner," Margaret says. "They had a band playing, and Gram sat in with them. He was singing 'Okie from Muskogee' and he was making up his own words, like, 'We all smoke marijuana in Muskogee.' The guy playing slide guitar couldn't play fast enough, and during the break he showed us why: He'd been shooting up meth into his arms. He could hardly move them. Gram was wearing overalls, and when the guy wouldn't play fast enough Gram would start to get undressed until the guy caught up.

"Then Gram said he wanted to do some heroin. We didn't have any. There was a girl living in the front room [at the Joshua Tree Inn] and she made the connection for him."

Gram drank steadily and downed an assortment of pills. Margaret is adamant that Gram had not been using heroin with any frequency. She insists that their shooting up in Joshua Tree was recreational—a spur-of-the-moment indulgence.

"The connection came down right about dark," Margaret says. "She was a girl. She had her two-year-old baby with her, which I didn't think was cool. She was older than me, thin, kind of tall, with blond hair sort of long, maybe medium length, wearing jeans and a shirt. She brought everything with her. She brought works—we didn't have works."

Gram and Margaret were staying in Room 8; they met the connection in Room 1. Neither Gram nor Margaret handled the needle; the connection—the blond girl with the two-year-old—injected them both. "She had these little vials of morphine sulfate in liquid. She said they'd ripped them off from the Marine base in Pendleton," Margaret says, referring to Camp Pendleton, near San Diego. "She hit me up and I got high. Then she shot

Gram up and he got high. We sat there for a while and Gram said he wanted to do some more. I said, 'That's probably not a good idea. Philip is going to be pissed about this.' He said, 'No, we can do some more.' I said, 'Well, I can't.'"

Morphine is chemically similar to heroin but not as strong. Although originally developed as a less addictive form of morphine, heroin is more than twice as potent. That may be why Gram, who had been using heroin intermittently, wanted more.

"She hit Gram up again and he was in trouble almost immediately," Margaret says. "She saw what was happening before I did and she was gone. She took the morphine and the works and her baby and she vanished. She was gone before I even realized Gram was in trouble. I tried to lift him up, but I couldn't do it—he was too big, too heavy. I thought, 'My God, he's OD'd!' so I went and got Dale. I'd never been around anyone in an OD state before. I had no way to compare what was happening to him to anything else. Dale didn't know anything about what to do. She was straight. Dale was not a druggie."

According to Margaret, Gram had consumed at least a fifth of whiskey and taken a handful of various pills, likely barbiturates, before topping off with morphine. Immediately after the connection fled—before Dale McElroy came into the room—Gram was nearly unconscious. With the two women holding him up, he could barely move his legs.

"I knew he was in trouble," Margaret says. "He was in control of his bodily functions, but he could hardly walk supported. He wasn't dead weight. But I was so scared. His head was nodding, like he was unconscious with his eyes open."

Though their stories differ in other respects, Dale and Margaret agree that they more or less carried Gram back to Room 8.

"One of the first times I hit up, I had OD'd," Margaret says. "When I came to, the guy told me how he brought me back. I thought, 'I have to do that right now.' I told Dale to go get ice, and I put Gram in the shower, put cold water on him, and put ice up his butt. He came around right away. He did seem to come back. He wasn't instantly not stoned, but I thought he was going to be okay. He was able to speak."

Dale's memory does not quite match Margaret's. In her version, they applied the ice as Gram lay on the floor. She was amazed when, moments later, Gram was conscious and making jokes about why they had taken his pants down. Both women agree that Dale returned to her room when Gram came around.

"He was stoned and slurry but, from my experience, what happened to him was exactly what happened to me," Margaret says. "In my experience he would be okay if I could keep him walking, keep him moving, and get some food and caffeine in him. So I left Dale to watch him."

The primary accusation against Margaret Fisher is that she panicked and abandoned Gram. That Gram died because she ran off. Margaret has been the scapegoat for more than thirty years. The popular version has it that Gram could have lived had Margaret been there. Fisher's detailed recall of what happened that night—and Dale McElroy's corroborating memories—make it clear that Gram was never abandoned.

"Nobody left him alone," Margaret says. "We did not leave him there to die. We did the freakin' best we could."

Margaret was high on morphine, but she was in love with Gram. She believed the ice cubes had worked, that the crisis was over. She left seeking a slightly longer-term solution: food and caffeine to get Gram through the night. Dale's version suggests that one of them was always by Gram's side. If Margaret had been more knowing, or less high, she might have sent McElroy to get coffee and stayed to walk Gram around or keep him under a cold shower. Dale McElroy, for all her traveling to tripped-out hippie destinations, knew little about hard drugs. She had even less basis for understanding the seriousness of Gram's condition than Margaret.

Margaret went to Dale's room and asked her to watch Gram while she went to get him coffee and food. Margaret looked intoxicated and Dale suggested that she go instead. Margaret was insistent. According to Dale, Margaret said, "Just go in there and sit with him until I get back."

"I drove down the road and got a mega thing of coffee at a restaurant and drove back," Margaret says. "There are differing stories of how long I was gone. I would say it was maybe twenty minutes. Maybe to Dale it seemed a lot longer. Time gets flexible when you're like that."

Margaret failed to tell Dale the protocol for dealing with an overdose—keep the victim awake and moving and never let him sleep. Dale went to Room 8 to babysit, carrying a book. Gram was on the bed, apparently sleeping, his breathing regular. Dale sat in a chair next to the bed and began to read.

Dale estimates she had been there about twenty minutes when Gram's breathing started to change, getting slower and weaker, then becoming a rasp. Dale was frightened. Should she leave him to get help, or stay and try to revive him? The Inn's office was closed and as far as she knew there was no one else staying at the motel. (The woman who hooked them up with the connection knew Margaret, not Dale.) Dale tried to revive Gram by pressing on his back to get him to breathe. She rolled him over and attempted mouth-to-mouth resuscitation.

Dale estimates this went on for as long as half an hour. She was panicky and exhausted. Gram was breathing, but laboring for breath. Dale was afraid to leave him. She didn't call for help. Later she wondered if Gram might have lived if she had. She kept trying to aid his breathing, feeling all the time that he was slipping away.

"When I got back," Margaret says, "Dale was giving him CPR. Having taken a CPR course, I know looking back that she was not giving him real CPR."

Gram might have survived if either woman had called an ambulance sooner. But the first impulse in the face of an illegal drug overdose is to keep outsiders away. No one accustomed to hard drugs would call the authorities until all home remedies had been exhausted. The lore of junkiedom is filled with close calls brought about by the overdose equivalent of chicken soup: ice cubes, walk-arounds, cold showers, caffeine. Junkie lore is also replete with accidental deaths. To ask why heroin users don't call an ambulance is to deny how addiction operates.

"Gram wasn't a junkie at the time," Margaret says. "That's why he died. If he'd been a junkie he could have done all that heroin." Gram shot morphine, in fact, but the two substances operate similarly in the body. "Junkies build up a tolerance," Margaret continues. "A junkie can do a lot of junk and not die. We didn't do that much morphine. Philip was mad at Gram around that time because Phil had found him doing heroin. That means that Gram wasn't doing it on a daily basis. He'd been clean to record *Grievous Angel*. It's hard to kill a junkie. Once you become addicted, your tolerance for drugs increases exponentially."

Gram suffered a classic relapse overdose. He had not injected heroin regularly for a while (although that interval is in dispute). He then took a dose of pure morphine at near his former level of consumption. Gram overestimated his capacity for opiates and underestimated—or was too high to remember—how much liquor and barbiturates he'd ingested.

"This was pure and simple error," Margaret says. "A mistake. He did not want to die. He was in a good mood."

As Dale was becoming convinced that it was useless for her to keep trying to revive Gram, Margaret arrived. "I was all pushed out of shape, scared out of my wits and furious for being left with him," Dale says. "I told her to go wake up the people in the office and get an ambulance down there fast."

Margaret came to the same conclusion: "I took one look at him and said, 'Call an ambulance.' He was unconscious on his bed, naked with a towel over him. Every so often you'd see his chest move, but it was obvious that he was in real trouble. I'd have a pulse on him sometimes and then I wouldn't. And he'd breathe sometimes, then he wouldn't. And I sat there.

"Dale was probably more blown away than I was. I was almost unnaturally calm."

It's not clear who made the call, but the police and an ambulance arrived. Dale remembers that they did not take long to get there.

"I told them, 'He's done heroin'—I didn't call it morphine," Margaret says. "There were cops that came with the ambulance but I don't remember who all was there. I was focused on one thing. I didn't care what was around me. I wanted Gram gotten to a hospital. They told me where the hospital was and they took him and I went to the hospital. I drove the Jaguar.

"I was not crying. I was upset but I was capable. I read somewhere that I was hysterical. I don't remember that. I was not."

The ambulance left with Gram; he was naked and unmoving. Neither Margaret nor Dale remembers any detail of Gram being taken from the room to the ambulance, nor any detail of the emergency care he received. "I didn't see them do one thing," Margaret says, "but put him on a stretcher and put him in an ambulance."

Margaret drove the seven miles from Joshua Tree to Yucca Valley, to the hospital on California Route 62—Twenty-Nine Palms Highway. She does not remember how Dale got to the hospital. "I didn't notice her," she says. "At that point I had extreme tunnel vision. It was like everything was going on around me was going on around me but I wasn't focusing on anything but this boy.

"It took me a while to get there, but I was calm the whole way. I drove fast and got there not long after the ambulance."

When she arrived, she was told Gram had died. She did not ask to see him. She didn't want to see his body; she had no doubt he was gone.

Gram Parsons was pronounced dead on arrival at High Desert Memorial Hospital in Yucca Valley, California, at 12:15 A.M. on Wednesday, September 19, 1973.

TWENTY-TWO
THE COFFIN

THE COPS WANTED TO TALK TO DALE AND MARGARET. THEY WERE QUESTIONED in adjoining rooms at the hospital. According to Dale, Margaret was obviously high. Dale wasn't sure what to do. She called Phil Kaufman. "I woke him up, told him we had a dead body on our hands, and that I believed it was one of his," she says. "Also that there was a man standing next to me with a dark blue uniform on who would like to know what the hell was going on."

Dale passed the phone to Margaret Fisher. "He was upset. He yelled at me for letting Gram do smack," Margaret says. "But he didn't tell me not to, you know?"

Crisis, however personal, was Kaufman's element. He knew what to do. He spoke to the cops, promising to clear up everything as soon as he got there. The police agreed to allow the two women to go back to the Inn until Kaufman arrived.

Kathy Fenton remembers getting Dale's call at midnight. Gram's body arrived at the hospital at 12:15 A.M., so the call probably came at closer to 12:30 A.M. "I answered the phone and Dale wouldn't talk to me," Kathy says. "I said, 'What's the matter?' and she said, 'I need to speak to Phil.' I gave him the phone and he listened and said, 'Are you sure? Are you positive?' He hung up the phone and said, 'Get dressed—we're going to Palm Springs.' I said, 'What happened?' He said, 'Gram's dead.'"

One of the cops told Margaret that she looked "pretty stoned." She answered, "I've watched a boy die. I guess I do look stoned or in shock, as the case may be." The police let her go.

"Walking out of the hospital, going into that cool air, all I could think of was that nothing is ever going to be the same," Margaret says. "Nothing in my whole life is ever going to be the same. This is an event that changes everything. This radically changes everything. Everything I know, everything I believe, everything, it's gone."

Somehow Margaret got back to the Joshua Tree Inn. She had the presence of mind to realize that the cops would be there shortly. "The first thing I did was go through the room and gather up every single pill bottle I possibly could, five or six, various stuff. I didn't even look at them. I started out the door and thought, 'I can't stand this. I can't do this.' I opened them and took two of everything. Then I went out and threw the rest in the desert. I buried the bottles in the sand."

She returned to Room 8. The rooms at the Inn are tiny, cinderblock squares with small windows. They offer little comfort in the best of times. Gram's clothes were scattered around.

"Everybody went to bed and left me alone," Margaret says. "I curled up there and felt so bad. I wanted to be unconscious. I don't think I wanted to die. That did not consciously materialize in my mind. On the other hand, I took a great many pills for somebody that was planning on living. By the time Phil got there, I was out of it."

"It's a two-hour trip down," Kathy Fenton says, "and in my Volkswagen van it was probably a two-and-a-half-hour trip because it was not a little speedster." Kathy didn't think either she or Phil slept on the way down. They were up all night, in and out of the motel room. "By the time we got the hotel room cleaned up," she says, "I'm sure it was five A.M., maybe six A.M."

"We were in shock," Kathy says. "Absolute shock. I'm good in emergency situations. I don't fall apart. Phil is the same way. It's like we are both on automatic pilot. There are certain things that we have to take care of and then we can take care of ourselves and our grief. Dale was in shock, and Margaret was probably hysterical. Dale was like a deer in headlights. She was the only responsible person there, so I know it weighed heavily on her."

Margaret is definite that she threw all the drugs out in the desert before

Phil arrived. Phil's story is that Margaret and Dale together went through the room and gave Phil the gathered stash. Phil says he took charge of cleaning up Gram's room and disposing of his pills. The irony that he was still hiding Gram's drugs didn't escape him.

If Margaret's is the definitive account of Gram's last night, Phil Kaufman has the last word on the morning after. Kaufman became famous for his role in the aftermath of Gram's death and has been living on that reputation ever since. In *Road Mangler*, Kaufman presents himself as he prefers to be seen: a tough-ass, nothing-sacred, seen-it-all mercenary.

Like Margaret Fisher, Kaufman has no other witnesses for much of what he did, and his account, whatever its flaws, has become the primary narrative. Kaufman's version was not published until twenty years after the fact, and it has the air of an oft-told barroom tale.

Kaufman worked the phones from the hospital. He wanted access to Gram's car before the cops opened it and found what Kaufman presumed would be more drugs. Kaufman didn't know whether there was heroin in the Jaguar.

"Philip had to go to the hospital and identify the body to make sure it was Gram," Kathy says. "We identified the body and made arrangements to transport his body up [to Los Angeles]. Philip first called Eddie [Tickner], and Eddie probably called [Bob] Parsons.

"The coroner's report said Gram died of a heart attack, but the hospital report said that he died of the alcohol content in his body. And I don't care what anybody says, I saw that report! And that's what the report said! Gram died of a combination of the alcohol and the morphine, but it was the alcohol content that killed him. It was not the amount of morphine in his body."

The autopsy does not attribute Gram's death to a morphine overdose. It found a significant amount of morphine in his body, but not enough to kill him. The cause of death is listed as: "Drug toxicity, days, due to multiple drug use, weeks." Morphine was the trigger, but Gram's death seems to have resulted from the long-term effects of Gram's drinking and pills.

One rumor has it that in the weeks prior to his death Gram had been diagnosed with heart problems. His bloated face and body have been described as resulting from medicine he took for his heart. But liver failure would cause bloating as well. No solid evidence of heart trouble ever emerged, and the coroner did not cite heart disease as a factor.

"I remember us getting Gram's car and getting the girls out of there," Kathy says. "Philip is such a fast talker. He could literally sell ice to an

Eskimo. He did some really fast talking. We had to do everything fast . . . get down there, take care of everything quickly, and put it in a box with a bow."

The police were looking for "two girls." Kaufman promised to bring the women in for questioning that afternoon. Instead, Kaufman drove Dale and Margaret straight to Los Angeles.

"Phil saved my ass in Joshua Tree," Margaret says. "The police said they wanted to talk to me down at the station. Philip said, 'Fine, soon as I get her breakfast I'll bring her down.' And he took me right back to L.A."

Confusion remains about how Gram's car got back to Los Angeles. The logical choice to drive it would have been Dale McElroy. But she remembers being whisked back to L.A. in Kathy's VW van.

"On the way back Philip was quizzing one of the girls," Kathy says. "I don't remember who-all was in my car. Someone drove Gram's car back. Maybe it was Dale. Maybe Gretchen went down and picked it up. I don't know.

"I don't remember the conversation coming back in the car. I was on automatic pilot and in shock. I'm sure Philip got tons of information and quizzed them up and down. I know he called Bruce Wolfe, our attorney and friend, and let him know what was going on."

"I was stoned. I was fucked-up. If I could talk I was probably slurring my words heavily," Margaret says. "Phil told me if he found out who the connection was he was going to kill him. That's all I needed, for him to go kill some chick. You can't blame the connection."

Kaufman wrote in his book that he believed the source of the morphine was the ex-wife of musician Scott McKenzie, the former Journeyman famous for the hit "San Francisco (Be Sure to Wear Flowers in Your Hair)." Kaufman thought McKenzie's ex was living near Joshua Tree at the time of Gram's death. Kaufman searched for her with revenge in his heart. Whether or not she was the connection, Kaufman never found her.

"I went to Philip's house and there were all these people," Margaret says. "I couldn't tell you who any of them were. I went to bed. I didn't know Philip. I'd been camping with him and his girlfriend and Gram once, but I didn't know them. I had given up trusting in a beneficent world. That was gone.

"When I woke up Philip put me on a plane for San Francisco. I flew back and went to bed."

ROBERT PARSONS MADE funeral arrangements without consulting Kaufman or Gretchen. He let Gram's friends know that the funeral would be in New Orleans. He made it clear that none of them was welcome.

"I know he tried very, very hard to get his body home and to have a decent burial for him," Bob's close friend Walter Lanaux says. "The rites of passage were something he was interested in doing the correct way."

"A bunch of us were sitting around the table after Gram died," Kathy Fenton says. "Phil found out that they were going to pick up Gram's body at LAX [the Los Angeles airport] and send it to New Orleans. Philip said, 'You know, Gram would hate that. He would absolutely hate that.'"

"Gram didn't want to go back to his stepfather, Bob Parsons, who was a bad guy," Kaufman says. "Gram used to refer to Bob Parsons as an 'alligator-shoe and pinkie-ring from New Orleans.'"

"We were all pissed off because the Parsons family were going to fly Gram's body by private plane to New Orleans and have a private ceremony with only the family and none of the friends," Kathy says. "They were going to have a closed little funeral service."

Kaufman felt bad. He had failed to protect Gram from himself. "I was sitting around the house playing shudda," Kaufman says. "*I shudda done this, I shudda done that* . . . and Kathy said, 'Well, shut your fucking mouth. Do it or shut up.' I said, 'You're right, toots.'"

"Somebody said, 'We can't let that happen," Kathy says. "Philip, you should go get him. Carry out his wishes! We promised! We made a pact!' They were loaded. They'd been drinking vodka and beer."

Kaufman called Dale McElroy; he told her he needed the hearse and Michael Martin to help drive. He told Martin they were going to snatch Gram's body. He spoke with the funeral home in Yucca Valley. Though suspicious, they confirmed to Kaufman that Gram's body would be leaving from LAX. He called Continental Mortuary Air Service and learned that the coffin would arrive from Yucca Valley at eight o'clock that evening.

"Philip goes into the bedroom and puts on this suit, a charcoal-gray pinstripe suit," Kathy says. "He looked ridiculous. He came out of the room all proud of himself and said, 'How do I look? I'm going to go pick up a coffin.' I said, 'You look ridiculous! You look unbelievable. Go put something else on!' So he went back and put his regular clothes on. He put his straw cowboy hat on, his cowboy boots, his Levi's, a T-shirt, and his Levi jacket.

"I'm sure they had a few little shots of whatever was around the house. He wasn't out of his mind drunk when they went to LAX, but he had a little nip. I don't remember us sitting around drinking, talking about it. Philip had one shot to get up the nerve. I know that he stopped at a liquor store and got a fifth of something, maybe scotch."

Michael Martin picked up Kaufman in McElroy's cherry-red hearse and drove to the loading station at Continental Mortuary. Kaufman warned Michael that he would do whatever was necessary to get Gram's body, including violence. As Kaufman climbed out of the hearse, a truck appeared with a coffin in the back. Kaufman confirmed with the driver that the coffin was "the Parsons remains." Kaufman told the driver the Parsons family had changed their plans and wanted the body flown out by private plane from Van Nuys Airport. They balked and Kaufman said, "Look, it's late in the night. We've got a couple of girls lined up and then we got this call. We want to do this quickly."

The driver agreed, offering to retrieve the necessary forms. Kaufman stood in the office putting a fake name—"Jeremy Nobody"—on the paperwork. A police car drove up.

"Just as they were about to get the coffin into the hearse a cop pulls up and blocks Philip's car," Kathy says. "Philip is sweating bullets. He tries to play it cool and says, 'Hey, buddy, help me get this coffin into the hearse. We're trying to get it to Burbank and the plane is leaving in twenty minutes.' The cop says, 'Oh, sure!' and helps Phil load the coffin into the back of the hearse. And off go Philip and Michael!"

The story of the helpful policeman fits a little too handily into the moronic-cop archetype of the off-the-pigs early seventies. Would any policeman in that time and place help any longhair with a load-out, never mind a full coffin? We have only Kaufman's word that it happened, and his version evokes Cheech and Chong.

As Michael Martin nervously pulled away with Gram's coffin in the back, he banged the hearse along the wall of Continental's hangar. Michael, Kaufman, and the cop all took a good look at the crumpled bodywork. The cop, unfazed, left without asking for license and registration or noticing that Michael and Kaufman were drunk, high, and practically vibrating with adrenaline.

Kaufman took the wheel from Michael and, after leaving the airport, stopped at a filling station to load up a jerry can with gas.

"They head off toward Joshua Tree," Kathy says, "and Philip calls me to let me know they had been successful in their mission. We had a code word, which was *ten*. Whatever you were doing, when you said the word *ten* it meant that you were doing the opposite. So he called and said, 'I've got my pal. We're headed north to San Francisco on 10.' Everyone knows that [Highway] 10 does not go to San Francisco, so I knew he wasn't going to

San Francisco because he was on ten. I knew he was going to Joshua Tree. That was the plan."

Kaufman and Martin drove out into the desert, singing and drinking. They played the radio as they drove into Cabazon, a desert town en route to Joshua Tree. They stopped to get a hamburger and more beer. When asked what they had in the car, Kaufman said that he answered, "Oh, some lucky stiff."

While Kaufman and Martin were on the road, Gretchen's father, Larry Burrell, showed up at Kaufman's house with the police. He had somehow learned that Gram's body never made it onto the plane. "Larry Burrell came knocking at my door with three or four cops at twelve-thirty at night," Kathy says. "Banging on the door. 'Open up! Open up! Kathy, it's Larry Burrell! Open up right now.' I looked out and there were three or four uniformed cops, Larry in a suit, and a detective in a suit. I didn't open the door. I called our attorney, Bruce Wolfe. He asked me one question: 'Do you have the body there?' I said no.

"Bruce told me to open the door and call if I needed him. I opened the door and they barreled into the house. They said, 'We're looking for Gram!' and I blanched. It freaked me out. I said, 'He's dead! Don't you know?' They said, 'We're going to search the house.' They must have [had a search warrant], because when I talked to Bruce he said, 'Let them look anywhere that is big enough to hide a body.' Thank God, because we had pot in the house, but I had hidden it well. They started looking around and I slammed a drawer closed in the kitchen, saying, 'You can't look there.' They said, 'We have a search warrant—we can look anywhere.' I told them, 'My attorney says you can only look in places big enough to hold a body.' They looked in the guesthouse where Gram had been living. They looked in the basement. They looked in all the closets . . . everywhere. I said, 'Hey, he's not here! Don't you know he's dead?'"

After finishing their burgers, Kaufman and Martin drove through the desert darkness. They passed the Joshua Tree Inn and, a couple miles down the road, turned into the Joshua Tree Monument—the national park. They wound around the pitch-black roads until Kaufman called a halt. It turned out they were near Cap Rock, a place the Joshua Tree LSD set maintained had a special vibratory power. Kaufman later wrote that he had no higher purpose in mind when he stopped there. He insists they were too drunk to keep driving. And that the parking lot allowed a quick escape.

Kaufman pulled the coffin toward him out the door at the back of the hearse. Together he and Martin lowered the front end until it rested on the dirt. Martin dragged the front of the coffin forward and the back end slid off the hearse and hit the ground with a crash. Kaufman reports that they both said, "Sorry, Gram."

In the middle of the desert in the middle of the night, with a stolen body at his feet, Martin was becoming increasingly nervous. He urged Kaufman to set the coffin on fire. He was horrified when Kaufman insisted on opening the lid. Inside, Gram lay naked, mutilated. His chest had been opened for the autopsy and was held together with surgical tape. According to his own account, Kaufman made a joke about the size of Gram's penis, then played "gotcha" with the corpse, pointing at Gram's wounded chest and then flicking his finger upward to Gram's nose. Kaufman's presentation of his own drunken antics with Gram's mutilated body brings the pang of a different grief: Did Gram have no one better to look after his interests than Philip Kaufman?

Car lights appeared in the distance. Fearing the lights might be the park police, Kaufman picked up the jerry can, poured gasoline over Gram's body, and threw in a match. The pooled gasoline in the casket ignited with a loud *whoosh* and a ball of flame lifted out of the coffin and rose into the sky. Kaufman and Martin watched Gram's corpse bubble as it burned.

Kaufman wrote that, in the intensity of the fire, Gram ceased to be Gram after only a moment. His identity melted away with his body. "He was very dead and very burned," Kaufman said. "There wasn't much left to recognize."

A dust devil rose out of the coffin, borne on the heat and rising flames. As Gram's ashes rose, Kaufman congratulated himself on fulfilling the promise he'd made—that Gram's ashes would be scattered in Joshua Tree.

Kaufman was admirably capable of bravado—of marching in and stealing Gram's body. But he has given no sign that he understood the implications of his actions. He's proven incapable of describing them as anything but a drunken, drug-soaked lark. Kaufman's narrative, in all its ugliness and crudity, tainted the memory of Gram's death for everyone who loved him.

The headlights were drawing nearer. Gram's bubbling flesh shot flames and gray smoke into the desert sky. Fearful of the cops, Kaufman and Martin slammed the back door of the hearse, jumped in, and raced away on the dusty road. The hearse left behind darkness and Gram's body blazing, alone.

When Lord Byron attended the seaside cremation of his friend and fellow poet Percy Bysshe Shelley in 1822, he gazed into the pyre and was astonished to see that Shelley's heart remained intact amid the flames. Martin and Kaufman were too drunk and stoned, and drove off too quickly, to record whether Gram Parsons' heart likewise refused to burn.

TWENTY-THREE
THE FUNERAL

PHIL AND MICHAEL RETURNED TO LOS ANGELES VIA A BACK ROUTE ALONG Big Bear Mountain. Kaufman remembers being too drunk to drive. He pulled over. He and Martin dozed through the night in the back of the hearse. In the morning the hearse was stuck in the sand. Michael went for a tow truck. He and Kaufman drank warm beer as the truck hauled the hearse free. With the hearse back on the road, they bought more beer and headed home.

When Kaufman later told the story to *Melody Maker* magazine, he claimed that forest rangers hurried to the spot when they saw the fireball created by Gram's burning corpse. "They chased us," he said, "but were encumbered by sobriety." This contradicts Kaufman's description of events in his 1993 book. Gram biographer Rick Cusick, who cited the *Melody Maker* interview, also wrote that a patrol helicopter that night "reported a black vehicle 'swerving away from the scene at high speed.'" Could the copter tell red from black at night? Or had someone else come by, seen a burning body, and driven away as fast as they could?

Gram's body was officially discovered at ten-thirty A.M. on Friday,

September 21. Campers reported a "burning log" near Cap Rock. All that remained of Gram Parsons was a smoking pile of charcoal and ash.

Bob Parsons, ill and walking with difficulty, flew to Los Angeles to reclaim what was left of his stepson and take the remains back to New Orleans for burial. He was disgusted by what had been done to Gram. "Bob tried to understand the environment Gram was living in, who his friends were," Walter Lanaux says. "They were all whacked-out, probably. Bob had no hatred in his heart for them. He thought they were wastrels and a bunch of idiots."

"I was absolutely fine with it because I knew that's what Gram wanted, so I didn't feel bad about it afterwards," Kathy Fenton says. "I was proud that we had done that. We kept that promise, and even though he had broken a promise to me"—his promise to stop using heroin—"we weren't breaking a promise to him."

Kaufman's stealing and burning Gram's body is a cornerstone of the Gram myth. People who have never heard a note of Gram's music know the story of the theft and immolation. "Phil Kaufman made Gram a star by burning him at Joshua Tree," Jimmi Seiter says. "Phil Kaufman wasn't Gram's manager. But Phil would have you believe that he was everything. The only thing Kaufman did was make Gram a household name."

"Once you're dead, you're dead," Billy Briggs says. "It's too bad all that happened, but it doesn't have a whole lot to do with Gram. He didn't have a whole lot to do with it—he was dead. It's a great story and all that, but I don't know how much it has to do with his life."

The context of the tale has remained as Kaufman told it. Kaufman was not only fulfilling a pact he'd made with Gram, but also keeping Gram's body and his wealth out of the clutches of Bob Parsons.

Gretchen Parsons and Little Avis later asserted that due to the eccentricities of Louisiana's Napoleonic Code, Bob Parsons would be in a stronger position to make a claim for Gram's estate if Gram's body were buried in Louisiana. Those assertions are mistaken. The location of Gram's body had no effect on any litigation Bob might pursue. Given that Gram was married, Bob Parsons had no standing.

Years before, the Snivelys whispered that Bob Parsons' adoption of Gram and Little Avis was financially motivated. Once again, no one trusted Bob's motives. The facts indicate that Bob's only desire was to do right by his dead stepson.

Despite the continued ill will between Bob Parsons and the Snivelys, both sides of the family were shocked by the desecration of Gram's body. They regarded it—and still do—as a heinous, self-serving, drug-fueled publicity stunt, one that robbed Gram's death of dignity and still pollutes their grief. They resent that Kaufman has constructed a legend starring himself as Gram's above-and-beyond friend.

Gram's service in New Orleans was a small family funeral. It took place at the Bultman Funeral Home on St. Charles Avenue, near Robert and Bonnie Parsons' home. Among those present were Aunt May Snively, Coon Dog's brother, Tom Connor, and sister, Pauline Wilkes, and Little Avis and her husband, Robert "Beau" Johnson. Gretchen was there with a friend, the singer and former Ikette Claudia Lennear. Nancy Ross and Polly Parsons did not attend.

"There was such a rift between all of [Gram's] guys back in California and the New Orleans contingent," Bonnie Parsons says. "It was mostly family and good friends. I can't remember if anyone came from Florida. It was a rough time. I was dealing with Gram's death badly and Bob was so sick. He was walking at a list. He was leaning wherever his liver was going. And he was still drinking."

"Why didn't Gram get buried in Winter Haven? What the hell did he have in Winter Haven?" Becky Gottsegen says. "Bob Parsons was not an interloper in their lives. Bob Parsons was a father to [Gram]."

"I called New Orleans, of course," Gram's childhood friend Jim Carlton says. "It was so similar to when Avis died. Bob was taking it all in stride, kind of matter of fact. I think Bob was trying to come to grips with his own life. I think he was trying to make his own way the best he could."

Gram was buried under a tiny plaque at Memorial Lawn Cemetery. "Bob and Gram are in separate cemeteries," Bonnie Parsons says. "I don't know how Bob picked Gram's. Gram's out in the country, in a pretty spot with a big tree. Maybe that's the way he'd like it."

Another knock against Bob Parsons, and a source of ironic amusement, is that he chose the encircling ring around Gram's tiny flush-mounted headstone that reads GOD'S OWN SINGER. Supposedly Bob, not knowing that "God's Own Singer" was written by Bernie Leadon, mistook it for a composition of Gram's and thus the perfect epitaph.

This part of the legend is questionable, too. There's no clear evidence of who placed the ring around Gram's stone. Lynyrd Skynyrd biographer Marley Brant, who coproduced *Gram Parsons and the Fallen Angels Live 1973*, asserts that she is responsible for the second encircling ring. She visited Gram's grave and found the tiny original marker inappropriately small and lacking in resonance. She knew full well that "God's Own Singer" was written by Leadon, but she was moved by the lyric "God's own singer of songs / Is going home."

The Snivelys' animus against Bob Parsons and his lifelong reputation as a hustler made Bob a convenient scapegoat for Gretchen as well. Her accusations about Bob's grasping distracted attention from her own actions. Gram died without a will. On September 20, the day after his death, Gretchen went to court to begin probate proceedings. As his wife, she sought control over Gram's estate.

"Gretchen opened Gram's succession in Los Angeles on September 20, when Gram's body was barely cold," a Snively family member says. "If there were ever statements made about someone moving fast to make sure they laid claim to Gram's estate, I think this makes it pretty obvious where that blame should lie."

The family member's terminology isn't precise. Succession refers to the order of inheritance when the deceased leaves no will. The spouse comes first, then children, then parents, and so on. Gram never prepared any document regarding his estate. Gretchen legally declared herself the surviving spouse, which she was.

"Therefore, by Gretchen going to court in Los Angeles the day after Gram's death and filing a petition opening his succession," the family member says, "she laid immediate claim to the most important role in controlling the distribution of his estate. She knew divorce was in the works, but no divorce documents had been filed. Legally, Gretchen was the surviving spouse."

According to court documents: "Following Parsons' death intestate [meaning that Gram died without a will], probate proceedings were opened on September 20, 1973, in the Los Angeles Superior Court. Parsons was survived by his wife, Gretchen Parsons, and his daughter from a prior marriage, Polly Parsons. Gretchen Parsons was appointed administrator of his estate."

Gram owned a house in California. He and Gretchen were still legally married when he died. She was therefore able to ask the probate court to put her in charge of his worldly goods. Robert Parsons might have administered part of Gram and Little Avis' trust, but everything else was in Gretchen's hands.

That couldn't have amounted to much. The Snivelys had fallen on hard times, Gram was burning through his trust and had seen only one royalty check in his lifetime. Gretchen would gain the house, their property, and any future money from Gram's music. Others might have preferred that Gretchen wait—given that the marriage no longer existed except on paper—but declaring herself the surviving spouse was entirely pro forma. The speed with which Gretchen moved has been regarded as unseemly and lacking in common hypocrisy, but nothing she did was underhanded or untoward.

KAUFMAN, AND MARTIN returned to Los Angeles on Monday, September 24. Three days later a film crew for the Arthur Penn film noir *Night Moves* began location shooting at Kaufman's house.

On September 26 the cops arrived to arrest Kaufman. He wasn't home. The policemen working as location cops on the *Night Moves* shoot found Kathy Fenton and told her. "I said, 'He's not here,'" Kathy remembers. "I went out and had a little chat with them. I said, 'I don't know where Phil is, but I think I can find him. If you give me a few minutes I will call him and let him know that you're here and I'll let you know what he's going to do.' The policeman said, 'When you contact him, tell him we will respect his space and not cause a scene, but if he starts playing any monkey business . . .'

"I called Philip and said, 'There are cops here and they want to arrest you. What do you want me to tell them?' He said, 'Tell them I'll be right there, but please respect the fact that Warner Brothers is shooting at our house. And not cause a scene.' I told him, 'They've already promised that if you come in peacefully they will not.' So he said, 'Okay, I will be there in about ten minutes.'"

"Phil called me while the police were coming," Margaret Fisher says. "I said, 'Fine, Phil.' I'd heard him make the promise [to burn Gram's body]—it was okay with me. Philip sounded a little hysterical, but I didn't doubt he'd done it."

"Phil drove up to the house and parked his car on the street," Kathy says. "He walked over and said, 'Hello, I'm Phil Kaufman. I understand you're looking for me. I understand you would like to arrest me and throw my ass in jail.' They said, 'Yes, we do!' So they handcuffed him [and] arrested him."

Kaufman maintains he was charged with stealing a coffin. He also claimed a cop said, "We had the damnedest time trying to figure out what to charge you with." Kaufman claims that one of the policemen joked that he was being charged with "Gram Theft Parsons." Such a perfect line in the mouth of a stranger seems suspicously convenient.

"Arthur Penn came up to me and he put his arm around me and he said, 'I have a feeling I'm directing the wrong movie,'" Kathy says.

Michael Martin turned himself in the following day.

On what would have been Gram's twenty-seventh birthday, Phil Kaufman and Michael Martin appeared in West Los Angeles Municipal Court. Both pleaded guilty to misdemeanor theft. They were fined three hundred dollars apiece, plus a $708 fee to the funeral home to replace the casket. According to Kathy Fenton, Kaufman also had to promise not to steal another body. Dale McElroy paid both fines and settled the casket fee. Kaufman's attorney, Bruce Wolfe, did not charge for his services. Neither did Harry Fradkin, Kaufman and Gram's favorite bail bondsman, whose motto went: "Don't wait in jail, call Harry for bail."

Kaufman was out of work and out of money. He and Martin threw a benefit for themselves in Kaufman's backyard. Kaufman and his neighbor, Al Swerdloff, designed custom labels for beer cans and T-shirts that read GRAM PILSNER: A STIFF DRINK FOR WHAT ALES YOU. The label featured a drawing of Gram looking far thinner than he had at the time of his death. DJ'ing was Dr. Demento, the soon-to-be-famous radio personality. The headlining act was Bobby "Boris" Pickett, the former leader of the Crypt Kicker 5, who was famous for the one-off hit "The Monster Mash." Also on the bill were Eddie Tickner's protopunk clients the Modern Lovers. (It's hard to imagine what those L.A. cowboys made of "Pablo Picasso" or "Road Runner.") A sign over the stage read, KA KA CONCERTS KAUFMAN'S KOFFIN KAPER CONCERT THANKS FOR COMING.

"I sold T-shirts. We had a bunch of them made up and charged money to get in," Kathy Fenton says. "The T-shirts were ten dollars. We made quite a bit of money. Everybody was there. Hundreds of people. The whole backyard was crowded with people, and the whole front yard. There were people in and out of the house. Many of the people that Gram had worked with." Kaufman maintains that Nudie showed up and gave him five hundred dollars.

"Emmylou wasn't [at the party]. She was on the East Coast," Kathy says. "She was too shocked. I think Philip recouped all the money he spent to buy the beer and make the T-shirts and stuff. I don't think he made a profit."

The day after Kaufman's arrest, *The Village Voice*, in New York City, ran an article headlined GRAM PARSONS DIES IN DESERT. The article described the theft and burning of Gram's body without identifying the perpetrators. "Authorities [seek] a battered black hearse . . . seen weaving . . . near . . . the funeral pyre," it reported. The story noted Gram's work with the International Submarine Band, the Byrds, and the Flying Burrito Brothers, then continued, "Cause of death has not been released, but people who knew Parsons presume it to have been due to an overdose. He was known to have been deeply involved with drugs, especially during his association with the Stones."

The *Voice* piece was the bell ringer for Gram's death. It told everyone outside of L.A. that Gram was dead.

"He wasn't planning what year to do a Hank Williams," Chris Hillman later said, "but it was a matter of time. With certain people, you figure there is nothing you can do. For that reason, it was more upsetting to lose Clarence White than Gram."

"He was my mate, and I wish he'd remained my mate for a lot longer," Keith Richards says. "It's not often that you can lie around on a bed with a guy doing cold turkey, in tandem, and still get along."

"Gram was a romantic," Bernie Leadon says. "He set out to become legendary by dying young. He saw that it worked for James Dean and Hank Williams. I think he thought it was a great idea, to live a tragically excessive life, die a tragic hero, and become immortal. And he pulled it off."

"He was a good Southern boy, loved to rock and roll, sad all the time," Chris Ethridge says. "He wanted to go out like Hank Williams, and he did. He rock and rolled out, and it was his fault."

"He was pretty far gone when I last saw him," Billy Briggs says. "He progressed after that to a stupor which killed him. It was too bad."

Jim Carlton remembers, "I was in Orlando and opened the paper. It said, BURNED BODY MAY BE SINGER. I immediately knew it was Gram. Instinctively, I knew it. Before I read the first word of copy. Because I said, This was the way he would do it. He would go out with a flair."

"He wanted to go out in a great flash of glory rather than fading away," Little Avis told an interviewer. "Look how beautifully he got himself together for that last album. Son of a bitch. I'm really pissed at him."

"I was living in Athens and Vickie Allen contacted me," Gram's childhood friend Dickey Smith says. "I was not surprised, but my first thought was, What a waste. I wondered what he could have been. It was a plain waste."

"The child was so pitiful to me," his aunt, Pauline Wilkes, says. "I mean the ending. To me, it's just sad to die from an overdose of drugs."

"When Gram died, I felt like I'd been amputated, like my life had been whacked off," Emmylou Harris says. "I'd only been with him a short time, but it was like everything had become clear to me in that short period."

On Oct. 23, 1973, *Rolling Stone* ran Eve Babitz' obituary of Gram Parsons. Babitz, the keenest observer of the Sunset Strip life, captured the enduring view of Gram with love and tenderness and just the right amount of mythology:

> Gram was a complicated Christian, an artist who bore . . . the magic seeds of the best and worst of our generation. . . . the fucked-up young lord zig-zagging . . . from purity to debauchery. . . . [P]eople like Gram don't last; [they] light their candles at both ends and sweep out the ashes in the morning.

Grievous Angel was released in January 1974. Gram had intended that he and Emmylou receive equal billing on the album jacket. He'd had a cover photo taken of him straddling Phil Kaufman's Harley, with Emmylou sitting behind. Gretchen Parsons and her father, Larry Burrell, objected. Emmylou's name was dropped. The cover photo that Gretchen approved was a headshot of an overweight, puzzled-looking Gram against a blue background.

Grievous Angel charted at a disappointing number 195. Gram's vision no longer needed explaining to critics, however. The album was reviewed generously. In part that was because Gram had died, suddenly and young. But Gram was also beginning to get his due.

"Gram Parsons had a vision of fusing all forms of American roots music," Tom Russell wrote in *Helix*. "His influence on bringing country music to rock and roll is as important as Bob Dylan's combining folk lyrics with rock."

"Both *GP* and *Grievous Angel* need no analysis," Allan Jones wrote in *Melody Maker*. "There are no words to describe the sense of desperation and the haunting quality of these last works. They just need to be listened to. 'Love Hurts' is a statement of pure pain. You can feel your nerve endings singing along to it. It's the same with 'Brass Buttons,' one of Gram's most tortured love songs. 'In My Hour of Darkness' says it all. Trapped beneath skies of uneasy dreams, maybe his death made some kind of sense. Perhaps he finally found a way out."

"Both of these albums justify the validity of Gram Parsons' contribution to the field of country music," journalist John Firminger wrote. "Gram Parsons is as important to country music as Jimmie Rodgers, Bob Wills, and Hank Williams."

Grievous Angel is not as strong an album overall as *GP.* The powerful cuts on it, though, are among the best of Gram's songs. The two LPs were released together as a CD two-fer in 1990. Since then the two records have merged into one for most listeners. But they were recorded at different times, under different circumstances, and are markedly different works.

Grievous Angel's first cut and title track establishes the tone and themes of the record. "Return of the Grievous Angel" is credited to Gram and Thomas Brown, the poet who approached Gram at the Fallen Angels show in Boston. The lyrics are almost entirely Brown's, but he was not credited for the song until 1976. Eddie Tickner believes that Brown's name was lost in the Laurel Canyon house fire.

The song is a saga of America, a road song, a poetic expression of the Beat ideal of discovering America through the window of a moving car. Brown's lyrics present a series of American journeys or mythological touchstones to which Americans have always traveled, either on the ground or in their imaginations.

Gram speak-sings the intro directly to the listener over a basic country arrangement. He's in fine, expressive voice, holding his notes and giving Emmylou a strong platform for harmonizing. He sounds happy and present; he gives a shout-out to James Burton as the guitarist launches a solo. Lyrically the song is a departure. It celebrates pleasures that are not sins and embraces a redemption attainable here on earth. In this narrative, experience nourishes the singer, giving him hope and convincing him that a place known as home exists, that there is a destination worth traveling to.

It's a remarkable performance by Gram, given that the song doesn't end in heartbreak, confession, or death. As Gram taught Emmylou, he keeps the emotion tamped down. Pathos rings out in the most unexpected places:

And the man on the radio won't leave me alone
He wants to take my money for something that I've never been shown

Gram sings these lines as if the fate of the world hangs in the balance. His performance is so unlikely yet so fitting, attuned to the deepest nuance of the poetry. The swindle, Gram's emphasis suggests, lurks at the heart of the American dream. By opening with the archetypal search for his and America's soul, Gram announces that *Grievous Angel* will address the themes of place, home, and identity.

"Hearts on Fire" is a song about love's brutal aftermath, written by Emmylou's boyfriend, Tom Guidera, and Walter Egan. Egan, a New York singer-songwriter, is best known for his 1978 platinum single, "Magnet and Steel."

Gram sounds weakened, like he's feeling his way through. He and Emmylou harmonize on every line. The blame of betrayal gets placed on both parties in the love affair. Each accuses the other of being untrue, of being the heartbreaker. Both recognize that the stakes are high:

> *Please take this heart of mine*
> *'Cause if you don't, the devil will*

The unbearable country heartache of Gram and Emmylou together becomes something more nihilistic, even more hopeless. No matter how entwined their voices, and thus their hearts, neither can find a way to forgive or to take the blame. Both yearn to reconnect; neither can. Coming on the heels of the redemptive "Grievous Angel," "Hearts" presents Gram's constant dilemma: how to break through the pain and accept love.

"I Can't Dance," by Tom T. Hall, was recommended by Barry Tashian. Hall's a lifelong Nashville hit-writing machine. He crafted seven number one singles, including "A Week in the County Jail" (1970), "The Year That Clayton Delaney Died" (1971), and "Old Dogs, Children, and Watermelon Wine" (1973). Gram's version is a ditty, with what sure sounds like Leon Russell on piano. The beat chugs and the piano provides rhythmic drive, but Gram's straight-up rockers never quite rock. That classic 4/4 beat is not Gram's thing. It's live as can be, with Gram hollering in the background over the guitar solos. Gram and Emmylou's voices form an unearthly union. Gram sounds neither high nor disengaged: He's having fun.

"$1000 Wedding" is all Gram's, words and music. This combination of Louvin Brothers doom and Gram's astonishingly dense, allusive, and literary storytelling suggests the sort of work he might have produced had he lived. It's a merciless, heart-wrenching story, worthy of the Louvin Brothers at their Old Testament–retribution grimmest. Gram almost speaks certain passages, his voice more than strong enough to bear his mournful enunciation. The structure is cinematic. A sung/spoken intro sets the scene, a bursting chorus with powerful drums carries us into the worst of the news, and the slowly sung words return. The structure repeats, invoking church-music dynamics: soft and spoken, then booming and sung in chorus.

On the day of a marriage, the bride "went away." Gram never specifies that she dies. He refuses to give us all the details, details the Louvins would have reveled in. Gram was taking a specific country storytelling tradition to the next level, a level of linguistic and narrative sophistication that no one has matched since. As with "Return of the Grievous Angel," the most moving lyrics do not contain any overtly tragic lines. The emotion derives from Gram's vocal intensity, the building arrangement, and what each line means to those that come before and after. No single couplet or verse strikes harder than another. The power of the songwriting resides in the whole.

Gram's vocals are firmly in the Bakersfield tradition he loved so. There's not a trace of folk music or rock and roll in the songwriting or structure. The song is not immediately identifiable as pure country. It's something new, richer, more complex, heretofore unseen, yet recognizable. In "Wedding" Gram embraced his own intelligence as a writer, singing as powerfully as he could around a band behind him every step—a band that clearly believes in his vision. For one blessed moment, Gram neither got in his own way nor sang of his own problems. He brings all his sensitivity to bear on the trials of another—an other that Gram invented. "Wedding" remains a breakthrough for Gram and a breakthrough in music.

"Medley Live from Northern Quebec" combines Ira and Charlie Louvin's "Cash on the Barrelhead" with Gram's own "Hickory Wind." This is a curiosity, one of Gram's smirking in-jokes that might have been better served by a straight-ahead presentation. Gram cut the song as a fake live recording with fake applause, fake concert ambience, and fake background hubbub. The songs make an awkward medley. "Cash," because it is a Louvin Brothers song, addresses the payment of some horrible dues. Here the dues are more manageable; they involve buying train tickets, coughing up the rent, and the like. The recurrent message aligns with all other Louvin Brothers songs: The universe and its guardians don't give a shit about your problems, so pay up. The slowdown into "Hickory Wind," a song dear to Gram's heart, seems inappropriate and reductive. Maybe Gram felt embarrassed by too much sincerity.

"Love Hurts" is arranged more like an Everly Brothers song than any other Gram recording. It was written by Boudleaux Bryant and his wife, Felice, who wrote "Bye Bye Love" and "Wake Up Little Susie" for the Everlys and who were inducted into the Country Music Hall of Fame in 1991. The band is mixed in the background for the early verses, save Al Perkins on the steel. As the bridge ascends, Gram and Emmylou's voices rise in the mix.

Added to their high lonesome is a lovely high whine, a mourning, keening reach for the suffering in the song. Neither overdoes it—they feel the pain, they show it to us, they make us feel every bit, but never go too far. Their sustain on the final "love hurts" demonstrates how they'd come together in emotion and technique. The Everlys, the Louvins, the Delmores, George Jones and Tammy Wynette: These are the benchmarks of country harmony. Gram studied them, and in the finest moments of *Grievous Angel* he and Emmylou equal them all.

The album ends with a prayer-cum-prophecy, "In My Hour of Darkness." The only song on the record cowritten by Gram and Emmylou Harris, it's an old-time white gospel plea for strength at one's weakest moment. The song is Gram's mourning for his three lost friends, Brandon De Wilde, Clarence White, and Sid Kaiser. After a churchy piano intro and massed voices begging the Lord for vision, Gram sings, in a preacher's deep tones, the verse referring—although not by name—to the death of Brandon De Wilde. The massed choir comes back in on the last line, suggesting that Gram does not suffer his grief alone. The arrangement is at once somber and jaunty, with its bluegrass roots showing clearly. Gram, still in those deeper, more bass tones, then sings of Clarence White.

Gram was not a prolific songwriter. But when he focused, his writing demonstrated his rather fine secondary education, his uncommon literacy, and his ability to directly address the issues at hand with grace and simplicity. The core of Gram's art was his courage in the face of emotional pain. While his life was consumed in fleeing or blunting that pain, his music addressed the most awful loss with singular clarity. For Gram, transcending pain meant staring it in the face, describing it in detail, owning the hurt without flinching. The verse for Sid Kaiser is the saddest, reflecting Gram's lifelong, unfulfilled search for a true father. It also reveals the most heartfelt urge of the secretive, the deceitful, the elusive, those who yearn to reveal themselves but cannot: to be truly seen and understood by another. The choir returns to buoy Gram up in the middle of the verse and does not desert him in the final chorus.

A lesser artist would have sung chorus after chorus, throwing in more and more arrangement, letting the song fade out after we'd all gotten sick of being in church. Master of song structure that he had become, Gram and the choir take one chorus only and, emphasizing the brevity of the lives they celebrate, stop.

Among the many puzzling questions in the face of this album, the foremost is: Why wasn't death a better career move for Gram Parsons?

It certainly worked out well for Jim Croce. The soft-voiced adult-oriented rock favorite died in a plane crash on September 21, 1973, two days after Gram overdosed. Immediately after Croce's death, his 1972 album *Don't Mess with Jim* shot to number one. His hit single "Bad, Bad Leroy Brown," originally released in the summer of 1973, went on to sell two million copies.

Croce had other things going for him, of course. He'd already had a hit, he died in a plane crash à la Buddy Holly and Otis Redding, and his music was as accessible as baby food.

Gram had things going for him, too: drugs and family money and body snatching and corpse burning. He was beautiful, glamorous, and tragic. He had produced a significant body of work. But the marketplace wasn't ready. Gram died before his time in so many ways.

In defiance of the usual pattern, Gram's early demise only made his music more negligible. Those who knew it loved it at its true worth. The broader world was not prepared to embrace Gram's art, dead or alive.

IT TOOK TIME for that readiness to ripen. As it did, there would come all the usual sordid cashing in and fighting over not only who owned Gram's music, but who owned Gram's legend. As that fighting, which began the day after Gram died, slowly heated up, a series of dramas emerged in the years that followed.

In death, Gram permanently abandoned his daughter, Polly. Her childhood was difficult and her adolescence tormented. She had been denied a father, but as she grew older she would learn to fight for her share of his legacy.

Another drama was the crushing of the spirit of Margaret Fisher, who never recovered from Gram's death and all the accusations leveled at her in its aftermath. A year after Gram's death, something happened to Margaret. Something that drove her back to Jacksonville forever, that perfectly typified the way she was misunderstood and typified how everyone thought they could scrape a buck off Gram Parsons. When it happened, she packed up her apartment and ran away, abandoning the scene she'd worked so hard to penetrate. She never left Florida again.

Margaret has spent the years since fighting her own demons, addictions, alcoholism, and health problems. She was always, like Gram, too sensitive a soul.

When Margaret got back to San Francisco the day after Gram died, she quit answering her phone and turned her attention to heroin. Margaret did a great deal of it and suffered ugly moments in its pursuit. When she couldn't get smack, she used codeine. In the depth of her junkiehood, she met Timothy Leary's son, Jack. He was an ironworker, clean as a whistle, and hated drugs. They fell in love. He helped Margaret get straight. Then, as she was slowly taking her first steps toward reengaging the world, there was a knock on her door.

When she opened it up, a youngish hippie stood there, holding something metal in his hand.

"Are you Margaret Fisher?" he asked.

She was.

"I have something here I thought you might want to buy."

Margaret said, "What is it?"

"It's a hinge."

"A hinge? Why would I want to buy a hinge?"

"Because," the hippie boy said, "it's the hinge from Gram's coffin."

EPILOGUE

There is no moral in this story; it is not bourgeois;
it does not say they were wrong to play when they should
have toiled; it just tells what the consequences are.

—PHILIP K. DICK, *A Scanner Darkly*

OF COURSE THE TEMPTATION TO GET ALL BOURGEOIS ON GRAM'S ASS IS IRRE-
sistible. To assert that he should have played less and toiled more. To look at
his life and try to find the crossroads at which he strayed . . . it's impossible
to say of someone consuming drugs at Gram's pace and volume when the
person ceased to exist and the drugs took over. Gram had the constitution
and the genetics for prodigious intake. His friends wrung their hands, but
rehab centers were few, and no aspiring star got any credit for quitting.

The myth of the Byronic genius pursuing Rimbaudian excess in the
service of his vision was rampant upon the land. To say no to a line or a drink
was not only bad manners, it was a violation of the social contract. The ability to drink and drug and hold your shit (and life) together remained a profound signifier of manhood. That Gram could afford outrageous custom
clothes and to create his own mythology and to buy the best-quality drugs
generated a community of resentment. That he did not function so well on
the fine dope he paid for granted that community a bitter satisfaction.
Caught between those poles, how was Gram to stop?

Gram spent his life proving his selfishness, unreliability, and lack of impulse control. Who would invest time, emotion, or trust in his personal problems? Gram's early trauma—the loss of his father foremost—generated a classic syndrome: He lied, he avoided intimacy, he feared the self and sought to obliterate it. Gram learned early on that nothing lasts, to trust no one, and that pleasure—or at least anesthetizing pain—was an available constant. Dee Dee Ramone said that addiction is for those who are terrified of a lack of control over their feelings. An addict, Dee Dee said—and he would have known—is at least certain how he's going to feel, even if he feels like shit. And for that blessing, an addict puts up with everything addiction brings.

AFTER GRAM'S DEATH, John Nuese, Emmylou Harris, Bill Keith, and Barry and Holly Tashian gathered at the Tashians' summer cabin in Connecticut. "The spirit was pretty low," John Nuese says. "That was the last time I saw Emmylou until she reestablished her own career."

"Shortly after Emmylou came up to Connecticut," Barry Tashian says, "she was kind of drifting. We jammed and she had a couple of tapes from the album. She played 'Brass Buttons.' I remember her crying. She was talking about wanting to start a band together."

Emmylou Harris went back to Washington, D.C. "I returned to Washington after Gram died," she says, "and I decided to keep working. I formed the Angel Band with my friend Tom Guidera. We toured around all these bluegrass clubs in Maryland and Washington."

Eddie Tickner, using Emmylou's harmonies on *Grievous Angel* as his leverage, convinced Warner Bros. to sign her as a solo act. Emmylou put together the ensemble that Gram wanted and Warners had refused to pay for a year earlier. James Burton signed up along with Glen D. Hardin, Ronnie Tutt, and Emory Gordy. Emmylou Harris dubbed them the Hot Band, and hired Phil Kaufman as her road manager.

"I was definitely gathering up everything that Gram had touched like they were holy relics," Emmylou continues. "I had just started to find my musical identity and my voice, but it was so closely associated with what he was doing. Then I was left in the lurch, so I figured, Okay, Gram picked this band to record with him, so they must be an important part of it!"

Emmylou Harris' debut album for Reprise, *Pieces of the Sky*, was released in 1975. Her cover of the Louvin Brothers' "If I Could Only Win Your Love" hit number four on the country charts. The album went to number seven.

Her follow-up album, *Elite Hotel*, came out the same year. It hit number one on the country charts and featured three Gram covers: "Ooh, Las Vegas," "Sin City," and "Wheels." Four songs charted: Buck Owens' "Together Again," which hit number one; "Sweet Dreams" by Don Gibson, which also reached number one; Earl Montgomery's "One of These Days" (number three); and Lennon-McCartney's "Here, There, and Everywhere" (number sixty-five).

Released in 1977, *Luxury Liner* included "She" as well as the title Gram track. The album went to number one. "It's impossible for me to talk about my music, or myself as a person, without talking about Gram," Emmylou said.

In 1985, Emmylou Harris released *The Ballad of Sally Rose*, which she described as a "country opera." The album tells the story of the singer Sally Rose and her lover-mentor, a musician who dies on the road.

Many albums later, Emmylou Harris reigns as a new saint of Nashville. Like all saints, she's tough as nails. Emmylou Harris has consistently refused to discuss her life with Gram Parsons.

BOB PARSONS NEVER RECOVERED from Gram's death, its sordid aftermath, and the efforts he expended to put things right by his standards. His drinking became pathological.

"On our last trip to St. Bart's," Bonnie Parsons says, "he found the bar in the room. I told him, 'You don't want to go down the way Avis did. Please don't.' It didn't stop him. I'd wake up in the middle of the night and he'd be sitting in the armchair with a glassful."

Not long after the second anniversary of Gram's death, Walter Lanaux had lunch with Bob. "He invited me for lunch at twelve," Walter Lanaux says. "I told him I could be there at twelve but I knew damn well he would not. I said, 'You've never been on time for lunch with me or anybody else in your life. If you don't show at twelve I'll be pissed—understand?' I showed up at twelve, and several martinis later here he comes, sixty minutes late, and sits down. No apologies—pure Bob. He ordered a big meal, a nice lunch, and never touched a bite of it. He had several rum drinks instead. We talked about a real estate venture.

"When we left he was walking so slowly. I asked if we could speed it up and he said no. He lifted up his trousers and his ankles were so swollen the flesh was hanging over his shoes. It was from some heart condition, a shocking sight. I said, 'Good God, man, you've got to do something about that.' He said, 'I know. I know I'm not supposed to drink.'

"We reached a corner. I was going in one direction, he was going in the other. He said, 'I'll give you a call.' The next time I saw him was in the hospital three weeks later, and he was close to death. Very close."

While Bob was in the hospital for the last time, his wife learned that, despite his deteriorating health, he remained an incorrigibly charming rake. Bob was so ill he could barely walk, but Bonnie discovered that he'd been having an affair with one of her college friends. Bob had set up the woman in an apartment "with money we didn't have," Bonnie said later, "because the IRS was sitting in the hospital waiting room, waiting for Bob to die or live, whichever.

"I sat on the bathroom floor crying and throwing up. Bob sat behind me on the tub and cried and cried and cried. He said he would stop immediately and didn't realize it would hurt me so much. I never thought Bob had the ability to stop behaving this way. I don't think he ever would have stopped."

Bob Parsons died of cirrhosis of the liver on November 11, 1975. He was fifty years old. Walter Lanaux, Gene Leedy, Alice Barre, and her daughters, Becky and Jan, attended his service at the Bultman Funeral Home along with a mob of the usual party guests. Bob's body was cremated, over the protests of his seventy-three-year-old mother, Lillian Parsons. She opposed cremation on religious grounds. His ashes were interred in Hope Mausoleum on Canal Street. "He's right at the end of Canal, so he can peer up and pretend he's going into the French Quarter," Bonnie Parsons says. Bonnie has a space reserved next to Bob for her own ashes.

The whole crowd went back to Bob's house after the service, just as he would have insisted they do.

Hanging in Bonnie's closet was a green brocade suit that had belonged to Big Avis Snively. Throughout their marriage, Bob had tried to get Bonnie to wear that suit. Not to become Avis, he insisted, but so Bonnie could dress in a more sophisticated way. Bonnie never wore it. One of the first things she did after Bob died was to throw it out.

LITTLE AVIS AND HER HUSBAND, Beau Johnson, moved to Virginia. They had a daughter, whom they named Flora. In 1991, Avis and Flora were out in a boat in the dead of night. Another boat collided with theirs.

"One of their closest friends bought a weekend at an old Coast Guard station on a barrier island off the coast of Virginia," Becky Gottsegen says, "and they invited several friends to come. They had to cross a channel with all of their gear, and the first boat broke down. By the time they crossed, it was dark and the boat had no running lights. A boat went over the top of the boat that Avis and Flora were in. Avis and Flora were thrown into the water and they managed to get them out and give them artificial resuscitation. They didn't live long after that."

Flora was sixteen. Avis was forty.

ELVIS COSTELLO WENT TO NASHVILLE in 1981 to record *Almost Blue*, an album of country covers. He chose veteran country producer Billy Sherrill, renowned for his smooth Nashville sound and swelling strings. Sherrill produced Tammy Wynette and cowrote Wynette's signature song, "Stand by Your Man." Costello included Gram's "Hot Burrito #2" and a heart-wrenching cover of "How Much I've Lied" that featured beautiful piano work by Costello's keyboardist Steve Nieve. *Almost Blue* persuaded the small percentage of Elvis Costello's audience that bought it to recognize the virtues of classic country. It helped trigger a new interest in Gram as well.

Early in his career, Elvis reprised Gram's Grand Ole Opry moment on *Saturday Night Live*. Elvis started one song, stopped after a few bars, and tore into another. Offstage, unknowingly channeling Tompall Glaser, *SNL* executive producer Lorne Michaels threw a total conniption. Screaming at Elvis, he repeated Tompall's very words: Elvis would never play SNL again. Later, of course, Elvis did, parodying his first appearance.

Gram's "Sin City" was included in 1981's *Smithsonian Collection of Classical Country Music*. In February of 1982, *Gram Parsons and the Fallen Angels Live 1973* was released by Sierra Records. Reprise released "Return of the Grievous Angel" and "Hearts on Fire" as a single. In 1983, "Love Hurts" from *Fallen Angels Live* was nominated for a Grammy.

In 1985, Sierra Records and Books published *Gram Parsons: A Music Biography* by Sid Griffin. Griffin was a rock journalist, singer-songwriter, and member of the band the Long Ryders, whose rave-up single "Looking for Lewis and Clark" features a shout-out to Gram in heaven. Griffin's book, a clear labor of love, contains interviews with musicians who knew and played with Gram. The book insisted that Gram's life, personality, and music were worth honoring and preserving.

In 1986 the Country Music Hall Foundation in Nashville chose "Luxury Liner" and "Blue Eyes" for inclusion in the Greatest Country Music Recordings of All Time, part of its official archive.

In 1990, *GP* and *Grievous Angel* were rereleased on one CD. Marley Brant and John Delgatto of Sierra Records wrote the liner notes. Uncle

Tupelo released their album *No Depression*, which is widely considered the first alt. country—alternative country—record.

"Before him I hear the Louvin Brothers, and I hear Hank Williams, and you know the Louvin Brothers were his obsession," Steve Earle says. "Even the stuff that he covered, [like the] Everly Brothers songs, those were all descendants of the Louvin Brothers. I certainly hear it in the Rolling Stones. It was really kinda funny coming back from the Eagles or the more accepted country-rock bands, because the less country they were, the more records they sold. Lyrically what I hear preceding him is Bob Dylan and that whole Cambridge folk scene. He was there at the tail end of it, and that [was when] songwriting became raised to the level of literature. The big thing about Gram is that the music itself was really, really hard country. It was influenced by really real country.

"There's the approach to harmonies and the fact that Gram didn't feel complete as a singer without them. By the time he made his solo record, he'd found Emmy—most of the time it's both of them singing on every note. The thing you gotta understand about successful country bands in the Louvin Brothers period is [that] they thought they were making pop records. They weren't making folk music, they were making pop records the best they knew how."

In 1991, Ben Fong-Torres' biography of Gram, *Hickory Wind: The Life and Times of Gram Parsons* was published. In 1992, Gram's name was added to the Country Music Hall of Fame Walkway of Stars. This incarnated a recognition and rehabilitation in the eyes of the country establishment. Perhaps Emmylou's rising stature, and her role as a new first lady of country, influenced the Nashville community. It took almost twenty years, but Gram had been accepted into a commercial music world that previously never had a lick of interest in him.

In 1993, Rhino Records released *Conmemorativo: A Tribute to Gram Parsons*. A collection of alt. country and post-punk bands—the Mekons, Uncle Tupelo, Sid Griffin's Coal Porters—covered what has now become a canonical collection of Gram songs. This was the first of the Gram tribute records.

1993 saw the publication of Phil Kaufman's memoir, *Road Mangler*. Kaufman's book fixed the burning of Gram's body in the public memory as the foremost identifying narrative of Gram's life and music.

IN JULY OF 1999 came the most serious evidence of Gram's critical and cultural resurgence. *Return of the Grievous Angel: A Tribute to Gram Parsons*, produced by Emmylou Harris, was released on Almo Sounds. The musicians chosen to cover Gram's songs were not only household names, but each had a unique sound and something of a reputation for eccentricity and authenticity: Elvis Costello, Wilco, Whiskeytown, Gillian Welch, Chris Hillman, Steve Earle, Emmylou Harris herself, and others. The record begat a live concert broadcast that was meticulously recorded, produced, and packaged. The quality, care, and presentation of this tribute positioned Gram as among the most significant songwriters and arrangers of the last thirty years.

In 2001 Sundazed Records released *Another Side of This Life*, the acoustic recordings Gram made in Jim Carlton's living room. In 2002 Australian Jason Walker published the biography *Gram Parsons: God's Own Singer.* 2003 saw the long-awaited rerelease of *Sweetheart of the Rodeo* as a double CD with Gram's deleted lead vocals and a couple of International Submarine Band tracks.

In 2004 Polly Parsons organized two tribute concerts to her father, one in Santa Barbara (where her mother, Nancy, lives) and another in Los Angeles. The lineup included Jim James, Jay Farrar, John Doe, Steve Earle, Dwight Yoakam, Norah Jones, Lucinda Williams, and, memorably, Keith Richards. James Burton played guitar, and Al Perkins steel. The evening yielded a DVD, *Return to Sin City: A Tribute to Gram Parsons*, and proved a great success and catharsis for Polly Parsons.

That same year also saw the theatrical debut of the film *Grand Theft Parsons*. The film, instigated by Phil Kaufman, was based on his memoir. It's an abomination, received uniformly horrified reviews, and sank without a trace. Don't rent it.

Fallen Angel, a documentary on Gram's life by Gandulf Hennig and cowritten by Sid Griffin, was released in 2005. Polly Parsons and Jessica Hundley published *Grievous Angel: An Intimate Biography of Gram Parsons.*

And in 2006, Rhino Records released a three-CD set of Gram's complete Reprise sessions, featuring radio promos, interviews, outtakes, and bonus tracks.

RESEARCHING AND WRITING this book has been a long, hard, lesson in the difference between facts and truth. Some facts, like what guitar Gram played or studio he recorded in, were fairly easy to find. Others, like the date of Gram's wedding, proved impossible. Rather than an indictment of a research method, these factual mysteries stand as metaphors for the foggy relationship Gram's contemporaries had with facts in the first place. The ensuing years have only made that fog thicker.

The people who grew up with and lived their lives connected to Gram, except for Eve Babitz and Pamela Des Barres, were not diarists. Most of Gram's contemporaries were high most of the time, and they never wrote anything down. Their memories for dates, times, and precise facts are sketchy. Their memories for the emotions of a moment are profound, if highly personal. As anyone who's dealt with the world of show business understands, there proved to be little point in asking rock stars anything. For stars, nothing ever happened if it didn't happen to them. If you want the details of the valence of a recording studio, don't ask the guitar hero, ask the guitar tech.

Moreover, the Gram world is split into numerous feuding camps and fiefdoms. Each strives to tip the story to its way of thinking. There were so many minefields to negotiate, each designed to protect a version of what happened or someone's vanity or agenda or incapacity for the truth. These competing versions might recall a similar sequence, but each teller strove for a monopoly on the meaning. From the fog of inexact memory and perverse competition has emerged this tale. This history is the overlap between facts and truth.

GRAM INCARNATES A beautiful culture that was discarded—thrown away in favor of drugs. Rock and roll is not a by-product of drugs, even though so much great rock was created on drugs. The drugs are a side effect of the culture, a toxic tail that wagged the dog. Everyone thought facing the demon of heroin was Byronic or Celine-ic or Miles Davis–like. Some just plain enjoyed the drug, like Keith. The early-seventies drug culture still resonated to the Beat-era smack ethos. White hipsters emulated the fifties' African American jazz culture notion of drugs, which regarded heroin as a rite of passage. Could you use and still play? Even John Coltrane went that route. Being John Coltrane, he got clean.

Those genetic avatars of consumption, Miles Davis, Keith Richards, and Lou Reed, not only survived but emerged pretty much intact. Few others used for years, remained productive on a high level, and came out the other side. Chet Baker, a voracious consumer, had the constitution of an immortal. But he was a shell of himself for decades before drugs finally killed him. Miles, Keith, and Lou eventually cleaned up to one extent or another.

The list of the dead from Gram's era is horrifying: Janis Joplin, Keith Moon, Brian Jones, Lowell George, Jimi Hendrix, Mike Bloomfield, Michael Cooper, Miss Christine of the GTOs, Rick Grech, Jesse Ed Davis, Bill Murcia of the New York Dolls, Al "Blind Owl" Wilson of Canned Heat, Jim Morrison, Elvis Presley, Danny Whitten of Crazy Horse, and many others.

This universe of overdoses holds no poetry. It's insane to regard these deaths as Byronic or Blakeian or exemplary of any other myth of finding wisdom on the path of excess. Every one came from liking drugs and doing them habitually until the drugs took over. They represent only the ultimate failure to get straight.

Years spent sifting through Gram Parsons' life, tracking the course of his years, listening to those who knew him, becoming ever more immersed in his music, make it clear to me that Gram's death offers not the slightest trace of romance. It was sordid. Gram liked drugs a lot, did more than he should, and drugs ate him up. His quite legitimate, piercing emotional suffering paralyzed any efforts at getting clean. Gram was such an elusive figure: a font of glamour—which always contains the aspect of being impossible to know—a pathological liar, an unreliable friend, a narcissistic husband and careless father. . . . All his worst qualities worsened when he was using.

Yet for all his weakness, Gram possessed such existential courage. He risked getting maimed every time he got up to sing in hardcore honky-tonks wearing satin pants and Moroccan slippers. He had the guts to seek out the guys with the toughest standards in rock and roll—the Nashville/L.A. session culture—not to mention the Rolling Stones and the Byrds; Gram had no qualms about inserting himself into scenes that were defined by the most rigorous levels of performance. He could be adventurous, gracious, and great company. He was capable of the unflinching gaze. His songwriting showcases the bravery with which he described the self he could not bear.

It's hard to get clean. For Gram, the clean moments of production, of making art, only underscored all the times he was unable to. What should have produced joy produced only more pain. And a greater need for anesthesia.

When Gram cleaned up even the slightest bit, he made some of the most exquisite, moving, thoughtful, and soulful music of the century. Operating at such a diminished capacity, and in the face of so little encouragement from the world, Gram produced so much. The quality of what he left behind is astounding, inspirational.

Gram's tragedy is that he had no choice. He threw it all away.

ACKNOWLEDGMENTS

Bruce Tracy, my editor at Villard Books, bought this book right away, then had to wait a long time to get it. He never complained nor expressed any doubts. I am, and will always be, grateful for his patience and support.

Jay Mandel, my agent at the William Morris Agency, sold this book right away, encouraged me, and left me alone. I'm grateful for his effort and his restraint.

Thanks to everyone at Random House and Villard, especially Ryan Doherty. Thanks to Janet Wygal and her staff, Will Georgantas, Tedd Prudhomme, and Will Rigby, for their graceful care and loving attention, and for saving me from my own carelessness many, many times. And thanks to David Stevenson for the beautiful cover and to Susan Turner for her lovely interior and page design.

Thanks to everyone who agreed to be interviewed, for their time, insight, patience, and willingness.

There is only one Jimmi Seiter. Thank you, dog.

Thanks to the indispensable Cypress Cowgirl. She shared her knowledge with enthusiasm and kindness.

Jim Carlton gave days of his time. He is a natural host and a truly funny man.

Margaret Fisher faced the demons of her past with courage, frankness, and humor. She was invaluable to this book. I'm proud to be her friend.

Thanks to Holly George-Warren for her generosity, wit, and for taking me to the best Mexican restaurant in California.

Thanks to Bonnie Muma, a brave, sensitive soul.

Thanks to Eve Babitz for her intelligence, grace, and insight.

Thanks to (Miss) Pamela Des Barres. And to Miss Mercy Peters.

Chris Ethridge looked after my research assistant, Jesi Khadivi, like she was family.

Thanks to Ian Dunlop.

Grant and Karen Lacerte of Winter Haven, Florida, were kindness incarnate.

Thanks to Bernie Leadon for his time, memories, and his illuminating lecture on the pedal steel guitar.

Thanks to James Austin and Rhino Records.

Thanks to Barry Feinstein for his wonderful photographs (www.barry feinsteinphotography.com).

And to Andee Nathanson for hers (www.andeenathanson.com).

Thanks to Dave Brolan for all his help (www.davebrolan.com).

Thanks to Kent LaVoie and the Dizzy Ramblers.

Thanks to Neal Skok, archivist extraordinaire.

Michael Vosse proved an invaluable, detailed resource.

Thanks to Becky Gottsegen.

Thanks to John Erstling and everyone at the Bolles School, especially Quinn Barton and Rufus McClure.

Thanks to Billy-Ray Herrin, Roger Williams, and everyone in Waycross.

Thank you: Robert Altman, Rick Cusick, John Einarson, Kathy Fenton, Marcia Katz, Judson Klinger, Peter Knobler, John Lomax, Versa Manos, Thea Stuart, and Ginny Winn.

Thanks also to: Susan Alexander, Earl Ball, David Barry, Bobby Braddock, Sid Griffin, Dr. Sam Hutt, a.k.a. Hank Wangford, Katy K, Polly Parsons, Johnny Rogan, Paul Surratt, Barry Tashian, Jet Thomas, Pauline Wilkes and Tom Wilkes.

To those who remain anonymous, thank you.

And if I forgot to thank anyone here who deserves it, please know you are appreciated.

I contemplated a Fuck You list of those who constantly lied or were pointlessly obstructionist or inflated their own value or demanded money before they would talk (nobody was paid for their interview—nobody), but those people already know who they are.

My community of friends gave me the strength to write this book. Thank you: Zachary Tumin and Laura Barbieri, Jay and Laura Sedrish, Jan

Cox, Cal Millar, Karl O'Toole, Ido Mizrahy, Guy Greenberg, Steve Fishman and Cristina Page, Cristina Seckinger, Greg Burk, Daniel Baird, Robert "Bob-O" Chapman, Megan Heuer, Richard Gowen, and Catherine Higham. Thanks to Jason Walker.

Thanks to all my students and colleagues at the New School.

Thanks to Jonathan Segal for his support and encouragement back in the day.

Julie Ardery of Austin, Texas, was the first girl I ever met who wore cowboy boots. She introduced me to the music of Gram Parsons, to the virtues of country music, and to so much music I would never have heard without her. She served, without knowing it, as the moral conscience of this book; I tried to hold myself to her standard of hard-earned truth.

Martha Kehoe understands country and every other form of music on the aesthetic, intellectual, spiritual, existential, sexual, and ass-shaking planes. And for someone who never succumbs, she's profoundly aware of and sympathetic to the processes of a writer getting in his own way. She remains the wittiest woman in Canada. She always believed.

Jesse Goldstein conducted and transcribed interviews and provided detailed, invaluable research. His easy manner and calm intelligence drew out significant memories from folks who would not have talked at all otherwise.

David Wilentz was great company, conducted and transcribed interviews, did research, and was a never-ending source of obscure, relevant music. When crises arose and tempers flared, we would always ask: "WWDWD?" And the answer always smoothed the way.

Finally, without the love, support, trust, and hard, hard work of Sarahjane Blum, Tessa DeCarlo, and Jesi Khadivi, this book would not exist. So, in alphabetical order:

Guess what, Sarahjane? You rock. Guess what else? You always will. Sarahjane conducted interviews, provided astonishing archival research, read each chapter in manuscript, argued fine points of rock, country, and culture, buoyed me up when I could not write and cheered me when I did. Her savoring of music, which shaped many of my opinions, is critically rigorous yet filled with joy. Her friendship is a pillar of my life.

What other people tell you about your writing will almost always tell you more about them than about your work. If you're lucky, you can find one person who understands your voice and what you're trying to say, and will strive to make your voice better without interference. In that realm and in others, Tessa DeCarlo is my rock. She edited this manuscript, communicated far into the night over every idea, and convinced me, in the face of the apparent facts, that this book would get done. Tessa's grammar is alive, elegant, and scholarly, her eye for nuance is unmatched, and she knows that the work will always provide the solution.

Jesi Khadivi was my research assistant and work partner for much of this book. We worked side by side all day every day and never had a harsh word (I swear). Her kind, soulful determination inspired me. Her ear for music is her heart; if Jesi tells you it's good, it's good. Jesi did the chores, the scut-work: research, dealing with jerks, fighting for print rights—all the tedious logistics upon which biographies feed. Jesi did numerous interviews, and the most recalcitrant souls would open like flowers to her questions. She is a rare gem and made this book possible. Thank you, Jesi.

SELECTED BIBLIOGRAPHY

Alterman, Lorraine. "Parsons Knows." *Melody Maker*, April 3, 1973.

Atlas, Jacoba. "Gram Parsons: The Burrito Ego Man." *Melody Maker*, July 25, 1970.

Babitz, Eve. "Ashes in the Morning." *Rolling Stone*, October 25, 1973.

———. *Eve's Hollywood*. New York: Seymour Lawrence, 1972.

———. *Sex and Rage: Advice to Young Ladies Eager for a Good Time*. New York: Knopf, 1979.

———. *Slow Days, Fast Company: The World, the Flesh, and L.A.* New York: Knopf, 1977.

Bangs, Lester, and John Morthland, ed. *Mainlines, Blood Feasts and Bad Taste: A Lester Bangs Reader*. New York: Anchor Books, 2003.

Bangs, Lester. *Psychotic Reactions and Carburetor Dung: The Work of a Legendary Critic: Rock 'n' Roll as Literature and Literature as Rock 'n' Roll*. New York: Vintage, 1987.

Bockris, Victor. *Keith Richards: The Biography*, third ed. Cambridge: Da Capo, 2003.

Booth, Stanley. *Keith: Standing in the Shadows*. New York: St. Martin's Press, 1995.

———. *The True Adventures of the Rolling Stones*. Chicago: A Cappella Books, 2000.

Bull, Debby. *Hillbilly Hollywood*. New York: Rizzoli, 2000.

Catwell, Robert. *When We Were Good: The Folk Revival*. Cambridge: Harvard University Press, 1997.

Charone, Barbara. *Keith Richards: Life as a Rolling Stone*. New York: Doubleday, 1982.

Christgau, Robert. *Any Old Way You Choose It: Rock and Other Pop Music 1967–1973*, expanded ed. New York: Cooper Square Press, 2000.

———. *Christgau's Record Guide: The '80s*. New York: Pantheon, 1990.

———. *Rock Albums of the '70s: A Critical Guide*. Cambridge: Da Capo, 1981.

Cusick, Richard. "Gram Parsons: The Story of the Grievous Angel Part One." *Goldmine*, September 1982.

———. "Gram Parsons: The Story of the Grievous Angel Part Two." *Goldmine*, December 1983.

———. "Gram Parsons: The Story of the Grievous Angel Part Three." *Goldmine*, January 1984.

———. "Gram Parsons: The Story of the Grievous Angel Conclusion." *Goldmine*, February 1984.

Davidoff, Nicholas. *In the Country of Country: A Journey to the Roots of American Music*. New York: Vintage, 1998.

Des Barres, Pamela. *I'm with the Band: Confessions of a Groupie*. New York: Jove, 1987.

———. *Rock Bottom: Dark Moments in Music Babylon*. New York: St. Martin's Press, 1996.

Doggett, Peter. *Are You Ready for the Country: Elvis, Dylan, Parsons and the Roots of Country Rock*. New York: Penguin, 2000.

Eddy, Chuck. *The Accidental Evolution of Rock 'n' Roll: A Misguided Tour Through Popular Music*. Cambridge: Da Capo, 1997.

Ehler, Jay. "Gram Parsons Sweeps out the Ashes." *Crawdaddy*, October 1973.

Einarson, John. *Desperados: The Roots of Country Rock*. New York: Cooper Square Press, 2001.

Faithfull, Marianne, and David Dalton. *Faithfull: An Autobiography*. New York: Cooper Square Press, 2000.

Firminger, John. "Gram Parsons." *Country Music Review*, December 1974.

"The Flying Burrito Brothers." *Circus*, March 1970.

George-Warren, Holly. "Gram Parsons: The Myth of the Grievous Angel." *No Depression*, July-August 1999.

George-Warren, Holly, and Michelle Freedman. *How the West Was Worn*. New York: Harry N. Abrams, 2001.

Goodman, Fred. *The Mansion on the Hill: Dylan, Young, Geffen, Springsteen and the Head-on Collision of Rock and Commerce*. New York: Vintage, 1998.

Green, Lloyd. Liner notes to *Sweetheart of the Rodeo*, Legacy Edition. New York: Sony Entertainment, Inc., 2006.

Greenberg, Alan. *Love in Vain: A Vision of Robert Johnson*. Cambridge: Da Capo, 1994.

Greenfield, Robert. "Goodbye Great Britain: The Rolling Stones on Tour." *Rolling Stone*, April 15, 1971.

———. *S.T.P.: A Journey Through America with the Rolling Stones*. Cambridge: Da Capo, 2002.

Griffin, Sid. *Gram Parsons: A Musical Biography*. Pasadena: Sierra Books, 1985.

Grissin, John. *Country Music: White Man's Blues*. New York: Paperback Library, 1970.

Groening, Matt, and Paul Bresnick, eds. *Da Capo Best Music Writing 2003: The Year's Finest Writing on Rock, Pop, Jazz, Country, and More.* Cambridge: Da Capo, 2003.

Hadju, David. *Positively 4th Street: The Lives and Times of Joan Baez, Bob Dylan, and Mimi Baez Fariña and Richard Fariña.* New York: Farrar, Straus, and Giroux, 2001.

Hebdige, Dick. *Cut 'N' Mix.* London: Methuen, 1987.

———. *Hiding in the Light.* New York: Routledge, 2002.

Hickey, Dave. *Air Guitar: Essays on Art and Democracy.* Los Angeles: Art Issues Press, 1997.

———. *The Invisible Dragon: Four Essays on Beauty.* Los Angeles: Art Issues Press, 1994.

Hillburn, Robert. "Gram Parsons—Straight Home to Us." *Los Angeles Times,* November 2, 1975.

Hornby, Nick, ed. *Da Capo Best Music Writing of 2004.* Cambridge: Da Capo, 2004.

Hoskyns, Barney. "The Good Old Boy." *Mojo,* July 1998.

———. *Hotel California: Singer-Songwriters and Cocaine Cowboys in the L.A. Canyons, 1967–1976.* London: Fourth Estate, 2005.

Johnson, David. "His Talent Died in the Desert." *Harvard Magazine,* July-August 1994.

Jones, Allan. "Burrito Deluxe." *Melody Maker,* February 8, 1975.

———. "Country Parsons." *Melody Maker,* July 27, 1974.

———. "Red Hot Burritos." *Melody Maker,* February 2, 1975.

Kaufman, Phil, and Colin White. *Road Mangler Deluxe,* second ed. Lafayette: White Boucke, 1998.

Kaye, Lenny. "The Rolling Stones: *Exile on Main St.*" *Rolling Stone,* July 6, 1972.

———. *You Call It Madness: The Sensuous Song of the Croon.* New York: Villard, 2005.

Klinger, Judson, and Greg Mitchell. "Gram Finale: The Profoundly Sick Life and Mysteriously Perverse Death of the Prince of Country-Rock." *Crawdaddy,* October 1976.

Leland, John. *Hip: The History.* New York: Ecco, 2004.

Marcus, Greil. *Lipstick Traces: A Secret History of the 20th Century.* Cambridge: Harvard University Press, 2000.

———. *Mystery Train: Images of America in Rock 'n' Roll,* fourth ed. New York: Plume, 1997.

———. *Ranters and Crowd Pleasers: Punk in Pop Music, 1977–1992.* New York: Doubleday, 1993.

———. *Stranded: Rock and Roll for a Desert Island.* New York: Knopf, 1979.

Meltzer, Richard. *A Whore Just Like the Rest: The Music Writings of Richard Meltzer.* Cambridge: Da Capo, 2000.

———. *The Aesthetics of Rock.* Cambridge: Da Capo, 1987.

Parsons, Gram. "Country Trip: A Talk with Gram Parsons." *Fusion*, March 26, 1969.

"Parsons: Wild in the Country." *Melody Maker*, June 26, 1976.

Patterson, Rob. "The Return of Gram Parsons." *Goldmine*, April 1982.

Phillips, John, and Jim Jerome. *Papa John*. New York: Dolphin Books, 1986.

"Race Dispute Splits Byrds Nest: Gram Parsons Refuses Gigs in South Africa." *Rolling Stone*, August 24, 1968.

Rogan, Johnny. *The Byrds: Timeless Flight Revisited, the Sequel*. London: Rogan House, 1998.

Rose, Mark. "Merle Haggard: Big Wheels Keep Rolling." *BAM*, October 24, 1980.

Roxon, Lillian. *Rock Encyclopedia*. New York: Grosset and Dunlap, 1978.

Russell, Tom. "Gram Parsons Remembered: In the Shadows of Joshua Tree." *Helix* 07.

Sackheim, Eric, ed. *The Blues Line: A Collection of Blues Lyrics from Leadbelly to Muddy Waters*. New York: Thunder's Mouth, 1969.

Sanchez, Tony. *Up and Down with the Rolling Stones*. Cambridge: Da Capo, 1996.

Sarig, Roni. *The Secret History of Rock: The Most Influential Bands You've Never Heard*. New York: Watson-Guptill, 1998.

Scoppa, Bud. "The L.A. Turnaround." *Country Music People*, September 1974.

Sullivan, Patrick. "Gram Parsons: The Mysterious Death—and Aftermath." *Rolling Stone*, October 25, 1973.

Tosches, Nick. *Country: The Biggest Music in America*. New York: Dell, 1979.

———. *Country: The Twisted Roots of Rock and Roll*. Cambridge: Da Capo, 1996.

———. *Dino: Living High in the Dirty Business of Dreams*. New York: Delta, 1992.

Unterberger, Richie. *Eight Miles High: Folk Rock's Flight from Haight-Ashbury to Woodstock*. San Francisco: Back Beat Books, 2003.

———. *Turn! Turn! Turn!: The '60s Folk Rock Revolution*. San Francisco: Back Beat Books, 2002.

Wald, Elijah. *Escaping the Delta: Robert Johnson and the Invention of the Blues*. New York: HarperCollins, 2004.

Walker, Jason. *God's Own Singer*. London: Helter Skelter, 2002.

Warhol, Andy, and Pat Hackett. *POPism: The Warhol Sixties*. San Diego: Harvest, 1990.

Wasserzieher, Bill. "Gram Parsons Dies in Desert." *The Village Voice*, September 27, 1973.

Wolfe, Charles K. *In Close Harmony: The Story of the Louvin Brothers*. Jackson: University Press of Mississippi, 1996.

Zimmerman, Keith and Kent. *Sing My Way Back Home*. San Francisco: Back Beat Books, 2004.

DISCOGRAPHY

The International Submarine Band, "Sum Up Broke" (Parsons-Nuese) b/w "One Day Week" (Parsons). Columbia, 1966.

———, "The Russians Are Coming" (Mandel) b/w "Truck Driving Man" (Fell). Ascot, 1966.

———, *Safe at Home*. LHI Records, 1968; reissued as *Gram Parsons*, Shiloh, 1976, *Safe at Home*, Sundown, 1996, and *Safe at Home*, Sundazed, 2004.

———, "Luxury Liner" (Parsons) b/w "Blue Eyes" (Parsons). LHI, 1968.

———, "Miller's Cave" (Clement) b/w "I Must Be Somebody Else You've Known" (Haggard). LHI, 1968.

The Byrds, *Sweetheart of the Rodeo*. Columbia, 1968.

———, "You Ain't Goin' Nowhere" (Dylan) b/w "Artificial Energy" (Hillman-McGuinn). Columbia, 1968.

———, "I Am a Pilgrim" (arr. McGuinn-Hillman) b/w "Pretty Boy Floyd" (Guthrie). Columbia, 1968.

The Flying Burrito Brothers, *Gilded Palace of Sin*. A&M, 1969.

———, "The Train Song" (Hillman-Parsons) b/w "Hot Burrito #1" (Ethridge-Parsons). A&M, 1969.

———, *Burrito Deluxe*. A&M, 1970.

———, "If You Gotta Go" (Dylan) b/w "Cody, Cody" (Parsons-Hillman). A&M, 1970.

———, "Older Guys" (Parsons-Hillman-Leadon) b/w "Down in the Churchyard" (Hillman-Parsons). A&M, 1970.

Gram Parsons, *GP*. Reprise, 1973.

———, "She" (Ethridge-Parsons) b/w "That's All It Took" (Edwards-Grier-Jones). Reprise, 1973.

———, "Cry One More Time" (Wolf-Justman) b/w "Streets of Baltimore" (Glaser-Howard). Reprise, 1973.

———, *Grievous Angel.* Reprise, 1974.

———, *Sleepless Nights*, PolyGram, 1976.

Gram Parsons & the Shilos, *The Early Years*, Sierra, 1979.

Gram Parsons and the Fallen Angels Live 1973, Sierra, 1982.

The Flying Burrito Brothers, *Dim Lights, Thick Smoke and Loud, Loud Music*, Edsel, 1987.

———, *Farther Along: The Best of the Flying Burrito Brothers*, A&M, 1988.

The Byrds, *The Byrds: Box Set*, Sony, 1990.

Gram Parsons, *GP/Grievous Angel*, Reprise, 1990.

———, *Warm Evenings, Pale Mornings, Bottled Blues 1963–1973*, Raven, 1991.

The Flying Burrito Brothers, *Out Of The Blue*, A&M, 1996.

Emmylou Harris, *Portraits: Box Set*, Reprise Archives, 1996.

The Byrds, *Sweetheart of the Rodeo—20 Bit Mastered Edition*, Columbia Legacy, 1997.

Gram Parsons, *Another Side of This Life*, Sundazed, 2000.

The Flying Burrito Brothers, *Hot Burritos!: Anthology 1969–1972*, A&M, 2000.

———, *The Best Of The Flying Burrito Brothers*, A&M: 20th Century Masters Series, 2001.

Gram Parsons, *Sacred Hearts and Fallen Angels: The Gram Parsons Anthology*, Rhino, 2001.

The Flying Burrito Brothers, *Sin City: The Very Best of the Flying Burrito Brothers*, A&M, 2002.

———, *The Gilded Palace of Sin & Burrito Deluxe*, Fontana, 2004.

TRIBUTES

Various Artists, *Conmemorativo: A Tribute to Gram Parsons*, Rhino, 1993.

———, *Return of the Grievous Angel*, Almo, 1999.

———, *The Gram Parsons Notebook: The Last Whippoorwill*, Shell Point, 2000.

UNDERGROUND RECORDINGS

The Byrds, *Sanctuary IV,* Columbia/Sundazed.

———, *Piper Club - Roma May 2, 1968*, Bulldog.

———, *Byrdaholics!*, Tendolar.

———, *Cosmic American Music: The Rehearsal Tapes 1972*, Magnum America; reissued as *The Lost Recordings*, Cowboy Music.

Gram Parsons, *Under Your Spell*, Colosseum.

The Flying Burrito Brothers, *Saddle Up the Palomino!*, Tendolar.

————, *The High Lonesome Sound of the Flying Burrito Brothers*, Scorpio; Seattle Pop Festival, Woodenville, Washington, July 27, 1969 and Winona, Minnesota, May 1970.

————, *Legendary Live 1973*, Weeping Goat, Live at Oliver's, Boston, March 19, 1973, Demo's, and Oliver's, Boston, March 20, 1973.

RECOMMENDED LISTENING

Following is a selective discography of music that influenced Gram Parsons, that was influenced by him, that was made by his contemporaries, and that he listened to avidly. The purpose of this list is to detail a context for Gram's music. There is no attempt here to create a music nerd's completist catalog, though the temptation is strong. Think of this as a condensed, wide-ranging record collection. The music listed is either the best or the most iconic of each performer. In a few cases—the Byrds, the Louvins, the Stones, Gene Clark—one or two albums isn't enough. Greatest-hits albums, however lacking in eccentricity, prove a more reliable purchase than original LPs that might have three good cuts and eight cuts of filler. The idea is to present each artist at his or her best.

The top twelve represents the first that should be listened to. Each in its own way reveals much about Gram's musical passions, and each exerted a broad musical influence beyond Gram. Taken together, the twelve form a primer of Cosmic American Music. The top twelve are in order of priority; the rest are alphabetical by artist and by album title within each artist's oeuvre. This list presumes you've already bought *GP/Grievous Angel*, *The Gilded Palace of Sin*, and *Sweetheart of the Rodeo*.

THE TOP TWELVE

1. *Satan Is Real*, The Louvin Brothers (Capitol, B000002U45)
2. *Modern Sounds in Country & Western Music*, Ray Charles (Rhino, B0000032B4)
3. *Exile on Main St.*, The Rolling Stones (Virgin, B000000W5L)
4. *Wynn Stewart's Greatest Hits* (Varèse Sarabande, 3020663212)
5. *The Essential George Jones: The Spirit of Country* (Sony, B000009RBG)
6. *Anthology of American Folk Music*, Various artists, edited by Harry Smith (Smithsonian Folkways, B000001DJU)
7. *Buck Owens' Greatest Hits Vols. I and II* (Curb, B000000CUY & B000000D48)
8. *Mendocino*, The Sir Douglas Quintet (Acadia, B00006JYVA)

9. *Flying High*, Gene Clark (Fontana International, B00000IHEP)
10. *Lefty's 20 Golden Hits*, Lefty Frizzell (Tee Vee, B000003OOA)
11. *Elvis Presley* (BMG Heritage, B0006TL9C8)
12. *The Great Twenty-Eight*, Chuck Berry (MCA, B000002Q61)

ROOTS

Cash, Johnny. *American Recordings* (Lost Highway, B000062X9D)

———. *At Folsom Prison* and *San Quentin* (Sony, B00000254Z)

———. *Greatest Hits Vol. I* (Sony, B0000024TG)

Cramer, Floyd. *Favorite Country Hits* (Ranwood, B000000B74)

The Delmore Brothers. *Fifty Miles to Travel* (Ace, B000ARHN8K)

Dixon, Floyd. *Marshall Texas Is My Home* (Specialty, B000000QMI)

Haggard, Merle. *The Lonesome Fugitive: The Merle Haggard Anthology (1963—1977)* (Razor & Tie, B000002Z8T)

Hartford, John. *Aereo-Plain* (Rounder Select, B0000002O7)

———. *Natural to Be Gone 1967–1970* (Raven, B000068R0X)

Johnson, Robert. *The Complete Recordings* (Sony, B000002ADN)

Jones, George, and Tammy Wynette. *16 Biggest Hits* (Sony, B000000JT4D)

Lewis, Jerry Lee. *25 All-Time Greatest Sun Recordings* (Varèse Sarabande, B00004TGT6)

Little Richard. *The Specialty Sessions* (Specialty, B000000QOG)

The Louvin Brothers. *Tragic Songs of Life* (Capitol, B000002U47)

———. *A Tribute to the Delmore Brothers* (Capitol, B000002U46)

———. *When I Stop Dreaming: The Best of the Louvin Brothers* (Razor & Tie, B000002Z94)

Monroe, Bill, and Doc Watson. *Live Duet Recordings 1963–1980* (Smithsonian Folkways, B000001DJ5)

Owens, Buck. *I've Got a Tiger by the Tail* (Sundazed, B000003GYA)

Price, Ray. *The Essential Ray Price 1951–1962* (Sony, B000002823)

———. *The Honky Tonk Years (1950–1966)* (Bear Family, B000001B3E)

Rich, Charlie. *The Complete Smash Sessions* (Polygram, B000008K01)

Rodgers, Jimmie. *The Essential Jimmie Rodgers* (RCA, B000002X3V)

Tillis, Mel. *The Best of Mel Tillis: The Columbia Years* (Collector's Choice, B0000EW05A)

Twitty, Conway. *The Conway Twitty Collection* (MCA Nashville, B000002OTE)

Various Artists. *The Big "D" Jamboree LIVE, Volumes 1 and 2* (Dragon Street, B00003TL83)

———. *The Complete Meteor Rockabilly & Hillbilly Recordings* (Ace, CDCH2885)

———. *Country Got Soul, Volume One* (Casual, B00009WNAU)

———. *Country Guitar Thunder* (CMH, B0000010QK)

———. *Down in the Basement: Joe Bussard's Treasure Trove of Vintage 78s 1926–1937* (Old Hat, B00009MGQU)

Williams, Hank. *40 Greatest Hits* (Polygram, B000001F76)

SOUL

Bland, Bobby "Blue." *Greatest Hits Volume One: The Duke Recordings* (RCA, B000007QE7)

———. *Greatest Hits Volume Two: The ABC-Dunhill/MCA Recordings* (RCA, B000009D21)

Booker T. & the MG's. *Hip Hug-Her* (Rhino, R271013)

Brown, James. *James Brown—20 All-Time Greatest Hits* (Polydor, B000001DUP)

———. *Live at the Apollo* (Polydor, B0001JXQ7O)

Carr, James. *You Got My Mind Messed Up* (Kent, B000069CIT)

Floyd, Eddie. *Chronicle: Greatest Hits* (Stax, B000000ZH5)

Franklin, Aretha. *Spirit in the Dark* and *Live at the Fillmore West with King Curtis* (Atlantic, B00000335K)

Pickett, Wilson. *Wilson Pickett's Greatest Hits* (Atlantic, B000002IKQ)

Redding, Otis. *The Dictionary of Soul: Complete and Unbelievable* (Atlantic, B000002JO2)

———. *Otis Blue: Otis Redding Sings Soul* (Elektra, B000002IHD)

———. *Otis Redding Live in Europe* (Elektra, B000002JKY)

Sledge, Percy. *It Tears Me Up: The Best of Percy Sledge* (Rhino, B0000032DQ)

Sly & The Family Stone. *Stand!* (Sony, B0000024VT)

Turner, Ike & Tina. *Dynamite!* (Collectables, B0000008P5)

———. *River Deep—Mountain High* (Polygram Int'l, B0000074LE)

Various Artists. *Chess Blues* (box set) (Chess, B000002OBW)

———. *Hitsville USA: The Motown Singles Collection 1959–1971* (Motown, B000006NUW)

———. *The Stax Story* (Stax, B00004Z3ZW)

Watson, Johnny "Guitar" and Larry Williams. *The Best of the Okeh Years* (Collectables, B00019JRB8)

Williams, Larry. *Larry Williams Show with Johnny "Guitar" Watson* (Edsel, B0000011SM)

GRAM'S L.A.

Buffalo Springfield. *Retrospective: The Best of Buffalo Springfield* (Elektra/WEA, B000002IAZ)

The Byrds. *Dr. Byrds and Mr. Hyde* (Sony, B000002AGG)

———. *Fifth Dimension* (Sony, B000002ACQ)

———. *Turn! Turn! Turn!* (Sony, B000002ACP)

———. *Younger Than Yesterday* (Sony, B000002ACR)

Cale, J. J. *Naturally* (Mercury/Universal, B000001FK3)

Clark, Gene. *Gene Clark with the Gosdin Brothers* (Edsel, B0000011XE)

———. *White Light* (Ume Imports, B000068PQ7)

Cooder, Ry. *Into the Purple Valley* (Reprise, B000002KBW)

Delaney & Bonnie and Friends. *The Best of Delaney & Bonnie* (Rhino, B0000032NK)

———. *On Tour with Eric Clapton* (Atco, B000002IAS)

Dillard & Clark. *The Fantastic Expedition of Dillard & Clark* and *Through the Morning Through the Night* (Polygram International, B00000JAYN)

The GTOs. *Permanent Damage* (Rhino, B000008G97)

Harris, Emmylou. *The Very Best of Emmylou Harris: Heartache and Highways* (Rhino, B0009NR7YU)

———. *Wrecking Ball* (Asylum, B000002HKI)

Hearts and Flowers. *The Complete Hearts and Flowers* (Collector's Choice, B00006RYJ7)

Little Feat. *Little Feat* (Warner Bros., B000002KBF)

———. *Sailing Shoes* (Warner Bros., B000002KE0)

Nesmith, Michael. *Magnetic South* and *Loose Salute* (BMG International, B00000IQ24)

Parks, Van Dyke. *Song Cycle* (Warner Bros., B000005JAT)

Penn, Dan. *Nobody's Fool* (Repertoire, B00000013G)

Poco. *Pickin' Up the Pieces* (Sony, B000002AP0)

The Rolling Stones. *Beggars Banquet* (Abkco, B00006AW2J)

———. *Let It Bleed* (Abkco, B00006AW2G)

———. *Sticky Fingers* (Virgin Records, B000000W5N)

Russell, Leon. *Leon Russell* (The Right Stuff, B000002TMY)

———. *Leon Russell and the Shelter People* (The Right Stuff, B000002TYO)

Various Artists. Performance: *Original Motion Picture Soundtrack* (Warner Bros., B000002LN5)

White, Clarence. *33 Acoustic Guitar Instrumentals* (Sierra, B00005QD5D)

Young, Neil, and Crazy Horse. *Everybody Knows This Is Nowhere* (Reprise/WEA, B000002KD7)

———. *Tonight's the Night* (Reprise/WEA, B000002KCC)

CONTEMPORARIES

The Band. *Music from Big Pink* (Capitol, B00004W50T)

Cocker, Joe. *Mad Dogs & Englishmen* (Interscope, B00001X58X)

Crazy Horse. *Crazy Horse* (Reprise/WEA, B000002KOY)

Dylan, Bob. *Blonde on Blonde* (Sony, B00026WU8M)

———. *Bringing It All Back Home* (Sony, B00026WU9Q)

———. *John Wesley Harding* (Sony, B00026WU5U)

———. *Nashville Skyline* (Sony, B00028HODG)

The Grateful Dead. *American Beauty* (Rhino, B00007LTIL)

———. *Workingman's Dead* (Rhino, B00007LTIK)

Great Speckled Bird. *Great Speckled Bird* (Stony Plain, B000001CW8)

Mahal, Taj. *Giant Step* and *The Old Folks at Home* (Columbia, B0000247RX)

Moby Grape. *Moby Grape* (San Francisco Sound, B000000DP9)

Neil, Fred. *The Many Sides of Fred Neil* (Collector's Choice, B00000IWN1)

Nelson, Rick. *Bright Lights & Country Music* and *Country Fever* (Ace, B0000O7O74)

The Rascals. *Time Peace: The Rascals' Greatest Hits* (Atlantic/Wea, B000008JSY)

COSMIC COWBOYS/OUTLAW COUNTRY

Clark, Guy. *Old No 1* and *Texas Cookin'* (BMG International, B0000250RY)

Nelson, Willie. *Phases and Stages* (Atlantic, WEA, B000002IQL)

———. *Shotgun Willie* (Atlantic/WEA, B000002175)

———. *Red Headed Stranger* (Sony, B00004U2G7)

Sahm, Doug. *The Best of Doug Sahm and Friends* (Rhino, B0000032UH)

———. *San Antonio Rock: The Harlem Recordings 1957–1961* (Norton, B00004RDS0)

Van Zandt, Townes. *The Late Great Townes Van Zandt* (Rhino, B00000330L)

———. *Road Songs* (Sugarhill, B000000EX1)

Walker, Jerry Jeff. *Viva Terlingua* (MCA Nashville, B00000ZNX9)

AFTERMATH

Costello, Elvis. *Almost Blue* (Rhino, B0002IQFDQ)

Earle, Steve. *El Corazón* (Warner Bros., B000002NIC)

———. *Guitar Town* (MCA Nashville, B00005V7G1)

Ely, Joe. *Down on the Drag* (MCA, B000002OG2)

Garing, Greg. *Alone* (Warner Bros., B000002L56)

Sun Volt. *A Retrospective: 1995–2000* (Rhino, B000803POA)

Uncle Tupelo. *89/93 An Anthology* (Sony, B000063CN9)

Various Artists, *Return of the Grievous Angel: A Tribute to Gram Parsons* (Almo Sounds, B00000JMXD)

Williams, Lucinda. *Car Wheels on a Gravel Road* (Mercury/Universal, B000007Q8J)

ENCYCLOPEDIA

The Aces Club: Country-western joint in City of Industry, California, known for its open-mike night, amphetamines, and bar brawls. Less hippie-friendly than the Topanga Corral. Earl Ball played piano in the house band.

Alexander, Susan: GP's maternal cousin. Daughter of John Snively Junior.

Allen, Vickie: GP's friend from Waycross, Georgia.

Alpert, Herb (b. 1935): Trumpet player/composer/bandleader/record producer/record executive. Cofounder of A&M Records. Signed the Flying Burrito Brothers to A&M. Front man of the wildly popular—fourteen gold records—Herb Alpert and the Tijuana Brass (1962–1969), a mariachi-influenced brass band playing Alpert's original compositions. Albums: *Going Places, Whipped Cream and Other Delights.*

Alpert, Richard (b. 1931): Professor/LSD avatar/former Harvard psychology and Eastern-philosophy explainer. Known for his controversial research program at Harvard studying the effects of LSD. Dismissed from Harvard in 1963. Traveled to India in 1967 and adopted the name Ram Das, meaning "servant of God." Became an early Western proponent of devotional yoga and meditation in the Theravadin, Mahayana Tibetan, and Zen Buddhist schools. Books: *The Psychedelic Experience* (coauthored with Timothy Leary and Ralph Metzner), *Be Here Now.*

Babitz, Eve (b. 1943): Los Angeles author, chronicler of the sixties Sunset Strip scene, friend of GP during his Chateau Marmont days. Former columnist for *Esquire* magazine. Books: *Eve's Hollywood, Slow Days, Fast Company, Two by Two.*

Baez, Joan (b. 1941): Protest-folkie singer known for strong, quavery voice, strident self-absorption, and being Bob Dylan's constant companion at the height of the folk era. Sister of folkie Mimi Fariña; covered GP and McGuinn's "Drug Store Truck Drivin' Man" at Woodstock music festival.

Ball, Earl: Country-rockabilly pianist extraordinaire; played on the ISB's *Safe at Home,* the Hollywood sessions of *Sweetheart of the Rodeo,* the lost GP sessions produced by Terry Melcher at A&M, and the Flying Burrito Brothers' third (post-GP) album. Veteran bandleader, session player, songwriter, and producer; member of Johnny Cash's band for over twenty years.

Barre, Alice: Robert Parsons' first wife; married in 1948. Mother of Jan Parsons and Becky Gottsegen.

Barry, David: Pianist/guitarist/L.A. session player. Harvard contemporary of GP, observer of the L.A. scene; played piano on Michael Nesmith's Country Time Records recordings.

Bartley, Jock (b. 1950): Guitarist. Replaced Tommy Bolin as lead guitarist in Zephyr (1968–1972); replaced original Fallen Angel guitarist Gerry Mule. Formed Firefall in 1974 with Mark Andes, Larry Burnett, and ex-Burritos Rick Roberts and Michael Clarke.

Barton, Quinn: Teacher and administrator at the Bolles School in Jacksonville, Florida.

Baxter, Dubie: GP's friend in Winter Haven. Brother of Jere Baxter. Neighbor of Patti Johnson, GP's high school girlfriend.

Beland, John (b. 1949): L.A. session guitarist. Member of the Flying Burrito Brothers from 1980–1985, when Sneaky Pete was the only remaining original member. In 1981 the group changed its name to Burrito Brothers and won *Billboard* magazine's award for "Best crossover group."

Bergman, Jo: Rolling Stones management factotum/social engineer during the Altamont and *Exile on Main Street* era and beyond.

Berline, Byron (b. 1944): Country fiddle master; played on *GP* and *Grievous Angel*. Best-known moment likely the fiddle-solo intro on the Rolling Stones' "Country Honk" on *Let It Bleed;* session and touring work includes Emmylou Harris, the Band, Willie Nelson. Known for his Double Stop Fiddle Shop in Guthrie, Oklahoma.

Bernal, Carlos: Byrds roadie; played guitar on Byrds' South African tour after GP quit the band.

Berry, Chuck (b. 1926): Foundational rock-and-roll songwriter-guitarist. GP covered his "Forty Days." The Rosetta stone of rock, Berry harnessed the rhythmic drive of R&B to epic, poetic teen narratives. Album: *The Great Twenty-Eight.*

Bland, Bobby "Blue" (b. 1930): Singer/songwriter. Schmoove-voiced R&B-blues vocalist regarded as key link between the big band sound and sixties soul (over thirty hits in the R&B top twenty). Known for powerful horn arrangements, apparently effortless swing, and white covers of his classic numbers "Further On up the Road" (covered by Eric Clapton) and "Turn On Your Love Light" (the Grateful Dead). Album: *Two Steps from the Blues.*

Booth, Stanley (b. 1942): Journalist/author. Friend of GP and Keith Richards. Book: *The True Adventures of the Rolling Stones.*

Braddock, Bobby (b. 1940): Witty, prolific country singer-songwriter from Polk County, Florida. A few years older than Gram, Braddock is best known for "D-I-V-O-R-C-E" (cowritten with Curly Putnam, taken to number one by

Tammy Wynette). "He Stopped Loving Her Today," also cowritten with Putnam, was a number one hit for George Jones.

Bragg, Charlie (b. 1931): Columbia staff engineer. Credits include *Sweetheart of the Rodeo, John Wesley Harding, Nashville Skyline,* and Johnny Cash's *At Folsom Prison.*

Brant, Marley: Biographer. Credited as coproducer on *Gram Parsons and the Fallen Angels Live 1973.* Wrote liner notes for original CD release of *GP/Grievous Angel.* Books include *Freebirds: The Lynyrd Skynyrd Story.*

Briggs, Billy: Keyboardist for the Remains. Briggs' heavy, rhythmic style complemented Barry Tashian's powerhouse lead guitar. Briggs and Tashian befriended GP and the ISB in New York; they formed the first incarnation of the FBB with ISB members in California.

Brown, Fred: GP's Bolles classmate and friend.

Brown, James (1933–2006): Singer/songwriter/producer/Godfather of Soul. As Chuck Berry is to rock, so James Brown is to soul, funk, and, via sampling, rap. Raised in Georgia, Brown brought Southern church music/Pentecostal hysteria and dynamics to R&B performance. His disciplined band, the Famous Flames, produced soul-funk luminaries William "Bootsy" Collins (bass), Maceo Parker (saxophone), and Fred Wesley (trombone), among others. Brown's heyday was characterized by precise arrangements and choreography, a steady funk beat, and chicka-chicka rhythm guitar over which James howled, grunted, spoke, and sang. At his peak, Brown's live performances were routinely transcendent. DVD: *The T.A.M.I. Show;* Albums: *Live at the Apollo; Make It Funky: The Big Payback, 1971–1975; 20 All-Time Greatest Hits!; Pass the Peas: The Best of the J.B.'s*

Bryant, Felice (1925–2003) and **Boudleaux** (1920–1987): Songwriters. Husband-and-wife team who wrote hit songs for the Everly Brothers, Roy Orbison, and Buddy Holly. GP recorded "Love Hurts" on *Grievous Angel* and *Gram Parsons and the Fallen Angels Live 1973.*

Buchanan, Bob: Guitarist. Member of the New Christy Minstrels in the mid-sixties. Met GP through singer-songwriter Fred Neil. Cowrote "Hickory Wind" with GP. Played on the sessions for the International Submarine Band's *Safe at Home.* Left Los Angeles in 1969, moved back to Michigan, and worked twenty-five years for General Motors.

Buffalo Springfield: 1960s L.A. folk-rock ensemble with psychedelic and country roots. Precursor to singer-songwriter supergroups of the early seventies. Founding lineup: Stephen Stills, Neil Young, Richie Furay, Bruce Palmer, and Dewey Martin. While not indicative of their sound, Stills' "For What It's Worth" is the song the group is best known for. Albums: *Buffalo Springfield, Buffalo Springfield Again.*

Burrell, Gretchen (b. 1953): GP's wife. Played bit role in Roger Vadim's 1971 *Pretty Maids All in a Row.* Later married Bob Carpenter of the Nitty Gritty Dirt Band.

Burrell, Larry: Right-wing L.A. television news anchor (Find Network). Also worked as an announcer for TV movies. Father of Gretchen Burrell.

Burroughs, William S. (1914–1997): Author. Proto-Beat, heroin avatar, American surrealist/halluciné. Burroughs wrote poetically of the drug experience and viewed

America through a prism of alienation and disgust, which was reflected in a prose style that rejected rationalism and social convention. Burroughs' views of drugs as a doorway to a more profound personal-political-cultural perception influenced Beat and countercultural mores. Book: *Naked Lunch*.

Burton, James (b. 1939): Guitarist, slide and dobro player; Elvis' guitarist and bandleader from 1969 on. Played lead guitar on *GP* and *Grievous Angel*; performed in 2004 GP tribute shows; quintessential session master for countless country, rock, and rockabilly artists from Ricky Nelson to Buffalo Springfield; defined the Bakersfield sound with Merle Haggard and Buck Owens; played lead guitar in the (Leon Russell–led) *Shindig!* house band, the Shindogs, with Glen D. Hardin, Delaney Bramlett, and others who would play with GP.

The Byrds: The American Beatles—if not the inventors of, then the popularizers of first-wave hippie fashion, folk rock, early hints of psychedelia, and country rock. Known for Dylan covers, multipart harmonies, constant infighting, and chiming Rickenbacker guitars. GP joined one incarnation to record *Sweetheart of the Rodeo*. Book: *Timeless Flight* by Johnny Rogan.

Cairns, Pam: Briefly GP's high school girlfriend in Winter Haven, Florida.

Cale, J. J. (b. 1938): Guitarist/songwriter. Part of the Leon Russell L.A. musical aggregation, the reclusive Cale hit nationally in 1971 with his album *Naturally* (released on Russell's Shelter Records), which included "After Midnight" (a hit for Eric Clapton in 1970), "Call Me the Breeze," and "Crazy Mama." Clapton also hit with Cale's "Cocaine." Cale's trademark whispery, slow vocals are echoed by his clean, distinct, laid-back picking. Cale also worked as an engineer and producer for legendary producer Snuff Garrett.

Campbell, Glen (b. 1936): Guitarist/singer/songwriter. Bland-faced virtuoso who played country, rock, and top-forty pop; sought as a session player for the Champs, Elvis Presley, and Frank Sinatra; was a onetime Beach Boy and did sessions with Gene Clark and the Gosdin Brothers; played (uncredited) on the ISB's *Safe at Home*. In 1968 Campbell scored an enormous country-pop crossover hit with "Wichita Lineman." Soon Campbell was hosting his own middle-of-the-road TV variety show. His MOR audience had barely an inkling of how Campbell's wide-ranging session work had shaped so much popular music of his time.

Carlton, Jim: Jazz guitarist/comedy writer for the Smothers Brothers, Jim Stafford, and others. A high school friend of GP, Carlton coproduced GP's *Another Side of This Life*, which was recorded in Carlton's living room in 1965 and 1966.

Carr, James (1942–2001): Singer. Overlooked R&B vocalist who translated lifelong severe depression into heart-wrenching, definitive Southern soul music. The FBB covered his magnum opus, "The Dark End of the Street," on *The Gilded Palace of Sin*. Carr's impassioned vocals have been described as "soul so deep you'll never find the bottom."

Cash, Johnny (1932–2003): Singer/songwriter/country-music icon/political activist/ drug addict/Jesus freak. Gravel-voiced, with a penchant for simple rhymes and simpler arrangements. His populist Man in Black persona stood as a beacon of perceived authenticity in the face of Nashville strings and sequins. After a

Beatles-like level of stardom that almost undid him, Cash dipped into relative obscurity in the eighties, focusing on battling addictions and missionary work. His 1990s Rick Rubin–produced *American Recordings* rebuilt his counterculture reputation. Albums: *At Folsom Prison* and *San Quentin, American Recordings.*

The Chad Mitchell Trio: Folk trio in Kingston Trio mold. Backup singers for Harry Belafonte at his May 1960 Carnegie Hall show. Sang satirical as well as conventional folk songs. John Denver replaced Chad Mitchell in 1965, though the group retained the Mitchell name. Albums: *Mighty Day on Campus, Singing Our Minds.*

Charles, Ray (1930–2004): Singer/pianist/composer. Lost sight as a child; learned music at a school for the deaf and blind and showed striking talent early on. A solo performing act led to a successful recording career that foretold the coming of rock and roll, but his breakthrough 1955 hit, "I Got a Woman," reshaped R&B music. Bridging religious and secular music, Charles reworked the gospel hymn "Jesus Is All the World to Me" into an R&B stomper, leading to the creation of soul music. His 1962 *Modern Sounds in Country & Western Music* proved not only another successful melding of musical styles, but also a major influence on the ISB, GP (and every other country singer), and the creation of country rock.

Clapton, Eric (b. 1945): Guitarist/songwriter. Once a blues virtuoso known for his work with John Mayall's Bluesbreakers, Cream, Blind Faith. Played in L.A. with Delaney & Bonnie; used core of Delaney & Bonnie's band for his masterpiece, *Layla and Other Associated Love Songs.*

Clark, Gene (1944–1999): Singer/songwriter/tambourine man. Founding member of the Byrds, founding member of Dillard & Clark. Best known for his brief tenure in the Byrds, Clark's melancholy harmonies shaped their early sound. Wrote early Byrds classics "Feel a Whole Lot Better," "Set You Free This Time," "Here Without You," "She Don't Care About Time," and the 1969 Turtles hit "You Showed Me," with Roger McGuinn. Clark's early solo work anticipates country rock through the prism of pop and psychedelia. Formed Dillard & Clark in 1968 with renowned bluegrass banjo picker Doug Dillard. Not quite country, not quite bluegrass, Dillard & Clark combined the mournful sentimentality of country with transcendent pop flourishes. Beset by serious health issues later in life, Clark died of complications from a bleeding ulcer aggravated by his alcohol abuse. Album: *Flying High.*

Clarke, Henry: GP's childhood friend in Waycross, Georgia.

Clarke, Michael (1946–1993): Drummer, born Michael Dick. Clarke joined the Byrds on the strength of his Brian Jonesesque haircut. Known as the "King of Common Time" and derided by fellow musicians as a hack, Clarke played with the Flying Burrito Brothers, Gene Clark, and Firefall. Died of liver failure.

Clevenger, Martin: Bass player in GP's Winter Haven band the Pacers.

Cocker, Joe (b. 1944): Singer. British white-boy soul shouter; scored hits with gritty R&B rearrangements of popular songs, including several Beatles tunes. Trademarked by intense physical performances, often appearing to be in the throes of an epileptic fit. Sang backups, along with GP, on Delaney & Bonnie sessions produced by Leon Russell. Album: *Mad Dogs & Englishmen.*

Cohn, Nudie (1902–1984): Tailor to country-music, western, and rodeo stars, born Nuta Kotlyarenko in the Ukraine. Nudie created Hank Williams concert suits, Elvis' gold lamé suit, Porter Wagoner's renowned rhinestone outfits, and various apparel for GP, including the infamous suit with LSD sugar cubes and Tuinals in rhinestones. A flamboyant character regarded as an anachronism until GP rediscovered Nudie as an icon of American entertainment style. Book: *How the West Was Worn* by Holly George-Warren and Michelle Freedman.

Colledge, Bill: GP's classmate and guitarist; casual musical partner at the Bolles School; brother of Shep.

Colledge, Shep: GP's classmate and casual musical partner at the Bolles School; brother of Bill. Regarded as a fine long-neck-banjo player.

Cone, Louise: Connor family hired help and playmate to Little Avis in Waycross. Sister to Sammy Cone.

Cone, Sammy: Connor family driver and household hired help in Waycross. Brother to Louise.

Connor, Ingram Cecil "Coon Dog": Father of GP and Little Avis; first husband of Avis Snively.

Cooper, Michael (1942–1973): Photographer. Friend of Keith Richards. Took iconic photographs of the Stones in Morocco and after the infamous Redlands bust. Befriended GP in England. Died of a drug overdose. Album covers: *Their Satanic Majesties Request, Sgt. Pepper's Lonely Hearts Club Band.*

Cordell, Denny: English producer/record executive. Began as head of Aladdin Records, a subsidiary of Island. Cordell's production company Straight Ahead worked with Procol Harum and Joe Cocker. Befriended Leon Russell while orchestrating Joe Cocker's 1970 Mad Dogs & Englishmen tour. Russell and Cordell formed Shelter Records that year. Cordell returned to Island in the early nineties and signed the Cranberries in 1991. Died in 1995. Also worked with the Moody Blues, T. Rex, Joe Cocker, Leon Russell, and Tom Petty.

Corneal, Jon (b. 1946): Drummer. GP's Winter Haven friend and bandmate. Played in the Legends with GP and Jim Stafford. Played on *Safe at Home* and *The Gilded Palace of Sin.* Played with Dillard & Clark and the Glaser Brothers.

The Corral: A Topanga Canyon club where the Flying Burrito Brothers gigged regularly. The most hippie-friendly of the Southern California C&W joints.

The Country Gazette: L.A. bluegrass band, 1971–1988. Contemporaries of the Flying Burrito Brothers and GP. Originally formed by fiddle player Byron Berline, known for their fusion of bluegrass and country rock. Precursor of the 1980s "newgrass" movement. Members included Alan Munde, Roland White, and Kenny Wertz. Album: *A Traitor in Our Midst* and *Don't Quit Your Day Job.*

Cowart, O. J.: Coon Dog Connor's employee at the Snively box plant in Waycross.

Cramer, Floyd (1933–1997): Pianist. Standout session player whose pedigree included being a cast member on the *Louisiana Hayride* radio show and playing with Webb Pierce, Elvis, Roy Orbison, the Everly Brothers, Patsy Cline, and Hank

Williams. Cramer's slip-note playing—wherein one note melded with the next—helped define the Nashville sound. "Slip-note" is the opposite of the hard, percussive, distinct playing of, say, Jerry Lee Lewis. Cramer hit with his 1960 instrumental, "Last Date." Emmylou Harris also had a hit in 1982 with her vocal version of the song. Album: *The Essential Floyd Cramer.*

Crosby, David (b. 1941): Singer/songwriter. Famously difficult and drug-addicted folkie turned rock star. Founding member of the Byrds and Crosby, Stills and Nash. Knew GP in L.A.

Davies, Hugh: Engineer. Engineered and mixed *GP* and *Grievous Angel.* GP chose Davies because of his association with Merle Haggard. Also worked with J. J. Cale and Glen Campbell.

Davis, Jesse Ed (1944–1988): Guitarist/pianist. Sought-after session musician who toured with Conway Twitty and was a member of Taj Mahal's band. Produced and played on Gene Clark's 1971 album *White Light.* Davis' solo album, *Jesse Davis!,* released in 1971, featured GP on backing vocals. Davis' long battle with drug and alcohol addiction ended when he died from an overdose in a Long Beach laundromat.

De Haven, Dorothy, a.k.a. Haney: GP's maternal grandmother, Big Avis' mother.

Delaney & Bonnie: Bonnie Bramlett (vocalist, b. 1944) and husband Delaney Bramlett (vocals and guitar, b. 1939) befriended GP in L.A.; the ever-changing lineup of their band included the core of Eric Clapton's *Layla* ensemble and musicians from Leon Russell's orbit. Eric Clapton and others utilized Delaney & Bonnie as a conduit to American blues and gospel-inflected roots music. Delaney & Bonnie, with Rita Coolidge, appear briefly in the echt road movie 1970's *Vanishing Point.* Their albums do not reflect the soulful camp-meeting seduction of their live performances. Albums: *Delaney & Bonnie on Tour with Eric Clapton, The Best of Delaney & Bonnie.*

Delgatto, John: Founder of Sierra Records and Books. Dedicated to preserving the legacy of Gram Parsons and Clarence White. Released *Gram Parsons and the Fallen Angels Live 1973* in 1982 and published Sid Griffin's book *Gram Parsons: A Musical Biography* in 1984. Wrote liner notes for Reprise's rerelease of *GP* and *Grievous Angel* in 1990.

Des Barres, Pamela (b. 1948): Groupie/author. Original L.A. supergroupie. Bridged the conservatism of the 1950s and the sexual liberation of the 1970s. Played in the Frank Zappa–produced GTOs (Girls Together Outrageously). Best-known for her memoir *I'm with the Band* and *Rock Bottom: Dark Moments in Music Babylon.*

De Wilde, Brandon (1942–1972): Actor and guitar player famous as boy Joey Starrett in 1953's *Shane.* Died in auto accident, age thirty. Friend of GP in New York City and L.A.

Dickson, Jim (b. 1931): Producer/music publisher/manager. Instrumental in the formation of the Byrds; encouraged them to record Dylan. Produced *Burrito Deluxe* at the behest of Chris Hillman. Credits include *The Best of Lord Buckley* and Hamilton Camp's *Paths of Victory.*

Dillard & Clark: Country-tinged folk-rock group led by Gene Clark and Doug Dillard. Contemporaries of the Flying Burrito Brothers. The Burritos often covered Clark's compositions and vice versa. Michael Clarke played with them before joining the Flying Burrito Brothers. Album: *Fantastic Expedition of Dillard & Clark.*

Dillard, Douglas (b. 1937): Banjo player. Among L.A.'s finest country-bluegrass pickers. Played with the Byrds on 1968's *Sweetheart of the Rodeo* European tour. Formed Dillard & Clark with Gene Clark.

The Dillards: Progressive bluegrass group. Founded by brothers Rodney and Douglas Dillard. Offended bluegrass purists with their use of echo. Doug Dillard's high-speed picking led to accusations that the band was speeding up their recordings. Albums: *Back Porch Bluegrass, Wheatstraw Suite.*

Doherty, Denny (1940–2007): Canadian singer-songwriter. Member of the mid-sixties folk-pop group the Mamas & the Papas.

Domino, Antoine "Fats" (b. 1928): Pianist/songwriter. Fats' loping New Orleans backbeat fueled fifties hits "Blueberry Hill," "Walking to New Orleans," "Ain't That a Shame" (which was emasculated by Pat Boone), and others. His immortal left hand helped bring New Orleans R&B to a white teen audience. Appeared (as did Little Richard) in 1957's *The Girl Can't Help It.* Album: *My Blue Heaven: The Best of Fats Domino.*

The Doors: Sixties L.A. band exploring Thanatos and Eros via a big beat and second-rate poetry. Renowned for asshole lead singer. Album: *The Doors.*

Dunlop, Ian: Bassist for the International Submarine Band. Lifelong friend of GP. Now a painter living in rural England.

Dylan, Bob (b. 1941): Singer/songwriter. Reinvigorated folk music with deeply personal, poetic, or political lyrics; created folk rock, offered early visions of country rock, gave the Beatles their first marijuana, and, in the words of a perceptive critic, used words not to generate meaning but to escape meaning. Least-known great album: *Soundtrack to Pat Garrett and Billy the Kid.*

The Eagles: The worst iconic band in American rock. In fact, much worse than that.

Earle, Steve (b. 1955): Singer/songwriter/producer/actor. Combines second-generation country-outlaw sensibility with unusual levels of lyric articulation, drug consumption, political awareness, musical archivism, and Hank Williams–style self-destruction in the face of astute self-knowledge. Earle's disparate songwriting and embrace of multiple musical forms make him, consciously or not, the leading practitioner of the notions of Cosmic American Music. Album: *The Mountain,* with the Del McCoury Band.

Emery, Ralph (b. 1933): Conservative Nashville DJ on WSM-AM. Interviewed the Byrds during the recording of *Sweetheart of the Rodeo* and insulted them on the air. GP and Roger McGuinn wrote "Drug Store Truck Drivin' Man" in retaliation.

Ethridge, Chris (b. 1947): Bassist for the Flying Burrito Brothers, popular 1970s L.A. session player. Cowriter with GP of "Hot Burrito #1," "Hot Burrito #2," and "She." Responsible for much of the soul influence in the first incarnation of the Flying Burrito Brothers.

The Everly Brothers: Singer/songwriters Don and Phil echoed the Louvin Brothers with their one-voiced close-harmony vocals, perhaps the most recognizable harmony singing in rock after the Beach Boys. They strummed acoustic guitars like folksingers, their cadences and melodies came from country music, and their lyrics reflected classic pop concerns. With twenty-six top forty singles (their greatest successes spanned 1957–1961), the Everlys influenced the Beatles, Simon and Garfunkel, the Beach Boys, GP, and thus pretty much everyone else mining profound emotion from harmony. Album: *The Definitive Everly Brothers: A Career Spanning Retrospective.*

Faithfull, Marianne (b. 1946): Singer/songwriter/autobiographer. English beauty and fixture on the London scene who hit with Jagger-Richards composition "As Tears Go By" in 1964. Performed in 1968's Rolling Stones Rock 'n' Roll Circus and Kenneth Anger's *Lucifer Rising.* Knew GP socially in England. Album: *Broken English.*

The Fallen Angels: GP's band in support of his solo tour after recording *GP.*

Fenton, Kathy: GP's friend. Former girlfriend of Phil Kaufman. Lived with GP and Kaufman in Van Nuys in the weeks preceding GP's death.

Fisher, Margaret: GP's friend from his Bolles days in Jacksonville; briefly GP's lover. With GP the night he died.

Flanz, Neil: Canadian pedal-steel player. Moved to Nashville in the mid-sixties and backed Charlie Louvin, Jean Shepard, Billy Walker, and Ray Pillow. GP's steel player for Fallen Angels tour. Later toured with Roy Drusky.

The Flying Burrito Brothers: GP's band after failure of the International Submarine Band. Early incarnation of country rock and rock-country fashion. Album: *The Gilded Palace of Sin.*

Fonda, Peter (b. 1940): Actor/director/screenwriter. Son of actor Henry Fonda, brother of Jane Fonda, Peter knew GP in L.A. and recorded GP's "November Nights." Starred in 1967 LSD film *The Trip;* produced, cowrote, and starred in 1969's cultural watershed *Easy Rider;* directed 1971's psychedelic western *The Hired Hand.* Model for, yet sole practitioner of, an iconic mode of laid-back L.A. sixties cool.

Foutz, Tony: Screenwriter and filmmaker. Friend of Keith Richards and Rolling Stones entourage. Befriended GP in England in 1968. Gram's roommate at the Chateau Marmont. Wrote and directed the film *Saturation '70,* starring GP, Michelle Phillips, Julian Jones, Stash Kosslowski, and Andee Nathanson. Screenplay: *Tales of Ordinary Madness.*

Freeman, Buddy (1934–2004): Friend of GP and family in Florida. Booked solo shows for GP and managed the Shilos.

Frey, Glenn (b. 1948): Singer/songwriter/guitarist. Founding member, the Eagles.

Furay, Richie (b. 1944): Singer/songwriter/guitarist. Founding member of Buffalo Springfield. Formed Poco, an early L.A. country-rock ensemble known for a sprightly sound and pop hooks (written by Jim Messina), in 1968. At the behest of Asylum Records president David Geffen, Furay teamed up with Chris Hillman and

J. D. Souther in 1974 to form the Souther-Hillman-Furay Band. Furay converted to Christianity in the late seventies and is pastor of a church in Colorado. Albums: *Buffalo Springfield, Pickin' Up the Pieces* (with Poco), *The Souther-Hillman-Furay Band.*

Ganahl, Ginny (1947–2003): Secretary to L.A. producer-songwriter-singer Terry Melcher. Knew GP in L.A.

Gauvin, Mickey: Drummer, the International Submarine Band.

Geffen, David (b. 1943): Music manager/film producer/media mogul. Rose to fame as manager of archetypal SoCal singer-songwriters Joni Mitchell, Jackson Browne, Crosby, Stills and Nash, and others. Helped assemble and launch the Eagles. Became top Hollywood talent manager, dealmaker, billionaire. Cofounded film studio Dreamworks SKG.

Glaser, Tompall (b. 1933): Country singer/songwriter. After vigorously expressing his outrage at the Byrds' appearance and behavior at the Grand Ole Opry (where he served as MC), Glaser saw the light and hopped on the Outlaw bandwagon. With Harlan Howard cowrote "Streets of Baltimore," which GP covered on *GP.*

Goldberg, Barry (b. 1941): Musician. Wrote "Do You Know How It Feels to Be Lonesome" with Gram.

The Gosdin Brothers: Singers/songwriters/country and bluegrass musicians. Active 1961–1973. Vern (b. 1934) and Rex Gosdin (1938–1983) played with Chris Hillman in the Southern California bluegrass ensemble the Golden State Boys. Sang on Gene Clark's debut solo album *Gene Clark with the Gosdin Brothers.* Vern Gosdin found success as a country solo artist through the 1980s and '90s. Album: *Sound of Goodbye.*

Gottsegen, Becky: GP's stepsister. Daughter of Robert Parsons and Alice Barre, sister of Jan.

Graves, Judson: GP's Bolles classmate.

Grech, Jenny: Wife of Rick Grech.

Grech, Rick (1946–1990): Bass player/songwriter/producer. Played bass in English bands Family, Blind Faith, and Traffic. Produced *GP;* wrote "Kiss the Children" on *GP.*

Green, Lloyd (b. 1937): Nashville session musician. Pedal-steel player on *Sweetheart of the Rodeo* and the Byrds' live show on the Grand Ole Opry.

Grossman, Albert (1926–1986): Music manager/producer. Bob Dylan's manager, cocreator of the Newport Folk Festival. At one time the very model of the inscrutable hip capitalist whose personal credibility sprang from a combination of native chutzpah and the artists on his roster. Considered signing GP's early band the Shilos. Grossman's wife and living room appear on the cover of Dylan's 1965 *Bringing It All Back Home.*

The GTOs (Girls Together Outrageously): Groupies/Whisky a Go Go scenemakers Miss Pamela, Miss Mercy, Sandra, Sparky, Cinderella, and Miss Christine were the queen band companions during the heyday of the Sunset Strip. Miss Pamela and Miss Mercy befriended GP. Album: *Permanent Damage.*

Guidera, Tom: Bassist/songwriter. Collaborated with Emmylou Harris early in her career. Cowrote "Hearts on Fire" with Walter Egan.

Haggard, Merle (b. 1937): Singer/songwriter/guitarist. Cocreator of the Bakersfield sound, Haggard brought the electric guitar to country music. Cranky, misanthropic, and reclusive, Haggard, with his quiet singing and self-obsession, lacks the soul of George Jones and the humor of Buck Owens. Many of a certain generation—for good reason—dismissed him entirely after his left-baiting, pro-Vietnam, anti-hippie anthems "Okie from Muskogee" and "The Fightin' Side of Me." Was to produce GP's first solo album but backed out at the last minute. Album: *Same Train, Different Train: A Tribute to Jimmie Rodgers.*

Halee, Roy: Producer/engineer. Engineer for the Byrds' *Sweetheart of the Rodeo.* Best known as producer and engineer for Simon and Garfunkel and on Paul Simon's *Graceland.* Also worked with the Lovin' Spoonful, Journey, and Blood, Sweat and Tears.

Hardin, Glen D. (b. 1939): Pianist/arranger. After playing in Buddy Holly's band the Crickets, became Elvis Presley's pianist and arranger and a widely sought-after session musician. Arranged band charts and backing vocals and played on *GP* and *Grievous Angel.*

Harris, Emmylou (b. 1947): Singer/songwriter. Gram's last, and most soulful, singing partner. Queen of Nashville after a thirty-year career of quality country and country-rock albums. Known for her high keening voice and unmatched harmony singing. Not a songwriter at heart, but demonstrated singular gift for selecting musicians, collaborators, and songwriters to cover. 1995's *Wrecking Ball* was a crossover success. Albums: *Luxury Liner, Elite Hotel.*

Hartford, John (1937–2001): Guitarist/banjo/fiddle virtuoso/singer/songwriter/producer. Genius Nashville cat, wrote "Gentle on My Mind" and served as multi-instrumentalist on *Sweetheart of the Rodeo.* Album: *Natural to Be Gone.*

Hazlewood, Lee (1929–2007): Singer/songwriter/producer. Famous for Nancy Sinatra's Hazlewood-produced hits and their duets ("These Boots Are Made for Walking," "Jackson," "Some Velvet Morning"). An Oklahoma tough-ass with a cultivated sinister air and distinctive half-singing, half-talking voice, Hazlewood released an early concept album, *Trouble Is a Lonesome Town,* in 1963. Signed the ISB and had his then-girlfriend, Suzi Jane Hokom, produce their one album.

Hearts and Flowers: 1967 L.A. band featuring Bernie Leadon and folk-flavored acoustic-guitar originals played in country time signatures that prefigure the SoCal sound of the early and mid-seventies. Band member Rick Cunha hosted Hoot Night at the L.A. club the Troubadour. Album: *The Complete Hearts and Flowers.*

Henriques, Peter: Member of the Bolles School faculty.

Hillman, Chris (b. 1944): Singer/songwriter/bass player/mandolinist/guitarist. Member of the Scottsville Squirrel Barkers, founding member of the Byrds, member of the Flying Burrito Brothers and the Souther-Hillman-Furay Band, and founder of Desert Rose Band. Innovative, wildly underestimated, historically significant bassist, songwriter, and harmony singer. Critical in creating signature Byrds sound and key figure in country rock. Collaborated with GP on Burrito Brothers classics "Sin City," "Wheels," and "Hippie Boy," among others. Album: *The Desert Rose Band*.

Hokom, Suzi Jane: Producer. Credited producer of the International Submarine Band's *Safe at Home*. Former girlfriend of Lee Hazlewood and Douglas Dillard.

Hopper, Dennis (b. 1936): Actor/director/photographer/art collector. A naturalist actor in the style of James Dean, Hopper cowrote, directed, and starred in *Easy Rider*. After years of drugs and madness (an eight-day marriage to Michelle Phillips included), Hopper returned to stardom with a self-parodying performance in David Lynch's *Blue Velvet* (1986). Forgotten in his subsequent twenty years of playing loonies is that Hopper is easily the finest screen actor of his generation and a visually subtle director capable of presenting emotional suffering with an unblinking eye on a par with GP's. Film, as actor: *The American Friend*; as director/actor: *Out of the Blue, Last Movie*.

Hoskins, Rob: GP's maternal cousin. Son of Evalyn (Dede) Snively.

Howard, Harlan (1927–2002): Songwriter. Active 1950–1990. Known as "the Irving Berlin of country music." In 1961, placed fifteen songs in the country top forty. Best known for "I Fall to Pieces" (Patsy Cline) and "I've Got a Tiger by the Tail" (Buck Owens). GP covered "Image of Me" (cowritten with Wayne Kemp) on *Burrito Deluxe* and "Streets of Baltimore" (cowritten with Tompall Glaser) on *GP*.

Hubbard, Robert: GP's English teacher and mentor at the Bolles School.

Sam Hutt, a.k.a. Hank Wangford (b. 1946): Musician/doctor. London rock-and-roll doctor who befriended GP during his time in Europe. In 1972, collaborated with GP and Rick Grech on a Grech solo album that was never released. In the 1990s, using the name Hank Wangford, Hutt created and starred in a country television and radio series for the BBC including episodes "Big Big Country," "The A to Z of C&W," "Ghengiz Khan Was a Cowboy Too," and "Looking for the Lonesome Yodel."

The International Submarine Band: Early country-rock band. Members included GP, guitarist John Nuese, Ian Dunlop on bass, and drummer Mickey Gauvin. First single: "The Russians Are Coming, the Russians Are Coming" (1966). Second single, the surprisingly pop "Sum Up Broke" (1966). Dunlop and Gauvin left and were replaced by Earl Ball and Winter Haven's Jon Corneal for the recording of their sole album, 1967's *Safe at Home*. Jay Dee Maness (pedal steel) also played on the album, which was produced by Lee Hazlewood's girlfriend Suzi Jane Hokom. *Safe at Home* remains a remarkably credible country record.

Iron Butterfly: Early heavy metal band. Signed to Atco in 1967, Butterfly released *In-A-Gadda-Da-Vida* in 1968. Featuring a 17:05 jam of the title song on side A, the album sold eight million copies and spent eighty-one weeks in the top ten and 140 weeks on the top-two-hundred chart. Moronic and catchy, the song introduced a mass audience to overlong drum and bass solos. Iron Butterfly demonstrated to record labels that the youth-psychedelic audience had more spending power than previously conceived. Album: *In-A-Gadda-Da-Vida*.

Jagger, Mick (b. 1943): Singer/songwriter/producer, the Rolling Stones. Empire-builder Jagger brought the Stones (and thus rock) into the corporate, jetset, and conventionally glamorous worlds. Jagger demonstrated how to maximize band earnings and status yet maintain credibility. To a point.

James, Jim: Singer/songwriter/guitarist for My Morning Jacket.

Johnson, Patti: Briefly GP's musical collaborator and high school girlfriend in Winter Haven. Dogged by rumors of pregnancy by, and planned elopement with, GP.

Jones, George (b. 1933): Country singer/songwriter. Regarded as the most expressive singer in country and one of its foremost madmen. Drugs, alcohol, love, manic depression: Jones gobbled all the pain each produced and came back for thirds. Goofy-looking, irritable, iconic. Album: *The Essential George Jones: The Spirit of Country*.

The Journeymen: 1960s folk trio known for stellar, if antiseptic, harmony arrangements. Members included John Phillips, Dick Weissman, and Scott McKenzie. Primary influence on GP's high school folk ensemble, the Shilos. John Phillips formed the Mamas & the Papas; Scott McKenzie sang Phillips' "San Francisco (Be Sure to Wear Flowers in Your Hair)." Album: *The Journeymen*.

Kelley, Kevin: Drummer for the Byrds during the *Sweetheart of the Rodeo* era. Also played with L.A. new-blues group the Rising Sons, featuring Ry Cooder and Taj Mahal.

Kelly, Joe: Acoustic bass player, the Shilos.

The Kentucky Colonels: Virtuoso bluegrass band featuring Clarence White and his brother Roland. Brought the acoustic guitar (played by Clarence) to prominence as a lead instrument in bluegrass. Album: *The Kentucky Colonels*.

Keys, Bobby (b. 1943): Saxophonist. An (improbably) living incarnation of rock-and-roll history, Keys recorded or toured with Buddy Holly, Mad Dogs & Englishmen, George Harrison, John Lennon, Delaney & Bonnie, Eric Clapton, and the Rolling Stones. His immediately recognizable ripping, rasping sound highlights "Brown Sugar." As famous for his prodigious appetites as for his legendary résumé.

The Kingston Trio: Folk trio. Instrumental in the popular folk revival. Had four albums in the top-ten charts in the early sixties. Spawned legion of button-down collegiate folk trios. Derided for being aggressively mainstream and lacking political consciousness. Best known for their rendition of "Tom Dooley," a number one hit in 1958. Album: *The Kingston Trio*.

Kleinow, "Sneaky" Pete (1934–2007): Pedal-steel guitarist/animator. Pedal-steel guitarist for the Flying Burrito Brothers. Known for eccentric tunings and instantly recognizable style, an amalgam of thoughtfully composed solos in the traditional country mode and near-psychedelic soundscapes reflecting a modern, more industrial, space-age sound. Animator on *Gumby* cartoons and others.

Lacerte, Grant: Winter Haven high school friend, confidant, and bandmate of GP. Husband of Karen Lacerte.

Lacerte, Karen: Winter Haven high school friend of GP; met her husband, Grant, through GP.

Lanaux, Walter: Friend of Robert Parsons.

LaVoie, Kent, a.k.a. Lobo (b. 1943): Singer/songwriter/guitarist. Winter Haven bandmate of GP and Jim Stafford. Wrote and sang hits "Me and You and a Dog Named Boo" and "I'd Love You to Want Me." LaVoie's cheesy lyrics and overwrought production do nothing to keep his choruses from burrowing into your head. And never leaving.

Lawrence, Linda: London and L.A. scenemaker. Briefly GP's girlfriend during his Chateau Marmont days. Mother of Julian Jones (father: Brian Jones). Later married Donovan and moved to Ireland.

Leadon, Bernie (b. 1947): Guitarist/multi-instrumentalist/songwriter. Rhythm and lead guitarist in later incarnation of the Flying Burrito Brothers; founding member of the Eagles (he named the band); played in SoCal ensembles the Scottsville Squirrel Barkers, Hearts and Flowers, and Dillard & Clark. Stellar rhythm guitarist of great understatement.

Leary, Timothy (1920–1996): LSD avatar; Harvard professor and public figure. Leary helped popularize the psychedelic lysergic acid diethylamide, LSD. His oft-repeated phrase, "Tune in, turn on, drop out," became a motto for the sixties. Regarded now not so much as a prophet of psychedelics but as a hustler whose publicity seeking led to widespread misunderstanding of the LSD experience and draconian laws suppressing its use.

Leedy, Gene: Architect; friend to Robert Parsons and Big Avis Snively.

The Legends: GP's Winter Haven band. Members came and went, but a representative lineup would be GP (guitar), Jim Carlton (bass), Jim Stafford (lead guitar), Jon Corneal (drums), and Jesse Chambers (bass).

Lewis, Jerry Lee (b. 1935): Pianist/songwriter/rock pioneer and Sun Records contemporary of Elvis. Lewis' deranged white Pentecostal rave-ups, accelerated blues-derived triplets, and sexually explicit lyrics made him the ne plus ultra of scary, transcendent speed-freak rednecks lost in the demonic lure of rock and roll. Shifted to more conventional country songs later in his career. Created an influential genre that seems to contain only him. Album: *25 All-Time Greatest Recordings.*

Lewy, Henry (1927–2006): Music engineer and producer. Joined A&M Records in 1967. Engineer for *The Gilded Palace of Sin.* Known for his association with Joni Mitchell. Also worked with Crosby, Stills and Nash, the Mamas & the Papas, Joan Baez, Van Morrison, Neil Young, and Leonard Cohen. Credits: *Blue, Crosby, Stills and Nash, Harvest.*

The Limeliters: Folk trio. Contemporaries of the Kingston Trio. In 1963 became the musical representatives of Coca-Cola and performed the jingle "Things Go Better with Coke." Albums: *The Limeliters, Tonight in Person.*

Little Feat: Seventies L.A. band led by former Mothers of Invention singer/song-writer/producer/slide-guitar and harmonica genius Lowell George (1945–1979). Characterized by literate, heartbreaking lyrics and a sound comprising traditional country, New Orleans, and blues elements filtered through George's unique syncopation. Someone said, presciently: "Wrote parodies of truck-stop songs that are the most moving truck-stop songs you ever heard." George died of a heart attack, apparently caused by years of drug and alcohol abuse. Albums: *Little Feat, Dixie Chicken*.

Little Richard (b. 1932): Pianist/songwriter, born Richard Penniman. As Jerry Lee Lewis provided the wigged-out white piano madman for early rock and roll, so Little Richard offered an even more wigged-out black version. His brief, soaring arc of hits was cut short in 1957 by a combination of cultural suppression (Pat Boone rerecording his hits in the blandest possible versions) and Little Richard's own religious epiphany, which led him to renounce the Satanism of rock and roll (an issue for Jerry Lee as well). His early records now sound impossibly frantic, tribal, and raw. Possessed, along with James Brown and Ike Turner, of the most enviable process/conk job in rock and roll. Album: *The Specialty Sessions*.

Lomax, John (1867–1948): American ethnomusicologist/writer/folk archivist–preservationist. Beginning in the 1930s, Lomax, later joined by son Alan, toured rural America and prisons recording—with cumbersome, early-generation portable equipment—ballads, blues, work songs, hymns, and hollers for the Archive of the American Folk Song. Credited with discovering Leadbelly (Huddie Ledbetter). Books: *American Folk Songs and Ballads, Cowboy Songs and Other Frontier Ballads*.

Lomax, John III: Rock journalist/manager. Represented Townes Van Zandt, Steve Earle. Author of *Nashville: Music City U.S.A.*

Longbranch Pennywhistle: Early incarnation of the SoCal sound featuring future Eagle Glenn Frey and L.A. singer-songwriter J. D. Souther.

The Louvin Brothers: Singer/songwriters Ira (1924–1965) and Charlie (b. 1927) Louvin, born Loudermilk, were among the most influential harmony singers in country music. Specialized in tales of tragedy, misfortune, damnation, and hard fate. Their tough, spare, rural sound evokes great emotion and they were hugely successful. GP covered their "Cash on the Barrelhead" on *Grievous Angel*. Album: *Tragic Songs of Life*.

Love: Cult stars of the sixties L.A. rock scene. Led by two gifted songwriters, acid-era genius-nutcase Arthur Lee and former Byrds roadie Bryan MacLean. Combining folk rock, protopunk, and orchestral ingredients, the trailblazing psychedelic unit released three breakthrough albums in two years before succumbing to drug abuse and paranoia. Lee carried on, reincarnating the group with different musicians for decades before serving a jail term on assault charges. Albums: *Love, Da Capo, Forever Changes*.

Mad Dogs & Englishmen: Joe Cocker's 1970 U.S. tour documented on an elaborate gatefold album on A&M records and a tour film of the same name. Leon Russell, who played on the tour, was enlisted as musical director and brought in many of his accomplished sidemen. The enormous forty-member band and chorus created a model for rock excess. Though ostensibly created as a tour to promote Cocker, Russell made the show a vehicle for himself, his band, and his signature sound.

Main Street Band: Loose jamming collective of L.A. musicians including J. J. Cale and Leon Russell. GP and Chris Hillman sat in occasionally as they were forming FBB.

Mallard, James: GP's Bolles School classmate.

Maness, Jay Dee: L.A. pedal-steel player. Played on *Safe at Home* and L.A. sessions for *Sweetheart of the Rodeo*. Played with Buck Owens, Dwight Yoakam, Beck, and Rod Stewart.

Manson, Charles (b. 1934): Cult leader. In 1969, young hippies who lived in Manson's "commune" invaded a house owned by producer Terry Melcher and killed movie star Sharon Tate and four others. Manson was convicted as the ringleader of those murders; he was not accused of being a participant. His minions also murdered Gary Hinman and Leno and Rosemary LaBianca. Many cite the Tate-LaBianca murders as the end of the sixties. Manson epitomized the old-school street wolf emerging from the jailbird underclass to prey on naïve, middle-class, hippie-kid sheep. A would-be musician, Manson thrust himself into the lives of Beach Boys Dennis and Brian Wilson, who introduced Manson to Melcher. Book: *Helter Skelter*.

Markland, Ted: Actor. Befriended GP in the late sixties. Supporting actor known for his roles in westerns and action films. Close friend of Steve McQueen, Jack Nicholson, and Peter Fonda. Popularized the mysticism of Joshua Tree and staged Timothy Leary's 1967 wedding to Rosemary Woodruff there. Was involved in Tony Foutz's film *Saturation '70*. Films: *One Flew Over the Cuckoo's Nest, Angels from Hell*.

Marks, Larry: Producer. Produced Flying Burrito Brothers album *The Gilded Palace of Sin*. Also worked with Phil Ochs and Chad and Jeremy.

Marquand, Christian (1927–2000): Actor/director. Befriended GP in L.A. through Tony Foutz and Andee Nathanson. Films, as actor: *Ciao Manhattan, Apocalypse Now Redux*; as director: *Candy*.

Martin, Michael: GP's valet on the Fallen Angels tour. Befriended GP through Phil Kaufman. Former boyfriend of Dale McElroy. With GP on his last trip to Joshua Tree.

McClure, Rufus: GP's instructor at the Bolles School.

McElroy, Dale: Heiress/scenemaker. Friend of Phil Kaufman's; present in Joshua Tree when GP overdosed.

McGuinn, Roger (b. 1942): Singer/songwriter/guitarist. Founder and leader of the Byrds; known for his distinctive quavering vocals, chiming Rickenbacker twelve-string guitar, early Dylan covers, and various religious conversions. Strangely anti-charismatic, McGuinn seems much smaller than his legacy. Album: *Sweetheart of the Rodeo*.

McNeer, Dickie: Winter Haven friend of GP. Played in the Village Vanguards with GP and Patti Johnson.

Melcher, Terry (1942–2004): Singer/songwriter/producer. The son of fifties actress-singer-superstar Doris Day, Melcher started out with prefab surf music, forming the Rip Chords with soon-to-be Beach Boy Bruce Johnston and scoring a hit with

"Hey Little Cobra." As a Columbia Records staff producer, Melcher shaped the Byrds' sound on *Mr. Tambourine Man* and *Turn! Turn! Turn!* Produced GP's solo sessions for A&M. After auditioning and rejecting Charles Manson, Melcher was led to believe he was the intended target of the Sharon Tate murders, which took place in his former home. Released an eclectic country-tinged solo album in 1974, coproduced by Johnston and featuring veteran session men and performers Hal Blaine, Michael Clarke, Ry Cooder, Sneaky Pete, Jay Dee Maness, and Spooner Oldham. Album: *Terry Melcher.*

The Modern Lovers: Formed by Velvet Underground–obsessed Jonathan Richman in 1970, the Modern Lovers presaged the stripped-down attack and sardonic attitude of punk. Managed by Eddie Tickner, the Lovers played "Gram Parsons' Funeral Party" at Phil Kaufman's house. Albums: *The Modern Lovers, Precise Modern Lovers Order.*

Moss, Jerry: Record executive. Cofounder of A&M Records.

Muma, Bonnie: Little Avis Snively's babysitter in Winter Haven; became Robert Parsons' third and final wife.

Nashville West: 1967 band featuring early aspects of country-rock sound. Members included Clarence White, Gene Parsons, Gib Guilbeau, and Wayne Moore. Band name came from an extended residency at an El Monte, California, bar of the same name.

Nathanson, Andee: Photographer/L.A. scenemaker/observer/muse. Close friend of GP during his Chateau days.

Neil, Fred (1936–2001): Singer/songwriter. Early Greenwich Village folksinger and twelve-string guitarist, best known for "Everybody's Talkin'," covered by Harry Nilsson as the theme song for the film *Midnight Cowboy* in 1969. Hit covers by Roy Orbison ("Candy Man") and Buddy Holly ("Come Back Baby") allowed Neil to indulge his interest in heroin and research into human communication with dolphins. Friend of GP, McGuinn, David Crosby. Album: *Fred Neil (Everybody's Talkin').*

Nelson, Rick (1940–1985): Guitarist/songwriter. Son of swing-era bandleader Ozzie Nelson, Rick grew up on television in a hit show starring his mother, father, and brother, *Ozzie and Harriet.* After teen pop success in the late fifties, Nelson became sincerely enthralled by country music. Neither pop nor country audiences granted him much credibility. His country albums *Bright Lights* and *Country Fever* featured Elvis' band (which GP later hired for his solo records). The best-known song from his adult career, "Garden Party," showcases Nelson's heartfelt bitterness that no one would listen to him play country. He died in a plane crash. Rumors—strongly denied by the Nelson family—persist that the crash was caused by an onboard fire resulting from someone with careless technique freebasing cocaine.

Nesmith, Michael (b. 1942): Singer/songwriter/guitarist. Heir to the Liquid Paper fortune, Nesmith came to fame as the ironic Monkee, the one who could actually play his instrument. A Texan with a deep sense of musical roots, Nesmith formed the First National Band, one of the earliest country-rock groups. He commissioned and collected a notable set of Nudie and other country-tailored rhinestone suits. Album: *Magnetic South*.

The New Christy Minstrels: Folk group. Formed by singer-guitarist Randy Sparks in 1961, the group's name refers to Edward Pearce Christy's mid-nineteenth-century blackface minstrel group. Their fresh-faced image, upbeat delivery, and lack of political engagement made them one of the most popular-yet-reviled folk ensembles of the early 1960s. Members included Gene Clark, John Denver, Barry McGuire, Kenny Rogers, and the Association's Larry Ramos. Album: *Ramblin'*.

Nuese, John: Guitarist with a penchant for roots music and rock and roll. Member of various Boston rock bands including the Trolls. Nuese and GP met in Cambridge, forming a musical partnership and lifelong friendship. Their first group, Gram Parsons and the Like, morphed into the ISB. Nuese and GP were the only original ISB members to play on *Safe at Home*. In 2000, Nuese put together the compilation album *The Gram Parsons Notebook*. Currently a guitar teacher in Nashville and upstate New York.

Ostin, Mo (b. 1927): Legendary president of Reprise Records and later Warner Bros. Responsible for signing Little Feat, Neil Young, Van Halen, Prince, the Beach Boys, and Prince, among others. Signed GP for his solo records.

Owens, Buck (1929–2006): Singer/songwriter/guitarist/bandleader. Though unfortunately most famous as the creepily animated cohost of the redneck comedy-variety show *Hee Haw* (and his fucking red-white-and-blue guitar), Owens defined the Bakersfield sound with his band the Buckaroos. Owens and lead guitarist Don Rich eschewed pedal steel, country fiddle, and backup orchestration. Steely, staccato, amplified guitar picking exemplified their sound and placed Owens precisely between country's rural roots and Nashville's glossy showbiz. The spare arrangements, which hark back to simple honky-tonk and rockabilly, reveal a sophisticated, deliberate reductivism played with discipline and rigor. Owens had twenty-one number one songs. Albums: *I've Got a Tiger by the Tail* and *Live at Carnegie Hall*.

The Pacers: GP's first Winter Haven band. Lineup: GP (guitar), Jimmy Allen (guitar), Martin Clevenger (bass), Skip Rosser (drums).

Pallenberg, Anita (b. 1944): Actress/model/fashion avatar/witch. Knew GP socially in L.A. and Europe. Best known for her romantic liaisons with the Rolling Stones. Dated Brian Jones; common-law wife of Keith Richards from 1967 to 1977, and briefly lovers with Mick Jagger. Often referred to as the sixth Rolling Stone. With Richards, an icon of wasted elegance. Mother of Marlon and Dandelion Richards. Films: *Performance, Barbarella, Dillinger Is Dead*.

The Palomino: North Hollywood club where the Flying Burrito Brothers gigged regularly. GP was one of the first longhairs to perform at its legendary talent night.

Parsons, Little Avis: GP's younger sister; daughter of Avis Snively and I. C. "Coon Dog" Connor.

Parsons, Diane: GP's youngest sister. Daughter of Avis Snively and Robert Parsons.

Parsons, Gene (b. 1944): Guitarist/banjoist/drummer/inventor. Byrds drummer from 1968's *Dr. Byrds and Mr. Hyde* to 1971's *Farther Along*. With Clarence White, invented the B-Bender, a device designed to enable a guitarist to evoke a sound similar to a pedal steel. Also played with Nashville West.

Parsons, Polly (b. 1967): GP's daughter with Nancy Ross. Producer of 2004 Gram Parsons tribute concerts in Santa Barbara and L.A. Coauthor of *Grievous Angel: An Intimate Biography of Gram Parsons.*

Parsons, Robert: GP's stepfather. Second husband to Avis Snively Connor Parsons; father of Becky Gottsegen, Jan Parsons, and Diane Parsons.

Paxton, Tom (b. 1937): Singer/songwriter/guitarist. Soft-voiced protest singer who also writes children's books. Best known for "The Last Thing on My Mind," as covered by Judy Collins. Album: *I Can't Help but Wonder Where I'm Bound: The Best of Tom Paxton.*

Pedrick, Edmund: Attorney. Friend of GP's parents in Waycross, Georgia.

Perkins, Carl (1932–1998): Guitarist/singer. Rockabilly pioneer who wrote and recorded classics of the genre. Perkins' cool-cat delivery of clever lyrics over a succinct blend of country and R&B influenced the Beatles, the Stones, and at least the first two decades of rock and roll. Scored a hit with "Blue Suede Shoes" (written on a potato sack), though a car accident hindered his success, leaving Elvis' cover version to rule the spotlight. With a far less metaphorical oeuvre and persona than his Sun Records labelmates Elvis, Johnny Cash, and Jerry Lee Lewis. In his later years, performed wearing the most tragic toupee in rock. Album: *Carl Perkins: Original Sun Greatest Hits.*

Peter, Paul & Mary: American folk trio. Bob Dylan's manager, Albert Grossman, put the group together in hopes of creating a "folk supergroup." Best known for their cover of Bob Dylan's "Blowin' in the Wind," Peter Yarrow's own composition "Puff the Magic Dragon," and "If I Had a Hammer."

Peters, Mercy: Groupie/scenemaker. Befriended GP in the Burrito Manor days. Performed with Frank Zappa–produced GTOs. Later married Shuggie Otis. Mother of Lucky Otis.

Phillips, John (1935–2001): Singer/songwriter/producer/entrepreneur. Founding member of the Journeymen and the Mamas & the Papas. Phillips' gifts as an arranger have their roots in folk, vaudeville, and pop. With Lou Adler, organized the Monterey Pop Festival. Befriended GP in New York City; renewed their friendship in L.A. Phillips was with GP during his bike wreck. Father of Mackenzie, Tamerlane, Bijou, and Chynna Phillips. Autobiography: *Papa John.* Album: *The Papas & the Mamas.*

Phillips, Michelle (b. 1944): Model/singer/actress. Ex-wife of John Phillips. Member of the folk-rock ensemble the Mamas & the Papas. Later Married Dennis Hopper for eight days. Mother of Chynna Phillips. Film: *Dillinger.*

Pickett, Wilson (1941–2006): Singer/songwriter. Pickett's raw delivery evoked his Southern gospel background and rejected the smoother soul traditions of Nat King Cole, Sam Cooke, and Smokey Robinson. Best known for hits "Mustang Sally" and "In the Midnight Hour," which was cowritten with Booker T. & the MGs guitarist Steve Cropper and Eddie ("Knock on Wood") Floyd. Album: *Wilson Pickett's Greatest Hits*.

Poco: Early L.A. country-rock band founded by Richie Furay of Buffalo Springfield. Contemporaries of the Flying Burrito Brothers and Dillard & Clark. Album: *Pickin' Up the Pieces*.

Pope, Dick: Entertainment entrepreneur who founded—with the help of Big John Snively—the destination amusement park Cypress Gardens in Florida.

Presley, Elvis (1935–1977): Singer/actor. For good or ill, the detonator of rock and roll in America. The canonical version presents Elvis as the white expression of R&B exultation, style, and sexuality, teaching young white America that pop music could be about fucking. Later historians paint him as the ultimate American tragedy: a naïve artist captive in a creative desert of oppressive management and drugs. His Vegas years raised self-parody to a deeply depressing, consistently lucrative art form. Elvis' early films showed sparks of talent to match his charisma, but his management kept him in hideously simpleminded roles. To see Elvis' 1968 comeback show is to understand the magic that was lost. DVD: *Elvis: The '68 Comeback Special*. Album: *Elvis: 30 #1 Hits*. Books: *Last Train to Memphis: The Rise of Elvis Presley* and *Careless Love: The Unmaking of Elvis Presley*, both by Peter Guralnick.

Rainero, Rosina: Big Avis Snively's sorority sister and lifelong friend.

Redding, Otis (1941–1967): The Macon, Georgia–raised Redding's heartfelt delivery and church-music timing helped make him the greatest American soul singer. His hits for Stax/Volt—backed by Booker T. & the MGs—defined Southern R&B. Redding's explosive (if pandering) performance at 1968's Monterey Pop Festival (and in the subsequent film *Monterey Pop*) made him a pop as well as soul star. "(Sittin' on) The Dock of the Bay," a crossover gesture when compared to Otis' signature work, was recorded days before his death in a plane crash. Released posthumously, it hit number one. Albums: *Otis Redding Live in Europe, Otis Blue*.

The Remains: Arguably the toughest sound to emerge from the East Coast in the sixties, the Boston-based Remains concluded their brief career as the warm-up act on the final Beatles tour. Barry Tashian and keyboardist Billy Briggs befriended GP and the ISB through guitarist John Nuese. Tashian played on GP's solo album and later with Emmylou Harris' Hot Band. Albums: *The Remains, A Session With. . . .*

Rhodes, Orville J. "Red" (1930–1995): Pedal-steel guitarist. Sought-after L.A. session musician. House pedal-steel player at the Palomino; crossed over with the Monkees, James Taylor, John Phillips, Seals and Crofts, and many others. Regular contributor to ex-Monkee Michael Nesmith's country-rock First National Band. Albums: *Red Rhodes' Steel Guitar, Fantastic Steel Guitar*.

Rich, Don (1941–1974): Guitarist/singer/songwriter/fiddle player. Bandleader of Buck Owens' Buckaroos and Buck's main vocal accompanist, right-hand man, and a key definer—via his clean picking and rigorously simple arrangements—of the Bakersfield sound. Fred Astaire said, "Elegance is refusal." Don Rich personified that elegance. Died in a motorcycle accident. Album: *Country Pickin': The Don Rich Anthology.*

Richards, Keith (b. 1943): Guitarist, Rolling Stones. In the immortal words of author Terry Southern: "The only man on earth who can play a Chuck Berry song worse than Chuck Berry."

Richardson, Perry: Stones factotum. Assistant to Rolling Stones photographer Michael Cooper. Befriended GP in England. Book: *The Early Stones: Legendary Photographs of a Band in the Making 1963–1973.*

Rivkin, David, a.k.a. David Z: Producer/engineer/mixer/songwriter. Friend of GP during Chateau Marmont days. Cowrote "How Much I've Lied" with GP. Best known for producing Prince's *Purple Rain.* Production credits: "She Drives Me Crazy" (Fine Young Cannibals), *Sister Sweetly* (Big Head Todd and the Monsters), and "Cradle of Love" (Billy Idol).

Roberts, Rick: Singer/songwriter/guitarist. Replaced GP in FBB. Founded execrable country soft-rock band Firefall in 1973, which included Michael Clarke and GP bassist Jock Bartley.

Ronstadt, Linda (b. 1946): Pure-voiced singer (but never songwriter) and influential folk and country-rock interpreter. Her beauty and wide-ranging cover songs made her one of the most visible popularizers of country rock. Sang background on GP's "In My Hour of Darkness" and has collaborated consistently with Emmylou Harris. Though her early records feature heartrending versions of "Desperado" and "Love Has No Pride," her smooth, overproduced records led her to be dismissed as the epitome of the plastic mid-seventies SoCal sound. Album: *Greatest Hits.*

Ross, Nancy: GP's live-in girlfriend in his early L.A. days; mother of Polly Parsons.

Russell, Leon (b. 1942): Session keyboardist/guitarist/songwriter/producer, born Claude Russell Bridges. Played on innumerable sixties hits for Phil Spector and a multitude of artists, and on both sides of the first Byrds single, "Mr. Tambourine Man." Performed on and helped produce *Gene Clark with the Gosdin Brothers;* played on the FBB's *Burrito Deluxe;* worked with Delaney & Bonnie and Joe Cocker (Cocker had a hit with Russell's "Delta Lady"); led the *Shindig!* TV show house band the Shindogs (members included James Burton and Glen D. Hardin). Russell's regular sidemen Bobby Keys and Junior Markham (also from Russell's native Tulsa, Oklahoma) played in the original version of the FBB. George Benson covered Russell's "This Masquerade"; it remains the only song to hit number one on the jazz, pop, and R&B charts. Played with Cocker, the Stones, George Harrison, Delaney & Bonnie, Eric Clapton, and almost anybody else you could think of. Later built a thriving career as nonexistent country star Hank Wilson. It is impossible to overestimate Russell's influence on L.A. rock and roll and pop from 1965 to 1972. Album: *Leon Russell.*

Sahm, Douglas (1941–1999): Guitarist/singer/songwriter. Sahm lived a life of Cosmic American Music. His oeuvre comprises a singular, irrepressible combination of rock, R&B, Tex-Mex, Cajun, Tejano, polka, blues, big band, and jam rock. Born in San Antonio, Sahm played mandolin, fiddle, and steel guitar on the radio by age five. As a child, Sahm shared a stage with Hank Williams. Released numerous records in his teens; formed the Sir Douglas Quintet with organist Augie Meyer and San Antonio music compadres. They hit with 1965's "She's About a Mover." Singlehandedly launched the Cosmic Cowboy movement by appearing on the November 23, 1968, cover of *Rolling Stone* sporting a huge cowboy hat, shoulder-length hair, and holding his young son (also in cowboy hat) in his arms. Later formed the Texas Tornados with Tex-Mex music star Freddy Fender and accordion god Flaco Jimenez. A deity of Texas music. Albums: *Mendocino; Doug Sahm and Friends.*

Sanchez, Tony: Rolling Stones factotum. Author of *Up and Down with the Rolling Stones.*

Sedaka, Neil (b. 1939): Pop singer/songwriter. A Brill Building staple and prolific songwriter, Sedaka wrote and sang the number one hits "Breaking Up Is Hard to Do" (1962) and "Laughter in the Rain" (1975). He wrote "Love Will Keep Us Together," a number one single for the Captain and Tennille in 1975. His life's work demonstrates the durability of the market for pop.

Seiter, Jimmi: Byrds/Flying Burrito Brothers/GP roadie and road manager.

The Shilos: Folk ensemble. GP's first professional band. Lineup included GP (guitar, vocals), Paul Surratt (banjo, guitar, vocals), Joe Kelly (upright bass, vocals), George Wrigley (lead vocals, guitar, banjo). Album: *Gram Parsons and the Shilos: The Early Years, Vol. 1.*

Slade, Larry: GP's Bolles School classmate.

Smart, N. D.: Drummer/songwriter. Drummer for the Remains and on GP's Fallen Angels tour. Appeared on *The Smothers Brothers Comedy Hour* as part of the Hello People and drummed for influential pre-country-rock Canadian ensemble Great Speckled Bird. Later played with Todd Rundgren.

Smith, Ben: Judge in Waycross, Georgia. Knew the Connors socially.

Smith, Dickie: GP's childhood friend from Waycross, Georgia.

The Smothers Brothers (Tommy and Dick): Singers/songwriters/comedians/ actors. Broke nationally in the early sixties with a mixture of Journeymen and Weavers–style folk music and stand-up comedy. Legendary for *The Smothers Brothers Comedy Hour,* which premiered on CBS in 1967 and featured anti-Vietnam and pro–civil rights politics, live performances by the Doors, Jefferson Airplane, et al., and a barrage of thinly veiled dope-culture comedy sketches. CBS canceled the show in 1969 over issues of censorship. Despite their aggressively clean-cut appearance, the brothers proved subversive purveyors of avant-sixties counter-culture to a national audience. Album: *Mom Always Liked You Best!*

Snively, Big Avis: GP's mother; wife of Ingram Cecil "Coon Dog" Connor and Robert Parsons.

Snively, Evalyn, a.k.a. Dede: GP's maternal aunt. Mother of Rob Hoskins.

Snively, Jack: GP's maternal cousin. Son of John Junior and May.

Snively, John A.: GP's maternal grandfather. Father of Big Avis Snively.

Snively, Martha: GP's maternal cousin. Daughter of John Junior and May.

Souther, J. D. (b. 1945): Singer/songwriter/producer. Pioneer of SoCal sound. Formed Longbranch Pennywhistle with future Eagle Glenn Frey, cowrote with Jackson Browne and James Taylor, wrote hits for the Eagles and Linda Ronstadt, and was a member, with former Byrd/FBB Chris Hillman and Poco founder Richie Furay, of the Souther-Hillman-Furay Band.

Spector, Larry: Notorious L.A. entertainment manager. GP's manager when he arrived in L.A. Clients included the Byrds, Dennis Hopper, Brandon De Wilde.

Spector, Phil (b. 1940): Producer/songwriter. Brill Building luminary and preeminent visionary producer of the 1960s and '70s. Creator of the Wall of Sound recording technique, which exploited monaural principles to create an operatic blast in which all instruments and vocals are mixed to equal, prominent volumes. Responsible for the era of the girl group. Inspired Brian Wilson in his production of the Beach Boys' mono masterpieces. Produced the Beatles' *Let It Be*, George Harrison's *All Things Must Pass*, John Lennon's *Plastic Ono Band* and *Imagine*, and the Ramones' *End of the Century*. Famously eccentric and violence prone. Played Fonda and Hopper's cocaine customer in *Easy Rider*. Album: *Back to Mono*.

Stafford, Jim (b. 1944): Guitarist/songwriter/producer/stand-up performer. GP's friend and bandmate in Winter Haven, Florida. Known for technical expertise as a guitarist, unquenchable work ethic, and first marriage to Bobbie Gentry, writer-singer of "Ode to Billy Joe." Worked with Lobo, cowrote and produced hits "Spiders and Snakes" and "My Girl, Bill." His TV variety show *The Jim Stafford Show* ran for the summer of 1975. Owns, operates, and performs in his theater in Branson, Missouri.

Stewart, Wynn (1934–1985): Singer/songwriter. Underrated pioneer of the Bakersfield sound; more influential than successful with a repertoire ranging from traditional country to honky-tonk to rockabilly to early rock and roll and pop. Backed by the stark sound of Lefty Frizzell's band, featuring Roy Nichols (guitar) and Ralph Mooney (pedal steel). Hit number one with 1967's "It's Such a Pretty World Today." Stewart's conversational but pain-wracked vocal delivery was a major influence on GP.

Stills, Stephen (b. 1945): Guitarist/songwriter/producer. Founding member—with Richie Furay and Neil Young—of Buffalo Springfield. Later founded Crosby, Stills and Nash and Manassas. Wrote hit "For What It's Worth" for Buffalo Springfield and solo single "Love the One You're With."

Stuart, Marty (b. 1958): Guitarist/mandolinist. Eclectic, genius picker with untouchable résumé: played with bluegrass legends Lester Flatt and Doc Watson and backed up Johnny Cash. Musical abilities at times overshadowed by mainstream posturing, his too-well-tended pompadour, and his collection of vintage Nudie and other country tailors' rhinestone outfits.

Surratt, Paul: Musician/archivist. Played banjo in GP's folk ensemble, the Shilos. Later founded Research Video, a musical-performance archive.

Taj Mahal (b. 1942): Guitarist/pianist/songwriter, born Henry St. Claire Fredericks. Wide-ranging musician known for vast repertoire in blues, rock, Caribbean, and African music. Early bands included Ry Cooder (the Rising Sons) and guitarist Jesse Ed Davis. Performs in *The Rolling Stones Rock and Roll Circus.* Album: *Giant Step.*

Talcott, Bruce: GP's classmate at the Bolles School.

Tashian, Barry: Guitarist/singer. Inspired by a summer in Europe when he discovered the Kinks and the Rolling Stones, Tashian founded superlative Boston band the Remains. Formed first incarnation of FBB with fellow Remain Billy Briggs and ex-ISB members Ian Dunlop, John Nuese, and Mickey Gauvin. Played on *GP* (including lead vocals on "Cry One More Time"). Guitarist in Emmylou's Hot Band from 1980 to 1989.

Thomas, Jet: GP's academic advisor at Harvard, lifelong friend, and confidant. Performed the wedding ceremony for GP and Gretchen Burrell.

Tickner, Eddie (1927–2006): Entertainment manager. GP's manager. Formed publishing agency Tickson Music with Jim Dickson in 1963. Managed the Byrds until 1967, when the group went with Larry Spector at the urging of David Crosby. Also managed Emmylou Harris.

The Troubadour: L.A.'s premier folk venue. By the early seventies, the Troub had become the clubhouse for L.A.'s burgeoning country-rock scene. Rick Cunha of Hearts and Flowers hosted a weekly Hoot Night on Mondays. Gene Clark, Linda Ronstadt, J. D. Souther, and Jackson Browne were frequent performers.

Tullis, Kyle (1948–2004): Musician. GP's bassist for Fallen Angels tour.

Tulsa Rhythm Review: A loose aggregation of L.A. session musicians who knew one another back home in Tulsa or connected via Leon Russell. Members included Taj Mahal, Jimmy "Junior" Markham, Jesse Ed Davis, Carl Radle, Jimmy Carstein, and, of course, Russell Bridges (Leon Russell).

Tutt, Ronnie: Drummer. From 1969 to 1977 played in Elvis' TCB (Taking Care of Business) backing band. Tour drummer for Neil Diamond and tireless session musician. Played on *GP* and *Grievous Angel.*

Tyner, McCoy (b. 1938): Jazz pianist. Pivotal pianist of unique sound bridging post-bop and free-jazz eras. Known for his groundbreaking work with John Coltrane Quartet and solo albums. Albums as solo artist: *Supertrios, Trident;* with the Coltrane Quartet: *My Favorite Things, Ballads, A Love Supreme.*

Usher, Gary (1938–1990): Producer/songwriter. Like Terry Melcher, Usher was a key craftsman of surf and folk-rock sounds. (A neighbor of the Wilson brothers, he produced and cowrote several songs for the Beach Boys, including the hits "In My Room" and "409.") Usher also shaped the sound of country rock. Produced the Byrds' *Sweetheart of the Rodeo* as well as *Younger Than Yesterday* and *The Notorious Byrd Brothers,* and coproduced *Gene Clark with the Gosdin Brothers.*

Vadim, Roger (1928–2000): Film director. Husband of Brigitte Bardot and Jane Fonda; directed Gretchen Burrell in *Pretty Maids All in a Row (1971).* Established early sixties salon in L.A. with Jane Fonda, whom he directed in 1968's camp space odyssey *Barbarella*, which costarred Brian Jones' and Keith Richards' paramour Anita Pallenberg.

The Ventures: Instrumental, guitar-driven, surf-space band, formed in 1959 and still playing. Key tunes that influenced rock include their cover of Johnny Smith's "Walk, Don't Run" and the commercial surf sound of the TV theme song "Hawaii Five-O." Played custom-made Mosrite guitars (as did Johnny Ramone) and, though pioneers in their use of effects such as fuzz pedals, showcased a clean, undistorted sound. Album: *Walk, Don't Run: The Best of the Ventures.*

The Village Vanguards: GP's acoustic folk trio in Winter Haven.

Vosse, Michael: A&R man for A&M Records. Instrumental in signing the Flying Burrito Brothers.

Wagoner, Porter (b. 1927): Singer/songwriter. Traditional Nashville country singer with Bakersfield overtones, known for his eye-popping Nudie suits and discovery of, and duets with, Dolly Parton. A lifelong regular on the Grand Ole Opry and host of his own syndicated TV variety show, *The Porter Wagoner Show*, which ran from 1960 to 1981. The ISB covered his "A Satisfied Mind." Album: *Satisfied Mind.*

Waite, Genevieve (b. 1948): South African actress/chanteuse. Moved to L.A. via Swinging London. Friend of GP during his Chateau Marmont days. Starred in Michael Sarne's 1968 film *Joanna*. Married John Phillips in the early seventies. Mother of Tamerlane and Bijou Phillips. Album: *Romance Is on the Rise.*

Wallace, Cornelia Snively: Widow of Alabama governor George Wallace, famed anti-integrationist and presidential candidate. Former wife of John "Jack" Snively III, GP's cousin.

Watson, Johnny "Guitar" (1935–1996): Pianist/guitarist/songwriter/producer. Precision player with a ferocious six-string attack, Watson proved to be ahead of his time, reinventing the R&B guitar sound as futuristic music ("Space Guitar," 1954). Coproduced Burritos' "Train Song" with musical partner (real-life pimp and drug dealer) Larry Williams. Reemerged in the mid-seventies as a pimp-styled funk guitarist, augmenting his innovative musical style with a raunchy and outrageous persona. Died onstage in Yokohama, Japan, in 1996. Albums: *Gangster of Love*, *A Real Mother for Ya.*

The Weavers: Prominent, hearty, left-leaning, early (formed 1947), popular folk group featuring Pete Seeger. Best-known for their interpretation of Leadbelly's "Goodnight, Irene," which sold two million copies. Their lineup—three men and a woman—set the model for folk ensembles throughout the fifties and early sixties. Regarded by purist folkies as careerist sellouts, they still suffered under the anti-Communist witch hunts and blacklists of the fifties. Album: *The Weavers' Greatest Hits.*

Whitaker, Dode: GP's maternal cousin.

White, Clarence (1944–1973): Guitarist. Inscrutable, widely venerated seminal bluegrass and country session player. Founded the Kentucky Colonels and Nashville West; credited with bringing acoustic-guitar picking to bluegrass. Played on 1966's *Gene Clark with the Gosdin Brothers;* played with the Byrds from 1968 to

1973. Invented the B-Bender with Byrds drummer Gene Parsons. Played on GP's "lost sessions," produced by Terry Melcher; toured briefly with GP, Emmylou Harris, and the Country Gazette in 1973. Killed by a drunk driver while loading out after a gig. Possessed of a unique sound, notable for his bluegrass picking and pedal-steel lines played on a Telecaster, and for blending his astonishing abilities into the group sound.

White, Roland (b. 1938): Mandolinist. Clarence White's brother. Played guitar with Bill Monroe, mandolin in the Kentucky Colonels with Clarence, and in Country Gazette with Byron Berline. Currently plays in Nashville Bluegrass Band. Album: *Livin' in the Past; Legendary Live Recordings.*

Whitehead, Susan: Briefly GP's high school girlfriend in Winter Haven.

Wilkes, Pauline: GP's paternal aunt.

Wilkes, Tom: Art director/photographer. Designer for Monterey Pop Festival. Head of the art department at A&M Records. Album credits include: *The Gilded Palace of Sin* (Flying Burrito Brothers), the original *Beggars Banquet* (Rolling Stones), *Decade* (Neil Young), and *All Things Must Pass* (George Harrison).

Williams, Hank (1923–1953): Singer/songwriter/guitarist. The creator of modern country music, Hank Williams = Elvis as far as seminal style and opening new worlds of commercial opportunity. Williams' alcoholism and addiction to painkillers and speed established him as an early model of the Dionysian poet-madman that GP and others in rock embraced. Williams' yelping, cutting—almost yodeling—vocals owed much to Jimmie Rodgers. But his songwriting, with its unflinching depiction of solitude ("I'm So Lonesome I Could Cry") set to jaunty, unforgettable melodies, owes nothing to nobody. Williams placed forty-one songs in the country top ten. Album: *The Complete Hank Williams.*

Williams, Larry (1935–1980): Singer/pianist/songwriter. New Orleans–born Williams' suave bravado and electric delivery, not as manic as Little Richard though equally powerful, defined the moment when R&B became rock and roll. When Richard abandoned rock and roll for religion in the late fifties, Williams stepped up. (Little Richard claims Williams once held a gun to his head in a drug dispute). Williams hit big with "Short Fat Fannie" and "Bony Maronie." Arrested for selling narcotics in 1959, Williams was dropped by Specialty Records. In the mid-sixties Williams formed a musical partnership with Johnny "Guitar" Watson and began producing. Watson and Williams produced the FBB's "Train Song." Williams died of a gunshot to the head. Though declared a suicide, speculation persists that he was shot over drugs and/or prostitution. Albums: *Here's Larry Williams, Larry Williams/Johnny Guitar Watson Two for the Price of One.*

Williams, Lucinda (b. 1953): Singer/songwriter. First overlooked and later overrated, Williams overtly recognized GP as a defining influence. After working as a Nashville songwriter through the 1980s and early 1990s, her 1998 *Car Wheels on a Gravel Road* found critical and commercial success. Its breakout sales and adult lyrical themes heralded maturation of the often GP-derivative alt. country genre. Perhaps the finest interpreter of GP's material. Album: *Car Wheels on a Gravel Road.*

Williams, Roger: GP's Bolles classmate and Waycross, Georgia, native.

Wrigley, George: GP's bandmate; guitarist for the Shilos.

Wynette, Tammy (1942–1998): Singer/songwriter. First lady of country music. With her 1960s and '70s streak of standout hits ("Stand by Your Man," "Your Good Girl's Gonna Go Bad," "D-I-V-O-R-C-E") and success, she represented—along with Loretta Lynn—a new paradigm for women in country music. After Tammy, women would sing about pain with as much rueful self-knowledge and hard-earned self-deception as men. Known for her definitive country duets with George Jones. Album: *Tammy Wynette's Greatest Hits.*

Young, Neil (b. 1945): Singer/songwriter/guitarist. Founding member of Buffalo Springfield; member of Crosby, Stills, Nash and Young; recorded many albums with backing band Crazy Horse. An anti-virtuosity virtuoso known for reductive, shockingly moving guitar solos, arrangements, and melodies and for his voice's distinctive rasping whine. Made several country-inflected albums utilizing pedal steel and banjo. Albums: *Tonight's the Night, Rust Never Sleeps, On the Beach.*

Zappa, Frank (1940–1993): Guitarist/composer/political activist/producer. Leader of the Mothers of Invention, a wildly intelligent sixties L.A. rock ensemble with avant-garde overtones. Via Zappa's compositions, the Mothers embodied the soon-to-be counterculturally dominant idea of the long-haired outsider as "freak" and sole sane observer of an America gone mad and in denial. Produced *Permanent Damage* for the groupie collective GTOs. Album: *Freak Out.*

Source Notes

ABBREVIATION KEY

AB	Alice Barre	GL	Gene Leedy
AN	Andee Nathanson	GrL	Grant Lacerte
BaT	Barry Tashian	GW	Genevieve Waite
BB	Bobby Braddock	HC	Henry Clarke
BC	Bill Colledge	ID	Ian Dunlop
BF	Buddy Freeman	JB	Jock Bartley
BG	Becky Gottsegen	JD	Jim Dickson
BiB	Billy Briggs	JdM	Jay Dee Maness
BL	Bernie Leadon	JG	Judson Graves
BM	Bonnie Muma	JiS	Jimmi Seiter
BoB	Bob Buchanan	JK	Joe Kelly
BS	Ben Smith	JM	James Mallard
BT	Bruce Talcott	JN	John Nuese
ByB	Byron Berline	JoB	John Beland
CB	Carlos Bernal	JS	Jack Snively
CE	Chris Ethridge	JT	Jet Thomas
CSN	Cornelia Snively Wallace	KF	Kathy Fenton
DaB	David Barry	KL	Karen Lacerte
DB	Dubie Baxter	KLV	Kent LaVoie
DM	Dickie McNeer	LC	Louise Cone
DS	Dickey Smith	LS	Larry Slade
DW	Dode Whitaker	MC	Martin Clevenger
EB	Earl Ball	MF	Margaret Fisher
EP	Edmund Pedrick	MK	Marcia Katz
EvB	Eve Babitz	MP	Mercy Peters
FB	Fred Brown	MS	Martha Snively

MV	Michael Vosse	RM	Rufus McClure
NF	Neil Flanz	RoM	Roger McGuinn
OC	O. J. Cowart	RR	Rosina Rainero
PC	Pam Cairns	SA	Susan Alexander
PDB	Pamela Des Barres	SE	Steve Earle
PeC	Peppy Castro	SH	Sam Hutt
PH	Peter Henriques	SK	Stash Klossowski
PW	Pauline Wilkes	SW	Susan Whitehead
QB	Quinn Barton	WL	Walter Lanaux
RH	Rob Hoskins		

ONE

Coon Dog Connor and Avis Snively

5 "We never listened to country": PW to author, 2002.

5 "We answered a question": ibid.

6 "an extremely popular boy": ibid.

7 "I didn't even get up": OC to author, 2003.

9 "But now you had better": DS to author, 2002.

10 "I would like to tell": Letter from George G. Kenny to Mrs. Connor, July 1943.

10 "I heard that most soldiers": PW to author, 2002.

10 "Malaria certainly zaps your strings": ibid.

10 "came to this country to escape religious": Polk County genealogical records.

11 "a woman of strong character": ibid.

12 "When a salesman": Anon to author, 2003.

13 "He was sitting": RH to author, 2003.

13 "Up until 1934": John Snively Senior, *Snively Groves.*

14 "Lease me this damn swamp": JC to author, 2003.

15 "He played golf": CSN to author, 2003.

15 "Five bedrooms, five baths": RH to author, 2003.

15 "He was a hard-ass": JS to author, 2003.

16 "The Snivelys were perceived": DW to author, 2003.

16 "He considered himself strictly": CSN to author, 2003.

16 "Mom, I guess": RH to author, 2003.

17 "When my mother divorced": ibid.

17 "John Senior was smart enough": DW to author, 2003.

17 "She didn't walk, she floated": ibid.

17 "Our house wasn't": RR to author, 2003.

17 "She could have": ibid.

18 "She told me about him": ibid.

18 "And then he called us": PW to author, 2002.

19 "I didn't have alcohol": ibid.

19 "My family were always suspicious": JS to author, 2003.

19 "Avis was absolutely gorgeous": DW to author, 2003.

19 "the dining table of antique": "Major Cecil Connor Weds Miss Snively in Beautiful Florida Home Setting." *Winter Haven Sentinel,* March 18, 1945.

TWO

22 "It was never": DW to author, 2003.

23 "well-liked, handsome fellow": BS to author, 2002.

24 "When she went up": RR to author, 2003.

24 "Everywhere you looked": DS to author, 2002.

24 "These people were": BS to author, 2002.

24 "They were a popular": EP to author, 2003.

25 "for our close friends": AS to author, 2003.

25 "You know, in the South": DS to author, 2002.

25 "Well, ye heard": AS to author, 2002.

25 "Have a party": ibid.

25 "He drank a lot": OC to author, 2003.

26 "was the biggest employer": ibid.

26 "The Snivelys had to": ibid.

26 "a real friendly boss": AS to author, 2003.

26 "We used to go quail hunting": ibid.

27 "There was a lot": Anon to author.

27 "Avis kind of": ibid.

27 "She participated in": DW to author, 2003.

27 "She was a strong woman": JS to author, 2003.

27 "I'd never seen": DS to author, 2002.

28 "Gram was a good boy": EP to author, 2003.

28 "We would go out": HC to author, 2002.

29 "Work was not": RR to author, 2003.

29 "Coon Dog and Avis": DW to author, 2003.

29 "It seems strange": LC to author 2003.

29 "But even though we": ibid.

30 "I wanted a bedroom": ibid.

30 "Gram had tons": DS to author, 2002.

30 "Gram had his own room": HC to author, 2002.

30 "I never told": DS to author, 2002.

30 "They were loving": ibid.

31 "Usually when Gram's mother drank": ibid.

31 "There was no comparing": DW to author, 2003.

31 "Gram was never disrespectful": DS to author, 2002.

31 "He could be a little rowdy": ibid.

31 "About the rowdiest thing": ibid.

31 "Most of us took": ibid.

31 "I'll never forget": ibid.

32 "Gram was a sweet child": LC to author, 2003.

32 "Gram's fingers were long": HC to author, 2002.

32 "Gram was amazing": ibid.

32 "One time Gram": DS to author, 2002.

32 "During the school year": ibid.

33 "Johnny Barnes would drive": HC to author, 2002.
33 "It was a service station": ibid.
33 "The one time Elvis": ibid.
33 "Gram bought a lot": ibid.
33 "You could see that": DS to author, 2002.
33 "When we did it": ibid.
34 "We knew where all": ibid.
34 "It didn't bother Gram": ibid.
34 "Another time we went": ibid.
34 "Gram tried to impress": ibid.
35 "Around fourth grade": ibid.
35 "The second year": ibid.
35 "In the daytime": ibid.
35 "When we wanted": ibid.
35 "The last time": ibid.
36 "They're no good": ibid.
36 "I don't know what": ibid.

THREE
December 23, 1958

37 "If she left": DS to author, 2002.
37 "I don't think that work": RR to author, 2003.
38 "We always used": LC to author, 2003.
38 "Avis was one": ibid.
38 "Mr. Connor drank": ibid.
38 "I guess his parents": DS to author, 2002.
38 "They usually went": ibid.
38 "He stopped at": OC to author, 2003.
39 "I know they swapped": Anon to author, 2002.
39 "You have to understand": EP to author, 2003.
39 "They had a circle": BS to author, 2002.
40 "I'm leaving my": RH to author, 2003.
40 "He predicted the year": DW to author, 2003.
40 "John Senior was one": RH to author, 2003.
40 "He started small": JS to author, 2003.
40 "The one thing that destroyed": ibid.
40 "Papa John stayed back": DW to author, 2003.
40 "If you ever wanted": RR to author, 2003.
40 "within the group": DW to author, 2003.
41 "The way you could": DS to author, 2002.
41 "He spent a lot": OC to author, 2003.
42 "Gram was getting": DS to author, 2002.
42 "He called my mother": PW to author, 2002.
42 "I'd been up": OC to author, 2003.
43 "Coroner A. J. Willis": *Waycross Journal-Herald*, December 24, 1958.
43 "When Coon Dog killed": RR to author, 2003.

43 "A pall came over": DW to author, 2003.
44 "Oh, I was hurt": LC to author, 2003.
44 "That whole Christmas": DW to author, 2003.
44 "I was at home": PW to author, 2002.
44 "When they finally": DW to author, 2003.
45 "I think it was December": PW to author, 2002.
45 "I'd been up to Baxley": OC to author, 2002.
45 "Everybody was shocked": BS to author, 2002.
45 "Maybe a day": DS to author, 2002.
45 "The Snivelys called": EP to author, 2003.
46 "Waycross is a place": Stanley Booth, *True Adventures of the Rolling Stones* (Chicago: A Cappella Books, 2000).
46 "We got in a taxi": PW to author, 2002.
46 "It was right there": ibid.
46 "We were sheltered kids": SA to author, 2003.
47 "The shock was terrible": RR to author, 2003.
47 "Ware County takes": EP to author, 2003.
47 "It was a turning point": SA to author, 2003.
47 "His mom lost": MS to author, 2003.
48 "In Waycross, Gram was": SA to author, 2003.
48 "Avis was a moody person": MS to author, 2003.
48 "He was bad": MS to author, 2002.
49 "He was a good kid": DB to author, 2003.
49 "Gram's IQ was up": RH to author, 2003.
49 "Back when we were kids": RH to author, 2003.
49 "Avis announced that": PW to author, 2002.

FOUR

Robert Parsons

50 "She was pursued": SA to author, 2003.
51 "Bob had a lot of charisma": Anon. to author, 2003.
51 "Did you jump": BM to author, 2003.
51 "That man is": RH to author, 2003.
51 "one of only two guys": GL to author, 2003.
52 "He was dapper": DW to author, 2003.
52 "When he met Avis": RR to author, 2003.
52 "The Snivelys didn't": GL to author, 2003.
52 "In my family": SA to author, 2003.
53 "He was involved": Anon to author, 2003.
53 "It was still so early": DW to author, 2003.
53 "I never thought": RR to author, 2003.
53 "when she was little": GL to author, 2003.
53 "Bob was basically": ibid.
53 "He demanded respect": JC to author, 2003.
53 "I wonder who": ibid.
54 "He was saying": ibid.

54 "Bob Parsons didn't help": MS to author, 2003.
54 "Bob was not mean": RR to author, 2003.
54 "I didn't like him": MS to author, 2003.
54 "My mother tried": RH to author, 2003.
54 "The family presented him": DW to author, 2003.
54 "It was a tough time": ibid.
55 "I tried to tell": ibid.
55 "Well, I wouldn't say": GL to author, 2003.
55 "I have never known": AB journal circa 1980s.
56 "He literally abandoned": BG to author, 2003.
56 "A government project": AB journal circa 1980s.
57 "He was a fabulous": BG to author, 2003.
57 "He was highly intelligent": AB journal circa 1980s.
57 "He joined Sigma Ki": ibid.
58 "Bob started his big": ibid.
58 "The Eisenhower campaign": WL to author, 2003.
58 "Everyone found their way": ibid.
59 "Baton Rouge was a small": ibid.
59 "Bob then was not": ibid.
59 "My grandmother": BG to author, 2003.
59 "And the women": WL to author, 2003.
59 "We moved because": AB journal circa 1980s.
60 "We called my dad": BG to author, 2003.
60 "I am no longer": JC to author, 2003.
60 "The family checked": SA to author, 2003.
60–61 "He waited on her": GL to author, 2003.
61 "a good husband": GL to author, 2003.
61 "Our first visit": BG to author, 2003.
61 "The Snivelys loved eating": GL to author, 2003.
61 "He was ambitious": ibid.
61 "Bob was spending": Anon to author, 2003.
62 "Leap Engineering invented": GL to author, 2003.
62 "I met Bob": ibid.
62 "Bob had a lot": ibid.
62 "When the Colombian": Anon to author, 2003.
63 "Avis would be": Anon to author, 2003.
63 "Bob ran into": GL to author, 2003.

FIVE

Winter Haven

64 "That room had": JC to author, 2003.
65 "His mother stayed": SW to author, 2003.
65 "It was neat": GrL to author, 2003.
65 "Polk County encompasses": BB to author, 2003.
66 "They were strangers": ibid.

66 "We couldn't get TV": DM to author, 2004.

67 "In the early 1950s": BB to author, 2003.

67 "Country was not": DM to author, 2004.

67 "The star of a show": BB to author, 2003.

67 "Florence Villa was": DB to author, 2003.

68 "Everybody's folks had": GrL to author, 2003.

68 "It wasn't the genteel": ibid.

69 "The youth centers promoted": ibid.

69 "The truckers were heavy": ibid.

69 "a lot of presence": ibid.

70 "We were all trying": MC to author, 2003.

70 "My family was always": JC to author, 2003.

71 "We had people": KL to author, 2003.

71 "The cabins were used": Anon to author, 2003.

71 "We used to go": DB to author, 2003.

72 "The rich had": GrL to author, 2003.

72 "Gram played piano": MC to author, 2003.

73 "We didn't have": GrL to author, 2003.

73 "I played this version": JC to author, 2003.

73 "We were all learning.": ibid.

73 "One of the little": ibid.

73 "not much of a band": ibid.

73 "I played in the Legends": GrL to author, 2003.

74 "People contradict one another": JC to author, 2003.

75 "He couldn't even drive": KLV to author, 2003.

75 "My first impression": SW to author, 2003.

75 "This may sound snobbish": ibid.

75 "This is boring": ibid.

76 "Even though he was": ibid.

76 "The moment our drummer": KLV to author, 2003.

76 "Rob was a little": ibid.

76 "We always considered": ibid.

76 "We weren't musicians": ibid.

77 "He always had": ibid.

77 "I was dumbfounded": ibid.

77 "It was an armory": ibid.

77 "Seven, no Gram": ibid.

77 "We wore these": ibid.

78 "My mind-set was": ibid.

78 "He was a Snively": BB to author, 2003.

78 "He'd go home": JC to author, 2003.

79 "For three days": ibid.

79 "My father thought": BB to author, 2003.

SIX
Vanguards and Legends

80 "Gram was a real": JC to author, 2003.
80 "We all looked": DB to author, 2003.
81 "We would go": JC to author, 2003.
81 "It was the Snively": GrL to author, 2003.
81 "My father-in-law": CSN to author, 2003.
81 "He was generous": GL to author, 2003.
81 "He sold off our groves": JS to author, 2003.
82 "Parsons talked Avis": RH to author, 2003.
82 "Parsons talked Avis": ibid.
82 "Hers was about $2.5 million": ibid.
83 "It was Avis' idea": RH to author, 2003.
83 "The one good thing": DW to author, 2003.
83 "They went to court": GL to author, 2003
83 "It was the distress": BF to author, 2003
83–84 "Later, the only arguments": GL to author, 2003.
84 "She drank much more": SA to author, 2003.
84 "She was the cutest kid": BF to author, 2003.
84 "For a fifteen-year-old": ibid.
84 "Gram was bored": ibid.
84 "The main thing": ibid.
85 "At this time folk": ibid.
85 "A couple people called": ibid.
85 "that little skinny girl": Anon to author, 2003.
85 "Bonnie was a bombshell": DB to author, 2003.
86 "When Bob walked": BM to author, 2003.
86 "So much of his life": BG to author, 2003.
86 "Avis said to me": WL to author, 2003.
87 "She'd come by": BM to author, 2003.
87 "She welcomed me": ibid.
87–88 "Gram was trying": ibid.
88 "I was doing this": ibid.
88 "Gram wanted to write": ibid.
88 "He was introspective": PC to author, 2003.
88 "He was a moody guy": ibid.
89 "He loved for other girls": ibid.
89 "Gram was leaning": ibid.
89 "Gram was raising": GrL to author, 2003.
89 "I was fond of Gram": ibid.
90 "He would go": SW to author, 2003.
90 "Bob and Gram got on": BM to author, 2003.
90 "I liked Bob Parsons": JC to author, 2003.
90 "Gram was important": BM to author, 2003.
90 "This huge guy pasted": JC to author. 2003.
90 "You have to stand": GL to author, 2003.

90 "Bob grew up": ibid.
91 "Where's the sonofabitch": ibid.
91 "Gram often got picked": JC to author, 2003.
91 "Gram's tendency to bullshit": GrL to author, 2003.
91 "It had to have been": ibid.
92 "One time after hearing": KL to author, 2003.
92 "Folk has always been": DM to author, 2003.
93 "Avis was an alkie": ibid.
93 "Gram was a loner": ibid.
93 "She had little": ibid.
93 "We drank Bob Parsons' beer": ibid.
94 "We asked Patti": ibid.
94 "Gram was head over": Anon to author, 2003.
94 "Today it would be": DB to author, 2003.
94 "Patti was the hottest": GrL to author, 2003.
95 "It all came easy": DM to author, 2003.
95 "We all went": ibid.
96 "Gram doing no schoolwork": KL to author, 2003.
96 "Women were after Bob": GL to author, 2003.
96 "We took off": BM to author, 2003.
96 "I asked him": ibid.
97 "One night I got up": ibid.
97 "And that's when": ibid.
97 "I do have": ibid.
97 "Anything negative": BG to author, 2003.
98 "we never, never": BM to author, 2003.
98 "He was honorable.": ibid.
98 "The dad's screwing": KL to author, 2003.
98 "It was a bad scene": SA to author, 2003.
99 "[The Johnsons] weren't": Anon to author, 2003.
99 "They wouldn't have": DM to author, 2003.
100 "When I got back": JC to author, 2003.

SEVEN
The Bolles School

103 "People like Gram": QB to author, 2003.
103 "They were the ugliest": MF to author, 2003.
103 "If you do not": RM to author, 2003.
103 "Bartram and Bolles": MF to author, 2003.
104 "It was a predominately": RW to author, 2003.
104 "Gram was definitely": PH to author, 2003.
104 "Gram arrived a good-looking": RM to author, 2003.
104 "I wonder how": RW to author, 2003.
105 "He couldn't go": ibid.
105 "Gram was different": JM to author, 2003.
105 "He was proper": BT to author, 2003.

105 "He was an attractive": ibid.

105 "People were intimidated": MF to author, 2003.

106 "Gram was noticeably": PH to author, 2003.

106 "Gram flourished at Bolles": RM to author, 2003.

106 "The faculty were close": FB to author, 2003.

106 "was the closest thing": ibid.

106 "You'd look across": RW to author, 2003.

106 "had his windows": ibid.

106 "never quite connected": FB to author, 2003.

107 "Gram wanted to be": LS to author, 2003.

107 "I was sitting": RW to author, 2003.

108 "He played JV": JM to author, 2003.

108 "He said, 'I see'": JK to author, 2003.

109 "The group we emulated": ibid.

109 "The Journeymen were": ibid.

110 "He sang 'You Know'": Sid Griffin, *Gram Parsons: A Musical Biography* (Pasadena: Sierra Books, 1985, 35.

110 "As a singer": ibid., 36.

110 "It wasn't like": JM to author, 2003.

111 "a covey of girls": ibid.

111 "Gram sang after": JG to author, 2003.

111 "He was playing": MY to author, 2003.

111 "After the girls": RW to author, 2003.

112 "Gram picked up": PH to author, 2003.

112 "He taught the English": FB to author, 2003.

112 "Gram was Hubbard's favorite": BT to author, 2003.

113 "It was a huge thing": FB to author, 2003.

113 "Gram liked her": ibid.

113 "Faculty members told": ibid.

113 "I think the faculty": ibid.

114 "He had seven kids": MF to author, 2003.

114 "I was the bottom": ibid.

114 "She was a waif": JG to author, 2003.

114 "Margaret was a beautiful": LS to author, 2003.

114 "It was a retreat": JG to author, 2003.

114 "It wouldn't have": MF to author, 2003.

115 "My first memory": ibid.

116 "I was in tenth": ibid.

116 "After that he would": ibid.

116 "We both had a clear idea": ibid.

116 "He said he was going": ibid.

116 "We never dated": ibid.

117 "He couldn't wait": BM to author, 2003.

117 "Only my mother": BF to author, 2003.

117 "Buddy?": BF to author, 2003.

117 "Apparently the band": ibid.

118 "We go to the hotel": ibid.

118 "I complimented": ibid.
118 "I so believed": ibid.
119 "It was a good product": JK to author, 2003.
120 "We were in the middle": ibid.
120 "sounded professional": GrL to author, 2003.
120 "Afterward he took": MF to author, 2003.
121 "That's what he's worn": JK to author, 2003.
121 "We could just look": ibid.
122 "Gram was a real charmer": ibid.
122 "He was comfortable with us": ibid.
122 "It wasn't that": ibid.
123 "But Gram had attracted": BF to author, 2003.
123 "Gram knew these folks": JK to author, 2003.
124 "By that time": ibid.
124 "Daytime was not": ibid.
125 "Anytime the Journeymen": ibid.
125 "That song of theirs": ibid.
126 "He was not": ibid.

EIGHT

Senior Year

127 "When Gram came back": MF to author, 2003.
127 "For me and girls": RW to author, 2003.
127 "We weren't tight": ibid.
127 "There were at least": ibid.
128 "It was an innocent": ibid.
128 "We'd have about": JM to author, 2003.
128 "We had some beer": BC to author, 2003.
129 "James had no pretensions": FB to author, 2003.
129 "I always complained": JM to author, 2003.
129 "He was open": ibid.
129 "There was always": ibid.
129 "There was a vulnerability": FB to author, 2003.
130 "Gram was smart": ibid.
130 "Gram didn't hold": ibid.
130 "We were eating": JM to author, 2003.
130 "It was the size": ibid.
130 "a big wild cat": LS to author, 2003.
131 "I remember his mother's": ibid.
131 "Gram had warm": JM to author, 2003.
131 "Gram tagged her up": ibid.
131 "On one of my visits": ibid.
131 "I don't remember Big Avis": SA to author, 2003.
132 "I began to see": DW to author, 2003.
132 "I never saw him": ibid.
133 "As for Gram": LS to author, 2003.

133 "We were and are still": RM to author, 2003.

133 "Gram's parents did": ibid.

133 "I wondered if": PH to author, 2003.

133 "I knew Gram": ibid.

133 "He had intellectual": QB to author, 2003.

134 "We thought we were": JM to author, 2003.

134 "We joked and called": ibid.

135 "I remember Big": DM to author, 2003.

135 "Bob had all these": GrL to author, 2003.

135 "Bob was a generous": ibid.

136 "He didn't think": JM to author, 2003.

136 "Carlton, that haircut": JC to author, 2003.

136 "It was a stereo": ibid.

139 "I didn't pay": MF to author, 2003.

139 "That was so cool": ibid.

139 "One night Avis got": GL to author, 2003.

139 "I knew that Avis": BF to author, 2003.

139 "Sick as she was": RR to author, 2003.

140 "It was a regular hospital": RH to author, 2003.

140 "The night before": JM to author, 2003.

140 "We were talking": FB to author, 2003.

140 "People missed us": ibid.

140 "Everybody said they": ibid.

141 "It was the next": MF to author, 2003.

141 "That afternoon was": FB to author, 2003.

141 "He left before": JM to author, 2003.

141 "It's the general": SA to author, 2003.

141 "he told the nurse": RR to author, 2003.

141 "when she was": JS to author, 2003.

141 "Gram's mother was dying": RH to author, 2003.

141 "I remember her": GL to author, 2003.

141 "If he made": BM to author, 2003.

142 "He said, about her": GL to author, 2003.

142 "She said that": DW to author, 2003.

142 "Bob called me": BM to author, 2003.

142 "He wasn't cavalier": JC to author, 2003.

143 "While we were waiting": ibid.

143 "He was probably numb": ibid.

143 "We all ended up": SA to author, 2003.

NINE

CAMBRIDGE

144 "I need the money": GL to author, 2003.

145 "I was blown away": John Einarson, *Desperados: The Roots of Country Rock* (New York: Cooper Square, 2001), 42.

145 "Brandon was getting": ID to author, 2005.

147 "I thought, 'I'd like'": Einarson, *Desperados*, 45.
148 "I came from": Richie Unterberger, *Turn! Turn! Turn!: The '60s Folk Rock Revolution* (San Francisco: Back Beat Books, 2002), 54.
150 "We rented a": ibid., 64.
151 "Gram was gone": JM to author, 2003.
151 "Halfway between Harvard": DaB to author, 2005.
152 "I had been": David W. Johnson, "His Talent Died in the Desert." *Harvard Magazine*, July-August 1994.
153 "you know, the alternative": ID to author, 2005.
153 "Both being from": JT to author, 2005.
153 "You wouldn't": ibid.
153 "Gram had strong ideas": ibid.
154 "I think I was there": Griffin, *Gram Parsons*, 56.
154 "He never met": JT to author, 2005.
154 "a group of people": JG to author, 2003.
155 "Gram got fucked-up": Johnson, "His Talent Died in the Desert."
155 "In the fall of 1965": ibid.
155 "The whole experience": ibid.
155 "They were educated": ID to author, 2005.
156 "She designed clothes": DaB to author, 2005.
156 "This was the sixties": ID to author, 2005.
156 "Desmond had": DaB to author, 2005.
157 "We got into jamming": JN to author, 2005.
157 "He was a smooth talker": ID to author, 2005.
157 "funky shoe stores": BiB to author, 2005.
157 "He was in": ID to author, 2005.
158 "I was floored by the guy": JN to author, 2005.
158 "an English psychiatrist's": Griffin, *Gram Parsons*, 56.
158 "I was living": ID to author, 2005.
159 "There was individuality": ibid.
160 "I remember Elvis": ibid.
160 "When the band got together": Griffin, *Gram Parsons*, 48.
160 "Country music formed": ibid., 56.
161 "I started right away": JN to author, 2005.
162 "Marty the Manager": ibid.
162 "We got more into": ibid.
162 "He said Harvard": BF to author, 2003.
163 "Gram had two choices": JT to author, 2005.
163 "I wish there was": letter from Gram Parsons to Avis Parsons, November 8, 1965.
163 "Gram had all": JC to author, 2003.

TEN
The International Submarine Band

165 "We did a bit": ID to author, 2005.
166 "One day, I'm hanging": MK to author, 2005.
166 "We went walking": ibid.

166 "Then one by one": ibid.

166 "a momentary hookup": ibid.

166 "John was private": ibid.

167 "They'd start rehearsing": ibid.

167 "His parents lived": BF to author, 2003.

167 "Mickey came out": ID to author, 2005.

167 "We did a lot": JN to author, 2005.

168 "Ray changed the feeling": ID to author, 2005.

168 "We sang a lot": ibid.

168 "The country industry": ibid.

168 "We were searching": ibid.

169 "I sat in at their": BaT to author, 2004.

169 "We'd go out": BiB to author, 2005.

169 "He liked my Hohner": ibid.

169 "I always thought": ibid.

169 "We'd drive out there": ibid.

169 "Mostly we used pot": BaT to author, 2004.

169 "Gram was not a druggie": ID to author, 2005.

170 "Gram had come": BaT to author, 2004.

170 "I wrote this last night": Barney Hoskyns, "The Good Ol' Boy," *Mojo*, July 1998, 74.

172 "It means *beneath*": ID to author, 2005.

173 "The ISB were": PeC to author, 2005.

173 "We didn't take that": ID to author, 2005.

173 "We couldn't have": ibid.

174 "So maybe we": ibid.

174 "They did cover": PeC to author, 2005.

174 "I would play": ibid.

174 "We played the music": JN to author, 2005.

174 "Tourists went there": ID to author, 2005.

174 "It was not a hip": DaB to author, 2005.

175 "The ISB showed up": ibid.

175 "We had a unit": JC to author, 2003.

175 "Gram dropped a little": ID to author, 2005.

176 "We went down": ibid.

177 "Suddenly there was": ibid.

177 "And we did": ibid.

177 "He wanted me": BM to author, 2003.

177 "She had gotten mad": ibid.

177 "I'm probably not": ibid.

178 "Daddy had gone": ibid.

178 "Bob said he": ibid.

178 "Honestly, it's funny": DB to author, 2003.

178 "Without one word": WL to author, 2003.

178 "a white dress": BM to author, 2003.

178 "I cried all": ibid.

179 "I think he": ibid.
179 "like a big movie": ID to author, 2005.
179 "The host was this": ibid.
179 "When Gram was into": JC to author, 2003.
179 "Gram always had": ibid.
180 "He got metaphysical": ibid.
180 "We simply did": JN to author, 2005.
180 "The Columbia session": ID to author, 2005.
180 "We cut an original": ibid.
181 "By the second": ibid.
182 "The ISB would": Hoskyns, "The Good Ol' Boy," 74.
182 "Brandon loved the": MK to author, 2005.
182 "We were restless": ID to author, 2005.
183 "Vito the Magnificent": JD to author, 2005.
183 "Their eyes met": JN to author, 2005.
184 "He came back": MK to author, 2005.
184 "We ran into some": ID to author, 2005.
184 "He came back": ibid.
184 "Gram was always": ibid.
185 "A lot of people": MK to author, 2005.
185 "this huge, fancy": JN to author, 2005.
185 "Some of the guys": MK to author, 2005.
185 "We kept the Bronx": ID to author, 2005.
185 "The Sub Band": PeC to author, 2005.

ELEVEN

Los Angeles

189 "While it could have": ID to author, 2005.
190 "Gram was kind": Griffin, *Gram Parsons*, 69.
190 "I wanted to give": ibid., 68.
190 "He taught me": ibid.
191 "She opened spiritual doors": MK to author, 2005.
191 "Gram got me": JT to author, 2005.
192 "After the initial": ID to author, 2005.
194 "We went to some funky": ibid.
194 "Ian will tell": BiB to author, 2005.
194 "Suddenly Mickey and I": ID to author, 2005.
195 "Whenever you go": BoB to author, 2005.
195 "He was casual": ibid.
195 "All those people doing": EB to author, 2005.
195 "If you played": DB to author, 2005.
196 "And that was not": ibid.
197 "Talent night at the": JdM to author, 2005.
197 "Gram usually went": BoB to author, 2005.
197 "Gram kept going": ibid.

197 "We recorded a mixed": ID to author, 2005.

198 "The ISB seemed": ibid.

198 "Gram and myself felt": JN to author, 2005.

199 "His only asset was": JD to author, 2005.

199 "Something happened with": ID to author, 2005.

199 "Gram and I were": BoB to author, 2005.

199 "Our approach to country": Einarson, *Desperados*, 63.

199 "seemed to be": MS to author, 2003.

200 "Nancy was a lovely": JC to author, 2003.

200 "I didn't get": ibid.

200 "Nancy was into him": ibid.

200 "We were at the": ibid.

200 "You're a very nice": ibid.

200 "They were the sunglasses": ibid.

200 "He brought home": ibid.

201 "Somebody onstage": ibid.

201 "One night Gram": ibid.

201 "And every day": ibid.

202 "We had family": BoB to author, 2005.

202 "We were having": ibid.

202 "She thrived on craziness": ibid.

203 "Say Gram was trying": ibid.

203 "At this time Gram": ibid.

203 "The Aces was rough": DaB to author, 2005.

203 "The toughness was part": ibid.

203 "Of course the Aces": ibid.

203 "Gram described sitting": ibid.

204 "I was down": Einarson, *Desperados*, 68.

204 "Jay Dee had": JN to author, 2005.

204 "I started playing": JdM to author, 2005.

204 "Jay Dee Maness came": EB to author, 2005.

205 "The ISB was the first": ibid.

205 "I thought, 'This'": JdM to author, 2005.

205 "I went to his": ibid.

205 "The country players": EB to author, 2005.

206 "We didn't record": EB to author, 2005.

206 "Jay Dee had": BoB to author, 2005.

206 "Jay Dee was far": ibid.

206 "I was a beer man": EB to author, 2005.

207 "She was bossy": JN to author, 2005.

207 "We had some real": Einarson, *Desperados*, 79.

207 "Suzi Jane Hokom": JdM to author, 2005.

207 "It was the Gram": BoB to author, 2005.

208 "I have some reservations": JN to author, 2005.

208 "You knew he wasn't": BoB to author, 2005.

208 "Money was not": Einarson, *Desperados*.

208 "I'd walk in": BoB to author, 2005.

209 "didn't want to": JN to author, 2005.

209 "We were there": ibid.

210 "There are those that say": JN to author, 2005.

212 "Ironically, the same isolation": Peter Doggett, *Are You Ready for the Country: Elvis, Dylan, Parsons and the Roots of Country Rock* (New York: Penguin, 2000), 53.

213 "is probably the best": GP to Chuck Cassell, "Big Mouth Blues" interview recording.

TWELVE
THE BYRDS

214 "Gene didn't add": Johnny Rogan, *The Byrds: Timeless Flight Revisited, the Sequel* (London: Rogan House, 1998), 168.

214 "Remember, you're only": RoM to author, 2001.

216 "Gene Clark was nervous": JD to author, 2005.

216 "Gene Clark was originally":

218 "The Byrds were a good brand name ": Roger McGuinn, rock clipping.

218 "we were both wearing": Griffin, *Gram Parsons*.

218 "Gram and I had": ibid., 83.

218 "I'd heard of the": Richard Cusick, "Gram Parsons: The Story of the Grievous Angel Part Two," *Goldmine*, December 1983.

218 "We already knew Gram": JiS to author, 2004.

218 "But he seemed like": ibid.

219 "We did some rehearsals": Anon to author, 2004.

219 "At the time Parsons": Rogan, *Timeless Flight*, 253.

219–220 "It wasn't a replacement": Griffin, *Gram Parsons*, 139.

220 "We hit it off right away": RoM to author, 2001.

220 "I knew this music": Cusick, "Grievous Angel Part Two."

220 "I sang harmony": ibid.

220 "We were in limbo": ibid.

221 "Gram's selling point": ibid.

221 "Along comes Gram": JiS to author, 2004.

221 "Roger and Chris had": CB to author, 2005.

221 "My original idea for *Sweetheart*": Cusick, "Grievous Angel Part Two."

221 "It wasn't my intention": RoM to author, 2001.

221 "People forget things": Griffin, *Gram Parsons*, 83.

222 "When Gram came": ibid., 84.

222 "There's a certain way": ibid.

222 "Hazlewood heard about": JN to author, 2005.

223 "Gram used the ISB": BoB to author, 2005.

223 "Gram was enthusiastic": ID to author, 2005.

223 "There was a unity": Cusick, "Grievous Angel Part Two."

223 "Chris and I, both": ibid.

224 "Nashville was where Bragg": CB to author, 2005.

224 "We were the first rock": JiS to author, 2004.

224 "Their hair was long": CB to author, 2005.

225 "I was aware": Lloyd Green, liner notes, *Sweetheart of the Rodeo*, Legacy Edition (New York: Sony Music Entertainment, Inc., 2006), 4.

225 "Gary Usher wasn't": JiS to author, 2004.

225 "He had a lot": CB to author, 2005.

225 "In Nashville the engineers": JiS to author, 2004.

225 "The technical capability": ibid.

226 "There was some snobbery": CB to author, 2005.

226 "I didn't have any country": Cusick, "Grievous Angel Part Two."

226 "There was never": CB to author, 2005.

227 "We got along okay": RoM to author, 2001.

227 "Players are players": JiS to author, 2004.

227 "The psychology of Gram": ibid.

227 "Nashville sessions are regimented": Green, *Sweetheart* liner notes.

229 "It was horrible": Anon to author, 2004.

229 "a redneck motherfucker": Anon to author, 2004.

229 "Gram would go": JiS to author, 2004.

230 "Gary Usher, our producer": Anon to author, 2004.

230 "Usher was on codeine": CB to author, 2005.

230 "We went to the": ibid.

230 "So we did that": ibid.

231 "The Grand Ole Opry": RoM to author, 2001.

231 "To let you know": Doggett, *Are You Ready for the Country*, 56.

231 "We had relatively short": RoM to author, 2001.

231 "like he's our old": JiS to author, 2004.

232 "Gram took the reins": Doggett, *Are You Ready for the Country*, 57.

232 "You could see Glaser": JiS to author, 2004.

232 "Gram decided, out of nowhere": Einarson, *Desperados*, 86.

THIRTEEN

SWEETHEART OF THE RODEO

234 "Gram has added": Doggett, *Are You Ready for the Country*, 57.

234 "He likes to work": Einarson, *Desperados*, 88.

234 "The first half will": Cusick, "Grievous Angel Part Two."

234–235 "When he first came": JiS to author, 2004.

235 "Gram played electric": Anon to author, 2004.

235 "They played 'Tambourine Man' ": Anon to author, 2004.

235 "For many people": Anon to author, 2004.

235 "He did a few shows": CB to author, 2005.

235 "I thought I hired": Doggett, *Are You Ready for the Country*, 55.

235 "the remains of": T. Wilym Grein interview with the Byrds; clipping from an unidentifiable publication.

236 "That's right": ibid.

236 "Gene was drunk": Rogan, *Timeless Flight*, 257.

236 "McGuinn's old lady": Anon to author, 2004.

236 "They appear secure": Jerry Hopkins, *Rolling Stone*, May 1968.

236 "I turned Gram": Anon to author, 2004.

237 "If you want to go": Einarson, *Desperados*, 87.

237 "A couple of times": JiS to author, 2004.

237 "Whoever sang lead": Rogan, *Timeless Flight*, 260.

238 "He was a rich kid": Barney Hoskyns, *Hotel California: Singer-Songwriters and Cocaine Coroboys* (London: Fourth Estate, 2005), 65.

238 "When you drive": EB to author, 2005.

238 "With Buck Owens": ibid.

238 "But I adapt": ibid.

238 "There were people": JdM, author interview, 2005.

238 "But I learned something": ibid.

238 "Roger McGuinn was": ibid.

238 "Gram was the boss": Einarson, *Desperados*, 87.

239 "There were a lot": EB to author, 2005.

239 "It was a great": Einarson, *Desperados*, 90.

239 "We would like to": LHI press release, 1968 (www.bsnpubs.com/abc/lhi.html).

239 "I look at that album": ibid., 89.

239 "Here we have a youthful": Pete Johnson, LA Times.

240 "The band is dealing": Einarson, *Desperados*, 89.

240 "The cover depicted": Doggett, *Are You Ready for the Country*, 52.

240 "People didn't take": JiS to author, 2004.

240 "Our fans were heartbroken": Hoskyns, *Hotel California*, 65.

241 "Gram and Chris took": Rogan, *Timeless Flight*, 257.

241 "Slowly Gram started": Anon to author, 2004.

241 "David Crosby used to talk": Anon to author, 2004.

241 "I had a snifter": CB to author, 2005.

241 "But it didn't matter": ibid.

242 "They started to drift": BoB to author, 2005.

242 "I used to say": JD to author, 2005.

242 "Gram would perform": JiS to author, 2004.

243 "In this way": Rogan, *Timeless Flight*, 258.

243 "I was really": Barbara Charone, *Keith Richards: Life as a Rolling Stone* (New York: Doubleday, 1982).

244 "Gram was like": Einarson, *Desperados*.

244 "He was a lovely": Hoskyns, "The Good Ol' Boy," 76.

244 "Gram immediately fell": Doggett, *Are You Ready for the Country*, 58.

244 "Since we obviously hooked": Cusick, "Grievous Angel Part Two."

244 "He has a great ear": ibid.

244 "The reason Gram": ibid.

245 "teaching him countless": Charone, *Keith Richards*.

245 "Parsons was one": ibid.

245 "I was sipping": Tony Sanchez, *Up and Down with the Rolling Stones* (Cambridge: Da Capo Press, 1996).

245 "There would be music": CB to author, 2005.

245 "I had heard": JiS to author, 2004.

245 "but he left forgetting": CB to author, 2005.

246 "They were playing": JiS to author, 2004.

246 "He seemed initially": CB to author, 2005.

246 "On dozens of occasions": ibid.

247 "I get to the hotel": JiS to author, 2004.

247 "Hillman's right there": ibid.

247–48 "She was pretty strung": BoB to author, 2005.

248 "As far as Nancy": ibid.

248 "He thought it": Rogan, *Timeless Flight*, 259.

248 "Things came out well": ibid., 260.

249 "Roger didn't help": Doggett, *Are You Ready for the Country*, 60.

249 "It is true": Rogan, *Timeless Flight*, 260.

249 "There was genuine concern": Rogan, *Timeless Flight*, 261.

249 "Columbia had thought": Griffin, *Gram Parsons*, 140.

249 "It becomes pretty obvious": Anon to author, 2004.

250 "I didn't enjoy": Cusick, "Grievous Angel Part Two."

250 "The Bay Area bands": Anon to author, 2004.

250 "Gram's the kind": JiS to author, 2004.

251 "Gram had a beautiful": CB to author, 2005.

251 "I had to take it": ibid.

251 "They had had number": CB to author, 2005.

251 "Everybody came": WL to author, 2003.

252 "I could have killed": BM to author, 2003.

252 "sort of hump": ibid.

252 "He was party-oriented": ibid.

252 "Saints tickets for sale": ibid.

252 "Bob and I had": ibid.

252 "She was protective": ibid.

252 "It was a cruise": ibid.

253 "And then they showed": ibid.

253 "Something people don't": Richard Cusick, "The Story of the Grievous Angel Part One," *Goldmine*, September 1982.

253 "He said that he": ibid.

253 "The way he left": CB to author, 2005.

254 "I'm going to stay": ibid.

254 "We put Gram's stuff": ibid.

254 "I knew right off": Rogan, *Timeless Flight*, 262.

254 "Gram pulled the race": RoM to author, 2001.

254 "He thought he was more important": Rogan, *Timeless Flight*, 262.

255 "I sometimes wonder": rock clipping.

FOURTEEN

THE FLYING BURRITO BROTHERS

260 "I was in Morocco": Anon to author, 2001.

261 "I had gone": e-mail from Tony Foutz to author 2002.

261 "And there he was": e-mail from Tony Foutz to author, 2002.

261 "Gram was ripe": Victor Bockris, *Keith Richards* (Cambridge: Da Capo, 2003), 147.

262 "We sat around": ibid., 120.

262 "Gram and I": ibid.

262 "Keith had to go": Cusick, "Grievous Angel Part Two."

262 "Nancy was getting despondent": MK to author, 2005.

262 "Gram would come": ibid.

263 "Joshua Tree is everybody's": Judson Klinger and Greg Mitchell, "Gram Finale," *Crawdaddy*, October 1976, 44.

264 "I showed Gram": Paul Cullum, "The Mayor of Joshua Tree," *L.A. Weekly*, October 3, 2001.

264 "They all seemed like": Hoskyns, *Hotel California*, 84.

264 "We had binoculars": ibid., 85.

264 "It was wonderful": Marianne Faithfull and David Dalton, *Faithfull* (New York: Cooper Square Press, 2001), 184.

264 "this unearthly sound": ibid.

265 "We never had": JiS to author, 2004.

265 "They try to sing": Doggett, *Are You Ready for the Country*, 58.

265 "in a super hip": rock clipping.

265 "We've always dabbled": Doggett, *Are You Ready for the Country*, 59.

266 "Gram turned me": Einarson, *Desperados*, 109.

266 "I saw Gram": ibid.

266 "Gram was trying": ibid.

266 "Gram decided he was": ibid., 110.

267 "You can't go on": Cusick, "Grievous Angel Part Two."

267 "When they came back": JiS to author, 2004.

267 "I don't know": Rogan, *Timeless Flight*, 277.

267 "At first Chris": Cusick, "Grievous Angel Part Two."

267 "My daddy wanted me": CE to author, 2006.

268 "I was playing": Cusick, "Grievous Angel Part Two."

268 "Sneaky uniquely played": BL to author, 2006.

269 "Pedal steel is": JoB to author, 2005.

269 "I borrowed the name": Cusick, "Grievous Angel Part Two."

269 "The Tijuana Brass": JD to author, 2005.

269 "That company hadn't": MV to author, 2006.

270 "My first thought": ibid.

270 "Then it got icky": ibid.

270 "There were a lot": "Country Trip: A Talk With Gram Parsons," *Fusion*, March 1969, 11.

270 "It was a bachelor": BL to author, 2005.

270–71 "Chris had a fur": PDB to author, 2004.

271 "There was never": JT to author, 2005.

271 "To this day": Griffin, *Gram Parsons*, 87.

271 "It's being familiar": ibid.

272 "The hippies in Southern California": DaB to author, 2005.

272 "One of the differences": ibid.

272 "But that was": ibid.

272 "Nudie was a character": CE to author, 2006.

272 "Gram really, really": ibid.

273 "Pamela had a connection": MP to author, 2004.

273 "I was captured": Griffin, *Gram Parsons*, 116.

273 "We drove to the outskirts": ibid., 116.

274 "He came to": PDB to author, 2004.

274 "They became my social": ibid.

274 "He had a sweetness": ibid.

275 "He hung back": AN to author, 2005.

275 "They would play": ibid.

275 "Gram had these after-hours clubs": ibid.

275 "The sixties is when": CE to author, 2006.

276 "There were no": Cusick, "Grievous Angel Part Two."

276 "Everything was recorded": JP Morrisett, Omaha Rainbow, Chris Hillman; from unidentifiable interview clipping.

276 "Larry Marks was": MV to author, 2006.

276 "I think Larry Marks": Cusick, "Grievous Angel Part Two."

276 "A&M opened their own": MV to author, 2006.

277 "To do the album": "Country Trip," *Fusion*, 10.

277 "There was a lot": MV to author, 2006.

277 "The original [drummer]": Griffin, *Gram Parsons*, 125.

277 "We did those live": ibid., 88.

277 "That was the merging": ibid., 87.

278 "Sneaky Pete provided magic": ibid., 129.

278 "We went through": "Country Trip," *Fusion*, 9.

279 "We kept saying": "Country Trip," *Fusion*, 9.

279 "Nancy became an instant": PDB to author, 2004.

279 "Nancy was a stunning": Pamela Des Barres, *I'm with the Band: Confessions of a Groupie* (New York: Jove, 1987), 114.

279 "Before he sat": ibid., 115.

279 "Nancy was a flower": PDB to author, 2004.

280 "We did everything": ibid.

280 "We smoked a lot of pot": ibid.

280 "We were such hippie": ibid.

280 "One afternoon Nancy": Pamela Des Barres, *Rock Bottom: Dark Moments in Music Babylon* (New York: St. Martin's Press, 1996), 233.

281 "I knew already": ibid., 234.

281 "It was pretty harrowing": PDB to author, 2004.

281 "I didn't have": Des Barres, *Rock Bottom*, 234.

281 "Gram was on his way": MP to author, 2004.

FIFTEEN

The Gilded Palace of Sin

283 "I designed my own": Einarson, *Desperados*, 142.

284 "The first couple of times I played the Palomino": Cusick, "Grievous Angel Part Two."

285 "They thought he": MP to author, 2004.

285 "The place was": MV to author, 2006.

285 "I cannot tell you": ibid.

285 "Usually they were": ibid.

286 "It was never horrible": ibid.

286 "I cannot recall": Einarson, *Desperados*, 137.

286 "On Monday nights": BL to author, 2005.

287 "I know Jon Corneal": Anon to author, 2004.

287 "I didn't work": MV to author, 2006.

287 "Gram was practically": Des Barres, *I'm with the Band*, 121.

287 "It was debauchery": Phil Kaufman and Colin White, *Road Mangler* (Lafayette: White Boucke, 1998), 85.

287 "because the Burritos": MV to author, 2006.

287 "Things were always": Cusick.

288 "The band found out": MV to author, 2006.

288 "I never saw Gram do": Anon to author, 2004.

288 "Woe unto anyone": MV to author, 2006.

288 "He had a little": ibid.

289 "Country-style music landed": Fred Kirby, *Billboard*.

290 "In Philly the shows": MV to author, 2006.

290 "The band felt good": ibid.

290 "Philly was the only": Anon to author, 2005.

290 "On the road": Anon to author, 2005.

290 "But in Philly": Anon to author, 2005.

291 "We got to New York": Cusick.

291 "Gram insisted that": JiS to author, 2004.

291 "This album quite clearly": John Firminger, "Gram Parsons," *Country Music Review*, December 1974, 20.

292 "The Flying Burrito Brothers. Boy, I love them": Cusick, "Grievous Angel Part Two."

292 "Let me discourse": Cusick, "Grievous Angel Part Two."

293 "one of the best": Stanley Booth, "*The Gilded Palace of Sin* and the Flying Burrito Brothers," *Rolling Stone*, May 17, 1969.

293 "They've let us": "Country Trip," *Fusion*, 11.

293 "When the Burrito Brothers": CB to author, 2006.

294 "He wanted to talk": EB to author, 2006.

294 "It was scary": Anon to author, 2005.

295 "No, we're not wife": *Circus*, March 1970, 24.

295 "I call this the butter": CE to author, 2005.

296 "It was terrible": JiS to author, 2004.

296 "Strange women coming": Klinger and Mitchell, "Gram Finale," 47.

296 "We were musical": Allan Jones, "Burrito Deluxe," *Melody Maker*, February 8, 1975.

296 "We're the only true": Cusick, "Grievous Angel Part Two."

297 "learned a lot about": Griffin, *Gram Parsons*, 91.

297 "They couldn't get booked": JiS to author, 2004.

297 "They could play": ibid.

297 "We played anywhere": Einarson, *Desperados*, 180.

297 "There is a good music scene": "Country Trip," *Fusion*, 3.

298 "We paid a lot": ibid., 10.

298 "We think sequins": ibid., 5.

299 "They're so uptight": ibid., 3.

299 "When I first met": EvB to author, 2005.

300 "The Chateau Marmont": ibid.

301 "The Garden of Allah": ibid.

301 "I once stayed next": Anthony Haden-Guest, "Castle Babylon," *The Independent*, July 16, 1994.

301 "The Chateau was hilarious": AN to author, 2005.

301 "It was like": EvB to author, 2005.

301 "It was rather": SK to author, 2005.

302 "The Chateau was": EvB to author, 2005.

302 "When I grew up": ibid.

302 "I was so into": ibid.

302 "I would make": ibid.

302 "had these incredible": GW to author, 2006.

302 "It was the end": AN to author, 2005.

303 "Mick didn't look": Booth, *True Adventures of the Rolling Stones*.

303 "When the three": Griffin, 101.

304 "I get a phone call": ByB to author, 2005.

304 "We have this idea": ibid.

304 "Now, getting ready": Booth, *True Adventures of the Rolling Stones*.

305 "Gram was so excited": AN to author, 2005.

305 "I would spend": EvB to author, 2005.

305 "Gram was as knowledgeable": Bockris, *Keith Richards*, 148.

305 "I decided that": Booth, *True Adventures of the Rolling Stones*.

306 "This whole generation": MP to author, 2004.

306 "Pharmaceuticals are for pussies": John Phillips, *Papa John: An Autobiography* (New York: Dell, 1986).

306 "Remember, I learned": Hoskyns, "Keith Richards: How Come He's Still Alive?," *The Independent*, June 5, 1999.

306 "We went to the recording": GW to author, 2006.

306 "Keith sent me": MP to author, 2004.

306 "John [Phillips] was not": GW to author, 2006.

307 "Gram and Keith": PDB to author, 2004.

307 "Gram got so overtaken": MP to author, 2004.

307 "He had a limp wrist": ibid.

307 "Keith scared me": PDB to author, 2004.

307 "The time he was": JT to author, 2005.

307 "Gram stuck out like a bleeding thumb": Cusick, "Grievous Angel Part Two."

307 "Gram wanted to be": Klinger and Mitchell, "Gram Finale," 47.

307 "Chris didn't like": JiS to author, 2004.

308 "The Rolling Stones": Bockris, *Keith Richards*, 148.

308 "Chris and I were": BL to author, 2005.

308 "Sometimes Gram was fine": Anon to author, 2004.

308 "[Gram and Hillman] both loved": JT to author, 2004.

308 "My only problem with": Stanley Booth, *Keith*, 108–109.

308 "I finally found him": Einarson, *Desperados*, 167.

309 "She was a gorgeous model": PDB to author, 2004.

309 "I met her once": GW to author, 2006.

309 "He was heavy into": MK to author, 2005.

309 "I had never realized": Griffin, *Gram Parsons*, 127.

309 "What we needed": ibid.

309 "I liked writing with him": ibid.

310 "The first album's momentum had been spent": BL to author, 2005.

310 "Gram was an incredibly": ibid.

310 "I was intrigued": ibid.

SIXTEEN
Burrito Deluxe

312 "Gram insisted that": JT to author, 2005.

312 "That was Gram's": BL to author, 2004.

312 "Sneaky Pete heads": ibid.

313 "I said, 'I'll go'": ibid.

313 "There was real anger": ibid.

314 "I was sitting": JT to author, 2004.

314 "As a matter": Des Barres, *I'm with the Band*, 158.

315 "We moved quickly": Booth, *True Adventures of the Rolling Stones*, 358.

315 "It didn't sound": ibid., 354.

315 "The reason that": BL to author, 2004.

315 "There was something": JT to author, 2005.

316 "Gram was kissing": Booth, *True Adventures of the Rolling Stones*, 373.

316 "The rest of the": BL to author, 2004.

316 "Mick kept saying": Des Barres, *I'm with the Band*, 159.

316 "I had a terrible": MF to author, 2003.

316 "The first six months": Einarson, *Desperados*, 178.

317 "Yes, out and out": *Circus*, March 1970, 23.

317 "Gram and I had": SK to author, 2005.

317 "It was about": AN to author, 2005.

318 "Tony shot great": ibid.

318 "We Cosmic Kitties": ibid.

318 "Gretchen Burrell has": Roger Vadim, *Playboy*, 155.

319 "*Pretty Maids*": SK to author, 2005.

319 "He knew who": AN to author, 2005.

319 "Denny rented the": ibid.

319 "We all went": SK to author, 2005.

319 "Gram was loving": AN to author, 2005.

319 "Keith was going": Cusick, "Grievous Angel Part Two."

319 "They were falling": JD to author, 2005.

320 "It was a horrendous": ibid.

320 "We had the Byrds": Cusick, "Grievous Angel Part Two."

320 "I brought in Eddie": JD to author, 2005.

320 "The Burritos weren't": BL to author, 2005.

321 "We started getting": BL to author, 2005.

321 "I couldn't get much": JD to author, 2005.

321 "After that brief": Cusick, "Grievous Angel Part Two."

321 "I think the Burritos": Einarson, *Desperados*, 180.

321 "Chris [Hillman] knew": Griffin, *Gram Parsons*, 126.

322 "The sessions weren't": JD to author, 2005.

322 "Chris was very professional": AN to author, 2005.

322 "[Dickson's] a good producer": Griffin, *Gram Parsons*, 127.

322 "We never had": JD to author, 2005.

322 "Gram wanted to be": ibid.

323 "So Gram sulked": ibid.

323 "Gram could sing": JiS to author, 2004.

323 "Some of the songs": JD to author, 2005.

323 "I don't think Gram had a car": BL to author, 2005.

323 "There was not": JD to author, 2005.

323 "Chris used to": ibid.

324 "They sucked up": ibid.

324 "We did an average": ibid.

324 "Bernie was a nice": ibid.

324 "Sneaky Pete would want": ibid.

325 "There was never": ibid.

325 "It was the first great": ibid.

325 "He was doing": ibid.

326 "The Stones sent": SK to author, 2005.

326 "The Stones said": JD to author, 2005.

326 "I met Gretchen": SK to author, 2005.

327 "She was angry": BG to author, 2003.

327 "Avie maybe slipped": BM to author, 2003.

327 "He had been performing": ibid.

328 "He had been feeding": BG to author, 2003.

328 "I saw Avie": BF to author, 2003.

328 "I had to get something": JD to author, 2005.

329 "The cover was Gram's": ibid.

329 "The second album": Griffin, *Gram Parsons*, 127.

329 "Of all the albums": JD to author, 2005.

329 "Nothin' on *Burrito*": Griffin, *Gram Parsons*, 130.

329 "Gram Parsons is all": *Circus*, March 1970.

331 "He was in a wheelchair": Klinger and Mitchell, "Gram Finale," 47.

331 "Perhaps the country": George Kneymeyer, rock clipping.

332 "pure redneck": Phillips, *Papa John*, 353.

332 "costing almost": JiS to author, 2004.

332 "Gram never ever": Anon to author, 2004.

332 "He was a little": Griffin, *Gram Parsons*, 93.
332 "Someone was watering": GW to author, 2005.
332 "John, take me": ibid.
332 "Neither of them": ibid.
332 "I remember thinking": ibid.
333 "When I found out": Anon to author, 2004.
334 "He was full": SK to author, 2005.
334 "I would read": GW to author, 2005.
334 "The bike wreck": MP to author, 2004.
334 "Went to see GP": Des Barres, *I'm with the Band*, 176.
334 "We didn't have": BL to author, 2004.
335 "We may be": Jacoba Atlas, "Gram Parsons: The Burrito Ego Man," *Melody Maker*, April 3, 1973.
335 "We were down in the Valley at some club": Einarson, *Desperados*, 181.
335 "It got to the": Griffin, *Gram Parsons*, 89.
335 "I may seem callous": ibid., 94.
335 "Chris Hillman never": JD to author, 2005.
335 "I found a newsstand": Des Barres, *I'm with the Band*, 185.
336 "I waited to see": Griffin, *Gram Parsons*, 128.
336 "Chris and I always": ibid.

SEVENTEEN
NELLCÔTE

339 "Terry liked witty": Hoskyns, *Hotel California*.
340 "Terry wanted to be hip": JD to author, 2005.
340 "Terry loved Gram": EvB to author, 2005.
340 "They would think up album titles": Klinger and Mitchell, "Gram Finale," 48.
340 "Working with Terry": JiS to author, 2004.
340 "Gram was a little punk": Klinger and Mitchell, "Gram Finale."
340 "If there were ever": Anon to author, 2004.
340 "I played on two": EB to author, 2005.
341 "I don't remember": ibid.
341 "I got a phone call": Anon to author, 2004.
341 "We were all kind": EB to author, 2005.
341 "About four-thirty in": JoB to author, 2005.
341 "Clarence did coke": ibid.
342 "The whole concept": Keith and Kent Zimmerman, *Sing My Way Back Home* (San Francisco: Back Beat Books, 2004), 34.
342 "I always knew": SK to author, 2005.
343 "Don't let Gretchen": GW to author, 2006.
343 "sort of hanging around": Richard Cusick, "Gram Parsons: The Story of the Grievous Angel Part Three," *Goldmine*, January 1984.
343 "I met William through": Jay Ehler, "Gram Parsons Sweeps out the Ashes," *Crawdaddy*, October 1973, 74.
343 "We did detox": Hoskyns, "The Good Ol' Boy," 83.

343 "Keith was battered": Sanchez, *Up and Down with the Rolling Stones*, 215.

343 "Methadone is *twice*": Ehler, "Gram Parsons Sweeps out the Ashes," 74.

344 "The company would be": Cusick, "Grievous Angel Part Three."

344 "I remember Gram": Hoskyns, "The Good Ol' Boy," 83.

344 "I did some preliminary": Ehler, "Gram Parsons Sweeps out the Ashes," 73.

344 "The doctors and the": SH to author, 2003.

345 "The clinic was started": ibid.

345 "I was a hippie": ibid.

345 "If you knew": ibid.

345 "While I consulted": ibid.

345 "He played 'You're'": ibid.

345 "They were a certain": ibid.

346 "He could be pale-faced.": ibid.

346 "We'd play together": ibid.

346 "He kept his inner": ibid.

346 "The chemical that people": Ehler, "Gram Parsons Sweeps out the Ashes," 74.

346 "I would prescribe": SH to author, 2003.

347 "slightly shamefaced": ibid.

347 "I dug their music": Ehler, "Gram Parsons Sweeps out the Ashes," 72.

347 "They were all of a sudden not in the studio": ibid., 73.

347 "I had a 1969 Rolls": SK to author, 2005.

347 "Mick and Bianca had": ibid.

348 "like pink talcum": Sanchez, *Up and Down with the Rolling Stones*, 230.

348 "They were two burly": ibid., 232.

348 "The food and drink were": ibid., 233.

349 "If you couldn't play": SK to author, 2005.

349 "A lot of people": ibid.

349 "In those days": ibid.

349 "He was on some": Stanley Booth, *Keith* (New York: St. Martin's Press, 1995), 130–31.

350 "There was music": ibid.

350 "Since the atmosphere": ibid.

350 "I was playing guitar": ibid.

351 "Okay, you will take": Klinger and Mitchell, "Gram Finale," 49.

351 "When I started to hang with Gram, it did alter my relationship with Mick": Booth, *Keith*, 108.

351 "moany and reproachful": Hoskyns, "The Good Ol' Boy," 83.

351 "He wouldn't leave me": ibid.

351 "There'd be times": SH to author, 2005.

351 "You worry and you": ibid.

351 "Well, I don't know": Hoskyns, "The Good Ol' Boy," 83.

352 "It was easy to get caught up in the world": ibid.

352 "I had started living": ID to author, 2004.

352 "England's a place": Ehler, "Gram Parsons Sweeps out the Ashes," 72.

352 "We were doing": ID to author, 2004.

353 "She was skinny": ibid.

353 "There was some manager": ibid.
353 "The first thing": Babitz, Klinger and Mitchell, "Gram Finale," 49.

EIGHTEEN
GP

354 "He was a little": BG to author, 2003.
354 "Gram was fat": Klinger and Mitchell, "Gram Finale," 49.
354 "I wouldn't have known": BM to author, 2003.
355 "Gretchen knew exactly": ibid.
355 "The stepfather had arranged": JT to author, 2005.
355 "Gram was in lust": BM to author, 2003.
355 "Gram and Gretchen": JT to author, 2005.
355 "I guess if you're": BM to author, 2003.
355 "He took her to": Klinger and Mitchell, " Gram Finale," 49.
356 "Gram met us down": ByB to author, 2005.
356 "Rick Roberts found Emmylou": Griffin, *Gram Parsons*, 94.
356 "I was pretty jaded": ibid., 154.
357 "Chris told me there was this girl": Ehler, "Gram Parsons Sweeps out the Ashes," 71.
357 "I got this phone call": Klinger, "Gram Finale," 50.
357 "He and Gretchen took": ibid.
357 "it's one of the hardest country duets I know": Ehler, "Gram Parsons Sweeps out the Ashes," 71.
357 "To make a confession": Klinger and Mitchell, "Gram Finale," 51.
357 "I found a chick": Griffin, *Gram Parsons*, 133.
357 "I don't know": ibid.
358 "I went with my hat": Lorraine Alterman, "Parsons Knows," *Melody Maker*, April 7, 1973.
358 "Warner Brothers arranged a meeting": Cusick, "Grievous Angel Part Three."
358 "Merle was stashed": Klinger and Mitchell, "Gram Finale," 50.
358 "Merle not producing": Hoskyns, "Good Ol' Boy," 84.
358 "He was a pussy": Mark Rose, "Merle Haggard: Big Wheels Keep Rolling" *BAM*, October 24, 1980, 23.
359 "Rick was hot": SH to author, 2003.
359 "Gram always followed": "Parsons/Grech," *Record Collector*, September 1994, 108.
360 "We unsuccessfully started": SH to author, 2003.
360 "We'd had great times": Hoskyns, "Good Ol' Boy," 84.
360 "Eddie Tickner arranged": KF to author, 2005.
361 "Phil was an unusual": BaT to author, 2004.
361 "I realized I'd had": Kaufman and White, *Road Mangler*, 61.
362 "We would hang out": BaT to author, 2004.
362 "Gram was getting": Anon to author, 2004.
362 "Gram never tried to clean up": Hoskyns, "Good Ol' Boy," 85.
362 "[Those rehearsals] were what": "Parsons/Grech," 109.
362 "There was plenty": Anon to author, 2004.

362 "Gram started berating": Anon to author, 2004.
362 "Gram was hungover": KF to author, 2005.
364 "Gram started calling": MF to author, 2003.
364 "We flew out": BaT to author, 2005.
364 "Let me apologize": Jason Walker, *God's Own Singer* (London: Helter Skelter, 2002), 160.
364 "We went back": BaT to author, 2005.
367 "I went out to": ibid.
368 "The first night Gram": ByB to author, 2005.
368 "He got so embarrassed": Klinger and Mitchell, "Gram Finale," 50.
368 "Gram would always": ByB to author, 2005.
368 "Most of the singing": ibid.
368 "Rick did pass": "Parsons/Grech," 109.
368 "It was Rick's": ibid.
369 "At first I figured": BaT to author, 2005.
370 "By singing with Gram": ELH to Holly George-Warren, 1999.
371 "I liked the music": Jason Walker, *God's Own Singer*, 163.
372 "Gram was inspiring, the way he spoke": BaT to author, 2004.
372 "I was the audience": ELH to Holly George-Warren, 1999.
373 "Gram had a vivid": Walker, *God's Own Singer*, 163.
373 "Gram showed me": ELH to Holly George-Warren, 1999.

NINETEEN
The Fallen Angels

377 "*GP* is unabashedly country": Warner Bros. Circular, 1972.
377 "brought a pure": Bud Scoppa, "The L.A. Turnaround," *Rolling Stone*, March 1971.
378 "After a few months": "Parsons/Grech," 109.
379 "I had no idea": NF to author, 2005.
379 "I used to tread": "Gram's Last Song," *Zig Zag*, c mid-1970s.
379 "I don't usually travel": NF to author, 2005.
379 "As for the band": ibid.
379 "It was a terrific": KF to author, 2005.
379 "Gram decided he wanted": ibid.
379 "It was a beautiful": ibid.
380 "We had some batiks": ibid.
380 "Kaufman had this country": Ehler, "Gram Parsons Sweeps out the Ashes," 70.
380 "Kaufman's house was": JBa to author, 2005.
381 "They'd pick me up": NF to author, 2005.
381 "Rehearsal for Gram": Walker, *God's Own Singer*, 170.
381 "As soon as six": NF to author, 2005.
381 "John said, 'That's'": GW to author, 2005.
381 "There is always": NF to author, 2005.
381 "[The bus] wasn't fancy": ibid.
382 "They were sitting": KF to author, 2005.
382 "Lance was secretly": Anon to author, 2005.

382 "We had a roadie named": KF to author, 2005.

382 "When the bus": NF to author, 2005.

383 "It was one of the": Klinger and Mitchell, "Gram Finale," 51.

383 "We didn't treat": NF to author, 2005.

383 "I was horrified": Klinger and Mitchell, "Gram Finale," 51.

383 "Gram was abusing": ibid., 50.

383 "I got a call": JBa to author, 2005.

383 "For some reason": NF to *Omaha Rainbow*.

383 "The first night when": JBa to author, 2005.

383 "Emmylou and Gram": ibid.

384 "Gram's band invites me": ibid.

384 "From the first night": ibid.

384 "Gretchen wasn't pleasant": KF to author, 2005

385 "Gretchen was never nice": ibid.

385 "On the bus there": JBa to author, 2005.

385 "'Progressive country' was a term": NF to author, 2005.

385 "Gram saw a bunch": JBa to author, 2005.

386 "We made up for": NF to author, 2005.

386 "Most of the places": ibid.

386 "At the Armadillo": ibid.

386 "The first night": JBa to author, 2005.

386 "Emmylou had never": ibid.

386 "The first night": ibid.

386 "Gram did not speak": NF to author, 2005.

387 "Gram ran the show": JBa to author, 2005.

387 "When he did": NF to author, 2005.

387 "Gram's singing brought": ibid.

387 "Gram was blasted": Hoskyns, "The Good Ol' Boy," 85.

388 "Gram's first solo": Walker, *God's Own Singer*, 175.

388 "That gig was one": JBa to author, 2005.

388 "They went *crazy*": KF to author, 2005.

388 "Gram also brought": rock clipping, 1973.

388 "Gram and Gretchen weren't": Hoskyns, "The Good Ol' Boy," 85.

389 "What was driving Gretchen": Anon to author, 2005.

389 "If I'd been": Hoskyns, "The Good Ol' Boy."

389 "Neil Young and Linda": JBa to author, 2005.

390 "We stayed up until": ibid.

390 "Gram's going, 'I got'": ibid.

390 "It got a bit loud": NF to author, 2005.

391 "There's Gram sitting": JBa to author, 2005.

391 "Phil told me": ibid.

391 "We get on the bus": ibid.

391 "Lance gets on the": ibid.

392 "There was this big": ibid.

392 "The big bottle of Jack": ibid.

392 "Phil and Gram got": KF to author, 2005.

392 "I went down": BoB to author, 2005.

393 "Emmy was supposed": ibid.

393 "We decided to go": ibid.

393 "Gram had no stage banter": ibid.

393 "He takes the first bite": JBa to author, 2005.

393 "After the show": ibid.

394 "I basically had to keep": KF to author, 2005.

394 "Gretchen's insecure": ibid.

394 "Sitting in a bar after": Klinger and Mitchell, "Gram Finale," 51.

394 "I had a short period": ibid.

394 "Dave Mason [from Traffic]": JBa to author, 2005.

394 "offering some of the best": Kirby, *Billboard*.

394 "Gram was more hefty": Scoppa, "The L.A. Turnaround."

395 "I was sitting": KF to author, 2005.

395 "We had a fabulous Chinese": NF to author, 2005.

397 "The majority of what": ibid.

397 "It was one of": Klinger and Mitchell, "Gram Finale," 49.

397 "We played 'Still Feeling'": ibid.

397 "By the time we": ibid.

398 "Warner Brothers threw": ibid.

398 "When Gram and Emmy": ibid.

398 "Watching Gram and Emmylou": JBa to author, 2005.

398 "Gram and Emmylou brought": Klinger and Mitchell, "Gram Finale," 50.

398 "I never heard": JBa to author, 2005.

398 "I think that Gram's": JT to author, 2005.

398 "The fight and feud": JBa to author, 2005.

399 "Eddie Tickner was on": ibid.

399 "There was a baseball": ibid.

400 "Gram was too high": Hoskyns, *Hotel California*, 155.

TWENTY

"FARTHER ALONG"

401 "The backyard backed": KF to author, 2005.

401 "Gram called and said": MF to author, 2003.

401 "We didn't go over": KF to author, 2005.

401 "He would call": MF to author, 2003.

402 "He had come very": WL to author, 2003.

402 "Bob yelled at them": BM to author, 2003.

402 "We had a good": ibid.

402 "Gram was a quiet one": ibid.

402 "Bob caught 'em": ibid.

404 "That's when the seizures": Ben Fong-Torres, *Hickory Wind* (New York: St. Martin's Griffin, 1998), 188.

404 "Jesus Christ, a seizure": KF to author, 2005.

404 "Phil decided he was": ibid.

405 "about the most fun": *Grass Scene*.

405 "I know everybody enjoyed it": Kleinow to the *Daily Planet*.

405 "What pure delight it was": Dennis Dyroff, *Rock Ravings and Musical Madness*.

405 "He called and said": MF to author, 2003.

405 "I met Gram at": ibid.

406 "But on that same trip": ibid.

406 "He might try to write": KF to author, 2005.

406 "I don't know if it was": ibid.

406 "Gram had a delivery": ibid.

407 "[Gram] was in a real state": "Parsons/Grech," 109.

407 "We used to hang": KF to author, 2005.

407 "He wasn't a man": ibid.

407 "He sent me a ticket": MF to author, 2003.

407 "Margaret was an airhead": KF to author, 2005.

407 "I liked Phil": MF to author, 2003.

407 "We went to Joshua": KF to author, 2005.

408 "We were sitting around": Doggett, *Are You Ready for the Country*, 182.

409 "Chris Ethridge called": ibid.

409 "We were sitting at": ibid.

409 "There wasn't anybody that": JD to author, 2005.

409 "It was a Catholic funeral": ByB to author, 2005.

409 "In the middle of": Cusick, "Grievous Angel Part Three."

410 "We went to the church": MF to author, 2003.

410 "I was standing right beside": ByB to author, 2003.

410 "Everybody felt the loss": JD to author, 2005.

411 "whereby the survivor": Kaufman and White, *Road Mangler*, 107.

411 "Gram and Phil Kaufman": ByB to author, 2005.

411 "We left the funeral": MF to author, 2003.

411 "Gram told me, 'I don't'": Klinger and Mitchell, "Gram Finale," 52.

411 "It was always our intention": KF to author, 2005.

411 "It wasn't a large group": JD to author, 2005.

412 "Gram said he had": MF to author, 2003.

412 "Near the end, Gram": Klinger and Mitchell, "Gram Finale," 51.

413 "[Gram] had split from his": Patrick Sullivan, "Gram Parsons: The Mysterious Death—and Aftermath," *Rolling Stone*, October 25, 1973.

413 "There was a lot": KF to author, 2005.

413 "We laid down all": "Grams Last Song."

413 "Every night we'd": Klinger and Mitchell, "Gram Finale," 51.

413 "He was in good shape": "Gram's Last Song."

413 "Gram's style was to start": ibid.

414 "Our singing came together": Klinger and Mitchell, "Gram Finale," 51.

414 "The song was done": "Gram's Last Song."

414 "None of the Americans": Parsons/Grech, 109.

414 "He said he's": MF to author, 2003.

414 "Philip wasn't home one": KF to author, 2005.

414 "I went running into": ibid.

415 "I said, 'What are'": ibid.
415 "I was absolutely": ibid.
415 "I kind of calmed down": ibid.

TWENTY-ONE
JOSHUA TREE

416 "He had his record": MF to author, 2003.
416 "I think Gram and I": MF to author, 2003.
417 "Everyone out here": Klinger and Mitchell, "Gram Finale."
417 "We talked about stuff": MF to author, 2003.
417 "We weren't using heroin": ibid.
418 "That guy could consume": Klinger and Mitchell, "Gram Finale," 58.
418 "During the day": MF to author, 2003.
418 "They had one song": ibid.
418 "Gram was surrounded": Klinger and Mitchell, "Gram Finale," 53.
419 "We went to a bar": MF to author, 2003.
419 "Then Gram said": ibid.
419 "The connection came down": ibid.
419 "She had these little": ibid.
420 "She hit Gram up again": ibid.
420 "I knew he was in": ibid.
420 "One of the first": ibid.
421 "He was stoned and": ibid.
421 "Nobody left him alone": ibid.
421 "Just go in there": Kaufman and White, *Road Mangler*, 325.
421 "I drove down": MF to author, 2003.
422 "When I got back": MF to author, 2003.
422 "Gram wasn't a junkie": ibid.
422 "Junkies build up a": ibid.
422 "This was pure": ibid.
422 "I was all pushed": Kaufman and White, *Road Mangler*, 326.
423 "I took one look": MF to author, 2003.
423 "Dale was probably": ibid.
423 "I told them, 'He's done'": ibid.
423 "I was not crying": ibid.
423 "I didn't see them": ibid.
423 "I didn't notice her": ibid.
423 "It took me a while": ibid.

TWENTY-TWO
THE COFFIN

424 "I woke him up": Kaufman and White, *Road Mangler*, 327.
424 "He was upset": MF to author, 2003.
424 "I answered the phone": KF to author, 2005.
425 "I've watched a boy": MF to author, 2003.
425 "Walking out of the hospital": ibid.

425 "The first thing I did": ibid.
425 "Everybody went to bed": ibid.
425 "It's a two-hour trip": KF to author, 2005.
425 "We were in shock": ibid.
426 "Philip had to go": ibid.
426 "The coroner's report": ibid.
426 "I remember us getting": ibid.
427 "Phil saved my ass": MF to author, 2005.
427 "On the way back": KF to author, 2005.
427 "I don't remember": ibid.
427 "I was stoned": ibid.
427 "I went to Philip's": MF to author, 2005.
427 "When I woke up": ibid.
428 "I know he tried": WL to author, 2005.
428 "A bunch of us": KF to author, 2005.
428 "Gram didn't want to": Kaufman and White, *Road Mangler*, 106.
428 "We were all pissed": ibid.
428 "I was sitting": Kaufman, *Road Mangler*, 107.
428 "Somebody said, 'We can't'": KF to author, 2005.
428 "Philip goes into": ibid.
428 "I'm sure they had a few": ibid.
429 "Look, it's late": ibid.
429 "Just as they were about": ibid.
429 "They head off toward": ibid.
430 "Larry Burrell came knocking": ibid.
430 "Bruce told me to": ibid.
431 "He was very dead": Kaufman and White, *Road Mangler*, 111.

TWENTY-THREE
The Funeral

433 "They chased us": Richard Cusick, "Gram Parsons: The Story of the Grievous Angel Conclusion," *Goldmine*, February 1984.
434 "Bob tried to understand": WL to author, 2003.
434 "I was absolutely fine": KF to author, 2005.
434 "Phil Kaufman made Gram": JiS to author, 2004.
434 "Once you're dead": BiB to author, 2004.
435 "There was such a rift": BM to author, 2003.
435 "Why didn't Gram get": BG to author, 2003.
435 "I called New Orleans": JC to author, 2003.
435 "Bob and Gram are": BM to author, 2003.
436 "Gretchen opened Gram's": Anon to author, 2003.
436 "Therefore, by Gretchen going": Anon to author, 2003.
437 "I said, 'He's not'": KF to author, 2005.
437 "I called Philip and": ibid.
437 "Phil called me while": MF to author, 2003.
437 "Phil drove up": KF to author, 2005.

437 "We had the damnedest": Sullivan, "Mysterious Death and Aftermath," 14.

438 "Arthur Penn came up": KF to author, 2005.

438 "I sold T-shirts": ibid.

438 "Emmylou wasn't [at the party]": ibid.

439 "Authorities [seek]": Bill Wasserzieher, "Gram Parsons Dies in Desert," *The Village Voice*, September 27, 1973.

439 "He wasn't planning what": Klinger and Mitchell, "Gram Finale," 53.

439 "He was my mate": Rolling Stones, *According to the Rolling Stones* (San Francisco: Chronicle Books, 2003), 155.

439 "Gram was a romantic": Einarson, *Desperados*, 264.

439 "He was a good Southern": Klinger and Mitchell, "Gram Finale," 56.

439 "He was pretty far": BiB to author, 2005.

439 "I was in Orlando": JC to author, 2003.

439 "He wanted to go out": Klinger and Mitchell, "Gram Finale," 56.

439 "I was living in Athens": DS to author, 2002.

440 "The child was so pitiful": PW to author, 2002.

440 "When Gram died": Hoskyns, "The Good Ol' Boy," 87.

440 "Gram was a complicated": Eve Babitz, "Ashes in the Morning," *Rolling Stone*, October 25, 1973, 14.

440 "Gram Parsons had a vision": Tom Russell, "Gram Parsons Remembered in the Shadows of Joshua Tree," *Relix* 07.

440 "Both *GP* and *Grievous Angel*": Allan Jones, "Country Parsons," *Melody Maker*, July 27, 1974, 30.

441 "Both of these albums": Firminger, "Gram Parsons."

446 "Are you Margaret": MF to author, 2003.

EPILOGUE

447 "*There is no moral*": Philip K. Dick, *A Scanner Darkly* (New York: Vintage, 1977), 277.

448 "The spirit was pretty": JN to author, 2005.

448 "Shortly after Emmylou": BaT to author, 2004.

448 "I returned to Washington": Doggett, *Are You Ready for the Country*, 187.

448 "I was definitely": ibid.

449 "It's impossible for me": Klinger and Mitchell, "Gram Finale," 50.

449 "On our last trip": BM to author, 2003.

449 "He invited me for": WL to author, 2003.

449 "When we left he": ibid.

450 "We reached a corner": ibid.

450 "I sat on the bathroom": BM to author, 2003.

450 "He's right at the end": ibid.

450 "One of their closest": BG to author, 2003.

452 "Before him I hear": SE to author, 2004.

452 "There's the approach": ibid.

ALBUM AND SONG INDEX

INDEX

ABOUT THE AUTHOR

DAVID N. MEYER's writing on film and music has appeared in *Entertainment Weekly*, *The New York Times*, *Wired*, *Glamour*, and *The Rocket*. His other books include *The 100 Best Films to Rent You've Never Heard Of* and *A Girl and a Gun: The Complete Guide to Film Noir on Video*. He teaches in cinema studies at the New School in New York City and is the film editor for the arts magazine *The Brooklyn Rail*. He contributed to the renowned underground humor classic *The Book of the SubGenius*. Mr. Meyer lives in New York City and Ketchum, Idaho.

ABOUT THE TYPE

The text of this book was set in Janson, a typeface designed in about 1690 by Nicholas Kis, a Hungarian living in Amsterdam, and for many years mistakenly attributed to the Dutch printer Anton Janson. In 1919 the matrices became the property of the Stempel Foundry in Frankfurt. It is an old-style book face of excellent clarity and sharpness. Janson serifs are concave and splayed; the contrast between thick and thin strokes is marked.